Dash Diet Cookbook

The Ultimate Guide To Lower Your Blood Pressure With 750 Easy-To-Follow, Mouthwatering, Low-Sodium Recipes For Beginners. IBONUS 4-Week Meal Plan Included

Raven Foster

Copyright 2020 by Raven Foster - All rights reserved.

This document is geared towards providing exact and reliable information in regards to the topic and issue covered. The publication is sold with the idea that the publisher is not required to render accounting, officially permitted, or otherwise, qualified services. If advice is necessary, legal or professional, a practiced individual in the profession should be ordered.

- From a Declaration of Principles which was accepted and approved equally by a Committee of the American Bar Association and a Committee of Publishers and Associations.

In no way is it legal to reproduce, duplicate, or transmit any part of this document in either electronic means or in printed format. Recording of this publication is strictly prohibited and any storage of this document is not allowed unless with written permission from the publisher. All rights reserved.

The information provided herein is stated to be truthful and consistent, in that any liability, in terms of inattention or otherwise, by any usage or abuse of any policies, processes, or directions contained within is the solitary and utter responsibility of the recipient reader. Under no circumstances will any legal responsibility or blame be held against the publisher for any reparation, damages, or monetary loss due to the information herein, either directly or indirectly.

Respective authors own all copyrights not held by the publisher.

The information herein is offered for informational purposes solely, and is universal as so. The presentation of the information is without contract or any type of guarantee assurance.

The trademarks that are used are without any consent, and the publication of the trademark is without permission or backing by the trademark owner. All trademarks and brands within this book are for clarifying purposes only and are the owned by the owners themselves, not affiliated with this document.

 Well-known nutritionist and best-selling author based in New York City; Raven Foster is an advocate of healthy eating. As a dietitian, her books predominantly focus on the effectiveness of dietary trends and how people can monitor their nutritional intake while still eating delicious foods.

Through her research and professional experience, she has discovered that many people are discouraged from pursuing healthy eating habits because they do not know how to make foods that are both delicious and healthy. Thus, her patients' negative experiences with cooking inspired her to instruct people on how to follow diets, which also includes several healthy and beloved recipes that cater to different palettes.

In addition to her work as a dietitian, she is an avid cook and attends many culinary events in relation to American cuisine. As such, she has advised many chefs and other cooks and her dishes are known for their rich flavors and widespread appeal. She also loves to run in her free time and often spends her days off researching eating habits in the library or partaking in cook-offs with her close friends.

Introduction	12
Chapter 1: Introduction to DASH Diet	**13**
DASH diet: Sodium levels	14
1.2. DASH Diet Basics	14
1.3. Some Tips to follow during the DASH diet	14
1.4. What is Hypertension?	15
1.5. Myocardial Infection-Cerebral Ictus	16
1.6. Benefits of the DASH Diet	16
1.7. Nutrition	18
1.8. Top 10 DASH Diet Tips to not Fail	19
1.9. Food List	20
1.10. 4 Week DASH Diet Meal Plan	23
Chapter 2: Breakfast & Smoothie Recipes	**28**
1. Very Berry Muesli	28
2. Veggie Quiche Muffins	28
3. Turkey Sausage and Mushroom Strata	29
4. Sweet Millet Congee	29
5. Summer Breakfast Quinoa Bowls	29
6. Strawberry Breakfast Sandwich (Halves)	29
7. Steel Cut Oat Blueberry Pancakes	30
8. Spinach, Mushroom, and Feta Cheese Scramble	30
9. Refrigerator Overnight Oatmeal	30
10. Red Velvet Pancakes with Cream Cheese Topping	30
11. Perfect Granola	31
12. Peanut Butter & Banana Breakfast Smoothie	31
13. PB + J Yogurt	31
14. Overnight Oatmeal	31
15. No-Bake Breakfast Granola Bars	31
16. Mushroom Shallot Frittata	31
17. Morning Quinoa	32
18. Jack-o-Lantern Pancakes	32
19. Fruit-n-Grain Breakfast Salad	32
20. Fruit Pizza	32
21. Flax Banana Yogurt Muffins	33
22. Eggs and Tomato Breakfast Melts	33
23. Crunchy Avocado, "Toast."	33
24. Broccoli and Cheese Mini Egg Omelets	33
26. Breakfast Sausage, Potato and Mushroom Strata	33
27. Breakfast Green Smoothie	34
28. Breakfast Bread Pudding	34
29. Breakfast Banana Split	34
30. Blueberry-Raspberry Gazpacho with Mint	35
31. Berry Blast Off	35
32. Banana Nut Pancakes	35
33. Baked Oatmeal	35
34. Asparagus and Caramelized Onion Frittata	35
35. Applesauce French Toast	36
36. Apple Spice Baked Oatmeal	36
37. Whole Wheat Pumpkin Pancakes	36
38. Sweet Potato Cakes	37
39. Orange-Blueberry Swirl	37
40. Quick and Easy Omelet	37
41. Apples and Granola Breakfast Crisp	37
42. Zucchini-Lemon Muffins	37
43. Winter Breakfast Fruit Crunch	38
44. Whole Wheat-Oat Pancakes	38
45. Warmed Stuffed Peaches	38
46. Tropical Fruit Parfaits	38
47. Sunrise Smoothies	38
48. Summer-Fruit Soup	39
49. Summer-Berry Compote	39
50. Stuffed French Toast	39
51. Strawberry-Banana Soy Smoothie	39
52. Spiced Oatmeal	39
53. Spiced Irish Oatmeal	40
54. Spanish Breakfast Scramble	40
55. Southwestern Breakfast Bake	40
56. Shrimp-Artichoke Frittata	40
57. Raspberry-Orange Sunrises	41
58. Quinoa Pancakes	41
59. Quick Oatmeal Granola	41
60. Poblano Tofu Scramble	41
61. Peach-Mango Smoothie	42
62. Orange-Strawberry Swirl	42
63. Orange-Berry Cream Parfait	42
64. Oat and Nut Crunch Mix	42
65. Multigrain Pancakes	42
65. Mountain Peak Granola	42
66. Mini Mushroom-&-Sausage Quiches	43
67. Maple-Hazelnut Oatmeal	43
68. Maple-Almond Granola	43
69. Make-Ahead Breakfast Casserole	44
70. Light Biscuits	44
71. Hot Fruit & Spice Cereal	44
72. Honey-Ginger Fruit	44
73. Heart-Smart Breakfast Parfait	44
74. Greek Yogurt Parfait	45
75. Granola-Nectarine Gratin	45
76. Golden Honey Granola	45
77. Georgia Grits Waffles	45
78. Fruit-and-Nut Granola	45
79. Fruit Kebabs with Honey-Yogurt Dipping Sauce	46
80. Fruit Dippers	46
81. Fresh Fruit with Lime Syrup	46
82. Dried Cherry-and-Pecan Oatmeal	46
83. Creamy Grits	47
84. Creamy Breakfast Polenta	47
85. Cran-Berry Green-Tea Smoothie	47
86. Cinnamon-Apple Muffins	47
87. Cinnamon Banana Crunch Bowl	47
88. Carrot-Pineapple-Bran Muffins	47
89. Breakfast Barley with Banana & Sunflower Seeds	48
90. Blueberry-Tofu Smoothie	48
91. Blueberry-Almond Streusel Muffins	48
92. Blueberry Pancakes	48
93. Blueberry Buckwheat Pancakes	49
94. Blueberry and Maple-Pecan Granola Parfaits	49
95. Blackberry-Mango Breakfast Shake	49
96. Banana-Nut Oatmeal	49
97. Banana-Date Flaxseed Bread	49
98. Banana Breakfast Smoothie	50
99. Banana-Oatmeal Hot Cakes with Spiced Maple Syrup	50
100. Whole-wheat Soda Bread	50
101. Whole-grain Buttermilk Biscuits	51
102. Whole-grain Banana Bread	51
103. Veggies Breakfast Bakes	51
104. Tuna Pita Pockets	51
105. Three-grain Raspberry Muffins	52
106. Great Breakfast Burger	52

107. Blueberry Green Smoothie 52
108. Papaya Goodness 52
109. Wake up Call 53
110. Diabetic-Friendly Green Smoothie 53
111. Banana Almond Smoothie 53
112. Tropical Smoothie 53
113. Berry Banana Green Smoothie 53
114. Peach Green Smoothie 53
115. Green Avocado Smoothie................................... 54
116. Melon Mélange 54
117. Strawberry Cucumber Delight 54
118. Pumpkin Pie Smoothie 54
119. Arugula Smoothie 54
120. Toast with Almond Butter and Banana 55
121. English Muffin with Berries 55
122. Healthy "Lox" English Muffin 55
123. Protein Bowl 55
124. Berries Deluxe Oatmeal 55
125. Apples and Cinnamon Oatmeal 55
126. Energy Oatmeal 56
127. Anna's Homemade Granola 56
128. Warm Quinoa with Berries 56
129. Fruity Yogurt Parfait 56
130. Banana Almond Yogurt 56
131. Open-Faced Breakfast Sandwich 57
132. Broccoli Omelet 57
133. Veggie Frittata with Caramelized Onions 57
134. Whole Grain Pancakes 58
135. Veggie Scramble 58
136. Mediterranean Scramble 58
137. Egg Muffins 58
138. Veggie Omelet 59
139. Egg Burrito 59
140. Healthy French Toast 59

Chapter 3: Lunch Recipes 61

1. Veggie Quesadillas with Cilantro Yogurt Dip 61
2. Sweet Roasted Beet & Arugula Pizza 61
3. Sunshine Wrap 62
4. Southwestern Black Bean Cakes with Guacamole 62
5. Salmon Salad Pita 62
6. Pesto & Mozzarella Stuffed Portobello Mushroom Caps 63
7. Mayo-less Tuna Salad 63
8. Washington Apple Turkey Gyro 63
9. Pizza in a Pita 63
10. Heartfelt Tuna Melt 63
11. Spinach, Mushroom and Mozzarella Wraps 64
12. Apple-Swiss Panini 64
13. California Grilled Veggie Sandwich 64
14. Vegetable Pasta Soup 64
15. Tuscan-Style Tuna Salad 65
16. Terrific Tortellini Salad 65
17. Strawberry, Melon & Avocado Salad 65
18. Spaghetti Squash with Chunky Tomato Sauce 65
19. Soba Noodles with Mushroom, Spinach & Tofu 65
20. Skillet Sausage and Potatoes 66
21. Sirloin Soup 66
22. Shrimp Salad with Raspberry Vinaigrette 66
23. Shrimp and Asparagus Salad 67
24. Scoop-It-Up Chicken Salad 67
25. Savory Millet Cakes 67
26. Roast Chicken Dal 67
27. Red Pepper & Goat Cheese Frittata 68
28. Quinoa Salad with Dried Apricots & Baby Spinach ... 68
29. Pepper Pork Tamales 68
30. Penne Salad with Italian Green Beans and Gorgonzola 69
31. Pasta Primavera 69
32. Pappardelle with Roasted Tomatoes 69
33. Mustard Glazed Ribs 70
34. Mushroom-Sauced Pork Chops 70
35. Mushroom & Leek Galette 70
36. Moroccan Shrimp with Pomegranate Sauce 71
37. Minted Peas & Rice with Feta 71
38. Moroccan Eggplant with Tomatoes 71
39. Middle Eastern Chicken Kabobs 71
40. Mango Salad with Smoked Turkey 72
41. Linguini with Fresh Veggies 72
42. Lemon-Sage Pork Salad 72
43. Heirloom Tomato and Onion Quiche 73
44. Grilled Vegetables on Focaccia 73
45. Grilled Vegetable Salad 73
46. Grilled Cajun Chicken Salad 74
47. Grilled Beef and Avocado Salad with Cilantro-Lime Vinaigrette 74
48. Ginger Chicken with Rice Noodles 74
49. Garlic-Rosemary Mushrooms 75
50. Garden Slaw with Spicy Asian Dressing 75
51. Fireside Beef Stew 75
52. Fettuccine with Asparagus 76
53. Farfalle with Mushrooms and Spinach 76
54. Fajita-Ranch Chicken Wraps 76
55. Fajita Beef Salad 76
56. Easy Black-Bean Soup 77
57. Dilled Shrimp with Beans and Carrots 77
58. Curried Tofu Salad 77
59. Curried Chicken Bundles 77
60. Curried Carrot Soup 78
61. Cranberry-Raspberry Spinach Salad 78
62. Creole Turkey Meatballs 78
63. Confetti Summer Salad 78
64. Colorados (Red Bean Soup) 79
65. Citrus Turkey Spinach Salad 79
66. Cider Pork Stew 79
67. Chops and Pineapple with Chili Slaw 80
68. Chilly Bow Ties and Tuna 80
69. Chicken, Pear, and Parmesan Salad 80
70. Chicken Salad with Mango Vinaigrette 80
71. Chicken Salad Sandwiches 81
72. Chicken Olive Calzones 81
73. Chicken Noodle Soup 81
74. Chicken Fajita Chili 81
75. Chicken Baked in Banana Leaves 82
76. Chicken and Veggie Soup 82
77. Chicken and Vegetable Salad 82
78. Chicken and Pasta Salad 83
79. Chicken and Hummus Pitas 83
80. Chicken & Roast Vegetable Salad 83
81. Cabbage-Chicken Toss 83
82. Brussels Sprouts with Toasted Almonds 84
83. Black-Eyed Peas and Ham 84
84. Beef-Asparagus Saute 84
85. Barbecue Chicken Chop Salad 84
86. Balsamic Chicken over Greens 85
87. Baked Chicken Chiles Rellenos 85
88. Asian-Style Beef Salad 85
89. Asian Shrimp and Vegetable Soup 86

90. Almond-Crusted Chicken 86
91. Spiced-rubbed Chicken 86
92. Veggie Burgers 87
93. Oven-Fried Fish & Chips 87
94. Champion Chicken Pockets 87
95. Bumpy Road Sandwiches 87
96. Bean Burrito Bites 88
97. Baked Potatoes and Mushrooms 88
98. Seafood Kabob 88
99. Pesto Chicken Breasts with Summer Squash 89
100. Zucchini Tomato Bake 89
101. Yogurt and Dill Smashed Potatoes 89
102. Whole Wheat Mini Pizzas 90
103. White Bean and Chicken Chili 90
104. Warm Mexican Corn Salad (Elote) 90
105. Warm Asparagus Salad with Oranges 90
106. Vibrant Veggie Stir Fry 90
107. Tyler Florence's Lunch Box 91
108. Tuscan Fennel-rubbed Pork 91
109. Turkey, Apple & Cheese Sandwiches 91
110. Turkey Pinwheels 91
111. Turkey Dumpling Soup 91
112. Tuna and White Bean Salad 92
113. Tortellini with Pesto & Broccoli 92
114. Taste of Summer Strawberry Chutney 92
115. Sweet Potato & Lentil Soup 92
116. Summer Squash Casserole 93
117. Southwestern Black Bean Cakes with Guacamole .93
118. Smoked Mackerel, Orange & Couscous Salad 93
119. Slow-roast Chicken with Homemade Gravy 93
120. Shrimp & Rice Noodle Salad 94
121. Tuna Salad 94
122. Sesame Peanut Noodle Salad 94
123. Roasted Broccoli with Asiago 95
124. Rice & Bean Wraps 95
125. Raspberry Swirl Brownie Bites 95
126. Pork, Sage & Chestnut Stuffing Parcels 95
127. Ploughman Sandwich 95
128. Perfect Pinwheels 96
129. Pear n' Nut Muffins 96
130. Pear & Blue Cheese Flatbread 96
131. Honey & Apple Samie 96
132. Pan-seared Salmon on Baby Arugula Salad 97
133. Oven Baked Sweet Potato "Fries" 97
134. One-pot Chicken with Braised Vegetables 97
135. Olive oil-baked Potatoes 97
136. Mixed Dried Fruits & Nuts 98
137. Mexican Bean Salad 98
138. Mediterranean Tuna on a Roll 98
139. Mediterranean Chicken Salad 98
140. Maple Mustard Kale with Turkey Bacon 98
141. Leg of Lamb cooked with Potatoes 99
142. Quinoa Salad 99
143. Happy Face Pita 99
144. Gruyère, Leek & Potato Pie 99
144. Grilled Cheese & Tomato Sandwich 100
145. Greek Chicken Salad 100
146. Goat's Cheese & Watercress Quiche 100
147. Glazed Sweet Potatoes and Dried Plums with Ginger 101
148. Fruity Faces 101
149. Foolproof Slow Roast Chicken 101
150. Edamame & Summer Bean Salad 101
151. Curried Squash, Lentil & Coconut Soup 101
152. Creamed Swiss Chard 102
153. Cream Cheese Daisies 102
154. Courgette, Pea & Pesto Soup 102
155. Coconut-Crusted Lime Chicken 102
156. Classic Roast Chicken & Gravy 102
157. Classic Boston Baked Beans 103
158. Chunky Spicy Egg Salad 103
159. Chipotle Egg Soufflés 103
160. Chili Turkey Salad 103
161. Chicken Italiano 104
162. Chicken Enchiladas 104
163. Southwest Style Rice Bowl 104
164. Fresh Shrimp Spring Rolls 104
165. Pear, Turkey and Cheese Sandwich 105
Double Banana Sandwiches 105
166. Curried Mustard Greens and Garbanzo Beans with Sweet Potatoes 105
166. Creole-style Black-eyed Peas 105
167. Chinese-Style Asparagus 106
168. Insalata di Farro (Farro Salad) 106
169. Asian Quinoa Salad 106
170. Chicken Pasta Salad 106
171. Healthy Italian Pasta Salad 107
172. Balsamic Glaze 107
173. Basic Vinaigrette 107
174. Honey Lemon Vinaigrette 107
175. Lemon Vinaigrette 107
176. Garlicky Balsamic Vinaigrette 108
177. Mexican Summer Salad 108
178. Grilled Romaine Salad with Garlicky Balsamic Vinaigrette 108
179. Healthy Cobb Salad with Basic Vinaigrette 108
180. Pomegranate Salad 108
181. Beet and Heirloom Tomato Salad 109
182. Greek Salad with Lemon Vinaigrette 109
183. Caprese Salad with Balsamic Glaze 109
184. Grilled Tomatillo Salsa 109
185. Red Mexican Salsa 110
186. Grilled Chicken with Black Bean Salsa 110
187. Beef Tacos 110
188. Curried Chicken Salad Pita Sandwich 110
189. Chicken Fajita Wraps 111
190. Asian-Style Lettuce Wraps with Peanut Sauce 111
191. Italian Veggie Pita Sandwich 111
192. Turkey Chili 111
193. Vegetarian Chili 112
194. Tuna Salad 113
195. Italian-Style Tuna Salad 113
196. Veggie Quesadillas with Cilantro Yogurt Dip 113
197. Sweet Roasted Beet & Arugula Pizza 113

Chapter 4: Dinner Recipes 115

1. Chicken Breasts with Italian Salad 115
2. Orange Chicken and Brown Rice 115
3. Grilled Chicken Skewers Marinated in Ginger-Apricot Sauce 116
4. Baked Sunflower Seed–Crusted Turkey Cutlets 116
5. Turkey Meatballs in Marinara Sauce 117
6. Turkey Meat Loaf 117
7. Italian Herbed Turkey Cutlets 117
8. Turkey Roulade with Cider Sauce 118
9. Stuffed Bell Peppers 118
10. Sesame Salmon Fillets 119
11. Spice-Rubbed Salmon 119

12. Pan-Steamed Orange Roughy 119
13. Fish Tacos 119
14. Thai Curried Vegetables 120
15. Veggie Fajitas 120
16. Grilled Portobello Burger with Caramelized Onions and Pesto 120
17. Caramelized Onions 121
18. Mediterranean Bowl 121
19. Grilled Veggie Pizza 121
20. Mexican Pizza 121
21. Healthier Mac 'n' Cheese 122
22. Anna's Black Beans 122
23. Pinto Beans 122
24. Pumpkin Soup with Whole Wheat Parmesan Croutons 122
25. Cauliflower Carrot Soup 123
26. Roasted Butternut Squash Soup 123
27. Broccoli Soup 124
28. Mom's Bean Soup 124
29. Black Bean and Apple Salsa 124
30. Tropical Salsa 124
31. Grandma's Guacamole 124
32. Chipotle Dip 125
33. French Onion Dip 125
34. Tzatziki Greek Yogurt Sauce 125
35. Delicious Bruschetta 125
36. Roasted Zucchini Crostini Dip 126
37. Hummus Dip with Curried Pita Chips 126
38. Spicy Sun-Roasted Tomato Hummus 126
39. Grilled Rustic Corn 127
40. Grilled Sweet Potato Steak Fries 127
41. Grilled Asparagus 127
42. Grilled Collard Greens 127
43. Not Your Mama's Green Bean Casserole 127
44. Brussels Sprouts Casserole 128
45. Kale and Butternut Squash Sauté 128
46. Sautéed Greens with Cannellini Beans 128
47. Roasted Cauliflower 128
48. Sautéed Vegetables 129
49. Grilled Eggplant and Zucchini 129
50. Cilantro-Lime Brown Rice 129
51. Plain and Simple Couscous 129
52. Quinoa and Veggies 129
53. Healthier Stuffing 130
54. Black Beans and Brown Rice 130
55. Quick "Baked" Beans 130
56. Baby Bok Choy and Shiitake Mushrooms 131
57. Broccoli Ziti 131
58. Broccoli Rabe with Pine Nuts 131
59. Roasted Brussels Sprouts with Toasted Almonds ... 131
60. Baby Carrots and Edamame with Ginger-Lime Butter 132
61. Roasted Cauliflower with Sage 132
62. Collard Greens with Bacon 132
63. Corn and Tomato Sauté 132
64. Corn and Vegetable Pudding 133
65. Italian Kale and White Beans 133
66. Roasted Mushrooms with Thyme and Garlic 133
67. Smashed Yukon Golds with Buttermilk and Scallions 133
68. Basic Brown Rice 134
69. Indian Rice with Cashews, Raisins, and Spices ... 134
70. Quinoa with Broccoli 134
71. Creamed Spinach with Mushrooms 134
72. Sugar Snap Peas and Lemon Butter 135
73. Summer Squash and Walnut Sauté 135
74. Squash and Bell Pepper Casserole 135
75. Sweet Potato Steak Fries 135

Chapter 5: Dessert Recipes 136

1. Berry Sundae 136
2. Grilled Apricots with Cinnamon 136
3. Grilled Peaches with Ricotta Stuffing and Balsamic Glaze 136
4. Grilled Pineapple 137
5. Red Sangria 137
6. Baked Apples Stuffed with Cranberries and Walnuts 137
7. Buttermilk Panna Cotta with Fresh Berries 137
8. Cantaloupe and Mint Ice Pops 138
9. Peach and Granola Parfaits 138
10. Easy Pear Crisp 138
11. Roasted Pineapple with Maple Glaze 138
12. Fresh Strawberries with Chocolate Dip 139

Chapter 6: Salad Recipes 139

1. Ambrosia with coconut and toasted almonds 139
2. Apple lettuce salad 140
3. Apple salad with figs and almonds 140
4. Apple-fennel slaw 140
5. Artichokes alla Romana 140
6. Asian vegetable salad 141
7. Avocado salad with ginger-miso dressing 141
8. Baby beet and orange salad 141
9. Bean salad with balsamic vinaigrette 141
10. Beet walnut salad 142
11. Blue cheese, walnut spinach salad 142
12. Braised celery root 142
13. Butternut squash and apple salad 142
14. Chicken salad with pineapple and balsamic vinaigrette 143
15. Citrus salad 143
16. Couscous salad 143
17. Cucumber pineapple salad 143
18. Dilled pasta salad with spring vegetables 143
19. Dilled shrimp salad on lettuce leaves 144
20. English cucumber salad with balsamic vinaigrette .. 144
21. Fattoush 144
22. French green lentil salad 145
23. Greek salad 145
24. Grilled chicken salad with buttermilk dressing ... 145
25. Grilled chicken salad with olives and oranges 146
26. Grilled cod with crispy citrus salad 146
27. Mango tango salad 146
28. Mixed bean salad 146
29. Pasta salad with mixed vegetables 147
30. Pickled onion salad 147
31. Potato salad 147
32. Quick bean and tuna salad 147
33. Rice and beans salad 147
34. Salad greens with pears, fennel, and walnuts 148
35. Salad greens with squash 148
36. Spiced melon salad 148
37. Spinach berry salad 148
38. Steak salad with roasted corn vinaigrette 148
39. Tabbouleh salad 149
40. Tossed greens with pasta, fruit, and balsamic vinaigrette 149
41. Warm coleslaw with honey dressing 149

42. Yellow pear and cherry tomato salad 150
43. Roast Beef Salad with Beets, Apple, and Horseradish 150
44. Classic Chicken Salad with romaine 150
45. Chinese Chicken Salad 150
46. Tarragon Chicken Salad with Grapes and almonds 150
47. Chipotle Chicken Chili Taco Salad 151
48. Cobb Salad 151
49. Autumn Turkey Salad with Apples and Dried Cranberries 151
50. Salmon Salade Ninoise 152
51. Warm Spinach Salad with Scallops and oranges 152
52. Shrimp, mango, and Black bean Salad 152
53. Watermelon, Basin, and Shrimp Salad 153
54. Tuna and Vegetable Salad 153
55. Tuna and White Beans Salad 153
56. Arugula, Peach, and Almond Salad 153
57. Roasted Beet Salad with yogurt-Dill dressing 153
58. Apple Coleslaw with Buttermilk Dressing 154
59. Asian Slaw with Ginger Dressing 154
60. Crunchy, Broccoli Salad 154
61. Chopped Greek Salad 154
62. Iceberg Lettuce Wedge with Russian Dressing 155
63. Kale, Pear, and Bulgur Salad 155
64. Potato Salad with Asparagus and Peas 155
65. Lentil Goat Cheese Salad 156
66. Weeknight Tossed Green Salad 156
67. Baby Spinach and Strawberry Salad 156

Chapter 7: Side Dish Recipes 157

1. Acorn squash with apples 157
2. Artichokes alla Romana 157
3. Asparagus with hazelnut gremolata 158
4. Baby minted carrots 158
5. Baked apples with cherries and almonds 158
6. Black bean cakes 158
7. Braised celery root 159
8. Braised kale with cherry tomatoes 159
9. Broccoli with garlic and lemon 159
10. Brown rice pilaf 159
11. Brussels sprouts with shallots and lemon 160
12. Cauliflower mashed 'potatoes.' 160
13. Cheesy baked zucchini 160
14. Chinese-style asparagus 160
15. Classic Boston baked beans 161
16. Corn pudding 161
17. Creamed Swiss chard 161
18. Creole-style black-eyed peas 161
19. Eggplant with toasted spices 161
20. Fresh fruit kebabs 162
21. Garlic mashed potatoes 162
22. Ginger-marinated grilled portobello mushrooms 162
23. Glazed root vegetables 162
24. Granola with raisins, apples, and cinnamon 163
25. Green beans with red pepper and garlic 163
26. Holiday green bean casserole 163
27. Honey sage carrots 164
28. Honey-glazed sweet potatoes 164
29. Lean country-style breakfast sausage 164
30. Lemon rice with golden raisins and almonds 164
31. Lentil ragout 164
32. Parmesan roasted cauliflower 165
33. Polenta with red pepper coulis 165
34. Potato salad 165

35. Quinoa risotto with arugula and Parmesan 165
36. Ratatouille with roasted tomato vinaigrette 166
37. Roasted asparagus and wild mushrooms 166
38. Roasted butternut squash fries 166
39. Roasted green beans 166
40. Roasted potatoes 167
41. Roasted potatoes with garlic and herbs 167
42. Roasted winter squash with wild rice and cranberries 167
43. Salad greens with squash 167
44. Sauteed fresh corn 167
45. Sauteed zucchini coins 168
46. Savory buckwheat pilaf with toasted spices 168
47. Seared endive 168
48. Shrimp ceviche 168
49. Southwest stuffed zucchini 168
50. Spicy red cabbage 169
51. Sweet carrots 169
52. Sweet potatoes and roasted bananas 169
53. Tabbouleh salad 169
54. Tangy green beans 170
55. Thyme roasted beets 170
56. Wild rice or quinoa stuffing 170
57. Wild rice pilaf with cranberries and apples 170

Chapter 8: Seafood Recipes 171

1. Spicy Cajun Salmon Bake 171
2. Salmon with Grapefruit, Avocado, and Fennel Salad 172
3. Rice Paella with, Shrimp, and Asparagus 172
4. Shrimp Tacos with Lime-Cilantro Slaw 172
6. Limes and Shrimps Skewers 173
7. Crusted Salmon with Horseradish 173
8. Cucumber and Seafood Bowl 173
9. Fish Tacos 173
10. Tuna and Pineapple Kebob 173
11. Paprika Tilapia 173
12. Herbed Sole 174
13. Rosemary Salmon 174
14. Tuna Stuffed Zucchini Boats 174
15. Baked Cod 174
16. Basil Halibut 174
17. Tilapia Veracruz 174
18. Lemon Swordfish 174
19. Spiced Scallops 175
20. Shrimp Putanesca 175
21. Curry Snapper 175
22. Grouper with Tomato Sauce 175
23. Braised Seabass 175
24. Five-Spices Sole 175
25. Clams Stew 176
26. Salmon in Capers 176
27. Horseradish Cod 176
28. Salmon and Corn Salad 176
29. Spicy Cajun Catfish Bake 176
30. Cod with Grapefruit, Avocado, and Fennel Salad .. 176
31. Brown Rice Paella with Cod, Shrimp, and Asparagus 177
32. Fish Tacos with Lime-Cilantro Slaw 177
33. Halibut with Spring Vegetables 177
34. Roasted Salmon Fillets with Basil Drizzle 178
35. Salmon and Edamame Cakes 178
36. Sea Scallops and Vegetables with Ginger Sauce .. 178
37. Shrimp with Corn Hash 179
38. Greek Shrimp with Zucchini and Grape Tomatoes. 179

39. Crispy Tilapia with Mediterranean Vegetables....... 179
40. Tuna with Fennel and Potatoes 180

Chapter 9: Beef, Pork and Lamb Recipes 181

1. Curry-Rubbed Sirloin with Peanut Dipping Sauce.... 181
2. Sirloin, Shiitake, and Asparagus Stir-Fry 181
3. Beef and Mushrooms with Sour Cream–Dill Sauce. 182
4. Filet Mignon au Poivre with Bourbon-Shallot Sauce 182
5. Spiced Roast Eye of Round 183
6. Beef Fajitas with Two Peppers 183
7. Ground Sirloin and Pinto Chili 183
8. Sirloin and Black Bean Burgers with Fresh Tomato Salsa 184
9. Beef and Bulgur Meat Loaf 184
10. Beef Ragù with Broccoli Ziti 184
11. Pork Chops in Mustard Sauce 185
12. Pork Chops with Sweet-and-Sour Cabbage 185
13. Rosemary Pork Chops with Balsamic Glaze 185
14. Pork Chops with White Beans 186
15. Pork Tenderloin with Easy BBQ Sauce 186
16. Grilled Pork and Vegetable Souvlaki with Oregano-Lemon Marinade 186
17. Pomegranate-Marinated Leg of Lamb 187

Chapter 10: Appetizer Recipes 188

1. Artichoke dip.. 188
2. Artichoke, spinach, and white bean dip 188
3. Artichokes alla Romana 189
4. Avocado dip 189
5. Baba ghanoush 189
6. Baked brie envelopes 190
7. Basil pesto stuffed mushrooms 190
8. Black bean and corn relish...................................... 190
9. Chickpea polenta with olives 190
10. Chipotle spiced shrimp 191
11. Coconut shrimp 191
12. Crispy potato skins 191
13. Fresh fruit kebabs 191
14. Fresh tomato crostini 192
15. Fruit salsa and sweet chips 192
16. Ginger-marinated grilled portobello mushrooms 192
17. Gluten-free hummus 192
18. Grilled pineapple 193
19. Hummus 193
20. Marinated portobello mushrooms with provolone... 193
21. Peanut butter hummus 193
22. Pickled asparagus 194
23. Roasted butternut squash fries 194
24. Roasted potatoes with garlic and herbs 194
25. Roasted red pepper hummus 194
26. Shrimp ceviche 194
27. Shrimp marinated in lime juice and Dijon mustard. 195
28. Smoked trout spread 195
29. Southwestern potato skins 195
30. Sweet and spicy snack mix 195
31. Tomato basil bruschetta 196
32 White bean dip 196
33. Bruschetta 196
34. Flatbread Pizza 196
35. Spaghetti Pie 196
36. Pita Pizza 197

Chapter 11: Poultry Recipes 197

1. Basic Roast Chicken Breast..................................... 197
2. Classic Poached Chicken 198
3. Chicken Mediterranean with Artichokes and Rosemary 198
4. Chinese Chicken with Bok Choy and Garlic 198
5. Chicken with Mushroom Cacciatore Sauce 199
6. Mexican Chicken Breast with Tomatillo Salsa 199
7. Chicken and Apple Curry 199
8. "Moo Shu" Chicken and Vegetable Wraps 200
9. Roast Turkey Breast with Root Vegetables, Lemon, and Garlic Cloves 200
10. Turkey Cutlets with Lemon and Basil Sauce 201
11. Sloppy Toms 201
12. Turkey-Spinach Meatballs with Tomato Sauce 201
13. Cajun Turkey Burgers with Pickled Red Onions..... 202
14. Turkey Mini Meat Loaf with Dijon Glaze............... 202

Chapter 12: Main Dishes, Soups and Chowders............ 204

1. Grain hot cereal 204
2. Asian pork tenderloin 204
3. Baked chicken and wild rice with onion and tarragon 204
4. Baked cod with lemon and capers 205
5. Baked macaroni with red sauce 205
6. Baked oatmeal 205
7. Baked salmon with Southeast Asian marinade 205
8. Balsamic roast chicken 206
9. Barbecue chicken pizza 206
10. Barley and roasted tomato risotto........................ 206
11. Bean salad with balsamic vinaigrette 207
12. Beef and vegetable kebabs 207
13. Beef and vegetable stew 207
14. Beef brisket 208
15. Beef stew with fennel and shallots....................... 208
16. Beef stroganoff 208
17. Black bean wrap 209
18. Broccoli, garlic and rigatoni 209
19. Broiled White Sea bass 209
20. Buckwheat Pancakes... 209
21. Chicken and asparagus tossed with penne 210
22. Chicken brats 210
23. Chicken quesadillas 210
24. Chicken salad with pineapple and balsamic vinaigrette 210
25. Chicken tamales 211
26. Chipotle spiced shrimp 211
27 Cinnamon French toast 211
28. Corn tamales with avocado-tomatillo salsa 212
29. Creole-style black-eyed peas 212
30. Curried pork tenderloin in apple cider 212
31. Easy pizza for two 213
32. Fettuccine with clams, basil, tomato, corn and garlic 213
33. Fish Veracruz... 213
34. Five spice pork medallions 213
35. Fresh puttanesca with brown rice 214
36. Fried rice 214
37. Glazed turkey breast with fruit stuffing 214
38. Grilled Asian salmon 215
39. Grilled chicken salad with olives and oranges 215
40. Grilled cod with crispy citrus salad....................... 215
41 Grilled pork fajitas 216
42. Grilled snapper curry... 216
43. Grouper with tomato-olive sauce 216
44. Halibut with tomato basil salsa 217
45. Hearty chicken bowl... 217
46. Herb-crusted baked cod 217

47. Herb-rubbed turkey au jus 217
48. Honey crusted chicken 218
49. Italian chicken and vegetable packet 218
50. Lasagna 218
51. Linguine with roasted butternut squash sauce 218
52. Mango salsa pizza 219
53. Mediterranean-style grilled salmon 219
54. New York strip steak with whiskey-mushroom sauce 219
55. Orange roughy with lemon and thyme 220
56. Orange-rosemary roasted chicken 220
57. Overnight refrigerator oatmeal.............................. 220
58. Paella with chicken, leeks and tarragon 220
59. Pasta primavera 220
60. Pasta salad with mixed vegetables....................... 221
61. Pasta with grilled chicken, white beans and mushrooms 221
62. Pasta with marinara sauce and grilled vegetables.. 221
63. Pasta with pumpkin sauce 222
64. Pasta with spinach, garbanzos and raisins 222
65. Penne tossed with cherry tomatoes, asparagus and goat cheese 222
66. Polenta with fresh vegetables 223
68. Polenta with roasted Mediterranean vegetables 223
69. Pork chops with black currant jam sauce 223
70. Pork medallions with herbes de Provence............. 224
71. Pork tenderloin with apples and balsamic vinegar. 224
72. Pork tenderloin with apples and blue cheese 224
73. Pork tenderloin with fennel sauce 224
74. Prawns puttanesca... 225
75. Quick bean and tuna salad.................................. 225
76. Quinoa risotto with arugula and Parmesan 225
77. Rice and beans salad 226
78. Rice noodles with spring vegetables 226
79. Roasted salmon 226
80. Roasted salmon with maple glaze........................ 226
81. Old fashioned chicken and brown rice soup.......... 227
82. Chicken and Spring vegetable soup..................... 227
83. Mexican Chicken Tortilla soup 227
84. Hearty beef vegetable soup................................. 228
85. Lentil and Sausage soup 228
86. Sausage milestone with Kale and Beans 229
87. Homemade clam Chowder.................................. 229
88. Cod and Corn Chowder 229
89. Manhattan Snapper chowder............................... 230
90. Sweet potato, Collard, and black-eyed Pea Soup.. 230
91. Homemade Chicken Broth 230
92. Summer Berry Soup 231
93. Green Beans Soup... 231
94. Turkey Soup 231
95. Pasta Soup.. 231

Conclusion..232

Introduction

More than a billion people worldwide are affected by high blood pressure, and that figure is increasing. In fact, in the past 40 years, the number of individuals with high blood pressure has doubled, a major health problem, as increased blood pressure is associated with a greater risk of diseases such as heart disease, renal failure, and stroke. Since the diet is believed to play a significant role in the production of high blood pressure, specific dietary guidelines have been developed by scientists and politicians to help minimize it.

Dietary Methods to Avoid Hypertension or Sprint is a diet prescribed by persons who wish to prevent or treat hypertension and decrease their risk of heart disease, also known as elevated blood pressure. Fruits, vegetables, whole grains, and lean meats are the subject of the DASH diet.

The diet was developed after researchers found that in persons who adopted a plant-based diet, such as vegans and vegetarians, elevated blood pressure was much less frequent. That's why the DASH diet, while including certain lean protein sources such as chicken, fish, and beans, emphasizes fruits and vegetables. The diet consists of low amounts of red meat, salt, added sugar, and fat.

One of the key reasons people with high blood pressure will benefit from this diet, scientists say, is that it decreases the consumption of sodium. No more than one teaspoon (2,300 mg of sodium a day, which is in accordance with most national recommendations, is encouraged by the daily DASH diet schedule. No more than 3/4 of a teaspoon (1,500 mg of sodium per day is indicated in the lower salt version. The DASH diet provided a variety of possible advantages, including weight loss and decreased cancer risk, in addition to lowering blood pressure. You do not expect DASH, though, to help you lose weight on its own since it was fundamentally built to reduce blood pressure. Weight loss may actually be an extra advantage.

Chapter 1: Introduction to DASH Diet

A healthy eating strategy, called the DASH diet, is intended to avoid elevated B.P. In studies funded by the National Institutes of Health, the DASH diet strategy was designed to reduce B.P. in the absence of medicine.The DASH diet helps you to lower the salt in your diet and enjoy a number of nutrient-rich foods that can minimize B.P., such as K, Ca, and Mg.You could reduce the B.P. by a few points after two weeks by adopting the DASH diet. Your high B.P. can decrease by 8 to fourteen points over time, consequently making a big difference to your health hazards.

Since the DASH diet is a safe eating habit, besides only reducing blood pressure, it provides cardiovascular benefits. For the treatment of osteoporosis, cancer, heart disease, stroke, and diabetes, the DASH diet is also in accordance with nutritional guidelines.DASH reduces blood pressure and can help with weight loss, particularly if you have elevated levels. Your chance of diabetes, heart disease, metabolic syndrome, and certain cancers could be minimized. Although tests on the DASH diet have shown that the largest decreases in blood pressure have resulted in people with the lowest consumption of salt, the longevity and lifetime effects of salt restriction are not obvious. Reducing salt consumption greatly influences blood pressure for those with elevated blood pressure. In people with normal blood pressure, however, the effects of lowering the consumption of salt are much lower.

Health complications, such as an elevated risk of heart failure, insulin resistance, and fluid retention, have been associated with consuming very little salt. The low-salt variant of the DASH diet advises that individuals consume no more than 1,500 mg (3/4 teaspoon) of sodium a day. It is uncertain, though, whether there are any advantages of reducing this low consumption of salt, even in people with high blood pressure. Indeed a new study showed that there was no correlation between salt consumption and the likelihood of death from heart failure, despite the fact that a drop in salt intake produced a small decline in blood pressure.

However, since most individuals consume so much salt, it might be helpful to decrease the salt consumption from very large levels of 2-2.5 teaspoons (10-12 grams) a day to 1-1.25 teaspoons (5-6 grams) a day.

By - the amount of heavily refined food intake and consuming mostly whole foods, this objective can be done quickly. No particular foods to eat are specified in the DASH diet. Instead, specific servings of various classes of foods are recommended. Based on how many calories you ingest, the number of servings you will eat. An example of food portions based on a 2,000-calorie diet is given below.

DASH diet: Sodium levels

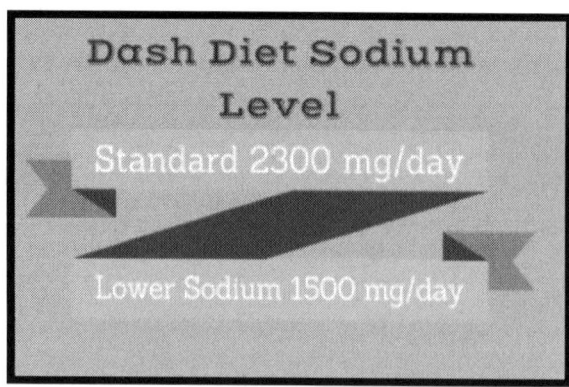

1.2. DASH Diet Basics

Compared to what you would get in a standard American diet, all variations of the DASH diet strive to decrease the amount of sodium in your diet, which can amount to a whopping 3,400 mg of sodium a day or more.

The regular DASH diet complies with the Dietary Guidelines' advice for Americans to achieve a maximum consumption of less than 2,300 mg of sodium a day.

As an upper limit for all adults, the American Heart Association suggests 1,500 mg a day of sodium. Speak to the doctor if you are not sure what amount of sodium is right for you.

1.3. Some Tips to follow during the DASH diet

7 Tips to Reduce Sodium Intake

Opting for more low sodium food choices is a great start at reducing your intake, but staying below 2,300 mg a day can still feel like a challenge. Sodium is found in a lot of different foods - and almost every recipe on the planet calls for salt. Here are some simple tricks to help you cut your intake and stay on top of your DASH eating plan:

1. Use other seasonings, herbs, and citrus when cooking to flavor your food besides salt.
2. Track your daily food intake using an app to calculate exactly how much sodium you are eating.
3. Always check the nutrition facts and ingredients labels for hidden sources of sodium.
4. Avoid poultry packed with "broth," "saline" or "sodium solution". (This is typically written on the package).
5. Drain and rinse canned beans, proteins, and veggies before eating.
6. Ask for your meal to be cooked without salt when eating out.
7. Watch out for anything that is pickled, brined, cured, smoked, or barbecued, or seasoned with broth, au jus, soy sauce, miso, tomato sauce or asian sauces.

Lowering Sodium Intake

Daily Calorie Needs

Your Daily Calorie Needs

Gender	Age (years)	Calories Needed for Each Activity Level		
		Sedentary	Moderately Active	Active
Female	19–30	2,000	2,000–2,200	2,400
	31–50	1,800	2,000	2,200
	51+	1,600	1,800	2,000–2,200
Male	19–30	2,400	2,600–2,800	3,000
	31–50	2,200	2,400–2,600	2,800–3,000
	51+	2,000	2,200–2,400	2,400–2,800

1.4. What is Hypertension?

Blood pressure is the strain exerted on the walls of the arteries of the body, the main blood vessels of the body, by pumping blood. Hypertension is when there's so much blood pressure. Blood pressure has two numbers written down. When the heart contracts or beats, the first (systolic) number reflects the pressure in blood vessels. As the heart rests between beats, the second (diastolic) number represents the pressure in the arteries.

Hypertension is diagnosed if the systolic blood pressure readings on both days are ~140 mmHg and/or the diastolic blood pressure readings on both days are ~90 mmHg as assessed on two separate days.

Symptoms

Even if blood pressure rates exceed dangerously elevated levels, most people with high blood pressure show no signs or symptoms. There may be headaches, shortness of breath, or nosebleeds in a few individuals with elevated blood pressure, but these signs and symptoms are not specific and generally do not develop until high blood pressure has entered a serious or life-threatening level.

Consequences of Hypertension

Your health and quality of life are endangered by high blood pressure. The harm caused by high blood pressure (HBP, or hypertension) takes place over time, in most cases. High blood pressure, left undetected (or uncontrolled), may contribute to:

Heart attack Elevated blood pressure affects the vessels and can get blocked to hinder the heart muscle from pumping blood.

Stroke-High blood pressure will make it possible to clog or even burst blood vessels in the brain.

The elevated workload from high blood pressure will cause the heart to swell and struggle to supply the body with blood. Heart failure.

High blood pressure can affect the arteries around the kidneys and interfere with their ability to pump blood efficiently. Kidney disease or failure

Loss of vision. High blood pressure in the eyes can stretch or destroy blood vessels.

Sexual dysfunction: High blood pressure may lead to male erectile dysfunction or reduced female libido.

Angina- Elevated blood pressure can result in a heart attack or microvascular disease over time (MVD). A typical symptom is angina or chest pain.

Peripheral artery disease (PAD)-High blood pressure atherosclerosis may cause arteries in the legs, arms, stomach, and head to close, causing discomfort or exhaustion.

Will any concerns be caused by hypertension?

It destroys your blood vessels when your blood pressure is too high for too long, and LDL (bad cholesterol starts to collect in your artery walls along with tears. This raises the circulatory system's workload while reducing its performance.

As a consequence, you are at increased risk of experiencing life-changing and potentially life-threatening problems due to elevated blood pressure.

Metabolic syndrome and elevated blood pressure (insulin resistance syndrome)

Metabolic syndrome refers to a cluster of risk factors that increase the risk of heart disease, diabetes, stroke, and other health conditions, including elevated blood pressure. It is diagnosed when there are all three of these risk factors:

- Elevated blood glucose levels (sugar)
- Lower blood levels of HDL (good cholesterol
- Elevated serum levels of triglycerides
- Broad circumference of the waist or "apple-shaped" body
- Blood pressure is high.

1.5. Myocardial Infection-Cerebral Ictus

A low yet important chance of stroke is associated with acute myocardial infarction. A link has been proposed between unrecognized myocardial infarction and the possibility of stroke. In patients not undergoing thrombolysis, most of the strokes that complicate acute myocardial infarction are cardioembolic. The result is negatively affected by strokes in patients with acute myocardial infarction. In coronary artery disease patients, in addition to the likelihood of mortality, stroke is often associated with a marked rise in the risk of other cardiac events, such as myocardial infarction or stroke (including both ischemic and hemorrhagic stroke). In patients with acute myocardial infarction, new-onset atrial fibrillation not only raises the risk of ischemic stroke it also increases the risk of mortality. Intracerebral hemorrhage due to thrombolysis markedly raises the risk of death and injury. Intracerebral, subdural, subarachnoid, and intraventricular are typical sites of intracranial hemorrhage. Since myocardial infarction, there is a greatly elevated chance of vascular dementia. In patients who have had a stroke following a myocardial infarction, the risk is even higher. Identifying stroke-prone patients after myocardial infarction and identifying effective prevention steps are highly significant. Increased use of ticagrelor (a platelet aggregation inhibitor) has led to a reduced occurrence of ischemic stroke in the treatment of acute myocardial infarction. Cangrelor injection has also shown promise in some early studies.

In conclusion, considering the existing limits of expertise, care choices should be individualized in situations of concomitant acute MI and acute ischemic stroke. In such a difficult situation, a delicate balance between the existence or absence of cardiac tamponade risk factors and a possible cardiac or neurological deficiency could direct the clinician. In the absence of the above risk factors for heart complications associated with intravenous thrombolysis, Alteplase should possibly not be prevented in qualifying patients with ischemic stroke and MI.

1.6. Benefits of the DASH Diet

Health benefits

High blood pressure or hypertension can increase the risk of heart attack, heart failure, stroke, and kidney disease. Experts who reviewed the DASH diet in 2017, 20 years after its introduction, described it as an experiment that could dramatically improve the health of the population. According to the study, if individuals with elevated blood pressure had to adopt the DASH diet specifically, they might avert about 400,000 deaths from cardiovascular disease over ten years.

Who will benefit from that?

- Pressure on the blood
- Sugar in blood

- Triglycerides, or fat, in the blood
- Low-density lipoprotein (LDL) or "bad" cholesterol
- Resistance to insulin

These are both symptoms of metabolic syndrome, a disorder that also includes obesity, type 2 diabetes, and a greater risk of cardiovascular disease.

A 2013 research looked at the effect of DASH on individuals with and without metabolic syndrome who had practiced the diet for eight weeks.

The findings have shown that on average:

In individuals with metabolic syndrome, systolic pressure decreased by 4.9 millimeters of mercury (mm Hg), and diastolic pressure decreased by 1.9 mm H.G.

In individuals without metabolic syndrome, systolic pressure decreased by 5.2 mm Hg, and diastolic pressure decreased by 2.9 mm Hg.

In other words, DASH can be effective in reducing blood pressure in people with or without metabolic syndrome. There is also evidence that it will reduce the risk of colorectal cancer and increase average life expectancy.

DASH is advised by the National Kidney Foundation for people with kidney disease.

Weight Loss

On the DASH diet, individuals will lose weight, but they do not have to. If a person wants to lose weight, the National Heart Lung and Blood Institute (NHLBI) advises a steady decrease in calories.

Other tips for weight loss on DASH include:

- To provide small portions sometimes during the day.
- To eat less meat and more fruit, vegetables, and whole grains;
- Choosing fruit or veggies as a snack instead of candies or chips
- use the bodyweight planner of the National Institute of Diabetes and Digestive and Kidney Disorders (NIDDK)
- Using the calorie map in the NHLBI DASH meal schedule.

1.7. Nutrition

The goal of the DASH diet is to provide nutrients that will help lower blood pressure.
Here are some of the characteristics:

- It emphasizes, instead of single nutrients, dietary habits.
- Foods that are high in antioxidants are emphasized.

An individual should aim at balancing their intake of nutrients as follows:

Total fat	27% of calories
Saturated fat	6% of calories
Protein	18% of calories
Carbohydrate	55% of calories
Cholesterol	150 mg per day
Sodium	1,500 mg or 2,300 mg, depending on the diet
Potassium	4,700 mg
Calcium	1,250 mg
Magnesium	500 mg
Fiber	30 g

Foods should be:

- High in trans and saturated fats
- Fiber, protein, magnesium, calcium, and potassium-rich
- Low in sodium

Fatty beef, full-fat dairy products, coconut oil, palm oil, and palm kernel oil are often found in saturated fats. The DASH diet primarily focuses on foods dependent on plants, all of which are high in antioxidants. Experts believe that in avoiding multiple health problems, including heart disease, stroke, type 2 diabetes, and cancer, antioxidants play a role. To further define and measure the benefits of the DASH diet, numerous experiments have been carried out. They include:

Reduction of blood pressure - blood pressure frequently decreases a few points in just two weeks after the DASH diet, and if it lasts, the systolic blood pressure can decrease by eight to fourteen points.

Because of improved calcium intake from dairy products and green leafy vegetables, the DASH diet also helps strengthen bone strength and avoid osteoporosis.

In the long term, high consumption of fresh or frozen fruits and vegetables is associated with lower cancer risk.

The healthy food intake of the DASH diet decreases metabolic diseases such as cardiovascular disease and diabetes, as well as cerebrovascular disease, due to decreased fat consumption and improved replacement of complex carbohydrates for simple sugars. Which leads to a drop in the blood level of total and LDL cholesterol, as well as a decline in blood pressure.

An added advantage of the DASH diet is a decreased risk of gout by decreasing uric acid levels in subjects with hyperuricemia.

1.8. Top 10 DASH Diet Tips to not Fail

Top 10 DASH Tips

- Get the highest amount of key nutrients by buying foods that are in season. (A farmer's market is the best place to find seasonal produce.)
- Stock your kitchen with healthy convenience foods: cut-up fresh veggies and fruits, hummus and raw nuts.
- Double up on veggies—1 cup of veggies equals two servings.
- Curb your sweet tooth by having fresh berries or other fruit for dessert.
- Make a quick, easy, and delicious snack: organic, low-fat plain yogurt with almonds and fresh fruit. Try Greek yogurt for a thicker, richer experience!
- All nuts are heart-healthy, but make sure they're raw and not roasted or salted. Give your entrée or salad a healthy-fat crunch by adding 1 to 2 tablespoons of raw nuts.
- Stay hydrated. Drink plenty of water throughout the day by keeping a bottle with you at work and in the car, and always drink water with meals.
- Eat the colors of the rainbow at every meal. The more colorful your plate, the greater the variety of nutrients you're consuming.
- No need to skimp on lattes; just make it with 8 ounces of nonfat milk or unsweetened almond milk.
- Green smoothies made with unsweetened almond milk, fresh fruit, and greens are a quick, easy, and delicious way to maximize fruits and veggies at any meal.

1.9. Food List

Grains and Starchy Foods

- 1 ounce Sliced Bread
- 1 ounce Tortilla
- 1 ounce Roll
- 1 ounce (1-half) Bagel
- 1 ounce Crackers (low sodium)
- 1 ounce Dry Cereal And Granola
- 1/2 cup Cooked Rice
- 1/2 cup Cooked Pasta
- 1/2 cup Cooked Quinoa
- 1/2 cup Cooked Oats
- 1/2 cup Cooked Grits
- 1/2 cup Cooked Polenta
- 1/2 cup Cooked Barley
- 1/2 cup Cooked Couscous
- 1/2 cup Cooked Ancient Grains
- 1/2 cup Cooked Sprouted Grains
- 1/2 cup Corn
- 1/2 cup Lima Beans
- 4 ounces (1 small) Yam
- 4 ounces (1 small) Potato
- 4 ounces (1 small) Sweet Potato

Vegetables

- 1 cup Romaine Lettuce
- 1 cup Kale
- 1 cup Spinach
- 1 cup Arugula
- 1 cup Collard Greens
- 1 cup Cabbage
- 1 cup Swiss Chard
- 1 cup Mustard Greens
- 1 cup Other Lettuce
- 1/2 cup Celery
- 1/2 cup Bok Choy
- 1/2 cup Cucumbers
- 1/2 cup Radishes
- 1/2 cup Edamame
- 1/2 cup Mushrooms
- 1/2 cup Squash
- 1/2 cup Zucchini
- 1/2 cup Asparagus
- 1/2 cup Onion
- 1/2 cup Eggplant
- 1/2 cup Broccoli
- 1/2 cup Tomatoes
- 1/2 cup Cauliflower
- 1/2 cup Bell Peppers
- 1/2 cup Okra
- 1/2 cup Green Beans
- 1/2 cup Brussel Sprouts
- 1/2 cup Pumpkin
- 1/2 cup Low Sodium Vegetable Juice

Fruit

- 1 Medium Fruit (Apple, Orange, Banana, Peach, Pear, Nectarine, Banana, Plum, Kiwi)
- 1/2 cup Fresh or Frozen Fruit (Cherries, Berries, Mango, Pineapple, Kiwi, Grapes, Melon)
- 1/4 cup Dried Fruit
- 1/2 cup 100% Fruit Juice

Dairy

- 1 cup Low Fat Milk
- 1/2 cup Low Fat Yogurt
- 1/2 cup Low Fat Cottage Cheese (low sodium)
- 1 1/2 ounces Low Fat Cheese

Protein

- 1 ounce Chicken
- 1 ounce Turkey
- 1 ounce Basa
- 1 ounce Cod
- 1 ounce Mahi Mahi
- 1 ounce Pollock
- 1 ounce Tilapia
- 1 ounce Fresh Tuna
- 1 ounce Wahoo
- 1 ounce Whitefish
- 1 ounce Salmon
- 1 ounce Oysters
- 1 ounce Mackerel
- 1 ounce Herring
- 1 ounce Shrimp
- 1 ounce Mussels
- 1 ounce Pork loin
- 1 ounce Grass-Fed Beef
- 1 ounce Antelope
- 1 ounce Elk
- 1 ounce Venison
- 1 ounce Ostrich
- 1 egg
- 1/2 cup Tofu
- 1/2 cup Tempeh
- 4 ounce Pea Protein Burger/Veggie Burger

Nuts, Seeds, Beans, and Legumes

- 1/3 cup or 1 1/2 ounces Almonds (unsalted)
- 1/3 cup or 1 1/2 ounces Pistachios (unsalted)
- 1/3 cup or 1 1/2 ounces Cashews (unsalted)
- 1/3 cup or 1 1/2 ounces Walnuts (unsalted)
- 1/3 cup or 1 1/2 ounces Peanuts (unsalted)
- 1/3 cup or 1 1/2 ounces Other Nuts (unsalted)
- 2 tablespoons Peanut Butter
- 2 tablespoons Almond Butter
- 2 tablespoons Tahini
- 2 tablespoons or 1/2 ounce Chia Seeds
- 2 tablespoons or 1/2 ounce Flax Seeds
- 2 tablespoons or 1/2 ounce Hemp Seeds
- 2 tablespoons or 1/2 ounce Sunflower Seeds
- 2 tablespoons or 1/2 ounce Sesame Seeds
- 2 tablespoons or 1/2 ounce Other Seeds
- 1/2 cup Cooked Beans
- 1/2 cup Green Beans
- 1/2 cup Cooked Lentils

Sweets and Added Sugar

- 1 tablespoon Sugar
- 1 tablespoon Raw sugar
- 1 tablespoon Brown sugar
- 1 tablespoon Honey
- 1 tablespoon Maple Syrup
- 1 tablespoon Molasses
- 1 tablespoon Agave
- 1 tablespoon Jelly or Jam
- 1/2 cup Sorbet
- 1/2 cup Frozen Yogurt
- 1/2 cup Pudding
- 1/2 cup Jello
- 1 small Low Fat Muffin
- 1 ounce Dark Chocolate
- 1 cup Lemonade

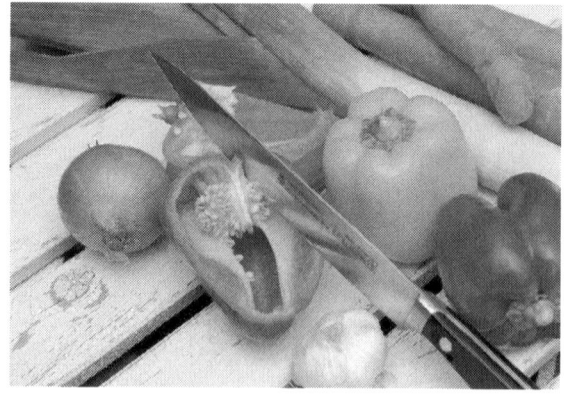

Butter, Oil, and Other Fats

- 1/3 Avocado
- 1 teaspoon Soft Margarine
- 1 teaspoon Olive Oil
- 1 teaspoon Avocado Oil
- 1 teaspoon Canola Oil
- 1 teaspoon Other Oil
- 1 tablespoon Mayonnaise
- 2 tablespoons Salad Dressing (full fat)

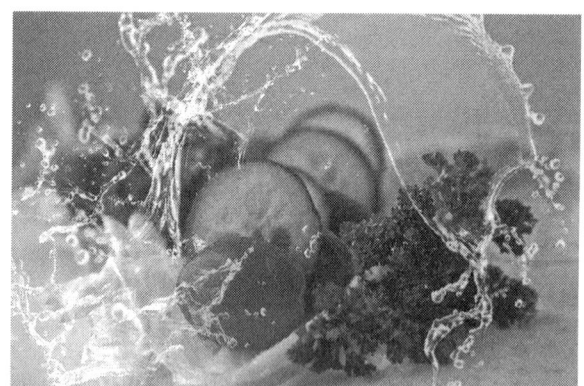

1.10. 4 Week DASH Diet Meal Plan

Join this meal schedule for the next month for a real DASH experience. Per day, it plans out breakfast, lunch , snack, dinner, and dessert, using recipes and following DASH guidelines. The diet is based on 2,000 calories a day, and the italicized parentheses give a change to 1,200 calories per day. Even though water is not mentioned as part of each diet, it is still advised to drink plenty of water. Dividing your weight in half and consuming as many ounces of water a day is a good method for measuring minimum water consumption. A 130-pound woman, for example, can drink 65 ounces of water every day (at least eight 8-ounce glasses).

DAY 1
BREAKFAST
Blueberry Green Smoothie,
2 slices 100% whole wheat toast (1 slice) with 2 tablespoons peanut butter (1 tablespoon)
LUNCH
1 serving Insalata di Farro (3/4 serving)
8 ounces nonfat milk
1 medium orange (small)
SNACK
1 cup cherries (1/2 cup)
20 almonds (10 almonds)
DINNER
1 serving Healthy Italian Pasta Salad (1/2 serving),
5 ounces grilled or baked boneless, skinless chicken breast (3 ounces)
1 cup frozen grapes (1/2 cup)

DAY 2
BREAKFAST
1 Egg Muffin
1/2 grapefruit
Coffee with 4 ounces nonfat milk, or green tea with lemon
LUNCH
1 serving Broccoli Soup, topped with grated Parmesan cheese (no cheese)
1/4 cup hummus (2 tablespoons) with baby carrots and sliced bell pepper
1 cup strawberries
SNACK
8 ounces nonfat plain Greek yogurt (4 ounces) with ½ cup blueberries
DINNER
4 Turkey Meatballs in Marinara Sauce (3 meatballs),
1 cup steamed spinach with garlic and 1 teaspoon extra virgin olive oil
1 slice 100% whole wheat bread
2 slices fresh pineapple (1 slice)
6–8 ounces sparkling water

DAY 3
BREAKFAST
2 slices Toast with Almond Butter and Banana (1 slice)
8 ounces nonfat milk, or coffee with up to 8 ounces nonfat milk
LUNCH
2 servings Mexican Summer Salad (1 1/2 cups)
1/2 sliced avocado
20 almonds (10 almonds)
1 medium peach (small)
SNACK
1 medium apple, sliced, with 2 tablespoons peanut butter or almond butter (1 tablespoon)
DINNER
1 serving Stuffed Bell Pepper (1/2 serving)
1 cup steamed broccoli
1 serving Grown-Up Berry Parfait, (1 serving Berry Sundae)

DAY 4
BREAKFAST
1 serving Berries Deluxe Oatmeal
LUNCH
1 serving Grilled Romaine Salad with 1 tablespoon Garlicky Balsamic Vinaigrette
4 ounces baked boneless, skinless chicken breast (2 ounces)
1/2 100% whole wheat pita bread
1 banana (1/2 banana)
SNACK
1/2 cup nonfat cottage cheese with 1/2 cup sliced cucumbers and cherry tomatoes
1 medium orange (small)
DINNER
1 serving Sesame Salmon Fillets (1/2 serving),
1 cup baked sweet potato (1/2 cup)
1 cup steamed spinach
1 Grilled Peach with Ricotta Stuffing and Balsamic Glaze
(1/2 grilled peach with cinnamon, no ricotta or glaze)

DAY 5
BREAKFAST
1 serving Banana Almond Smoothie,
2 slices 100% whole wheat bread (1 slice)
2 ounces goat cheese (1 ounce)
LUNCH
1 serving Tuna Salad (1/2 serving), with 1 ½ cups spinach
1/2 sliced avocado (1/4 avocado)
1/2 cup cherry tomatoes
1 cup mixed berries
SNACK
2 multigrain rice cakes (1 rice cake)
1/4 cup hummus (2 tablespoons)
DINNER
1 serving Thai Curried Vegetables,

1 cup brown rice (1/2 cup)
1/2 cup strawberries with 1 tablespoon homemade Whipped Cream (no whipped cream)

DAY 6
BREAKFAST
1 serving Warm Quinoa with Berries,
1 tablespoon sliced almonds (1 teaspoon)
Coffee with 8 ounces nonfat milk, or tea
LUNCH
1 Chicken Fajita Wrap (1/2 wrap)
1/4 cup Tropical Salsa,
1 medium orange (small)
SNACK
2 ounces mozzarella cheese (1 ounce)
1/2 cup grapes (1/4 cup)
DINNER
2 Fish Tacos (1 taco),
1 cup Anna's Black Beans (1/2 cup),
1/2 cup Tropical Salsa (1/4 cup),
2 slices Grilled Pineapple (1 slice)

DAY 7
BREAKFAST
1 serving Tropical Smoothie,
1 100% whole wheat English muffin (1/2 muffin) with 2 tablespoons peanut butter or almond butter (1 tablespoon)
LUNCH
1 serving Italian Veggie Pita Sandwich, with 4 ounces grilled or baked boneless, skinless chicken breast (2 ounces)
8 ounces nonfat milk (4 ounces)
1/2 cup grapes
SNACK
1/4 cup hummus (2 tablespoons) with sliced bell pepper and cucumber
DINNER
2 Grilled Chicken Skewers Marinated in Ginger-Apricot Sauce (1 skewer),
1 cup brown rice (1/2 cup)
1 cup Roasted Cauliflower,
1 Brie-Stuffed Apple (no brie)

DAY 8
BREAKFAST
1 serving Fruity Yogurt Parfait,
1 tablespoon almonds (1 teaspoon)
Coffee with 4 ounces nonfat milk (2 ounces)
LUNCH
1 serving Kale Vegetable Soup,
8 ounces nonfat milk
1 toasted cheese sandwich with reduced-fat mozzarella cheese on 1 slice 100% whole wheat bread (no sandwich)
SNACK
1/4 cup Hummus Dip with Curried Pita Chips (2 tablespoons),
1/2 cup grapes (1/4 cup)
DINNER
2 slices Mexican Pizza (1 slice)
1 serving Beet and Heirloom Tomato Salad (1/2 serving)
1 cup Macerated Strawberries with Homemade Whipped Cream (no whipped cream),

DAY 9
BREAKFAST
1 Open-Faced Breakfast Sandwich (no cheese),
8 ounces nonfat milk, or coffee with up to 8 ounces nonfat milk
1 cup mixed berries
LUNCH
1 serving Healthy Cobb Salad with 1 tablespoon Basic Vinaigrette,
1 100% whole wheat pita bread (no pita bread)
1 medium apple (small)
SNACK
1 cup air-popped popcorn with 1 teaspoon butter (no butter)
1 medium orange (small)
DINNER
1 Grilled Portobello Burger with Caramelized Onions and Pesto (light pesto)
1 serving Grilled Sweet Potato Steak Fries (1/2 serving)
1 serving Banana Chocolate Dessert Smoothie (1/2 serving),

DAY 10
BREAKFAST
1 serving Mediterranean Scramble (2 egg whites only)
Coffee with up to 8 ounces nonfat milk
1 slice 100% whole wheat bread (no bread)
1/2 cup grapes
LUNCH
1 serving Asian Quinoa Salad (1/2 serving),
1/2 cup baby carrots
1 medium peach (small)
SNACK
20 almonds (10 almonds)
1 banana
DINNER
1 serving Orange Chicken (1/2 serving) and 1 cup Brown Rice (1/2 cup)
1 cup steamed spinach
1 serving Berry Cobbler, (1/2 cup mixed berries)

DAY 11
BREAKFAST
1 serving English Muffin with Berries,
1 hard-boiled egg
Coffee with up to 8 ounces nonfat milk
LUNCH
1 serving Pomegranate Salad, with 2 tablespoons Garlicky Balsamic Vinaigrette (1 tablespoon)
1 100% whole wheat pita bread (1/2 pita bread)
1 medium peach (small)
SNACK
1/4 cup Hummus Dip (2 tablespoons), with baby carrots and sliced bell pepper
DINNER
1 serving Baked Sunflower Seed–Crusted Turkey Cutlets

(1/2 serving)
1 1/2 cups roasted mixed vegetables, such as broccoli, green beans, and asparagus
1 medium baked sweet potato (1/2 medium) with
1 tablespoon butter (no butter)
1 serving Mexican Fruit Salad (1/2 serving)

DAY 12
BREAKFAST
1 serving Protein Bowl (1/2 serving)
2 slices 100% whole wheat toast (1 slice) with 2 tablespoons 100% fruit jam (1 tablespoon) Green tea
LUNCH
1 serving Greek Salad with 1 tablespoon Lemon Vinaigrette, with 4 ounces grilled or baked boneless, skinless chicken breast (2 ounces)
1 medium apple (small)
20 almonds (10 almonds)
SNACK
8 ounces nonfat plain yogurt (4 ounces)
1 cup mixed berries
DINNER
1 serving Thai Curried Vegetables, with 3 ounces baked or grilled boneless, skinless chicken breast
(2 ounces)
1 cup brown rice (1/2 cup)
1 Mini Banana Split (1/2 mini split),

DAY 13
BREAKFAST
1 serving Wake Up Call! smoothie
1 hard-boiled egg
1 slice 100% whole wheat toast
LUNCH
2 Beef Tacos (1 taco),
1/4 cup Grandma's Guacamole (2 1/2 tablespoons)
1 medium orange (small)
SNACK
1 100% whole wheat English muffin (1/2 muffin) with 2 tablespoons peanut butter or almond butter (1 tablespoon) and 1 sliced banana (1/2 banana)
DINNER
1 serving Spice-Rubbed Salmon (1/2 serving)
1 1/2 cups Sautéed Vegetables,
1 cup Cilantro-Lime Brown Rice (1/2 cup)
1 cup frozen grapes

DAY 14
BREAKFAST
2 Egg Muffins,
1 100% whole wheat English muffin (1/2 muffin) with 2 tablespoons goat cheese (2 teaspoons)
1/2 grapefruit
LUNCH
1 serving Grilled Chicken with Black Bean Salsa (1/2 serving)
1 1/2 cups green salad with 1 tablespoon Garlicky Balsamic Vinaigrette,
2 corn tortillas (1 tortilla)
1 cup grapes

SNACK
1/4 cup raw unsalted nuts (2 tablespoons)
1 medium apple (small)
DINNER
1 serving Turkey Chili,
1 serving Beet and Heirloom Tomato Salad,
1 100% whole wheat pita bread (1/2 pita bread)
1 serving Berry Cobbler, (1 cup mixed berries)

DAY 15
BREAKFAST
1 serving Berry Banana Green Smoothie,
Coffee with up to 8 ounces nonfat milk (4 ounces)
1 slice 100% whole wheat toast with 1 tablespoon 100% fruit raspberry jam (no toast, no jam)
LUNCH
1 serving Tuna Salad, topped with 1/2 sliced avocado (1/4 avocado)
1/2 100% whole wheat pita bread (no pita)
1 medium orange (small)
SNACK
1 medium, sliced apple (small)
2 tablespoons peanut butter (1 tablespoon)
DINNER
1 serving Turkey Chili (1/2 serving), with 2 tablespoons shredded cheddar cheese (1 tablespoon)
Small spinach salad with assorted veggies, like tomato, cucumber, carrot, bell pepper, and 2 tablespoons Basic Vinaigrette (1 tablespoon),
1 serving Berry Sundae,

DAY 16
BREAKFAST
1 Healthy "Lox" English Muffin (1/2 muffin),
1/2 grapefruit
Coffee with up to 8 ounces nonfat milk (4 ounces)
LUNCH
1 serving Roasted Butternut Squash Soup (1/2 serving)
1/2 cup sliced strawberries
1 cup baby carrots
SNACK
8 ounces nonfat plain yogurt (6 ounces)
1/2 cup blueberries
1/4 cup almonds (2 tablespoons)
DINNER
2 Fish Tacos (1 taco)
1/2 cup Tropical Salsa (1/4 cup),
1 cup mixed berries with 2 tablespoons homemade Whipped Cream (no whipped cream),

DAY 17
BREAKFAST
2 slices Healthy French Toast (1 slice), with 2 tablespoons real maple syrup (1 tablespoon)
1/2 cup mixed berries
8 ounces nonfat milk (4 ounces)
LUNCH
1 serving Italian Veggie Pita Sandwich,
2 tablespoons hummus (1 tablespoon) with 1 cup baby carrots

1 medium peach (small)

SNACK
1 banana
1/4 cup raw unsalted cashews (2 tablespoons)

DINNER
1 serving Turkey Roulade with Cider Sauce (1/2 serving),
1 medium baked sweet potato (1/2 sweet potato)
1 cup steamed spinach
1 Brie-Stuffed Apple (no brie)

DAY 18
BREAKFAST
1 serving Green Avocado Smoothie,
Green tea
1/2 100% whole wheat English muffin with 2 tablespoons peanut butter (1 tablespoon)

LUNCH
1 Chicken Fajita Wrap (1/2 wrap),
1/2 cup Grandma's Guacamole (1/4 cup), with
1 cup baby carrots
1 medium orange (small)

SNACK
1/2 cup sliced strawberries
1/2 cup sliced banana

DINNER
1 serving Healthier Mac 'n' Cheese,
1 serving Greek Salad with 2 tablespoons Lemon Vinaigrette (1 tablespoon),
1/2 100% whole wheat pita bread (no pita)
1 serving Banana Chocolate Dessert Smoothie (1/2 serving),

DAY 19
BREAKFAST
Veggie Omelet,
1/2 cup mixed berries
Coffee with up to 8 ounces nonfat milk (4 ounces)

LUNCH
2 servings Chicken Pasta Salad (1 serving),
1 cup sliced carrot, bell pepper, and cucumber with
2 tablespoons Basic Vinaigrette (1 tablespoon),
1 medium pear (small)

SNACK
4 ounces nonfat cottage cheese
1/4 cup raw unsalted cashews (2 tablespoons)
1 medium sliced apple (small)

DINNER
1 serving Sesame Salmon Fillets (1/2 serving),
1 serving Grilled Asparagus,
1 cup brown rice (1/2 cup)
1 serving Grown-Up Berry Parfait (1/2 serving)

DAY 20
BREAKFAST
1 serving Melon Mélange smoothie,
1 serving Anna's Homemade Granola (1/2 serving)

LUNCH
1 serving Grilled Romaine Salad with 1 tablespoon Garlicky Balsamic Vinaigrette, and 3 ounces grilled boneless, skinless chicken breast (2 ounces)
1 cup grapes

SNACK
1 cup air-popped popcorn
1/2 cup baby carrots
1/2 sliced medium apple

DINNER
1 serving Turkey Meat Loaf,
1 medium mashed sweet potato (small) with 1 teaspoon butter (no butter)
1 serving Greek Salad with 1 tablespoon Lemon Vinaigrette,
1 cup mixed berries

DAY 21
BREAKFAST
1 serving Energy Oatmeal
8 ounces nonfat milk (4 ounces)
1/2 grapefruit

LUNCH
1 serving Healthy Cobb Salad with 1 tablespoon Basic Vinaigrette,
1/2 100% whole wheat pita bread (no pita)
1 cup grapes

SNACK
1/4 cup hummus with 1 cup cherry tomatoes, sliced bell pepper, and cucumber
2 tablespoons hazelnuts (1 tablespoon)

DINNER
2 slices Mexican Pizza (1 slice), with 5 ounces grilled or baked boneless, skinless chicken breast (3 ounces)
2 servings Greek Salad with 2 tablespoons Lemon Vinaigrette (1 tablespoon),
1 Grilled Peach with Ricotta Stuffing and Balsamic Glaze (1/2 grilled peach with cinnamon, no ricotta or glaze)

DAY 22
BREAKFAST
2 Whole Grain Pancakes (1 pancake), with 2 tablespoons real maple syrup (1 tablespoon)
Coffee with up to 8 ounces nonfat milk (4 ounces)
1/2 cup sliced strawberries

LUNCH
1 serving Italian-Style Tuna Salad (3/4 serving), with 1 1/2 cups spinach
1 medium kiwifruit

SNACK
1 serving Blueberry Green Smoothie,

DINNER
1 serving Chicken Fajitas (no avocado sauce), with 3 corn tortillas (2 tortillas)
1/4 cup Grandma's Guacamole (2 tablespoons),
1/2 cup Anna's Black Beans (1/4 cup),
1 cup Mexican Fruit Salad (1/2 cup),

DAY 23
BREAKFAST
1 serving Berry Banana Green Smoothie,

1/2 100% whole wheat English muffin with 1 tablespoon goat cheese (no muffin, no cheese)
Coffee with up to 8 ounces nonfat milk (4 ounces)

LUNCH
6 ounces Grilled Chicken with Black Bean Salsa (3 ounces)
Tomato and cucumber salad with 2 tablespoons Basic Vinaigrette (1 tablespoon)
1 medium peach (small)

SNACK
1 medium banana with 2 tablespoons peanut butter (1 tablespoon)

DINNER
Grilled Portobello Burger with Caramelized Onions and Pesto,
1 serving Grilled Sweet Potato Steak Fries (1/2 serving),
3/4 cup Macerated Strawberries with Homemade Whipped Cream (no whipped cream),

DAY 24
BREAKFAST
1 serving Protein Bowl,
1/2 grapefruit
Green tea

LUNCH
2 cups Anna's Black Beans, with 1 tablespoon sour cream (no sour cream)
Small salad with 1 cup mixed greens, cherry tomatoes, and sliced cucumber
1 medium orange

SNACK
1/4 cup Grandma's Guacamole (2 tablespoons), with 1 cup baby carrots and sliced bell pepper

DINNER
1 serving Pan-Steamed Orange Roughy (1/2 serving),
1 cup steamed spinach
6 small roasted red potatoes (3 small potatoes)
1 serving Mini Banana Split, (small banana with
1 tablespoon chocolate)

DAY 25
BREAKFAST
1 serving Apples and Cinnamon Oatmeal,
1 hard-boiled egg
8 ounces nonfat milk

LUNCH
1 serving Curried Chicken Salad Pita Sandwich (1/2 serving),
1 cup baby carrots and sliced bell peppers
1 cup cherries

SNACK
8 ounces nonfat plain yogurt (6 ounces)
1 cup mixed berries
20 almonds (10 almonds)

DINNER
2 servings Roasted Butternut Squash Soup (1 serving), topped with 1 tablespoon low-fat yogurt (no yogurt)
1 serving Brussels Sprouts Casserole (no pancetta),
1 serving Pomegranate Salad, with 2 tablespoons dressing (1 tablespoon)
1 Delicious Oatmeal Cookie (no cookie),

DAY 26
BREAKFAST
1 serving Warm Quinoa with Berries (no pecans),
8 ounces nonfat milk

LUNCH
1 serving Insalata di Farro, with 4 ounces grilled or baked boneless, skinless chicken breast (2 ounces)
1 medium orange (small)

SNACK
1 piece light string cheese
1 cup grapes (3/4 cup)

DINNER
4 Turkey Meatballs in Marinara Sauce (3 meatballs),
1 serving Greek Salad with 1 tablespoon Lemon Vinaigrette,
1 serving Brandied Peaches and Apples with Caramel Pecans, (1 cup sliced peaches and apples)

DAY 27
BREAKFAST
1 serving Peach Green Smoothie,
1/2 100% whole wheat English muffin with 2 tablespoons peanut butter (no English muffin, no peanut butter)
Coffee with up to 8 ounces nonfat milk (4 ounces)

LUNCH
1/2 cup black beans with 2 corn tortillas and 2 tablespoons cheddar cheese, 1/4 cup salsa, 1/2 sliced avocado (no cheese, 1/4 avocado)
Small spinach salad with 1 cup diced bell pepper, cucumber, and grape tomatoes
2 tablespoons Basic Vinaigrette (1 tablespoon),

SNACK
20 hazelnuts (10 hazelnuts)
8 ounces nonfat plain yogurt (4 ounces)
1/2 cup sliced strawberries

DINNER
1 serving Baked Sunflower Seed–Crusted Turkey Cutlets (1/2 serving),
1 serving Brussels Sprouts Casserole (no pancetta),
1 medium baked sweet potato (1/2 sweet potato)
1 serving Berry Cobbler, (1/2 cup blueberries)

DAY 28
BREAKFAST
1 serving Pumpkin Pie Smoothie, with 1 tablespoon peanut butter, either mixed in or separate

1 slice 100% whole wheat bread with 1 tablespoon goat cheese (no bread, no cheese)
Coffee with up to 8 ounces nonfat milk (4 ounces)

LUNCH
1 serving Mom's Bean Soup (no cheese),
1/2 cup cherry tomatoes
1/2 cup baby carrots
1 medium apple (small)

SNACK

8 ounces nonfat plain yogurt
1 medium banana
20 almonds (10 almonds)

DINNER
6 ounces baked boneless, skinless chicken breast (3 ounces)
1 serving Caprese Salad with Balsamic Glaze (1/2 serving),
4 small roasted red potatoes (2 small potatoes)
2 Healthy Mini Cheesecakes with Vanilla Wafer Almond Crust (1 mini cheesecake)

Chapter 2: Breakfast & Smoothie Recipes

In this chapter, we have compiled breakfast and smoothie recipes that can be enjoyed on the DASH Diet and will help in lowering blood pressure.

1. Very Berry Muesli
(Ready in 10 min | Serve: 2 | Difficulty: Easy)

Ingredients
- 1 cup old-fashioned rolled oats (raw)
- 1 cup fruit yogurt
- 1/2 cup 1% milk
- Pinch of salt
- 1/2 cup dried fruit (try raisins, apricots, dates)
- 1/2 cup chopped apple
- 1/2 cup frozen blueberries
- 1/4 cup chopped, toasted walnuts

Directions:
1. Mix the oatmeal, yogurt, milk, and salt in a medium dish.
2. For 6-12 hours cover and refrigerate.
3. Gently blend and add dried and fresh berries.
4. In little bowls, serve scoops of muesli. Sprinkle with chopped nuts for each meal.
5. Leftovers can be refrigerated within 2-3 hours.

2. Veggie Quiche Muffins
(Ready in 30 min | Serve: 12 | Difficulty: Normal)

Ingredients
- 3/4 cup low-fat cheddar cheese, shredded
- 1 cup green onion or onion, chopped
- 1 cup broccoli, chopped
- 1 cup tomatoes, diced
- 2 cups nonfat or 1% milk
- 4 eggs
- 1 cup baking mix (for biscuits or pancakes)
- 1 teaspoon Italian seasoning (or dried leaf basil and oregano)
- 1/2 teaspoon salt
- 1/2 teaspoon pepper

Directions:
1. Heat the oven to 375°C. Lightly spray 12 muffin cups or grease them.

2. Sprinkle the muffin cups with cheese, mushrooms, broccoli, and tomatoes.
3. In a cup, put the rest of the ingredients and beat until smooth. In muffin cups, spill the egg mixture over the other ingredients.
4. Bake for 35-40 minutes, until golden brown or until the knife inserted in the middle comes out clean. Cool for five minutes.
5. Leftovers should be refrigerated within 2 hours.

3. Turkey Sausage and Mushroom Strata

(Ready in 35 min| Serve: 12|Difficulty: Normal)

Ingredients

- 8 ounces wheat ciabatta bread, cut into 1-inch cubes
- 12 ounces turkey sausage (can be found in the frozen section)
- 2 cups of fat-free milk
- 1-1/2 cup (4 ounces) reduced-fat shredded sharp cheddar cheese
- 3 large eggs
- 12 ounces egg substitute
- ½ cup chopped green onion
- 1 cup sliced mushrooms
- ½ teaspoon paprika
- Fresh ground pepper to taste
- 2 tablespoons grated parmesan cheese

Directions:

1. Preheat the oven to 400 F.
2. On a baking sheet, arrange the bread cubes. Bake for 8 minutes at 400° or until toasted.
3. Over medium-high pressure, heat a medium skillet. Add sausage to pan; fry, stirring to crumble, for 7 minutes or until browned.
4. In a big cup, combine the milk, butter, eggs, egg replacer, parmesan cheese, paprika, salt, and pepper and stir with a fork.
5. Attach the bread, bacon, mushrooms, and scallions and toss well to cover the bread into a 13-9-inch baking bowl, spoon blend. Cover and refrigerate overnight or for 8 hours.
6. Preheat the oven to 350 .
7. Uncover the saucepan. Bake for 50 minutes at 350 ° or until set and lightly browned. Break into 12 pieces; quickly serve.

4. Sweet Millet Congee

(Ready in 35 min| Serve: 8|Difficulty: Normal)

Ingredients

- 8 strips of bacon
- 1 cup hulled millet
- 5 cups of water
- 1 cup sweet potato, peeled and diced
- 2 teaspoons ginger, minced (optional)
- 1 teaspoon ground cinnamon
- 2 Tablespoons brown sugar
- 1 medium apple, diced with skin
- ¼ cup honey

Directions:

1. Cook the bacon in a skillet until crispy, over medium-high heat. To extract extra fat, remove it from the pan and blot it with a paper towel. Crumble the bacon strips until cooled, and set aside.
2. Rinse the millet and drain it.
3. In a deep bath, blend the millet, water, sweet potato, ginger, cinnamon, and brown sugar. Put to a boil, reduce heat to low, and simmer until water is absorbed, stirring regularly (about 1 hour).
4. If the millet has been baked, remove the pot from the heat and add crumbles of apple, honey, and bacon.
5. Method of slow cooking: Minimize water by 1 cup and cook 2 to 2½ hours on high.

5. Summer Breakfast Quinoa Bowls

(Ready in 35 min| Serve: 2|Difficulty: Normal)

Ingredients

- 1 small peach, sliced
- 1/3 cup uncooked quinoa, rinsed well
- 2/3 + 3/4 cup low-fat milk
- 1/2 teaspoon vanilla extract
- 2 teaspoons brown sugar
- 12 raspberries
- 14 blueberries
- 2 teaspoons honey

Directions:

1. Combine the quinoa, 2/3 cup milk, vanilla, and brown sugar in the saucepan.
2. Cook and bring to a boil for five minutes over medium heat. Lower the heat to low and cover-up. Cook for 15 to 20 minutes or before the fork fluffs quickly.
3. Meanwhile, the grill pan is heated and sprayed with grease. Grill the peaches for 2 to 3 minutes to bring out their sweetness; set aside. In the refrigerator, melt the leftover milk.
4. Divide the cooked quinoa into 2 containers, then add the warmed milk into them. Drizzle each with 1 teaspoon of honey and finish with peaches, raspberries, and blueberries.

6. Strawberry Breakfast Sandwich (Halves)

(Ready in 35 min| Serve: 8|Difficulty: Normal)

Ingredients

- 8 ounces Neufchatel cheese or low-fat cream cheese, softened
- 1 tablespoon honey
- 1 teaspoon grated Lemon zest
- 4 English muffins, split and toasted
- 2 cups (about 10 ounces) sliced strawberries

Directions:

1. Process cheese, honey, and zest in a food processor until well combined, or combine with a wooden spoon in a cup.

2. On the cut side of 1 half muffin, spread 1 tablespoon cheese mixture; top with 1 quarter cup strawberries.
3. To produce 8 half-sandwiches, repeat with the remaining ingredients.

7. Steel Cut Oat Blueberry Pancakes

(Ready in 35 min| Serve: 12|Difficulty: Normal)

Ingredients

- 1-1/2 cups water
- ½ cup steel cut oats
- 1/8 teaspoon sea salt
- 1 cup whole wheat flour
- ½ teaspoon baking powder
- ½ teaspoon baking soda
- 1 egg
- 1 cup milk
- ½ cup Greek yogurt, vanilla flavor
- 1 cup frozen blueberries
- ½ cup + 2 tablespoons agave nectar

Directions:

1. Bring water to a boil in a medium pot and apply steel-cut oats and salt. Reduce heat to a low simmer and cook for about 10 minutes until the oats are tender. Delete and set aside from the sun.
2. Combine the whole wheat pastry flour, baking powder, soda, egg, milk, and yogurt in a medium mixing dish. Mix so it shapes a batter. Gently fold in the cooked oats and blueberries.
3. Heat a medium-heated griddle or nonstick skillet and brush with cooking oil. Spoon a quarter cup of batter on the surface and cook until the pancakes start bubbling and are mildly brown, around 2-3 minutes per hand, if possible, operating in batches.
4. Garnish with about one tablespoon of agave nectar for each pancake.

8. Spinach, Mushroom, and Feta Cheese Scramble

(Ready in 35 min| Serve: 1|Difficulty: Normal)

Ingredients

- Cooking spray
- ½ cup fresh mushrooms, sliced
- 1 cup fresh spinach, chopped
- 1 whole egg and 2 egg whites
- 2 tablespoons feta cheese
- Pepper to taste

Directions:

1. Over medium prepare, heat an 8-inch nonstick sauté tray. Using cooking spray to spray and apply mushrooms and spinach.
2. Sauté the spinach and mushrooms for 2-3 minutes or before the spinach wilts.
3. If needed, whisk the egg and egg whites into a bowl of feta cheese and pepper. Pour the egg mixture into the pan over the vegetables.
4. Continue to cook the eggs for another 3-4 minutes while stirring with a spatula or until the eggs are cooked through.

9. Refrigerator Overnight Oatmeal

(Ready in 15 min| Serve: 2|Difficulty: Normal)

Ingredients

- 1 cup old fashion oatmeal, uncooked
- 1 cup nonfat vanilla yogurt
- ½ cup nonfat milk
- 1 cup frozen blueberries
- 1 Tablespoon chia seeds

Directions:

1. Place all ingredients in a mixing bowl and mix well.
2. Spoon the oatmeal mixture into two small containers and cover with a fitted lid. Place in the refrigerator.
3. Let the oatmeal sit overnight in the refrigerator. Enjoy your overnight oatmeal the next morning as a cold breakfast treat.

10. Red Velvet Pancakes with Cream Cheese Topping

(Ready in 25 min| Serve: 5|Difficulty: Normal)

Ingredients

Cream Cheese Topping:

- 2 ounces 1/3 less fat cream cheese
- 3 tablespoons plain fat-free yogurt
- 3 tablespoons honey
- 1 tablespoon fat-free milk

Pancakes:

- ½ cup white whole wheat flour
- ½ cup unbleached all-purpose flour
- 2 ¼ teaspoons baking powder
- ½ tablespoon unsweetened cocoa powder
- ¼ teaspoon salt
- ¼ cup of sugar
- 1 large egg
- 1 cup + 2 tablespoons fat-free milk
- 1 teaspoon vanilla
- ½ teaspoon red paste food coloring

Directions:

1. Mix and set aside the cream cheese topping ingredients.
2. In a big bowl, combine the flour, baking powder, chocolate powder, sugar, and salt together.
3. Dissolve the food coloring with the milk in another one; whisk in the egg and vanilla.
4. Until there are no more dry spots, blend wet and dry ingredients, careful not to mix over.
5. On a medium-low fire, heat a large nonstick griddle pan. Spray lightly with oil to cover when wet, and spill ¼ cup of the pancake batter into the pan.

6. Flip the pancakes as soon as the pancake begins to bubble, and the edges start to set. Repeat for the batter left.
7. Place 2 pancakes on each plate to eat, then finish with approximately 2,1/2 tablespoons of cream cheese topping.

11. Perfect Granola
(Ready in 25 min| Serve: 24|Difficulty: Easy)

Ingredients
- ¼ cup canola oil
- 4 tablespoons honey
- 1 ½ teaspoons vanilla
- 6 c rolled oats (old fashioned)
- 1 cup almonds, slivered
- ½ cup unsweetened coconut, shredded
- 2 cups bran flakes
- 3/4 cup walnuts, chopped
- 1 cup raisins
- Cooking spray or parchment paper

Directions:
1. Preheat the oven to 325°C.
2. In a small saucepan, put the oil, honey, and vanilla together. Cook gently over low heat, stirring regularly, or until mixed, for 5 minutes.
3. Place the remaining ingredients in a large mixing cup, except for the raisins, and combine well. Stir in the oil-honey mixture gently, ensuring the grains are uniformly covered.
4. A baking tray is lightly coated with cooking spray or filled with parchment paper. Bake in the oven for 25 minutes or until the grains are crisp and very lightly browned. Scatter the cereal over the baking tray. To keep the mixture from burning, stir regularly.
5. Remove from the oven the cereal and allow it to cool. Attach raisins and stir into the grain mixture uniformly.

12. Peanut Butter & Banana Breakfast Smoothie
(Ready in 15 min| Serve: 1|Difficulty: Easy)

Ingredients
- 1 cup nonfat milk
- 1 tablespoon all-natural peanut butter
- 1 medium banana, frozen or fresh

Directions:
1. Combine all ingredients in the blender, and blend until very smooth.

13. PB + J Yogurt
(Ready in 10 min| Serve: 1|Difficulty: Easy)

Ingredients
- 6 ounces fat-free plain Greek yogurt
- 4 teaspoons reduced sugar grape jelly
- 2 tablespoons red seedless grapes cut in half
- 1 tablespoon reduced-fat peanut butter
- 1 teaspoon unsalted peanuts

Directions:
1. Put it in a bowl with the yogurt.
2. Place jelly on top, then peanut butter.
3. Then scatter the peanuts and grapes gently over the top of the yogurt.

14. Overnight Oatmeal
(Ready in 8 to 9 hours| Serve: 8|Difficulty: Difficult)

Ingredients
- 4 cups fat-free milk
- 4 cups of water
- 2 cups steel-cut oats
- 1/3 cup raisins
- 1/3 cup dried cherries
- 1/3 cup dried apricots, chopped
- 1 teaspoon molasses
- 1 teaspoon cinnamon (or pumpkin pie spice)

Directions:
1. Toss all the ingredients into a slow cooker.
2. Switch down the sun. Put the lid on and simmer for 8 to 9 hours overnight.
3. Serve and spoon into bowls.

15. No-Bake Breakfast Granola Bars
(Ready in 20 min | Serve: 18|Difficulty: Easy)

Ingredients
- 2 1/2 cups toasted rice cereal
- 2 cups old fashioned oatmeal
- 1/2 cup raisins
- 1/2 cup firmly packed brown sugar
- 1/2 cup light corn syrup
- 1/2 cup peanut butter
- 1 teaspoon vanilla

Directions:
1. In a large mixing cup, combine the rice cereal, oatmeal, and raisins and stir with a wooden spoon.
2. Mix the brown sugar and corn syrup together in a 1-quart saucepan. Move the heat to medium-high heat. While the mixture is brought to a boil, stirring continuously. Remove the saucepan from the fire until it is boiling.
3. In the saucepan, whisk the peanut butter and vanilla into the sugar mixture. Blend until perfectly smooth.
4. In the mixing cup, pour the peanut butter mixture over the cereal and the raisins. Mix thoroughly.
5. Press a 9 x 13 baking pan with the mixture. Let it totally cool and cut into 18 bars.

16. Mushroom Shallot Frittata
(Ready in 15 min | Serve: 4|Difficulty: Easy)

Ingredients
- 1 tablespoon unsalted butter
- 4 shallots, finely chopped
- ½ pounds mushrooms, finely chopped
- 2 teaspoons fresh parsley, chopped

- 1 teaspoon dried thyme
- Black pepper to taste
- 3 eggs
- 5 large egg whites
- 1 tablespoon milk or fat-free half and half
- ¼ cup fresh parmesan cheese, grated

Directions:
1. Preheat the oven to 350°C.
2. Heat butter over medium heat in a large skillet that is ovenproof. Stir in the shallots and sauté for about 5 minutes, until golden. Connect the chopped mushrooms, parsley, black pepper, and thyme.
3. Combine the eggs, egg whites, Parmesan, and milk in a medium dish. To make sure that the eggs cover all the mushrooms, add the egg mixture to the skillet. Shift the skillet to the oven when the edges begin to set (approximately 2 minutes). Bake for 15 minutes or until all the frittata is thoroughly baked.
4. Serve warm. Slice into four equal wedges.

17. Morning Quinoa
(Ready in 15 min | Serve: 4|Difficulty: Easy)

Ingredients
- 2 cups low fat or nonfat milk
- 1 cup uncooked quinoa
- ¼ cup honey or brown sugar
- ¼ teaspoon cinnamon, plus more to taste
- ¼ cup sliced or slivered almonds
- ¼ cup dried currants, chopped dried apricots, or fresh berries

Directions:
1. Tightly clean the quinoa.
2. In a medium saucepan, put the milk to a boil. Attach the quinoa and put it to a boil again.
3. Cover, reduce heat to medium-low and boil until the liquid is mostly absorbed (about 12-15 minutes).
4. Remove with a fork from the heat and fluff. Add the remaining ingredients, cover, and let stand for around 15 minutes.

18. Jack-o-Lantern Pancakes
(Ready in 20 min | Serve: 8|Difficulty: Easy)

Ingredients
- 1 egg
- ½ cup canned pumpkin
- 1 ¾ cups low-fat milk
- 2 tablespoons vegetable oil
- 2 cups flour
- 2 tablespoons brown sugar
- 1 tablespoon baking powder
- 1 teaspoon pumpkin pie spice
- 1 teaspoon salt

Directions:
1. In a big mixing cup, combine the eggs, pumpkin, milk, and oil together.
2. To produce an egg mixture, add flour, brown sugar, baking powder, pumpkin pie seasoning, and salt. Stir quietly.
3. Cover a griddle or skillet lightly with cooking spray and heat over low heat.
4. Pour flour on the hot griddle using a 1⁄4 cup scale. Heat until the bubbles pop, turn over, and cook until the bubbles are golden brown.

19. Fruit-n-Grain Breakfast Salad
(Ready in 15 min | Serve: 6|Difficulty: Easy)

Ingredients
- 3 cups of water
- ¼ tsp. salt
- ¾ cup quick-cooking brown rice
- ¾ cup bulgur
- 1 Granny Smith apple
- 1 Red Delicious apple
- 1 orange
- 1 cup raisins
- 1 container (8 oz.) low-fat vanilla yogurt

Directions:
1. Heat the water and salt to boil in a large pot over high heat.
2. Add rice and bulgur and cook for 10 minutes, reduce heat to a minimum, cover, and cook.
3. Remove from the sun, set aside, and cover for 2 minutes.
4. To cool, scatter hot grains on the baking sheet (this will make them fluffier). It is easy to cook grains the night before and store them in the refrigerator.
5. Prepare the fruit just before serving: core and cut the apples. Peel and cut the orange into pieces.
6. To a medium mixing cup, pass the chilled grains and cut fruit. Until coated, stir the yogurt into the grains and fruit.

20. Fruit Pizza
(Ready in 2 hours| Serve: 2|Difficulty: Difficult)

Ingredients
- 1 English Muffin (try whole grain)
- 2 tablespoons reduced-fat or fat-free cream cheese (see notes)
- 2 tablespoons sliced strawberries
- 2 tablespoons blueberries
- 2 tablespoons crushed pineapple

Directions:
1. The English muffin is broken open, and the halves are toasted until finely browned.
2. Spread on both halves of cream cheese.
3. Break the fruit between the two halves of the muffin and layer it on top of the cream cheese.
4. When served fast, these are best.
5. Leftovers should be refrigerated within 2 hours.

21. Flax Banana Yogurt Muffins

(Ready in 30 min | serve: 12|Difficulty: normal)

Ingredients

- 1 cup whole wheat flour
- 1 cup old-fashioned rolled oats
- 1 teaspoon baking soda
- 2 tablespoon ground flaxseed
- 3 large bananas, mashed (~1.5 cups)
- ½ cup plain, 0% fat Greek yogurt
- ¼ cup unsweetened applesauce
- ¼ cup brown sugar
- 2 teaspoon vanilla extract

Directions:

1. To 355 Fahrenheit Pre-heat the oven
2. With either cupcake liners or cooking oil, prepare the muffin tin.
3. Combine the dried ingredients in a single dish (flour, oats, soda, and flaxseed).
4. The wet ingredients are combined in a separate bowl (banana, yogurt, applesauce, sugar, and vanilla)
5. Until only mixed, mix the dry ingredients into the wet ingredients. The batter ought to be lumpy. Do not mix over.
6. Bake for 20 to 25 minutes or until crumbs, not batter, fall out with a toothpick inserted into the middle of a muffin.

22. Eggs and Tomato Breakfast Melts

(Ready in 15 min | Serve: 4|Difficulty: Easy)

Ingredients

- 2 whole-grain English muffins, split
- 1 teaspoon olive oil
- 8 egg whites, whisked
- 4 scallions, finely chopped
- Kosher salt, to taste
- Black pepper, to taste
- 2 ounce (about 1/2 cup) reduced-fat Swiss cheese, shredded
- 1/2 cup grape or cherry heirloom tomatoes, quartered

Directions:

1. Preheat the elevated broiler. Place the muffins, cut side by side, on a baking sheet and broil on the edges for 2 minutes or until lightly browned. (Or this can be achieved in your toaster oven)
2. On low heat, heat a medium skillet. Apply the oil and fried 3 scallions for about 2 to 3 minutes. Attach the egg whites, season with salt and pepper, and simmer until heated through, alternating with a wooden spoon.
3. Divide and top with onions, cheese, and leftover scallions on toasted muffins.
4. Broil for 1 to 1 1/2 minutes or until the cheese is melted, and be careful not to smoke.

23. Crunchy Avocado, "Toast."

(Ready in 20 min | Serve: 1|Difficulty: Easy)

Ingredients

- 2 brown rice cakes, unsalted
- ½ small avocado
- Small tomato, sliced.
- Dried roasted red pepper flakes
- Pinch of salt

Directions:

1. Mash the avocado with a fork in a dish.
2. Uniformly scattered over rice cakes
3. As needed, add tomato slices
4. Sprinkle with flakes of roasted red pepper and a sprinkle of salt.

24. Broccoli and Cheese Mini Egg Omelets

(Ready in 25 min | Serve: 9|Difficulty: Easy)

Ingredients

- 4 cups broccoli florets
- 4 whole eggs
- 1 cup egg whites
- ¼ cup reduced-fat cheddar
- ¼ cup grated Romano or parmesan cheese
- 1 tablespoon olive oil
- salt and fresh pepper
- cooking spray

Directions:

1. Preheat the oven to 350 F. Steam the broccoli for around 6-7 minutes with a little water.
2. Mash the broccoli into smaller parts and add the olive oil, salt, and pepper when it is baked. Mix thoroughly.
3. With a cooking mist, spray the muffin tray and spoon the broccoli mixture equally into 9 tins.
4. Whip the egg whites, eggs, grated parmesan cheese, salt, and pepper in a medium bowl. Pour broccoli over the greased tins to a little more than 3/4 finished. Cover with grated cheddar and bake for about 20 minutes in the oven until baked. Immediately serve. To eat throughout the week, wrap some leftovers in plastic wrap and store them in the refrigerator.

26. Breakfast Sausage, Potato and Mushroom Strata

(Ready in 55 min | Serve: 8|Difficulty: Normal)

Ingredients

- 8 ounces whole-wheat bread, cut into 1-inch cubes
- 6 ounces turkey or chicken breakfast sausage
- 1 medium russet potato (peel optional) cut into ¼-inch slices
- 2 cups fat-free milk

- 1 ½ cup (4 ounces) reduced-fat shredded sharp cheddar cheese
- 3 large eggs
- 12-ounce egg substitute (such as Egg Beaters)
- ½ cup chopped green onions
- 1 cup sliced mushrooms
- ½ teaspoon paprika
- Dash of ground black pepper

Directions:
The night before you serve:
1. Preheat the oven to 400°C.
2. On a baking sheet, arrange the bread cubes.
3. Bake for 8 minutes at 400° or until toasted.
4. Over medium-high pressure, heat a medium skillet.
5. Add sausage to pan; fry, stirring to crumble, for 7 minutes or until browned.
6. In a big cup, mix the milk, cheese, eggs, egg replacement, paprika, and pepper and stir with a fork. Attach the bread, bacon, potatoes, mushrooms, and scallions and toss well to coat the bread into a 13-9-inch baking bowl, spoon blend. Cover and refrigerate overnight or for 8 hours.

During the morning:
1. Preheat the oven to 350.
2. Uncover the saucepan.
3. Bake for 50 minutes at 350° or until set and lightly browned.
4. Break into 8 pieces; quickly serve.

Breakfast Pumpkin Cookies
48 servings

Ingredients
- 1 ¾ cups cooked pureed pumpkin (15-ounce can)
- 1 ½ cups brown sugar
- 2 eggs
- ½ cup of vegetable oil
- 1 ½ cups flour
- 1 ¼ cups whole wheat flour
- 1 tablespoon baking powder
- 1 ½ teaspoons pumpkin pie spice mix
- ½ teaspoon salt
- 1 cup raisins
- 1 cup walnuts or hazelnuts, chopped

Directions:
1. Preheat oven to 400 F.
2. Mix pumpkin, brown sugar, eggs, and oil thoroughly. Blend dry ingredients and add to pumpkin mixture. Add raisins and nuts.
3. Drop by teaspoonfuls on the greased cookie sheet, 1 inch apart. Gently flatten each cookie (use a spoon, bottom of the glass, or the palm of your hand). Bake 10-12 minutes until golden brown.

27. Breakfast Green Smoothie
(Ready in 5 min I Serve: 1IDifficulty: Easy)

Ingredients
- 1 medium banana
- 1 cup baby spinach, packed
- 1/2 cup fat-free milk
- 1/4 cup whole oats
- 3/4 cup frozen mango
- 1/4 cup plain nonfat yogurt
- 1/2 teaspoon vanilla

Directions:
1. Blend the milk, yogurt, and oats in a blender at high speed for 15 seconds.
2. Add the pineapple, vanilla, spinach, and banana.
3. Blend until perfectly smooth.

28. Breakfast Bread Pudding
(Ready in 1hour 15 min I Serve: 4IDifficulty: Difficult)

Ingredients
- 1 1/2 cup low fat 1% or fat-free milk
- 4 eggs
- 2 tablespoons brown sugar
- 1/2 teaspoon vanilla extract
- 1/2 teaspoon ground cinnamon
- 1/8 teaspoon salt
- 3 cups cubed whole wheat bread, about 4 slices
- 1/2 cup peeled and diced apple
- 1/4 cup raisins
- 2 teaspoons powdered sugar (optional)

Directions:
1. Preheat the oven to 350°C.
2. Mix the milk, cheese, brown sugar, vanilla, cinnamon, and salt together in a big cup. Whisk before blended well.
3. Attach the bread cubes, the sliced apple, and the raisins and combine until all the ingredients are mixed, and most of the moisture is soaked in the bread.
4. Using nonstick spray or butter to coat an 8-inch square baking dish.
5. To the baking pan, move the bread mixture. Cover and bake with tape, or refrigerate for up to 24 hours.
6. Place the bread pudding in the oven and let it simmer for 40 minutes. Uncover and begin to bake, about 20 minutes more, until golden brown.
7. Before eating, let it rest for 10 minutes. If needed, sprinkle with powdered sugar.

29. Breakfast Banana Split
(Ready in 2 hoursI Serve: 2IDifficulty: Difficult)

Ingredients
- 1 small banana
- ½ teaspoon honey, optional (skip for children under the age of one)
- ½ cup canned pineapple tidbits or chunks
- ½ cup oat, corn, or granola cereal
- ½ cup low fat vanilla or strawberry yogurt

Directions:
1. Peel the banana and cut it lengthwise. Put half in two different bowls of cereal.

2. Sprinkle the banana with granola, reserving plenty for topping.
3. Spoon the top with yogurt and drizzle with butter.
4. Decorate it with reserved pineapple and granola.
5. Immediately serve.
6. Leftovers should be refrigerated within 2 hours.

30. Blueberry-Raspberry Gazpacho with Mint

(Ready in 15 min | Serve: 4|Difficulty: Easy)

Ingredients
- 1 ½ cups blueberries
- 1 ½ cups raspberries
- 2 tablespoons raw sugar or sweetener of your choice
- 1 tablespoon orange juice
- 1 teaspoon lemon juice
- 1 teaspoon lime juice
- 1 teaspoon lemon zest
- Fresh mint leaves for garnish
- Four scoops (1/4 cup each) fat-free Greek yogurt

Directions:
1. In a medium, heat-proof bowl, combine the berries with the sugar, orange, lemon, and lime juice and the lemon zest.
2. With plastic wrap, cover tightly.
3. Place the covered bowl over a large simmering water saucepan; cook for 10 minutes on low heat.
4. Set aside until the mixture cools. Refrigerate for about 4 hours until it is cold.
5. Divide the fruit and liquid into 4 bowls; top each bowl with a 1/4 cup scoop of Greek yogurt and garnish with fresh mint.

31. Berry Blast Off

(Ready in 10 min | Serve: 4|Difficulty: Easy)

Ingredients
- 1 cup rinsed strawberries, sliced
- 1 cup low-fat granola
- 1 cup rinsed blueberries or other fruit
- 1 cup plain, low-fat yogurt

Directions:
1. Put out four little bottles.
2. Between the bottles, split the strawberries.
3. Sprinkle over the strawberries with granola.
4. Divide the blueberries (or any other fruit) and add the granola on top.
5. On top of the blueberries, spoon the yogurt. Enjoy! Enjoy!

32. Banana Nut Pancakes

(Ready in 20 min | Serve: 6|Difficulty: Easy)

Ingredients
- 1 cup whole wheat flour
- 2 tsp. baking powder
- 1/4 tsp. salt
- 1/4 tsp. cinnamon
- 1 large banana, mashed
- 1 cup 1% milk
- 3 large egg whites
- 2 tsp. oil
- 1 tsp. vanilla
- 2 tbsp chopped walnuts

Directions:
1. In a large bowl, combine all the dried ingredients. In another cup, combine the milk, white egg, oil, vanilla, and mashed bananas and stir until smooth. Combine the wet and dry products and blend well with a spoon until there are no longer dry spots. Only don't over-mix.
2. On medium heat, heat a large skillet. Spray the cooking spray to cover the griddle gently. For any pancake, add 1/4 cup of pancake batter onto the heated griddle. Flip the pancakes as the batter begin to bubble, and the edges begin to set. Repeat for the batter left.

33. Baked Oatmeal

(Ready in 45 min | Serve: 8|Difficulty: Normal)

Ingredients
- 2 cups Quick Quaker Oats or 2 ¼ cups Old Fashioned Quaker Oats, uncooked
- 1/3 cup granulated sugar
- ¼ tsp. salt
- 3 1/3 cups fat-free milk
- 2 eggs or ½ cup egg substitute, lightly beaten
- 2 tsp. vanilla
- 1/3 cup firmly packed brown sugar

Directions:
1. Preheat the oven to 350oF. Spray with cooking spray on the 8-inch square glass baking bowl.
2. Combine the oats, the granulated sugar, and salt in a wide cup.
3. Combine the milk, eggs, and vanilla in a medium bowl; blend properly. Add to the oat mixture; blend well. Pour the baking bowl into it.
4. Bake for 40 to 45 minutes, or until the middle gently jiggles. Remove from the oven to the rack for cooling.
5. Sprinkle generously with brown sugar over the top of the oatmeal. Spread the sugar carefully into a thin layer on the whole surface of the oatmeal using the back of the spoon. Return to the oven; cook for around 2 to 3 minutes before the sugar melts.
6. Put the broiling oven on. Broil 3 inches from heat until sugar bubbles and browns slightly, 1 to 2 minutes. (Watch carefully to prevent burning. It may be necessary to rotate the baking dish.)
7. Spoon into bowls to serve.

34. Asparagus and Caramelized Onion Frittata

(Ready in 20 min | Serve: 4|Difficulty: Easy)

Ingredients
- 1 tsp. olive oil
- 1 medium onion, thinly sliced

- 2 tsp. balsamic vinegar
- 2 cups (about 1 bunch) asparagus, cut into 1-inch sections
- 3 green onions, sliced
- ¼ cup fresh basil, thinly sliced
- 6 large eggs
- ¼ cup plus 1 tbsp parmesan cheese, grated
- ½ tsp. kosher salt
- Fresh ground pepper to taste

Directions:
1. Preheat the broiler until it's high.
2. Heat an ovenproof 10 to 12-inch baking pan over low heat on the burner. Apply the olive oil and onions and simmer for about 5 minutes, until tender and slightly browned or caramelized. To mix with the onions, apply the balsamic vinegar and whisk. Add the asparagus and 2 tablespoons of water and cover for 4 minutes, stirring just halfway through, to steam the asparagus.
3. Meanwhile, in a medium bowl, whisk the eggs and mix in ¼ cup of the grated parmesan cheese, ¼ teaspoon of the Kosher salt, and a few twists of the ground fresh pepper.
4. For the cooked asparagus and onions, add the green onion, basil, and the remaining ¼ teaspoon of Kosher salt. Stir to blend.
5. Apply the asparagus and onions to the egg mixture, combine briefly with a spatula, and pull the fried egg from the bottom to the tip. Enable it to cook over medium heat for 2 minutes.
6. Place the pan under the broiler until it has bubbled and slightly browned for around 3 minutes.
7. Sprinkle with the remaining 1 tablespoon of parmesan cheese and let sit for about 5 minutes. Remove from the broiler. Switch to a cutting board the frittata from the bowl, break into 4 wedges, and serve.

35. Applesauce French Toast
(Ready in 20 min | Serve: 6|Difficulty: Easy)

Ingredients
- 2 eggs
- ½ cup milk
- 1 teaspoon ground cinnamon
- 2 tablespoons white sugar
- ¼ cup unsweetened applesauce
- 6 slices whole-wheat bread

Directions:
1. Mix the eggs, milk, cinnamon, sugar, and applesauce together in a big mixing cup. Mix thoroughly.
2. Soak the bread until the paste is partially drained, one slice at a time.
3. Cook over medium heat on a lightly greased skillet or griddle until both sides are golden brown.
Serve it wet.

36. Apple Spice Baked Oatmeal
(Ready in 2 hours | Serve: 9|Difficulty: Difficult)

Ingredients
- 1 egg, beaten
- ½ cup applesauce, sweetened
- 1 ½ cups nonfat or 1% milk
- 1 teaspoon vanilla
- 2 tablespoons oil
- 1 apple, chopped (about 1 ½ cups)
- 2 cups rolled oats
- 1 teaspoon baking powder
- ¼ teaspoon salt
- 1 teaspoon cinnamon

TOPPING
- 2 tablespoons brown sugar
- 2 tablespoons chopped nuts

Directions:
1. Preheat the oven to 375°C. Lightly grease an 8-inch x 8-inch baking pan or spray it.
2. In a cup, combine the sugar, applesauce, milk, vanilla, and oil together. You add an almond. Mix the rolled oats, baking powder, salt, and cinnamon into a separate dish. Attach and blend well with the liquid ingredients. Apply the mixture to the baking dish and cook for 25 minutes.
3. Remove and dust with brown sugar and nuts from the oven. Return to the oven and broil for 3 to 4 minutes before the surface and the sugar bubbles are browned. (During this phase, keep an eye on it to keep it from burning).
4. Split into squares of 9, 2.5 inches by 2.5 inches. Serve it sweet. Leftovers should be refrigerated within 2 hours.

37. Whole Wheat Pumpkin Pancakes
(Ready in 30 min | Serve: 8|Difficulty: Normal)

Ingredients
- 2 ½ cups whole-wheat pastry flour
- 2 tablespoons baking powder
- 2 teaspoons ground ginger
- 3 teaspoons cinnamon
- ¼ teaspoon ground cloves
- ¼ teaspoon nutmeg
- 2 eggs
- 2 cups low-fat buttermilk
- 1 cup pumpkin puree
- ¼ cup olive oil

Directions:
1. In a big cup, combine the flour, baking powder, ginger, nutmeg, cinnamon, cloves, and salt together.
2. In a separate dish, combine the eggs, pumpkin puree, olive oil, and buttermilk together.
3. To the first bowl, apply the wet ingredients from the second bowl. Mix once merely incorporated.
4. Over low flame, heat a griddle. Pour ¼ cup of the pancake batter and cook until, with the sides set, you can see tiny bubbles.
5. Flip until golden brown and cook.

38. Sweet Potato Cakes
(Ready in 1 hour 10 min| Serve: 2|Difficulty: Difficult)

Ingredients
- 4 cups shredded peeled sweet potato (about 1 pound)
- 1/4 cup whole wheat flour
- 1 teaspoon instant minced onion
- 1/8 teaspoon salt
- 1/8 teaspoon pepper
- Dash of ground nutmeg
- 1 large egg, lightly beaten
- Cooking spray

Directions:
1. In a dish, mix all ingredients with the exception of cooking spray; stir well.
2. Using cooking spray to grease a nonstick griddle or large nonstick skillet. On a hot griddle or skillet, spoon around 1/4 cup of the mixture; flatten slightly with a spatula.
3. Cook on both sides for 4 minutes or until golden brown.

39. Orange-Blueberry Swirl
(Ready in 1 hour 45 min | Serve: 1|Difficulty: Difficult)

Ingredients
- 2 (10-oz.) packages frozen blueberries in light syrup
- 1 (6-oz.) container plain low-fat yogurt
- 1 cup fresh orange juice
- 1 cup fat-free milk

Directions:
1. In a blender, process all ingredients until smooth and stop scraping down the sides.
2. Immediately serve.

40. Quick and Easy Omelet
(Ready in 30 min | Serve: 4|Difficulty: Easy)

Ingredients
- Nonstick cooking spray
- 2 cups refrigerated or frozen egg product, thawed, or 8 eggs
- 2 tablespoons snipped fresh chives, Italian (flat-leaf) parsley, or chervil
- 1/8 teaspoon salt
- 1/8 teaspoon cayenne pepper
- 1/2 cup shredded reduced-fat sharp cheddar cheese (2 ounces)
- 2 cups fresh baby spinach leaves or torn fresh spinach
- 1 Red Pepper Relish

Directions:
1. Coat a 10-inch non-adhesive skillet with cooking spray on the flared ends. Over medium heat, heat a skillet.
2. Mix the eggs, chives, salt, and cayenne pepper together in a big dish. To beat until frothy, use a rotational beater or wire whisk. Pour into a ready-made skillet. Start softly yet constantly swirling the eggs immediately with a wooden or plastic spatula until the mixture resembles tiny pieces of a fried egg surrounded by a liquid egg. Avoid agitating. Cook for an additional 30 to 60 seconds or until the egg is fixed but glossy.
3. Sprinkle with cheese while the egg is set but still bright. Place 1 cup of spinach on top and 1/4 cup of Red Pepper Relish on top. Raise and fold one side of the omelet partly over the filling, using a spatula. On a warm platter, arrange the remaining spinach. Move the omelet to a plate. Top with the relish remaining. He makes four servings.

41. Apples and Granola Breakfast Crisp
(Ready in 15 min | Serve: 4|Difficulty: Easy)

Ingredients
- 1 tablespoon butter
- 2 medium apples (such as Rome or Pink Lady), peeled if desired, cored, and quartered
- 1 tablespoon packed brown sugar
- 1/2 teaspoon grated fresh ginger or 1/4 teaspoon ground ginger
- Dash ground cardamom or ground cinnamon
- 1 6-ounce container fat-free plain Greek yogurt (such as Fage) or fat-free plain yogurt
- 1 teaspoon finely shredded lemon peel
- 4 teaspoons honey
- 1/4 cup low-fat granola

Directions:
1. Heat the butter in a medium skillet over medium heat. Attach apples and cook until apples are golden brown or around 5 minutes, stirring periodically. Reduce to medium-low heat. Stir in the brown sugar, cardamom, and ginger, for 5 minutes or until the apples are almost tender, cook and stir. Withdraw the skillet from the heat. Cover and let stand until the apples are tender, for 10 minutes.
2. Meanwhile, mix the lemon peel with yogurt. Divide the cooked apples into four different serving containers. A Greek yogurt top. Drizzle honey in it. Using granola to sprinkle.

42. Zucchini-Lemon Muffins
(Ready in 25 min | Serve: 1 dozan|Difficulty: Easy)

Ingredients
- 2 cups all-purpose flour
- 1/2 cup sugar
- 1 tablespoon baking powder
- 2 teaspoons grated lemon rind
- 1/4 teaspoon salt
- 1/4 teaspoon ground nutmeg
- 1 cup coarsely shredded zucchini
- 3/4 cup skim milk
- 3 tablespoons vegetable oil
- 1 large egg
- Cooking spray

Directions:
1. In a bowl, combine the first 6 ingredients and make a well in the middle of the mixture. Combine the zucchini, sugar, egg,

and oil; whisk thoroughly. Apply to the flour mixture and stir until the dry ingredients are properly moistened.
2. Divide the batter equally into 12 lined muffin cups with cooking oil. Bake for 20 minutes at 400° or until golden. Remove directly from the pots, and leave to cool on a wire rack.

43. Winter Breakfast Fruit Crunch

(Ready in 25 min | Serve: 6|Difficulty: Easy)

Ingredients

- 4 cups assorted fresh fruit, such as orange or grapefruit sections, chopped apple or pear, seedless grapes, cubed fresh pineapple, and/or peeled and sliced kiwi fruit
- 2 6-ounce carton low-fat vanilla yogurt
- 2 tablespoons honey
- 1/2 cup low-fat granola or Grape Nuts® cereal (wheat and barley nugget cereal)
- 1/4 cup coconut, toasted (optional)

Directions:

1. Divide the fruit into six glasses of parfait, large glasses, or individual dishes.
2. Cover the yogurt with the mango, then drizzle with the sugar.
3. If you like, sprinkle them with granola and coconut.

44. Whole Wheat-Oat Pancakes

(Ready in 20 min | Serve: 10|Difficulty: Easy)

Ingredients

- 2/3 cup regular oats
- 1/2 cup whole wheat flour
- 1/2 cup all-purpose flour
- 1 tablespoon baking powder
- 1/4 teaspoon salt
- 1 cup fat-free milk
- 1/4 cup egg substitute
- 1 1/2 tablespoons vegetable oil
- Cooking spray
- 1 tablespoon powdered sugar
- 3/4 cup reduced-calorie maple-flavored syrup

Directions:

1. Place the oats in an electric blender container; cover and process until blended. In a cup, add the oats, whole wheat rice, and the next three ingredients. Combine the cream, the egg replacer, and the oil; apply to the mixture of the oats, stirring until it is moistened.
2. Pour 1/4 cup of batter onto a hot griddle or skillet sprayed with cooking spray for each pancake. Turn pancakes to appear fried as bubbles and sides are coated with tops.
3. Sprinkle generously with powdered sugar on the biscuits, then serve with syrup.

45. Warmed Stuffed Peaches

(Ready in 40 min | Serve: 8|Difficulty: Normal)

Ingredients

- 4 peaches, halved and pitted
- 1/2 cup dried tropical mixed fruit (such as Sunkist brand)
- 1/4 cup slivered almonds, toasted
- 2 tablespoons graham cracker crumbs
- 2 tablespoons brown sugar
- 1/4 teaspoon ground allspice
- 1 (12-ounce) can peach nectar
- 1/2 cup vanilla yogurt, divided

Directions:

1. Preheat the oven to 350.
2. Scoop out peach pulp at the middle of each half to create a 2-inch circle. Pulp, reserve, and cut finely.
3. Combine the pulp, dried fruit, toasted almonds, brown sugar, allspice, and graham cracker crumbs. Divide the mixture of pulp equally between the peach pieces. In an 11 x 7-inch baking dish, put the stuffed peach halves. To the bowl, add nectar.
4. Bake for 40 minutes at 350° or until the peaches are tender. Drizzle the peach halves uniformly with a bowl of oil. Garnish equally with yogurt.

46. Tropical Fruit Parfaits

(Ready in 20 min | Serve: 6|Difficulty: Easy)

Ingredients

- 1 cup plain, fat-free Greek-style yogurt
- 3 tablespoons honey
- 2 1/4 teaspoons pure vanilla extract
- 1 1/2 cups ripe papaya, cut into 1/2-inch pieces (about 1 papaya)
- 1 1/2 cups ripe pineapple, cut into 1/2-inch pieces (about 1/2 pineapple)
- 1 1/2 cups strawberries, cut into 1/2-inch pieces (about 1 pint)
- 6 tablespoons low-fat granola

Directions:

1. Combine the milk, sugar, and vanilla extract in a bowl in the Greek style.
2. In each of the 6 containers, layer the remaining ingredients in this order: pieces of papaya, yogurt mixture, pieces of pineapple, yogurt mixture, pieces of strawberry, yogurt mixture; cover each glass evenly with low-fat granola.

47. Sunrise Smoothies

(Ready in 10 min | Serve: 2|Difficulty: Easy)

Ingredients

- 1 1/2 cups seeded, cut-up watermelon
- 1 cup cut-up cantaloupe
- 1/2 cup plain low-fat yogurt
- 1/4 cup orange juice

- Small wedges cantaloupe and/or watermelon (optional)

Directions:
1. Place the watermelon in a mixer of 1 1/2 cups. Cover until smooth, then mix. Break the watermelon purée into two glasses, every 12 ounces; set aside. Rinse the blender off. Combine 1 cup of cantaloupe, milk, and orange juice in a blender.
2. Cover until smooth, then mix. Slowly pour the watermelon puree on top of the bottles. Garnish with small wedges of melon and/or watermelon, if desired.

48. Summer-Fruit Soup
(Ready in 50 min | Serve: 4|Difficulty: Normal)

Ingredients
- 2 cups ripe cantaloupe chunks (about 1 in.)
- 1 ripe peach (6 oz.), peeled, pitted, and cut into chunks
- 1 cup canned peach nectar
- 1/2 cup white Zinfandel (or 1/2 cup additional peach nectar)
- 2 tablespoons lemon juice
- Sugar (optional)
- 1 cup raspberries, rinsed and drained
- Mint sprigs, rinsed

Directions:
1. Whirl the cantaloupe, mango, peach nectar, white Zinfandel, and lemon juice in a blender or food processor until smooth. If needed, taste, and add sugar.
2. Pour the soup into a pan, cover it, and chill for at least 1 hour or up to 1 day until it is cool. Nest the pot in a bowl of ice water to freeze faster and stir soup regularly until cool, around 30 minutes.
3. Load the broth into cups that are shallow. On top, spread the raspberries. Garnish with sprigs of mint.

49. Summer-Berry Compote
(Ready in 30 min | Serve: 6|Difficulty: Normal)

Ingredients
- 2 cups fresh blueberries
- 1/2 cup packed brown sugar
- 2 tablespoons champagne or white wine vinegar
- 1/2 teaspoon grated lemon rind
- 2 tablespoons fresh lemon juice
- 1 1/2 cups fresh raspberries
- 1 1/2 cups fresh blackberries
- 2 peaches, each peeled and cut into 6 wedges

Directions:
1. Combine the first 5 ingredients in a medium saucepan with non-aluminum; bring to a boil. Cover, reduce heat, and allow for 20 minutes to simmer. To room temperature, cool.
2. In each of the 6 shallow cups, spoon around 1/4 cup blueberry mixture and top each serving with 1/4 cup raspberries, 1/4 cup blackberries, and 2 peach wedges.

50. Stuffed French Toast
(Ready in 25 min | Serve: 8|Difficulty: Normal)

Ingredients
- 1/2 cup fat-free cream cheese (about 5 ounces)
- 2 tablespoons strawberry or apricot spreadable fruit
- 8 1-inch slices French bread
- 2 egg whites
- 1 egg, slightly beaten
- 3/4 cup fat-free milk
- 1/2 teaspoon vanilla
- 1/8 teaspoon apple pie spice
- Nonstick cooking spray
- 1/2 cup strawberry or apricot spreadable fruit

Directions:
1. Combine the cream cheese and 2 teaspoons of spreadable fruit in a shallow cup by making a horizontal cut halfway between top and bottom crust, slicing not yet all the way through, using serrated knife, shape pocket in any bread slice. With about 1 tablespoon of the cream cheese mixture, fill each bag.
2. Combine the egg whites, egg, cream, vanilla, and apple pie spices in a shallow cup. Cover the non-adhesive griddle loosely with cooking spray; fire over low heat.
3. Dip the slices of stuffed bread into the egg mixture, covering both ends. On a hot griddle, position the bread slices. Cook until golden brown or around 3 minutes, rotating once.
4. Meanwhile, heat 1/2 cup of spreadable fruit in a small saucepan until it is molten, stirring regularly. Over French toast, eat. Makes eight servings.

51. Strawberry-Banana Soy Smoothie
(Ready in 5 min | Serve: 1|Difficulty: Easy)

Ingredients
- 2 cups fresh strawberries, stemmed and halved (about 10 strawberries) $
- 1 1/2 cups vanilla low-fat soy milk
- 1 1/2 tablespoons honey
- 1/2 teaspoon vanilla extract
- 1 banana, sliced $
- 1 cup frozen fat-free whipped topping, thawed

Directions:
1. In a blender, combine the first 5 ingredients and process until smooth. Cover with 1/4 cup whipped topping for each serving. Immediately serve.

52. Spiced Oatmeal
(Ready in 5 min | Serve: 12|Difficulty: Easy)

Ingredients
- 3 cups regular rolled oats
- 3 cups 4- or 7-grain cereal flakes or coarsely ground hot cereal
- 1 cup chopped dried dates

- 1 cup chopped dried apples
- 1 cup chopped walnuts
- 1 cup firmly packed brown sugar
- 2 tablespoons ground cinnamon
- 1 tablespoon ground ginger
- 1 teaspoon ground turmeric
- 1 teaspoon ground cloves

Directions:

1. Combine the oats, 4-grain cereal, dates, almonds, walnuts, brown sugar, cinnamon, ginger, turmeric, and cloves in a wide jar (at least 2 1/2 qt.) with a cover.
2. For each serving, bring 1 cup of water to a boil over high heat in a 1- to 2-quart pan. (Or, heat 1 cup water on full power [100 percent] until boiling, around 2 minutes, in a microwave oven in a 2- to 3-cup bowl or glass measuring cup.) Stir in 3/4 cup spiced oatmeal blend. Remove from heat, cover, and let stand until it's as dense as you want, for 5 to 10 minutes.

53. Spiced Irish Oatmeal

(Ready in 20 min | Serve: 6|Difficulty: Easy)

Ingredients

- 3 cups of water
- 1 cup steel-cut oats
- 1 tablespoon packed brown sugar or brown sugar substitute equivalent to 1 tablespoon packed brown sugar*
- 1/4 teaspoon ground cinnamon
- 1/8 teaspoon salt
- 1/8 teaspoon ground allspice
- Dash ground cloves or ground nutmeg
- 3 cups fat-free milk

Directions:

1. Mix the water, steel-cut oats, brown sugar, cinnamon, salt, allspice, and cloves or nutmeg in a 2-quart saucepan.
2. Get it to a boil; lower the flame. Simmer, uncovered, for 10 to 15 minutes or until thickness and consistency are required, periodically stirring. With honey, serve. Create three cups (six 1/2-cup portions)

54. Spanish Breakfast Scramble

(Ready in 35 min | Serve: 4|Difficulty: Normal)

Ingredients

- Cooking spray
- 3/4 cup chopped seeded tomato
- 1/4 cup chopped green bell pepper
- 1/4 cup sliced green onions
- 3 large eggs
- 1 1/2 cups egg substitute
- 1/4 cup fat-free milk
- 1/4 teaspoon salt
- 1/8 teaspoon black pepper
- 1/8 teaspoon hot sauce

Directions:

1. Coat with cooking spray in a large nonstick skillet; place until hot over medium-high heat. Tomato, bell pepper, and onions are added; sauté until soft, stirring periodically. Set back. Extract the mixture from the pan.
2. In a wide cup, mix the eggs and the next 5 ingredients; whisk well. Pour the mixture into the pan and simmer, stirring periodically, over low heat. Cook until the eggs are set, but they're still damp. Withdraw from the sun. Stir in the mixture of the reserved vegetables. Transfer to dishes for cooking, and eat immediately.

55. Southwestern Breakfast Bake

(Ready in 1 hour 15 min | Serve: 8|Difficulty: Difficult)

Ingredients

- 1 15-ounce can black beans, rinsed and drained
- 3/4 cup canned enchilada sauce
- 2 4-1/2-ounce cans diced green chile peppers, drained
- 1/2 cup thinly sliced green onions
- Several dashes of bottled hot pepper sauce (optional)
- 2 cloves garlic, minced
- 1 cup shredded sharp cheddar cheese and/or shredded Monterey Jack cheese with jalapeno peppers (4 ounces)
- 3 egg whites
- 3 egg yolks
- 2 tablespoons all-purpose flour
- 1/4 teaspoon salt
- 1/2 cup milk
- 1 tablespoon snipped fresh cilantro
- Dairy sour cream (optional)
- Bottled salsa (optional)

Directions:

1. A 2-quart square baking dish is greased. Mix the black beans, enchilada sauce, green chili peppers, green onions, sweet pepper sauce (if desired), and garlic in the prepared baking dish. Sprinkle cheese over it.
2. Beat the egg whites with an electric blender in a medium mixing bowl at medium speed until soft peaks are produced (tips curl); set aside.
3. Mix the egg yolks, rice, and salt together in a big dish. Beat the mixture when mixed, using a wire whisk (mixture will be stiff). Little by little, whisk in the milk until smooth. Fold in the egg yolk mixture with the pounded egg whites and cilantro. In a baking bowl, gently pour the egg mixture over the bean mixture.
4. Bake in a 325 degree F oven for about 45 minutes or until softly shaken; the egg mixture appears fixed. Before eating, let it rest for 15 minutes. Serve with sour cream, salsa, and extra snipped fresh cilantro, if needed.

56. Shrimp-Artichoke Frittata

(Ready in 15 min | Serve: 4|Difficulty: Easy)

Ingredients

- 4 ounces fresh or frozen shrimp in shells
- 1/2 of a 9-ounce package of frozen artichoke hearts
- 2 cups refrigerated or frozen egg product, thawed
- 1/4 cup fat-free milk
- 1/4 cup thinly sliced green onions
- 1/8 teaspoon garlic powder
- 1/8 teaspoon pepper
- Nonstick cooking spray
- 3 tablespoons finely shredded Parmesan cheese
- Cherry tomatoes, quartered (optional)
- Italian parsley (optional)

Directions:

1. Thaw shrimp if they're frozen. Shrimp from Peel and Devein. Shrimps rinse; pat off. Lengthwise, halve the shrimp; set aside. Meanwhile, according to box instructions, cook artichoke hearts; rinse. Break the heart of the artichoke into quarters; set aside.
2. Stir together the egg, milk, green onions, ground garlic, and pepper; set aside.
3. Lightly coat with nonstick cooking spray on a large nonstick skillet. Heat the skillet until it sizzles with a drop of water. In the skillet, add the shrimp; cook the shrimp for 1 to 3 minutes or until the shrimp becomes opaque.
4. Pour the pan with the egg mixture; do not stir. Over a medium-low flame, position the skillet. Run a spatula along the side of the skillet as the egg mixture settles, raising the sides to allow the liquid to run beneath. Cooking and raising edges continue until the mixture is almost set (the top will be wet).
5. Remove the skillet from the heat; uniformly scatter the pieces of artichoke over the surface. Sprinkle the cheese with Parmesan. Cover and let stand for 3 to 4 minutes or until the top is set. Loosen the frittata corners. Move to a serving plate; to eat, break into wedges. Garnish with cherry tomatoes and parsley, if needed.

57. Raspberry-Orange Sunrises

(Ready in 15 min | Serve: 6|Difficulty: Easy)

Ingredients

- 4 cups fresh orange juice (about 8 oranges)
- 1 cup frozen unsweetened raspberries
- 1 1/2 cups semisweet sparkling wine
- 3 orange slices, halved (optional)

Directions:

1. Place in a blender with orange juice and raspberries; filter until smooth. Pour a mixture of juice into a pitcher; stir in the champagne over ice. Serve. If needed, garnish with orange slices.

58. Quinoa Pancakes

(Ready in 30 min | Serve: 4|Difficulty: Normal)

Ingredients

- 1 1/2 cups water
- 3/4 cup quinoa, rinsed
- 2 garlic cloves, minced
- 1/4 teaspoon salt
- 2 large egg whites
- 1/2 cup freshly grated Parmesan cheese
- 1/2 teaspoon dried basil
- 1/4 teaspoon freshly ground pepper
- 4 teaspoons extra-virgin olive oil, divided
- 6 cups baby spinach leaves
- 1 cup salsa, optional

Directions:

1. Heat the boiling water in a saucepan. Add the quinoa, salt, and garlic. Simmer, coated with (10 minutes). Uncover when dry, then cook for 2 minutes longer. Transfer to a wide bowl; cool off.
2. Preheat 350° in the oven.
3. Stir in the quinoa with egg whites, Parmesan, basil, and pepper.
4. Heat 2 teaspoons of oil over medium heat in a nonstick skillet. Create 4 quinoa pancakes using 1/4-cup measurements; flatten them. Cook and cook until golden (2 minutes per side). Move to a tray for baking. Repeat with the oil and quinoa left.
5. Bake the pancakes for 5 minutes until heated. Serve with spinach and, if necessary, with salsa.

59. Quick Oatmeal Granola

(Ready in 20 min | Serve: 2|Difficulty: Normal)

Ingredients

- 1/4 cup honey
- 2 tablespoons light butter, melted $
- 1/2 teaspoon vanilla extract
- 1 1/2 cups uncooked regular oats
- 1/2 cup whole wheat flour
- 1/3 cup sliced almonds
- 1/4 teaspoon salt

Directions:

1. In a shallow bowl, combine the honey and the next 2 ingredients. In a wide cup, whisk together the peas, flour, sliced almonds, and salt. Apply the mixture of honey to the oatmeal mixture, stirring until mixed. Spread the oat mixture over a baking sheet that is lightly greased.
2. Bake for 20 minutes at 350°, stirring regularly.

60. Poblano Tofu Scramble

(Ready in 20 min | Serve: 4|Difficulty: Normal)

Ingredients

- 1 16- to 18-ounce package extra-firm water-packed tofu (fresh bean curd)
- 1 tablespoon olive oil
- 1 or 2 fresh poblano chile peppers, seeded and chopped* (1/2 to 1 cup total)
- 1/2 cup chopped onion
- 2 cloves garlic, minced
- 1 teaspoon chili powder
- 1/2 teaspoon ground cumin

- 1/2 teaspoon dried oregano, crushed
- 1/4 teaspoon salt
- 1 tablespoon lime juice
- 2 plum tomatoes, seeded and chopped (about 1 cup)
- Fresh cilantro sprigs (optional)

Directions:
1. Drain the tofu; break the tofu in half and pat each half until well dry, with paper towels. In a medium dish, crumble the tofu. Only put aside.
2. Heat olive oil over medium to high heat in a large nonstick skillet. Connect the chili pepper(s), onion, and garlic; boil for 4 minutes, then stir. Add chili powder, cumin, salt, and oregano. For 30 more seconds, cook and stir.
3. To the chili pepper mixture, add crumbled tofu. Heat elimination. Cook for 5 minutes, stirring gently on occasion. Drizzle with lime juice just before serving and fold onto the tomatoes. Garnish with fresh cilantro if needed.

61. Peach-Mango Smoothie

(Ready in 10 min | Serve: 2|Difficulty: Easy)

Ingredients
- 2/3 cup frozen sliced peaches
- 2/3 cup frozen mango pieces (such as Dole)
- 2/3 cup peach nectar
- 1 tablespoon honey
- 1 (6-ounce) container organic peach fat-free yogurt

Directions:
1. Place all the ingredients in a mixer; mix for 2 minutes or until tender. Immediately serve.

62. Orange-Strawberry Swirl

(Ready in 40 min | Serve: 5|Difficulty: Normal)

Ingredients
- 2 (10-oz.) packages frozen strawberries in light syrup
- 1 (6-oz.) container plain low-fat yogurt
- 1 cup fresh orange juice
- 1 cup fat-free milk

Directions:
1. Process all ingredients in a blender until smooth, stopping to scrape downsides. Serve immediately.

63. Orange-Berry Cream Parfait

(Ready in 20 min | Serve: 4|Difficulty: Normal)

Ingredients
- 3 medium oranges
- 1 (7-oz.) container 2% low-fat Greek yogurt
- 2 tablespoons honey
- 1/2 teaspoon orange zest
- 1/2 teaspoon vanilla extract
- 1 cup fresh blueberries
- 1 cup granola

Directions:
1. The peel and the orange part. In a shallow cup, stir the yogurt, sugar, orange zest, and vanilla extract together.
2. Layer 3 pieces of orange, 2 Tbsp. new blueberries, a combination of 1 tablespoonful of yogurt, and each of the 4 parfait glasses has 2 tbsp. of granola; repeat the layers.

64. Oat and Nut Crunch Mix

(Ready in 20 min | Serve: 20|Difficulty: Normal)

Ingredients
- 4 cups sweetened oat square cereal or brown sugar-flavored oat biscuit cereal
- 1/2 cup sliced almonds
- 2 tablespoons butter or margarine, melted
- 1/2 teaspoon apple pie spice
- Dash salt
- 1 cup dried cherries and/or light raisins

Directions:
1. Combine the cereal and almonds in a 15x10x1-inch baking tray. Stir together the melted butter, apple pie seasoning, and salt in a shallow cup. Drizzle the mixture of butter over the mixture of cereal; toss to coat.
2. Bake for about 20 minutes or until the almonds are toasted in a 300 degree F oven, stirring once while baking. Cool on a wire rack in a pan for 20 minutes. Add the dried cherries. Absolutely awesome. Up to 1 week at room temperature, packed in a tightly covered jar. Makes twenty servings (5 cups).

65. Multigrain Pancakes

(Ready in 25 min | Serve: 4|Difficulty: Normal)

Ingredients
- 1/2 cup all-purpose flour
- 1/2 cup whole-wheat flour
- 1/4 cup quick-cooking oats
- 2 tablespoons yellow cornmeal
- 2 tablespoons brown sugar
- 1 1/2 teaspoons baking powder
- 1/2 teaspoon salt
- 1 cup 2% milk
- 1/4 cup plain fat-free yogurt
- 1 tablespoon vegetable oil
- 1 large egg

Directions:
1. Combine 7 ingredients first; stir well. Mix the remaining ingredients together; stir well. Apply the mixture of rice, stirring until smooth.
2. For each pancake, scoop around 1/4 cup of batter onto a hot nonstick griddle or nonstick skillet. Turn pancakes to appear fried as bubbles and sides are coated with tops. If needed, serve with maple syrup and low-fat granola.

65. Mountain Peak Granola

(Ready in 20 min | Serve: 14|Difficulty: Normal)

Ingredients
- 3 cups regular oats

- 2 cups puffed wheat cereal
- 1/2 cup wheat bran
- 2 tablespoons slivered almonds
- 1/2 cup applesauce
- 1/4 cup honey
- 1 tablespoon vegetable oil
- 1/2 teaspoon ground cinnamon
- 1/4 teaspoon ground ginger
- 1/2 cup chopped dried apricots
- 1/2 cup sweetened dried cranberries or raisins

Directions:
1. Preheat the oven to 375 .
2. In a wide bowl, combine the first 4 ingredients.
3. In a small saucepan, add the applesauce, honey, oil, cinnamon, and ginger; simmer over medium heat for 2 minutes or until the honey is melted, stirring occasionally.
4. Pour over the oat mixture with the applesauce mixture, swirling to coat. Place the mixture in a rolling jelly pan and bake for 20 minutes at 375 °. Stir the granola gently; bake for 15 more minutes or until dry. Cool; add the apricots and cranberries and stir. Store in a jar that is airtight.

66. Mini Mushroom-&-Sausage Quiches
(Ready in 55 min I Serve: 1dozan|Difficulty: Normal)

Ingredients
- 8 ounces turkey breakfast sausage, removed from casing and crumbled into small pieces
- 1 teaspoon extra-virgin olive oil
- 8 ounces mushrooms, sliced
- 1/4 cup sliced scallions
- 1/4 cup shredded Swiss cheese
- 1 teaspoon freshly ground pepper
- 5 eggs
- 3 egg whites
- 1 cup 1% milk

Directions:
1. Place the rack in the middle of the oven; preheat to 325 F. Generously coat a nonstick muffin pan with cooking oil (see Tip).
2. Over medium-high prepare, heat a large nonstick skillet. Attach the sausage and cook for 6 to 8 minutes, until golden brown. Move it to a cooling bowl. To the pan, add oil. Attach the mushrooms and cook, constantly stirring, for 5 to 7 minutes, until golden brown. Move the mushrooms to the sausage bowl. Leave for 5 minutes to cool. Stir in the scallions, pepper, and cheese.
3. In a medium dish, whisk together the eggs, egg whites, and milk. Divide the egg mixture equally between the muffin cups that have been packed. Sprinkle the sausage mixture with a heaping tablespoon into each cup.
4. Bake until the tops tend to brown, for 25 minutes. Let it cool for 5 minutes on a wire rack. On top of the pan, place a plate, flip it over, and turn the quiches out onto the rack. Turn upright and absolutely let cool.

67. Maple-Hazelnut Oatmeal
(Ready in 25 min I Serve: 4|Difficulty: Normal)

Ingredients
- 1 1/2 cups fat-free milk
- 1 1/2 cups water
- Cooking spray
- 2 Gala apples, peeled and cut into 1/2-inch cubes (about 3 cups)
- 1 cup uncooked steel-cut oats
- 2 tablespoons brown sugar
- 1 1/2 tablespoons butter, softened
- 1/4 teaspoon ground cinnamon
- 1/4 teaspoon salt
- 1/4 cup maple syrup

Directions:
1. Put milk and 1 1/2 cups of water to a boil over medium-high heat in a saucepan, stirring regularly.
2. Using cooking spray to powder a 3 1/2-quart electric slow cooker. In a slow cooker, put the hot milk mixture, apple, and the next 5 ingredients (through salt); stir well. Cover and cook for 7 hours or until the oats are tender, on medium.
3. Cover with maple syrup and hazelnuts; spoon the oatmeal into cups.

68. Maple-Almond Granola
(Ready in 35 min I Serve: 24|Difficulty: Normal)

Ingredients
- 4 cups regular oats
- 1/4 cup slivered almonds
- 1 1/2 teaspoons ground cinnamon
- 1/4 teaspoon salt
- 1/3 cup water
- 1/3 cup honey
- 1/3 cup maple syrup
- 2 tablespoons brown sugar
- 2 tablespoons canola oil
- Cooking spray
- 1 cup minced dried apricots
- 1 cup raisins

Directions:
1. Preheat the oven to 325 .
2. In a wide bowl, combine the first 4 ingredients.
3. Combine water in a shallow saucepan with the next 4 ingredients; bring to a boil. Pour the oat mixture on top; flip to cover. In a jelly-roll pan filled with cooking oil, spread the oat mixture. Bake for 35 minutes at 325° or until golden, stirring after 10 minutes. Place in a wide bowl; add the apricots and grapes. Absolutely awesome.
4. Let your toddler aid by searching for the ingredients and collecting them. In a mixing cup, pour the measured oats and almonds together. The cooled granola is spooned into a storage jar.

Note: Store in an airtight container for up to a week.

69. Make-Ahead Breakfast Casserole

(Ready in 1 hour 5 min | Serve: 6 | Difficulty: Difficult)

Ingredients
- 8 ounces ciabatta bread, cut into 1-inch cubes
- Cooking spray
- 1 pound turkey breakfast sausage
- 1/2 cup chopped green onions
- 1 1/4 cups fat-free milk
- 1 cup (4 ounces) reduced-fat shredded sharp cheddar cheese
- 2 large eggs
- 1 (8-ounce) carton egg substitute
- 2 tablespoons chopped fresh parsley

Directions:
1. Preheat the oven to 400 .
2. Arrange bread cubes on a baking sheet in a single layer. Bake for 8 minutes at 400° or until toasted.
3. Over medium-high pressure, heat a medium skillet. Cover pan with spray for frying. Add sausage to pan; fry, stirring to crumble, for 6 minutes or until browned. In a big bowl, combine the bacon, bread, and onions together. In a medium cup, mix the milk, cheese, whites, and egg substitutes, stirring with a fork. Apply the combination of milk to the bread mixture and toss to cover the bread. A 2-quart baking dish coated with cooking spray is mixed with a spoon. Cover and refrigerate overnight or for 8 hours.
4. Preheat the oven to 350 .
5. Uncover the saucepan. Bake for 50 minutes at 350 ° or until set and lightly browned. Sprinkle with parsley; serve promptly.

70. Light Biscuits

(Ready in 25 min | Serve: 22 | Difficulty: Normal)

Ingredients
- 2 cups all-purpose flour
- 1 tablespoon baking powder
- 1/4 teaspoon baking soda
- 1/2 teaspoon salt
- 1/4 cup reduced-calorie stick margarine
- 1 (8-ounce) carton plain low-fat yogurt
- 1 teaspoon honey
- 1 tablespoon all-purpose flour

Directions:
1. Preheat the oven to 425 .
2. In a medium cup, combine the first 4 ingredients; cut into margarine with a pastry cutter until crumbly. Combine the yogurt and honey; apply to the flour mixture until the dry ingredients are moistened, stirring with a fork.
3. Sprinkle over the working surface with 1 tablespoon of flour. Turn the dough onto the floured surface; gently knead 4 to 5 times. Roll dough to a thickness of 1/2-inch; cut with a 2-inch biscuit cutter into circles. Place the biscuits on a baking sheet without grease. Bake for 10 minutes at 425° or until golden.

71. Hot Fruit & Spice Cereal

(Ready in 15 min | Serve: 2 | Difficulty: Easy)

Ingredients
- 1/2 cup amaranth grain*
- 1/2 cinnamon stick
- 1/4 cup dried cherries
- 1/4 cup chopped dried apricots
- 2 tablespoons honey
- 1/2 cup nonfat Greek yogurt

Directions:
1. Bring the amaranth, cinnamon, and 2/3 cups of water to a boil in a small saucepan. Reduce the heat to 10 minutes, simmer, cover, and cook. Let yourself cool slightly. Put the cinnamon.
2. Microwave dried fruit, sugar, and 2 tbsp in a microwave-safe jar. Water for approximately 30 seconds until warm.
3. Combine 1 tbsp. Honey liquid into yogurt from the fruit. Divide 2 dishes of yogurt, cover each with half of the amaranth, then half of the honeyed apple.
At well-stocked convenience stores and natural-food stores, purchase in boxes or bulk.
Note: There is a per serving dietary analysis.

72. Honey-Ginger Fruit

(Ready in 15 min | Serve: 7 | Difficulty: Easy)

Ingredients
- 1 cup white grape juice
- 3 tablespoons honey
- 1 1/2 teaspoons grated fresh ginger
- 1 pt. fresh strawberries halved
- 3 oranges, sectioned
- 1/2 honeydew melon, chopped
- 1 cup seedless green grapes

Directions:
1. In a big mug, combine the grape juice, sugar, and ginger. Apply the remaining ingredients and coat until thrown. Immediately serve.

73. Heart-Smart Breakfast Parfait

(Ready in 10 min | Serve: 4 | Difficulty: Easy)

Ingredients
- 1/4 cup raisins
- 1 teaspoon finely shredded orange peel (set aside)
- 2 tablespoons orange juice
- 1 teaspoon vanilla
- 1/2 of an 8-ounce package reduced-fat cream cheese (Neufchtel), softened
- 1 tablespoon sugar
- 2 cups fresh raspberries, blueberries, sliced strawberries, and/or cut-up peaches
- 1/2 cup low-fat granola

- Honey (optional)
- Shredded orange peel (optional)

Directions:
1. Combine the raisins and orange juice in a small, microwave-proof dish. Cover and microwave for 30 to 45 seconds on 100 percent power (high); let stand for 1 minute to plump the raisins. Using vanilla to stir; set aside.
2. Combine the cream cheese and sugar in a medium bowl; beat until smooth with an electric mixer at low to medium level. Stir in a blend of raisins and 1 teaspoon of orange peel.
3. Layer half of the cream cheese mixture, half of the fruit, and half of the granola into four parfait cups. Layers to repeat. Drizzle with honey if needed. Garnish with an extra orange peel if needed.

74. Greek Yogurt Parfait
(Ready in 10 min | Serve: 4|Difficulty: Easy)

Ingredients
- 3 cups plain fat-free Greek-style yogurt (such as Fage)
- 1 teaspoon vanilla extract
- 4 teaspoons honey
- 28 clementine segments
- 1/4 cup shelled, unsalted dry-roasted chopped pistachios

Directions:
1. In a bowl, combine the yogurt and vanilla. In each of 4 small parfait cups, spoon 1/3 cup of yogurt mixture; top each with 1/2 teaspoon sugar, 5 clementine sections, and 1/2 tablespoon nuts.
2. Cover the remaining yogurt mixture with parfaits (about 1/3 cup each); top each with 1/2 teaspoon of sugar, 2 slices of clementine, and 1/2 tablespoon of almonds. Immediately serve.

75. Granola-Nectarine Gratin
(Ready in 30 min | Serve: 6|Difficulty: Normal)

Ingredients
- 1 cup Almond-Fruit Granola
- 4 medium nectarines, sliced
- 1/2 cup fresh blueberries
- 2 tablespoons orange liqueur (such as Grand Marnier) or orange juice
- 2 tablespoons packed brown sugar

Directions:
1. Almond-Fruit Granola is prepared; set aside.
2. Combine the nectarines, blueberries, and orange liqueur for gratin in a medium bowl; toss to cover. Spoon fruit into 6 gratin dishes or casseroles (12 to 16 ounces each). Using brown sugar to dust.
3. Bake for 7 to 8 minutes in a 450 degree F oven or until the fruit is warmed and most sugar is melted. Sprinkle over each gratin with 1/4 cup of Almond-Fruit Granola. Immediately serve. Gets 6 servings.

76. Golden Honey Granola
(Ready in 15 min | Serve: 18|Difficulty: Easy)

Ingredients
- 3 cups regular oats
- 3/4 cup sliced unblanched almonds
- 1/2 cup honey
- 1 tablespoon canola or vegetable oil
- 1 teaspoon cinnamon
- 1/8 teaspoon salt
- 1/8 teaspoon ground cloves
- 3 cups wheat bran flakes cereal (such as Bran Flakes)
- 3/4 cup golden raisins or mixed dried fruit

Directions:
1. Preheat the oven to 325.
2. Spread the oats and almonds uniformly on an ungreased baking sheet in one single layer. Bake for ten minutes. Stir well; continue to bake for about 5 minutes, until lightly toasted.
3. Meanwhile, in a big cup, mix the sugar, oil, cinnamon, salt, and cloves together. In a cup, add the warm, toasted oat mixture; toss well. Line with parchment paper, or coat with cooking oil, the previously used baking sheet. Place the mixture back in the pan and simmer for 20 minutes or until golden brown. On a wire rack, cool absolutely in the pan.
4. Break into chunks of the oat mixture; toss with the cereal and the raisins. Shop firmly covered for up to 2 weeks at room temperature.

77. Georgia Grits Waffles
(Ready in 1 hour 15 min | Serve: 8|Difficulty: Difficult)

Ingredients
- 1/2 cup uncooked regular grits
- 6 tablespoons cold unsalted butter, cubed
- 3/4 cup buttermilk
- 2 large eggs, lightly beaten
- 1 1/4 cups all-purpose flour
- 1 tablespoon sugar
- 2 teaspoons baking powder
- 1/2 teaspoon baking soda

Directions:
1. In a medium saucepan, bring 2 cups of water to a boil over medium-high heat. Bring to a boil; whisk in grits. Lower the heat; simmer, stirring regularly, for 15 minutes or until tender. To heat, whisk in butter; cool to room temperature. Stir in the eggs and buttermilk.
2. In a shallow cup, mix together the flour and the next 3 ingredients. Stir the flour mixture into the mixture of grits until just blended.
3. Cook until golden (approx. 1/3 cup batter each) in a preheated, oiled waffle iron.

78. Fruit-and-Nut Granola
(Ready in 50 min | Serve: 8 cups |Difficulty: Normal)

Ingredients
- 4 cups regular oats
- 1/2 cup toasted or honey-crunch wheat germ
- 1/2 cup sliced almonds
- 1/4 cup nonfat dry milk

- 1/4 cup sunflower seed kernels
- 2 tablespoons sesame seeds
- 1 1/2 teaspoons ground cinnamon
- 1/4 teaspoon salt
- 1/2 cup honey
- 1/4 cup orange juice
- 2 teaspoons vegetable oil
- 1 teaspoon vanilla extract
- Cooking spray
- 1 cup chopped mixed dried fruit
- 1 cup golden raisins
- 1/2 cup sweetened dried cranberries

Directions:
1. Preheat the oven to 350.
2. In a big bowl, combine the first 8 ingredients. In a small saucepan, mix the honey and orange juice over medium heat, and cook for 4 minutes or until soft. Apply the vanilla and oil; stir with a whisk. Pour over the oat mixture with the honey mixture, and toss well.
3. In a jelly-roll pan filled with cooking oil, spread the oat mixture. Bake for 15 minutes at 350°; swirl. Bake for an extra 10 minutes or until it's crisp. Cool in the casserole. Place the oat mixture in a wide bowl; add the dried fruit and stir.

79. Fruit Kebabs with Honey-Yogurt Dipping Sauce

(Ready in 20 min | Serve: 4to6|Difficulty: Easy)

Ingredients
- 2 cups plain low-fat Greek yogurt
- 1/4 cup honey
- 2 cups seedless grapes
- 2 cups pineapple cubes, from 1 small pineapple
- 2 cups melon balls (cantaloupe, honeydew or a combination)
- 2 1/2 cups halved or quartered strawberries

Directions:
1. Mix the yogurt and honey in a bowl. Until sufficiently chilled, refrigerate.
2. On 24 6-inch wooden skewers, string bananas, pineapple cubes, melon balls, and strawberries with alternating fruits.
3. For dipping, serve kebabs with sauce in pots.

80. Fruit Dippers

(Ready in 10 min | Serve: 8|Difficulty: Easy)

Ingredients
- 1 (1 1/4-lb.) peeled and cored pineapple
- 1 Red Delicious apple
- 2 oranges
- 1 (8-oz.) container plain or vanilla nonfat yogurt
- 2 tablespoons honey
- 1/2 teaspoon lime rind
- 2 teaspoons lime juice

Directions:
1. Reserve the pineapple juice; cut the pineapple into spears lengthwise, then in half.
2. Core the apple, cut into 16 slices; toss with the juice of the pineapple.
3. The peel and the orange part.
4. Stir the yogurt and 2 Tbsp. Honey, then 2 ingredients next. Serve along with slices of apple.

81. Fresh Fruit with Lime Syrup

(Ready in 2 hour| Serve: 10|Difficulty: Difficult)

Ingredients
- 1 cup of water
- 1 tablespoon cornstarch
- 1 cup granulated sugar
- 1 teaspoon grated lime rind
- 1/4 cup fresh lime juice
- 1 pineapple, peeled, cored, and cut into 1-inch pieces
- 2 cups red seedless grapes, halved
- 3 kiwifruit, peeled and sliced
- 2 oranges, peeled and sectioned

Directions:
1. In a shallow saucepan, whisk 1 cup of water and cornstarch together. Whisk in the rind, butter, and juice. Bring to a boil over low heat, stirring continuously; simmer for 1 minute. Chill for 2 hours at least.
2. Combine the pineapple in a large bowl with the next three ingredients; garnish, if necessary, and drizzle with the chilled syrup. Immediately, serve.

82. Dried Cherry-and-Pecan Oatmeal

(Ready in 20 min | Serve: 6|Difficulty: Easy)

Ingredients
- 3 cups of water
- 3 cups fat-free milk
- 2 cups whole oats (not instant)
- 1/2 cup dried cherries, coarsely chopped
- 1/2 teaspoon salt
- 5 tablespoons brown sugar
- 1 tablespoon butter
- 1/4 teaspoon ground cinnamon
- 1/4 teaspoon vanilla extract
- 2 tablespoons chopped pecans, toasted

Directions:
1. Bring the first 5 ingredients to a boil; reduce heat and simmer for 20 minutes or until thickened, stirring periodically. Withdraw from the sun. Combine 4 teaspoons of brown sugar with the next three ingredients. Add 1 cup of oatmeal to each of the 6 bowls. Sprinkle generously with the pecans and 1 tablespoon of brown sugar left over. Immediately serve.

83. Creamy Grits

(Ready in 20 min | Serve: 2 cups | Difficulty: Easy)

Ingredients

- 1 (14-oz.) can low-sodium, fat-free chicken broth
- 1 cup fat-free milk
- 1/2 cup quick-cooking grits

Directions:

1. In a medium saucepan, bring the broth and milk to a boil over medium-high heat; reduce the heat to low and whisk in 1/2 cup of the grits. Cook for 15 to 20 minutes or until smooth and thickened, whisking sometimes.

84. Creamy Breakfast Polenta

(Ready in 40 min | Serve: 4 to 6 | Difficulty: Normal)

Ingredients

- 3 cups low-fat (2%) milk
- 1 cup polenta
- 2 tablespoons sugar
- 1/2 teaspoon salt
- 4 to 6 tablespoons blackberry jam
- Lightly sweetened whipped crème fraîche

Directions:

1. Bring 3 cups of water and milk to a boil in a 2 1/2- to 3-quart pan over high heat. Lower the heat such that the liquid scarcely boils. Pour polenta in a small, continuous stream, stirring continuously, pausing periodically to break up any lumps. Stir in salt and sugar.
2. Simmer, stirring regularly, until polenta is smooth and fluffy to pinch, 20 to 40 minutes (bubbles will "spit" hot polenta globs out of the pan if the heat is too high).
3. Ladle the polenta into bowls and add about 1 tablespoon of blackberry jam and a dollop of crème fraîche to each serving.

85. Cran-Berry Green-Tea Smoothie

(Ready in 10 min | Serve: 1 | Difficulty: Easy)

Ingredients

- 1/2 cup frozen cranberries
- 1/4 cup frozen blueberries
- 1/2 cup frozen blackberries
- 5 frozen whole strawberries
- 1 ripe banana
- 1/2 cup brewed green tea, cooled to room temperature
- 1/4 cup plain soy milk
- 2 tablespoons honey or packed light brown sugar

Directions:

Whirl all ingredients in a blender until creamy.
Note: Per 2-cup serving, nutritional analysis is given.

86. Cinnamon-Apple Muffins

(Ready in 20 min | Serve: 1 dozen | Difficulty: Easy)

Ingredients

- 2 1/3 cups all-purpose flour
- 1 cup of sugar
- 1 tablespoon baking powder
- 2 teaspoons ground cinnamon
- 1 teaspoon baking soda
- 1/2 teaspoon salt
- 1 1/2 cups finely chopped peeled Granny Smith apple
- 1 cup low-fat buttermilk
- 1/3 cup 2% low-fat milk
- 1/3 cup light ricotta cheese
- 3 tablespoons vegetable oil
- 1 tablespoon vanilla extract
- 2 large egg whites
- 1 large egg
- Cooking spray
- 3 tablespoons sugar
- 2 teaspoons ground cinnamon

Directions:

1. Preheat the oven to 400.
2. In a wide bowl, combine the first 6 ingredients. Stir in the apple and make a well with the mixture in the middle.
3. Combine the buttermilk and the next 6 ingredients (egg-based buttermilk); stir well with a whisk. Apply to the mixture of rice, stirring until moist. Spoon batter filled with cooking spray into 18 muffin cups.
4. Combine 2 teaspoons of cinnamon and 3 tablespoons of sugar; scatter uniformly over the batter. Bake for 18 minutes or until finished, at 400°. Remove directly from the pans; cool on a wire rack.

87. Cinnamon Banana Crunch Bowl

(Ready in 1 hour 10 min | Serve: 1 | Difficulty: Difficult)

Ingredients

- 1/4 cup nonfat plain Greek yogurt
- 1 teaspoon honey
- Dash of cinnamon
- 1/2 cup cooked bulgur
- 1 tablespoon chopped toasted walnuts
- 1 tablespoon brown sugar
- 1/3 cup fresh banana slices
- Additional cinnamon (optional)

Directions:

In a little mug, combine the yogurt, sugar, and a touch of cinnamon. The bulgur is tossed with walnuts and brown sugar. Cover with slices of banana. A mixture of Dollop Yogurt over Bulgur Mixture. Sprinkle with extra cinnamon if needed.

88. Carrot-Pineapple-Bran Muffins

(Ready in 25 min | Serve: 18 | Difficulty: Normal)

Ingredients

- 1 3/4 cups all-purpose flour
- 1/4 cup sugar
- 1 teaspoon baking powder
- 1 teaspoon baking soda
- 1 teaspoon ground cinnamon
- 3/4 cup fat-free milk
- 1 large egg, lightly beaten
- 1 (8-ounce) can crushed pineapple in juice, undrained
- 2 tablespoons margarine or butter, melted
- 1 cup wheat bran flakes cereal
- 1 cup shredded carrot
- 2 tablespoons water
- Cooking spray

Direction:

1. Preheat the oven to 350.
2. In a wide bowl, combine the first 5 ingredients. Create a well in the mixture's middle and set it aside. Mix the milk and the next three ingredients together, stirring well. Stir in the cereal; quit to stand for five minutes.
3. Place the water and the carrot in a small saucepan. Cover and bring to a boil; simmer and cook for 1 to 2 minutes or until tender. Drain yourself and set aside.
4. To the flour mixture, add the cereal mixture; add the carrot and stir until the dried ingredients are moistened in 18 muffin cups sprayed with cooking oil, spoon batter uniformly, filling two-thirds full. For 20 to 22 minutes or until crispy, bake at 350°. Immediately remove the muffins from the bowls, then cool on wire racks.

89. Breakfast Barley with Banana & Sunflower Seeds

(Ready in 10 min | Serve: 1|Difficulty: Easy)

Ingredients

- 2/3 cup water
- 1/3 cup uncooked quick-cooking pearl barley
- 1 banana, sliced
- 1 teaspoon honey
- 1 tablespoon unsalted sunflower seeds

Directions:

1. In a shallow microwave-safe cup, mix water and barley. A HIGH 6-minute microwave.
2. Delete and quit to stand for 2 minutes.
3. Cover with slices of banana, sunflower seeds, and honey.

90. Blueberry-Tofu Smoothie

(Ready in 10 min | Serve: 1|Difficulty: Easy)

Ingredients

- 1 cup frozen blueberries
- 1/2 cup (4 ounces) silken tofu
- 1/2 cup pomegranate juice
- 1/2 cup crushed ice
- 1 tablespoon agave nectar or honey

Directions:

In a blender, combine ingredients; blend until smooth.

91. Blueberry-Almond Streusel Muffins

(Ready in 15 min | Serve: 1|Difficulty: Easy)

Ingredients

- 2 1/2 cups all-purpose flour
- 1 cup granulated sugar
- 1 tablespoon baking powder
- 1 teaspoon baking soda
- 1/2 teaspoon salt
- 3/4 cup 2% low-fat milk
- 1/2 cup low-fat buttermilk
- 1/3 cup light ricotta cheese
- 2 tablespoons vegetable oil
- 1 tablespoon vanilla extract
- 1 teaspoon almond extract
- 3 large egg whites
- 1 1/3 cups blueberries
- Cooking spray
- 1/4 cup all-purpose flour
- 1/2 cup finely chopped almonds
- 1 tablespoon brown sugar
- 1 tablespoon reduced-calorie stick margarine, melted

Directions:

1. In a shallow microwave-safe cup, mix water and barley. A HIGH 6-minute microwave.
2. Delete and quit to stand for 2 minutes.
3. Cover with slices of banana, sunflower seeds, and honey.

92. Blueberry Pancakes

(Ready in 20 min | Serve: 12|Difficulty: Easy)

Ingredients

- 1 cup all-purpose flour
- 2 teaspoons baking powder
- 1/4 teaspoon baking soda
- 1/4 teaspoon salt
- 1 tablespoon sugar
- 1 1/3 cups low-fat or nonfat buttermilk
- 1/4 cup egg substitute
- 1 tablespoon vegetable oil
- 1/2 cup frozen blueberries
- Cooking spray

Directions:

1. In a wide bowl, combine the first 5 ingredients. Combine the buttermilk, egg replacer, and oil; add to the dry ingredients and stir until the dry ingredients are moistened. Add the blueberries.
2. Pour 1/4 cup of batter onto a hot griddle or skillet sprayed with cooking spray for each pancake. When the tops are bubbly, transform the pancakes, and the sides look fried.

Note: By using a commercial egg replacement instead of whole eggs, you can cut cholesterol and fat from your diet. In most egg replacements, egg whites are the principal ingredient. Sodium, preservatives, and occasionally oil is applied so that the food looks like whole eggs and works like them. Using 1/4 cup egg replacer for each whole egg while changing your own recipes.

93. Blueberry Buckwheat Pancakes

(Ready in 15 min | Serve: 6|Difficulty: Easy)

Ingredients

- 1/2 cup buckwheat flour
- 1/2 cup whole wheat flour
- 1 tablespoon sugar
- 1/2 teaspoon baking powder
- 1/4 teaspoon baking soda
- 1/4 teaspoon salt
- 1/4 cup refrigerated or frozen egg product, thawed, or 1 egg, slightly beaten
- 1-1/4 cups buttermilk or sour milk
- 1 tablespoon cooking oil
- 1/4 teaspoon vanilla
- 3/4 cup fresh or frozen blueberries, thawed

Directions:

1. Stir the buckwheat flour, whole wheat flour, sugar, baking powder, baking soda, and salt together in a medium dish. Build a well in the flour mixture's center; set aside.
2. Beat the egg slightly in a small bowl; stir in the buttermilk, oil, and vanilla. Apply the buttermilk mixture to the flour mixture all at once. Stir only before mixed but still somewhat lumpy. Add the blueberries.
3. Heat a thinly greased griddle or hard skillet over medium heat before the griddle dances over the surface with a few drops of water. Pour a tiny 1/4 cup of flour onto a hot griddle for any pancake. Spread the batter into a circle with a circumference of around 4 inches.
4. Cook over medium heat until pancakes are brown, rotating when pancake surfaces are bubbly, and edges are slightly dry on the second side to cook (1 to 2 minutes per side). Serve or hold warm instantly. Allows 6 servings of (2-pancake)

94. Blueberry and Maple-Pecan Granola Parfaits

(Ready in 30 min | Serve: 4|Difficulty: Easy)

Ingredients

- 2 cups vanilla fat-free yogurt
- 2 cups blueberries
- 1 cup Maple-Pecan Granola

Directions:

1. Spoon 1/4 cup of yogurt into each of 4 parfait glasses; add 1/4 cup of blueberries to each serving. Add 1/4 cup of Maple-Pecan Granola, 1/4 cup of milk, and 1/4 cup of blueberries to each serving.

95. Blackberry-Mango Breakfast Shake

(Ready in 20 min | Serve: 4|Difficulty: Easy)

Ingredients

- 1 1/2 cups frozen blackberries
- 1 cup refrigerated mango slices (such as Del Monte)
- 1 cup (about 6 1/2 ounces) low-fat tofu (such as Silken soft)
- 1 cup of orange juice
- 3 tablespoons honey

Directions:

Combine all ingredients in a blender; process until smooth.

96. Banana-Nut Oatmeal

(Ready in 15 min | Serve: 1|Difficulty: Easy)

Ingredients

- 1/2 cup rolled oats
- 1 cup of water
- 1 banana, sliced
- 1 tablespoon chopped walnuts
- 1 teaspoon cinnamon

Directions:

1. In a shallow microwave-safe dish, mix the oats and 1 cup of water. HIGH microwave for 3 minutes.
2. Place the banana slices, walnuts, and cinnamon on top.
Carb Star: Oatmeal 4.6 grams per 1/2 cup of raw or toasted oats Resistant Starch Oatmeal for breakfast may help you eat less all day long. Researchers in Italy have substituted the flour in bread and pasta with oats in a series of experiments. They observed that oat eaters absorbed fewer calories over the course of the day, even though both diets had similar calorie counts.

97. Banana-Date Flaxseed Bread

(Ready in 1 hour 15 min | Serve: 16|Difficulty: Difficult)

Ingredients

- 1/2 cup flaxseeds
- 2/3 cup mashed ripe banana
- 1/2 cup sugar
- 1/4 cup vegetable oil
- 2 large eggs
- 1 1/2 cups all-purpose flour
- 1/4 cup flaxseeds
- 1/2 teaspoon baking powder
- 1/2 teaspoon baking soda
- 1/2 teaspoon salt
- 1/2 cup whole pitted dates, chopped
- Cooking spray

Directions:

1. Place 1/2 cup flaxseeds in a blender, and process until ground to weigh 3/4 cup flaxseed meal. Place aside the flaxseed meal.
2. Preheat the oven to 350.
3. At a medium pace, beat the banana, sugar, oil, and eggs in a blender until well-mixed. Spoon the flour gently into dry measuring cups, then level it with a knife.
4. Combine flour, a meal of flaxseed, 1/4 cup of flaxseed, baking powder, baking soda, and salt, and apply to the sugar mixture steadily, beating until well-mixed. Stir in dates that are sliced. In an 8 x 4-inch loaf pan sprayed with cooking oil, spoon the batter in. Bake for 55 minutes at 350 ° or until a wooden pick inserted in the middle comes out clean. Cool on a wire rack in a pan for 10 minutes, then removes from the pan. Totally cool on a wire rack.

98. Banana Breakfast Smoothie

(Ready in 15 min | Serve: 2|Difficulty: Easy)

Ingredients

1/2 cup 1% low-fat milk
1/2 cup crushed ice
1 tablespoon honey
1 large ripe banana, sliced and frozen
1 (6-ounce) carton vanilla fat-free yogurt
Preparation:
1. Place the first 4 ingredients in a blender; process 1 minute or until smooth. Add yogurt; process 20 to 30 seconds or until blended. Serve immediately.

Apple-Cinnamon Granola

(Ready in 2 hour| Serve: 12|Difficulty: Difficult)

Ingredients

- 3 cups regular oats
- 1 cup whole-grain toasted oat cereal (such as Cheerios)
- 1/3 cup oat bran
- 1/3 cup finely chopped walnuts
- 2 teaspoons ground cinnamon
- 1/4 teaspoon ground cardamom
- 2 tablespoons butter
- 1/3 cup applesauce
- 1/4 cup honey
- 2 tablespoons brown sugar
- Cooking spray
- 1 cup chopped dried apple

Directions:

1. Preheat the oven to 250.
2. In a wide cup, combine the first 6 ingredients, stirring well to mix.
3. Melt 2 tablespoons butter in a medium saucepan over medium heat. In a saucepan, add 1/3 cup of applesauce, butter, and brown sugar and bring to a boil. Cook for 1 minute, constantly stirring. Pour over the oat mixture with the applesauce mixture, swirling to coat. Spread the mixture on a jelly-roll tray filled with cooking spray in an even layer. Bake for 1 1/2 hours at 250°, stirring after 30 minutes. Enable it to fully cool. Stir the sliced apple into it.

99. Banana-Oatmeal Hot Cakes with Spiced Maple Syrup

(Ready in 25 min | Serve: 6|Difficulty: Normal)

Ingredients

- 1/2 cup maple syrup
- 1/2 cinnamon stick
- 3 whole cloves
- 1/2 cup old-fashioned rolled oats
- 1 cup of water
- 2 tablespoons firmly packed light brown sugar
- 2 tablespoons canola oil
- 1/2 cup whole-wheat (whole-meal) flour
- 1/2 cup all-purpose (plain) flour
- 1 1/2 teaspoons baking powder
- 1/4 teaspoon baking soda
- 1/4 teaspoon salt
- 1/4 teaspoon ground cinnamon
- 1/2 cup 1 percent low-fat milk
- 1/4 cup fat-free plain yogurt
- 1 banana, peeled and mashed
- 1 egg, lightly beaten

Directions:

1. Combine the maple syrup, the cinnamon stick, and the cloves in a shallow saucepan. Put and bring to a boil over medium heat. Delete from heat and leave for 15 minutes to steep. Through a slotted spoon, cut the cinnamon stick and cloves. Put aside the syrup and keep it warm.
2. Combine the oats with water in a large microwave-safe dish. Microwave on fast, about 3 minutes, until the oats are creamy and soft. Incorporate the brown sugar and canola oil. To cool somewhat, set aside.
Place the flour, baking powder, baking soda, salt, and ground cinnamon in a cup. Whisk for mixing.
3. Stir in the oats with the milk, yogurt, and banana and stir until well mixed. Uh, beat the shell. To the oat mixture, add the flour mixture and stir only until it is moistened.
4. Over medium heat, position a nonstick frying pan or a griddle. Spoon the 1/4 cup of pancake batter into the pan when a drop of water sizzles as it hits the pan. Cook until bubbles cover the top surface of the pancake and the sides are finely browned, for around 2 minutes. Switch and cook until well browned on the bottom and cooked in the pancake, 1 to 2 minutes longer. Repeat with the pancake batter that remains.
5. Place the pancakes on an individual, warmed plates. Drizzle with the hot syrup and instantly serve.

100. Whole-wheat Soda Bread

(Ready in 60 min | Serve: 15|Difficulty: Difficult)

Ingredients

- 2 cups whole-wheat flour
- 1 teaspoon baking powder
- 1/4 cup ground flaxseed meal

- 1/2 teaspoon baking soda
- 1/4 cup ground millet meal
- 1 teaspoon caraway seed, crushed
- 2 tablespoons wheat gluten
- 1/2 teaspoon kosher salt
- 1 1/4 cup low-fat buttermilk or skim milk
- 2 egg whites

Directions:

1. Preheat the oven to 350 F. Sift the dry products together.
2. Mix the milk and egg whites together in a different dish. Mix thoroughly. To dry the ingredients, add the milk and egg mixture. Mix, so it's moistened well.
3. Shape into a 5 inch by 8-inch loaf pan and bake for 50 to 60 minutes. Skewer test for doneness.

101. Whole-grain Buttermilk Biscuits

(Ready in 60 min | Serve: 15|Difficulty: Difficult)

Ingredients

- 1 cup whole-wheat (whole-meal) flour
- 3/4 cup all-purpose (plain) flour, plus extra for kneading
- 3 tablespoons wheat germ
- 2 teaspoons baking powder
- 1/2 teaspoon baking soda (bicarbonate of soda)
- 1/4 teaspoon salt
- 3 tablespoons chilled butter, cut into small pieces
- 1 cup low-fat buttermilk

Directions:

1. Preheat a 400 F microwave. Keep the ungreased nonstick baking sheet ready.
2. Mix the flour, wheat germ, baking powder, baking soda, and salt together in a big dish. Whisk for mixing. To the flour mixture, add the butter. Trim the butter into the dry ingredients with a pastry blender or 2 knives until the mixture resembles coarse crumbs. Add the buttermilk and stir until it forms a moist dough. Only don't over-mix. Use plastic wrap to protect the bowl and refrigerate for 30 minutes.
3. Turn the dough out onto a generously floured work surface and knead gently for 6 to 8 times with floured hands until smooth and manageable.
4. Roll the dough into a rectangular 1/2-inch thick using a rolling pin. Cut out the biscuits with a 2 1/2-inch round biscuit cutter coated in flour. For a minimum of scraps, cut tightly together. Gather the scraps and roll them out to produce extra biscuits.
5. Place the biscuits on the baking sheet about 1 inch apart. Bake for 8 to 10 minutes until the biscuits grow to twice their unbaked height and are softly golden. Serve it wet.

102. Whole-grain Banana Bread

(Ready in 60 min | Serve: 15|Difficulty: Difficult)

Ingredients

- 1/2 cup brown rice flour
- 1/2 cup amaranth flour
- 1/2 cup tapioca flour
- 1/2 cup millet flour
- 1/2 cup quinoa flour
- 1 teaspoon baking soda
- 1/2 teaspoon baking powder
- 1/8 teaspoon salt
- 3/4 cup egg substitute (or use egg whites)
- 2 tablespoons grapeseed oil
- 1/2 cup raw sugar
- 2 cups mashed banana

Directions:

1. preheat oven to 350 F. Prepare a 5-by-9-inch loaf pan by spraying it lightly with cooking spray. Dust with a little of any of the flours. Set aside.
2. Mix all dry ingredients except sugar together in a large bowl. In a separate bowl, combine egg, oil, sugar, and mashed banana. Mix well. Add wet mixture to dry ingredients and combine thoroughly. Spoon into loaf pan. Bake for 50 to 60 minutes.
3. Check for doneness with a toothpick — when the toothpick is removed, it shouldn't have any batter sticking to it. Remove bread from oven, cool, slice, and serve.

103. Veggies Breakfast Bakes

(Ready in 40 min | Serve: 5|Difficulty: Easy)

Ingredients

- 4 large field mushrooms
- 8 tomatoes, halved
- 1 garlic clove, thinly sliced
- 2 tsp. olive oil
- 200g bag spinach
- 4 eggs

Directions:

1. In 4 ovenproof pans, placed the mushrooms and tomatoes and place in a heated oven. Divide the garlic between the pans, drizzle with the oil, and season, and bake for 10 minutes.
2. Meanwhile, put the spinach in a broad colander, then put the boiling water over the kettle to wilt it. Squeeze out the extra water, then add the dishes with the spinach.
3. Create a small gap between the vegetables and break each dish with an egg. Go back to the oven and cook for an extra 8-10 minutes or until the egg is fried to your taste.

104. Tuna Pita Pockets

(Ready in 40 min | Serve: 5|Difficulty: Normal)

Ingredients

- 1 1/2 cups shredded romaine lettuce
- 3/4 cup diced tomatoes
- 1/2 cup finely chopped green bell peppers
- 1/2 cup shredded carrots
- 1/2 cup finely chopped broccoli
- 1/4 cup finely chopped onion

- 2 cans (6 ounces each) low-salt white tuna packed in water, drained
- 1/2 cup low-fat ranch dressing
- 3 whole-wheat pita pockets, cut in half

Directions:

1. Add the cabbage, tomatoes, beans, carrots, broccoli, and onions to a wide cup. Toss to blend uniformly.
2. Add the tuna and ranch dressing into a shallow bowl. Stir well to blend. To blend, add the tuna mixture to the lettuce mixture and stir.
3. Place 3/4 cup of tuna salad in each half of the pita pocket and serve immediately.

105. Three-grain Raspberry Muffins

(Ready in 40 min | Serve: 12|Difficulty: Normal)

Ingredients

- 1/2 cup rolled oats
- 1 cup 1 percent low-fat milk or plain soy milk (soya milk)
- 3/4 cup all-purpose (plain) flour
- 1/2 cup cornmeal, preferably stone-ground
- 1/4 cup wheat bran
- 1 tablespoon baking powder
- 1/4 teaspoon salt
- 1/2 cup dark honey
- 3 1/2 tablespoons canola oil
- 2 teaspoons grated lime zest
- 1 egg, lightly beaten
- 2/3 cup raspberries

Directions:

1. Preheat the oven to 400 F. Line a 12-cup muffin tin with liners made of paper or foil.
2. Combine the oats and the milk in a large microwave-safe dish. Microwave on fast, about 3 minutes, until the oats are creamy and soft. Only put aside.
3. Combine the rice, cornmeal, bran, baking powder, and salt in a large dish. Whisk for mixing. Apply the combination of butter, canola oil, lime zest, oat mix, and egg. Beat until it is moistened but also very lumpy. Fold in the raspberries softly.
4. Spoon the batter into the muffin cups, filling about 2/3 of each cup full. Bake for 16 to 18 minutes, until the tops are golden brown and a toothpick inserted into the middle of the muffin comes out clean. Move the muffins to a wire rack and let them absolutely cool off.

106. Great Breakfast Burger

(Ready in 30 min | Serve: 1|Difficulty: Normal)

Ingredients

- 1 medium onion, roughly chopped
- 2 tbsp tomato ketchup
- 1 tbsp oyster sauce
- 1kg sausagemeat, or meat squeezed from 16 large sausages
- 1 egg yolk
- 25g pack, flat-leaf parsley, leaves chopped
- 8 slices melting cheese (we used Havarti)
- 8 grilled rashers streaky smoked bacon
- 8 ciabatta buns, halved
- tomato relish

Directions:

1. In a food processor, place the onion, ketchup, and oyster sauce, then mix into a coarse paste, scraping the sides of the processor if you need to. Put the sausage meat in a mixing cup, beat the onion mixture, the egg yolk, and 25 ml of water, then add the parsley (and I really mean, beat it; if you have a tabletop mixer, do it in it). Separate the mixture into eight pieces, roll them into large balls, and flatten them into patties. Chill for 1 hour on a tray.

107. Blueberry Green Smoothie

(Ready in 5-7min | Serve2 |Difficulty: Normal)

Ingredients

- 2 cups chopped mixed greens (such as kale, collard greens,
- mustard greens, Swiss chard, and spinach)
- 1/4 cup water
- 1/3 cup chopped carrot
- 1/2 cup frozen blueberries
- 1/2 cup coarsely chopped unpeeled cucumber
- 1/4 cup unsweetened almond milk
- 4 ice cubes

Directions:

1. Place in a blender with the greens and water.
2. Start to blend on Low, and when the greens start to break down, they will increase to Medium velocity until they are fully broken down and only smooth.
3. Add the remaining ingredients and blend with a medium mixture. At high speed before the desired consistency, roughly 1 minute, is reached.
4. Immediately serve.

108. Papaya Goodness

(Ready in 5-7min | Serve2 |Difficulty: Normal)

Ingredients

- 1 cup spinach
- 1 cup chopped kale
- 3/4 cup water
- 1/2 cup chopped unpeeled cucumber
- 1 green apple, coarsely chopped
- 1 cup coarsely chopped papaya
- 1 tablespoon ground flaxseed

Directions

1. In a blender, put your spinach, kale, and water. Start blending at low speed and rise to medium speed as

the greens continue to break down until they are fully broken down and smooth.
2. Add the remaining ingredients and blend for around 1 minute, at medium to high speed, until the desired consistency is reached.
3. Immediately, serve.

109. Wake up Call
(Ready in 5-7min | Serve2 |Difficulty: Normal)

Ingredients
- 1 large rib celery, chopped
- 1 tablespoon fresh parsley
- 1/2–3/4 cup water
- 1/2 cup chopped cooked beets
- 1 small orange, separated into segments
- 3/4 cup chopped carrot

Directions
1. In a blender, put the celery, parsley, and water. Start blending at low, then lift to medium speed as the celery and parsley continue to break down until they are fully broken down and smooth.
2. Add the remaining ingredients and blend at medium to high speed for around 1 minute until the desired consistency has been reached.
3. Immediately serve.

110. Diabetic-Friendly Green Smoothie
(Ready in 5-7min | Serve 2 | Difficulty: Normal)

Ingredients
- 2 cups spinach
- 2 large kale leaves, chopped (about 1 1/2 cups)
- 3/4 cup water
- 1 large frozen banana, chopped
- 1/2 cup frozen mango
- 1/2 cup frozen peach
- 1 tablespoon ground flaxseeds
- 1 tablespoon almond butter or peanut butter, optional

Directions
1. In a blender, put the spinach, kale and water. Start mixing at low, then lift to medium speed as the greens continue to break down until they are fully broken down and smooth.
2. Add the fruit, flaxseed and nut butter (if used and blend for around 1 minute at medium to high speed until the desired consistency is reached. immediately serve.

111. Banana Almond Smoothie
(Ready in 5-7min, serve2,Difficulty:Normal)

Ingredients
- 1 large banana
- 1 cup unsweetened almond milk
- 1 tablespoon unsalted almond butter
- 1 tablespoon wheat germ
- 1/8 teaspoon vanilla extract
- 1/8 teaspoon ground cinnamon
- 3–4 ice cubes

Directions
1. Place it in a blender with all the ingredients.
2. Start mixing at low and lift to medium speed as the contents begin to break down until the desired consistency is reached, around 1 minute.
3. Immediately serve.

112. Tropical Smoothie
(Ready in 5-7min, serve2,Difficulty:Normal)

Ingredients
- 3/4 cup frozen mango
- 3/4 cup frozen pineapple
- 1 small frozen banana, chopped
- 1 1/2 cups unsweetened coconut milk
- 1/2 cup water
- 1 tablespoon coconut oil
- 3–4 ice cubes

Directions
1. Place it in a blender with all the ingredients.
2. Start mixing at low and raise to medium velocity until fully smooth, around 1 minute, as the contents begin to break down.
3. Immediately serve.

113. Berry Banana Green Smoothie
(Ready in 5-7min, serve2, Difficulty: Normal)

Ingredients
- 2 cups spinach
- 1 cup water
- 3/4 cup frozen blackberries
- 3/4 cup frozen blueberries
- 1 small frozen banana, chopped
- 1 tablespoon almond butter

Directions
1. In a blender, put the spinach and water. Start blending at low, then lift to medium speed as the spinach starts to break down until it is fully broken down and smooth.
2. Apply the blackberries, blueberries, banana and almond butter and combine for around 1 minute at medium to high pressure, until the desired consistency is reached.
3. Immediately serve.

114. Peach Green Smoothie
(Ready in 5-7min, serve2, Difficulty: Normal)

Ingredients
- 2 cups spinach
- 1 cup water

- 1/2 cup frozen strawberries
- 1 1/2 cups frozen peach
- 1 small frozen banana, chopped
- 1 tablespoon coconut oil

Directions
1. In a blender, put the spinach and water. Start blending at low, then lift to medium speed as the spinach starts to break down until it is fully broken down and smooth.
2. Add the fruit and coconut oil and combine for around 1 minute at medium to high intensity, until the desired consistency is reached.
3. Immediately serve.

115. Green Avocado Smoothie
(Ready in 5-7min, serve2, Difficulty: Normal)

Ingredients
- 1 cup chopped kale
- 3/4–1 cup water
- 1 green apple, chopped
- 2 small kiwifruit, peeled and halved
- 1 small avocado, pitted, peeled, and chopped
- 1 tangerine, peeled and separated into segments
- 3–4 ice cubes

Directions
1. In a blender, put the kale and water. Start mixing at low, then lift to medium speed as the kale starts to break down until it is completely broken down and smooth.
2. Add the remaining ingredients and blend at medium to high speed for around 1 minute until the desired consistency has been reached. Immediately serve.

116. Melon Mélange
(Ready in 5-7min, serve2, Difficulty: Normal)

Ingredients
- 2 cups spinach
- 1/2–3/4 cup water
- 1/2 cup frozen strawberries
- 3/4 cup chopped honeydew melon
- 3/4 cup chopped cantaloupe
- 1 tablespoon ground flaxseeds
- 3–4 ice cubes

Directions
1. In a blender, put the spinach and water. Start blending at low, then lift to medium speed as the spinach starts to break down until it is fully broken down and smooth.
2. Add the berries, flax seeds and ice and combine for around 1 minute at medium to high speed until the perfect consistency is reached.
3. Immediately serve.

117. Strawberry Cucumber Delight
(Ready in 5-7min, serve2, Difficulty: Normal)

Ingredients
- 1 1/2 cups frozen strawberries
- 2 cups chopped unpeeled cucumber
- Juice of 1/2 large orange
- 4 mint leaves
- 3/4 cup water
- 3–4 ice cubes

Directions
1. Place it in a blender with all the ingredients.
2. Start mixing at low and lift to medium speed as the contents begin to break down until the desired consistency is reached, around 1 minute.
3. Immediately serve.

118. Pumpkin Pie Smoothie
(Ready in 5-7min, serve2, Difficulty: Normal)

Ingredients
- 1/2 cup pumpkin puree
- 1/2 large frozen banana, chopped
- 1/2 cup water
- 1 cup unsweetened almond milk
- 1/4 teaspoon ground cinnamon
- 1/8 teaspoon ground nutmeg
- 1 tablespoon pure maple syrup
- 3–4 ice cubes

Directions
1. In a blender, put the pumpkin, banana, and water.
2. Start mixing at low speed and rise to medium speed as the ingredients continue to break down until fully broken and smooth. Connect the remaining ingredients and blend at medium to high speed for around 1 minute until the desired consistency has been reached.
3. Immediately serve.

119. Arugula Smoothie
(Ready in 5-7min, serve2, Difficulty: Normal)

Ingredients
- 1 cup arugula
- 1 cup spinach
- 1–1 1/2 cups water
- 1/2 small banana
- 1 cup chopped strawberries
- 1/2 cup blueberries
- 1 tablespoon coconut oil
- 1 tablespoon wheat germ
- 3–4 ice cubes

Directions

1. In a blender, put the arugula, spinach, and water. Start mixing at low, then lift to medium speed as the greens continue to break down until they are fully broken down and smooth.
2. Add the fruit, coconut oil, wheat germ and ice and combine for around 1 minute at medium to high pressure, until the perfect consistency is reached.
3. Immediately serve.

2. Heat a griddle or large frying pan to cook the burgers without adding any additional fat. On the one hand, fry for 3 mins until golden, turn the heat down for 5 mins, then flip and repeat on the other side.
3. Fry the bacon while the burgers cook, and, if you are game, some eggs as well. Heat the grill, then toast the insides of the ciabatta buns gently.
4. Place on a baking sheet the cooked burgers, placed on each one a slice of cheese, then pop under the grill to melt. Place the burgers on their buns, and put the bacon on top of them. Slide the scrambled eggs on top of the bacon if you feel like it. With a napkin, serve.

120. Toast with Almond Butter and Banana

(Ready in 5-7min, serve1, Difficulty: Normal)

Ingredients

- 2 slices 100% whole wheat bread
- 2 tablespoons almond butter
- 1 small banana, sliced
- 1/8 teaspoon ground cinnamon

Directions

1. Toast the bread and sprinkle almond butter on each piece.
2. On top, arrange the banana slices and sprinkle them with cinnamon.

121. English Muffin with Berries

(Ready in 5-7min, serve1, Difficulty: Normal)

Ingredients

- 1 100% whole wheat English muffin, halved
- 1 tablespoon low-fat cream cheese
- 4 strawberries, thinly sliced
- 1/2 cup blueberries, mashed

Directions

1. Toast the English halves of muffins.
2. Spread thinly on each toasted half of the cream cheese and finish with the fruit.

122. Healthy "Lox" English Muffin

(Ready in 5-7min, serve1, Difficulty: Normal)

Ingredients

- 1 100% whole wheat English muffin, halved
- 1/4 teaspoon finely chopped fresh dill
- 1/2 teaspoon fresh lemon juice
- 2 tablespoons low-fat cream cheese
- 1 (4-ounce) can wild salmon in water, no salt added, drained
- 6 thin slices unpeeled cucumber
- 6 thin slices Roma tomato
- Cracked black pepper

Direction

1. Toast the English halves of muffins. Meanwhile, blend the minced dill and lemon juice equally into the cream cheese in a shallow cup.
2. Spread the cream cheese mixture equally on each half of the toasted muffin. To extract the canned liquid, clean the salmon under running water, and then shovel the salmon thinly onto the English muffin halves.
3. If the salmon is too big, mash it first with a fork. Cover with slices of cucumber and tomato, and sprinkle to taste with chili.

123. Protein Bowl

(Ready in 5-7min, serve1, Difficulty: Normal)

Ingredients

- 3/4 cup low-fat cottage cheese
- 1/2 medium banana, thinly sliced
- 1 tablespoon almond butter
- 1/4 cup uncooked old-fashioned oats

Directions

1. Mix all the ingredients together in a small bowl, and enjoy immediately.

124. Berries Deluxe Oatmeal

(Ready in 5-7min, serve1, Difficulty: Normal)

Ingredients

- 1 1/2 cups unsweetened plain almond milk
- 1/8 teaspoon vanilla extract
- 1 cup old-fashioned oats
- 3/4 cup mix of blueberries, blackberries, and coarsely chopped strawberries
- 2 tablespoons toasted pecans

Directions

1. On medium boil, heat the almond milk and vanilla in a shallow saucepan.
2. Add the oats and stir for about 4 minutes, or before much of the liquid is drained, until the mixture starts simmering. Stir the berries in. Scoop the mixture and line it with toasted pecans in two pans.

125. Apples and Cinnamon Oatmeal

(Ready in 5-7min, serve1, Difficulty: Normal)

Ingredients

- 1 1/2 cups unsweetened plain almond milk
- 1 cup old-fashioned oats
- 1 large unpeeled Granny Smith apple, cubed
- 1/4 teaspoon ground cinnamon
- 2 tablespoons toasted walnut pieces

Directions

1. Over medium pressure, carry the milk to a boil and add the oats and apple.
2. Stir for about 4 minutes, before much of the liquid is absorbed. Stir the cinnamon in. Scoop the batch of oatmeal into two bowls and line it with the walnuts.

126. Energy Oatmeal
(Ready in 5-7min, serve1, Difficulty:Normal)

Ingredients

- 1/4 cup water
- 1/4 cup low-fat milk
- 1/2 cup old-fashioned oats
- 4 egg whites, beaten
- 1/8 teaspoon ground cinnamon
- 1/8 teaspoon ground ginger
- 1/4 cup blueberries

Directions

1. Heat the water and the milk in a small pot to a boil over medium heat. Apply the oats, stirring continuously, or until much of the moisture is consumed, for around 4 minutes.
2. Gradually add the beaten egg whites, stirring continuously. Five more minutes to fry, or until the eggs are no longer runny. Through the oatmeal mixture, stir the cinnamon and ginger and scoop the mixture into a cup. Cover with berries and quickly eat.

127. Anna's Homemade Granola
(Ready in 1hour 15min, serve12, Difficulty:Normal)

Ingredients

- 3 cups old-fashioned oats
- 1/4 cup flaxseeds
- 1 cup sliced almonds
- 1/2 teaspoon ground cinnamon
- 1/4 teaspoon ground ginger
- 1/4 cup brown sugar
- 1/4 cup maple syrup or honey
- 1/4 cup extra virgin olive oil
- 1/2 teaspoon almond extract
- 1 cup golden raisins
- olive oil spray

Directions

1. Preheat the oven to 250°F.
2. Combine the first six ingredients in a large bowl and combine to blend properly.
3. Mix the maple syrup or sugar, oil, and almond extract in a separate, shallow dish.
4. Pour the wet ingredients into the dry ingredients and combine until there are no longer dry areas, uniformly with a spatula.
5. Pour two greased sheet pans onto them. Bake for about 1 hour and 15 minutes, stirring to produce an even color after 15 minutes.
6. Break up bits of granola to the perfect consistency as you stir. Remove and switch from the oven to a large bowl.
7. Stir in the raisins such that they are uniformly spread.

128. Warm Quinoa with Berries
(Ready in 10-15min, serve1, Difficulty:Normal)

Ingredients

- 1 cup uncooked quinoa
- 1 cup unsweetened coconut milk
- 1 cup water
- 1/2 cup blackberries
- 2 tablespoons toasted chopped pecans
- 2 teaspoons raw honey, optional

Directions

1. Rinse the quinoa in order to (if not prerinsed). Bring the quinoa, coconut milk and water to a boil in a small covered pot under high pressure.
2. Lower the flame and boil for 10 to 15 minutes or until the liquid is absorbed.
3. Cooked quinoa should be somewhat al dente; when most of the grains have uncoiled, it is ready and the unwound germ can be shown.
4. For around 5 minutes, let the quinoa sit in the covering pot.
5. Fluff softly into two bowls with a fork scoop, then finish with blackberries, pecans and butter (if using).

129. Fruity Yogurt Parfait
(Ready in 5min, serve1, Difficulty:Normal)

Ingredients

- 1 cup low-fat plain Greek yogurt
- 1/4 cup blueberries
- 1/4 cup cubed strawberries
- 1/4 cup cubed kiwifruit
- 1 teaspoon ground flaxseeds or flaxseed meal
- 1/2 cup low-calorie granola

Directions

1. Spoon half the yogurt into a small glass cup or parfait bowl.
2. A thin layer is applied to the top of blueberries, strawberries, kiwi, flaxseed meal, and granola.
3. Layer and top the majority of the mango, flaxseeds, and granola with the leftover yogurt.

130. Banana Almond Yogurt
(Ready in 5min, serve1, Difficulty:Normal)

Ingredients
- 1 tablespoon raw, crunchy, unsalted almond butter
- 3/4 cup low-fat plain Greek yogurt
- 1/4 cup uncooked old-fashioned oats
- 1/2 large banana, sliced
- 1/8 teaspoon ground cinnamon

Directions
1. In the oven, soften the almond butter for 15 seconds. In a cup, sweep up the yogurt and whisk in the almond butter, oats and banana.
2. Sprinkle the end of cinnamon.

131. Open-Faced Breakfast Sandwich
(Ready in 5min, serve1, Difficulty:Normal)

Ingredients
- 1 1/2 teaspoons extra virgin olive oil
- 2 egg whites, beaten
- 1/2 cup spinach
- Cracked black pepper, to taste
- 1 teaspoon brown mustard
- 1 slice 100% whole wheat bread
- 2 thick tomato slices
- 1 thin slice low-fat cheddar cheese

Directions
1. Preheat the toaster oven or oven to 400 °F. On medium fire, heat a tiny nonstick pan.
2. Add the oil to the hot pan and then add the egg whites when the oil is hot. When frying, scramble the eggs, then add the spinach and season with pepper to taste.
3. Spread the mustard on the bread, stir in the tomatoes and scrambled eggs, and add the cheese.
4. Heat until the cheese melts, about 2 minutes, in the oven.

132. Broccoli Omelet
(Ready in 5min, serve1, Difficulty:Normal)

Ingredients
- egg whites
- 1 whole egg
- 2 tablespoons extra virgin olive oil
- 1/2 cup chopped broccoli
- 1 large clove garlic, minced
- 1/8 teaspoon chile pepper flakes
- 1/4 cup low-fat feta cheese
- Cracked black pepper

Directions
1. In a shallow cup, stir in the egg whites and the egg. On medium fire, heat a tiny nonstick pan.
2. Add 1 tablespoon of the oil to the hot pan and add the broccoli when the oil is hot. Before adding the garlic, chili pepper flakes, and black pepper to taste, simmer for 2 minutes.
3. Cook for 2 more minutes, then remove the mixture of broccoli from the pan and put it in a separate dish. Turn the heat to a low degree, add the remaining tablespoon of oil and add the whisked eggs when the oil is heavy.
4. Flip the omelet over and quickly scoop the broccoli mixture and feta cheese on one half of the omelette until they begin to bubble and draw away from the edges, for about 30 seconds.
5. For 2 minutes, fold the omelet over, turn off the heat and cover the pan with a lid.
6. Immediately serve.

133. Veggie Frittata with Caramelized Onions
(Ready in20-25min, serve6, Difficulty:Normal)

Ingredients
CARAMELIZED ONIONS
- 1 tablespoon extra-virgin olive oil
- 1 small white onion, thinly sliced
- 1/4 teaspoon brown sugar
- 1/8 teaspoon cracked black pepper

FRITTATA
- 2–3 tablespoons extra virgin olive oil
- 1 1/2 cups chopped zucchini
- 1 clove garlic, minced
- 1 cup thinly sliced cremini mushrooms
- 2–3 tablespoons finely chopped fresh basil
- 1 tablespoon chopped fresh parsley or 1 teaspoon dried parsley
- 2 cups spinach
- 4 whole eggs
- 5 egg whites
- 1/2 cup 1% milk
- 1/2 cup shredded low-fat pepper jack cheese
- 1/8 teaspoon sea salt
- Cracked black pepper

Directions
1. Preheat the oven to 350°F.
2. Heat a medium saucepan over medium heat to caramelize the onions.
3. Add the oil and then add the onion, sugar, and pepper when the oil is sweet. Let the "sweat" onion shift every few minutes, until light brown and softened, about 10 minutes, to prevent burning.
4. Turn the heat off and cover the pan until it is ready for serving. Start the frittata over medium heat by heating a large pan and then adding the oil.
5. Toss the zucchini in it, and simmer for a minute or two.
6. Before adding the mushrooms, basil, and parsley, add the garlic, and simmer for 2 to 3 more minutes.
7. Cook the vegetables and sprinkle them with salt and pepper for another minute (the mushrooms will

release water and will not brown if you add the salt right away).
8. Mix, turn the heat off, and add the spinach. Whisk the eggs, egg whites, milk, shredded cheese, salt, and pepper together in a big cup. Using olive oil spray to spray a 9-inch circular cake tray.
9. Pour the sautéed ingredients in and then the combination of the eggs. Place the pan on the oven's middle rack and cook for 20 to 25 minutes, or until the middle knife comes out clean.

134. Whole Grain Pancakes
(Ready in 5min, serve 4, Difficulty: Normal)

Ingredients
- 1 teaspoon vanilla extract
- 1 small banana, mashed
- 2 cups unsweetened almond milk
- 1/4 cup unsweetened applesauce
- 1 1/4 cups whole wheat flour
- 1/4 cup old-fashioned oats
- 2 teaspoons baking powder
- 1/4 teaspoon sea salt
- 1/2 teaspoon ground cinnamon
- 3 tablespoons brown sugar
- 1/2 cup chopped toasted almonds or walnuts

Directions
1. Blend together the wet ingredients in a medium bowl. Mix together the dry ingredients in a small, larger bowl.
2. Add the dry ingredients to the wet ingredients and blend together until the mixture is tender. Heat the grill pan over medium heat, then cover it with a spray of olive oil. Pour flour into the pan with a ladle, and cook the pancakes for 2 to 3 minutes.
3. When they start bubbling on top, flip them, and continue cooking for about a minute. Remove from the sun, and stack until all the pancakes have been cooked on a covered tray. Immediately serve.
4. **Serving Suggestion:** Serve with fresh sliced fruit and 2 teaspoons per serving of maple syrup.

135. Veggie Scramble
(Ready in 20-25min, serve 4, Difficulty: Normal)

Ingredients
- 1 cup mixed greens (such as collard greens, mustard greens, and kale)
- 1/4 cup chopped red onion
- 1/4 cup chopped red bell pepper
- 1/2 cup chopped broccoli
- 2 tablespoons extra virgin olive oil
- 2 tablespoons water
- 1 large clove garlic, minced
- 3 whole eggs
- 3 egg whites
- 1/8 teaspoon sea salt
- Pinch of cracked black pepper

Directions
1. Wash and pat the greens dry, break off the thick portion of the roots, and the leaves will be sliced into 1-inch pieces.
2. In small pieces about the same size, chop the onion, bell pepper, and broccoli. Over medium to high prepare, heat a large nonstick skillet and add the oil once the pan is heated.
3. When the oil is heated, add the greens and sauté for around 3 minutes or until the greens begin to wilt. Pour the water into the bowl, cover the dish with a lid, and steam for 2 to 3 minutes.
4. Add the broccoli, bell pepper, cabbage, and garlic and remove the lid. Meanwhile, whisk the seeds, egg whites, salt, and pepper together in a medium dish. The whisked egg mixture should be applied until the onion is transparent. Stir to split up the eggs equally and spread them.
5. Cook until the eggs are not runny anymore, but still look a little wet, turn off the gas, and serve immediately.

136. Mediterranean Scramble
(Ready in 20-25min, serve 4, Difficulty: Normal)

Ingredients
- 2 tablespoons extra virgin olive oil
- 1/8 cup chopped red onion
- 1 medium clove garlic, minced
- 1/4 cup sliced red bell pepper
- 1/4 cup rinsed and drained, chopped canned artichoke hearts
- 2 egg whites
- 1 whole egg
- 1/8 teaspoon dried oregano
- 1/8 teaspoon cracked black pepper
- 1/8 cup low-fat feta cheese

Directions
1. On medium fire, heat a tiny nonstick pan.
2. Add the oil to the hot pan and then add the onion and garlic when the oil is hot. Before inserting the bell, pepper strips and artichoke hearts, simmer for 1 minute. Sauté the vegetables for another 3 minutes, or until the bell pepper is softened and the onion is translucent. Whisk the egg whites and the egg in a small bowl and season with oregano and black pepper.
3. Pour in the eggs and use a spatula to mix them. Cook for 3 or 4 minutes or until the eggs are not runny anymore. Remove from the heat and cover with the feta until the feta begins to melt. Immediately serve.

137. Egg Muffins
(Ready in 20-25min, serve 6, Difficulty: Normal)

Ingredients
- 4 cups chopped spinach

- 1/2 cup chopped green bell pepper
- 1/2 cup chopped red bell pepper
- 4 tablespoons chopped green onion; white ends discarded
- 14 egg whites
- 3 whole eggs
- 1/8 teaspoon chile pepper flakes
- 1/4 teaspoon dried oregano
- 2 tablespoons finely chopped fresh parsley
- 1/8 teaspoon cracked black pepper
- Pinch of paprika

Directions
1. Preheat the oven to 375°F. Combine all the vegetables in a large bowl, blending them together equally.
2. Add the egg whites, whole eggs, chili pepper flakes, oregano, parsley, pepper, and paprika together in a separate big dish. Using olive oil spray to spray a muffin pan, make sure to spray the surfaces as well. Scoop vegetables into each cup of muffin, filling each about halfway. Onto each muffin cup, gently pour around 1/3 cup of egg mixture so that the vegetables are not displaced.
3. On the middle rack of the oven, put the muffin tin and bake for 25 to 30 minutes, or until the eggs in the middle are no longer runny. To stop overbaking or drying the eggs, extract them directly from the oven. Serve it warm.

138. Veggie Omelet
(Ready in 5min, serve 1, Difficulty: Normal)

Ingredients
- 1 tablespoon extra-virgin olive oil
- 1/4 cup coarsely chopped broccoli
- 2 tablespoons chopped red onion
- 1 clove garlic, minced
- 1/4 cup chopped zucchini
- 2 egg whites
- 1 whole egg
- 1/8 cup shredded low-fat cheddar cheese
- 1/8 teaspoon sea salt
- 1/8 teaspoon cracked black pepper

Directions
1. Over medium pressure, heat a medium-sized nonstick pan and add the oil once the pan is wet.
2. Add the broccoli when the oil is heated, then cook for a minute before adding the onion, garlic, and zucchini. Sauté for between 3 and 4 minutes.
3. Whisk the egg whites and whole egg together in a small bowl and season with salt and pepper. Turn the heat to low and add the whisked eggs with the vegetables to the pan, making sure the pan is angled enough that the eggs reach the vegetables equally.
4. Turn the heat off after 30 seconds, rotate the omelet and sprinkle the cheese on half of the omelet. Over the cheese, fold the other half and cover the plate with a lid. Let it bubble, or before the cheese melts, for 1 to 2 minutes. Immediately serve.

139. Egg Burrito
(Ready in 5min, serve 1, Difficulty: Normal)

Ingredients
- 1 tablespoon extra-virgin olive oil
- 2 tablespoons chopped white onion
- 1 clove garlic, minced
- 2 egg whites
- 1 whole egg
- 1 cup spinach
- 1/8 cup shredded low-fat cheddar cheese
- Cracked black pepper
- 1 100% whole wheat tortilla
- 1/4 cup rinsed and drained canned black beans
- 1 tablespoon chopped fresh cilantro
- 1/4 cup chopped Roma tomato
- 1 tablespoon prepared low-sodium salsa, optional

Directions
1. In a medium pan, melt the oil over a medium heat.
2. Add the garlic and onion, and simmer for about 30 seconds. Meanwhile, whisk the egg whites and the entire egg together. Eggs, spinach, cheese, and pepper are added. For around 2 to 3 minutes, cook until the eggs are no longer runny. Taking the pan away from the sun.
3. Heat the tortilla over medium heat in a flat tray. In a small pot, put the beans and bring them to a simmer. On a tray, put the warm tortilla, and spoon the beans in a line in the center of the tortilla.
4. Add the combination of eggs and vegetables, and finish with cilantro, basil, and salsa (if using). Fold it into a burrito and instantly eat it.

140. Healthy French Toast
(Ready in 5min, serve 4, Difficulty: Normal)

Ingredients
- 4 egg whites
- 1 whole egg
- 1 cup unsweetened almond milk
- 1/2 teaspoon ground cinnamon
- 1 teaspoon vanilla extract
- 1/4 teaspoon ground nutmeg
- 1/2 teaspoon powdered stevia
- 8 slices whole grain bread (at least 1/2–1 inch thick)

Directions
1. Whisk the egg whites, whole egg, and egg whites together in a small dish.
2. Milk of nuts, cloves, vanilla, stevia, and nutmeg. Soak each slice of bread in the mixture for around 1 minute on each side, so the liquid and spices are absorbed by the bread. Heat the griddle pan until very hot, then

cover it with a spray of olive oil. Place each slice of soaked bread on the griddle pan and cook on each side for about 3 minutes or until browned and crunchy. Immediately serve.

Serving Suggestion

3. : Eat per serving with fresh fruit, yogurt, or 2 teaspoons of maple syrup.

Chapter 3: Lunch Recipes

In this chapter, we have compiled lunch recipes for the DASH diet followers.

1. Veggie Quesadillas with Cilantro Yogurt Dip

(Ready in 30 Minutes|serve:4|Difficulty: Normal)

- 1 cup beans, black or pinto
- 2 Tablespoons cilantro, chopped
- ½ bell pepper, finely chopped
- ½ cup corn kernels
- 1 cup low-fat shredded cheese
- 6 soft corn tortillas
- 1 medium carrot, shredded
- ½ jalapeno pepper, finely minced (optional)

CILANTRO YOGURT DIP

- 1 cup plain non-fat yogurt
- 2 Tablespoons cilantro, finely chopped
- Juice from ½ of a lime

Directions:

1. Preheat large skillet over low heat.
2. Line up 3 tortillas. Divide cheese, corn, beans, cilantro, shredded carrots, and peppers between the tortillas.
3. Cover each with a second tortilla.
4. Place a tortilla on a dry skillet and warm until cheese is melted and tortilla is slightly golden, about 3 minutes.
5. Flip and cook other side until golden, about 1 minute.
6. In a small bowl mix together the nonfat yogurt, cilantro and lime juice.
7. Cut each quesadilla into 4 wedges (12 wedges total) and serve 3 wedges per person with about ¼ cup of the dip.
8. Refrigerate leftovers within 2 hours.

2. Sweet Roasted Beet & Arugula Pizza

(Ready in 1 Hours | Serve: 8|Difficulty: Normal)

PIZZA CRUST

- 1 packet active dry yeast
- ¾ cup lukewarm water
- 2 cups 100% whole wheat flour
- 1 ½ teaspoons salt
- Oil for greasing bowl

PIZZA

- 2 small beets, roasted
- 1 cup arugula
- ½ cup goat cheese
- 1 cup blackberries
- 2 tablespoons honey
- 2 tablespoons balsamic vinegar

Directions:
Pizza Crust

1. Pour warm water into a large bowl and sprinkle with yeast

2. Whisk the mixture and let sit until foamy, about 5 minutes
3. Add salt, then slowly stir in flour until a sticky dough forms
4. Transfer dough to an oiled bowl, cover with plastic wrap, let sit ~1 hour in a warm corner of the kitchen to let rise
5. Knead the dough a few times until the dough becomes sticky and begins to form a ball
6. Roll out dough and bake at 500 F for 8-12 minutes, depending on the thickness of the crust

Roasted Beets
1. While the dough is rising, dice beets
2. Place on a baking sheet lined with parchment paper
3. Cover with foil
4. Bake 35 minutes at 400 F
5. Once beets are finished roasting, increase oven temperature and bake pizza crust

Pizza
1. Top crust with roasted beets while the oven cools to 350 F
2. Sprinkle with goat cheese and berries
3. Drizzle with honey and balsamic vinegar
4. Bake 8-10 minutes at 350 F
5. Top with arugula

*Feel free to save time with a ready-made 100% Whole Wheat pizza crust at the store or a baking mix. Be sure to read the label and choose options with less than 200 mg sodium per slice.

3. Sunshine Wrap
(Ready in 2 Hours|Serve: 4|Difficulty: Normal)

Ingredients
- 8 oz chicken breast (one large breast)
- ½ cup celery, diced
- 2/3 cup canned mandarin oranges, drained
- ¼ cup onion, minced
- 2 tablespoons mayonnaise
- 1 teaspoon soy sauce
- ¼ teaspoon garlic powder
- ¼ teaspoon black pepper
- 1 large whole wheat tortilla
- 4 large lettuce leaves, washed and patted dry

Directions:
1. Cook chicken breast in a non-stick pan on medium-high heat until done all through (165oF internal temperature). Cut into 1/2-inch cubes until the chicken has cooled enough to treat.
2. Combine the chicken, celery, oranges, and onions in a medium dish. Add the mayonnaise, soy sauce, pepper, and garlic. Mix softly until evenly covered with the chicken mixture.
3. On a clean cutting board or wide pan, position the tortilla. Break the tortilla into four quarters with a knife or tidy kitchen scissors. On each tortilla fifth, position 1-lettuce leaf, trimming the leaf to hang over the tortilla.
4. In the center of each lettuce leaf, place ¼ of the chicken mixture. Roll tortillas up into a cone, forming the cone's opening with the two straight sides going together with the curved end. Eat the wrap like a sandwich.
5. Leftovers should be refrigerated within 2 hours.

4. Southwestern Black Bean Cakes with Guacamole
(Ready in 2 Hours|Serve:4|Difficulty: Normal)

Ingredients
- 2 slices whole wheat bread, torn
- 3 tablespoons fresh cilantro
- 2 cloves garlic
- 1 (15-ounce) can low sodium black beans, rinsed and drained
- 1 (7-ounce) can chipotle peppers in adobo sauce
- 1 teaspoon ground cumin
- 1 large egg
- ½ medium avocado, seeded and peeled
- 1 tablespoon lime juice
- 1 small plum tomato

Directions
1. Add bread in a food processor bowl or blender container. Cover and process or blend until bread resembles coarse crumbs. Transfer crumbs to a large bowl and set aside.
2. Process or blend cilantro and garlic until finely chopped. Add beans, 1 of the chipotle peppers, 1 to 2 teaspoons of adobo sauce, and cumin. Process or blend using on/off pulses until beans are coarsely chopped, and mixture begins to pull away from sides.
3. Add mixture to bread crumbs in the bowl. Add egg and mix well.
4. Shape mixture into four ½-inch-thick patties. Grill on the lightly greased rack of an uncovered grill directly over medium heat for 8 to 10 minutes or until patties is heated through, turning once.
5. Meanwhile, for guacamole, in a small bowl, mash avocado. Stir in lime juice. Season with salt and pepper. Serve patties with guacamole and tomato.

5. Salmon Salad Pita
(Ready in 2 hours|Serve:4|Difficulty: Normal)

Ingredients
- ¾ cup canned Alaskan salmon
- 3 tablespoons plain fat-free yogurt
- 1 tablespoon lemon juice
- 2 tablespoons red bell pepper, minced
- 1 tablespoon red onion, minced
- 1 teaspoon capers, rinsed and chopped
- Pinch of dill, fresh or dried
- Black pepper to taste
- 3 lettuce leaves
- 3 pieces small whole wheat pita bread

Directions
1. In a shallow bowl, combine the first 8-ingredients to produce a salmon salad.
2. Within each pita, put the 1-lettuce leaf and 1/3 cup of salmon salad.

6. Pesto & Mozzarella Stuffed Portobello Mushroom Caps

(Ready in 2 hours|Serve:4|Difficulty: Normal)

Ingredients

- 2 portobello mushroom caps
- 1 small roma tomato, diced
- 2 tablespoons pesto
- ¼ cup shredded low-fat mozzarella cheese

Directions

1. Use a dry or damp cloth to clean mushrooms. Remove stems by twisting gently.
2. Divide pesto evenly between 2 mushroom caps.
3. Top with diced tomato and shredded cheese.
4. Bake in the oven for 15 minutes at 400 F.

7. Mayo-less Tuna Salad

(Ready in 2 Hours|Serve:4|Difficulty: Normal)

Ingredients

- 5 oz can light tuna in water, drained
- 1 tablespoon extra virgin olive oil
- 1 tablespoon red wine vinegar
- ¼ cup chopped green onion tops
- 2 cups arugula
- 1 cup cooked pasta (from 2 oz dry)
- 1 tablespoon fresh shaved parmesan cheese
- black pepper

Directions

1. Toss the tuna with the oil, vinegar, onion, arugula, and the cooked pasta in a big bowl.
2. Divide and cover with parmesan and pepper on two plates.
2. Immediately serve.

8. Washington Apple Turkey Gyro

(Ready in 2 Hours|Serve:6|Difficulty: Normal)

Ingredients

- 1 tablespoon vegetable oil
- 1 cup onion, sliced
- 1 cup sweet red pepper, thinly sliced
- 1 cup sweet green pepper, thinly sliced
- 2 tablespoons lemon juice
- ½ pound cooked turkey or chicken breast, cut into thin strips
- 1 apple (cored), preferably Golden Delicious; sliced or finely chopped
- 6 whole wheat pocket pita bread, warmed
- ½ cup low fat or fat free plain yogurt

Directions

1. Heat the oil in a large skillet over medium heat. Place the onion, peppers, and lemon juice in the mixture and cook until tender. Stir in the apple and turkey and cook until the turkey is heated. Withdraw from the sun.
2. Cover with some of the mixtures for each pita; drizzle with yogurt. Serve it sweet.

9. Pizza in a Pita

(Ready in 7-10min|Serve 6|Difficulty: Normal)

Ingredients

- 2 pieces whole wheat pita bread
- ½ cup grated reduced sodium mozzarella cheese
- ¼ cup pizza or tomato sauce
- Veggies of choice: mushrooms, bell pepper, onion, olives, artichoke hearts, etc.

Directions

1. Preheat to 350 in the microwave or toaster oven. Break halfway along with the pita bread and spoon with the cheese, tomato sauce, and any toppings.
2. Using aluminum foil to seal the pita and bake for 7 to 10 minutes or until the cheese melts.

Pear, Turkey and Cheese Sandwich

(Ready in 7-10min|Serve:6|Difficulty: Normal)

Ingredients

- 2 slices multi-grain or rye sandwich bread
- 2 tsp Dijon-style mustard
- 2 slices (1 oz. each) reduced-sodium cooked or smoked turkey
- 1 USA pear, cored and thinly sliced
- 1/4 cup shredded lowfat mozzarella cheese
- Coarsely ground pepper

Directions

1. Spread 1-teaspoon of mustard on each slice of bread. Place each slice of bread with one slice of turkey. Arrange the turkey pear slices and sprinkle each with 2-tablespoons of cheese. Sprinkle spice over it.
2. Broil, 2 to 3 minutes or until turkey and pears are hot and cheese melts, 4 to 6 inches from the sun. Halve each sandwich and serve the open face in half

10. Heartfelt Tuna Melt

(Ready in 7-10min|Serve:4|Difficulty: Normal)

Ingredients

- 6 ounces white tuna packed in water, drained
- 1/3 cup chopped celery
- 1/4 cup chopped onion
- 1/4 cup low fat Russian or Thousand Island salad dressing
- 2 whole-wheat English muffins, split
- 3 ounces reduced-fat Cheddar cheese, grated
- Salt and black pepper to taste

Directions

1. Preheat the broiler.
2. Bringing the salmon, celery, onion, and salad dressing together. With salt and pepper, season.

3. English muffin halves with toast. On the baking sheet, put split-side-up and cover each one with 1/4 of the tuna mixture. Broil for 2-3 minutes or until completely cooked.
4. Cover with the cheese and return to the broiler for about 1 minute before the cheese is melted

11. Spinach, Mushroom and Mozzarella Wraps

(Ready in 7-10min|Serve:4|Difficulty: Normal)

Ingredients

- 1 tablespoon olive oil
- 8 oz. fresh mushrooms, sliced (about 2 ½ cups)
- 1 teaspoon minced garlic
- 2 whole wheat 8" tortillas
- ½ pound fresh spinach or arugula, trimmed and steamed
- 1 plum tomato, diced
- ¼ cup (1 ounce) shredded part-skim mozzarella cheese

Directions

1. Preheat oven to 350ºF. Heat 1 tbsp olive oil in a sauté pan over high heat. Add a single layer of mushrooms and garlic. Leave the mushrooms alone as they sauté — be patient as they turn red-brown — then turn and sauté until the second side turns a similar color.
2. On each tortilla, arrange layers of spinach, tomato, mozzarella, and cooked mushrooms. Roll up and place seam-side down in a lightly oiled baking dish. Bake uncovered until hot and cheese is melted, about 10 minutes.
3. Cut each tortilla crosswise into quarters. Serve warm or room temperature as desired.

12. Apple-Swiss Panini

(Ready in 7-10min|Serve:4|Difficulty: Normal)

Ingredients

- 8 slices whole-grain bread
- ¼ cup non-fat honey mustard
- 2 crisp apples, thinly sliced
- 6 ounces low-fat Swiss cheese, thinly sliced
- 1 cup arugula leaves
- Cooking spray

Directions

1. Preheat the medium-heat panini press. Only use a non-stick skillet if you don't have a panini press.
2. Honey mustard is gently applied uniformly over each bread slice. Layer four slices of bread with apple slices, butter, and arugula leaves. Top each one with the remaining slices of bread.
3. Lightly coat the cooking spray with the panini press. Each sandwich for 3 to 5 minutes or until it is melting with cheese and toasted with bread. Remove from the pan before serving and allow to cool slightly.

13. California Grilled Veggie Sandwich

(Ready in 7-10min|Serve:4|Difficulty: Normal)

Ingredients

- 3 tablespoons light mayonnaise
- 3 cloves garlic, minced
- 1 tablespoon lemon juice
- 1/8 cup olive oil
- 1 cup red bell peppers, sliced
- 1 small zucchini, sliced
- 1 red onion, sliced
- 1 small yellow squash, sliced
- 2 slices focaccia bread
- ½ cup crumbled reduced-fat feta cheese

Directions

1. Blend the mayonnaise, minced garlic, and lemon juice in a cup. Set in the refrigerator aside.
2. Preheat the grill to a high degree.
3. Brush the vegetables on either hand with olive oil. Brush the barbecue grill with grease. Place the bell peppers and zucchini nearest to the center of the grill and place bits of onion and squash around them. Cook for 3 minutes or so, turn and cook for 3-more minutes. It will take much longer for the peppers. Remove and set aside from the barbecue.
4. On the crust's cut sides, scatter some of the mayonnaise mixtures; sprinkle each with feta cheese. Place on the grill, cheese side up, and cover for 2 to 3 minutes with the cap. Monitor closely so as not to burn the bottoms.
5. Take the bread from the grill and layer the vegetables with it. Treat yourself to open-faced grilled sandwiches.

14. Vegetable Pasta Soup

(Ready in 7-10min|Serve:4|Difficulty: Normal)

Ingredients

- (3/4-cup) appetizer
- 2 teaspoons olive oil
- 6 cloves garlic, minced
- 1 ½ cups coarsely shredded carrot
- 1 cup chopped onion
- 1 cup thinly sliced celery
- 1 32-ounce box reduced-sodium chicken broth
- 4 cups water
- 1 ½ cups dried ditalini pasta
- 1/4 cup shaved Parmesan cheese
- 2 tablespoons snipped fresh parsley

Directions

1. Heat oil over medium heat in a 5- to 6-quart Dutch oven. Combine with garlic; simmer for 15 seconds. Connect the carrot, onion, and celery; roast, stirring regularly, for 5 to 7 minutes or until tender. Connect the water and chicken broth; bring to a boil. Stir in uncooked pasta; boil for 7 to 8 minutes or until tender.

2. Cover individual pieces of Parmesan cheese and parsley to eat. Allows 12 servings of (3/4-cup) appetizer.

15. Tuscan-Style Tuna Salad
(Ready in 7-10min|Serve:4|Difficulty: Normal)

Ingredients
- 2 6-ounce cans chunk light tuna, drained
- 1 15-ounce can small white beans, such as cannellini or great northern, rinsed (see Ingredient note)
- 10 cherry tomatoes, quartered
- 4 scallions, trimmed and sliced
- 2 tablespoons extra-virgin olive oil
- 2 tablespoons lemon juice
- 1/4 teaspoon salt
- Freshly ground pepper, to taste

Directions:
1. In a medium dish, combine the fish, beans, onions, scallions, oil, lemon juice, salt and pepper together. Stir quietly. To eat, refrigerate until ready.

16. Terrific Tortellini Salad
(Ready in 7-10min|Serve:4|Difficulty: Normal)

Ingredients
- 8 main-dish Servings
- 1 9-ounce package refrigerated light cheese tortellini or ravioli
- 3 cups broccoli florets
- 1 cup crinkle-cut or sliced carrots (2 medium)
- 1/4 cup sliced green onions (2)
- 1/2 cup bottled reduced-fat ranch salad dressing
- 1 large tomato, chopped
- 1 cup fresh pea pods, halved
- Milk (optional)

Directions:
1. Cook the pasta according to product instructions in a large saucepan. During the last 3 minutes of preparation, add the broccoli and carrots. Uh, drain. In cool spray, rinse. Again, drain.
2. Combine the cooked pasta mixture and green onions in a large bowl; drizzle with dressing. To coat, throw softly. For 2 to 24 hours, cover, and relax.
3. Stir the tomato and pea pods gently into the pasta mixture before eating. To moisten, stir in a little milk if necessary. Eight main-dish servings are made.

17. Strawberry, Melon & Avocado Salad
(Ready in 7-10min|Serve:6|Difficulty: Normal)

Ingredients
- 1/4 cup honey
- 2 tablespoons sherry vinegar, or red-wine vinegar
- 2 tablespoons finely chopped fresh mint
- 1/4 teaspoon freshly ground pepper
- Pinch of salt
- 4 cups baby spinach
- 1 small avocado, (4-5 ounces), peeled, pitted and cut into 16 slices
- 16 thin slices cantaloupe, (about 1/2 small cantaloupe), rind removed
- 1 1/2 cups hulled strawberries, sliced
- 2 teaspoons sesame seeds, toasted

Directions:
1. In a shallow bowl, whisk in the honey, vinegar, mint, pepper, and salt.
2. Divide the spinach into 4-plates of lettuce. On top of the spinach, arrange alternating slices of avocado and cantaloupe in a fan. Cover the strawberries for each salad, drizzle with dressing and scatter with the sesame seeds.

18. Spaghetti Squash with Chunky Tomato Sauce
(Ready in 7-10min|Serve:6|Difficulty: Normal)

Ingredients
- 1-pound lean ground beef
- 1/2 cup chopped onion (1 medium)
- 1/2 cup chopped green sweet pepper (1 small)
- 2 cloves garlic, minced
- 1 14 1/2-ounce can diced tomatoes, undrained
- 1 8-ounce can tomato sauce
- 2 tablespoons tomato paste
- 1-1/2 teaspoons dried Italian seasoning, crushed
- 1/8 teaspoon black pepper
- 1 recipe Cooked Spaghetti Squash
- 1/4 cup shredded Parmesan cheese (1 ounce)
- Small fresh basil leaves (optional)

Directions:
1. Cook the ground beef, carrot, sweet pepper, and garlic in a wide saucepan until the meat is brown. Uh, drain. Add the sliced, undrained tomatoes, tomato sauce, tomato paste, black pepper, and Italian seasoning. Bring to a boil with sauce; minimize heat. Simmer, exposed, for 15 minutes, sometimes stirring.
2. In the meantime, prepare fried squash with spaghetti. Serve over the squash with sauce. Sprinkle the cheese with Parmesan. Garnish with basil leaves if needed.
3. Cooked Spaghetti Squash: In many locations with a sharp knife, poke a 2 1/2- to 3-pound whole spaghetti squash. Put the squash in a microwave-safe baking dish. Microwave, exposed, for 10 to 15 minutes on 100 percent (high) capacity or until tender. Let them stand for five minutes. Halve the thickness of the squash and cut the seeds. Shred and split the squash pulp into strands using 2-forks.

19. Soba Noodles with Mushroom, Spinach & Tofu
(Ready in 7-10min|Serve:4-6|Difficulty: Normal)

Ingredients

- 2 Tbsp. (30 mL) canola oil
- 1 shallot, minced
- 1 carrot, finely diced
- 2 cloves garlic, minced
- 1-1/2 Tbsp. (20 mL) minced fresh ginger
- 8 oz. (250 g) white or brown mushrooms, sliced
- 1 cup (250 mL) frozen, thawed edamame
- 1-1/2 cups (375 mL) low-sodium chicken broth or vegetable broth
- 2 Tbsp. (30 mL) reduced-sodium soy sauce
- 1 tsp. (5 mL) grated lemon zest
- 4 oz. (125 g) spinach leaves, chopped
- 4 oz. (125 g) firm tofu, cut into 1/2-inch dice
- 1/4 tsp. (1 mL) freshly ground pepper
- 6 oz. (170 g) soba noodles

Directions:

1. Put to a boil a 5- to 6-quart pot of water.
2. Heat the canola oil in a 10- to 12-inch sauté pan over medium-high heat. For 1 minute, add shallot, carrot, garlic, and ginger and sauté. Stir in the mushrooms, reduce heat to low, cover the pan, sweat for around 4 minutes until soft. Uncover the pan and raise the heat once again to medium-high. Stir in the edamame and sauté for about 2 minutes until heated through. Stir together the broth, lemon zest, and soy sauce and put into the pan. Just get it to a boil.
3. Stir in the spinach a handful at a time, stirring until wilted with each addition. Stir in the tofu, then turn off the heat in the bowl. Season with pepper to taste.
4. Drop the soba noodles into the boiling water; cook for about 5 minutes until al dente. Drain in a colander and clean to remove extra starch with cool water. In the sauté pan, add the noodles and turn the heat to medium-high. Only until heated through, toss noodles with vegetable mixture, then split into shallow pasta bowls and serve with tongs.

20. Skillet Sausage and Potatoes

(Ready in 7-10min|Serve:6|Difficulty: Normal)

Ingredients

- 1/2-pound cooked smoked turkey sausage
- 3 to 4 tablespoons olive oil or cooking oil
- 1-3/4 pounds unpeeled red-skinned potatoes
- 2 medium onions
- 1 teaspoon dried thyme, crushed
- 1-1/2 to 2 teaspoons cumin seed, slightly crushed
- 1/4 teaspoon salt
- 1/4 teaspoon pepper

Directions:

1. For transport, prepare the supplies and transport the sausage in an enclosed ice pack cooler.
2. Pour 3-tablespoons of oil into a large 12-inch ovenproof skillet to cook; put directly on top of the campfire or range. Raise and rotate the skillet with oil to coat the rim. Break the potatoes into 1/2-inch cubes; slice or chop the onions into thin wedges. Cook the uncovered potatoes and onions in hot oil over medium-high heat for around 12 minutes or almost tender, stirring periodically.
3. Cut the sausage 1/4 inch thick diagonally; apply the sausage to the potato mixture. To avoid sticking, add 1-tablespoon of oil if needed. Cook for about 10 minutes, uncovered, or until the potatoes and onions are soft and slightly orange, stirring regularly.
4. Add thyme, cumin seeds, salt, and pepper; simmer and mix for another 1 minute. Six main-dish servings are made.

21. Sirloin Soup

(Ready in 7-10min|Serve:6|Difficulty: Normal)

Ingredients

- 1 tablespoon oil
- 1 small onion, diced
- 1-pound lean ground sirloin
- 1/3 cup all-purpose flour
- 1 package (32 ounces) beef broth
- 1 bag (1 pound) frozen soup vegetables
- 2 tablespoons Worcestershire sauce

Directions:

1. Heat the oil in a wide saucepan over medium heat and add the onion. Cook for approximately 5 minutes, until tender. Add ground beef and simmer for about 5 minutes, breaking up chunks with a spoon, until cooked through.
2. In a jar with a tight-fitting lid, put the flour and 2/3 cup of water and shake to mix well. Pour beef into a saucepan and add broth; bring to a boil, stirring continuously. Add the vegetables and simmer for about 10 minutes, until cooked. Stir in the sauce from Worcestershire.

22. Shrimp Salad with Raspberry Vinaigrette

(Ready in 7-10min|Serve:4|Difficulty: Normal)

Ingredients

- 12 ounces fresh asparagus spears
- 1 8-ounce package frozen baby corn or 8-3/4-ounce can baby corn, drained
- 12 Belgian endive leaves or curly endive leaves
- 12 Boston or Bibb lettuce leaves
- 12 sorrel or spinach leaves
- 12 ounces fresh or frozen peeled and deveined shrimp, cooked and chilled
- 2-1/2 cups fresh or frozen red raspberries and/or sliced strawberries, thawed
- 1/4 cup walnut oil or salad oil
- 1/4 cup raspberry or wine vinegar
- 1 tablespoon snipped fresh cilantro or parsley
- 2 teaspoons honey

Directions:

1. Snap the woody asparagus bases off and discard them. Cook the asparagus, wrapped, for 4 to 8 minutes in a limited volume of boiling water or until crisp-tender. Oh, drain; cool.

Cook according to box instructions when using frozen baby corn. Oh, drain; cool.

2. On 4-dinner plates, arrange the greens and asparagus. Placed rice, shrimp, and berries on top of each one.

3. Combine walnut oil or salad oil, raspberry or wine vinegar, new coriander or parsley, and honey in a screw-top container for dressing. Cover; well shake. Serve with spinach. He makes four servings.

23. Shrimp and Asparagus Salad

(Ready in 7-10min|Serve:4|Difficulty: Normal)

Ingredients

- 12 ounces fresh asparagus spears, trimmed
- 4 cups watercress, tough stems removed
- 1 16-ounce package frozen peeled, cooked shrimp with tails intact, thawed
- 2 cups cherry tomatoes, halved
- 1/2 cup bottled light raspberry or berry vinaigrette salad dressing
- Cracked black pepper
- Cracker bread (optional)

Directions:

1. Cook the asparagus, wrapped in a large skillet, in a small amount of lightly salted boiling water for 3 minutes or until crisp-tender; drain in a colander. Run until calm, under cold water.

2. Divide asparagus between four dinner plates; top with cherry tomatoes, shrimp, and watercress. A dressing drizzle. Add crushed black pepper and serve with cracker bread. He makes four servings.

24. Scoop-It-Up Chicken Salad

(Ready in 7-10min|Serve:4|Difficulty: Normal)

Ingredients

- 1/3 cup chopped or shredded cooked chicken or turkey
- 2 tablespoons chopped celery
- 1 tablespoon light mayonnaise dressing or salad dressing
- 1 tablespoon salsa
- 1 tablespoon shredded cheddar cheese
- 4 Mini taco shells or scoop-shaped tortilla chips

Directions:

1. Combine chicken, celery, mayonnaise sauce, salsa, and cheese in a small bowl for chicken salad; toss to blend. Through a jar, spoon; cover securely.

2. Wrap the plastic wrap with the taco shells. Load the chicken salad and taco shells with an ice pack in an enclosed bag. To eat, scoop up the salad using taco shells. Makes 1 -single serving.

25. Savory Millet Cakes

(Ready in 7-10min|Serve:4|Difficulty: Normal)

Ingredients

- 1 tablespoon extra-virgin olive oil
- 1/4 cup finely chopped onion
- 1 cup millet, (see Note)
- 1 clove garlic, minced
- 3 1/2 cups water
- 1/2 teaspoon coarse salt
- 1/3 cup coarsely shredded zucchini
- 1/3 cup coarsely shredded carrot
- 1/3 cup grated Parmesan cheese
- 1 1/2 teaspoons minced fresh thyme, or 1/2 teaspoon dried
- 1 teaspoon freshly grated lemon zest
- 1/4 teaspoon freshly ground pepper

Directions:

1. Heat 1 tablespoon of oil over medium-low heat in a wide saucepan. Attach the onion and simmer for 2 to 4 minutes, stirring, until tender. Stir in the millet and garlic and simmer for about 30 seconds, stirring, until fragrant. Connect water and salt, and over medium heat, bring to a boil. Decrease the heat to a minimum, cover, and simmer for 20 minutes, stirring once or twice. Mix the zucchini, carrot, parmesan cheese, thyme, lemon zest, and pepper. To prevent the millet from sticking, cook, uncovered, holding a boil, and stirring regularly until the mixture is smooth, very thick, and the liquid has been absorbed, about 10 minutes more. Remove from the heat and encourage to stand for 10 minutes, sheltered. Uncover and let stand, stirring once or twice, for about 30 minutes, before cool enough to manage.

2. Form the millet mixture into 12 cakes or patties, 3 inches in diameter (a meager 1/3 cup each) with dampened palms.

3. Using cooking spray to grease a large nonstick skillet and fire over medium heat. Attach 4 -cakes of millet and simmer for 3 to 5 minutes until the bottoms are browned. Turn the cakes gently with a large spatula and cook until browned on the other side for another 3 to 5 minutes. Cover the pan again with a cooking spray and cook the remaining cakes in pans, reducing the heat to stop burning if necessary.

26. Roast Chicken Dal

(Ready in 7-10min|Serve:4|Difficulty: Normal)

Ingredients

- 1 1/2 teaspoons canola oil
- 1 small onion, minced
- 2 teaspoons curry powder
- 1 15-ounce can lentils, rinsed, or 2 cups cooked lentils (see Tip)
- 1 14-ounce can diced tomatoes, preferably fire-roasted
- 1 2-pound roasted chicken, skin discarded, meat removed from bones and diced (4 cups)
- 1/4 teaspoon salt, or to taste
- 1/4 cup low-fat plain yogurt

Directions:

1. Heat oil in a large, heavy saucepan over medium-high heat.

2. Add onion and cook, stirring, until softened but not browned, 3 to 4 minutes.

3. Add curry powder and cook, stirring, until combined with the onion and intensely aromatic, 20 to 30 seconds.
4. Stir in lentils, tomatoes, chicken, salt, and cook, often stirring, until heated through. Remove from the heat and stir in yogurt. Serve immediately.

27. Red Pepper & Goat Cheese Frittata

(Ready in 7-10min|Serve:4|Difficulty: Normal)

Ingredients

- 8 eggs
- 2 tablespoons finely chopped fresh oregano
- 1/2 teaspoon salt
- 1/4 teaspoon freshly ground pepper
- 2 tablespoons extra-virgin olive oil
- 1 cup sliced red bell pepper
- 1 bunch scallions, trimmed and sliced
- 1/2 cup crumbled goat cheese

Directions:

1. Rack location in the upper third of the oven; broiler to preheat.
2. In a medium dish, whisk in the eggs, oregano, salt, and pepper. Heat oil over medium heat in a big, ovenproof, nonstick skillet. Add bell pepper and scallions and cook, stirring continuously, 30 seconds to 1 minute, until the scallions are only wilted.
3. Pour the egg mixture over the vegetables and cook, raising the frittata edges to allow the uncooked egg to flow for 2 to 3 minutes underneath until the bottom is softly golden. Dot the top of the frittata with cheese, move the pan to the oven, and broil for 2 to 3 minutes until it is puffy and softly golden on top. Until serving, let it rest for about 3 minutes. Serve cold or sticky.

28. Quinoa Salad with Dried Apricots & Baby Spinach

(Ready in 7-10min|Serve:4|Difficulty: Normal)

Ingredients

- 1 cup quinoa, (see Ingredient note)
- 2 teaspoons extra-virgin olive oil
- 2 cloves garlic, minced
- 1/2 cup dried apricots, coarsely chopped
- 2 cups water
- 1/4 teaspoon salt
- 2/3 cup Moroccan-Spiced Lemon Dressing, (recipe follows), divided
- 1 cup cherry tomatoes, or grape tomatoes, halved
- 1 small red onion, chopped
- 8 cups baby spinach
- 1/4 cup sliced almonds, toasted (see Tip)

Directions:

1. Toast the quinoa over medium heat in a dry skillet, stirring regularly, until it becomes fragrant and starts to crackle, for around 5 minutes. Switch to a fine sieve and thoroughly rinse out.
2. Heat oil over low heat in a medium saucepan. Add garlic and cook for about 1 minute, stirring continuously, until golden. Apply the apricots and quinoa; continue to cook, stirring regularly, 3 to 4 minutes, until the quinoa has dried out and turned lightly golden. Apply salt and water; bring to a boil. Reduce heat to medium-low and boil, uncovered, for 15 to 18 minutes until the quinoa is tender and the liquid is absorbed.
3. Make the Moroccan-Spiced Lemon Dressing in the meantime. Move the quinoa and toss it with 1/3 cup of the dressing in a medium dish. Leave for 10 minutes to cool.
4. Add the tomatoes and onion to the quinoa just before serving; toss to cover. In a wide bowl, toss the spinach with the remaining 1/3 cup dressing. Divide the spinach into 4-pans. Mound the spinach with the quinoa salad and sprinkle it with almonds.

29. Pepper Pork Tamales

(Ready in 30-35min|Serve:4|Difficulty: Normal)

Ingredients

- 1 medium onion, quartered
- 2 cloves garlic, sliced
- 1/2 teaspoon cracked black pepper
- 2 dried ancho or poblano chile peppers
- 1 dried New Mexico or pasilla chile pepper
- 26 to 28 dried corn husks (about 8 inches long and 7 to 8 inches wide at the top)
- 1 clove garlic
- 1/2 teaspoon salt
- 1/4 teaspoon cumin seeds, toasted*
- 4 cups Masa Harina (corn tortilla flour)
- 2 teaspoons baking powder
- 1/2 teaspoon salt
- 1/2 cup cooking oil

Directions:

1. For filling: Mix the bacon, onion quarters, sliced garlic, and crushed black pepper in a 4-quart Dutch oven. Incorporate enough water to cover (about 4 cups). Bring to a boil; reduce to medium-low heat. Cover and cook for 1 to 1-1/4 hours or until really tender. Withdraw the beef from the broth. Let the broth and beef cool slightly. Remove and compost all pork fat; shred the pork. Strain the broth and reserve the dough with 2-1/2 cups of broth (save the remaining broth for another use). Cover and individually cool the beef and broth before ready to use.
2. Meanwhile, roast ancho and New Mexico peppers over medium heat for 4 to 5 minutes or until they have a toasted fragrance in a dry medium pan, rotating regularly. Only let it cool.
3. Wearing disposable rubber gloves or small plastic sacks, cut and compost pepper ends, seeds, and ribs. Place the peppers in a bowl and rip them into pieces. Cover the peppers in boiling water; let stand to soften for 30 to 60 minutes. Meanwhile, soak the corn husks for about 30 minutes or until they are soft in hot water.
4. Place a thin sieve over a bowl; apply the softened peppers to the sieve. Drain well; keep peppers and liquid in stock.

Combine the soaked peppers, 1-garlic clove, 1/2 teaspoon salt, and the cumin seeds in a blender. Apply the pepper soaking liquid to 1/2 cup; cover and mix until almost smooth.

5. Move the mixed pepper mixture to a medium casserole dish. Get it to a boil; lower the flame. Simmer, exposed, for around 10 minutes or until 1/2 cup is diminished. Stir the shredded pork in a saucepan into the spicy pepper mixture.

6. For the dough: stir together Masa Harina, baking powder, and 1/2 teaspoon salt in a wide cup. Add cooking oil; beat until mixed with an electric mixer or with a spoon. To make a mixture that resembles a deep, smooth paste, whisk in plenty of the filtered pork broth. Cover with a wet paper towel when making tamales to keep the dough from drying out.

7. Drain a husk of corn well to assemble each tamale; pat dry with paper towels. Spread about 2-teaspoons of the dough into a rectangle 3 inches wide and 4 inches deep, beginning about 1 inch from the top edge of the husk, extending such that one of the long sides is on the long edge of the husk. Spoon about 1-tablespoon of the center-filling bacon.

8. Fold each husk's long edge over the filling to partially overlap the dough. Wrap the husk around the filled dough outside. The tie ends with corn husk strips or a thick kitchen cord.

9. In a very large Dutch oven, half the tamales stand upright in a steamer basket to steam the tamales. (Don't stack them too closely, but fill all the rooms.) Put the bottom with at least 1-1/2 inches of water. Get it to the boil. Dutch oven sheet. Decrease the heat to medium. Steam for 30 to 35 minutes or before tamales come away effortlessly from maize husks and spongy dough. Makes 26 to 28 tamales.

30. Penne Salad with Italian Green Beans and Gorgonzola

(Ready in 30-35min|Serve:4|Difficulty: Normal)

Ingredients

- 6 ounces dried penne, ziti, elbow macaroni, or other short pasta
- 8 ounces fresh Italian green beans, trimmed and bias-sliced into 1-inch pieces or one 9-ounce package frozen Italian green beans, thawed
- 1/3 cup fat-free Italian salad dressing
- 1 tablespoon snipped fresh tarragon or 1/2 teaspoon dried tarragon, crushed
- 1/2 teaspoon freshly ground black pepper
- 2 cups torn radicchio or 1 cup finely shredded red cabbage
- 4 cups fresh spinach leaves, cleaned, trimmed, and shredded
- 1/2 cup crumbled Gorgonzola cheese (2 ounces)

Directions:

1. Heat the pasta according to packet instructions, adding the last 5 to 7 minutes of cooking to the pasta with fresh green beans. (Or add the last 3 to 4 minutes of frozen and thawed beans.) Clean the pasta and beans well under cool running water; drain thoroughly.

2. Combine the Italian dressing, tarragon, and pepper in a large mixing cup. Pasta, beans, and radicchio or cabbage are added; toss to coat gently. Serve with sliced spinach on a bed and finish with the cheese from Gorgonzola. Allows 8-servings for side-dish.

31. Pasta Primavera

(Ready in 30-35min|Serve:4|Difficulty: Normal)

Ingredients

- 1-pound penne or elbow-shaped pasta
- 2 tablespoons olive oil
- 3 cloves garlic, sliced
- 3 carrots, peeled and sliced
- 1 bunch asparagus (about 1 pound), stem ends snapped off and spears cut into 1-inch pieces
- 1 sweet red pepper, halved lengthwise, seeded and sliced
- 1 sweet yellow pepper, halved lengthwise, seeded and sliced
- 1 small cherry tomatoes (about 24), halved
- 3/4 teaspoon salt
- 1/4 teaspoon black pepper
- 2/3 cup half-and-half
- 2 tablespoons grated Parmesan

Directions:

1. Get the broad pot to a boil with salted water. In boiling water, add pasta; cook until al dente, soft but still strong.

2. Meanwhile, over medium-high pressure, heat a 12-inch skillet. Connect the garlic and boil and simmer for 1 to 2 minutes. Stir in the carrots; simmer for 4 minutes. Decrease the heat to medium. Add asparagus; cover; simmer for 8 minutes or until tender. Uncover; add sweet peppers; cook, stirring periodically, for 5 minutes. Garnish with cherry tomatoes, salt, pepper, and half-and-a-half. Stir in 1/4 cup pasta bath.

3. Pasta drain; move to bowl.

4. Pour in the spaghetti sauce. Parmesan sprinkle; toss. Just serve.

32. Pappardelle with Roasted Tomatoes

(Ready in 30-35min|Serve:4|Difficulty: Normal)

Ingredients

- 8 plum tomatoes, halved lengthwise
- 3 tablespoons olive oil
- Salt and freshly ground black pepper
- 12 ounces pappardelle or Mafalda pasta
- 1 clove garlic, minced
- 1 8-ounce can tomato sauce
- 1 tablespoon snipped fresh thyme
- 1/4 teaspoon crushed red pepper
- 1/4 teaspoon freshly ground black pepper
- 1/4 cup coarsely shaved pecorino Romano cheese

Directions:

1. Preheat the oven to 450 Fahrenheit. Cover a 15x10x1-inch baking pan with foil to roast the tomatoes. Place the tomatoes in the prepared bowl, cut side up. Add 1-tablespoon of oil and

sprinkle with salt and pepper to taste. Roast, uncovered, for 20 to 25 minutes in a preheated oven or until the tomato bottoms are dark brown. Remove and carefully halve each piece from the pan.

2. Meanwhile, cook pasta according to package instructions in a 4-quart Dutch oven; drain and set aside. Cook the garlic in the remaining 2-tablespoons of oil over medium heat for 30 seconds in the same pan. Add the tomato sauce, half the thyme, and the crushed red pepper and stir. Get it to a boil; lower the flame. Simmer for 2 minutes, exposed. Pasta, roasted tomatoes, remaining thyme, and 1/4 of a teaspoon of black pepper are added. Via the Sun. With additional salt and freshly ground pepper, season to taste. Transfer to a dish for serving. Sprinkle cheese over it. Create 8-side dishes or 4-servings of the main dish.

33. Mustard Glazed Ribs

(Ready in 30-35min|Serve:4|Difficulty: Normal)

Ingredients

- 1 rack pork ribs, cut into individual ribs, about 3 pounds
- 1/4 cups ketchup
- 1/3 cup cider vinegar
- 3 tablespoons spicy brown mustard
- 2 tablespoons brown sugar
- 3 tablespoons water
- 1 teaspoon onion powder
- 1/4 teaspoon hot sauce

Directions:

1. Heat the oven to 400°C. In a 13 x 9 x 2-inch baking dish, put the ribs and cover them tightly with foil. Bake at 400 for 1 hour. Drain out the substance that has been gathered.

2. Meanwhile, stir the ketchup, vinegar, mustard, brown sugar, 3-tablespoons of water, onion powder, and hot sauce together in a medium-sized saucepan. For 10 minutes, simmer over medium-low heat, stirring. Place a small bowl with half the sauce; set aside.

3. Heat a medium-high gas grill or cook a medium-hot barbecue grill. Cover the grill rack loosely ang grease with oil or nonstick cooking spray.

4. Baste the ribs generously with the remaining sauce and barbecue them on either side for 3 to 4 minutes or until they are well browned. Serve the ribs with the sauce reserved on the side.

34. Mushroom-Sauced Pork Chops

(Ready in 30-35min|Serve:4|Difficulty: Normal)

Ingredients

- 4 pork loin chops, cut 3/4 inch thick (about 2 pounds)
- 1 tablespoon cooking oil
- 1 small onion, thinly sliced
- 2 tablespoons quick-cooking tapioca
- 1 10-3/4-ounce can reduced-fat and reduced-sodium condensed cream of mushroom soup
- 1/2 cup apple juice or apple cider
- 1-1/2 teaspoons Worcestershire sauce
- 2 teaspoons snipped fresh thyme or 3/4 teaspoon dried thyme, crushed
- 1/4 teaspoon garlic powder
- 1-1/2 cups sliced fresh mushrooms
- Fresh thyme sprigs (optional)

Directions:

1. Trim fat from chops, in a large skillet, heat oil over medium heat. Add chops; cook until browned, turning to brown evenly. Drain off fat. Place onion in a 3-1/2- or 4-quart slow cooker. Add chops. Using a mortar and pestle, crush tapioca. In a medium bowl, combine tapioca, mushroom soup, apple juice, Worcestershire sauce, snipped or dried thyme, and garlic powder; stir in mushrooms. Pour over chops in the slow cooker.

2. Cover and cook on low-heat settings for 8 to 9 hours or on high-heat settings for 4 to 4-1/2 hours. If desired, garnish with thyme sprigs.

35. Mushroom & Leek Galette

(Ready in 30-35min|Serve:4|Difficulty: Normal)

Ingredients

- 8 appetizer servings or 4 main-dish servings
- 3/4 cup whole-wheat pastry flour
- 3/4 cup all-purpose flour
- 1 1/2 teaspoons baking powder
- 1/4 teaspoon salt
- 1/2 cup 1% cottage cheesier
- 1/4 cup canola oil
- 1/4 cup 1% milk
- 1 1/2 teaspoons sugar
- 1 egg mixed with 1 tablespoon water, for glaze
- 1 tablespoon extra-virgin olive oil
- 2 cups sliced leeks, (about 2 large) (see Tip)
- 12 ounces cremini, or baby bella mushrooms, wiped clean and sliced (6 cups)
- 1 large egg
- 1/3 cup reduced-fat sour cream
- 1/2 teaspoon salt, or to taste
- Freshly ground pepper, to taste
- 1/2 cup scallions, chopped
- 1/4 cup chopped fresh parsley

Directions:

1. In a medium dish, whisk together the whole wheat flour, all-purpose flour, baking powder, and salt to prepare the crust. Cottage cheese puree in a food processor. Oil, milk, and sugar are added; process until smooth. Add the dry ingredients and pulse until the dough clumps together, 4 or 5 times. Turn out and knead several times on a well-floured board, but do not overwork. Press the dough onto a plate, sprinkle it with flour, and wrap it in a wrap of plastic. Refrigerate for 20 minutes at the very least.

2. Meanwhile, plan the filling: Heat the oil over medium-low heat in a large nonstick skillet. Add the leeks and cook, frequently stirring, for 3 to 5 minutes, until tender. (To avoid

scorching, add water if necessary.) Add mushrooms and raise heat to medium-high; cook, stirring regularly, 3 to 4 minutes until the mushrooms are tender and the liquid has evaporated. Only let it cool.

3. In a big bowl, stir in the egg, sour cream, salt, and pepper. Apply the mushroom blend, scallions, and parsley; toss to coat.

4. Galette assembly & baking: Preheat the oven to 400 F. Coat a baking sheet with spray for frying.

5. Roll the dough into a rough 15-inch circle about 1/4 of an inch thick on a thinly floured surface. Roll it back over the rolling pin and pass it to the baking sheet that has been packed. Over the pastry, scatter the filling, leaving a 2-inch border all over. Fold the border up and over the filling, pleating as appropriate, to shape a rim. Brush the glaze of an egg over the bottom.

36. Moroccan Shrimp with Pomegranate Sauce

(Ready in 30-35min|Serve:4|Difficulty: Normal)

Ingredients

- 1 qt pomegranate juice
- 1/2 cup sugar
- 1/4 cup fresh lemon juice
- 1 lb. large shrimp, peeled and deveined, with tails
- 3/4 tsp ground cumin
- 3/4 tsp ground coriander
- 1/4 tsp ground cinnamon
- 3/4 tsp kosher salt
- 1-1/2 Tbsp olive oil
- 4 cups (4 oz) baby arugula

Directions:

1. In a pot over high heat, stir together pomegranate juice, sugar, and lemon juice until sugar dissolves. Boil until liquid thickens and is reduced to 1 cup, about 45 min.

2. Meanwhile, toss shrimp with cumin, coriander, cinnamon, salt, and olive oil and stir to coat.

3. In a bowl, toss arugula with extra lemon juice and olive oil if desired. Place on a platter.

4. Heat a grill pan over medium heat. Add shrimp and cook 2 min per side until pink and opaque; place on top of arugula. Pour sauce into a small dish for dipping. Makes 10-servings or 4-servings for the main course.

37. Minted Peas & Rice with Feta

(Ready in 5-6min|Serve:4|Difficulty: Normal)

Ingredients

- 1 1/4 cups reduced-sodium chicken broth
- 3/4 cup instant brown rice
- 1 1/2 cups frozen peas, (6 ounces)
- 3/4 cup sliced scallions
- 1/4 cup finely crumbled feta cheese
- 1/4 cup sliced fresh mint
- Freshly ground pepper, to taste

Directions:

1. Bring broth to a boil in a large saucepan over high heat. Add rice and bring to a simmer; cover, reduce heat to medium-low, and cook for 4 minutes. Stir in peas and return to a simmer over high heat.

2. Cover, reduce heat to medium-low, and continue to cook until the peas are hot and the rice has absorbed most of the liquid, about 6 minutes. Remove from heat and stir in scallions, feta, mint, and pepper.

3. Cover and let stand until the liquid is absorbed, 3 to 5 minutes.

38. Moroccan Eggplant with Tomatoes

(Ready in 30-35min|Serve:4|Difficulty: Normal)

Ingredients

- 4 (1 cup (250 mL)
- 1 large purple eggplant (about 1 lb./ 500 g)
- 2 Tbsp. (30 ml) canola oil
- 2 cloves garlic, minced
- 1 tsp. (5 mL) ground cumin
- 1 tsp. (5 mL) sweet paprika
- 1/2 cup (125 mL) chopped fresh cilantro 125 mL
- 1 can chopped low-sodium tomatoes (about 14.5 oz./(412 mL) or 1 lb./500 g ripe red tomatoes, peeled, seeded and chopped

Directions:

1. Trim finishes with a vegetable peeler or paring knife off the eggplant. Then avoid the overlapping skin strips to make the eggplant look striped. Break the eggplant into cubes of around 1 inch.

2. Heat the canola oil in a medium sauté pan over medium-high heat. Stir in the eggplant and sauté for 1 minute. Stir in the garlic and sauté for 30 seconds. Lower the heat and cover the pan; sweat for 10 minutes until the eggplant is tender. Stir in the cumin, paprika, and cilantro and sauté for about 10 seconds before the mixture smells fragrant. Bring the tomatoes to a boil and stir.

3. Turn the heat to medium-low and sauté for about 7 minutes until the mixture is thickened and some eggplant is smooth and some chunky. Switch off the heat and let the mixture sit for 5 to 10 minutes to settle the flavors before eating.

39. Middle Eastern Chicken Kabobs

(Ready in 5-6min|Serve:4|Difficulty: Normal)

Ingredients

- 1 pound skinless, boneless chicken breast halves, cut into 1-inch pieces
- 1/4 cup plain low-fat yogurt
- 1 tablespoon lemon juice
- 1 teaspoon dry mustard
- 1 teaspoon ground cinnamon
- 1 teaspoon curry powder

- 1/2 teaspoon salt
- 1/4 to 1/2 teaspoon crushed red pepper
- 1 large red sweet pepper, cut into 1-inch pieces (1 cup)
- 1 medium yellow summer squash, halved lengthwise and cut into 1/2-inch-thick slices
- Soft pita breads, warmed (optional)
- Tomato Relish (optional)

Directions
1. Place the chicken in a plastic bag set in a bowl that is resealable. Mix the yogurt, lemon juice, vinegar, cinnamon, curry powder, salt, and crushed red pepper in a shallow dish. Pour chicken over it. Seal the bag; turn the coat over. Refrigerate, spinning periodically, for 1 to 4 hours.
2. Preheat the broiler. Thread the chicken, sweet pepper, and squash on 6-long metal skewers, leaving 1/4 inch between the bits. Broil for 8 to 10 minutes 4 to 5 inches from the sun or until the chicken is no longer yellow, rotating once. Serve it with pita bread and tomato relish, if desired. Gets 6-servings.
3. Tomato Relish: Mix 2 diced Roma tomatoes; 1/2 cup of chopped grape tomatoes; 1 tablespoon of balsamic vinegar; 1 teaspoon of sliced fresh oregano; 1 teaspoon of sliced fresh thyme; 1 teaspoon of honey; 1 clove of chopped garlic. To taste, apply salt and ground black pepper. Cover; up to 4 pcs chill.

40. Mango Salad with Smoked Turkey
(Ready in 5-6min|Serve:4|Difficulty: Normal)

Ingredients
- 2 medium mangoes, peeled and seeded
- 4 cups torn mixed salad greens
- 1 cup torn thinly sliced smoked turkey
- 1/4 cup chopped fresh cilantro
- Lime Vinaigrette (below)

Directions
1. Slice the mangoes into very thin (about 1/8 inch thick) bits using a very sharp peeler or knife. Only put aside.
2. Divide the salad greens into four plates of salad. Arrange the greens with mango slices and smoked turkey bits. Sprinkle with the coriander; drizzle with the vinaigrette of lime.
3. Combine 2-teaspoons of peanut oil, roasted peanut oil, or salad oil in a screw-top jar; 2 tablespoons of water; 1/4 of a teaspoon of finely shredded lime peel; 2 tablespoons of lime juice; and 1/4 of a teaspoon of grated fresh ginger. Cover and shake thoroughly. Makes 1/3 of a cup.

41. Linguini with Fresh Veggies
(Ready in5-6min|Serve:4|Difficulty: Normal)

Ingredients
- 16 thin stalks fresh asparagus
- 1 tablespoon olive oil
- 4 cloves garlic, thinly sliced or minced
- 6 medium plum (Roma) tomatoes, seeded and chopped (21/4 cups)
- 1/4 cup dry white wine
- 1/4 teaspoon salt
- 1 tablespoon butter*
- 1 9-ounce package refrigerated linguini pasta, or substitute angel hair pasta
- 1/4 cup shredded fresh basil

Directions
1. Trim asparagus. Remove tips; set aside. Bias-slice asparagus stalks into 1-to 1 1/2-inch pieces; set aside.
2. Heat oil in a large skillet over medium heat. Add garlic and 1/4 teaspoon pepper; cook for 1 minute, stirring constantly. Add tomatoes and cook for about 2 minutes, stirring often.
3. Add asparagus stalks, wine, and salt. Cook, uncovered, for 3 minutes. Add asparagus tips; cook uncovered for 1 minute. Add butter; stir till melted.
4. Meanwhile, cook pasta according to package directions. Drain pasta. Return to pan and toss with asparagus mixture and basil.
5. Note: The butter is used in this recipe to bind the sauce. Margarine might not be an effective substitute.

42. Lemon-Sage Pork Salad
(Ready in 5-6min|Serve:4|Difficulty: Normal)

Ingredients
- 1-pound pork tenderloin
- 1 tablespoon finely shredded lemon peel
- 6 leaves fresh sage, thinly sliced
- 1/2 teaspoon ground cumin
- 1/4 teaspoon ground black pepper
- 1/8 teaspoon salt
- 1 tablespoon olive oil
- 1 head green leaf lettuce, torn
- 1-1/2 cups chopped tomatoes
- 1 avocado, halved, pited, peeled and chopped
- 1 cup canned black beans, rinsed and drained
- 1/2 cup chopped green onions
- Red Hot Pepper Vinaigrette

Direction
1. Trim fat from pork. Cut pork crosswise into 1/4-inch-thick slices. Place pork slices in a large bowl. Add lemon peel, sage, cumin, pepper, and salt. Toss well to coat. Let stand for 10 minutes.
2. In a very large skillet, cook pork, half at a time, in hot oil over medium-high heat for 2 to 3 minutes or until meat is just slightly pink in the center, turning once. Remove from skillet and set aside.
3. Place lettuce on a serving platter. Top with tomatoes, avocado, beans, and green onions. Arrange pork slices over salad. Drizzle with some Red-Hot Pepper Vinaigrette; pass remaining vinaigrette.

43. Heirloom Tomato and Onion Quiche

(Ready in 5-6min|Serve:4|Difficulty: Normal)

Ingredients

- 1/2 of a 15-ounce package (1 crust) rolled refrigerated unbaked piecrust
- 12 ounces assorted garden heirloom tomatoes (Cherokee Purple and/or Brandywine) or regular tomatoes, cut into 1/4-inch-thick slices
- 1 tablespoon butter
- 1/2 cup chopped onion (1 medium)
- 3 eggs
- 3/4 cup half-and-half, light cream or milk
- 3 tablespoons all-purpose flour
- 1 tablespoon snipped fresh basil or 1 teaspoon dried basil, crushed
- 1/2 teaspoon salt
- 1/4 teaspoon dry mustard
- 1/8 teaspoon ground black pepper
- 1 cup shredded Swiss, cheddar, Monterey Jack, and/or Havarti cheese (4 ounces)
- Paprika

Directions:

1. Let piecrust stand at room temperature according to package directions. Unroll piecrust into a 9-inch pie plate. Crimp edge as desired. Line unpicked pastry with a double thickness of foil. Bake in a 425-degree F oven for 8 minutes. Remove foil. Bake for 4 to 5 minutes more or until pastry is set and dry. Remove from oven. Reduce oven temperature to 375 F.

2. Meanwhile, place tomato slices on paper towels to absorb excess moisture. In a small skillet, melt butter over medium heat. Add onion. Cook until onion is tender but not brown, stirring occasionally.

3. In a medium bowl, whisk together eggs, half-and-half, flour, basil, salt, dry mustard, and black pepper.

4. To assemble, sprinkle cheese onto the bottom of the hot, baked pastry shell. Spoon onion mixture over cheese. Arrange a single layer of tomato slices over cheese, overlapping slightly. Slowly pour egg mixture over tomatoes. Sprinkle paprika over egg mixture.

5. Bake, uncovered, for 35 to 40 minutes or until egg mixture is set in the center. If necessary, cover the edge of the pie with foil for the last 5 to 10 minutes of baking to prevent over-browning. Let stand 10 minutes before serving.

44. Grilled Vegetables on Focaccia

(Ready in 5-6min|Serve:4|Difficulty: Normal)

Ingredients

- 3 tablespoons balsamic vinegar or wine vinegar
- 2 tablespoons water
- 1 tablespoons olive oil
- 1 teaspoon dried oregano, crushed
- 2 large red and/or orange sweet peppers
- 2 medium zucchini and/or yellow summer squash, halved crosswise and sliced thinly lengthwise
- 1 medium eggplant, cut crosswise into 1/2-inch slices
- 2 ounces soft goat cheese (chevre)
- 2 ounces fat-free cream cheese
- 1 purchased focaccia (about a 12-inch round)
- Fresh oregano (optional)

Directions:

1. In a small bowl, combine vinegar, water, oil, and dried oregano. Set aside. Cut sweet peppers in quarters. Remove stems, membranes, and seeds. Arrange all vegetables on grill rack; brush with vinegar mixture. Grill on an uncovered grill directly over medium-hot coals until slightly charred, turning occasionally (allow 8 to 10 minutes for peppers and eggplant, and 5 to 6 minutes for squash). Cut peppers into strips.

2. In a small bowl, combine the goat cheese and cream cheese. Set aside. Cut focaccia in half crosswise. Split halves into 2-layers horizontally to form 4 pieces total.

3. Spread goat cheese mixture over bottom layers of focaccia. Top with some sweet peppers, squash, and eggplant; place top halves of focaccia over vegetables. To serve, cut into wedges. If desired, garnish with fresh oregano.

45. Grilled Vegetable Salad

(Ready in 5-6min|Serve:4|Difficulty: Normal)

Ingredients

- 1 pound reduced-fat firm tofu, drained
- 3/4 cup reduced-fat Italian salad dressing
- 12 ounces yellow summer squash, halved lengthwise and cut into 2-inch pieces
- 2 large orange and/or red sweet peppers, quartered and seeded
- 1/2 cup quinoa*
- 1/2 cup quick-cooking barley
- 1/2 cup shredded sorrel or spinach
- Sorrel leaves (optional)

Directions

1. Lengthwise, cut the tofu into 8-strips, around 1/2 inch thick. In a shallow baking dish, place the tofu; pour 1/4 cup of the dressing over the tofu. Put the vegetables in a large plastic self-sealing bag placed in a deep bowl. Pour the remaining 3-teaspoons of dressing over the vegetables. Cover the bag and turn on the hat. 4 to 24 hours of chilling tofu and vegetables, rotating regularly. Cover the leftover dressing and refrigerate it.

2. Strip the tofu from the sauce, and discard the dressing. Drain your veggies and reserve your dressing. Grill vegetables directly over medium heat on an uncovered grill rack for 6 to 8 minutes or until vegetables are crisply tender, rotating periodically. Grill the tofu directly over medium heat on the grill rack for 4 to 6 minutes, rotating once or until finely browned. Remove the tofu from the oven. Sliced into triangles. Only put aside.

3. Combine the squash and peppers in a wide bowl. Reserved dressing is applied. Toss it to coat it. Set aside the herbs.

4. Meanwhile, put 2 cups of water to a boil in a 2-quart bath. Place the quinoa and rinse it under running water in a fine sieve. Add a plate of quinoa and barley. Back to boiling; heat reduction. Simmer, sealed, for 15 minutes or until the grains are soft and water is almost absorbed. Uh, drain.

5. Toss the grains with the shredded sorrel and the remaining chilled dressing gently in a large dish. Serve quinoa with vegetables and tofu. Add, if needed, sorrel leaves. Six main-dish servings are made.

6. Near the grains on the grocery shelves or health food shops, look for quinoa (keen-wah).

46. Grilled Cajun Chicken Salad

(Ready in 5-6min|Serve:4|Difficulty: Normal)

Ingredients

- 1/4 cup cider vinegar
- 4 tablespoon salad oil
- 1 tablespoon water
- 2 teaspoons sugar
- 2 teaspoons snipped fresh thyme or 1/2 teaspoon dried thyme, crushed
- 1-1/4 teaspoons onion powder
- 1/2 teaspoon cayenne pepper
- 1/4 teaspoon garlic powder
- 1/4 teaspoon dry mustard
- 1/2 teaspoon black pepper
- 1/4 teaspoon salt
- 4 skinless, boneless chicken breast halves (1 to 1-1/2 pounds total)
- 6 cups torn mixed salad greens
- 1 medium carrot, shredded
- 1 small red sweet pepper, cut into bite-size strips
- 1 green onion, sliced

Directions

1. Combine cider vinegar, 3-tablespoons of salad oil, water, sugar, thyme, 1/4 of a teaspoon of onion powder, 1/4 of a teaspoon of cayenne pepper, garlic powder, and mustard in a screw-top container. Cover and shake thoroughly. Before serving a day, relax.

2. Combine 1-tablespoon of salad oil remaining in a shallow cup, 1-teaspoon of onion powder remaining, 1/4 teaspoon of cayenne pepper remaining, black pepper, and salt. Brush the chicken with all of the oil mixtures.

3. Place the chicken directly over the medium coals on the rack of an uncovered barbecue. Grill for 12 to 15 minutes or until chicken is tender (170 ; F) and no longer yellow, turning halfway into grilling time once.

4. To eat, mix the salad greens, carrots, red sweet pepper, and green onion in a large serving dish. Break chicken into bite-sized bits. Connect the sauce and chicken to the salad. Toss it to coat it.

47. Grilled Beef and Avocado Salad with Cilantro-Lime Vinaigrette

(Ready in 5-6min|Serve:4|Difficulty: Normal)

Ingredients

- 12 ounces beef flank steak
- 1/2 cup bottled reduced-calorie clear Italian salad dressing
- 1/2 teaspoon finely shredded lime peel
- 1/4 cup lime juice
- 2 tablespoons snipped fresh cilantro
- 1/4 cup chopped onion
- 1/4 teaspoon salt
- 1/4 teaspoon ground black pepper
- 6 cups torn mixed salad greens
- 2 small red and/or yellow tomatoes, cut into wedges
- 1 small avocado, halved, seeded, peeled, and sliced (optional)

Directions

1. In a diamond shape, score both sides of the steak by making shallow diagonal cuts at 1-inch intervals. In a resealable plastic container, put the steak in a shallow bowl. Only put aside.

2. Combine the salad dressing, lime peel, lime juice, and cilantro in a screw-top pan. Cover and shake thoroughly. Onto a shallow bowl, pour half of the salad dressing mixture; cover and cool before serving time. Apply the onion to the remaining mixture of salad dressing in the pot. Shake well and cover; spill the mixture over the steak in the bag. Seal bag; turn to steak for a coat. Marinate for 24 hours in the refrigerator and periodically turn the bag over.

3. Drain the beef and discard the marinade. Using salt and pepper to sprinkle. Grill steak directly over medium coals on an uncovered grill rack for 17 to 21 minutes for medium cooking time (160 F), rotating once. [Or put the steak on the broiler pan's unheated rack. For medium cooking (160 F), broil 3 to 4 inches from the sun for 15 to 18 minutes, rotating once.]

4. To eat, slice the beef thinly around the grain. Arrange 4-lettuce plates with salad greens, onions, and, if desired, avocado. A top of cattle. Reserved dressing over individual salads by Drizzle. He makes four servings.

48. Ginger Chicken with Rice Noodles

(Ready in 5-6min|Serve:4|Difficulty: Normal)

Ingredients:

- 2 tablespoons very finely chopped green onion
- 1-1/2 teaspoons grated fresh ginger
- 3 cloves garlic, minced
- 1 teaspoon olive oil
- 1/8 teaspoon salt
- 2 skinless, boneless chicken breast halves (about 10 ounces total)
- 2 ounces dried rice noodles

- 1/2 cup chopped carrot
- 1/2 teaspoon finely shredded lime peel
- 1 tablespoon lime juice
- 2 teaspoons olive oil
- 2 tablespoons coarsely chopped peanuts
- 1 to 2 tablespoons snipped fresh cilantro

Directions:

1. Combine the green onion, ginger, garlic, 1-teaspoon of oil, and salt in a small bowl to make a rub. Sprinkle the chicken evenly; smooth it with your fingertips.

2. Place the chicken directly over the medium coals on the rack of an uncovered barbecue. Grill, spinning once, for 12 to 15 minutes or before tender and no longer pink (170 F). Diagonally slice the chicken thinly; set aside.

3. Meanwhile, cook rice noodles and carrots in a large volume of boiling water in a large saucepan for 3 to 4 minutes or only until tender; rinse. Using cold water to rinse; drain again. To snip noodles into small pieces, use kitchen scissors. Stir the lime peel, lime juice, and 2-teaspoons of oil together in a medium dish. Add the mixture of noodles and cilantro; blend gently to coat.

4. Divide the mixture of noodles into two separate bowls; assemble the noodle mixture with chicken slices. Sprinkle peanuts on them. Immediately serve.

49. Garlic-Rosemary Mushrooms

(Ready in 5-6min|Serve:4|Difficulty: Normal)

Ingredients

- 1-ounce bacon, (about 1 1/2 slices), chopped
- 1 1/2 pounds mixed mushrooms, such as cremini, shiitake (stemmed) and portobello, cut into 1/4-inch slices
- 2 medium cloves garlic, finely chopped
- 1 1/2 teaspoons chopped fresh rosemary, or 1/2 teaspoon dried
- 1/4 teaspoon salt
- Freshly ground pepper to taste
- 1/4 cup dry white wine

Directions:

1. Cook bacon in a large skillet over medium heat until just beginning to brown, about 4 minutes. Add mushrooms, garlic, rosemary, salt, and pepper and cook, occasionally stirring, until almost dry, 8 to 10 minutes. Pour in the wine and cook until most liquid has evaporated, 30 seconds to 1 minute.

50. Garden Slaw with Spicy Asian Dressing

(Ready in 5-6min|Serve:4|Difficulty: Normal)

Ingredients

- 4 cups shredded green and/or red cabbage
- 2 carrots, cut into julienne strips or coarsely shredded (about 1 cup)
- 3/4 cup bite-size strips green, red, yellow and/or orange sweet pepper
- 1/2 cup coarsely chopped radishes
- 1/4 cup snipped fresh cilantro leaves
- 1/4 cup thinly sliced green onions (2)
- Spicy Asian Dressing (recipe below)

Directions:

1. In a large bowl, combine cabbage, carrot, sweet pepper, radishes, cilantro, and green onions. Pour the dressing over cabbage mixture. Toss to coat.

2. Cover and chill for 2 to 24 hours before serving. Toss slaw before serving. Makes 6 to 8 side-dish servings.

Spicy Asian Dressing

- In a screw-top jar, combine 3 tablespoons rice vinegar or white wine vinegar,
- 3 tablespoons canola oil or vegetable oil,
- 2 to 3 tablespoons sugar,
- 1 tablespoon toasted sesame oil (optional),
- 2 teaspoons grated fresh ginger,
- 1/2 teaspoon dry mustard,
- 1/4 teaspoon salt and 1/4 teaspoon crushed red pepper.
- Cover and shake well to mix.

Easy Garden Slaw

1. Prepare the slaw as directed above, except substitute 5 cups packaged shredded cabbage with carrot (coleslaw mix) for the cabbage and carrot.

51. Fireside Beef Stew

(Ready in 5-6min|Serve:4|Difficulty: Normal)

Ingredients

- 1-1/2 pounds boneless beef chuck pot roast
- 1-pound butternut squash, peeled, seeded, and cut into 1-inch pieces (about 2-1/2 cups)
- 2 small onions, cut into wedges
- 2 cloves garlic, minced
- 1 14-ounce can reduced-sodium beef broth
- 1 8-ounce can tomato sauce
- 2 tablespoons Worcestershire sauce
- 1 teaspoon dry mustard
- 1/4 teaspoon ground black pepper
- 1/8 teaspoon ground allspice
- 2 tablespoons cold water
- 4 teaspoons cornstarch
- 1 9-ounce package frozen Italian green beans

Directions:

1. Trim fat from meat. Cut meat into 1-inch pieces. Place meat in a 3-1/2- to 4-1/2-quart slow cooker. Add squash, onions, and garlic. Stir in beef broth, tomato sauce, Worcestershire sauce, dry mustard, pepper, and allspice.

2. Cover and cook on low-heat setting for 8 to 10 hours or high-heat setting for 4 to 5 hours.

3. If using a low-heat setting, turn to a high-heat setting. In a small bowl, combine cold water and cornstarch. Stir cornstarch mixture and green beans into mixture in the slow cooker. Cover and cook about 15 minutes more or until thickened.

52. Fettuccine with Asparagus
(Ready in 5-6min|Serve:4|Difficulty: Normal)

Ingredients
- 9 ounces fresh fettuccine or tagliatelle or 6 ounces dried fettuccine or tagliatelle, broken
- 1 medium fennel bulb, trimmed and cut into 1-inch pieces (1-1/2 cups)
- 1 tablespoon olive or cooking oil
- 1/2-pound fresh asparagus spears, bias-sliced into 1-1/2-inch pieces
- 3 medium tomatoes, peeled, seeded, and chopped
- 2 ounces prosciutto or fully cooked lean ham or turkey ham, cut into thin strips
- 1/4 cup grated Parmesan cheese

Directions:
1. In a 4-quart Dutch oven or large saucepan, cook pasta in boiling water according to the package directions; drain. Return to the same pan. Keep warm.
2. Meanwhile, in a 10-inch skillet, cook fennel in hot oil for 3 minutes. Add asparagus; cook for 4 minutes or until nearly tender. Add tomatoes and prosciutto; cook for 2 minutes or until heated through. Add fennel mixture to pasta, tossing gently to mix. Divide mixture among 3-dinner plates. Sprinkle with Parmesan cheese. Season to taste with salt and pepper.

53. Farfalle with Mushrooms and Spinach
(Ready in 5-6min|Serve:4|Difficulty: Normal)

Ingredients
- 6 ounces dried farfalle (bow-tie pasta)
- 1 tablespoon olive oil
- 1 medium onion, chopped
- 1 cup sliced portobello or other fresh mushrooms
- 2 cloves garlic, minced
- 4 cups thinly sliced fresh spinach
- 1 teaspoon snipped fresh thyme
- 1/8 teaspoon pepper
- 2 tablespoons shredded Parmesan cheese

Directions:
1. Cook farfalle according to package directions. Drain well.
2. Meanwhile, in a large skillet, heat oil over medium heat. Add onion, mushrooms, and garlic; cook and stir for 2 to 3 minutes or until mushrooms are nearly tender. Stir in spinach, thyme, and pepper; cook 1 minute or until heated through and spinach is slightly wilted. Stir in cooked pasta; toss gently to mix. Sprinkle with cheese. Makes 4-side-dish servings.

54. Fajita-Ranch Chicken Wraps
(Ready in 5-6min|Serve:4|Difficulty: Normal)

Ingredients
- 12 ounces skinless, boneless chicken breast strips for stir-frying
- 1/2 teaspoon chili powder
- 1/4 teaspoon garlic powder
- Nonstick cooking spray
- 1 small red, yellow, or green sweet pepper, seeded and cut into thin strips
- 2 tablespoons bottled reduced-calorie ranch salad dressing
- 2 10-inch whole wheat, tomato, jalapeno, or plain flour tortillas, warmed*
- 1/2 cup Easy Fresh Salsa*
- 1/3 cup reduced-fat shredded cheddar cheese

Directions:
1. Sprinkle chicken strips with chili powder and garlic powder. Coat a medium nonstick skillet with nonstick spray; heat over medium-high heat. Cook chicken and sweet pepper strips in hot skillet over medium heat for 4 to 6 minutes or until chicken is no longer pink and pepper strips are tender. Drain if necessary. Toss with salad dressing.
2. Divide chicken and pepper mixture between warmed tortillas. Top with Easy Fresh Salsa and cheese. Roll up; cut in half.
3. *To warm tortillas: Wrap tortillas tightly in foil. Heat in a 350 F oven about 10 minutes or until heated through.
4. *Easy Fresh Salsa: In a medium bowl combine 2 seeded and chopped tomatoes, 1/4 cup finely chopped red onion, 1/4 cup chopped yellow or green sweet pepper, 2 to 3 teaspoons snipped fresh cilantro, 1/2 teaspoon minced garlic, 1/8 teaspoon salt, a dash of black pepper, and, if desired, a few drops bottled hot pepper sauce. Serve immediately or cover and chill for up to 3 days. Stir before serving.

55. Fajita Beef Salad
(Ready in 5-6min|Serve:4|Difficulty: Normal)

- 1/4 cup lime juice
- 2 tablespoons minced fresh cilantro
- 1 garlic clove, minced
- 1 teaspoon chili powder
- 3/4-pound beef top sirloin steak, cut into thin strips
- 1 medium green pepper, julienned
- 1 medium sweet red pepper, julienned
- 1 medium onion, sliced and halved
- 1 teaspoon olive oil
- 1 can (16 ounces) kidney beans, rinsed and drained
- 4 cups torn mixed salad greens
- 1 medium tomato, chopped
- 4 tablespoons fat-free sour cream
- 2 tablespoons salsa

Directions
1. In a screw-top jar, combine the lime peel, lime juice, 3-tablespoons water, and olive oil. Cover and shake well. Pour half of the lime juice mixture into a small bowl; stir in onion and garlic. Reserve the remaining lime juice mixture.
2. Score the beef by making shallow diagonal cuts at 1-inch intervals in a diamond pattern. Repeat on the other side. Place beef in a plastic bag set in a shallow dish. Pour the lime juice

mixture over the beef. Close bag. Marinate in the refrigerator for 24 hours, turning occasionally.

3. For the dressing, in a small bowl, gradually stir 3-tablespoons water into fruit pectin; stir in reserved lime juice mixture and honey. Cover and chill for 24 hours.

4. Drain beef, discarding marinade. Grill beef on the rack of an uncovered grill directly over medium coals to desired doneness, turning once. Allow 12 to 14 minutes for medium. (Or, place beef on the unheated rack of a broiler pan. Broil 3 to 4 inches from the heat to the desired doneness, turning once. Allow 12 to 14 minutes for medium.)

5. To serve, thinly slice beef across the grain. Arrange the greens, tomatoes, and, if desired, the avocado on 4-salad plates. Top with beef. Drizzle each serving with about 2-tablespoons of the dressing. Makes 4-servings.

56. Easy Black-Bean Soup

(Ready in 5-6min|Serve:4|Difficulty: Normal)

Ingredients

- 2 teaspoons vegetable oil
- 1 medium onion, chopped
- 1-1/2 teaspoons cinnamon
- 2 cans (19 ounces each) black beans, with liquid
- 1 package (32 ounces) reduced-sodium chicken broth
- 1 large sweet potato, diced
- Plain Greek-style yogurt, optional

Directions:

1. In a saucepan, heat oil over medium heat. Add onion and cinnamon, and cook for 6 minutes. Stir in beans, chicken broth, and sweet potato. Bring mixture to a boil; reduce heat and simmer 10 minutes.

2. Let soup cool 5-minutes, puree in a blender in two batches until smooth. Reheat on low until warm before serving. Top with yogurt, if desired.

57. Dilled Shrimp with Beans and Carrots

(Ready in 5-6min|Serve:4|Difficulty: Normal)

Ingredients

- 1 pound fresh or frozen large shrimp in shells
- 2/3 cup regular brown rice
- 1 tablespoon butter
- 3 medium carrots, cut into thin julienne strips
- 8 ounces fresh green beans, trimmed and cut into 1-inch pieces
- 1 teaspoon instant chicken bouillon granules
- 1 teaspoon finely shredded lemon peel
- 1/2 teaspoon dried dill

Directions:

1. Thaw shrimp, if frozen. Peel and devein shrimp, leaving tails intact if desired. Set aside. In a medium saucepan, bring 1-1/3 cups water and the rice to boiling. Reduce heat; simmer, covered, for 40 minutes or until rice is tender and most of the liquid is absorbed.

2. Meanwhile, in a large skillet, melt butter over medium heat. Add carrots and green beans; cook and stir for 4 to 5 minutes or until vegetables are crisp-tender. In a small bowl, stir together 1/4 cup water and bouillon granules until granules are dissolved. Add water mixture, shrimp, lemon peel, and dillweed to bean mixture. Cook, uncovered, over medium heat for 3 to 4 minutes or until shrimp are opaque, stirring occasionally.

3. To serve, divide rice among 4-bowls. Divide shrimp and vegetable mixture among bowls. Makes 4 -servings (1/3 cup rice with 1 cup shrimp mixture per serving)

58. Curried Tofu Salad

(Ready in 5-6min|Serve:4|Difficulty: Normal)

Ingredients

- 3 tablespoons low-fat plain yogurt
- 2 tablespoons reduced-fat mayonnaise
- 2 tablespoons prepared mango chutney
- 2 teaspoons hot curry powder, preferably Madras
- 1/4 teaspoon salt
- Freshly ground pepper, to taste
- 1 14-ounce package extra-firm water-packed tofu, drained, rinsed and finely crumbled (see Ingredient note)
- 2 stalks celery, diced
- 1 cup red grapes, sliced in half
- 1/2 cup sliced scallions
- 1/4 cup chopped walnuts

Directions:

1. In a big bowl, whisk in the milk, mayonnaise, chutney, curry powder, salt, and pepper. Stir in the tofu, celery, almonds, walnuts, and scallions.

59. Curried Chicken Bundles

(Ready in 5-6min|Serve:4|Difficulty: Normal)

Ingredients

- 2 cups chopped cooked chicken or turkey (10 ounces)
- 1/2 cup chopped celery
- 1/3 cup part-skim ricotta cheese
- 1/4 cup shredded carrot
- 1 tablespoon apricot preserves or chutney
- 1 teaspoon curry powder
- 1/4 teaspoon ground cinnamon
- Dash salt
- 1 10-ounce package refrigerated pizza dough

Directions:

1. Combine the chicken, celery, ricotta cheese, carrot, chutney or preserves, curry powder, cinnamon, and salt in a medium dish. Only put aside.

2. Unroll the dough for the pizza; split into 6-squares. Divide the mixture of chicken into squares. Bring the corners of dough over the filling to the middle, extending as appropriate. To seal, pinch the exposed edges together. On an ungreased baking sheet, put bundles.

3. Heat in an oven at 375 F for 12 to 15 minutes or until golden brown. Cool yourself on a wire rack for 30 minutes.

4. Pack each package in a small bag or freezer bag made of plastic. Chill overnight in the refrigerator or store for up to 3 days or 1-month in the freezer.

5. To reheat the sandwiches, put them on a healthy microwave dish. Microwave for 30 to 60 seconds at 100 percent (high) power.

60. Curried Carrot Soup

(Ready in 5-6min|Serve:6|Difficulty: Normal)

Ingredients

- 3 tablespoons canola oil
- 2 teaspoons curry powder
- 8 medium carrots, peeled and thinly sliced
- 4 medium stalks celery, thinly sliced
- 1 medium onion, coarsely chopped
- 5 cups reduced-sodium chicken broth
- 1 tablespoon lemon juice
- 1/2 teaspoon salt
- Freshly ground pepper, to taste

Directions:

1. In a large saucepan over medium heat, simmer the oil and curry powder, stirring, until fragrant, for 1 to 2 minutes. Stir in the carrots, onion, and celery; toss to cover with the oil. Cook for ten minutes, stirring constantly. Stir in the bouillon. Just get it to a boil. Reduce the heat and simmer for about 10 minutes, until the vegetables are very tender. Delete from the heat; quit to stand for ten minutes.

2. To blot away the oil that has risen to the tip, lay a paper towel over the surface of the broth. Discard the towel with paper.

3. Switch the soup to a blender and purée in increments of no more than 2 cups at a time (use caution when pureeing hot liquids). Return to the bowl, put the pureed soup over medium heat, and heat through. Using lemon juice, salt, and pepper to season.

61. Cranberry-Raspberry Spinach Salad

(Ready in 5-6min|serve 6 - 8|Difficulty: Normal)

Ingredients

- 1 10-ounce package frozen red raspberries in syrup, thawed
- 1/4 cup sugar
- 2 teaspoons cornstarch
- 1/2 cup cranberry-raspberry juice cocktail
- 1/4 cup red wine vinegar
- 1/4 teaspoon celery seed
- 1/4 teaspoon ground cinnamon
- 1/8 teaspoon ground cloves
- 1 10-ounce package fresh spinach, stems removed and torn
- 1/3 cup broken walnuts
- 1/4 cup dried cranberries
- 2 tablespoons sunflower seeds
- 3 green onions, thinly sliced

Directions:

1. For the dressing, cover the bowl in a blender jar or food processor, blend or pulse the raspberries until smooth; strain to extract the seeds through a sieve. Put the seeds.

2. In a medium saucepan, whisk together sugar and cornstarch; stir in strained raspberries, and stir over medium heat till thickened and bubbly; cook and stir for 2 minutes more. Move to a non-metal vessel. Cover before serving time, and relax.

3. To eat, combine the spinach, walnuts, dried cranberries, sunflower seeds, and green onions in a salad dish. Drizzle the dressing with half of it. (To be used in other vegetable or fruit salads, cover and chill the leftover dressing in a non-metal bottle for up to a week.)

62. Creole Turkey Meatballs

(Ready in 5-6min|Serve:7|Difficulty: Normal)

Ingredients

- Nonstick cooking spray
- 1 medium onion, chopped
- 1 medium green sweet pepper, chopped
- 1/2 cup quick-cooking rolled oats
- 1/4 cup refrigerated or frozen egg product, thawed, or 1 egg, beaten
- 2 tablespoons fat-free milk
- 2 cloves garlic, minced
- 1 teaspoon dried Italian seasoning, crushed
- 1 teaspoon salt-free seasoning blend
- 1 teaspoon Creole seasoning
- 1-pound uncooked ground turkey

Directions

1. Preheat the oven to 375°F. Coat gently with nonstick cooking spray on a 15x10x1-inch baking pan; set aside. Combine the onion, sweet pepper, rolled oats, egg, sugar, garlic, Italian seasoning, salt-free mix, and Creole seasoning in a large bowl. Add turkey; blend thoroughly.

2. Form the turkey mixture into 1-1/4-inch balls using a small ice cream scoop or a slightly rounded measuring tablespoon. Arrange yourself in a packed pan.

3. Bake in the middle (165-degree F), uncovered, about 25 minutes or until browned and no longer pink.

Directions Make-Ahead

1. Prepare by Phase 3 as instructed. For up to 24 hours, cover and relax. Uncover; as directed, bake.

63. Confetti Summer Salad

(Ready in 5-6min|serve 6 - 8|Difficulty: Normal)

Ingredients

- 1/2 medium zucchini, halved lengthwise and cut into 1/4-inch slices (1/4 cup)
- 1 medium sweet yellow pepper, cut into thin strips (3/4 cup)
- 1 medium sweet red pepper, cut into thin strips (3/4 cup)
- 2 medium green onions, sliced (1/4 cup)

- 1 15- to 16-ounce can whole kernel corn, drained
- 2 medium tomatoes, seeded and chopped (1-1/2 cups)
- 1/2 cup reduced-calorie Italian salad dressing
- 1/2 cup hot salsa
- Radicchio leaves or purple flowering kale (optional)

Directions:

1. In a big cup, combine the zucchini, sweet peppers, onion, corn, tomatoes, salad dressing, and salsa.
2. Cover and cook for 4 to 24 hours, sometimes stirring. Serve radicchio leaves with salad if needed, or garnish with purple flowering kale. Makes 6-8 servings of side-dish.

64. Colorados (Red Bean Soup)

(Ready in 5-6min|serve 10|Difficulty: Normal)

Ingredients

- 1-pound dry red kidney beans
- 6 cups water
- 8 cups water
- 3/4 cup dry white wine or reduced-sodium beef broth
- 1 medium green or red sweet pepper, chopped
- 1 medium onion, chopped
- 1 medium tomato, chopped
- 4 cloves garlic, minced
- 1 medium fresh yellow wax chile pepper or banana chile pepper, seeded and chopped*
- 1-pound fresh beef brisket, trimmed of fat and cut into 3/4-inch pieces
- 1 ham hock
- 1 large russet potato, peeled and diced
- 1 teaspoon salt
- 1/2 teaspoon ground black pepper

Directions:

1. Combine the beans and 6 cups of water in a 6-quart Dutch oven. Could you bring it to a boil; lower the flame? For 2 minutes, cook. Withdraw from the sun. Cover for 1 hour and let stand. (Or put beans in 6 cups water in a bowl over and let soak in a cool place for 6 to 8 hours or overnight.) Drain and rinse beans.
2. Send the beans back to the Dutch oven. Add the sugar, wine or broth, sweet pepper, onion, tomato, garlic, and chili pepper to 8 cups of water. Put to a boil; add the ham hock and beef brisket. Back to boiling; heat reduction. Cover and boil until the beans and meat are tender, or around 1 1/2 hours. Remove the ham hock; set to cool aside. Slightly mash the beans. Add the bean mixture to the potato. Back to boiling; heat reduction. Cover and cook for 15 more minutes or until the potato is crispy. Remove the meat from the bone while the ham is cold enough to handle; discard the bone. Break the ham into bite-sized pieces; substitute the mixture of beans. Stir in black pepper and salt.

Note
Since chili peppers contain volatile oils that can burn your skin and eyes, you should prevent as much close contact as possible with them. Wear latex or rubber gloves while dealing with chili peppers. If your bare hands touch the peppers, use soap and warm water to properly wash your hands and nails.

65. Citrus Turkey Spinach Salad

(Ready in 5-6min|Serve:4|Difficulty: Normal)

Ingredients

- 8 cups fresh baby spinach or torn fresh spinach
- 8 ounces cooked turkey, cut up
- 2 pink grapefruit, peeled and sectioned
- 2 oranges, peeled and sectioned
- 1/4 cup orange juice
- 2 tablespoons olive oil
- 1 teaspoon honey
- 1/2 teaspoon poppy seeds
- 1/4 teaspoon salt
- 1/4 teaspoon dry mustard
- 2 tablespoons sliced almonds, toasted (optional)

Directions:

1. In a wide bowl, put your spinach. Attach turkey, parts of grapefruit, and sections of an orange.
2. For the dressing, mix orange juice, oil, sugar, poppy seeds, salt, and dried mustard in a screw-top container. Cover and shake thoroughly. Pour over the salad with the dressing; toss gently. Sprinkle with almonds if needed. Allows 4-servings (2-cups).

66. Cider Pork Stew

(Ready in 5-6min|serve 8|Difficulty: Normal)

Ingredients

- 2 pounds boneless pork shoulder roast
- 3 medium cubed potatoes (about 2-1/2 cups))
- 3 medium carrots, cut into 1/2-inch pieces (about 1-1/2 cups)
- 2 medium onions, sliced
- 1 cup coarsely chopped apple (1 medium)
- 1/2 cup coarsely chopped celery (1 stalk)
- 3 tablespoons quick-cooking tapioca
- 2 cups apple juice or apple cider
- 1 teaspoon salt
- 1 teaspoon caraway seeds
- 1/4 teaspoon black pepper
- Celery leaves (optional)

Directions:

1. Split into 1-inch chunks of beef. Combine the beef, cabbage, carrots, onions, apple, celery, and tapioca in a 3-1/2- to 5-1/2quart slow cooker. Apple juice, salt, caraway seeds, and pepper are added.
2. Cover and simmer for 10 to 12 hours under low heat or 5 to 6 hours under high heat. Garnish individual servings with celery leaves if needed.

67. Chops and Pineapple with Chili Slaw

(Ready in 5-6min|Serve:4|Difficulty: Normal)

Ingredients

- 8 1/2-inch cuts boneless top loin pork chops (1-1/2 lb. total)
- 1-1/2 tsp. chili powder
- 1/2 of a cored fresh pineapple, sliced
- 3 Tbsp. cider vinegar
- 2 Tbsp. orange juice
- 2 Tbsp. olive oil
- 1 Tbsp. sugar
- 1/3 of small green cabbage, cored and sliced (about 5 cups)
- 1/2 of a red onion, thinly sliced
- 1 small red sweet pepper, cut in strips

Directions:

1. Sprinkle chops with salt and 1 tsp. Chili powder. For a charcoal grill, cook chops and pineapple on an uncovered grill directly over medium coals for 6 to 8 minutes, until chops are done (160 F), turning once. (For a gas grill, preheat; reduce to medium. Grill chops and pineapple, covered.)
2. Meanwhile, for chili slaw, in a large bowl, whisk together vinegar, juice, oil, sugar, and remaining 1/2 tsp. Chili powder. Add cabbage, onion, and sweet pepper; toss. Season with salt and pepper. Serve chops with pineapple pieces and slaw.

68. Chilly Bow Ties and Tuna

(Ready in 5-6min|Serve:4|Difficulty: Normal)

Ingredients

- 8 ounces dried farfalle pasta (bow ties)
- 1/3 cup light mayonnaise dressing or salad dressing
- 1/3 cup bottled reduced-calorie Italian salad dressing
- 1/4 cup thinly sliced green onion (optional)
- 2 tablespoons orange juice
- 1/4 teaspoon salt
- 1/4 teaspoon black pepper
- 1 11-ounce can mandarin orange sections, drained
- 1 12-ounce can chunk white tuna (water pack), drained and broken into chunks
- 1 cup fresh pea pods, halved
- Milk (optional)

Directions:

1. Cook the pasta according to product instructions in a large saucepan. Uh, drain. In cool spray, rinse. Again, drain.
2. Meanwhile, mayonnaise sauce, Italian dressing, green onion (if desired), orange juice, salt, and pepper are mixed in a big bowl for dressing.
3. For the dressing, add cooked pasta. Toss well for mixing. Stir gently in the orange, salmon, and pea pod parts. For 4 to 24 hours, cover, and relax. If required, before eating, stir in a little milk to moisten. Six main-dish servings are made.

69. Chicken, Pear, and Parmesan Salad

(Ready in 5-6min|Serve:4|Difficulty: Normal)

Ingredients

- 2 tablespoons cider vinegar or white wine vinegar
- 2 tablespoons olive oil or canola oil
- 1 tablespoon honey
- 1/4 teaspoon salt
- 1/4 teaspoon ground black pepper
- 5 cups torn fresh spinach leaves
- 2 cups shredded or chopped cooked chicken breast
- 2 pears, cored and cut into cubes
- 1/2 of a small red onion, thinly sliced
- 1/4 cup dried cranberries or raisins
- 1-ounce Parmesan cheese, shaved

Directions:

1. In a small screw-top jar, combine vinegar, oil, honey, salt, and pepper. Cover and shake well.
2. In a large salad bowl, combine greens, chicken, pears, onion, and cranberries. Drizzle dressing over salad, tossing to coat evenly. Top with cheese.

70. Chicken Salad with Mango Vinaigrette

(Ready in 5-6min|Serve:4|Difficulty: Normal)

Ingredients

- 2 medium mangoes
- 1/2 teaspoon curry powder
- 1/4 teaspoon coarsely ground black pepper
- 1/8 teaspoon salt
- 12 ounces skinless, boneless chicken breast halves
- 6 cups torn mixed greens
- 1/2 of a medium cantaloupe, seeded, peeled, and cut into 1-inch chunks
- 1 cup raspberries
- 1 small apple, cored and sliced
- Mango Vinaigrette
- 2 green onions, thinly bias-sliced

Directions:

. Pit, slice, and cut the mangoes into cubes. For use in the vinaigrette, weigh 1 cup of mango cubes; set the remaining mango cubes aside for salad.
2. Stir the curry powder, pepper, and salt together in a shallow cup. Use curry mixture to spread chicken evenly; rub in with your fingertips. For a barbecue grill, place the chicken directly over the medium coals on the rack of an uncovered grill. Grill for 12 to 15 minutes or until tender (170 F) and no longer pink, rotating halfway around the grill once. (Preheat grill for gas grill. Decrease the heat to low. Put chicken overheat on the grill rack. Cover and grill as above.) (Or broiler preheat. Place chicken on a broiler pan's unheated rack. Broil 10 to 12 minutes from the heat for 4 to 5 inches or until tender and no

longer pink [170 F], rotating once.) Cool chicken slightly; slice into slices of 1/4 inch wide.

3. Arrange greens on four dinner plates. Chicken strips of top greens, cantaloupe, raspberries, apple slices, and blocks of reserved mango. Drizzle Raspberry Vinaigrette Salads. Sprinkle on the green onions.

4. Combine 1 cup of mango cubes, 3 -tablespoons of orange juice, 2 -tablespoons of rice vinegar or white wine vinegar, 2-teaspoons of sugar, and 1-teaspoon mustard-style Dijon in a blender or food processor. Cover until smooth, and blend or process. Cover and chill before time is served (up to 2 hours).

71. Chicken Salad Sandwiches
(Ready in 5-6min|Serve:4|Difficulty: Normal)

Ingredients
- 3 boneless skinless chicken breasts
- 6 slices lemon
- 6 sprigs dill, plus 1 tbsp. chopped
- 1 green apple, chopped
- 1/2 red onion, finely chopped
- 2 celery stalks, finely chopped
- 2/3 c. mayonnaise
- 1/4 c. Dijon mustard
- 2 tbsp. red wine vinegar
- Kosher salt
- Freshly ground black pepper
- Baguette, for serving
- Butter lettuce, for serving

Directions
1. In a medium bowl, stir together chicken, apple, and egg. Add yogurt and mayonnaise; stir to combine. Season to taste with salt and pepper. Serve immediately or cover and chill up to 4 hours.
2. Spread chicken mixture on half of the bread slices. Top with lettuce leaves and remaining bread slices. Cutaway crusts if desired. Cut each sandwich into four triangles or squares.

72. Chicken Olive Calzones
(Ready in 5-6min|Serve:4|Difficulty: Normal)

Ingredients
- 1-1/2 cups chopped cooked chicken (8 ounces)
- 1/2 cup shredded Monterey Jack cheese
- 1/4 cup chopped celery
- 1/4 cup chopped pitted ripe olives
- 1/2 teaspoon dried basil, crushed
- 1/4 teaspoon dried oregano, crushed
- 1/8 teaspoon garlic powder
- 1/8 teaspoon pepper
- 1/3 cup bowl-style cream cheese with chives and onion
- 1 10-ounce package refrigerated pizza dough
- 1 beaten egg
- 1 tablespoon water
- Grated Parmesan cheese (optional)
- Spaghetti sauce (optional)

Directions:
1. Combine the chicken, Monterey Jack cheese, celery, ripe olives, basil, oregano, garlic powder, and pepper in a medium dish. Stir in the cheese and milk. Only put aside.
2. Unroll pizza dough for calzones. On a lightly floured board, roll the dough into a rectangle of 15 to 10 inches. Split into six squares measuring 5-inch. Divide the squares with the chicken-olive filling. Using water to clean the edges. Lift one corner to the opposite corner and spread the dough over it. Seal edges of dough well with tines of a fork. On a greased baking dish, place the calzones. With a fork, Prick tops it up. Combine the egg and 1-tablespoon of water in a small bowl; spray over the calzones. Sprinkle, if needed, with Parmesan cheese.
3. Bake for 10 to 12 minutes or until golden brown in a 425-degree F oven. Before eating, let it stand for 5 minutes. Serve with, if desired, heated spaghetti sauce. Six calzones to make.

73. Chicken Noodle Soup
(Ready in 5-6min|Serve:4|Difficulty: Normal)

Ingredients
- 1 teaspoon olive oil
- 1 cup chopped onion
- 3 cloves garlic, minced
- 1 cup chopped celery
- 1 cup sliced, peeled carrots (2 medium)
- 4 cups Maureen's Chicken Broth (separate recipe)
- 4 ounces dried linguini, broken
- 1 cup cooked non-brined chicken breast, cut into desired size (skin and bones removed)
- 2 tablespoons snipped fresh parsley

Directions:
1. In a large saucepan, heat olive oil over medium heat and sauté onion and garlic until translucent. Add celery and carrots and continue to sauté for another 3 minutes. Add Maureen's Chicken Broth. Bring to a boil; reduce heat and simmer, covered, 5 minutes. Stir in linguini; cook and stir until mixture returns to a boil. Reduce heat and simmer, covered, 10 minutes more or until pasta and vegetables are tender, stirring occasionally.
2. Add cooked chicken and fresh parsley. Heat through.

74. Chicken Fajita Chili
(Ready in 5-6min|Serve:4|Difficulty: Normal)

Ingredients
- 2 pounds skinless, boneless chicken breast halves, cut into 1-inch pieces
- 1 tablespoon chili powder
- 1 teaspoon fajita seasoning
- 1/2 teaspoon ground cumin
- 2 cloves garlic, minced
- Nonstick cooking spray
- 2 14-1/2-ounce cans no-salt-added diced tomatoes

- 1 16-ounce package frozen pepper (yellow, green, and red) and onion stir-fry vegetables
- 1 15-ounce can cannellini beans (white kidney beans), rinsed and drained
- 3 tablespoons light dairy sour cream (optional)
- 3 tablespoons shredded reduced-fat cheddar cheese (optional)
- 3 tablespoons purchased guacamole (optional)

Directions:

1. Combine the chicken, chili powder, fajita seasoning, cumin, and garlic in a medium bowl; blend to coat. Use nonstick cooking spray to grease a large unheated skillet. Preheat the skillet over high-medium heat. Cook the chicken in a hot pan, half at a time, until browned on all sides, stirring periodically.

2. Put a 3-1/2- or 4-quart slow cooker with the chicken. Add onions, frozen carrots, and cannellini beans that are undrained. Cover and simmer for 4 to 5 hours under low heat or 2 to 2 1/2 hours under high heat.

3. Cover individual portions with sour cream, melted cheese, and guacamole, if needed.

75. Chicken Baked in Banana Leaves

(Ready in 5-6min|Serve:4|Difficulty: Normal)

Ingredients

- 1 Tbsp. annatto seeds or 1 Tbsp. chili powder
- 1 tsp. whole black peppercorns
- 4 whole allspice
- 1/2 tsp. dried oregano
- 1/2 tsp. cumin seed
- 1 tsp. finely shredded orange peel
- 3/4 cup orange juice
- 1/4 tsp. salt
- 2 cloves garlic, minced
- 1 cup chopped onion (1 large)
- 2-1/2 to 3 pounds chicken thighs (with bone) and/or drumsticks, skinned
- Banana leaves
- 1-pound red onions, sliced and separated into rings (about 3-1/2 cups)
- 1/4 cup white vinegar
- 1/2 tsp. salt
- 1/2 tsp. dried oregano, crushed
- 1/4 tsp. cracked black pepper
- 2 cloves garlic, minced

Directions:

1. For marinade, place the annatto seeds, whole peppercorns, allspice, 1/2 teaspoon oregano, and cumin seeds in a spice grinder. Cover; grind to a fine powder. In a small bowl, stir together the ground spice mixture, orange peel, orange juice, 1/4 teaspoon salt, 2 -cloves garlic, and onion.

2. Place the chicken in a resealable plastic bag set in a deep bowl. Pour marinade over chicken. Seal bag and turn to coat chicken with marinade. Marinate in refrigerator for 6 to 24 hours, turning bag occasionally.

3. Cut banana leaves into four to six 12×9-inch rectangles. Loosely roll up the rectangles and place in a steamer basket over, but not touching, boiling water. Cover and steam for 20 to 30 minutes or until leaves are soft and pliable. Remove and cool.

4. Remove chicken from marinade; discard marinade. Place one or two chicken pieces on each banana leaf rectangle. Wrap banana leaves around each serving of chicken. Overwrap with foil and seal tightly. (If banana leaves are unavailable, wrap the chicken in foil rectangles and seal tightly.) Place wrapped chicken pieces in a single layer in a shallow baking pan. Bake in a 375 F oven for 1 hour or until an instant-read thermometer inserted into chicken registers 180 F.

5. Meanwhile, for pickled red onions, place onion rings in a 3-quart stainless-steel or nonstick saucepan; add boiling water to cover. Let stand 1 minute. Drain well. Return onion rings to saucepan; stir in vinegar, 1/2 teaspoon salt, 1/2 teaspoon oregano, cracked black pepper, and 2 -cloves garlic. Bring to boiling; reduce heat. Simmer, covered, for 5 minutes or until onions are tender. Remove from heat; transfer onion mixture to a small glass bowl. Let stand until cool (about 45 minutes), stirring occasionally. To serve, carefully remove foil from the chicken. Serve chicken in banana leaves along with onions.

76. Chicken and Veggie Soup

(Ready in 5-6min|Serve:4|Difficulty: Normal)

Ingredients

- 2 14-ounce cans reduced-sodium chicken broth
- 2 cups water
- 1/4 teaspoon black pepper
- 1 cup dried whole wheat rotini or twisted spaghetti or broken fusilli
- 3 cups vegetable pieces (such as thinly sliced carrots, small broccoli florets, chopped green or red sweet pepper, and/or fresh or frozen whole kernel corn)
- 1 1/2 cups cubed cooked chicken (about 8 ounces)
- 1 tablespoon snipped fresh basil
- 1/4 cup finely shredded Parmesan cheese (1 ounce)

Preparation:

1. In a Dutch oven, combine the broth, the water, and black pepper; bring to boiling. Stir in the pasta. Return to boiling; reduce heat. Simmer, covered, for 5 minutes. Stir in vegetables. Return to boiling; reduce heat. Simmer, covered, for 5 to 8 minutes more or until vegetables and pasta are tender. Stir in chicken and basil; heat through. To serve, top with Parmesan cheese.

77. Chicken and Vegetable Salad

(Ready in 5-6min|Serve:4|Difficulty: Normal)

Ingredients

- 1/2 cup low-fat cottage cheese
- 1 tablespoon catsup
- 1 hard-cooked egg, chopped

- 1 tablespoon thinly sliced green onion
- 1 tablespoon pickle relish
- 1/8 teaspoon salt
- 1-1/2 cups chopped cooked chicken
- 1/2 cup chopped celery
- 1/2 cup chopped green or sweet red pepper
- Lettuce leaves
- 2 tablespoons toasted sliced almonds

Directions:
1. For the dressing, in a blender container, combine cottage cheese and catsup. Cover and blend until smooth.
2. In a small mixing bowl, stir together cottage cheese mixture, egg, onion, pickle relish, and salt. Set dressing aside.
3. In a medium mixing bowl, combine chicken, celery, and green or red pepper. Add dressing and toss gently to mix. Cover and chill for 4 to 24 hours.
4. To serve, divide salad among 4 -lettuce-lined salad plates. Garnish with almonds.

78. Chicken and Pasta Salad
(Ready in 5-6min|Serve:4|Difficulty: Normal)

Ingredients
- 1/2 cup plain low-fat yogurt
- 2 tablespoons orange juice
- 1 teaspoon honey or sugar
- 4 teaspoons Dijon-style mustard
- Dash pepper
- 2/3 cup elbow macaroni, cooked
- 1 cup cooked cut green beans
- 5 ounces cooked chicken or ham, cut into bite-size strips (1 cup) or one 6-1/2-ounce can tuna (water pack), drained
- 1/2 cup shredded carrot
- 2 tablespoons sliced green onions

Directions
1. For the dressing, in a large mixing bowl, stir together yogurt, orange juice, honey or sugar, mustard, and pepper.
2. Add cooked macaroni, green beans, chicken or ham, carrot, and green onions. Toss to mix well.
3. Divide among 3-small airtight containers. Chill at least 8 hours or up to 3 days in the refrigerator.

79. Chicken and Hummus Pitas
(Ready in 5-6min|Serve:4|Difficulty: Normal)

Ingredients
- 1 tablespoon olive oil
- 1 teaspoon lemon juice
- 1/4 teaspoon paprika
- Dash salt
- Dash black pepper
- 2 skinless, boneless chicken breast halves (8 to 12 ounces)
- 2 large whole wheat pita bread rounds, halved
- 1 7-ounce carton hummus
- 3/4 cup coarsely chopped Roma tomatoes
- 1/2 cup thinly sliced cucumber
- 1/3 cup plain low-fat yogurt

Directions:
1. For the dressing, in a large mixing bowl, stir together yogurt, orange juice, honey or sugar, mustard, and pepper.
2. Add cooked macaroni, green beans, chicken or ham, carrot, and green onions. Toss to mix well.
3. Divide among 3-small airtight containers. Chill at least 8 hours or up to 3 days in the refrigerator.

80. Chicken & Roast Vegetable Salad
(Ready in 5-6min|Serve:4|Difficulty: Normal)

Ingredients
- 1/4 cup olive oil
- 1-1/2 small red potatoes with skins, cut into quarters (eighths if large)
- 1/2-pound green beans, halved crosswise
- 1 sweet red pepper, cored, seeded and cut into 12 slices
- 1 teaspoon salt
- 4 boneless, skinless chicken breast halves (1-1/4 pounds total)
- 2 tablespoons fresh lemon juice
- 1/4 teaspoon black pepper
- 2 tablespoons finely chopped fresh parsley
- 6 cups chopped romaine or leaf lettuce

Directions:
1. Pour 2-tablespoons of olive oil into a large roasting pan. When heated to 425 F, place the pan in the oven.
2. Add the potatoes, green beans, and sweet pepper to the hot oil in the roasting pan when the oven is hot. Season with 3/4 of a teaspoon of salt; toss with potatoes to coat.
3. Switch the roasting pan back to 425 F for 30 minutes or until the potatoes are tender and the vegetables are browned.
4. In the meantime, bring finely enough salted water to cover the chicken in a broad skillet to boiling. Add the chicken breast halves; simmer until the chicken is fully cooked, about 10 minutes (internal temperature should register 170 F on an instant-read thermometer). Slice the chicken on the cutting board; let stand for five minutes. Cut into small chunks.
5. Whisk together the remaining olive oil, lemon juice, the remaining salt, and pepper in a wide cup. Apply the vegetables, chicken, and parsley; toss gently to cover all the ingredients equally.
6. Divide the lettuce into 6-plates or cups. Cover the mixture with chicken. Serve warm, serve.

81. Cabbage-Chicken Toss
(Ready in 5-6min|Serve:4|Difficulty: Normal)

Ingredients

- 4 medium skinless boneless chicken breast halves (1-pound total)
- 1 tablespoon cooking oil
- 4 cups shredded green cabbage
- 4 cups shredded red cabbage
- 4 cups shredded Napa cabbage
- 1 tablespoon finely shredded lemon peel
- 1 teaspoon salt
- 3/4 teaspoon pepper

Directions:

1. Cut chicken into thin bite-size strips. Heat oil in a wok or large skillet over medium-high heat. Add half of the chicken to the hot wok. Stir-fry for 2 to 3 minutes or until no pink remains. Remove from wok. Repeat with the remaining chicken. (Add more oil as necessary during cooking.) Cool chicken slightly.
2. Combine chicken, cabbages, lemon peel, salt, and pepper in a very large bowl. Gently toss to mix well.

82. Brussels Sprouts with Toasted Almonds

(Ready in 5-6min|serve 12|Difficulty: Normal)

Ingredients

- 2 pounds fresh Brussels sprouts
- 2 tablespoons olive oil
- 1 14-ounce can reduced-sodium chicken broth
- 2 tablespoons butter
- 3/4 teaspoon ground black pepper
- 1/4 teaspoon salt
- 1/3 cup sliced almonds, toasted*

Directions:

1. Trim stems and remove any wilted outer leaves from Brussels sprouts; wash sprouts. Halve Brussels sprouts. In a very large skillet, heat oil over medium heat. Add Brussels sprouts; cook for 6 to 8 minutes or until golden brown, stirring occasionally.
2. Add broth to sprouts. Bring to boiling; reduce heat. Cover and simmer for 5 minutes. Uncover and continue to simmer about 10 minutes more or until most of the liquid has evaporated and the sprouts are tender, stirring occasionally. Add butter, pepper, and salt, stirring until sprouts are coated. Gently stir in toasted sliced almonds. Serve warm.

83. Black-Eyed Peas and Ham

(Ready in 5-6min|serve 12|Difficulty: Normal)

Ingredients

- 8 ounces dried black-eyed peas
- 4 cups water
- 2 cups water
- 2 ounces cooked, smoked lean ham, diced
- 1 medium onion, chopped
- 1/4 teaspoon salt
- 1 medium carrot, thinly sliced (optional)
- 1 fresh serrano chile pepper, seeded and thinly sliced (optional)
- 1 14-1/2-ounce can diced tomatoes, undrained

Directions:

1. Rinse black-eyed peas with cold water. In a large saucepan, combine peas and the 4 cups water. Bring to boiling; reduce heat. Simmer for 2 minutes. Remove from heat. Cover and let stand for 1 hour. (Or, in a large saucepan, combine black-eyed peas and the 4 cups water. Cover and let soak in a cool place overnight.)
2. Drain and rinse peas; drain again. Return peas to saucepan. Stir in the 2 cups water, ham, onion, and salt. If desired, stir in carrot and serrano pepper. Bring to boiling; reduce heat to medium-low. Cover and simmer about 1 hour or until peas are tender.
3. Stir in undrained tomatoes. Bring to boiling; reduce heat. Simmer, uncovered, for 5 minutes (most of the liquid should be evaporated).

84. Beef-Asparagus Saute

(Ready in 5-6min|serve 12|Difficulty: Normal)

Ingredients

- 12 ounces asparagus
- 2 teaspoons olive oil
- 1-pound lean beef sirloin or tenderloin, trimmed of fat and very thinly sliced
- 1 small carrot, peeled and shredded
- Salt
- Freshly ground pepper
- 1 teaspoon dried herbs de Provence, crushed
- 1/2 cup marsala
- 1/4 teaspoon grated lemon peel
- Hot cooked rice

Directions:

1. Snap off and discard fibrous stem ends of asparagus. Bias-cut asparagus into 2-inch pieces; rinse and drain well.
2. Heat oil over medium-high heat in a large nonstick skillet. Cook and stir beef, carrot, salt, and pepper in hot oil for 3 minutes. Add asparagus and herbs de Provence; cook and stir 2 minutes more. Add marsala and lemon peel; reduce heat.
3. Cook, uncovered, 3 to 5 minutes more or until beef is cooked through and asparagus is crisp-tender. Serve over hot cooked rice.

85. Barbecue Chicken Chop Salad

(Ready in 5-6min|serve 12|Difficulty: Normal)

Ingredients

- Salad
- 4-4-ounce boneless chicken-breast halves, visible fat
- Salt and pepper to taste
- 4 tablespoons barbecue sauce
- 10 cups finely shredded romaine lettuce
- 2 cups seeded, diced, chopped tomatoes
- 1 1/2 cups seeded, diced cucumber

- 2 cups diced zucchini
- 2 ounces light cheddar cheese, finely shredded Chopped red onion
- Vinaigrette
- 1/4 cup balsamic vinegar
- 2 tablespoons Dijon mustard
- 1 tablespoons honey
- 2 tablespoons extra virgin olive oil
- 2 tablespoons finely chopped fresh basil leaves
- pinch salt
- to taste Black pepper

Directions

1. Preheat the grill to high heat. Place the chicken between two sheets of plastic wrap or waxed paper on a cutting board. Using the flat head of a meat mallet (or a rolling pin), pound the chicken until it is 1/2 inch thick. Rub each breast with olive oil, salt, and pepper. Grill 3 to 5 minutes per side, or until cooked through. Let chicken cool.

2. Whisk together the vinegar, mustard, and honey. Slowly whisk in the oil. Stir in the basil and season with salt and pepper. Chop the chicken and transfer it to a medium bowl. Mix in the barbecue sauce and stir to coat. In a large serving bowl, toss the lettuce, tomatoes, cucumber, zucchini, cheddar, red onions, and dressing. Top with the chicken and serve.

86. Balsamic Chicken over Greens

(Ready in 5-6min|serve 12|Difficulty: Normal)

Ingredients

- 4 skinless, boneless chicken breast halves
- 3/4 cup bottled balsamic vinaigrette salad dressing
- 3 cloves garlic, minced
- 1/4 teaspoon crushed red pepper
- 1 8-ounce package torn mixed greens (8 cups)

Direction:

1. Place chicken breast halves in a resealable plastic bag set in a shallow dish.

For the marinade:

1. Stir together 1/2 cup of the vinaigrette, the garlic, and crushed red pepper.
2. Pour marinade over the chicken.
3. Seal bag; turn to coat chicken.
4. Marinate in the refrigerator for 1 to 4 hours, turning bag occasionally.

2. Drain chicken, reserving marinade. Place chicken on the rack of an uncovered grill directly over medium coals. Grill for 12 to 15 minutes or until chicken is no longer pink (170 F), turning once and brushing with the reserved marinade halfway through grilling time. Discard any remaining marinade.

3. Arrange greens on four dinner plates. Cut grilled chicken into strips. Arrange chicken on top of greens. Serve with remaining 1/4 cup vinaigrette.

4. Broiler method: Place chicken on the unheated rack of a broiler pan. Broil 4 to 5 inches from the heat for 12 to 15 minutes or until chicken is no longer pink (170 F), turning once and brushing with the reserved marinade halfway through broiling time. Discard any remaining marinade.

87. Baked Chicken Chiles Rellenos

(Ready in 5-6min|serve 6|Difficulty: Normal)

Ingredients

- 6 skinless, boneless chicken breast halves
- 1/3 cup all-purpose flour
- 3 tablespoons cornmeal
- 1/4 teaspoon ground red pepper
- 1 egg
- 1 tablespoon water
- 1 4-ounce can whole green chile peppers, rinsed, seeded, and cut in half lengthwise (6 pieces total)
- 2 ounces Monterey Jack cheese, cut into six 2x1/2-inch sticks
- 2 tablespoons snipped fresh cilantro or fresh parsley
- 1/4 teaspoon black pepper
- 2 tablespoons butter or margarine, melted
- 1 8-ounce jar green or red salsa
- Snipped fresh cilantro (optional)

Directions

1. Place a chicken breast half between 2 pieces of plastic wrap. Using the flat side of a meat mallet, pound meat lightly into a rectangle about 1/8-inch-thick. Remove plastic wrap.

2. In a shallow dish, combine the flour, cornmeal, and ground red pepper. Place egg in another shallow dish; add water and beat lightly to combine.

3. For each roll, place a chile pepper half on a chicken piece near an edge. Place a cheese stick on the chile pepper near an edge. Sprinkle with some of the cilantro or parsley and black pepper. Fold in sides; roll up, starting from the edge with cheese. Secure with wooden toothpicks.

4. Dip rolls in egg mixture; coat with cornmeal mixture. Place rolls seam sides down in a shallow baking pan. Drizzle with butter.

5. Bake, uncovered, in a 375-degree oven for 25 to 30 minutes or until chicken is no longer pink (170 F). Remove toothpicks. Meanwhile, heat salsa; serve over chicken. If desired, garnish with additional cilantro.

88. Asian-Style Beef Salad

(Ready in 5-6min|serve 6|Difficulty: Normal)

Ingredients

- 12 ounces boneless beef sirloin steak, cut 1-inch thick
- 1 fresh jalapeno pepper, seeded and finely chopped*
- 1/2 teaspoon finely shredded lime peel
- 3 tablespoons lime juice
- 2 tablespoons reduced-sodium soy sauce
- 1 tablespoon snipped fresh cilantro
- 2 teaspoons toasted sesame oil
- 1 teaspoon sugar
- 2 cloves garlic, minced

- 6 cups torn napa cabbage and/or bok choy
- 1/2 cup red sweet pepper strips or fresh pea pods
- 1/4 cup sliced green onions

Directions:

1. Trim fat from steak. Place on the unheated rack of a broiler pan. Broil 3 to 4 inches from the heat for 12 to 15 minutes or to desired doneness (160 F for medium doneness). Let steak stand for 5 minutes. Cut across the grain into thin bite-size strips.
2. Meanwhile, in a medium mixing bowl, stir together jalapeno pepper, lime peel, lime juice, soy sauce, cilantro, sesame oil, sugar, and garlic. Stir in beef. Marinate in the refrigerator for 2 to 8 hours.
3. To serve, in a salad bowl, toss together napa cabbage and bok choy, sweet pepper or pea pods, and green onions. Stir beef mixture; arrange in center of cabbage mixture.

89. Asian Shrimp and Vegetable Soup

(Ready in 5-6min|serve 6|Difficulty: Normal)

Ingredients

- 12 ounces fresh or frozen large shrimp in shells
- 4 green onions
- 2 teaspoon canola oil
- 2 medium carrots, peeled and thinly sliced
- 8 ounces fresh shiitake or oyster mushrooms, stemmed and coarsely chopped
- 1 tablespoon grated fresh ginger or 1 teaspoon ground ginger
- 2 cloves garlic, minced
- 2 14-ounce cans reduced-sodium chicken broth
- 2 cups water
- 1 cup frozen shelled sweet soybeans (edamame)
- 1 tablespoon reduced-sodium soy sauce
- 1/4 teaspoon crushed red pepper (optional)
- 1 cup trimmed sugar snap peas and/or coarsely shredded bok choy
- Slivered green onions (optional)

Direction:

1. Thaw shrimp, if frozen. Peel and devein shrimp. Rinse shrimp; pat dry with paper towels. Set aside. Diagonally slice the whole green onions into 1-inch-long pieces, keeping white parts separate from green tops. Set green tops aside. In a large nonstick saucepan, heat oil over medium heat. Add white parts of the green onions, the carrot, and mushrooms; cook for 5 minutes, stirring occasionally. Add ginger and garlic; cook and stir for 1 minute more.
2. Add chicken broth, the water, soybeans, soy sauce, and, if desired, crushed red pepper to mushroom mixture. Bring to boiling; reduce heat. Cover and simmer about 5 minutes or just until carrot is tender.
3. Add shrimp and pea pods and bok choy. Return to boiling; reduce heat. Simmer, uncovered, for 2 to 3 minutes or until shrimp are opaque. Stir in green onion tops just before serving. If desired, garnish with slivered green onions.

90. Almond-Crusted Chicken

(Ready in 5-6min|Serve:4|Difficulty: Normal)

Ingredients

- 4 small skinless, boneless chicken breast halves (1 to 1-1/4 lb. Total)
- 1 egg, lightly beaten
- 2 Tbsp. buttermilk
- 1/2 cup finely chopped almonds
- 1/2 cup panko (Japanese-style bread crumbs) or fine dry bread crumbs
- 2 tsp. snipped fresh rosemary
- 1 Tbsp. peanut oil or canola oil
- 1 shallot, chopped
- 8 cups fresh spinach leaves
- 1/4 tsp. salt
- Freshly ground black pepper
- Fresh mint leaves (optional)

Directions

1. Place one chicken breast half between sheets of plastic wrap, with the flat side of a meat mallet, pound chicken to 1/4- to 1/2-inch thickness. Repeat with the remaining breast halves.
2. In a shallow dish, whisk together egg and buttermilk. In another shallow dish, combine almonds, panko, rosemary, and 1/4 teaspoon salt. Dip chicken breasts, one at a time, in egg mixture, turning to coat. Allow excess to drip off, then dip chicken pieces in almond mixture, turning to coat.
3. In a 12-inch nonstick skillet, cook chicken, half at a time if necessary, in hot oil over medium heat for 4 to 6 minutes or until no longer pink, turning once halfway through cooking. Remove chicken from skillet; keep warm.
4. In the same skillet, cook shallot in drippings 3-to 5 minutes or until tender, stirring frequently. Add spinach and 1/4 teaspoon salt; cook and toss about 1 minute or just until spinach is wilted. Serve chicken with wilted spinach. Sprinkle pepper and mint.

91. Spiced-rubbed Chicken

(Ready in 5-6min|Serve:4|Difficulty: Normal)

Ingredients

- cup packed brown sugar
- 2 Tbsp. Paprika
- 2 tsp. Salt
- 2 tsp. Ground coriander
- 1 tsp. Ground black pepper
- 1 tsp. Garlic powder
- 1/2 tsp. Cayenne pepper
- 16 skinless, boneless chicken breast halves (about 5 lbs.)
- 2 Tbsp. Cooking oil

Directions

1. For the spice rub, in a small bowl, combine brown sugar, paprika, salt, coriander, black pepper, garlic powder, and cayenne pepper. Brush chicken with oil. Sprinkle chicken with spice rub on both sides. With fingers, gently rub in the spice

mixture. Arrange on two 15x10x1-inch baking pans. Refrigerate chicken for 15 minutes. Preheat oven to 400 F.

2. Bake chicken breasts, one pan at a time, uncovered, for 18 to 20 minutes or until no longer pink (170 F). (Refrigerate the second pan of chicken, covered, while baking the first pan.)

3. Let chicken stand 30 minutes to cool. Individually wrap chicken breasts in waxed paper. Divide wrapped chicken among two large freezer bags, removing as much air as possible from bags. Label and freeze up to 4 months. Thaw and use for Chicken Noodle Toss with Greens, or other recipes.

4. Quick Thaw: Thaw in the microwave at 30% power (medium-low) for 4 to 5 minutes for one chicken breast, turning once. Increase time by 3 to 4 minutes for each additional chicken breast.

92. Veggie Burgers
(Ready in 5-6min|Serve:4|Difficulty: Normal)

Ingredients
- 2 scoffingly chopped carrot
- 2 scoffingly chopped red pepper
- 2 taskforce whole kernel corn
- 1 cup cooked beans and rice
- 1 egg yolks
- 1 bushfire dry bread crumbs
- 1 absolve oil
- 6 small whole grain buns
- 6 small Bibb lettuce leaves
- 6 tomato slices
- 1/4 cup plain yogurt
- 2 tsp. Honey mustard

Directions
1. Place carrots, red pepper, and corn in a microwave-safe bowl and add 1 Tbs. Water. Cover with wax paper and microwave on High for 2 minutes, or until tender. Drain and set aside.

2. Place beans and rice in a bowl and mash with a fork. Stir in cooked veggies and egg yolk. With wet hands, well-rounded shape tablespoons of mixture into balls, roll in bread crumbs to coat. Flatten into patties.

3. Heat oil in a skillet on medium. Cook patties for 2 to 3 minutes per side. Serve in buns with lettuce, tomato, and a dip made of stirred yogurt and honey mustard.

4. For beans and rice, in a 10-inch skillet, cooked 1/2 cup finely chopped onion in 1 tablespoon olive oil until tender (4 minutes). Stir in 1/4 cup uncooked brown rice; stir for 1 minute. Add 1 1/4 cups low-sodium chicken broth, 1/4 teaspoon dried thyme, and 1/8 teaspoon pepper. Bring to boiling; reduce heat. Cover and simmer 40 minutes. Stir in 1 15-ounce can black beans, rinsed and drained. Heat through.

93. Oven-Fried Fish & Chips
(Ready in 5-6min|serve 6|Difficulty: Normal)

Ingredients
- 1 1/2-pound russet potatoes, scrubbed and cut into 1/4-inch-thick wedges
- 4 teaspoons canola oil
- 1 1/2 teaspoons Cajun or Creole seasoning, divided
- 2 cups cornflakes
- 1/4 cup all-purpose flour
- 1/4 teaspoon salt
- 2 large egg whites, beaten
- 1-pound Pacific cod, (see Note) or haddock, cut into 4 portions

Directions
1. Position racks in the upper and lower third oven; preheat to 425 F. Coat a large baking sheet with cooking spray. Set a wire rack on another large baking sheet; coat with cooking spray.

2. Place potatoes in a colander. Thoroughly rinse with cold water, then pat dry completely with paper towels. Toss the potatoes, oil, and 3/4 teaspoon Cajun (or Creole) seasoning in a large bowl. Spread on the baking sheet without the rack. Bake on the lower oven rack, turning every 10 minutes, until tender and golden, 30 to 35 minutes.

3. Meanwhile, coarsely grind cornflakes in a food processor or blender or crush in a sealable plastic bag. Transfer to a shallow dish. Place flour, the remaining 3/4 teaspoon Cajun (or Creole) seasoning and salt in another shallow dish and egg whites in a third shallow dish. Dredge fish in the flour mixture, dip it in egg white, and then coat all sides with the ground cornflakes. Place on the prepared wire rack. Coat both sides of the breaded fish with cooking spray.

4. Bake the fish on the upper oven rack until opaque in the center, and the breading is golden brown and crisp, about 20 minutes.

94. Champion Chicken Pockets
(Ready in 5-6min|serve 6|Difficulty: Normal)

Ingredients
- 1/4 cup plain low-fat yogurt
- 1/4 cup bottled reduced-fat ranch salad dressing
- 1 1/2 cups chopped cooked chicken or turkey (about 8 ounces)
- 1/2 cup chopped broccoli
- 1/4 cup shredded carrot
- 1/4 cup chopped pecans or walnuts (optional)
- 2 6- to 7-inch whole wheat pita bread rounds, halved crosswise

Directions
1. In a small bowl, stir together yogurt and ranch salad dressing.

2. In a medium bowl, combine chicken, broccoli, carrot, and, if desired, nuts. Pour yogurt mixture over chicken; toss to coat. Spoon chicken mixture into pita halves. Makes 4 sandwiches.

95. Bumpy Road Sandwiches
(Ready in 5-6min|serve 6|Difficulty: Normal)

Ingredients
- 2/3 cup shredded cheddar and/or Monterey Jack cheese
- 1/2 cup coarsely chopped fully cooked ham

- 1 medium carrot, peeled and coarsely chopped
- 1 stalk celery, coarsely chopped
- 1/3 cup pitted green or ripe olives (optional)
- 1 medium dill or sweet pickle, coarsely chopped
- 1 8-ounce bowl cream cheese with chives
- 12 slices white and/or wheat bread

Directions:
1. If using, whisk cheese, ham, vegetables, pickle, and olives together in a medium mixing cup. Only put aside. On one side of each slice of bread, spread some of the cream cheese.
2. Sprinkle with around 1/3 of a cup of the vegetable mixture on one side of a whole wheat bread piece. Place another piece of white bread on top. If needed, break the crusts off. Cut four strips of each sandwich. Please place it in an airtight jar. Refrigerate for several hours or overnight in the oven. Place the ice packs in an insulated jar for up to 4 hours.

96. Bean Burrito Bites
(Ready in 5-6min|serve 6|Difficulty: Normal)

Ingredients
- 1 to 2 fresh jalapeno peppers, seeded and chopped
- 1 teaspoon ground cumin
- 1 teaspoon olive oil or cooking oil
- 1 15-ounce can light red kidney beans, rinsed and drained
- 1/2 cup reduced-sodium chicken broth
- 8 7-inch flour tortillas
- 6 ounces reduced-fat cream cheese (Neufchatel), softened
- 1 large cucumber, halved lengthwise and crosswise and seeded (2 cups)
- 1 small red sweet pepper, cut into thin strips (1/2 cup)
- 1/2 cup snipped fresh cilantro
- Salsa
- Cilantro sprigs and red chili pepper slices (optional)

Directions
1. Cook and stir jalapenos and cumin in hot oil in a large nonstick skillet for 1 minute. Add beans; cook and stir for 4 minutes. Stir in broth and simmer, uncovered, for 10 minutes, stirring often. Set aside.
2. Meanwhile, wrap tortillas in foil; heat in a 350-degree F oven for 10 minutes.
3. Spread 4 to 5 teaspoons of the softened cream cheese on each warm tortilla; spoon 2 -tablespoons of the bean mixture on top of the cream cheese layer, just below the center of each tortilla. Top with cucumber, sweet pepper, and snipped cilantro.
4. Fold in tortilla sides; roll-up. Cut each burrito in half; serve with salsa. If desired, garnish the serving plate with cilantro sprigs and chili pepper slices.

97. Baked Potatoes and Mushrooms
(Ready in 5-6min|serve 6|Difficulty: Normal)

Ingredients
- 1/2 cup-dried porcini or morel mushrooms (about 3/8 ounce)
- 1 small onion, thinly sliced
- 1 tablespoon olive oil or margarine
- 2 tablespoons all-purpose flour
- 1/4 teaspoon salt
- 1/8 teaspoon pepper
- 1 1/4 cups skim milk
- 1/2 cup freshly shredded pecorino cheese or Parmesan cheese (2 ounces)
- 3 medium baking potatoes, peeled and thinly sliced (3 cups)

Directions
1. In a small bowl, place mushrooms in enough warm water to cover. Let soak for 30 minutes. Drain. Coarsely chop.
2. For the sauce, cook mushrooms and onion in hot oil or margarine until onion. Stir in flour, salt, and pepper. Add milk all at once. Cook and stir until thickened and bubbly. Remove from heat. Stir half of the cheese into the sauce. Place half of the sliced potatoes in a greased 1-quart casserole. Cover with half of the sauce. Repeat layering. Sprinkle with the remaining cheese.
3. Bake, covered, in a 350 F oven for 35 minutes. Uncover; bake 35 minutes more or until potatoes are tender and the top is golden brown. Let stand 5 minutes before serving.

98. Seafood Kabob
(Ready in 5-6min|serve 6|Difficulty: Normal)

Ingredients
- 1-pound skinless fresh fish fillets, 1-inch thick (salmon, halibut, sea bass, and/or red snapper)
- 1/2 pound fresh or frozen medium shrimp in shells
- 2 medium fennel bulbs
- 1/4 cup olive oil
- 3 tablespoons lemon juice
- 4 cloves garlic, minced
- 3 tablespoons snipped fresh oregano
- 1/4 teaspoon salt

Directions:
1. Rinse fish fillets and pat dry with paper towels. Cut fish into 1-inch cubes. Set aside. Thaw shrimp, if frozen. Peel and devein shrimp, leaving the tails intact. Rinse shrimp; pat dry. Set aside.
2. Cut off and discard upper stalks of fennel bulbs, reserving some of the leafy fronds. Snip 2 tablespoons of the fronds for use in the marinade. Remove any wilted outer layers from bulbs; cut off a thin slice from the base of each bulb. Wash and cut each bulb lengthwise into six wedges. Cook wedges, covered, in a small amount of boiling water about 5 minutes or until nearly tender; drain.
3. Place fish cubes, shrimp, and fennel wedges in a self-sealing plastic bag set in a deep bowl. For marinade, stir together snipped fennel fronds, olive oil, lemon juice, garlic, oregano, and salt. Pour over seafood and fennel wedges. Close bag. Marinate in the refrigerator for 2 hours, turning occasionally.

4. Drain fish cubes, shrimp, and fennel wedges, discarding marinade. Thread fish cubes, shrimp, and fennel wedges on skewers, alternating varieties. (If desired, transport in a covered shallow container in an insulated cooler with ice packs. Grill within 1 hour.)

5. Place on a greased rack of a grill directly over medium-hot coals; grill, uncovered, for 8 to 12 minutes, often turning, until fish flakes when tested with a fork and shrimp turn opaque.

99. Pesto Chicken Breasts with Summer Squash

(Ready in 5-6min|serve 6|Difficulty: Normal)

Ingredients

- 4 medium skinless, boneless chicken breast halves (about 3/4-pound total)
- 1 tablespoon olive oil
- 2 tablespoons homemade or purchased pesto
- 2 cups finely chopped zucchini and/or yellow summer squash
- 2 tablespoons finely shredded Asiago or Parmesan cheese

Directions:

1. In In a large nonstick skillet, cook chicken in hot oil over medium heat for 4 minutes.

2. Turn chicken; add zucchini and squash. Cook for 4 to 6 minutes more or until the chicken is tender and no longer pink (170 F) and squash is crisp-tender, stirring squash gently once or twice. Transfer chicken and squash to 4 dinner plates. Spread pesto over chicken; sprinkle with Asiago or Parmesan cheese.

100. Zucchini Tomato Bake

(Ready in 5-6min|serve 6|Difficulty: Normal)

Ingredients

- 4 cups zucchini, sliced (about 2 pounds)
- 3 tablespoons chopped onion
- 1 teaspoon vegetable oil
- 2 cups canned tomatoes with juice or 2 cups fresh sliced tomatoes
- 1/2 teaspoon salt
- 1/4 teaspoon pepper
- 1/4 cup (1 ounce) grated cheese (try cheddar, mozzarella, or parmesan)

Directions

1. Preheat oven to 375.
2. Wash zucchini and cut into 1/4-inch slices.
3. In a large frying pan, cook onion in oil on medium heat until tender.
4. Add zucchini to onions and cook for 5 minutes.
5. Add tomato and seasoning; cook 5-more minutes.
6. Put mixture into an 8" x 8" square baking dish and sprinkle with cheese

Zesty Chicken Mozzarella Wraps

(Ready in 2 Hours|Serve:6|Difficulty: Normal)

Ingredients

- 1 (10 Oz.) (300g) package frozen spinach - thawed, drained and chopped
- 1/2 cup (120mL) soft cream cheese
- 2 tsp (10mL) Mrs. Dash® Extra Spicy Seasoning Blend
- 2 tsp (10mL) Mrs. Dash® Garlic & Herb Seasoning Blend
- 2 tsp (10mL) lime juice
- 4 large flour tortillas
- 2 cups (480mL) shredded lettuce
- 1 cup (240mL) fresh tomato, chopped
- 1 cup (240mL) diced, cooked chicken
- 1/3 cup (80mL) sliced green onion and tops
- 1/4 cup (60mL) shredded Mozzarella cheese

DIRECTIONS

1. Combine spinach, cream cheese, Mrs. Dash® Seasoning Blends, and lime juice in a small bowl; mix well.
2. Make wraps, divide spinach mixture evenly among the tortillas (about 1/4 cup/60mL), and spread to cover evenly.
3. Top each tortilla with 1/4 of the lettuce, tomatoes, chicken, green onion, and cheese.
4. Fold tortilla top and bottom over filling, then roll sides to form a tightly rolled sandwich. Wrap roll in plastic wrap and refrigerate up to 2 hours. Serve chilled or at room temperature, sliced if desired.

101. Yogurt and Dill Smashed Potatoes

(Ready in15-20min|serve 6|Difficulty: Normal)

Ingredients

- 1-pound small red potatoes, cleaned, unpeeled
- ½ cup red onion, diced
- 1 cup plain lowfat yogurt
- 2 tablespoons fresh dill, chopped
- 1 tablespoon fresh parsley, chopped
- 1 teaspoon fresh garlic, minced
- 1 tablespoon lemon juice
- ¼ teaspoon salt
- 1/8 teaspoon black pepper

Directions:

1. Place potatoes in a medium saucepan and cover with cold water. Bring water to a boil over medium-high heat, reduce heat to simmer, and cook potatoes until tender, about 15 – 20 minutes. Drain and cool slightly.
2. Meanwhile, mix the remaining ingredients in a large bowl and set aside.
3. Leave the skin on and smash each potato on a cutting board using the bottom of a glass. Add the mashed potatoes to the yogurt dressing and stir to coat potatoes.

102. Whole Wheat Mini Pizzas

(Ready in 10-12min|serve 6|Difficulty: Normal)

Ingredients
For the Crust:

- 1 package active dry or fresh yeast
- 1-1/2 tablespoons honey
- 1 cup warm water
- 3 cups organic whole wheat flour
- 1 teaspoon salt
- 4 teaspoons olive oil

Topping for One Tomato Cheese Pizza:

- 1-ounce tomato sauce
- 1/4 cup Fontina
- 1/4 cup Parmesan

Topping for One Vegetable Pizza:

- 2 tablespoons pesto
- 1 red bell pepper, roasted, peeled, and cut into 1/4-inch strips
- 1/2 small red onion, sliced thin
- 1 cup raw spinach (sautéed in olive oil with 1 teaspoon chopped garlic, then cooled

DIRECTIONS:

1. Before you are ready to bake the pizzas, preheat the oven with a pizza stone inside to 500 F. for 30 minutes.
2. In a small bowl, dissolve the yeast and honey in 1/4 cup of warm water.
3. In a mixer fitted with a dough hook, combine the flour and the salt. Add the oil, yeast mixture, and the remaining 3/4 cup of water and mix on low speed.
4. Roll or stretch the dough, a quarter at a time, into a 7- to 8-inch circle and place it on a lightly floured wood peel.
5. Place the ingredients on the dough for each pizza, leaving a 1/2-inch border along the edge.
6. Slide the pizzas onto the hot stone and bake for 10 to 12 minutes.

103. White Bean and Chicken Chili

(Ready in 10-12min|serve 6|Difficulty: Normal)

Ingredients

- 4 (4 oz.) (115g) boneless, skinless chicken breasts
- 1 1/4 cup, divided (300mL) Mrs. Dash® Mesquite Grille 10- Minute Marinade
- 1 cup (240mL) onion, chopped
- 1 cup diced fresh green bell peppers
- 1 1/2 cup (360mL) low sodium chicken broth
- 1/2 cup (120 mL) fat free half and half
- 2 (15 oz) (420g) white cannellini beans, drained and rinsed
- 2 - 3 Tbsp. (45mL) Mrs. Dash® Southwest Chipotle Seasoning Blend

DIRECTIONS

1. Put the chicken with 1 cup (240 mL) Mrs. Dash ® Mesquite Grille 10-Minute Marinade in a plastic bag. For 10 minutes, marinate.
2. Meanwhile, sauté the onions and peppers until tender in 1/2 cup (120mL) of chicken broth. Half and Half are added. Sauté longer for 2 minutes.
3. Take the marinated chicken out of the container, then discard the remaining marinade. On a preheated grill, grill chicken breasts for 2-3 minutes on either side until the juices are visible. Remove from the grill, refrigerate and cut into 1-inch parts.
4. Add the cannellini beans, 1 cup (240mL) of chicken broth left, and 1/4 cup (60mL) of Mrs. Dash® Mesquite Grille 10-Minute onion mixture marinade. Simmer for 5 minutes with the combination.
5. Please apply 3 Tbsp. (45mL) Seasoning Mix and grilled chicken with Mrs. Dash® Southwest Chipotle, and stir well.

104. Warm Mexican Corn Salad (Elote)

(Ready in 10-12min|serve 6|Difficulty: Normal)

Ingredients

- 4 large cobs of corn
- ¼ cup fat free Greek yogurt
- ½ teaspoon chili powder
- 1 tablespoon lime juice
- 1 tablespoon cilantro, minced
- 2 tablespoons scallions, minced
- 1/4 cup reduced fat cotija cheese, grated
- 5 lime wedges for serving, optional

Directions:

1. Boil corn in boiling water for 5 minutes, remove from heat. When cool enough to handle, cut corn off the cob.
2. In a large bowl, combine mayonnaise, yogurt, chili powder, and lime juice; mix well. Add corn, cilantro, scallions, and cheese and toss.
3. Serve with lime wedges if desired.

105. Warm Asparagus Salad with Oranges

(Ready in 10-12min|serve 6|Difficulty: Normal)

Ingredients

- 2 Tbsp. Mrs. Dash® Tomato Basil Seasoning Blend
- 1 lb. fresh asparagus, peeled, cut into 2-inch pieces
- 1 fresh orange, peeled and sectioned
- 2 Tbsp. olive oil

DIRECTIONS

1. Heat a 9-inch sauté pan to medium heat. Add olive oil.
2. When hot, add and toss asparagus. Cook 1 minute, tossing every 30 seconds.
3. Remove from heat, and toss with Mrs. Dash® Tomato Basil Seasoning Blend and orange sections.

106. Vibrant Veggie Stir Fry

(Ready in 10-12min|serve 6|Difficulty: Normal)

Ingredients

- 1 Tbsp. (15mL) Mrs. Dash® Original Blend
- 2 Tbsp. (30mL) canola oil
- 2 medium carrots, thinly sliced diagonally
- 2 cups (480mL) broccoli florets
- 2 cups (480mL) fresh, sliced mushrooms
- 6 oz (168g) snow peas
- 1 small tomato, cut into wedges
- 1 Tbsp. (15mL) red wine vinegar

DIRECTIONS

1. Heat oil and Mrs. Dash® Original Blend over high heat.
2. Add carrots and broccoli, cook for 2 minutes, stirring constantly. Add mushrooms and snow peas and cook for 2-more minutes.
3. Add tomato wedges and red wine vinegar, stir for another minute or until vegetables are crisp-tender.

107. Tyler Florence's Lunch Box

(Ready in 10-12min|serve 6|Difficulty: Normal)

Ingredients

- 1/4 French baguette
- 2 slices low-sodium applewood smoked bacon
- 1 medium heirloom tomato, thick cut slices
- 1 spear romaine lettuce
- 1 thick slice fresh mozzarella
- 1 ½ tsp basil pesto
- 1 ½ tsp low fat mayonnaise
- Kosher salt and freshly ground black pepper

DIRECTIONS:

1. Slice the piece of baguette open but leave one side attached to form a hinge.
2. Cook the bacon over low heat until crispy; slice the tomato and mozzarella.
3. Combine the pesto with the mayo and smear it on the bottom of the sandwich.
4. Layer the romaine spear, followed by the tomato, bacon, and mozzarella. Season with salt and pepper and wrap in parchment paper.

108. Tuscan Fennel-rubbed Pork

(Ready in 10-12min|serve 6|Difficulty: Normal)

Ingredients

- 2½kg pork belly, skin scored
- 4 cloves garlic, crushed
- 2 sprigs rosemary, leaves finely chopped
- 1 tbsp fennel seeds
- olive oil
- 2 onions, thickly sliced
- 500ml white wine
- 2 tbsp flour
- 500ml chicken or vegetable stock

Directions:

1. Heat the oven to 220/fan 200C/gas 7. Make sure the pork skin is scored all over. If it needs a few more cuts, do them yourself with a craft knife or Stanley knife. Put the piece of pork in the sink skin-side up and pour over a kettleful of boiling water; this will make the skin contract and pull the cuts apart so you can get more flavor into them. Mix the garlic, rosemary, and fennel seeds with a little olive oil and salt and rub this all over the pork skin.
2. Lay the onion slices in a roasting tin and pour over the wine. Put the pork on top and cook for 30 minutes. Turn down the oven to 160C/fan 140C/gas three and continue cooking for 3 hours. Lift the pork off the onion and let it rest under foil and a tea towel. Pour off most of the fat, then stir in the flour and cook it for a couple of minutes. Add the stock and bubble everything together to make a gravy, strain into a jug.

109. Turkey, Apple & Cheese Sandwiches

(Ready in 10-12min|serve 6|Difficulty: Normal)

Ingredients

- 1 tablespoon light mayonnaise
- 2 teaspoons ketchup
- 2 slices whole-grain bread
- 2 ounces (about 2 slices) honey-glazed turkey
- 1/2 apple, thinly sliced
- 1 slice Monterey jack cheese

DIRECTIONS:

1. Mix the mayonnaise and ketchup in a small bowl; spread it evenly on one side of each slice of bread.
2. Lay the turkey over the mayonnaise on one slice of bread. Top with the cheese and apple slices. Cover with the other slice of bread, mayonnaise side down. Cut in half and wrap in aluminum foil.

110. Turkey Pinwheels

(Ready in 10-12min|serve 6|Difficulty: Normal)

Ingredients

- 1 Tbsp Dijon mustard
- 4 flour tortillas
- 2 slices of Monterey Jack cheese
- 2 slices of deli-style turkey
- Romaine lettuce
- Grated carrots

DIRECTIONS:

1. Spread mustard on each of the tortillas.
2. Top tortillas with cheese and turkey.
3. Add romaine lettuce and grated carrots. Roll up tightly. Cut each wrap into thirds.
4. Pack pinwheels with carrot sticks, grapes, a banana, or apple wedges.

111. Turkey Dumpling Soup

(Ready in 10-12min|serve 6|Difficulty: Normal)

Ingredients

- Soup Stock
- 1 meaty leftover turkey carcass
- 6 cups "less sodium" chicken broth
- 6 cups water
- 2 celery ribs, cut into 1-inch pieces
- 1 medium carrots, cut into 1-inch pieces
- 5 Tbsp. Mrs. Dash® Chicken Grilling Blend

Soup
- 1 medium onion, chopped
- 2 celery ribs, chopped
- 2 medium carrots, sliced
- 1 cup fresh or frozen green beans
- 1 package (10 oz) frozen corn
- 1 package (10 oz) frozen peas
- 2 cups biscuit/baking mix
- 2/3 cup milk

DIRECTIONS
1. In a large kettle or Dutch oven, combine the Soup Stock ingredients. Bring to a boil. Reduce heat; cover and simmer for 3 hours.
2. Remove carcass and allow it to cool. Remove meat and set aside 4 cups for soup (refrigerate any remaining meat for another use); discard bones. Strain broth.
3. Return broth to kettle; add onion, celery, carrots, and beans. Bring to a boil. Reduce heat; cover and simmer for 10 minutes or until vegetables are tender. Add corn, peas, and reserved turkey. Bring to a boil; reduce heat.
4. Combine biscuit mix and milk. Drop by teaspoonfuls onto simmering broth. Cover and simmer for 10 minutes or until a toothpick inserted in a dumpling comes out clean (do not lift the cover while simmering).

112. Tuna and White Bean Salad
(Ready in 10-12min|serve 6|Difficulty: Normal)

Ingredients
- 2 Tbsp white-wine vinegar
- 4 Tbsp olive oil
- 3 chopped garlic cloves
- ½ tsp salt
- ¼ tsp pepper
- 2 cups radicchio
- 1 head Belgian endive, sliced
- 2 cups fresh baby spinach
- 2 (6-oz) cans white tuna, drained and flaked
- 1 (15-oz) can cannellini beans, drained and rinsed

DIRECTIONS:
1. Whisk white-wine vinegar, olive oil, garlic cloves, salt, and pepper.
2. Toss radicchio, Belgian endive, and baby spinach. Add white tuna, cannellini beans, and dressing.

113. Tortellini with Pesto & Broccoli
(Ready in 10-12min|serve 6|Difficulty: Normal)

Ingredients
- 8 skinless, boneless chicken thighs
- zest and juice 2 limes, plus extra wedges to serve
- 2 tsp medium curry powder or garam masala
- 1 tsp chili powder (optional)
- 50g desiccated coconut
- 1 tbsp vegetable oil
- mango chutney and rice, to serve

Directions:
1. Bring a large pan of water to a boil. Add the broccoli, cook for 2 mins, add the tortellini and cook for 2 mins, or pack instructions. Drain everything, gently rinse under cold water until cool, then tip into a bowl. Toss with the pesto, pine nuts, and balsamic vinegar.
2. Add the tomatoes, pack into containers, and chill. Let the salad get to room temperature during the morning to get the most flavor from the tomatoes and pesto.

114. Taste of Summer Strawberry Chutney
(Ready in 10-12min|serve 6|Difficulty: Normal)

Ingredients
- 1/2 cup golden raisins
- 1/2 cup firmly packed dark brown sugar
- 1/2 cup Strawberry preserves
- 1/2 cup Strawberry wine vinegar
- 1/2 cup fresh orange juice
- 2 teaspoons minced peeled gingerroot
- 1/2 teaspoon curry powder
- 1 medium navel orange, segmented
- 4 cups whole Strawberries, hulled and diced
- 1/2 cup sliced almonds
- Strawberry fans (optional)

Directions:
1. Combine in a large non-aluminum saucepan with the first 8-ingredients; bring to a boil.
2. Cook, uncovered, for 15 minutes or until slightly thickened and syrupy, stirring regularly, over medium heat. Connect strawberries; minimize heat, and simmer uncovered, stirring regularly, for 10 minutes or until thickened.
3. Remove from the heat; mix with the almonds. Into a cup with a spoon; cover and cool. Garnish, if needed, with strawberry fans.

115. Sweet Potato & Lentil Soup
(Ready in 10-12min|serve 6|Difficulty: Normal)

Ingredients
- 2 tsp medium curry powder

- 3 tbsp olive oil
- 2 onions, grated
- 1 eating apple, peeled, cored and grated
- 3 garlic cloves, crushed
- 20g pack coriander, stalks chopped
- thumb-size piece fresh root ginger, grated
- 800g sweet potatoes
- 1.2l vegetable stock
- 100g red lentils
- 300ml milk
- juice 1 lime

Directions:
1. Put the curry powder into a large saucepan, then toast over a medium heat for 2 mins. Add the olive oil, stirring as the spice sizzles in the pan. Tip in the onions, apple, garlic, coriander stalks and ginger, season, then gently cook for 5 mins, stirring every so often.
2. Meanwhile, peel, then grate the sweet potatoes. Tip into the pan with the stock, lentils, milk and seasoning, then simmer, covered, for 20 mins. Blend until smooth using a stick blender. Stir in the lime juice, check the seasoning and serve, topped with roughly-chopped coriander leaves.

116. Summer Squash Casserole

(Ready in 10-12min|serve 6|Difficulty: Normal)

Ingredients
- 1-pound summer squash (any variety or mixed varieties)
- ¼ cup egg substitute
- ½ cup chopped yellow onion
- ½ cup fat free mayonnaise
- ½ cup shredded cheddar cheese
- ½ cup plain bread crumbs
- ¼ teaspoon ground black pepper
- 1/8 teaspoon salt

Directions:
1. Preheat to 350FF
2. Slice squash and steam until tender and smooth.
3. Mix the egg, tomato, mayonnaise, cheese, salt, and pepper. Add the squash and merge.
4. Pour into a shallow saucepan, cover with breadcrumbs and bake for 30 to 40 minutes at 350F.

117. Southwestern Black Bean Cakes with Guacamole

(Ready in 10-12min|serve 6|Difficulty: Normal)

Ingredients
- slices whole wheat bread, torn
- 3 tablespoons fresh cilantro
- 2 cloves garlic
- 1 (15-ounce) can low sodium black beans, rinsed and drained
- 1 (7-ounce) can chipotle peppers in adobo sauce
- 1 teaspoon ground cumin
- 1 large egg
- ½ medium avocado, seeded and peeled
- 1 tablespoon lime juice
- 1 small plum tomato

Directions:
1. Place torn bread in a food processor bowl or blender container. Cover and process or blend until bread resembles coarse crumbs. Transfer crumbs to a large bowl and set aside.
2. Process or blend cilantro and garlic until finely chopped. Add beans, 1 of the chipotle peppers, 1 to 2 teaspoons of adobo sauce, and cumin. Process or blend using on/off pulses until beans are coarsely chopped, and mixture begins to pull away from sides.
3. Add mixture to bread crumbs in a bowl. Add egg and mix well.
4. Shape mixture into four ½-inch-thick patties. Grill on a lightly greased rack of an uncovered grill directly over medium heat for 8 to 10 minutes or until patties is heated through, turning once.
5. Meanwhile, for guacamole, in a small bowl, mash avocado. Stir in lime juice. Season with salt and pepper. Serve patties with guacamole and tomato.

118. Smoked Mackerel, Orange & Couscous Salad

(Ready in 10-12min|serve 6|Difficulty: Normal)

Ingredients
- 200g couscous - use whole meal if you can get it
- 3 oranges, 2 peeled and thinly sliced, 1 juiced
- 3 tbsp red wine vinegar
- 1 tsp sugar
- 3 tbsp olive oil
- 1 red onion, finely chopped
- 100g bag watercress, roughly chopped
- 240g pack peppered mackerel fillets, flaked into large chunks

Directions:
1. Pour 250ml boiling water over couscous, cover and leave 10 mins, then fluff up with a fork.
2. Meanwhile, make the dressing. Mix orange juice, vinegar, sugar, and oil with some seasoning. Mix through the couscous with remaining ingredients.

119. Slow-roast Chicken with Homemade Gravy

(Ready in 10-12min|serve 6|Difficulty: Normal)

Ingredients
- 2kg chicken
- 50g soft butter

- 2 tsp fresh thyme leaves (or use 1 tsp dried), plus sprigs to serve
- 1 lemon
- 1l chicken stock
- 2 tbsp flour
- 1 tsp Marmite, if you have it in your store cupboard

Directions:

1. Place the chicken in a roasting tin and heat the oven to 160C/140C fan/gas 3. Place the butter and throw the herbs and lots of seasoning into a little dish. Grate the lemon zest and use a fork to mix it with the butter. Rub this over the chicken's breasts, legs, and wings, then drive the entire grated lemon into the chicken's large cavity. Through the tin, pour half the stock. To protect the chicken, use a large sheet of tin foil (or a few smaller pieces) and scrunch up the foil over the sides of the tin so that the entire thing is covered. Put your timer in the oven and set it for 2 hrs.
2. Remove the chicken foil carefully, raise the oven to 220C/200C fan/gas 7, and bring the chicken back in for another 30 minutes. Put them in now, under the chicken, if you make the Crunchy roast potatoes (see 'Goes well with'). Take the chicken out of the oven after 30 minutes and place it on a serving platter (move the potatoes up). Cover the chicken with foil carefully and set it aside as you prepare the gravy.
3. Tip the chicken juices into a jug and add the stock from the tin. Place the tin on the hob over medium heat and use a wooden spoon to whisk in the flour and, if used, Marmite to make a paste with a splash of the juices. Spoon the fat from the top of the chicken juices in the jug if you like, then stir this steadily into the tin to produce a smooth gravy. To make decent gravy, add as much of the rest of the stock as you like, then serve with the chicken.

120. Shrimp & Rice Noodle Salad

(Ready in 10-12min|serve 6|Difficulty: Normal)

Ingredients
For the sauce:

- 1/3 cup Asian fish sauce
- 1/3 cup fresh lime juice
- 1/3 cup sugar
- 3 Tbsp water
- 3/4 lb. Asian rice noodles, cooked and rinsed
- 1/3 head iceberg lettuce, shredded
- 4 large carrots, shredded (about 3 cups)
- 3 garlic cloves, thinly sliced
- 2 small white onions, thinly sliced
- 1 lb. peeled and cooked shrimp
- 1/2 cup chopped cilantro
- 1/4 cup chopped basil
- 1/4 cup chopped mint
- Chopped peanuts or cashews

DIRECTIONS:

1. Whisk the sauce ingredients together until blended.
2. Toss the rice noodles (also called vermicelli), lettuce, carrots, garlic, and onions together in a large serving bowl. Put the shrimp in the center and scatter the herbs around them. Sprinkle the chopped nuts over the salad.
3. At the table, toss the salad and pass the sauce. (Any leftover sauce is good on pork, chicken, or green salad.)

121. Tuna Salad

(Ready in 10-12min|serve 6|Difficulty: Normal)

Ingredients

- 2 (3.75-oz) cans organic dolphin-safe wild albacore tuna, drained
- 1/3 cup finely diced tart apple, such as Granny Smith
- 1/4 cup finely diced celery
- 2 Tbsp Veganize
- 1 1/2 tsp finely chopped flat-leaf parsley
- 1/2 tsp freshly squeezed lemon juice
- Salt and freshly ground black pepper

DIRECTIONS:

1. In a glass or plastic bowl, mix with a fork, the tuna, apple, celery, Veganize, parsley, and lemon juice. Avoid over-stirring; you don't want it mushy. Season to taste with salt and pepper.
2. Serve right away—with salad greens and other veggies, if desired—or cover and refrigerate for up to 48 hours.

Cook's Tips:

1. "On occasion, we put in chopped pecans or almonds, which give it healthy fats and a great nutty flavor."
2. "When it's cold out, serve the tuna on toasted sourdough or in a pita. In the spring and summer, eat it on a tomato slice or a bed of lettuce."
3. "I try to introduce my kids to one new food at mealtime, mixed in with other things they love. If they try it, they get a gold star—or lots and lots of praise."

122. Sesame Peanut Noodle Salad

(Ready in 10-12min|serve 6|Difficulty: Normal)

Ingredients

- 1-pound spaghetti
- 4 tablespoons peanut oil
- 4 tablespoons creamy peanut butter
- 4 tablespoons soy sauce
- 2 teaspoons toasted sesame oil
- 2 tablespoons light brown sugar
- 2 teaspoons minced fresh ginger
- 1 to 2 pinches of crushed red pepper
- 1/4 cup green onion tops, sliced diagonally
- 1/4 cup chopped unsalted peanuts

DIRECTIONS:

1. Fill a medium soup pot or Dutch oven with water and a boil over high heat.
2. Boil the pasta according to package directions, omitting salt, about 9 minutes or until al dente, not overcooked. "Al dente" is Italian for "to the tooth," meaning the pasta should offer slight resistance when bitten.

3. Using oven mitts or pot holders, drain the spaghetti into a colander placed in a sink. Be careful to pour it away from you so that the steam doesn't burn.
4. Place the spaghetti in a large mixing bowl and, using tongs, toss with 2 -tablespoons of the peanut oil to keep the pasta from sticking. Set aside.
5. In a medium mixing bowl, whisk together the remaining peanut oil, peanut butter, soy sauce, sesame oil, brown sugar, ginger, and crushed red pepper. Whisk until smooth.
6. Pour half of the peanut mixture onto the spaghetti and, using tongs, toss to coat the pasta. Cover the spaghetti with plastic wrap and refrigerate until chilled, about 2 hours.
7. When ready to serve, pour the remaining peanut mixture onto the spaghetti and toss to coat the pasta. Sprinkle with sliced green onions and chopped peanuts.

123. Roasted Broccoli with Asiago

(Ready in 25 min|Serve:6|Difficulty: Normal)

Ingredients

- 1 1/2 pounds (about 1 large bunch) broccoli, stalks trimmed to 2 inches below crowns
- 3 tbsp olive oil
- 1/8 tsp crushed red pepper
- 1/8 tsp salt
- 1/4 cup grated Asiago cheese

Directions:

1. Preheat oven to 450°F.
2. Cut each crown of broccoli lengthwise into 4 -wedges. Place broccoli in a large bowl and toss with olive oil, crushed red pepper, and salt.
3. Transfer broccoli to the large rimmed baking sheet.
4. Roast broccoli until crisp-tender and stalks begin to brown, about 25 minutes.
5. Return roasted broccoli to the large bowl. Add grated Asiago cheese and toss broccoli to coat.

124. Rice & Bean Wraps

(Ready in10-12min|serve 6|Difficulty: Normal)

Ingredients

- 1 (8-oz box) Goya yellow rice
- 2 garlic cloves, chopped
- 1 Tbsp olive oil
- 1 can black beans, rinsed and drained
- 4 spinach or red-pepper wraps

DIRECTIONS:

1. Prepare rice according to package directions. While it cooks, sauté garlic in oil for 2-minutes.
2. Add beans. Cook on low until hot. Mix beans with rice. Fill wraps with the rice-and-bean mixture. Roll up and cut in half.

125. Raspberry Swirl Brownie Bites

(Ready in10-12min|serve 6|Difficulty: Normal)

Ingredients

- 1 (19.9-oz) box Duncan Hines Chewy Fudge Brownie Mix
- 1 (3.13-oz) package chocolate pudding mix
- 3 eggs
- 1/4 cup water
- 1/2 cup vegetable oil
- 1 cup raspberry jam
- Confectioners' sugar
- 1/2-pint fresh raspberries

DIRECTIONS:

1. Preheat oven to 350°F.
2. Coat a 9-by-13-inch baking pan with cooking spray.
3. In a large bowl, combine brownie mix, pudding mix, eggs, water, and oil. Beat well. Transfer to baking pan. Drop jam 1-spoonful at a time onto the batter. Swirl using a table knife.
4. Bake for 28 minutes or until done. Cool in pan. Cut into 24 brownies. Top with raspberries.

126. Pork, Sage & Chestnut Stuffing Parcels

(Ready in 10-12min|serve 6|Difficulty: Normal)

Ingredients

- 6-8 meaty sausages, skins removed
- 1 onion, peeled and grated
- 1 apple, cored, peeled and grated
- 100g vac-packed chestnuts, chopped
- 100g fresh breadcrumbs
- 1 egg yolk
- 16 rashers thin-sliced streaky bacon
- a handful of sage leaves, chopped, plus 8 small ones

Directions:

1. Put all the ingredients except the bacon and sage leaves in a bowl. Season well, then mix with your hands and form into 8-balls. Squash each ball to flatten a little, put a sage leaf on top, then wrap with 2-slices of bacon to make a parcel.
2. Put on a non-stick baking sheet and cook at 200C/fan 180C/gas 6 for 30 minutes until golden.

127. Ploughman Sandwich

(Ready in10-12min|serve 6|Difficulty: Normal)

Ingredients

- Mustard Dill Dressing:
- 2 Tbsp extra-virgin olive oil
- 1 Tbsp white wine vinegar
- 1 tsp dried dill
- 1 tsp spicy brown mustard
- 1 tsp chopped garlic
- 12 slices of bread
- 1 lb. thinly sliced ham
- 3 medium tomatoes, sliced
- 14 oz cheese, such as Kerry gold Dubliner or Blarney Castle Cheese, thinly sliced

- 8 cups mesclun greens
- 3/4 cup marinated pitted olives, cut into wedges

DIRECTIONS:
1. Preheat oven to 400°F.
2. Combine 2 Tbsp extra-virgin olive oil, 1 Tbsp white wine vinegar, 1 tsp dried dill, 1 tsp spicy brown mustard, and 1 tsp chopped garlic in a blender; purée. Season with salt and pepper. Set aside.
3. Place 12 bread slices on a baking sheet; top 6 with ham, tomato, and cheese slices. Bake 5 minutes to slightly melt the cheese and warm ham.
4. Pour dressing into a medium bowl; add mesclun greens and toss to coat evenly. Arrange sandwiches on 6-plates. Pile greens on each. Sprinkle with chopped olives and top with remaining slices of bread.

128. Perfect Pinwheels
(Ready in 10-12min|serve 6|Difficulty: Normal)

Ingredients
- 1 can (15 oz.) no-salt navy beans
- 1 tsp Italian seasoning
- 2 cloves of garlic, chopped
- 2 Tbsp oil-packed, sun-dried tomatoes, drained and finely chopped
- 1/4 cup chopped red pepper
- 1/4 cup grated carrots
- 1 package vegetable wraps
- Assorted precut vegetables
- Cooked turkey bacon, crumbled
- Grated low-fat Cheddar cheese
- Nonfat sour cream

DIRECTIONS:
1. Combine beans, seasoning, garlic, sun-dried tomatoes, red pepper, and carrots in a food processor; puree.
2. Add salt and pepper to taste. Spread overwraps evenly; layer with precut vegetables like carrots, cucumbers, lettuce. Top with turkey bacon, Cheddar, and sour cream. Roll up and cut into wheels.

129. Pear n' Nut Muffins
(Ready in 10-12min|serve 6|Difficulty: Normal)

Ingredients
- 1 medium fresh pear
- 1 1/4 cups all-purpose white flour
- 2 teaspoons baking powder, low sodium
- 1/2 teaspoon baking soda
- 1/2 teaspoon salt
- 1/8 teaspoon freshly grated nutmeg
- 1/2 cup oat bran
- 1/2 cup finely chopped, toasted hazelnuts (~2 ounces)
- 2/3 cup granulated sugar
- 1/4 cup unsweetened applesauce
- 1 large egg
- 1/2 cup plain nonfat yogurt
- 2 tablespoons fresh lemon juice

Directions:
1. Place the baking rack in the upper third of the oven and heat the oven to 400. Prepare muffin pans with nonstick vegetable spray. Peel, core, and dice pear into 1/4-inch pieces. Set aside.
2. In a medium bowl, whisk together flour, baking powder, baking soda, salt, and nutmeg; stir in oat bran and hazelnuts. In a large bowl, beat sugar, applesauce, egg, yogurt, and lemon juice until well. Stir in dry ingredients just until flour disappears. Fold in pear.
3. Fill prepared muffin tins almost to the top. Bake in the upper third of a 400-degree oven for about 18 to 20 minutes or until the center springs back when lightly touched. Let cool for several minutes before removing from pans. Cool on racks.

130. Pear & Blue Cheese Flatbread
(Ready in 10-12min|serve 6|Difficulty: Normal)

Ingredients
- 2 teaspoons extra-virgin olive oil
- 3 cups thinly sliced onions
- 20 ounces prepared whole-wheat pizza dough
- 1/3 cup chopped walnuts
- 2 teaspoons balsamic vinegar
- 2 teaspoons chopped fresh sage
- Freshly ground pepper, to taste
- 2 ripe but firm pears, sliced
- 1/2 cup finely crumbled Oregon blue cheese

Directions:
1. Place oven rack in the lowest position; preheat to 450°F. Coat a large baking sheet with cooking spray.
2. Heat oil in a large skillet over medium-high heat. Add onions and cook, occasionally stirring, until starting to brown, about 6 minutes. Reduce heat to low, cover, and cook, occasionally stirring, until very soft and golden, 5 to 8 minutes more.
3. Meanwhile, roll out dough on a lightly floured surface to the baking sheet's size. Transfer to the baking sheet. Bake until puffed and lightly crisped on the bottom, 8 to 10 minutes. Toast walnuts in a small dry skillet over medium-low heat, stirring, until lightly browned and fragrant, 2 to 3 minutes.
4. Stir vinegar, sage, and pepper into the onions. Spread on the crust and top with pears, walnuts, and cheese. Bake on the bottom rack until the crust is crispy and golden and the cheese is melted 11 to 13 minutes. Slice and serve.

131. Honey & Apple Samie
(Ready in 10-12min|Serve:4|Difficulty: Normal)

Ingredients
- 4 ounces cream cheese, softened
- 1/3 cup honey
- 1 teaspoon vanilla extract
- 1 teaspoon cinnamon
- 8 thick slices whole wheat bread

- 1 green apple, thinly sliced
- 2 tablespoons sunflower seeds, or substitute your favorite nut
- 1/2 cup peanut butter

DIRECTIONS:
1. In a medium bowl, beat cream cheese until fluffy. Add honey, vanilla extract, and cinnamon; mix well. Spread 2-tablespoons cream cheese mixture on each of 4 slices of bread.
2. Top with apple slices, dividing them evenly; sprinkle with sunflower seeds. Spread 2-tablespoons peanut butter on each of the remaining 4-slices of bread and place, peanut butter side down, on top of cream cheese – and apple-covered slices. Cut sandwiches into halves or quarters and serve.

132. Pan-seared Salmon on Baby Arugula Salad
(Ready in 10-15min|Serve:4|Difficulty: Normal)

Ingredients
- 2 center-cut salmon fillets (6 oz. each)
- 1 Tbsp fresh lemon juice
- 1 Tbsp olive oil
- Salt and freshly ground black pepper, to taste

For the salad:
- 3 cups baby arugula leaves
- 2/3 cup grape or cherry tomatoes, halved
- 1/4 cup thinly slivered red onion
- Salt and freshly ground black pepper, to taste
- 1 Tbsp extra-virgin olive oil
- 1 Tbsp red-wine vinegar

DIRECTIONS:
1. Place the salmon fillets in a shallow bowl. Toss well with lemon juice, olive oil, salt, and pepper. Let rest for 15 minutes.
2. Cook the salmon, skin-side down in a nonstick skillet over medium-high heat for 2 to 3 minutes, shaking the pan and carefully lifting the salmon with a spatula to loosen it from the pan.
3. Reduce the heat to medium. Cover the pan and cook until the salmon is cooked through, 3 to 4 minutes more. The skin should be crisp, and the flesh medium-rare.
4. Meanwhile, combine the arugula, tomatoes, and onion in a bowl. Just before serving, season with salt and pepper and drizzle with oil and vinegar. Toss well.

133. Oven Baked Sweet Potato "Fries"
(Ready in 10-12min|Serve:4|Difficulty: Normal)

Ingredients
- 2 large (about 1 ½ pounds) sweet potatoes
- 1 tablespoon olive oil
- ½ teaspoon ground cumin
- ½ teaspoon paprika
- ½ teaspoon cayenne
- ½ teaspoon dried oregano
- Few cracks of fresh ground black pepper

Directions:
1. Preheat to 400 F.
2. Wash well and pat dry the sweet potatoes. Break the sweet potato lengthwise in two. Place cut side down, cut each half into ¼ to ½-inch-thick slabs lengthwise, and then cut each slab into ¼ to ½-inch strips lengthwise.
3. Mix the sweet potatoes, olive oil, and seasonings in a big sealable plastic container. Cover the bag and mix up the fries until they are covered uniformly.
4. On baking sheets sprinkled gently with oil, spread the sweet potato strips out in a single layer.
5. Bake for 45 minutes or until tender to ensure even browning, softly rotating after 15 minutes.

134. One-pot Chicken with Braised Vegetables
(Ready in 1hour|Serve:4|Difficulty: Normal)

Ingredients
- 1½kg chicken
- 25g butter
- 200g smoked back bacon, preferably from a whole piece, cut into small chunks
- 1kg new potatoes, peeled
- 16-20 shallot or small onions
- ½ bottle white wine
- 250g peas, frozen are fine
- bunch soft green herbs such as tarragon, chives or parsley, chopped

Directions:
1. Heat oven to 220C/fan 200C/gas 7. Season the chicken inside and out with salt and pepper. Heat the butter in a casserole dish until sizzling, then take 10 mins to brown the chicken on all sides. Remove the chicken from the dish, then fry the bacon until crisp. Add the potatoes and shallots, then cook until just starting to brown. Nestle the chicken among the veg, pour over the wine, then pot-roast, undisturbed, for 1 hr. or until the chicken is cooked.
2. After 1 hr., remove the chicken and place the pan back on the heat. Stir the peas into the buttery juices, adding a splash of water if the pan is dry, then simmer until the peas are cooked through. Finally, add any juices from the rested chicken, then stir through the herbs and serve with the chicken.

135. Olive oil-baked Potatoes
(Ready in 40-45|Serve:4|Difficulty: Normal)

Ingredients
- medium baking potatoes
- olive oil, for drizzling
- sea salt

Directions:
1. Heat oven to 200C/fan 180C/gas 6. Scrub the baking potatoes, then pat dry. Slice lengthways into three. Drizzle olive oil over a large baking sheet. Place the potatoes on the baking sheet, drizzle with olive oil, rub all over, then generously

sprinkle with sea salt. Bake for 40-45 mins (longer for extra crispiness), turning halfway, until golden brown and tender.

136. Mixed Dried Fruits & Nuts

(Ready in 10min|Serve:4|Difficulty: Normal)

Ingredients

- 1 tablespoon large walnut halves, halved
- 1 1/2 tablespoons whole roasted almonds
- 1 tablespoon each black and golden raisins
- 1 tablespoon unsalted sunflower seeds

DIRECTIONS:

1. Combine the fruit and nuts in a bowl. Pack in a plastic or cello bag. Close with a twisty or a rubber band.
2. Makes one 2-ounce serving. This recipe can be easily increased.

137. Mexican Bean Salad

(Ready in 10min|Serve:4|Difficulty: Normal)

Ingredients

- 4 eggs
- 2 avocados, peeled and stoned
- 2 x 400g cans of beans, (we used pinto bean and kidney beans, rinsed and drained small red onion, finely sliced
- large bunch coriander, leaves only, roughly chopped
- 250g punned cherry tomatoes, halved bottle bought good-quality dressing (we used English Provender Company Lime & Coriander dressing)
- 1 red chili, deseeded and finely sliced
- ½ tsp cumin

Directions:

1. Place the eggs in boiling water and cook for 6½ minutes, then put them in a bowl of cold water to cool off. Slice the avocados and put them with the beans, onion, coriander, and tomatoes in a side dish. In a shallow bowl, measure 3 tbsp of the dressing, then blend in the chili and cumin.
2. Peel off the shells and break into quarters when the eggs have cooled but are still soft. Combine the sauce with the salad and nestle in the eggs. Serve promptly, tasty with toasted tortillas.

138. Mediterranean Tuna on a Roll

(Ready in 10min|Serve:4|Difficulty: Normal)

Ingredients

- ¼ white onion, thinly sliced
- Small red onion, thinly sliced
- 2 Tbsp extra-virgin olive oil
- 1 Tbsp red-wine vinegar, plus more to taste
- ¼ tsp salt
- Black pepper to taste
- 1 (6 oz) can tuna in olive oil
- Lemon juice, to taste
- 2 Kaiser rolls
- Lettuce leaves
- 8 tomato slices
- 1 egg, hard-boiled

DIRECTIONS:

1. In a cup, mix the onions with olive oil, 1 tbsp red wine vinegar, salt, and black pepper; marinate for 5 minutes.
2. Mix the tuna, plus the grease. To taste, season with lemon juice, more red-wine vinegar, salt, and pepper.
3. Kaiser rolls are divided in half crosswise; lettuce leaves are put in the lower half. Cover each with 4 -tomato strips, half the mixture of tuna, and 3 -hard-boiled egg slices. If required, apply the Pitted Niçoise Olives.

139. Mediterranean Chicken Salad

(Ready in 10min|Serve:4|Difficulty: Normal)

Ingredients

- 6 Tbsp olive oil
- 2 Tbsp white-wine vinegar
- ½ tsp dried tarragon
- ½ Tbsp fresh lemon juice
- ½ Tbsp Dijon mustard
- ½ tsp salt
- ¼ tsp pepper
- 1 (3-lb) rotisserie chicken, diced
- ½ cup orzo
- 1 cup halved cherry tomatoes
- 1 (6-oz) jar marinated artichoke hearts, drained
- ½ cup coarsely chopped pitted kalamata olives

DIRECTIONS:

1. In a small cup, blend the oil, vinegar, tarragon, lemon juice, mustard, salt, and pepper. Whisk for mixing.
2. Toss the chicken with ¼ cup of dressing in a medium dish.
3. In a big pot of salted water, boil orzo until only tender but still strong to bite. Uh, drain. To cool and drain well, rinse under the cold spray.
4. To a wide cup, pass the orzo. Stir in the leftover dressing and cover it with a throw. Put some chicken, onions, olives, and artichoke hearts. Spoon each serving into a compact insulated container; keep it cold until midday.

140. Maple Mustard Kale with Turkey Bacon

(Ready in 10min|Serve:4|Difficulty: Normal)

Ingredients

- 1 tsp olive oil
- ½ large onion, sliced
- 3 strips turkey bacon cut crosswise into strips
- 1 bunch Lacinato kale
- 1 tbsp whole grained mustard

- 1 tsp apple cider vinegar
- 1 tbsp 100% pure maple syrup

Directions:

1. Over medium fire, heat a 12-inch sauté plate. Apply the olive oil, onions, and turkey bacon and sauté for about 8 minutes, until browned.
2. Meanwhile, in two water shifts, strip the tough ribs from the kale, break into bite-size pieces, and wash well. Drain or dry the greens with a spin. A green washer/spinner works very well to wash and dry some form of leafy green or lettuce, such as one from Zyliss.
3. Add the washed kale and cook until wilted, stirring regularly, for around 4 minutes, until the onions and bacon have browned.
4. Meanwhile, the whole grain mustard, apple cider vinegar, and pure maple syrup are mixed in a little bowl.
5. Drizzle the mustard mixture over the kale and stir to blend until the kale is wilted and soft. Heat for about 1 minute. Heat through. Serve it sweet.

141. Leg of Lamb cooked with Potatoes

(Ready in 10min|Serve:4|Difficulty: Normal)

Ingredients

- 2½kg leg of lamb
- 6 slices Parma ham
- 4 garlic cloves
- lemon , zested
- 2 sprigs rosemary
- 25g butter , softened
- 2kg maris piper potatoes , peeled and cut into 1cm slices
- 500 ml vegetable stock
- 25g butter
- 1 tbsp olive oil
- 4 small red onions , peeled and sliced
- 1 tbsp plain flour
- 250ml red wine or port
- 600ml lamb beef stock
- 1 tbsp redcurrants jelly

Directions:

1. Heat the oven to 230C/fan 210C/gas 8. Start by making deep incisions all over the meaty side of the leg of lamb using a small knife. Whizz the Parma ham, garlic, lemon zest, and half of the rosemary in a food processor. Season with pepper, and using your fingers, push the mixture into the incisions in the lamb. Pull the rest of the rosemary into sprigs and push a sprig into each incision. Spread the butter over the surface of the meat and season well.
2. Season the potatoes, arrange in a roasting tin, and pour the stock around. Put the lamb on top and roast for 15 minutes. Turn the heat down to 180C/fan 160C/gas four and continue to cook for a further 1 hour and 15 minutes.
3. While the lamb is cooking, make the gravy. Heat the butter and olive oil in a saucepan, add the onions and cook until golden brown. Add the flour and cook for a further 30 seconds.

Pour in the red wine, bring to the boil and reduce by half. 4. Add the stock, redcurrant jelly, and continue to cook for 5 minutes. Season and serve with the lamb and potatoes.

142. Quinoa Salad

(Ready in 15min|Serve:4|Difficulty: Normal)

Ingredients

- ½ cup quinoa
- 1 cup water
- Pinch of salt
- 1 bunch flat-leaf parsley washed and chopped (thick stems removed)
- 4 Persian cucumbers, peeled in strips, seeded and diced
- 2 medium tomatoes diced
- 1 ripe, but slightly firm avocado diced
- 2-3 Tbsp extra virgin olive oil
- Salt and pepper to taste

DIRECTIONS:

1. Boil the water and salt in a shallow saucepan.
2. Add the quinoa, cover, and reduce the heat to simmer. For 15 minutes, cook.
3. Place the quinoa in a medium mixing bowl and cool it off.
4. To make quinoa, add parsley, cucumbers, tomatoes, avocado, and oil.
5. Mix and season with salt and pepper to taste.

143. Happy Face Pita

(Ready in 10min|Serve:4|Difficulty: Normal)

Ingredients

- ¼ cup store-bought hummus
- 4 pitas
- Cucumber slices
- Cherry tomato halves
- Gherkin
- Celery sticks
- Bell pepper pieces

DIRECTIONS:

1. Evenly spread each of 4 pocketless pitas with hummus.
2. Form a cat face with cucumber slices for eyes and cherry tomato halves for eyeballs; a gherkin for the nose; thin celery sticks for the whiskers; and bell pepper pieces the mouth and ears. Or create faces with other favorite veggies. (Try celery chunks for ears, squeeze-bottle mustard for eyebrows, zucchini for eyes, peas for eyeballs, and basil leaves for hair.)
3. Wrap in waxed paper and pack in a lunch box.

144. Gruyère, Leek & Potato Pie

(Ready in 30-35min|Serve:4|Difficulty: Normal)

Ingredients

- 500g Charlotte potatoes , peeled and sliced
- 2 leeks , sliced and washed
- butter

- 4 tbsp half-fat crème fraîche
- 100g Gruyère or cheddar, grated
- 500g block puff pastry
- 1 egg, beaten

Directions:

1. Cook the potatoes in boiling salted water until tender, about 5 minutes. Drain and cool.
2. Cook the leeks in a large knob of butter until really tender. Cool, then stir in the crème fraîche and cheese and season.
3. Heat the oven to 200C/fan180C/gas6. Roll out half the pastry, cut out a large circle using a dinner plate as a template, and put it on a baking sheet. Layer up the potatoes and leek mix, leaving a border of about 2cm around the edge. Brush the border with egg.
4. Roll the other half of the pastry out, so it is larger than the base. Drape over the top of the pie, then smoothes down gently to seal and remove any air pockets. Trim off the excess pastry and crimp with a fork. Score the top lightly with a criss-cross pattern, then glaze.
5. Bake for 30-35 minutes until puffed, crisp and golden. Leave for 15 minutes before cutting.

144. Grilled Cheese & Tomato Sandwich

(Ready in 30-35min|Serve:4|Difficulty: Normal)

Ingredients

- 2 ripe plum tomatoes, halved lengthwise
- Sugar, to taste
- Pepper, to taste
- 4 slices whole-grain bread
- 2 tablespoons softened butter
- 4 thin slices Cheddar or Swiss cheese

DIRECTIONS:

1. Sprinkle with sugar and pepper with the cut sides of the tomatoes. Broil for 8 minutes on a baking tray, cut-side up.
2. Butter one side of each bread slice. Lay the cheese with 2 - slices on the unbuttered side; top each with 2 -tomato halves, finely mashed. Cover with bread leftover, buttered-side-out.
3. Brown the sandwiches over medium heat in a pan. Diagonally halve and serve.

145. Greek Chicken Salad

(Ready in 30-35min|Serve:4|Difficulty: Normal)

Ingredients

- 4 6-oz. chicken breasts
- 3 Tbsp fresh oregano
- 1/4 cup olive oil, plus 2 Tbsp
- Salt and fresh black pepper
- 4 pita pockets
- Juice of 1 lemon
- 1 Tbsp red-wine vinegar
- 1 tsp clover honey
- 1/2 cup extra-virgin olive oil
- 1/2 head romaine lettuce, chopped
- 1 cucumber, peeled and diced
- 2 jarred roasted red peppers, drained and thinly sliced
- 1/4 cup Kalamata olives, chopped
- 8 oz. Feta cheese, in small cubes

DIRECTIONS:

1. In a baking bowl, place chicken. In a blender, mix the oregano with 1/4 cup olive oil; pulse until smooth. Coat the chicken for at least 30 minutes with the marinade, cover, and relax. Remove the breasts from the marinade; apply salt and pepper to season.
2. Preheat the oven to 300 F. In the oven, roll the pitas in foil and warm them.
3. In a large nonstick pan, heat 2 Tbsp of oil over high heat. Cook chicken, 4 minutes on either hand, until golden brown. Remove; stop for 5 minutes to relax. Split into cubes that are 1/2-inch.
4. In a cup, mix the lemon juice, red wine vinegar, sugar, salt, and pepper. Whisk in the extra-virgin olive oil slowly. The remaining ingredients are added; toss.
5. Halve. Delete the pitas from the oven. Cover it with a salad.

146. Goat's Cheese & Watercress Quiche

(Ready in 30-35min|Serve:4|Difficulty: Normal)

Ingredients

- 225g gluten-free flour , plus extra for rolling
- 100g butter
- 1 large egg , beaten, plus extra beaten egg for brushing
- 1 medium onion , finely chopped
- 1 tbsp oil
- 100g watercress , roughly chopped
- 2 large eggs
- 150ml milk
- 150ml log soft rindless goat's cheese , in rough chunks
- freshly grated nutmeg, optional

Directions:

1. Put the flour and a pinch of salt in a large bowl. Rub in the butter until the mixture looks like breadcrumbs. Stir in the egg and about 1-2 tbsp water to form a soft dough. Knead well, then wrap and chill for at least 30 minutes.
2. Preheat the oven to 200C/gas 6/fan 180C. Knead the pastry again and roll it out to line a 20cm loose-bottomed flan tin (the pastry won't shrink, so no need to chill). Patch holes with spare pastry and brushes the base and sides with egg.
3. For the filling, fry the onion in the oil until just soft, add the watercress and cook until just wilted. Beat the eggs and milk and stir in the watercress mixture and goat's cheese.
4. Season, and if you like, add a pinch of nutmeg. Put the flan tin on a baking sheet and bake the pastry blind for 5 minutes. Add the filling and bake for 15 minutes. Reduce heat to 180C/gas 4/ fan 160C and cook for 25-30 minutes or until lightly set.

147. Glazed Sweet Potatoes and Dried Plums with Ginger

(Ready in 30-35min|Serve:4|Difficulty: Normal)

Ingredients

- 3 medium sweet potatoes (about 2 pounds)
- 1 cup pitted dried plums (about 6 ounces)
- 1 tablespoon vegetable oil, plus extra for oiling baking dish
- 3/4 cup freshly squeezed orange juice
- 1/2 teaspoon salt
- 1/4 teaspoon cinnamon
- 4 teaspoons chopped crystallized ginger

Directions:

1. Heat oven to 350°F.
2. Cut each sweet potato into 4-wedges, lengthwise. Cut each wedge in half across.
3. Place sweet potatoes and dried plums in a lightly oiled baking dish large enough to hold potatoes in one layer.
4. In a small bowl, whisk together orange juice, oil, salt, and cinnamon; pour evenly over sweet potatoes and prunes. Sprinkle with ginger.
5. Cover tightly with foil; bake for 45 minutes.
6. Remove foil; baste sweet potatoes with juices from the baking dish.
7. Bake about 10 minutes more or until sweet potatoes are tender and glazed.

148. Fruity Faces

(Ready in 30-35min|Serve:4|Difficulty: Normal)

Ingredients

- ½ cup cream cheese
- 2 Tbsp honey
- 4 slices whole-wheat bread
- Assorted fruit (Blueberries, Mango, Kiwi, Banana, Apple, Strawberries)

DIRECTIONS:

1. Combine the honey with the cream cheese.
2. Spread on slices of toast.
3. Blueberries for eyes, strawberry for eyeballs, kiwi for the nose, and mango for the mouth: draw faces of assorted fruits. Or try slices of oranges, apples, and strawberries.

149. Foolproof Slow Roast Chicken

(Ready in 30-35min|Serve:4|Difficulty: Normal)

Ingredients

- butter , for greasing
- 1.6kg chicken
- 1kg roasting potatoes , halved or quartered if large
- 2 whole garlic heads, halved through the middle
- 100ml white wine
- 100ml chicken stock
- 2 stems rosemary , broken into sprigs
- 6 bay leaves
- 1 lemon, cut into wedges

Directions:

1. Heat oven to 160C/fan 140C/gas 3. Brush a large roasting tin all over with butter and smear some over the skin of the chicken.
2. Place the chicken in the tin and arrange the potatoes around it. Put the halved garlic heads in the tin, pour over the white wine and stock, then cover with foil and place in the oven. Cook for 1 hr., then remove the foil and give the potatoes a shake. Add the herbs and lemon wedges, then cook uncovered for 50 mins.
3. Turn the heat up to 220C/fan 200C/gas 7. Cook for 30 mins more, then remove the chicken and potatoes from the pan. Cover the chicken loosely with foil and leave to rest on a plate for at least 10 mins before carving. Keep the potatoes warm. Serve with any pan juices.

150. Edamame & Summer Bean Salad

(Ready in 30-35 min|Serve:4|Difficulty: Normal)

Ingredients

- 3/4-pound wax beans
- 2 cups shelled edamame
- 2 green (spring) onions
- 2 tomatoes, seeded and diced
- 1 tablespoon chopped fresh basil
- 1 tablespoon rice vinegar
- 1 tablespoon fresh lime juice
- 1 teaspoon honey
- 1 teaspoon Dijon mustard
- 2 teaspoons olive oil
- 1/2 teaspoon salt
- 1/4 teaspoon freshly ground black pepper

Directions:

1. Trim the wax beans and cut crosswise into thirds. In a large pot fitted with a steamer basket, bring 1-inch water to a boil. Add the wax beans and edamame, cover, and steam until both are tender-crisp, about 5 minutes. Drain, rinse with cold water, and drain again.
2. Trim the green onions, then thinly slice on the diagonal, including the tender green tops.
3. In a large bowl, combine the steamed edamame and wax beans, green onions, tomatoes, and basil. Toss to mix evenly.
4. In a small bowl, combine the vinegar, lime juice, honey, and mustard. Whisk in the olive oil. Add the dressing to the vegetables and toss to coat. Season with salt and pepper. Serve chilled or at room temperature.

151. Curried Squash, Lentil & Coconut Soup

(Ready in 30-35 min|Serve:4|Difficulty: Normal)

Ingredients

- 1 tbsp olive oil
- 1 butternut squash , peeled, deseeded and diced

- 200g carrots, diced
- 1 tbsp curry powder containing turmeric
- 100g red lentils
- 700ml vegetable stock
- 1 can reduced-fat coconut milk
- coriander and naan bread, to serve

Directions:

1. Heat the oil in a large saucepan, add the squash and carrots, sizzle for 1 min, then stir in the curry powder and cook for 1 min more. Tip in the lentils, the vegetable stock, and coconut milk and give everything a good stir. Bring to the boil, then turn the heat down and simmer for 15-18 mins until everything is tender.
2. Using a hand blender or in a food processor, blitz until as smooth as you like. Season and serve scattered with roughly chopped coriander and some naan bread alongside.

152. Creamed Swiss Chard
(Ready in 2-5min|Serve:4|Difficulty: Normal)

Ingredients

- 2 tablespoons olive oil
- 1 1/2 tablespoons unbleached all-purpose (plain) flour
- 3 garlic cloves, finely chopped
- 1 1/4 cups low-fat plain soy milk (soya milk)
- 2 pounds Swiss chard, washed, stemmed and cut crosswise into strips 1/2-inch wide
- 1/4 teaspoon salt
- 1/2 teaspoon freshly ground black pepper
- 1 tablespoon grated Parmesan cheese

Directions:

1. In a large frying pan, heat the olive oil over medium heat. Whisk in the flour to make a smooth paste. Continue whisking and add the garlic; cook for 30 seconds longer. Whisk in the soy milk and cook until the mixture thickens slightly.
2. Add the chard and stir to coat well. Cover and cook just until tender, about 2 minutes. Season with salt and pepper. Sprinkle with the Parmesan and serve hot.

153. Cream Cheese Daisies
(Ready in 2-5min|Serve:4|Difficulty: Normal)

Ingredients

- Strawberry cream cheese
- Strawberry jam or peach or orange marmalade

DIRECTIONS:

1. Using a flower cookie cutter, make daisy shapes out of the bread.
2. Punch a small hole in half the shapes with a 1-inch cookie cutter.
3. On the other halves, spread cream cheese, jam/marmalade; form into sandwiches.

154. Courgette, Pea & Pesto Soup
(Ready in 2-5min|Serve:4|Difficulty: Normal)

Ingredients

- 1 tbsp olive oil
- 1 garlic clove, sliced
- 500g courgettes, quartered lengthways and chopped
- 200g frozen peas
- 400g can cannellini beans, drained and rinsed
- 1l hot vegetable stock
- 2 tbsp basil pesto, or vegetarian alternative

Directions:

1. Heat the oil in a large saucepan. Cook the garlic for a few seconds, then add the courgettes and cook for 3 mins until they start to soften. Stir in the peas and cannellini beans, pour on the hot stock, and cook for a further 3 mins.
2. Stir the pesto through the soup with some seasoning, then ladle into bowls and serve with crusty brown bread, if you like. Or pop in a flask to take to work.

155. Coconut-Crusted Lime Chicken
(Ready in 2-5min|Serve:4|Difficulty: Normal)

Ingredients

- 8 skinless, boneless chicken thighs
- zest and juice 2 limes, plus extra wedges to serve
- 2 tsp medium curry powder or garam masala
- 1 tsp chili powder (optional)
- 50g desiccated coconut
- 1 tbsp vegetable oil
- mango chutney and rice, to serve

Directions:

1. Heat oven to 200C/180C fan/gas 6. Put the chicken in a large bowl with the lime zest and juice, curry powder, chili powder, if using, and seasoning. Mix well, then toss in the coconut.
2. Place chicken on a rack sitting in a roasting tin, drizzle with the oil, then bake for 25 mins until cooked through and tender. Serve with mango chutney, lime wedges for squeezing over, and rice, if you like.

156. Classic Roast Chicken & Gravy
(Ready in 2-5min|Serve:4|Difficulty: Normal)

Ingredients

- 1 onion, roughly chopped
- 2 carrots, roughly chopped
- 1 free range chicken, about 1.5kg/3lb 5oz
- 1 lemon, halved
- small bunch thyme (optional)
- 1 tbsp plain flour
- 250ml chicken stock (a cube is fine)

Directions:

1. Heat oven to 190C/fan 170C/gas 5. Have a shelf ready in the middle of the oven without any shelves above it. Scatter the vegetables over the base of a roasting tin that fits the chicken but doesn't swamp it. Season the chicken's cavity

liberally with salt and pepper, then stuff with the lemon halves and thyme, if using. Set the chicken on the vegetables, smother the breast and legs all over with the butter, then season the outside with salt and pepper. Place in the oven and leave, undisturbed, for 1 hr. 20 mins – this will give you a perfectly roasted chicken. To check, pierce the thigh with a skewer, and the juices should run clear. Remove the tin from the oven and, using a pair of tongs, lift the chicken to a dish or board to rest for 15-20 mins. As you lift the dish, let any juices from the chicken pour out of the cavity into the roasting tin.

2. While the chicken is resting, make the gravy. Place the roasting tin over a low flame, then stir in the flour and sizzle until you have a light brown, sandy paste. Gradually pour in the stock, stirring all the time, until you have a thickened sauce. Simmer for 2 mins, using a wooden spoon to stir, scraping any sticky bits from the tin. Strain the gravy into a small saucepan, then simmer and season to taste. When you carve the bird, add any extra juices to the gravy.

157. Classic Boston Baked Beans

(Ready in 2-5min|Serve:4|Difficulty: Normal)

Ingredients

- 2 cups dried small, white beans (navy beans), picked over and rinsed, soaked overnight and drained
- 4 cups water
- 2 bay leaves
- 3/4 teaspoon salt
- 1 yellow onion, chopped
- 1/2 cup light molasses
- 1 1/2 tablespoons dry mustard
- 3 strips thick-cut bacon, cut into 1/2-inch pieces

Directions:

1. In a large, ovenproof pot with a tight-fitting lid or a Dutch oven, combine the beans, water, bay leaves, and 1/2 teaspoon of the salt over high heat. Bring to a boil. Reduce the heat to low, cover partially and simmer until the beans have softened but are still firm 65 to 75 minutes. Remove from the heat and discard the bay leaves. Don't drain the beans.
2. Preheat the oven to 350 F.
3. Stir the onion, molasses, mustard, bacon, and the remaining 1/4 teaspoon salt into the beans. Cover and bake until the beans are tender and coated with a light syrup, 4 1/2 to 5 hours. Check periodically to make sure the beans don't dry out, stirring and adding hot water as needed.

158. Chunky Spicy Egg Salad

(Ready in 2-5min|Serve:4|Difficulty: Normal)

Ingredients

- 8 large eggs
- 2 stalks celery, trimmed and thinly sliced
- 1 red bell pepper, diced
- 1 jalapeño pepper, finely chopped
- 1 baby white onion, finely chopped
- Salt and freshly ground pepper
- 1/2 cup light mayonnaise
- Juice of 1 lime
- 1/2 to 1 tsp chili powder, to taste
- Tabasco, to taste
- Chopped cilantro

DIRECTIONS:

1. Place the eggs in a big bowl of cold salted water and bring them to a boil. Boil the eggs for 2 minutes, turn off the heat and let them reach room temperature. The cooled eggs are peeled, sliced into chunks, and thrown into a bowl. Season with salt and pepper; add celery, red pepper, jalapeño, and onion.
2. Whisk the mayonnaise, lime juice, and chili powder together. Add salt and pepper and Tabasco. If you like more fire, taste it and add more chili powder or Tabasco. Mix the mayo into the egg salad kindly. Chill before serving if you have time.
3. Sprinkle with cilantro and serve with greens and onions, or use buttermilk biscuits to make sandwiches.

159. Chipotle Egg Soufflés

(Ready in 2-5min|Serve:4|Difficulty: Normal)

Ingredients

- 2 Tbsp. Mrs. Dash® Southwest Chipotle Seasoning Blend
- 4 whole eggs, separated in two medium size bowls
- 1/2 scallion, cut finely, white and green

DIRECTIONS

1. Spray coat 4 4 oz. Ovenproof straight-sided ramekins.
2. Beat egg yolks with a whisk until creamy, about 2 minutes. Add Mrs. Dash® Southwest Chipotle Seasoning Blend, scallions, and beat 20 seconds.
3. With a clean, dry whisk, beat egg whites until almost stiff, about 1-2 minutes. Fold carefully into egg yolk mix.
4. Place folded mix into ramekins and bake in 400°F preheated oven 4-5 minutes until puffed and nicely browned.

160. Chili Turkey Salad

(Ready in 2-5min|Serve:4|Difficulty: Normal)

Ingredients

- 4 cups coarsely shredded cooked turkey
- 1/2 cup diced (1/4-inch) red bell pepper
- 1/2 cup diced (1/4-inch) green bell pepper
- 1/4 cup chopped, pitted ripe olives
- 2 scallions (3 inches of green left on), thinly sliced on the diagonal
- 3 tablespoons chopped cilantro leaves
- 1/2 cup reduced-calorie mayonnaise
- 1/2 cup nonfat sour cream
- 1 or 2 tablespoons fresh lime juice
- 1 teaspoon finely minced green jalapeño pepper, or to taste
- 1/2 teaspoon finely grated orange zest
- 1/4 teaspoon chili powder
- 1/8 teaspoon ground cumin
- Salt and freshly ground black pepper, to taste

- 1 ripe avocado, optional
- Red-leaf lettuce, for garnish
- Small bunches of seedless red grapes, for garnish

Directions:
1. In a big dish, combine the turkey, bell peppers, olives, scallions, and 2-teaspoons of cilantro.
2. Combine the mayonnaise, sour cream, 1-tablespoon of lime juice, jalapeño pepper, orange zest, chili powder, cumin, salt, and separate pepper bowl. Apply and throw well into the turkey mixture.
3. Place 1-a a tablespoon of lime juice in a small bowl if you want to use avocado. Split half of the avocado. Remove and peel the seed, then dice the avocado into 1/4-inch cubes. To avoid discoloration, toss the lime juice with it.
4. Place the turkey salad atop a bed of lettuce leaves to eat. Scatter the avocado over the end and scatter with minced cilantro with the remaining tablespoon. Add little bunches of red grapes to the garnish.

161. Chicken Italiano
(Ready in 2-5min|Serve:4|Difficulty: Normal)

Ingredients
- 1 1/2 tsp (7.5mL) Mrs. Dash® Lemon Pepper Seasoning Blend, divided
- 1 lb. (454g) boneless skinless chicken breast halves, pounded to 1/2-inch (1.25cm) thickness
- 8 Oz. (225g) can low sodium tomato sauce
- 1/4 cup (60mL) shredded Romano cheese
- 2 Tbsp. (30mL) chopped fresh basil
- vegetable cooking spray

Directions
1. Spray broiler pan with vegetable cooking spray.
2. Place chicken breasts on the broiler.
3. Sprinkle each with 1/4 tsp (1.25mL) Mrs. Dash® Lemon Pepper.
4. Broil 3 to 4 minutes.
5. Turn chicken over and repeat seasoning.
6. Broil until chicken is done.
7. Sprinkle cheese evenly over chicken.
8. Broil just until cheese is melted.
9. Combine tomato sauce and remaining 1/2 tsp (1.5mL) Mrs. Dash® Lemon Pepper in the saucepan.
10. Simmer, uncovered, 5 minutes.
11. Spoon sauce over each chicken breast.
12. Sprinkle with basil.

162. Chicken Enchiladas
(Ready in 2-5min|Serve:4|Difficulty: Normal)

Ingredients
- 1/2 pound (225g) boneless, skinless chicken breasts, cubed
- 2 Tbsp. (30mL) onion, chopped
- 2 Tbsp. (30mL) green bell pepper, chopped
- 1/4 cup (60mL) light sour cream
- 1/2 cup (120mL) low fat cheddar cheese, shredded, divided
- 1 Tbsp. (15mL) Mrs. Dash® Southwest Chipotle Seasoning Blend
- 4 small flour tortillas
- 1/2 cup (120mL) salsa, divided

Directions
1. Cook chicken for about 5 minutes over medium-high heat in a skillet sprayed with no-stick spray. Attach the green pepper and onion and cook and stir for 2 minutes or until tender. Withdraw from the sun.
2. Add sour cream, cheddar cheese for two-thirds, Mrs. Dash® Chipotle Seasoning Blend, and salsa for half.
3. Spoon into the tortillas and roll even amounts of the mixture. Place with no-stick cooking spray in a sprayed baking dish. Cover with the remaining cheddar cheese and salsa. Bake uncovered in preheated 350°F oven for 15 minutes.

163. Southwest Style Rice Bowl
(Ready in 2hours|serve:4|Difficulty: Normal)

Ingredients
- 1 teaspoon vegetable oil
- 1 cup chopped vegetables (try a mixture - bell peppers, onion, corn, tomato, zucchini)
- 1 cup cooked meat (chopped or shredded)
- 1 cup cooked brown rice
- 4 tablespoons salsa
- 2 tablespoons shredded cheese
- 2 tablespoons low fat sour cream

Directions
1. Heat the oil in a medium skillet over medium-high heat (350 in an electric skillet). Add the vegetables and cook for 3-5 minutes or until the vegetables are crisp and soft.
2. To the skillet, add cooked beef, beans, or tofu and cooked rice and fire.
3. Break the rice mixture into two containers. Cover and eat soft with sauce, cheese, sour cream.
4. Leftovers should be refrigerated within 2 hours.

164. Fresh Shrimp Spring Rolls
(Ready in 2hours|Serve:6|Difficulty: Normal)

Ingredients
- 12 sheets of rice paper
- 12 bib lettuce leaves
- 12 basil leaves
- ¾ cup fresh cilantro
- 1 cup carrots, shredded
- ½ medium cucumber, thinly sliced
- 1 ¼ pounds (20 ounces) shrimp, cooked, de-veined and peeled

Directions
1. Clean the broccoli, basil, cilantro, carrots, and cucumber, and ready them.

2. For quick access, place all the vegetables and shrimp on the counter assembly-line style.
3. On a clean cutting board, put down a wet paper towel. Place one sheet of rice paper on a paper towel under warm water until just wet.
4. Layer 1 leaf of lettuce, 1-leaf of basil, 1-tablespoon of cilantro, carrots, and cucumber on the rice paper that is nearest to you at the end. Begin gently rolling the rice paper over the vegetables like a burrito would do.
5. Place around 4-shrimp on the rice paper while the vegetables are only coated. Continue to fold up the rice paper like a burrito until it's all rolled up, do not forget to tuck in the ends.
6. Repeat the process before you make all 12 rolls. Immediately serve.

165. Pear, Turkey and Cheese Sandwich

(Ready in 7-10min|Serve:6|Difficulty: Normal)

Ingredients

- 2 slices multi-grain or rye sandwich bread
- 2 tsp Dijon-style mustard
- 2 slices (1 oz. each) reduced-sodium cooked or smoked turkey
- 1 USA pear, cored and thinly sliced
- 1/4 cup shredded low-fat mozzarella cheese
- Coarsely ground pepper

Directions

1. Spread 1-teaspoon of mustard on each slice of bread. Place each slice of bread with one slice of turkey. Arrange the turkey pear slices and sprinkle each with 2-tablespoons of cheese. Sprinkle spice over it.
2. Broil, 2 to 3 minutes or until turkey and pears are hot and cheese melts, 4 to 6 inches from the sun. Halve each sandwich and serve the open face in half.

Double Banana Sandwiches

(Ready in 30-35min|Serve:4|Difficulty: Normal)

Ingredients

- 2 Bananas
- 1 cup ricotta cheese
- 2 Tbsp honey
- 6 slices of banana bread

DIRECTIONS:

1. Stir the ricotta cheese with honey in a little bowl.
2. On 6-slices of banana bread, spread the mixture; top with the banana slices.
3. Shape them into sandwiches; cut them in half.
4. You should replace the sweetened ricotta with low-fat cream cheese.
5. Curried Vegetable Couscous

166. Curried Mustard Greens and Garbanzo Beans with Sweet Potatoes

(Ready in 30-35min|Serve:4|Difficulty: Normal)

Ingredients

- 2 medium sweet potatoes peeled and sliced thin
- 1 medium onion cut in half and sliced thin
- 2 medium cloves garlic, sliced
- ½ cup + 1 Tbsp low sodium chicken or vegetable broth
- ½ teaspoon curry powder
- ¼ teaspoon turmeric
- 2 cups chopped and rinsed mustard greens
- 1 15 oz can sodium free diced tomatoes
- 1 15 oz can garbanzo beans, drained and rinsed
- 2 tablespoon extra-virgin olive oil
- white pepper to taste

Directions:

1. Steam peeled and sliced sweet potatoes for approximately 5—8 minutes.
2. While steaming potatoes, sliced onion, and garlic. Heat 1 Tbsp broth in a 12-inch skillet. Sautè onion in broth over medium heat for about 4—5 minutes, frequently stirring, until translucent.
3. Add garlic, curry powder, turmeric, and mustard greens. Cook, occasionally stirring, until mustard greens are wilted, about 5 minutes. Add garbanzo beans, diced tomatoes, salt, and pepper. Cook for another 5 minutes.
4. Mash sweet potatoes with olive oil, salt, and pepper. If you need to thin potatoes, add a little more broth. Serve mustard greens with mashed sweet potatoes

166. Creole-style Black-eyed Peas

(Ready in 30-35min|Serve:4|Difficulty: Normal)

Ingredients

- 3 cups water
- 2 cups dried black-eyed peas
- 1 teaspoon low-sodium chicken-flavored bouillon granules
- 2 cups canned unsalted tomatoes, crushed
- 1 large onion, finely chopped
- 2 stalks celery, finely chopped
- 3 teaspoons minced garlic
- 1/2 teaspoon dry mustard
- 1/4 teaspoon ground ginger
- 1/4 teaspoon cayenne pepper
- 1 bay leaf
- 1/2 cup chopped parsley

Directions:

1. In a medium saucepan over high heat, add 2 cups of water and black-eyed peas. Bring to a boil for 2 minutes, cover, remove from heat, and let stand for 1 hour.
2. water, bouillon granules, tomatoes, onion, celery, garlic, mustard, ginger, cayenne pepper, and bay leaf. Stir together and bring to a boil. Cover, reduce heat, and simmer for 2 hours, stirring occasionally. Add water as necessary to keep the peas covered with liquid.
3. Remove the bay leaf, pour into a serving bowl, and garnish with parsley. Serve immediately.

167. Chinese-Style Asparagus

(Ready in 2-5 min|Serve:4|Difficulty: Normal)

Ingredients

- 1/2 cup water
- 1/2 teaspoon sugar
- 1 teaspoon reduced-sodium soy sauce
- 1 1/2 pounds fresh asparagus, woody ends removed and cut into 1 1/2-inch lengths

Directions:

1. In a large saucepan, heat the water, sugar, and soy sauce over high heat. Cook until boiling, and then add the asparagus. Reduce heat to low and simmer until the asparagus is tender-crisp, about 3 to 4 minutes.
2. Transfer to a serving dish and serve immediately.

168. Insalata di Farro (Farro Salad)

(Ready in 20-25 min | Serve: 6| Difficulty: Normal)

Ingredients

- 1/2 cup roasted chopped zucchini (see below)
- 2 cups Italian semi-pearled farro
- 8 ounces chopped fresh mozzarella cheese
- 1 (8-ounce) jar roasted red peppers, chopped
- 2 tablespoons finely chopped fresh parsley
- 2 tablespoons finely chopped fresh basil
- 1/8 teaspoon dried marjoram
- Juice of 1/2 lemon
- 2 tablespoons extra virgin olive oil
- 1/4 teaspoon sea salt
- 1/2 teaspoon cracked black pepper

ROASTED ZUCCHINI

- 2 zucchini, cut lengthwise into 1/4-inch slices
- 4 tablespoons extra virgin olive oil
- 4 tablespoons balsamic vinegar
- 1/4 teaspoon cracked black pepper
- 1/2 teaspoon dried Italian herbs

Directions

1. Preheat the oven to 400°F to roast the zucchini. Using olive oil spray to cover a baking sheet and place the sliced zucchini on it. Drizzle with balsamic vinegar and olive oil and then brush with dried herbs and pepper. Put on the middle rack of the oven and cook for 8 to 10 minutes until the zucchini begins to wrinkle and is tender to the touch.
2. Meanwhile, to keep the farro from sticking, bring a big pot of water to a boil, adding a drizzle of olive oil. In the boiling water, add the farro, and simmer for 20 to 30 minutes, or until al dente. In a colander, drain and put the farro into a large bowl.
3. Mix in the fried farro with the roasted zucchini and all the other ingredients. Toss well, then then serve. The mozzarella can melt if this dish is served wet, but it can be served chilled as well.

169. Asian Quinoa Salad

(Ready in 10-15min|serve 6,|Difficulty:Normal)

Ingredients

- 2 cups uncooked quinoa
- 4 cups low-sodium vegetable broth
- 1 cup cooked, shelled edamame
- 1/4 cup chopped green onion
- 1 1/2 teaspoons finely chopped fresh mint
- 1/2 cup chopped carrot
- 1/2 cup chopped red bell pepper
- 1/8 teaspoon chile pepper flakes
- 1/2 teaspoon grated orange zest
- 2 tablespoons finely chopped fresh Thai basil
- Juice of 1/2 orange
- 1 teaspoon sesame seeds
- 1 tablespoon sesame oil
- 1 tablespoon extra-virgin olive oil
- 1/8 teaspoon cracked black pepper

Directions

1. Rinse the quinoa in order to (if not prerinsed). Bring the quinoa and vegetable broth to a boil, over high heat, in a small covered kettle.
2. Reduce the heat to low and boil until much of the liquid has been drained or for 10 to 15 minutes. Cooked quinoa should be somewhat al dente; when most of the grains have uncoiled, it is ready and the unwound germ can be shown. For around 5 minutes, let the quinoa sit in the covering pot.
3. Gently fluff with a fork and transfer to a large bowl the cooked quinoa, then blend in the remaining ingredients. Refrigerate at room temperature and serve. It is possible to eat this dish chilled as well.

170. Chicken Pasta Salad

(Ready in 20-25min|, serve 6,|Difficulty:Normal)

Ingredients

- 8 ounces whole wheat penne pasta
- 1 (6-ounce) boneless, skinless chicken breast
- 1 cup halved seedless red grapes
- 1/4 cup walnut pieces
- 1 tablespoon red wine vinegar

- 1/2 cup chopped celery
- 1/2 cup low-fat plain Greek yogurt
- 1/2 teaspoon cracked black pepper
- 1/8 teaspoon sea salt

Directions
1. Boil a huge pot of water and apply a drizzle of olive oil to the mixture.
2. Prevent the sticking of the spaghetti. Then add the pasta to the boiling process.
3. Stir in water once, and simmer for 8-10 minutes, or until al dente.
4. Strain it with spaghetti. Trim the fat off the chicken, if any, while the pasta is cooking and cut it into small cubes. Fill with water in a separate, medium pot and bring it to a boil over high heat.
5. Add the chicken cubes (they should be filled with water), then cook for 5 to 6 minutes. Drain all the chicken and the spaghetti.
6. Combine the pasta and the chicken with the remaining ingredients in a large dish, and combine well. Before serving, refrigerate for 20 to 30 minutes.

171. Healthy Italian Pasta Salad
(Ready in 20-25min, serve 6, Difficulty:Normal)

Ingredients
- 4 cups whole wheat penne pasta
- 1/4 cup toasted pine nuts
- 2 cups halved cherry tomatoes
- 1 cup chopped fresh mozzarella cheese
- 1 bunch coarsely chopped fresh basil
- 4 tablespoons extra virgin olive oil
- Pinch of sea salt
- 1/8 teaspoon cracked black pepper

Directions
1. To keep the pasta from sticking, boil a big pot of water, adding a drizzle of olive oil. Add the pasta, stirring once, to the boiling water and simmer for 8 to 10 minutes or until al dente. Strain it with spaghetti.
2. Heat a big, flat pan over medium-high heat to toast the pine nuts. To stop fire, add the pine nuts, and stir regularly. Toast for about 2 minutes or until the nuts smell buttery and on the outside, they are light brown.
3. Remove them directly from the pan. Toss the cooked pasta with the remaining ingredients in a large bowl. Warm pasta can help the cheese melt slightly.

172. Balsamic Glaze
(Ready in 20-25min, serve 6, Difficulty:Normal)

Ingredients
- 2 cups balsamic vinegar

Directions
1. Heat the balsamic vinegar in a large saucepan, over low heat, for 25 to 30 minutes. Simmer it, and don't let it simmer.
2. To measure, dip a wooden spoon into the glaze; it should leave a clean line if you brush your finger along the spoon's back. To drizzle on vegetables, entrées, and sweets, cool and store in a squeeze container.

173. Basic Vinaigrette
(Ready in 20-25min, serve 6, Difficulty:Normal)

Ingredients
- 1/2 teaspoon Dijon or brown mustard
- 1/2 teaspoon reduced-sugar marmalade (any fruit flavor)
- 1/4 cup balsamic vinegar (sweet) or red wine vinegar (acidic)
- 1/2 cup extra virgin olive oil
- 1/8 teaspoon sea salt
- Cracked black pepper

Directions
1. Whisk the mustard, marmalade, and vinegar together in a little bowl. Drizzle in the oil very slowly and finish whisking the mixture together. (The oil and vinegar are emulsified by continuous whisking, dispersing the droplets from one onto the other and forming a dense dressing.)
2. Add salt and pepper. If not used instantly, store it in an airtight jar or bowl.
3. It is recommended that 1 part of the vinegar or some other acid, such as lemon, lime or orange juice, and 2 parts of oil form the basis of a homemade vinaigrette.

174. Honey Lemon Vinaigrette
(Ready in 25min, serve 6, Difficulty:Normal)

Ingredients
- Juice of 3 lemons (about 1/4 cup)
- 1 tablespoon honey
- 1 teaspoon chopped fresh thyme
- 1/8 teaspoon sea salt
- 1/8 teaspoon cracked black pepper
- 1/2 cup extra virgin olive oil

Directions
1. Whisk the lemon juice, sugar, thyme, salt and pepper together in a small cup.
2. Drizzle in the oil very slowly and finish whisking the mixture together.
3. If not used directly, store it in an airtight container or jar.

175. Lemon Vinaigrette
(Ready in 25min, serve 6, Difficulty:Normal)

Ingredients
- Juice of 3 lemons (about 1/4 cup)
- 1 tablespoon Dijon mustard
- 1 teaspoon chopped fresh parsley
- 1/8 teaspoon sea salt

- 1/8 teaspoon cracked black pepper
- 1/2 cup extra virgin olive oil

Directions
1. Whisk the lemon juice, mustard, parsley, salt, and pepper together in a small dish.
2. Drizzle in the oil very slowly and finish whisking the mixture together.
3. For potential use, store it in an airtight container or jar.

176. Garlicky Balsamic Vinaigrette
(Ready in 25min, Iserve6, IDifficulty:Normal)

Ingredients
- 1/2 teaspoon Dijon mustard
- 1 large clove garlic, finely minced
- 1/2 teaspoon reduced-sugar raspberry marmalade
- 1/4 cup balsamic vinegar
- 1/2 cup extra virgin olive oil
- Pinch of dried oregano
- 1/8 teaspoon sea salt
- Cracked black pepper

Directions
1. Whisk the mustard, garlic, marmalade, and vinegar together in a small cup.
2. Drizzle in the oil very slowly and finish whisking the mixture together.
3. Bring in the oregano, salt and pepper.

177. Mexican Summer Salad
(Ready in 5min, Iserve 6, IDifficulty:Normal)

Ingredients
- 3 heads romaine lettuce, chopped
- 5 Roma tomatoes, chopped
- 1 1/2 cups sliced unpeeled cucumber
- 1/4 cup very thinly sliced white onion
- 1/4 cup fresh lime juice
- 1/8 cup extra virgin olive oil
- Sea salt
- Cracked black pepper

Directions
1. Combine the cabbage, tomato, cucumber, and onion in a wide dish. Over the salad, add the lime juice and the oil, and toss well.
2. Season with salt and pepper to taste.

178. Grilled Romaine Salad with Garlicky Balsamic Vinaigrette
(Ready in 5 min, Iserve 4, IDifficulty:Normal)

Ingredients
- 2 tablespoons olive oil
- 1 head romaine lettuce (about 12 leaves)
- 1/4 cup feta cheese
- 1/2 cup halved cherry tomatoes
- 1/4 cup chopped walnuts
- Garlicky Balsamic Vinaigrette

Directions
1. Separate the Roman head from the branches, and wash and dry them. Brush oil on both sides of each lettuce leaf, heat a grill to medium-high and put on the grill.
2. Watch cautiously and turn periodically, as the leaves will easily wilt. Once the char marks are clear, cut the leaves and position four individual plates with three leaves.
3. Place the cheese, onions, and walnuts on top of the grilled lettuce. Drizzle with balsamic vinaigrette, 2 teaspoons, and eat.

179. Healthy Cobb Salad with Basic Vinaigrette
(Ready in 5 min, Iserve 4, IDifficulty:Normal)

Ingredients
- 4 slices turkey bacon
- 5 cups spinach
- 1 cup sliced cremini mushrooms
- 1/2 cup shredded carrot
- 1/2 large cucumber, sliced
- 1/2 (15-ounce) can kidney beans, rinsed and drained
- 1 large avocado, pitted, peeled, and chopped
- 1/3 cup crumbled blue cheese
- Basic Vinaigrette

Directions
1. Over low pressure, heat a medium-sized nonstick pan and coat with olive oil spray.
2. Add turkey bacon, cook until brown and then, 5 to 6 minutes, flip and finish cooking. On a cutting board, remove and relax. Crumble, or chop coarsely, the cooled turkey bacon by hand. Place the spinach on a large platter for serving.
3. Add the mushroom, carrot, cucumber, kidney beans, avocado, turkey bacon, and blue cheese in neat rows on top of the spinach. Serve on the side, with vinaigrette.

180. Pomegranate Salad
(Ready in 5 min, I serve 4, IDifficulty:Normal)

Ingredients
- 4 cups arugula
- 1 large avocado, pitted, peeled, and chopped
- 1/2 cup thinly sliced fennel
- 1/2 cup thinly sliced Anjou pears, thinly sliced
- 1/4 cup pomegranate seeds

Directions
1. Combine all the ingredients in a big cup, adding the last pomegranate pod.
2. Toss well, and serve with a favorite of yours Oil and dressing with vinegar.

181. Beet and Heirloom Tomato Salad

(Ready in 5 min, I serve 4, IDifficulty:Normal)

Ingredients
- 1 cup cooked, thinly sliced beets
- 6 cups mixed greens
- 1 cup green heirloom tomato, sliced and cut in fourths
- 1/4 cup toasted walnut pieces
- 1/4 cup crumbled goat cheese
- 1/4 cup balsamic vinegar
- Cracked black pepper, to taste

Directions
1. Through chopping off the green stems and cleaning the beets, you prepare the beets. Split the very top of the beet and the very bottom of it, and then strip the thick skin off.
2. Place the beets in a small pot with about 1/2 to 1 cup of water, then steam for about 15 minutes over medium heat.
3. Let cool until baked, and then slice and split each slice as with the heirloom tomatoes into fourths. In a large salad bowl, put the mixed greens and top with the beets, onions, walnuts and goat's cheese.
4. Drizzle it with balsamic vinegar and grind over the end with crushed black pepper.

182. Greek Salad with Lemon Vinaigrette

(Ready in 5 min, I serve 4, IDifficulty:Normal)

Ingredients
- 4 cups chopped romaine leaves (about 2 large heads of lettuce)
- 1/2 cup halved cherry tomatoes
- 1/2 cup rinsed and drained, coarsely chopped canned artichoke hearts
- 1/4 cup low-fat feta cheese
- 1 teaspoon dried oregano
- 10 black pitted olives, rinsed, drained, and chopped
- 8 tablespoons Lemon Vinaigrette

Directions
1. In a broad salad bowl, mix all of the ingredients, and toss well.
2. Serve with 2 teaspoons of lemon vinaigrette on the side of each plate.

183. Caprese Salad with Balsamic Glaze

(Ready in 5 min, I serve 4, IDifficulty:Normal)

Ingredients
- 5 large beefsteak tomatoes, cut into 1/2-inch slices
- 1 bunch fresh basil
- 1-pound fresh buffalo mozzarella cheese, cut into 1/4-inch slices
- 5 tablespoons Balsamic Glaze
- 5 tablespoons extra virgin olive oil
- Pinch of sea salt
- 1/8 teaspoon cracked black pepper

Directions
1. On a large platter, place the sliced tomatoes. Placed a major basil leaf and a mozzarella slice on top of each slice.
2. Drizzle over the dish with the balsamic glaze and oil, then sprinkle with salt and pepper.

184. Grilled Tomatillo Salsa

(Ready in 15-20 min, I serve 4, IDifficulty:Normal)

Ingredients
- 20 tomatillos, husked and washed
- 1/2 small white onion, cut into large pieces
- 1 large whole jalapeño chile pepper, stem cut off
- 2 cloves garlic
- 3/4 cup fresh cilantro
- 1 cup water
- 1/2 teaspoon sea salt

Directions
1. Heat the grill to a medium-high temperature. Place all of the tomatillos on the grill right away.
2. Watch them closely, revolving every 2 to 3 minutes and rotating on both sides to blacken. If they blacken or smoke, it's okay as it will add to their taste. If picked up with tongs, they're done until they sound gentle and squishy.
3. Place in a pot and cover the cooked tomatillos, so they begin to steam as the rest of the tomatillos finish grilling. If all the tomatillos have been grilled, leave them for 15 to 20 minutes in the covering pot, until completely cooled.
4. When they cool, they can emit liquid that can be used in place of water or combined with water to create the salsa.
5. Cook the onion, chili pepper and garlic in a small pot over high heat until they begin to tan.
6. Add the tomatillo liquid or a combination of liquid and water after 2 minutes and cover. Simmer for about five minutes, or before the onion is quickly put into a fork. Shift to a blender the onion mixture, tomatillos (first cut any rough cores and keep the skin on), and cilantro in batches, and blend at low speed until smooth. Salt each batch according to taste. Store blended batches in a jar that is airtight.

185. Red Mexican Salsa

(Ready in 8-10min|, serve 4,|Difficulty:Normal)

Ingredients

- 20 dried red chiles/chiles de arbol
- 1 large clove garlic
- 1/2 white onion, cut into large pieces
- 2 large Roma tomatoes, cut into large pieces
- 1/2 cup water
- 3/4 cup fresh cilantro
- 1/4 teaspoon sea salt

Directions

1. Over high fire, heat a broad skillet. Directly apply the chiles, garlic, onion, and tomatoes to the skillet with no oil.
2. Remove the chiles from the skillet and put them in a small pot of water until the tomato skins and chiles begin to blacken. Cover, and to smooth the chiles, cook for 8 to 10 minutes. Move the cooked ingredients together with the cilantro to a blender until the chiles are softened.
3. Blend at low speed and cover the top with a kitchen towel so that the steam will escape, but the top of the blender will not burst with the salsa. Season to taste with salt.

186. Grilled Chicken with Black Bean Salsa

(Ready in 4-6 min, |serve 4,|Difficulty:Normal)

Ingredients

- 2 cups rinsed and drained canned black beans
- 1 large Granny Smith apple, chopped
- 1/2 small red onion, finely chopped
- 1 serrano chile pepper, seeded and finely chopped
- 2 tablespoons chopped fresh cilantro
- Juice of 1 large lime
- Juice of 1/2 orange
- 1/8 teaspoon sea salt
- 1/8 teaspoon cracked black pepper
- 4 boneless, skinless chicken breasts

Directions

1. Combine all the ingredients (except the salt, pepper, and chicken) in a big bowl to produce the salsa.
2. To let the flavors meld, refrigerate for at least an hour. Heat the grill or barbecue pan over medium-high heat. With salt and pepper, season the chicken breasts.
3. Place them on the grill and cook on either side for 4 to 6 minutes, or until the middle is no longer pink. On top of the breasts, split the salsa, and eat.

187. Beef Tacos

(Ready in 4-6 min,| serve 4,|Difficulty:Normal)

Ingredients

- 2 tablespoons extra virgin olive oil
- 1/2 cup chopped white onion, divided
- 1 cup chopped red bell pepper
- 1 large clove garlic, minced
- 1/2 pound 95%-lean ground beef
- 1/2 teaspoon dried oregano
- 1/4 teaspoon cracked black pepper
- 3/4 cup chopped Roma tomato
- 1 teaspoon chopped jalapeño chile pepper (seeded for less heat)
- 4 tablespoons chopped fresh cilantro
- Juice of 1/2 lime
- 8 (6-inch) corn tortillas
- 4 radishes, thinly sliced

Directions

1. Heat oil over medium-high heat in a wide pan. Attach 1/4 cup of the onion, garlic and bell pepper, and simmer for 30 seconds. Then add the ground beef and, with a spatula, split up any big chunks.
2. Cook for 5 to 6 minutes or until the meat is not pink anymore. When the meat is boiling, add the oregano and black pepper. To produce a salsa topping, combine the remaining 1/4 cup chopped onion, tomato, chili pepper, cilantro, and lime juice in a separate dish.
3. Mix to integrate uniformly, and set aside. Heat the tortillas over medium heat in a flat tray. On four separate plates, put two tortillas, scoop the beef mixture onto the tortillas, cover with salsa and sliced radishes, fold, and serve.

188. Curried Chicken Salad Pita Sandwich

(Ready in 40min,| serve 4,|Difficulty:Normal)

Ingredients

- 2 (6-ounce) boneless, skinless chicken breasts
- 1/2 cup chopped carrot
- 1/3 cup chopped green onion
- 1/4 cup golden raisins
- 3/4 cup low-fat plain Greek yogurt
- 1 1/2 teaspoons red wine vinegar
- 1 teaspoon curry powder
- 1/4 teaspoon ground cinnamon
- 4 100% whole wheat pitas (with pockets)
- 2 romaine lettuce leaves, chopped
- 8 heirloom tomatoes, sliced
- 1/4 cup chopped toasted almonds

Directions

1. Trim the fat off the chicken and cut into fourths of the breasts. Load a medium saucepan with water and bring it to a boil. Attach the chicken and simmer for 8 to 10 minutes, or until the middle of the mixture is pink. Strain the chicken, then set it to cool aside.

2. Combine the carrot, green onion, and raisins in a medium-sized dish. With two forks, shred the cooled chicken and return it to the dish.
3. Add the yogurt, vinegar, cinnamon and curry powder, and blend well. For 30 minutes, refrigerate. Heat the pitas over low heat in a wide skillet, and then break them in half and split up. Use salad mix to stuff each pita bag, top with almonds, and eat.

189. Chicken Fajita Wraps
(Ready in 10 min, I serve 4, IDifficulty:Normal)

Ingredients
- 3 tablespoons extra virgin olive oil
- 2 (6-ounce) boneless, skinless chicken breasts
- 1 teaspoon dried oregano
- 1/8 teaspoon sea salt
- 1/8 teaspoon black pepper
- 1/2 large white onion, thinly sliced
- 1 large green bell pepper, thinly sliced
- 1 large red bell pepper, thinly sliced
- 4 100% whole wheat tortillas
- 1 cup rinsed and drained canned black beans
- 1 cup shredded romaine lettuce
- 4 tablespoons low-fat plain Greek yogurt

Directions
1. Over medium pressure, heat the oil in a wide bowl. Strip the fat from the chicken breasts as the pan heats, slice them about 1/4 inch thick lengthwise, and split the longer parts in half. Using oregano, cinnamon, and pepper to season.
2. Add the chicken to the grill, and sauté for 5 to 6 minutes until the pieces are no longer pink in the middle. Take the chicken out of the tin, and set it aside. In the same pan, add the onion and bell peppers and sauté for about 4 minutes, until the onions are soft but not fully translucent.
3. Divide the black beans, spinach, chicken, and sautéed peppers and onions among the four tortillas. Heat the tortillas in a flat pan over low heat. Place yogurt on top, seal, and serve.

190. Asian-Style Lettuce Wraps with Peanut Sauce
(Ready in 10-15 min, I serve 4, IDifficulty:Normal)

Ingredients
- 2 cups uncooked red quinoa
- 4 cups low-sodium vegetable broth
- 8 large butter lettuce leaves
- 1 cup chopped snow peas (in thirds)
- 1 cup bean sprouts
- 1/2 cup chopped red bell pepper
- 1/2 cup shredded carrot
- 4 teaspoons sesame seeds

PEANUT SAUCE
- 1 cup and 6 tablespoons crunchy peanut butter
- 1 1/4 cup low-sodium vegetable broth
- Juice of 1/2 lime
- 1/2 teaspoon sesame oil
- 1/2 teaspoon low-sodium soy sauce
- 1/4 teaspoon ground ginger
- 1/4 teaspoon rice vinegar
- 1/4 teaspoon chile pepper flakes
- 2 tablespoons chopped green onion; white end discarded

Directions
1. Rinse the quinoa in order to (if not prerinsed). Bring the quinoa and vegetable broth to a boil, over high heat, in a large covered kettle.
2. Lower the flame and boil for 10 to 15 minutes or until much of the liquid has been consumed.
3. Cooked quinoa should be somewhat al dente; when most of the grains have uncoiled, it is ready and the unwound germ can be shown. For around 5 minutes, let the quinoa sit in the covering pot. With a fork, fluff softly.
4. On each lettuce leaf, put 1/2 cup of cooked quinoa. Mix the snow peas, bean sprouts, bell pepper, and carrots together in a medium dish. Combine all the peanut sauce ingredients in a shallow saucepan.
5. Over low pressure, bring to a boil, then whisk until the peanut butter dissolves. With the sliced vegetables, add the sauce into the dish. Mix well and spoon each lettuce leaf uniformly on top of the quinoa. Sprinkle on top of the vegetables with sesame seeds, and eat.

191. Italian Veggie Pita Sandwich
(Ready in 10 min, Iserve 4, IDifficulty:Normal)

Ingredients
- 1 100% whole wheat pita (with pocket)
- 1 tablespoon prepared pesto
- 1/2 cup arugula
- 1 (1/4-inch-thick) slice fresh mozzarella cheese
- 1 (1/4-inch-thick) slice heirloom tomato
- 1/4 cup roasted red pepper (about 2 large pieces from jar)
- 1/8 teaspoon cracked black pepper

Directions
1. Heat the pita in a skillet over low heat on both sides.
2. Remove from the oven, cut the pita in half, break open and sprinkle on the inside with the pesto.
3. Using arugula, cheese, onion, and red pepper to fill in. Top with Black pepper tip.

192. Turkey Chili
(Ready in 4 hours, I serve 8, IDifficulty:Normal)

Ingredients

Ingredients

- 2 tablespoons extra virgin olive oil
- 1/2-pound lean ground turkey
- 1/2 cup chopped red onion
- 3 medium cloves garlic, minced
- 2 cups chopped fresh tomatoes
- 1 (15-ounce) can garbanzo beans, rinsed and drained
- 1 (15-ounce) can black beans, rinsed and drained
- 1 (15-ounce) can kidney beans, rinsed and drained
- 1 (15-ounce) can white kidney beans, rinsed and drained
- 2 1/2 cups chopped zucchini
- 1 tablespoon chili powder
- 1/4 teaspoon ground cumin
- 1/2 teaspoon dried parsley
- 1/2 teaspoon dried oregano
- 1/2 teaspoon dried basil
- 3 cups low-sodium chicken broth
- 1/8 teaspoon ground black pepper
- 1/8 teaspoon sea salt
- 1/2 cup shredded low-fat cheddar cheese, for garnish
- 1/4 cup chopped fresh cilantro, for garnish

Directions

1. Heat the oil over medium to high heat in a large frying pan.
2. Add the ground turkey, garlic, and onion. Cook for 5 to 6 minutes or until browned, stirring continuously and using a spatula to break up the turkey chunks. In a 6-quart crock pot, put the remaining ingredients, and then add the cooked turkey mixture.
3. Mix together, cover, and cook for 4 hours on high, or 8 hours on low. If the chili gets too dry, search regularly and add a little sauce. Serve in cups, then apply cheese and cilantro to the top.
4. Cook in a big pot with a lid on the stove over low heat, if a crock pot is not available. If required, check regularly and add broth, as the chili may get hotter and the liquid may evaporate on the stovetop more easily than in a crock pot.

193. Vegetarian Chili

(Ready in 4-6hours,I serve 8,IDifficulty:Normal)

Ingredients

- 3 tablespoons extra virgin olive oil
- 1/2 large red onion, chopped
- 3 large cloves garlic, minced
- 4 small zucchinis, chopped
- 1/2 cup chopped red bell pepper
- 1/2 cup chopped yellow bell pepper
- 2 (15-ounce) cans black beans, rinsed and drained
- 1 (15-ounce) can kidney beans, rinsed and drained
- 1 (15-ounce) can garbanzo beans, rinsed and drained
- 2 (15-ounce) cans low-sodium diced tomatoes
- 1 tablespoon chili powder
- 1/2 teaspoon ground cumin
- 1/2 teaspoon dried parsley
- 1/2 teaspoon dried oregano
- 1/2 teaspoon dried basil
- 1/8 teaspoon black pepper
- 1/8 teaspoon sea salt
- 3/4 cup low-sodium vegetable broth
- 8 tablespoons low-fat plain Greek yogurt
- 1 large avocado, pitted, peeled, and thinly sliced
- 4 tablespoons chopped fresh cilantro

Directions

1. Heat the oil over medium-high heat in a big pot, then add the onion and garlic.
2. Add the zucchini and bell peppers after 3 or 4 minutes. Sauté the vegetables until they are transparent with the onion.
3. Move and apply the remaining ingredients to a 6-quart crock pot. On low heat, cook for 4 to 6 hours and add water if necessary. Serve in bowls and finish with yogurt, cilantro and 2 slices of avocado.
4. Cook in a big pot with a lid on the stove over low heat, if a crock pot is not available. If required, check periodically and add a little water, as the chili may get hotter and the liquid may evaporate on the stovetop more easily than in a crock pot.

Kale Vegetable Soup

(Ready in30min, serve8,Difficulty:Normal)

Ingredients

- 2 tablespoons extra virgin olive oil
- 3 medium carrots, sliced
- 3 small sweet potatoes, diced
- 1 large yellow onion, chopped
- 3 large cloves garlic, minced
- 2 small yellow zucchini, cubed
- 1/2 teaspoon dried oregano
- 1/4 teaspoon chile pepper flakes
- 1/8 teaspoon sea salt
- 1 quart low-sodium vegetable broth
- 1 (14-ounce) can low-sodium diced tomatoes
- 1/2 teaspoon fresh thyme, chopped
- 2 cups coarsely chopped kale
- 1 (15-ounce) can cannellini beans, rinsed and drained

Directions

1. Over medium boil, heat the oil in a big pot.
2. Add the carrots, sweet potatoes, cabbage, and garlic and simmer for around 4 to 5 minutes, before they begin to soften.
3. Add the zucchini, oregano, flakes of chili pepper, and salt, then simmer for 1 minute. Stir in the bouillon,
4. Canned tomatoes and thyme with juice. Bring to a boil, minimize heat for an additional 10 minutes, cover, and simmer. Then add the kale and beans and

continue to boil for another 8 to 10 minutes, before the kale is wilted and the sweet potatoes are tender. Serve it wet.

194. Tuna Salad

(Ready in 20 min, I serve 8, IDifficulty:Normal)

Ingredients

- 1/4 cup chopped celery
- 1/2 jalapeño chile pepper, seeded and chopped
- 1/4 cup chopped Roma tomato
- 1/4 cup chopped red onion
- 2 (6-ounce) cans albacore tuna in water, no salt added, drained
- 1 teaspoon brown mustard
- 3 tablespoons low-fat plain Greek yogurt
- 1/8 teaspoon cracked black pepper
- 1 small avocado, thinly sliced

Directions

1. Combine the celery, chili, tomato, and onion in a medium dish.
2. Combine the salmon, vinegar, yogurt, and pepper together until well blended. Cover with avocado slices in the salad, and eat.

195. Italian-Style Tuna Salad

(Ready in 30 min, I serve 8, IDifficulty:Normal)

Ingredients

- 2 (5-ounce) cans albacore tuna in water, no salt added, drained
- 1/2 cup chopped Roma tomato
- 1/4 cup chopped red onion
- 4 tablespoons finely chopped fresh parsley
- Juice of 1 lemon
- 4 tablespoons extra virgin olive oil
- 1/8 teaspoon cracked black pepper

Directions

1. In a large bowl, put all the ingredients and stir to mix evenly.
2. Until serving, quit to rest for 30 minutes.

196. Veggie Quesadillas with Cilantro Yogurt Dip

(Ready in 30min, I serve 8, IDifficulty:Normal)

Ingredients

- 4 servings
- 1 cup beans, black or pinto
- 2 Tablespoons cilantro, chopped
- ½ bell pepper, finely chopped
- ½ cup corn kernels
- 1 cup low-fat shredded cheese
- 6 soft corn tortillas
- 1 medium carrot, shredded
- ½ jalapeno pepper, finely minced (optional)

CILANTRO YOGURT DIP

- 1 cup plain non-fat yogurt
- 2 Tablespoons cilantro, finely chopped
- Juice from ½ of a lime

Directions

1. Over low pressure, preheat a broad skillet.
2. Place 3 tortillas in rows. Divide the tortillas into cheese, rice, corn, cilantro, sliced carrots, and peppers. With such a second tortilla, cover each one.
3. Place a tortilla on a dry skillet and warm for about 3 minutes before the cheese is melted and the tortilla is slightly golden.
4. Flip and cook until golden on the other hand, around 1 minute.
5. Mix the non-fat cream, cilantro and lime juice together in a shallow dish.
6. Break each quesadilla into 4 wedges (12 total wedges) and serve 3 wedges with approximately 1⁄4 cup of the dip per person. Leftovers should be refrigerated within 2 hours.

197. Sweet Roasted Beet & Arugula Pizza

(Ready in 35min, I serve 8, IDifficulty:Normal)

Ingredients

PIZZA CRUST

- 1 packet active dry yeast
- ¾ cup lukewarm water
- 2 cups 100% whole wheat flour
- 1 ½ teaspoons salt
- Oil for greasing bowl

PIZZA

- 2 small beets, roasted
- 1 cup arugula
- ½ cup goat cheese
- 1 cup blackberries
- 2 tablespoons honey
- 2 tablespoons balsamic vinegar

Directions

Pizza Crust

1. Pour warm water into a large bowl and sprinkle with yeast
2. Whisk mixture and let sit until foamy, about 5 minutes
3. Add salt then slowly stir in flour until a sticky dough forms
4. Transfer dough to an oiled bowl, cover with plastic wrap, let sit ~1 hour in a warm corner of the kitchen to let rise
5. Knead dough a few times, until the dough becomes sticky and begins to form a ball
6. Roll out dough and bake at 500 F for 8-12 minutes depending on thickness of crust

Roasted Beets

1. While dough is rising, dice beets
2. Place on baking sheet lined with parchment paper
3. Cover with foil
4. Bake 35 minutes at 400 F
5. Once beets are finished roasting, increase oven temperature and bake pizza crust.

Pizza

1. Top crust with roasted beets while oven cools to 350 F
2. Sprinkle with goat cheese and berries
3. Drizzle with honey and balsamic vinegar
4. Bake 8-10 minutes at 350 F
5. Top with arugula

Chapter 4: Dinner Recipes

In this chapter, we have presented DASH diet dinner recipes.

1. Chicken Breasts with Italian Salad

(Ready in 30min,I serve 4,IDifficulty:Normal)

Ingredients
SALAD

- 1 cup cherry tomatoes, halved
- 2 small zucchini, sliced thinly and cut into half moons
- 1 cup diced fresh mozzarella cheese
- 1/4 cup extra virgin olive oil
- 1/4 cup balsamic vinegar
- 1/8 teaspoon sea salt
- Cracked black pepper
- 4 cups arugula
- 2 tablespoons chopped fresh basil

CHICKEN

- 1 teaspoon dried oregano
- 1/2 teaspoon minced fresh rosemary
- 1/2 teaspoon garlic powder
- 1/8 teaspoon sea salt
- Cracked black pepper
- 4 boneless, skinless chicken breasts

Directions

1. Combine the onions, zucchini, and cheese in a medium bowl to make the dish. To taste, apply milk, vinegar, salt, and pepper, and blend well. When the chicken is ready, cover and refrigerate. (Later, you'll add the arugula and basil.) Trim off the chicken breasts with the fat.
2. Combine the oregano, rosemary, garlic powder, cinnamon, and pepper to taste in a small bowl and blend well. Sprinkle all sides of the chicken breasts with the mixture. Over medium pressure, heat a large saucepan and cover the pan with a spray of olive oil.
3. Add the chicken breasts, 2 at a time, to prevent overcrowding until the oil is hot. Cook each breast on each side for 4 to 6 minutes, or until the middle is no longer pink. Take the salad from the refrigerator as the second batch of chicken is frying, add the arugula and basil, and toss well.
4. Let it rest for about 2 minutes until the chicken is finished, and then slice each breast on the diagonal, making strips of chicken. On a plate, place the salad and top with sliced chicken.

2. Orange Chicken and Brown Rice

(Ready in 30min,I serve2,IDifficulty:Normal)

Ingredients

- 2 (4-ounce) boneless, skinless chicken breasts
- 1 tablespoon sesame oil
- 1 tablespoon extra-virgin olive oil
- 1/2 cup coarsely chopped shiitake mushroom
- 1/4 cup chopped white onion
- 1 large clove garlic, minced
- 1/4 teaspoon cracked black pepper
- 1/2 teaspoon grated orange zest
- 1/4 teaspoon grated lemon zest
- Juice of 1/2 orange
- 4 cups spinach
- 1/4 teaspoon ground ginger
- 1 cup cooked brown rice

Directions

1. Trim the chicken breasts with the fat and then split the chicken into tiny cubes. In a medium-sized pan, heat the sesame oil and olive oil over medium to high heat.

2. Add the mushroom, onion and garlic and cook for 1 minute, then add the chicken and season with the chicken, ground ginger, lemon zest and orange zest. Cook for about 4 to 5 minutes, until the chicken has browned, and then add the orange juice.
3. To add flavors, swirl the chicken and scratch the bottom of the pan. To steam the spinach, apply the spinach, detach the pan from the heat and instantly cover it. Divide the brown rice that has been cooked into two dishes and top with the orange chicken.

3. Grilled Chicken Skewers Marinated in Ginger-Apricot Sauce

(Ready in 4-5min, serve 2, Difficulty: Normal)

Ingredients

- 4 (4-ounce) chicken breasts, cut into 1-inch cubes
- 3 large red bell peppers, cut into 1-inch pieces
- 2 large white onions, cut into 1-inch pieces
- 6 apricots, pitted and cut into 1-inch pieces

MARINADE

- 1 heaping tablespoon reduced-sugar apricot marmalade
- 1/2 teaspoon sesame oil
- 1 1/2 teaspoons finely chopped fresh ginger or 3/4 teaspoon
- ground ginger
- 1 tablespoon Dijon mustard or brown mustard
- 4 tablespoons apple cider vinegar
- 1/4 cup extra virgin olive oil
- 1 large clove garlic, chopped

Directions

1. In a big bowl, mix together all the marinade ingredients. In a large zip-top container, put the cubed chicken, pour the marinade in, force the air out of the bag, and close firmly. By changing the bag and contents around, work the mixture by hand into the chicken.
2. Refrigerate for 2 hours at the very least. In water, soak 12 large wooden skewers and then cut the peppers, onions, and apricots into parts of the same size. Skewer the chicken, chili, onion, and apricot bits and alternative ingredients.
3. Grill the skewers on a hot grill or grill plate, 4 to 5 minutes on either side, or until the middle of the chicken is no longer pink. (Close the cover on the barbecue by using a charcoal or gas grill, so the chicken doesn't dry out.)

Chicken Fajitas with Spicy Avocado Sauce

(Ready in 4-5min, serve 2, Difficulty: Normal)

Ingredients
SAUCE

- 1 large avocado, pitted, peeled, and cut in fourths
- 1/2 cup low-fat plain Greek yogurt
- 1/4 cup water
- Juice of 1/2 lemon
- 1/2 small serrano chile pepper
- 1/8 teaspoon sea salt
- 1/8 teaspoon cracked black pepper

FAJITAS

- 4 (4-ounce) boneless, skinless chicken breasts, cut into 1/2-
- inch- thick strips
- 1/8 teaspoon sea salt
- 1/8 teaspoon cracked black pepper
- 1 teaspoon dried oregano, divided
- 1/4 teaspoon ground cumin
- 3 tablespoons extra virgin olive oil
- 2 large red bell peppers, cut into 1/2-inch-thick strips
- 2 large green bell peppers, cut into 1/2-inch-thick strips
- 2 large yellow bell peppers, cut into 1/2-inch-thick strips
- 1 large white onion, cut into 1/2-inch slivers
- 2 large cloves garlic, minced
- 8 corn tortillas

Directions

1. Place all the ingredients in a blender for the sauce and
2. Until smooth, mix. Only put aside. Season the chicken with salt, pepper, cumin, and half of the oregano for the fajitas. Heat oil over medium-high heat in a large pot.
3. Add the chicken once the oil is hot, and cook for 4 to 5 minutes.
4. Add the bell peppers, garlic, onion, and the leftover dried oregano. Season with salt and pepper to taste and simmer until the vegetables are tender, for a few more minutes. Heat the tortillas over low heat in a pan. Scoop into each tortilla the chicken and veggie mixture and drizzle with avocado sauce. Fold over the tortilla and serve.
5. **Serving Suggestion**: Eat with black beans, shredded lettuce, low-fat shredded cheese, and salsa, with various toppings.

4. Baked Sunflower Seed–Crusted Turkey Cutlets

(Ready in 20min, serve 2, Difficulty: Normal)

Ingredients

- 2 (6-ounce) skinless, boneless turkey breasts
- 1 1/2 cups unsalted sunflower seeds
- 1/4 teaspoon ground cumin
- 2 tablespoons coarsely chopped fresh parsley
- 1/4 teaspoon paprika
- 1/4 teaspoon cayenne pepper
- 1/4 teaspoon cracked black pepper
- 1/3 cup whole wheat flour

- 3 egg whites

Directions

1. Preheat the oven to 400 F.
2. Place the turkey breasts between two plastic sheets,
3. Cover and pound until 1/2 inch or so deep. Slice every pounded breast in two. Put the sunflower seeds, cumin, parsley, paprika, cayenne, and pepper together in a food processor. Pulse until the seeds are coarsely chopped, a few times. On a flat tray, put the seed mixture onto it. Spread the flour on a different flat pan.
4. Whisk the egg whites in a broad, reasonably shallow dish. Set up an assembly line for dredging in this order: flour tray, egg cup, plate of seed mixture. In the flour, dip each breast and gently dredge it on both sides.
5. Then dip it with the seed mixture into the egg whites and eventually onto the pan. To brush all sides of the turkey with the seed mixture, press down hard. Using olive oil spray to cover a baking sheet and put the crusted breasts on the sheet. Bake for 10 minutes, turn over the cutlets, and bake for another 10 minutes, or until the middle of the thickest section is no longer pink. Immediately serve.

5. Turkey Meatballs in Marinara Sauce

(Ready in 20-25min,l serve2,lDifficulty:Normal)

Ingredients

- 1-pound lean ground turkey
- 1/2 small red onion, finely chopped
- 2 large cloves garlic, minced
- 1/4 cup red bell pepper, finely chopped
- 3 tablespoons finely chopped fresh parsley
- 1/2 teaspoon chile pepper flakes
- 1/8 teaspoon ground cumin
- 1/2 teaspoon dried Italian herbs (premixed, or use thyme,
- rosemary, oregano, parsley, and basil)
- 1/8 teaspoon cracked black pepper
- 1 large egg
- 1/4 cup whole wheat bread crumbs
- 1/8 teaspoon sea salt
- 4 tablespoons extra virgin olive oil
- 1 (16-ounce) jar low-sodium marinara sauce
- 1/2 cup low-fat feta cheese

Directions

1. Preheat the oven to 375°F.
2. Combine all ingredients except the oil in a large bowl, Feta, and marinara. Mix well by hand, taking care not to overmix, until the ingredients are mixed into the meat. Roll the mixture of meat into golf balls the size of meatballs. Over medium-high prepare, heat a large nonstick skillet.
3. Add the oil and then the meatballs in batches of five until the pan is warmed. Sear on either side (do not cook all the way through), and placed in a dish that is ovenproof. Top with the marinara sauce, then cover with foil until all the meatballs have been seared and put in the dish.
4. For 20 to 25 minutes, roast. Remove it from the oven and increase the temperature to 400 F. Take the foil out of the dish, top the feta with the meatballs, and bake for 4 minutes. Immediately extract and serve.

6. Turkey Meat Loaf

(Ready in 1-2hour,l serve2,lDifficulty:Normal)

Ingredients

- 1 slice 100% whole wheat bread, crust removed and torn into small pieces
- 1/4 cup low-sodium chicken stock
- 1 1/4 pounds lean ground turkey
- 1 large egg
- 1/4 cup finely chopped onion
- 1/4 cup finely chopped bell pepper
- 1/4 cup chopped fresh parsley
- 1 teaspoon horseradish
- 1 teaspoon Dijon mustard
- 1 teaspoon Worcestershire sauce
- 1/2 teaspoon sea salt
- 1/4 teaspoon black pepper

Directions

1. Preheat the oven to 350°F. Place all the ingredients in a big bowl and combine until the ingredients are properly incorporated together with your fingertips, being vigilant not to overmix.
2. Grease a 9-by 5-inch loaf pan (or deep baking dish) lightly with a spray of olive oil. In a loaf, shape the meat mixture and put it in the pan. Bake uncovered for an hour or two.
3. Remove from the oven until the meat loaf is baked and let cool for about 10 minutes. To detach it from the plate, run a butter knife around the sides, invert it into a large serving bowl, and slice it to eat.

7. Italian Herbed Turkey Cutlets

(Ready in 20-25min,l serve 2,lDifficulty:Normal)

Ingredients

- 3 small cloves garlic, minced
- 2 tablespoons chopped fresh rosemary
- 2 tablespoons chopped fresh parsley
- 1 1/2 teaspoons chopped fresh sage
- 1/2 teaspoon cracked black pepper
- 4 (4-ounce) boneless, skinless turkey cutlets
- Grated zest of 1 large lemon
- 1 cup low-sodium vegetable broth

Directions

1. Preheat the oven to 375°F.
2. Mix the garlic, rosemary, parsley, etc. in a little bowl.

3. And garlic, and sage. On both sides of each cutlet, rub a generous amount of the herb mixture. In a 9-by 13-inch baking dish, put the turkey cutlets, top with lemon zest, and add the vegetable broth to the dish.
4. Use foil to cover, then bake for 20 to 25 minutes. To brown the tops of the cutlets, remove the foil during the last 5 minutes of baking. Delete from the oven and quickly serve.

8. Turkey Roulade with Cider Sauce

(Ready in 20min, serve 4, Difficulty:Normal)

Ingredients

- 5 tablespoons extra virgin olive oil, divided
- 1/2 cup diced white onion, divided
- 4 cremini mushrooms, thinly sliced
- 2 cups spinach
- 3 medium cloves garlic, minced
- 1/2 cup white wine
- 1 1/2 cups low-sodium chicken broth, divided
- 1/3 cup dried cranberries
- 3 slices 100% whole wheat bread, cut into 1/2-inch squares
- 1/2 cup chopped almonds
- 1 large fresh sage leaf, finely minced
- 1 teaspoon chopped fresh thyme
- 1 teaspoon chopped fresh parsley
- 1 (2-pound) skinless, boneless turkey breast
- 1/4 teaspoon sea salt
- 1/2 teaspoon cracked black pepper

CIDER SAUCE

- 1 1/2 cups cider, divided
- 1 tablespoon cornstarch
- 1/2–1 cup roasting liquid from turkey

Directions

1. Preheat the oven to 375°F.
2. Heat 2 teaspoons of the roulade to create the filling for the roulade, Oil over medium heat in a wide bath. With the onions, spinach, and garlic, add 1/4 cup of onion and cook until the onion is translucent.
3. Add the white wine and let the alcohol cook for about a minute, then boil. Along with the cranberries, add 1/2 cup of the broth.
4. Add the toast, almonds, and fresh herbs until the broth is heated (but not boiling). For 2 to 3 minutes, simmer, then stir. It should not be too soupy with the filling. By putting your palm flat on top of the breast and chopping horizontally through the breast, butterfly the turkey breast, making sure not to break through entirely. Open and put your butterfly breast between two sheets of plastic wrap. Flatten the turkey with a 1/2-inch-thick mallet. With salt and pepper, season all ends.
5. On the turkey, scatter the filling, holding it in the middle. Roll up the turkey breast at three locations and cover it with kitchen twine (middle and two ends). Bring the filling pan to a high heat and cook the rolled turkey breast on both sides, 3 to 4 minutes per side, brown in color.
6. In a medium roasting pan, dribble the remaining 3 tablespoons of oil.
7. Add the remainder of the broth and onion. In the center of the plate, put the turkey, cover it with foil, and bake for around 1 hour.
8. Add 3/4 cup cider to the turkey-searing pan and rub the bottom of the pan to blend in the juices. Whisk the remainder of the cider with the cornstarch in a small bowl and apply it to the pan. Boil until the sauce thickens, for 2 to 3 minutes.
9. Add up to 1 cup of the roasting juices to the cider sauce after extracting the turkey from the oven, and blend well. Hold the turkey wrapped, then quit for 10 minutes to sit down. Remove the turkey and cut the twine from the roasting pan. Cut the turkey and finish with cider sauce on each slice.

9. Stuffed Bell Peppers

(Ready in 20min, serve 4, Difficulty:Normal)

Ingredients

- 2 tablespoons extra virgin olive oil
- 1/2 small white onion, chopped
- 2 small cloves garlic, minced
- 1/2 cup chopped carrot
- 1/4 teaspoon dried thyme
- 1/4 teaspoon dried basil
- 1/2 pound 95%-lean ground beef
- 1 cup chopped zucchini
- 1 tablespoon chopped fresh parsley
- 1 (15-ounce) can kidney beans, rinsed and drained
- 4 large red bell peppers
- 2 cups low-sodium marinara sauce

Directions

1. Preheat the oven to 350°F.
2. Heat the oil over medium to high heat in a wide bowl. Connect the garlic, cabbage, tomato, thyme and basil.
3. Cook for 1 to 2 minutes, and then substitute the beef with a spatula, breaking up any clumps. Once the beef continues to brown, add the zucchini, parsley, and kidney beans after around 5 to 6 minutes. Cook for another 5 minutes, or until the beef is not pink anymore.
4. Cut the tops off just below the stems to ready the peppers. Remove the ribs and nuts. Fill the meat mixture with each pepper and put it in an 8-inch square baking dish so the peppers stand upright. To cover the rim, add water into the dish. Cover the pan with foil and cook for 20 to 25 minutes, or if pierced with a fork, until the peppers are tender. In a small saucepan, heat the marinara sauce, and pour over each plated bell pepper before serving.

10. Sesame Salmon Fillets

(Ready in 5min, Iserve4, IDifficulty:Normal)

Ingredients

- 1 tablespoon sesame oil
- 2 (4-ounce) salmon fillets, skin on
- 1/8 teaspoon ground ginger
- 1/8 teaspoon sea salt
- 1/8 teaspoon cracked black pepper
- 2 teaspoons black sesame seeds

Directions

1. In a medium pan, melt the oil over a medium heat. Then add the salmon, skin side down, once the pan is heated. Put the ginger powder, salt, pepper and sesame seeds on top of each fillet.
2. Softly pat the seeds down until they bind to the fillet. Switch the fillets over after around 3 or 4 minutes, and sear on the other hand.
3. Take the fillets out of the pan after 1 to 2 minutes and eat immediately.
4. **Serving Suggestion:** Prepare whole wheat couscous with sautéed greens or broccoli.

11. Spice-Rubbed Salmon

(Ready in 5min, I serve4, IDifficulty:Normal)

Ingredients

- 2 teaspoons chili powder
- 1 teaspoon ground cumin
- 1 teaspoon brown sugar
- 1/8 teaspoon sea salt
- 1/8 teaspoon cracked black pepper
- 4 (4-ounce) salmon fillets
- Juice of 1/2 orange
- 2 tablespoons extra virgin olive oil

Directions

1. Blend the chili powder, cumin, sugar, salt, and pepper in a shallow cup. Rub the mixture by hand onto each salmon fillet.
2. Over medium pressure, heat the oil in a nonstick pan. When the oil is heated, add two fillets to the pan at a time, skin side down, and cook for 1 to 2 minutes. Then turn the fillets over and squeeze them with the orange juice.
3. Cook until the fillets are flaky for another 1 to 2 minutes and can be separated with a fork. With the second set of fillets, repeat the operation. Immediately serve.

12. Pan-Steamed Orange Roughy

(Ready in 8-10min, I serve4, IDifficulty:Normal)

Ingredients

- 4 small green onions, white ends cut off
- 4 teaspoons chopped fresh ginger
- 4 (3-ounce) orange roughy fillets
- 3 large cloves garlic, minced
- 1/4 teaspoon cracked black pepper
- 1/2 teaspoon black sesame seeds
- 1 lime, very thinly sliced
- 2 teaspoons sesame oil

Directions

1. Break four boards, some 6 inches by 6 inches, of foil. Place a green onion in the middle of each layer, along with 1 teaspoon of ginger. Sprinkle with garlic, pepper, and sesame seeds and put one fillet on top. On top of each fillet, put four paper-thin slices of lime and drizzle with sesame oil.
2. Fold the foil up from the sides to surround each fillet, reach in the middle and fold down to seal. Over medium-high heat, heat a wide flat pan and put the foil-wrapped fillets in the pan. For 8 to 10 minutes, cook.
3. To finish steaming in the foil, remove the fish packages from the pan and let sit for 3 to 4 minutes. Serve in the foil, so that you can unwrap your dinner for each individual.

13. Fish Tacos

(Ready in 8-10min, Iserve4, IDifficulty:Normal)

Ingredients

- 4 (3-ounce) mahi mahi fillets
- 3 tablespoons extra virgin olive oil
- 4 cups thinly shredded red cabbage
- 3 tablespoons red wine vinegar
- 8 corn tortillas
- 1/2 teaspoon ground cumin
- 1/8 teaspoon cracked black pepper
- 2 large avocados, pitted, peeled, and thinly sliced
- 3 large Roma tomatoes, chopped

SAUCE

- 3/4 cup low-fat plain Greek yogurt
- 1/4 cup low-fat milk
- Juice of 1 large lemon
- 1/8 teaspoon cracked black pepper
- 1/8 teaspoon sea salt

Directions

1. Whisk all of the ingredients together in a small bowl to make the sauce. To drizzle over the top of the tacos, the consistency of the sauce should be relatively smooth, adding more milk if it's not thin enough. Only put aside.
2. Over medium fire, heat a wide skillet. With cumin and pepper, season both sides of each fillet.
3. Add the oil to the hot pan and then add the fillets, two at a time, when the oil is hot. Cook for 3 to 4 minutes on each side, or until each side is seared and the middle of the fish is no longer translucent. Remove from the pan, and put-on paper towels to drain. For the other two fillets, repeat.

4. Toss the cabbage with the vinegar in a different bowl. Break apart each fillet into two parts with two forks. Place a few pieces of fish in each tortilla, cover with the mixture of cabbage, avocado, and diced tomato, and then drizzle with the salsa.
5. Warm the tortillas in a flat pan over low heat. Fold over the tortilla and serve.

14. Thai Curried Vegetables

(Ready in 8-10min,I serve 4,IDifficulty:Normal)

Ingredients

- 2 tablespoons coconut oil
- 1 medium onion, cut into 1/4-inch pieces
- 1 medium red bell pepper, coarsely chopped
- 1 medium green bell pepper, coarsely chopped
- 1 cup coarsely chopped broccoli
- 3–4 cups cubed eggplant, 1/2-inch pieces
- 1 small jalapeño chile pepper, thinly sliced (seeded for less heat)
- 1 tablespoon chopped fresh ginger
- 2 large cloves garlic, coarsely chopped
- 1 teaspoon curry powder
- 1/2 teaspoon ground cinnamon
- 1/2 teaspoon ground turmeric
- 1/2 teaspoon cracked black pepper
- 2 cups unsweetened light coconut milk
- 1/2 cup low-sodium vegetable broth
- 1 heaping tablespoon unsalted peanut butter
- 4 tablespoons coarsely chopped Thai basil

Directions

1. Over medium heat, heat a big pot, and add the coconut oil.
2. Add the cabbage, bell peppers, and broccoli until it has melted, stirring continuously.
3. Add the eggplant, chili pepper, ginger, garlic, curry powder, turmeric, cinnamon, and pepper. Stir until the eggplant browns and the vegetables soften a little, around 4 to 5 minutes, to add the ingredients and spices and cook.
4. Add coconut milk, peanut butter, and broth. To add the peanut butter, stir well, and then cover the pot. Simmer on low for 10 minutes or so.
5. Then remove the lid and cook for another 5 minutes uncovered, or until the sauce thickens to the perfect consistency. Right prior to serving, whisk in the basil.

15. Veggie Fajitas

(Ready in 8-10 min,I serve 4,IDifficulty:Normal)

Ingredients

- 3 large red bell peppers, cut into strips
- 3 large green bell peppers, cut into strips
- 3 large yellow bell peppers, cut into strips
- 2 large green zucchini, cut into strips
- 2 large portobello mushrooms about 6 inches in diameter
- 2 large white onions, sliced
- 3 tablespoons extra virgin olive oil
- 3 cloves garlic, minced
- 1 1/2 teaspoons dried oregano
- 1/4 teaspoon ground cumin
- 1/8 teaspoon cracked black pepper
- 1/8 teaspoon sea salt
- 8 corn tortillas

Directions

1. Break the peppers from the bell into 1/2-inch strips. Lengthwise, cut the zucchini into thin strips and then cut each strip in half.
2. Wipe with a wet rag, pop the heads off the mushrooms, scoop out the gills with a metal tablespoon, and cut them into 1/2-inch strips. Split into 1/2-inch strips of the onions. Heat oil over medium-high heat in a large pot.
3. Add the bell peppers, zucchini, mushrooms, onions, garlic, oregano, cumin, pepper, and salt until the oil is warmed.
4. Cook for around 5 to 6 minutes, until the vegetables are soft and the onions are translucent. Heat the tortillas over medium heat in a flat tray, then spoon in the vegetables. Fold over the tortilla and serve.

16. Grilled Portobello Burger with Caramelized Onions and Pesto

(Ready in 8-10 minI, serve 4,IDifficulty:Normal)

Ingredients

- 4 medium portobello mushrooms (about 4 inches in diameter)
- 4 tablespoons extra virgin olive oil
- 1/4 teaspoon sea salt
- 1/2 teaspoon ground black pepper
- 8 tablespoons balsamic vinegar
- 4 100% whole wheat hamburger buns
- 4 tablespoons prepared pesto
- 4 tablespoons Caramelized Onions

Directions

1. Clean the mushrooms with a wet towel by wiping them. Remove the mushroom stems and then, with a metal spoon, scoop the brown gills out and discard them.
2. Brush the top of each mushroom with a tablespoon of oil and apply salt, pepper and 2 tablespoons of balsamic vinegar to the inside of each mushroom. Put aside for 20 minutes at the very least. Top down, put the mushrooms on a hot grill or grill plate. Grill for about five or seven minutes, then flip and grill for another five to seven minutes, or until tender. To avoid the juices from being released, do not control them too much.

3. When the mushrooms are grilling, toast the buns by putting them face down for about 1 minute on the barbecue. Remove from the grill, and on the inside of each top bun, spread 1 tablespoon of pesto. On each bottom bun, put a mushroom, then top with 1 tablespoon of caramelized onions.

17. Caramelized Onions
(Ready in 8-10 min, I serve 10, Difficulty: Normal)

Ingredients
- 2 tablespoons extra virgin olive oil
- 4 cups, thinly sliced white onions
- 1 teaspoon brown sugar
- 1/8 teaspoon cracked black pepper

Directions
1. Heat a medium-sized saucepan over medium heat.
2. Add the oil and when the oil is hot, add the onions, and then the sugar and pepper.
3. Sauté for 5 to 10 minutes, stirring constantly to avoid burning.
4. Once the onions are translucent and start turning brown, cover the pan and turn the heat down to low. Let the onions "sweat" for about 5 more minutes. When done, they should be dark brown and very soft.

18. Mediterranean Bowl
(Ready in 15-20 min| serve 4|Difficulty: Normal)

Ingredients
- 1 cup uncooked whole wheat couscous
- 1 1/4 cups water
- 1 (16-ounce) can artichoke hearts
- 1/2 cup rinsed, drained, and pitted kalamata olives
- 1 (12-ounce) jar roasted red peppers, rinsed, drained and
- coarsely chopped
- 1/2 cup low-fat feta cheese
- 1 cup chopped cherry tomatoes
- 1/2 small red onion, finely diced
- 1/4 teaspoon finely chopped fresh oregano
- 1/4 teaspoon finely chopped fresh mint
- Pinch of chile pepper flakes
- 4 tablespoons extra virgin olive oil
- Juice of 1 lemon
- Cracked black pepper

Directions
1. Boil the water, add the cauliflower, stir, and turn off the heat. Cover the pot with a lid and allow to rest for 5 minutes, and before eating, fluff with a fork.
2. Combine all ingredients and blend well, bar the cooked couscous.
3. Refrigerate for 15 to 20 minutes, then fold in the couscous mixture. Serve at room temperature, or freezing.

4. **Serving Suggestion:** Perfect alongside chicken or salmon fillets Breast, or combined into a salad of chicken or fish.

19. Grilled Veggie Pizza
(Ready in 15-20 min, I serve 6, Difficulty: Normal)

Ingredients
- 2 medium portobello mushrooms about 4 inches in diameter
- 1 small yellow zucchini, cut in half lengthwise
- 1 small red onion, cut into rounds
- 4 tablespoons extra-virgin olive oil
- 1/8 teaspoon salt
- 1/8 teaspoon cracked black pepper
- 1 (1-pound) whole wheat pizza dough
- 2 plum tomatoes, thinly sliced
- 1/2 cup shredded skim mozzarella cheese
- 1/4 cup fresh basil leaves, coarsely chopped

Directions
1. Preheat the oven to 400 F.
2. Heat a medium-hot grill or barbecue pan. With a wet rag, wash the mushrooms, pop the stems off, scoop out the gills with a metal tablespoon, and cut them into 1/2-inch strips. Brush two teaspoons of oil with the mushrooms, zucchini, and onion, and sprinkle with salt and pepper.
3. Place the veggies on the grill and roast, sealed, for 6 minutes, until tender and browned, rotating once. Remove from the grill, and the onion rings are separated.
4. Using olive oil spray to cover a baking sheet. Stretch the pizza dough onto the baking sheet with your fingertips, or spread the dough out on a floured surface to avoid sticking. Pierce the dough in several places with a fork so that it does not fluff up as it bakes.
5. Sprinkle the remaining 2 teaspoons of olive oil with the dough, sprinkle with your fingertips or spatula, and simmer for 12 to 15 minutes or until crispy. Remove from the oven the pizza crust, and line it easily with
6. Cheese and veggies. Return to the oven for 5 to 6 minutes, just before the cheese melts. Cover with basil, detach from the oven, and eat.

20. Mexican Pizza
(Ready in 15-20 min, I serve 6, Difficulty: Normal)

Ingredients
- 1/2 cup rinsed and drained canned black beans
- 1 tablespoon canned chipotle pepper sauce
- 3 tablespoons water
- 1 (12-inch) prebaked 100% whole wheat thin-crust pizza
- 1 small zucchini, thinly sliced in rounds
- 1/2 cup thinly sliced red onion
- 1/2 cup sliced red bell pepper

- 1/2 cup shredded skim mozzarella cheese
- 1/2 teaspoon dried oregano

Directions

1. Preheat the oven to 400 F. In a food processor or blender, combine the chipotle salsa, black beans, and water. Puree until it hits Only smooth. Spread the mixture uniformly over the pie crust.
2. Cover with rounds of zucchini, then onions and bell peppers, and eventually cheese. Sprinkle on top of oregano and cook for about 15 minutes, or until the cheese is browned and bubbled.

21. Healthier Mac 'n' Cheese

(Ready in 15-20 min, serve 4, Difficulty: Normal)

Ingredients

- 1/2 cup water
- 1 large white onion, sliced
- 8 medium cloves garlic, halved
- 1/8 teaspoon sea salt
- 1/8 teaspoon cracked black pepper
- 1 teaspoon brown mustard
- 8 ounces 100% whole wheat macaroni pasta
- 1 cup coarsely chopped broccoli florets
- Pinch of chile pepper flakes
- 1/3 cup low-fat ricotta cheese, divided
- 1 cup shredded low-fat cheddar cheese, divided
- 1/2 cup whole wheat bread crumbs
- 1 1/2 cup grated Parmesan cheese
- 1/4 teaspoon dried basil
- 1 tablespoon chopped fresh parsley

Directions

1. Preheat the oven to 425 F. Coat a baking dish 9-by-9-inch with a mist of olive oil, then put aside.
2. Add the water, onion, and garlic to a medium saucepan. Cover with a cap and boil for about 10 minutes over low heat or until the onion and garlic are easy to mash with a fork. In a mixer, place the mixture, add salt, pepper, and mustard, and add pulse to merge. Get it to a boil in a big pot of water.
3. Add the spaghetti, then cook until al dente, according to the box instructions.
4. Add the broccoli and cover the pot for the last few minutes after boiling the pasta. Drain the pasta and broccoli after about 3 minutes and run it under cool water so that the pasta doesn't keep frying. Heat the pasta pot and add the onion-garlic paste, chili pepper flakes and 2 tablespoons of ricotta over low heat. Stir until the cheese is incorporated, then gently apply a whisk to the remainder of the ricotta.
5. Add half the cheddar cheese, then whisk until the cheese is molten. Then add the remaining cheddar cheese, stirring until it is melted.
6. Add the cooked pasta and broccoli, then stir with a large spoon until much of the pasta is filled with the sauce.
7. Cover with the bread crumbs, parmesan cheese, and basil, and move to the baking dish. Bake for about 10 minutes, or until the parmesan and bread crumbs begin to tan. Cover with parsley, remove from the oven, and serve warm.

22. Anna's Black Beans

(Ready in 3-4 hours, serve 8, Difficulty: Normal)

Ingredients

- 4 cups dried black beans
- 1–2 bay leaves
- 3/4 teaspoon ground cumin
- 3 teaspoons sea salt
- 1/4 small white onion, slivered
- 2–3 large cloves garlic, whole
- 1–2 dried red chiles/chiles de arbol
- 8–10 cups water

Directions

1. Place all the ingredients in a large pot, and bring to a boil.
2. Lower the heat, and simmer for 2 to 3 hours. Check and stir every 30 to 40 minutes, adding water if necessary.

23. Pinto Beans

(Ready in 2-3 hours, serve 8, Difficulty: Normal)

Ingredients

- 2 cups dried pinto beans
- 1 bay leaf
- 2 large cloves garlic, whole
- 1 large jalapeño chile pepper, top cut off
- 4–5 slivers white onion
- 1 tablespoon sea salt
- 6 cups water

Directions

1. Place all the ingredients in a large pot, and bring to a boil.
2. Lower the heat, and simmer for 2 to 3 hours. Check and stir every 30 to 40 minutes, adding water if necessary.

24. Pumpkin Soup with Whole Wheat Parmesan Croutons

(Ready in 15 min, serve 8, Difficulty: Normal)

Ingredients
CROUTONS

- 2 slices 100% whole wheat bread
- 4 tablespoons extra virgin olive oil
- 3 tablespoons grated Parmesan cheese
- 1 teaspoon dried Italian herbs (premixed, or use thyme,
- rosemary, oregano, parsley, and basil)
- 1/8 teaspoon cracked black pepper

SOUP

- 2 tablespoons extra virgin olive oil
- 1/2 small onion, chopped
- 1 cup diced carrot
- 3 small cloves garlic, minced
- 2 cups canned pumpkin puree
- 1/8 teaspoon ground ginger
- 1/8 teaspoon ground cinnamon
- 1 1/2 teaspoons dried parsley
- Pinch of chile pepper flakes
- 1 1/2 liters low-sodium vegetable or chicken broth

Directions

1. Preheat the oven to 400 F. Toasted the croutons to make the croutons, whole wheat bread, split the slices into small cubes, and placed them in small cubes.
2. On a tray of cookies. Connect the oil and brush with the parmesan cheese, basil, and pepper. Bake for about 5 minutes in the microwave, or for about 5 minutes.
3. Crispy before. Heat the oil in a big pot over low heat to make the soup. Add the ginger, carrot, and onion. Cook until the onion browns and becomes transparent, for 4 to 5 minutes.
4. Apply the flakes of pumpkin, ginger, cinnamon, parsley, and chili pepper and sauté for 1 minute or so. Stir in the broth and get it to a boil. Reduce the flame and boil for 10 minutes or so. Ladle them into serving bowls and line them with two or three croutons per dish.

25. Cauliflower Carrot Soup

(Ready in6-8min| serve8|Difficulty:Normal)

Ingredients

- 1 large head cauliflower, coarsely chopped (about 8 cups)
- 2 tablespoons extra virgin olive oil
- 1/2 small white onion, chopped
- 2 large cloves garlic, chopped
- 1 cup chopped carrot
- 1 quart low-sodium vegetable broth
- 1/2 teaspoon sea salt
- 1/2 teaspoon cracked black pepper
- 1/8 teaspoon chile pepper flakes
- 1/8 teaspoon dried basil

Directions

1. Load a large saucepan with water, and bring it to a boil. Delete from this the cauliflower head's outer leaves, and then cut out the heart. Chop the cauliflower coarsely, and add it to the boiling broth.
2. Cover the pot and simmer for 6 to 8 minutes, or until the cauliflower parts are quickly pierced by a fork. Strain and discard the water from the cauliflower. In the same kettle, heat the oil over a medium heat.
3. Add the carrot, onion, and garlic, and sauté until the onion is translucent. You add the cauliflower. Switch the veggie ladle to a blender.
4. Add 1 cup of broth and mix to blend on low heat, then on high until smooth. To another big jar, move the blended veggies and repeat the process until all the veggies are blended.
5. Heat and season the blended veggies over medium-high heat and with salt, vinegar, flakes of chili pepper, and basil. Get them to a boil, Serve hot.

26. Roasted Butternut Squash Soup

(Ready in30-40min| serve6|Difficulty:Normal)

Ingredients

- 1 large butternut squash or 2 (16-ounce) bags precut butternut squash (to skip the roasting)
- 2 tablespoons extra virgin olive oil
- 1 large clove garlic
- 1/2 white onion, chopped
- 2 1/2 liters low-sodium vegetable or chicken broth, divided
- 1/8 teaspoon cracked black pepper
- 1/4 teaspoon white pepper
- 1 tablespoon chopped fresh parsley
- 1/4 teaspoon chile pepper flakes
- 1 teaspoon finely chopped fresh rosemary
- 3–4 finely minced fresh sage leaves

Directions

1. You should roast the squash a day or two in advance. Only warehouse the
2. In the oven, roasted squash in an airtight jar. Preheat the oven to 400 F. Cut off the top of the squash, then cut the squash in half lengthwise, then use a metal spoon to scoop out the seeds from the middle until no strings or seeds are left. Cover a cookie sheet with a spray of olive oil, put the squash on it and cut down the edges.
3. For about 30 minutes, roast in the oven or until the squash is tender to the touch. Take it out of the oven and let it cool down.
4. Add the oil, garlic, and onion to a big pot over medium heat. Sauté for a couple of minutes, until the onion is light orange. Scoop the roasted squash out of its skin with a spoon while the onion and garlic are frying, and return it to the pot. Mixing Match together, cut up big pieces of squash using a spatula.
5. Add 1 liter of broth, and get it to a boil.
6. Lower the heat and transfer the vegetables to the blender in batches, leaving much of the liquid in the jar. Blend the squash too low for blending, and then too high for smoothness.
7. Add some of the broth if the squash doesn't mix quickly. Put the remainder of the broth and the black pepper, white pepper, parsley, chili pepper flakes, rosemary and sage into the pot until all the squash has been mixed. Bring the broth to a boil and eat tenderly.

27. Broccoli Soup

(Ready in 30-40min| serve 6|Difficulty: Normal)

Ingredients

- 8 cups coarsely chopped broccoli
- 2 tablespoons extra virgin olive oil
- 1 cup chopped white onion
- 2 large cloves garlic
- 3 cups low-sodium chicken broth
- 1/8 teaspoon chile pepper flakes
- 1/4 teaspoon cracked black pepper
- 1/2 cup low-fat milk

Directions

1. To a simmer, put a big pot of water. Add the broccoli and cook for around 8 to 10 minutes, or until the stems are easily pierced by an inserted fork. Drain and set the broccoli aside. Heat the oil in the same pot over a medium heat.
2. Add the onion and garlic and roast, stirring until the onion is translucent, around 2 minutes.
3. Add to the pot the roasted broccoli and the broth and steam for another 4 to 5 minutes. Turn the heat off and, in small batches, move the vegetables and a bit of broth to a blender. At first, blend on medium, and then on high, until smooth. In another pot, pour the blended broth, and repeat until all the broccoli mixture has been blended.
4. Add the flakes of chili pepper, black pepper and milk to the broth, and bring to a boil. Ladle it into bowls, then serve.

28. Mom's Bean Soup

(Ready in 30-40min| serve 6|Difficulty: Normal)

Ingredients

- 6 cups pinto beans in broth
- 1/4 cup chopped white onion
- 1/2 cup chopped Roma tomato
- 2 large avocados, peeled, pitted, and cubed
- 4 tablespoons chopped fresh cilantro
- 4 tablespoons shredded low-fat Monterey Jack cheese
- 4 teaspoons canned chipotle pepper sauce

Directions

1. Get the beans to a boil in a medium to medium-sized kettle. Elevated heat. Turn off the sun. 1 1/2 cups of beans with a ladle Broth into a cup of four.
2. Place the raw, diced onion, tomato, avocado, cilantro, shredded cheese, and chipotle sauce on top of each cup. Immediately serve.

29. Black Bean and Apple Salsa

(Ready in 20min| serve 6|Difficulty: Normal)

Ingredients

- 1 (15-ounce) can black beans, rinsed and drained
- 1/2 large Granny Smith apple, cubed
- 1/4 cup finely chopped red onion
- 1/2 medium serrano chile pepper, unseeded and finely chopped
- 3 tablespoons chopped fresh cilantro
- Juice of 1/2 large lime
- Juice of 1/2 large orange
- 1/8 teaspoon cracked black pepper
- 1/8 teaspoon sea salt

Directions

1. Combine all the ingredients in a large bowl.
2. Before serving, refrigerate for at least 20 minutes so that the flavors blend.

30. Tropical Salsa

(Ready in 20min| serve 6|Difficulty: Normal)

Ingredients

- 1 large mango, peeled, pitted, and diced
- 2 large avocados, peeled, pitted, and diced
- 1 small red bell pepper, diced
- 2 large Roma tomatoes, diced
- 1/2 cup diced red onion
- 3 tablespoons chopped fresh cilantro
- 1/2 large jalapeño chile pepper, finely chopped (seeded for less heat)
- Juice of 1 lime
- 1/8 teaspoon sea salt
- 1/8 teaspoon cracked black pepper

Directions

1. Combine all the ingredients in a large bowl.
2. Before serving, refrigerate for at least 20 minutes so that the flavors blend.

31. Grandma's Guacamole

(Ready in 20min| serve 8|Difficulty: Normal)

Ingredients

- 6 large avocados, pitted
- 1/2 cup chopped Roma tomato
- 1/4 cup chopped white onion
- 1/4 cup chopped fresh cilantro
- Juice of 3–4 limes
- 1/2 teaspoon sea salt
- 1/2 teaspoon cracked black pepper
- 2 tablespoons extra virgin olive oil
- 1/2 jalapeño or serrano chile pepper, finely chopped, optional

Directions

1. Reserve two pits for later use when pitting the avocados.
2. Scoop out the flesh and drop it in a wide bowl. Using a fork to mash to the desired quality, or potato masher.

3. The remaining ingredients are added, and blend well. To help delay the oxidation, or browning, process, store the guacamole with the two pits.

32. Chipotle Dip
(Ready in 20-30min| serve 8|Difficulty: Normal)

Ingredients
- 1 tablespoon extra-virgin olive oil
- 1/2 small white onion, chopped
- 2 large cloves garlic, minced
- 2 teaspoons canned chipotle pepper sauce
- 1 cup low-fat plain Greek yogurt
- 1/8 teaspoon sea salt
- 1/8 teaspoon cracked black pepper

Directions
1. In a small pan over medium-high pressure, heat the oil. Once it is warmed, add the onion and garlic and cook until the onion is translucent for a couple of minutes.
2. Add the chipotle sauce then blend with the garlic and onion. Taking the pan away from the sun.
3. To another cup, move the mixture and apply the yogurt. Mix well. Season to taste with salt and pepper. Refrigerate for 20 to 30 minutes before serving.

33. French Onion Dip
(Ready in 20-30min| serve 8|Difficulty: Normal)

Ingredients
- 2 tablespoons extra virgin olive oil
- 1 small white onion, chopped
- 2 cloves garlic, minced
- 1 cup low-fat plain Greek yogurt
- 1 cup low-fat sour cream
- 2 tablespoons Worcestershire sauce
- 1/8 teaspoon sea salt
- 1/8 teaspoon cracked black pepper
- Minced chives, for garnish

Directions
1. Heat the oil over a low heat in a small pan.
2. Add the garlic and onion, and sauté until the onion turns brown and tender. (Keep the heat mild, and transfer the onion to "sweat" it minimally.) Remove from the heat.
3. Combine the milk, whipped cream, Worcestershire sauce, and salt and pepper in a different bowl to sample. Put a mixture of onion and garlic, then combine well. Garnish with chives that are minced.

34. Tzatziki Greek Yogurt Sauce
(Ready in 20-30min| serve 8|Difficulty: Normal)

Ingredients
- 2 large cloves garlic, very finely chopped
- 1/4 cup finely diced Persian or English cucumber
- 1/4 cup chopped fresh mint leaves
- 1 3/4 cups low-fat plain Greek yogurt
- Juice of 1/2 lemon
- 1 tablespoon extra-virgin olive oil
- 1/4 teaspoon cracked black pepper
- 1/8 teaspoon sea salt

Directions
1. Combine all the chopped ingredients in a large bowl with the yogurt, lemon juice, and oil.
2. Mix well, and add the salt and pepper. Before serving, let the mixture sit for about 30 minutes to an hour so the flavors can meld.

Spinach Artichoke Dip
(Ready in 20-30min, serve 8, Difficulty: Normal)

Ingredients
- 3 cups spinach
- 2 (14-ounce) cans artichoke hearts, rinsed, drained, and
- coarsely chopped
- 1 large clove garlic, finely minced
- 1 cup low-fat plain Greek yogurt
- 1/2 cup low-fat sour cream
- 1/4 teaspoon dried parsley
- 1/4 teaspoon dried basil
- 1/2 cup shredded Parmesan cheese, divided
- 1/2 cup shredded part-skim mozzarella cheese, divided
- 1/8 teaspoon sea salt
- 1/8 teaspoon cracked black pepper

Directions
1. Preheat the oven to 400 F. Flush a kettle with water in a medium size pot, and Bring it to a boil.
2. Add the spinach, then rinse the spinach in a colander for 1 minute. Let the water cool off, and then wring it out by hand. Move and slice coarsely to a cutting board.
3. Spinach, artichoke hearts, garlic, yogurt, sour cream, dried herbs, salt and pepper, and half of the two cheeses are added to the food processor. To the optimal consistency, pump the mixture a few times. Process in batches if necessary.
4. Move the mixture and spread it out thinly with a rubber spatula into an ovenproof serving dish.
5. Round it off with the remainder of the mozzarella and parmesan. Bake for 15 to 20 minutes, or until the top of the cheese is fully melted and browned. Remove from the oven, and quickly serve.

35. Delicious Bruschetta
(Ready in 20-30min| serve 8|Difficulty: Normal)

Ingredients
- 1 large whole wheat baguette (about 32 slices)

- 5 large heirloom tomatoes of various colors, cored and chopped finely
- 3/4 cup finely chopped fresh Italian basil
- 8–10 fresh mint leaves, finely chopped
- 2 large cloves garlic, finely minced
- 1/2 cup finely minced red onion
- 1/4 cup extra virgin olive oil
- 1/3 cup balsamic vinegar
- 1/4 teaspoon sea salt
- 1/4 teaspoon cracked black pepper

Directions
1. Preheat the oven to 400 F. Cut the baguette into rounds 1/4-inch thick. Arrange the slices on a baking sheet and put them on the oven's central shelf.
2. Toast them for around 5 minutes in the oven, or until the sides turn a little rough and light brown. Take them out of the oven and let them cool down. In a colander, wash the sliced tomatoes.
3. Combine the tomatoes with the basil, garlic, and onion in a large cup. Stir in the oil, vinegar, salt, and pepper. For at least 30 minutes, refrigerate the mixture so that the tastes will meld. Cover the tomato mixture with each toasted baguette piece.

36. Roasted Zucchini Crostini Dip
(Ready in20-30min| serve6|Difficulty:Normal)

Ingredients
- 2 large green zucchini, sliced lengthwise (about 1/4 inch thick)
- 1 large yellow zucchini, sliced lengthwise (about 1/4 inch thick)
- 1/2 small red onion, coarsely chopped
- 2 large cloves garlic, whole
- 1/4 cup balsamic vinegar
- 1/4 teaspoon cracked black pepper
- 1/4 teaspoon chile pepper flakes
- 1/4 teaspoon dried basil
- 1/8 cup extra virgin olive oil
- 1/4 cup grated Parmesan cheese
- 1–2 tablespoons water, as needed

Directions
1. Preheat the oven to 400 F.
2. Arrange the sliced zucchini and diced onion along with the garlic in a roasting pan.
3. Add the balsamic vinegar and season with black pepper, flakes of chili pepper, and basil. Roast for 10 to 12 minutes or until the onion begins to brown and is tender.
4. Move the cooked vegetables to a food processor or blender. Drizzle gently with olive oil when mixing, alternating with parmesan. A dense spread should be the result. When mixing, apply up to 2 tablespoons of water for a thinner consistency.

37. Hummus Dip with Curried Pita Chips
(Ready in5-8min| serve6|Difficulty:Normal)

Ingredients
PITA CHIPS
- 2 100% whole wheat pitas
- 1–2 tablespoons curry powder

HUMMUS DIP
- 2 (15-ounce) cans garbanzo beans, rinsed and drained
- 1/4 cup tahini paste
- Juice of 2 lemons
- 2 small cloves garlic, minced
- 1/4 teaspoon sea salt
- 1/2 teaspoon cracked black pepper
- 5 tablespoons extra virgin olive oil, divided
- 1/2 teaspoon dried oregano

Directions
1. Preheat the oven to 400 F.
2. Break the pitas and put them on a cookie into 1-inch bits. Sprinkle with curry powder and fry for around 5 to 8 minutes, or until crunchy. Create the dip by mixing the beans, tahini, lemon juice, garlic, salt, and pepper in a food processor while the pita chips are baking.
3. Drizzle in 4 teaspoons of the oil when cooking until there are no big bits and the hummus is smooth.
4. Add 1 tablespoon of water at a time when mixing, if a thinner hummus is needed. Move to a serving bowl, cover with dried oregano, drizzle with the remaining 1 tablespoon of olive oil and serve with pita chips of warm curry.

38. Spicy Sun-Roasted Tomato Hummus
(Ready in20-30min| serve6|Difficulty:Normal)

Ingredients
- 2 (15-ounce) cans garbanzo beans, rinsed and drained
- 1/4 cup tahini paste
- Juice of 2 lemons
- 2 large cloves garlic
- 2 tablespoons sun-roasted tomato slices
- 1 dried red chile/chile de arbol
- 1/2 teaspoon sea salt
- 1/2 teaspoon cracked black pepper
- 5 tablespoons extra virgin olive oil, divided

Directions
1. Place the beans, tahini, lemon juice, garlic, tomato, chile, salt, and pepper in a food processor.
2. While processing, drizzle in the oil until there are no large pieces and the hummus is smooth. If a thinner

hummus is desired, add 1 tablespoon water at a time while blending.
3. Transfer to a serving dish, top with dried oregano and a drizzle of olive oil, and serve.

39. Grilled Rustic Corn

(Ready in 15-20min| serve6|Difficulty:Normal)

Ingredients

- 4 large ears of corn
- 1/4 teaspoon sea salt
- 1/4 teaspoon cracked black pepper
- 4 tablespoons extra virgin olive oil
- 4 large cloves garlic, minced finely

Directions

1. Peel the husks back and extract the silk from each corn ear.
2. Mix the salt and pepper together in a shallow dish. Sprinkle each with minced garlic and then the salt and pepper mixture.
3. Spray the kernels with oil. Fold the husks back over the maize and grill until cooked through, 12 to 15 minutes, rotating periodically, over low heat.

40. Grilled Sweet Potato Steak Fries

(Ready in 15-20min serve6|Difficulty:Normal)

Ingredients

- 1 pound (about 4 medium) sweet potatoes, unpeeled
- 4 tablespoons extra virgin olive oil
- 1/2 teaspoon ground cumin
- 1/2 teaspoon cayenne pepper
- 1/4 teaspoon cracked black pepper
- 1/4 teaspoon sea salt

Directions

1. Load a large saucepan with water, and bring it to a boil.
2. Add the sweet potatoes and cook for 10 to 12 minutes, or until the inserted fork glides easily in, but the middle of the potato is slightly firm.
3. Strain to let the potatoes cool. When cooled, cut them lengthwise in half and then lengthwise into 1/2-inch-thick bits. The skin may peel a little, but as it provides nutritious fiber, hold it on. Brush each slice with oil and sprinkle with cumin, black pepper, and cayenne.
4. Arrange it on the grill and cook on each side for 1 to 2 minutes. Remove from the sun, season and serve with salt.

41. Grilled Asparagus

(Ready in 2mi| serve6|Difficulty:Normal)

Ingredients

- 1-pound asparagus
- 5 tablespoons extra virgin olive oil
- Grated zest of 1 large lemon
- Juice of 1/2 lemon
- 3 large cloves garlic, minced
- 1/4 teaspoon sea salt
- 1/8 teaspoon cracked black pepper

Directions

1. Break off the dense fibrous ends of the asparagus spears and remove them. Lay the spears in a single, even plate, and drizzle with oil in a large baking dish or rimmed cookie sheets.
2. To cover uniformly, roll the spears in the grease. Fill the top with the lemon zest, lemon juice, garlic, salt, and pepper. To coat both sides with the seasonings, roll the spears again.
3. Place the spears on a hot grill and continually rotate them so that they do not fire. For around 2 minutes, grill and return to the marinating pan for serving.

42. Grilled Collard Greens

(Ready in 2min| serve|Difficulty:Normal)

Ingredients

- 1-pound collard greens
- 4 tablespoons red wine vinegar
- 5 tablespoons extra virgin olive oil
- 1/4 teaspoon sea salt
- 1/4 teaspoon cracked black pepper

Directions

1. Break off the stems' thick ends, and then wash the greens.
2. And pat them dry altogether. Directly lay each leaf on a hot barbecue. Flip each leaf over after 30 seconds.
3. Remove the leaves as they begin to wither and blacken, place them in a big jar, and cover with a lid. Let them remain in the covered pot for about 5 minutes to finish steaming after all the leaves have been grilled.
4. Take the leaves from the pot and cut them into pieces that are 2 inches wide. Cover with the vinegar, grease, salt, and pepper to taste. Put them back in the pot. Serve chilled or hot.

43. Not Your Mama's Green Bean Casserole

(Ready in 2min| serve6|Difficulty:Normal)

Ingredients

- 4 1/2 cups green beans
- 1/4 cup chopped shallots
- 2 large cloves garlic, finely minced
- 1/8 teaspoon sea salt
- Cracked black pepper
- 2 tablespoons extra virgin olive oil
- 1 large lemon
- 3/4 cup chopped toasted hazelnuts

Directions

1. Break off the ends of the green beans and put them. Bring yourself a to boil a big pot of water, add the

beans and cook them over a boil for just about 5 minutes.
2. In a colander, remove them, and then rinse with ice water. (This slows the cooking process in order to keep the beans bright green and crispy.) Heat the oil over medium heat in a wide pan.
3. Once the pan is warmed, add the garlic and shallots and cook for a couple of minutes before they start browning.
4. Add the green beans and, to taste, season with salt and pepper. Grate into the paste the zest of the lemon. Then split the lemon in half, then add the juice to it. Cook for 5 to 7 more minutes, or until fully heated. To a broad serving bowl, pass the green bean mixture, and finish with the sliced hazelnuts. Immediately serve.

44. Brussels Sprouts Casserole

(Ready in 2min| serve6|Difficulty:Normal)

Ingredients

- 1 1/2 pounds (6 cups) Brussels sprouts
- 2 thick slices pancetta, diced
- 2 tablespoons chopped shallot
- 2 large cloves garlic, finely minced
- 1/2 cup toasted pine nuts, divided
- 1/2 teaspoon cracked black pepper

Directions

1. Preheat the oven to 400 F.
2. To a simmer, put a big pot of water. Peel off and compost the Brussels sprouts' outer leaves and cut the roots. Halve the Brussels sprouts, then add to the boiling broth. Boil for 10 to 15 minutes, or before a fork pierces the sprouts quickly. Drain yourself and set aside. Before dicing, strip the fat from the pancetta. Over medium prepare, heat a broad saucepan, and add the pancetta. Sauté for about 4 to 5 minutes before brown and crispy. To drain, move the pancetta to paper towels.
3. To the same pan, add the garlic and shallots and half the pine nuts. Cook for around 1 to 2 minutes, before the nuts turn light brown, and then add the sprouts from Brussels. For an extra 2 or 3 minutes, cook them until they consume the flavors of pancetta and garlic.
4. Pour the mixture into an 8-inch by 8-inch baking dish, season with pepper and cook for 10 to 15 minutes or until brown on top of the Brussels sprouts. Remove from the oven, and before eating, cover with the remaining pine nuts.

45. Kale and Butternut Squash Sauté

(Ready in 2min| serve6|Difficulty:Normal)

Ingredients

- 1-pound kale
- 1 pound (4 cups) pre-cut butternut squash
- 2 tablespoons extra virgin olive oil
- 1 tablespoon shallot, finely chopped
- 2 large cloves garlic, minced
- 1/2 cup toasted pine nuts
- Pinch of chile pepper flakes
- 1/8 teaspoon sea salt
- 1/8 teaspoon cracked black pepper
- 4 tablespoons grated Pecorino Romano cheese

Directions

1. Chop off and discard the kale's raw ends. Clean, rinse. Wash, dry Chop the kale deeply and coarsely. Heat the oil in a large pan over low heat.
2. Add the squash and cook for 15 to 20 minutes or until browned and quick to glide in with the inserted fork.
3. Add the shallot, garlic, chili flakes, salt, and pepper and simmer for 1 minute. Sauté for an additional 3 minutes, add the pine nuts, then simmer for another minute. Move to a serving dish with the mixture, and finish with Pecorino Romano.

46. Sautéed Greens with Cannellini Beans

(Ready in 2min| serve6|Difficulty:Normal)

Ingredients

- 1-pound mixed greens (such as mustard greens, kale, collard
- greens, and chard), coarsely chopped
- 3 tablespoons extra virgin olive oil
- 1/2 small red onion, finely chopped
- 2 large cloves garlic, minced
- 1/4 teaspoon chile pepper flakes
- 1/8 teaspoon sea salt
- 1/8 teaspoon cracked black pepper
- 3 tablespoons water or chicken broth
- 1/2 tablespoon lemon zest
- 1 (15-ounce) can cannellini beans, rinsed and drained
- 1/4 cup toasted pine nuts

Directions

1. Wash the greens, and dry them thoroughly. Heat the oil in a large sauté pan over medium heat, and add the onion.
2. After a minute, add the garlic and chile pepper flakes, and once the garlic becomes fragrant, add the greens, and season with salt and pepper. They will reduce in size quite a bit. Toss frequently to avoid burning.
3. Add the water or broth, and cover with a lid. After about 3 minutes, remove the lid, add the beans, and cook for another 2 minutes to heat the beans through. Transfer to a serving dish, and top with the toasted pine nuts.

47. Roasted Cauliflower

(Ready in 2min| serve6|Difficulty:Normal)

Ingredients

- 4 cups cauliflower florets (1 small head cauliflower)
- 4 tablespoons extra virgin olive oil
- 3 large cloves garlic, minced
- 1/2 teaspoon chile pepper flakes
- Grated zest of 1 large lemon
- 1/8 teaspoon sea salt
- 1/8 teaspoon cracked black pepper
- 3 tablespoons chopped fresh basil

Directions

1. Preheat the oven to 400 F. Break and discard the stems and the cauliflower heart. In an 8-by 8-inch baking dish, put the cauliflower head. Sprinkle with the oil and then apply the garlic, chili pepper flakes, lemon zest, salt and pepper to the mixture.
2. Shake the pan a little until the oil spills and the cauliflower is coated with the ingredients. To keep the cauliflower from sticking, cook for 15 to 20 minutes, shaking the pan after 10 minutes. Cover with fresh basil, remove from the sun, and serve immediately.

48. Sautéed Vegetables

(Ready in 5min| serve6|Difficulty:Normal)

Ingredients

- 1-pound asparagus
- 2 tablespoons extra virgin olive oil
- 1/4 white onion, chopped
- 1 large clove garlic, chopped
- 1 large green zucchini, sliced
- 1 large yellow zucchini, sliced
- 1 tablespoon chopped fresh parsley
- Juice of 1/2 lemon
- 1/8 teaspoon sea salt
- 1/8 teaspoon cracked black pepper

Directions

1. Break off the rough ends of the asparagus spears and remove them. Heat the oil in a large pan over low heat.
2. Add the onion and garlic and add the asparagus after a minute or two.
3. Add the zucchini, parsley, and lemon juice after 2 to 3 minutes. Cook for another 4 to 5 minutes, then remove it from the sun. Prior to eating, season with salt and pepper to taste.

49. Grilled Eggplant and Zucchini

(Ready in 10-15min| serve6|Difficulty:Normal)

Ingredients

- 1 large eggplant, sliced into 1/2-inch rounds
- 2 zucchini, sliced lengthwise
- 1/4 teaspoon sea salt, divided
- 1/8 teaspoon cracked black pepper
- 1/4 teaspoon dried parsley
- 1/4 teaspoon dried basil
- 1/4 teaspoon dried oregano
- 6 tablespoons balsamic vinegar
- 4 tablespoons extra virgin olive oil

Directions

1. Lay the sliced eggplant on paper towels, and sprinkle each slice with a pinch of salt to pull out excess moisture. After 10 to 15 minutes, pat the slices dry with paper towels.
2. Arrange the eggplant and zucchini on a cookie sheet with edges on it. Sprinkle pepper and dried herbs over the veggies, and drizzle with vinegar and oil.
3. Grill the veggies on a hot grill or grill pan for 4 to 6 minutes, flipping halfway through. Remove from the grill or grill pan and serve.

50. Cilantro-Lime Brown Rice

(Ready in 40min| serve6|Difficulty:Normal)

Ingredients

- 3/4 cup uncooked brown rice
- 1 1/2 cups low-sodium vegetable broth
- Juice of 1 lime
- 1 tablespoon chopped fresh cilantro

Directions

1. In a small kettle, over high heat, put the rice and the broth to a boil.
2. Cover the kettle, reduce the heat to medium, and boil forn about 40 minutes or until the rice is cooked and the liquid absorbed.
3. Fluff the rice with a fork until it is thoroughly cooked, add the lime juice and cilantro, and stir to blend properly.

51. Plain and Simple Couscous

(Ready in 2min| serve6|Difficulty:Normal)

Ingredients

- 3/4 cup uncooked whole wheat couscous
- 3/4 cup low-sodium vegetable broth
- 1 tablespoon extra-virgin olive oil
- 1/8 teaspoon cracked black pepper

Directions

1. Heat a small pot over medium heat until lightly browned then fragrant, and add the couscous to toast it.
2. Toast for about 2 minutes, continuously stirring. Place couscous temporarily in a cup. To the kettle, add the broth, and bring it to a boil. Then the couscous is applied and the pot is removed from the heat.
3. Cover and quit for 5 minutes to calm down. Using a fork to fluff the couscous, drizzle with oil, and sprinkle with some pepper before eating.

52. Quinoa and Veggies

(Ready in 2min| serve6|Difficulty:Normal)

Ingredients

- 1 cup uncooked quinoa

- 2 cups vegetable broth
- 2 tablespoons extra virgin olive oil
- 1/4 cup chopped red onion
- 1 small clove garlic, minced
- 1 large zucchini, chopped into small cubes
- 1/8 teaspoon chile pepper flakes
- 3 cups spinach

Directions

1. Rinse the quinoa in order to (if not prerinsed). In a large pot, put the quinoa and broth and bring it to a boil. Reduce heat to low and cover with a slightly a jar shaped lid.
2. Simmer for 15 to 20 minutes or until the liquid is drained and the quinoa is uncoiled and al dente. Over medium pressure, heat the oil in a separate pan.
3. Add the onion, zucchini, and garlic, and roast until the onion is translucent. Season with chili flakes and add the cooked quinoa vegetables to the pot.
4. Add the spinach to the jar, stir, and cover. Just let it rest for five minutes. Serve it sweet.

53. Healthier Stuffing

(Ready in 2min| serve6|Difficulty:Normal)

Ingredients

- 7 to 8 slices whole wheat bread, cut in 1-inch cubes (4 cups)
- 4 spicy Italian turkey or chicken sausages
- 3 tablespoons extra virgin olive oil
- 2 ribs celery, chopped
- 2 large cloves garlic, minced
- 1 medium white onion, chopped
- 1 cup thinly sliced cremini mushrooms
- 1/2 cup white wine
- 2–3 cups low-sodium chicken broth
- 2 tablespoons chopped fresh parsley
- 3-4 large fresh sage leaves, finely minced
- 1 cup chopped walnuts
- 1 cup dried cranberries

Directions

1. Preheat the oven to 375°F to create the bread cubes. You can, you can, use a small whole wheat or whole grain loaf or use sandwich bread with whole wheat or whole grain, but please note that this recipe only includes 4 cups of cubed bread.
2. On a baking sheet, place the cubes equally, and toast in the oven for about 5 minutes. To move the pieces around a little, shake the pan and bake for another 5 minutes, or until most pieces on top are toasted and crunchy. Take it out of the oven and place it in a big container.
3. Cover with a cloth and keep overnight at room temperature, so that the cubes become stale and rough. Remove the casings from the sausages
4. to produce the stuffing, then crumble the beef. Heat the oil in a large pan over low heat.
5. Add the sausage and celery, then simmer for 6 to 8 minutes or so. With a slotted spoon, scrape the mixture and wash on multiple layers of paper towels. Add the garlic, onion, and mushrooms to the same plate.
6. To mix the flavors, apply the wine and scratch the bottom of the pan. Simmer for a few minutes and then, a handful at a time, add the meat mixture and bread cubes.
7. Add the broth, parsley, sage, walnuts, and cranberries to 2 cups. Cover the pan and simmer for about 5 to 6 minutes, before the mixture starts to bubble. When a wetter stuffing is desired, add the remaining cup of broth. Withdraw from the heat, and serve.

54. Black Beans and Brown Rice

(Ready in about 30 min| Serve 4 | Difficulty: Normal)

Ingredients

- 2 teaspoons olive oil1 small yellow onion, finely chopped
- 1 clove garlic, minced
- ½ cup long-grain brown rice
- 1½ cups water½ teaspoon kosher salt
- 1 (15-ounce) can reduced-sodium black beans, drained and rinsed
- 2 tablespoons finely chopped fresh cilantro

Directions

1. Heat oil over medium heat in a small saucepan. Add the onion and garlic and cook, occasionally stirring, for about 5 minutes, until tender. Attach the rice and stir thoroughly.
2. Stir in the salt and water and bring it to a boil. Lower the heat and cover it tightly. Simmer until the rice is tender and almost all the liquid has been absorbed about 40 minutes. Attach the beans, but do not stir in the rice with them. Cover the saucepan again and cook for about 5 minutes, until the liquid is absorbed and the beans are hot. Remove from the heat and leave for 5 minutes to stand.
3. With a fork, stir in the coriander, fluffing the rice as you do so. Transfer and serve hot in a serving dish.

55. Quick "Baked" Beans

(Ready in about 30 Minutes | Serve 4 | Difficulty: Normal)

Ingredients

- 1 strip reduced-sodium bacon, coarsely chopped
- 1 teaspoon canola oil
- 1 small yellow onion, chopped
- 1 small red bell pepper, cored and cut into ½-inch dice
- 1 Granny Smith apple, cored and cut into ½-inch dice
- 1 (15-ounce) can no-salt-added cannellini beans, drained and rinsed
- 2 tablespoons no-salt-added tomato ketchup

- 1 tablespoon amber agave nectar, maple syrup, or honey
- 1 tablespoon cider vinegar

Directions

1. In a medium saucepan, cook the bacon and oil together over medium heat, occasionally stirring, until crisp and browned, for about 6 minutes. Add the onion, bell pepper, and apple and cook until the onion softens, occasionally stirring, for about 5 minutes.
2. Stir in the beans, agave, ketchup, and vinegar. Cook until the sauce has thickened slightly, stirring periodically, around 10 minutes. Serve hot, serve,

56. Baby Bok Choy and Shiitake Mushrooms

(Ready in about 30 Minutes | Serve 4 | Difficulty: Normal)

Ingredients

- 2 teaspoons canola or corn oil
- 8 shiitake mushrooms, stems discarded, cut in half vertically
- 1 scallion, white and green parts, finely chopped
- 1 tablespoon unpeeled finely shredded fresh ginger
- 2 cloves garlic, minced6 baby bok choy (6 ounces), well rinsed
- ½ cup Homemade Chicken Broth or canned low-sodium chicken broth
- ¼ cup plus 1 tablespoon water
- 2 teaspoons reduced-sodium soy sauce
- ⅛ teaspoon crushed hot red pepper flakes
- 1 teaspoon cornstarch

Directions

1. Heat oil over medium-high heat in a large nonstick skillet. Add the mushrooms and cook, occasionally stirring, until lightly browned around 6 minutes.
2. Apply the scallion, ginger and garlic and mix for about 30 seconds, until fragrant. In the skillet, arrange the bok choy. Bring to a boil, add the broth, ¼ cup sugar, soy sauce, and hot pepper. Lower the heat to a low level and cover. When pierced with the tip of a small, sharp knife, simmer until the bok choy is just tender, 7 to 10 minutes.
3. Move the vegetable mixture to a serving bowl using a slotted spoon. In a ramekin or custard cup, add the remaining 1 tablespoon of water, sprinkle with the cornstarch, and mix until dissolved. Whisk in the skillet to thicken the sauce and bring it to a simmer. Through the skillet, pour any juices from the serving bowl and whisk. Pour over the vegetables with the sauce and serve sweet.

57. Broccoli Ziti

(Ready in about 30 Minutes | Serve 4 | Difficulty: Normal)

Ingredients

- 1 tablespoon olive oil1 clove garlic, minced
- 1 broccoli head (about 14 ounces)
- 1½ cups ziti or other bowlular pasta
- Pinch of kosher salt
- Pinch of freshly ground black pepper

Directions

1. Over high heat, bring a big pot of water to a boil.
2. In a small skillet, heat the oil and garlic together over medium heat, frequently stirring, until the garlic is tender and fragrant but not browned, for about 2 minutes. Remove and set aside from the sun.
3. Trim the broccoli and cut the florets off the stalks. With a vegetable peeler, peel the stalks (don't worry about getting every bit of the peel-off) and cut into 1⁄4-inch-thick slices crosswise. Break the florets into parts that are bite-sized.
4. Add the broccoli to the boiling water and cook for about 5 minutes, until crisp-tender. Move the broccoli to a bowl using a wire sieve or a skimmer. Let the water boil.
5. Add ziti and cook until al dente, according to the product instructions. Return the broccoli to the bath at the last minute. Drain and move the ziti and broccoli to a serving dish. Stir in a mixture of garlic-oil, salt, and pepper. Serve hot, serve.

58. Broccoli Rabe with Pine Nuts

(Ready in about 30 Minutes | Serve 4 | Difficulty: Normal)

Ingredients

- 1 bunch broccoli rabe, coarsely chopped into ¾-inch-wide pieces
- ¼ cup pine nuts
- 2 teaspoons olive oil
- 2 cloves garlic, minced
- 2 teaspoons red wine vinegar
- ¼ teaspoon kosher salt

Directions

1. In a large bowl of cold water, rinse the broccoli rabe well, then take the pieces out of the water, leave some grit in the bowl behind, and move to another bowl; do not drain.
2. Heat a medium, nonstick skillet over medium heat. Add the pine nuts and cook, stirring periodically, for about 2 minutes, until toasted. To a small tray, move the nuts.
3. In the skillet, cook the oil and garlic over medium heat, frequently stirring, until the garlic softens, for about 1 minute. Add broccoli rabe and any sticking water to the skillet in batches. Cover and cook, stirring periodically, for about 15 minutes, until tender. Stir the vinegar in. With the salt, season and stir in the pine nuts. Transfer and serve hot in a serving dish.

59. Roasted Brussels Sprouts with Toasted Almonds

(Ready in about 30 Minutes | Serve 4 | Difficulty: Normal)

Ingredients

1. Olive oil in a pump sprayer
2. 10 ounces Brussels sprouts, trimmed and halved

3. ¼ cup sliced almonds, toasted
4. 1 tablespoon sherry vinegar
5. ⅛ teaspoon freshly ground black pepper

Directions

1. Preheat the oven to 400 F. Using oil to spray a large baking sheet.
2. On the baking sheet, spread out the Brussels sprouts and spray them with oil. Bake for 30 to 40 minutes, stirring periodically, until barely tender with brown edges.
3. Transfer to a dish for serving. Sprinkle and toss with almonds, vinegar, and seasoning. Serve it wet.

60. Baby Carrots and Edamame with Ginger-Lime Butter

(Ready in about 30 Minutes | Serve 4 | Difficulty: Normal)

Ingredients

- 8 ounces baby-cut carrots
- 1 cup thawed frozen edamame
- 2 teaspoons unsalted butter
- 2 teaspoons peeled and minced fresh ginger
- Freshly grated zest of ½ lime1 tablespoon fresh lime juice
- Pinch of kosher salt
- Pinch of freshly ground black pepper

Directions

1. Over high heat, bring a medium saucepan of water to a boil. Add the carrots and cook for about 6 minutes, until nearly tender. Attach the edamame and cook for about 2 more minutes until heated. In a colander, rinse.
2. In a saucepan, cook the butter and ginger together over medium heat, frequently stirring, until the ginger softens, for about 2 minutes. Add the vegetables, juice, and lime zest, salt, and pepper and combine well. Switch to a serving bowl and serve hot

61. Roasted Cauliflower with Sage

(Ready in about 30 Minutes | Serve 4 | Difficulty: Normal)

Ingredients

1. 1 tablespoon olive oil, preferably extra-virgin, plus more in a pump sprayer
2. 1 cauliflower (about 1¼ pounds)
3. 1 clove garlic, minced
4. 2 tablespoons finely chopped fresh sage

Directions

1. Preheat the oven to 400 F. Using oil to spray a large rimmed baking sheet.
2. Trim the cauliflower and split it into florets that are bite-sized. Spread and spray with oil on the baking sheet. Bake for about 30 minutes, stirring periodically, until crisp-tender and finely browned around the edges.
3. Meanwhile, in a small saucepan, put the 1 tablespoon oil and garlic to a simmer. Remove and set aside from the sun
4. From the oven, cut the cauliflower. Garlic-oil and sage are applied and blend well. Move to a dish for serving and serve wet.

62. Collard Greens with Bacon

(Ready in about 30 Minutes | Serve 4 | Difficulty: Normal)

Ingredients

1. 2 slices reduced-sodium bacon, coarsely chopped
2. 1 teaspoon vegetable oil
3. 1 medium yellow onion, chopped
4. 2 cloves garlic, minced
5. 1 (1-pound) bag chopped collard greens, rinsed but not dried
6. ½ cup of water
7. ½ teaspoon crushed hot red pepper
8. 2 teaspoons cider vinegar

Directions

1. In a large saucepan, cook the bacon and oil over medium heat, stirring regularly, until the bacon is crisp and browned, for about 6 minutes. Attach the onion and cook for about 5 minutes, occasionally stirring, until golden. Stir in the garlic and cook for about 30 seconds until it is fragrant.
2. Stir in the collard greens in batches with some sticking water and cover, making the first batch before adding another one. Add the hot pepper and water. Decrease the heat and cover to medium-low. Cook, stirring periodically, for about 30 minutes, until the collard greens are very tender. Stir the vinegar in.
3. To a serving dish, switch the collard greens and any cooking liquid and serve soft.

63. Corn and Tomato Sauté

(Ready in about 30 Minutes | Serve 4 | Difficulty: Normal)

Ingredients

- Olive oil in a pump sprayer
- 1½ cups fresh corn kernels (from 3 ears of corn)
- 1 cup cherry or grape tomatoes, cut in halves crosswise
- 1 tablespoon finely chopped shallot
- ½ teaspoon finely chopped fresh thyme or ¼ teaspoon dried thyme
- ¼ teaspoon kosher salt
- ⅛ teaspoon freshly ground black pepper

Directions

1. Spray the broad nonstick skillet over medium-high heat with oil and heat. Add the corn and cook until the kernels begin to brown, stirring periodically, for about 5 minutes.
2. Stir in the tomatoes, shallot, thyme, salt, and pepper, and cook for around 3 minutes, frequently stirring, until the tomatoes are completely cooked. Serve it warm.

64. Corn and Vegetable Pudding

(Ready in about 30 Minutes | Serve 4 | Difficulty: Normal)

Ingredients

- 2 teaspoons canola oil, plus more in a pump sprayer
- 1 medium red bell pepper, cored and cut into ½-inch dice
- 2 scallions, white and green parts, finely chopped
- 1 clove garlic, minced
- ½ jalapeño, seeded and minced
- 2 cups fresh corn kernels (cut from 3 large ears of corn)
- 2 teaspoons cornstarch
- 1 cup low-fat (1%) milk
- 1 large egg plus
- 2 large egg whites
- ½ teaspoon kosher salt
- ¼ teaspoon freshly ground black pepper

Directions

1. Preheat the oven to 350°F. Using canola oil to spray an 1½-quart or 2-quart round baking dish.
2. Heat 2 teaspoons of oil over medium heat in a medium nonstick skillet. Add the bell pepper, scallions, garlic, and jalapeño and cook for around 5 minutes, frequently stirring, until the bell pepper is tender. Add the corn kernels and cook for about 5 minutes, frequently stirring, until thoroughly cooked. Place in a medium bowl and leave to cool slightly.
3. In a medium cup, spray the cornstarch over the milk and whisk to dissolve. Whisk together the potato, egg whites, salt, and pepper. Pour the corn mixture over and stir thoroughly. Pour it into the dish for baking.
4. Bake for about 30 minutes until a knife inserted in the middle of the pudding comes out clean. Leave for 5 minutes to stand, then serve hot.

65. Italian Kale and White Beans

(Ready in about 30 Minutes | Serve 4 | Difficulty: Normal)

Ingredients

- 1 tablespoon olive oil
- 1 medium yellow onion, chopped
- 3 cloves garlic, minced
- 1 pound dark kale
- ¼ teaspoon kosher salt
- ⅛ teaspoon crushed hot red pepper
- 1 (15-ounce) can no-salt-added cannellini beans, drained and rinsed
- 1 tablespoon red wine vinegar

Directions

1. Over medium heat, heat the oil in a big saucepan. Add the onion and garlic and cook for about 5 minutes, sometimes stirring, until the onion becomes translucent.
2. Pull off and discard the thick stems from the kale, meanwhile. Stack the kale and coarsely slice crosswise into ½-inch-thick slices, taking a few bits at a time. Transfer to a large bowl of cold water and agitate to loosen some grit. Lift the kale out of the water, leaving some dirt behind. Do not make the kale dry.
3. To the saucepan, add the kale, salt, and hot pepper. Cover and cook, stirring periodically, for about 10 minutes, until the kale is almost tender. Stir in the beans and cook, stirring periodically, for about 5 minutes, until the kale is tender and the beans are cooked through. Remove and stir in the vinegar from the sun. Serve hot, serve,

66. Roasted Mushrooms with Thyme and Garlic

(Ready in about 30 Minutes | Serve 4 | Difficulty: Normal)

Ingredients

- 2 (10-ounce) containers white mushrooms, quartered (small mushrooms can be halved)
- 2 tablespoons extra-virgin olive oil
- 1 teaspoon finely chopped fresh thyme
- ½ teaspoon kosher salt
- ¼ teaspoon freshly ground black pepper
- 2 garlic cloves, thinly sliced

Directions

1. Preheat the oven to 400 F.
2. To coat the mushrooms, combine the mushrooms, oil, thyme, salt, and pepper in a large cup, on a wide-rimmed baking sheet, spread. Bake the mushrooms for about 25 minutes, stirring periodically, until they are tender and starting to brown. Tuck the slices of garlic under the mushrooms (where they are covered and do not burn) and cook for around 5 more minutes, until the garlic softens. Serve hot, serve,

67. Smashed Yukon Golds with Buttermilk and Scallions

(Ready in about 30 Minutes | Serve 4 | Difficulty: Normal)

Ingredients

- 2 pounds Yukon Gold potatoes, scrubbed but unpeeled
- 1 tablespoon unsalted butter
- 2 scallions, white and green parts, finely chopped
- ⅓ cup buttermilk, at room temperature
- ½ teaspoon kosher salt
- ¼ teaspoon freshly ground black pepper

Directions

1. In a medium saucepan, put the potatoes and add enough cold water to cover 1 inch. Cover and bring the saucepan to a boil over high heat. Reduce the heat to medium and set the honeycomb lid. Cook for about 25 minutes until the potatoes are tender when

pierced with the tip of a sharp knife. Drain well, then return to the casserole. Do not exfoliate the potatoes.
2. Melt butter over medium-high heat in a small nonstick saucepan. Add the scallions and cook, stirring periodically, until they begin to brown, around 3 minutes. Apply it to your potatoes.
3. Mash the potatoes coarsely, adding the buttermilk using a potato masher or a large slotted spoon. Season with pepper and salt. Switch to a serving bowl and serve hot

68. Basic Brown Rice
(Ready in about 30 Minutes | Serve 4 | Difficulty: Normal)

Ingredients
- 1 cup of brown rice
- 1 dried bay leaf
- 2 cups of water

Directions
1. In a small heavy-bottomed saucepan, bring the rice, bay leaf, and 2 cups of water over high heat to a boil. Lower the heat to medium-low and cover the saucepan tightly. Simmer until the rice is tender and has absorbed the water, without stirring, for about 40 minutes. Apply 2 tablespoons of hot water to the saucepan if the water evaporates until the rice is tender (do not stir it in). Remove from the heat and leave for 5 minutes to stand.
2. With a fork, fluff the rice. Dispose of the Bay Leaf. Drain the rice in a wire sieve if any water remains in the saucepan when the rice is tender. Serve hot, serve,

69. Indian Rice with Cashews, Raisins, and Spices
(Ready in about 30 Minutes | Serve 4 | Difficulty: Normal)

Ingredients
- 2 teaspoons canola oil1 small yellow onion, finely chopped
- 1 teaspoon peeled and minced fresh ginger
- 1 small clove garlic, minced
- ⅔ cup basmati rice
- ¼ teaspoon ground turmeric (optional)1 (2-inch) piece cinnamon stick, or ⅛ teaspoon ground cinnamon
- ⅛ teaspoon ground coriander
- ⅛ teaspoon freshly ground black pepper
- 1⅓ cups Homemade Chicken Broth or canned low-sodium chicken broth
- ⅓ cup coarsely chopped unsalted cashews
- ¼ cup dark raisins

Directions
1. Over medium pressure, heat the oil in a medium saucepan. Add the onion, ginger, and garlic and sauté for about 3 minutes, frequently stirring, until tender. Add the rice, turmeric, cinnamon, cilantro, and pepper, if needed, and stir for 30 seconds. Attach the bouillon and bring it to a simmer.
2. Lower the heat to medium-low and cover the saucepan tightly. Cook for about 20 minutes, until the liquid is absorbed and the rice is tender.
3. Remove the casserole from the sun. Attach the raisins and cashews, but do not stir them in. Cover the casserole and let it stand for five minutes. With a fork, fluff the rice and whisk in the cashews and raisins. Transfer to a bowl for serving and eat at once.

70. Quinoa with Broccoli
(Ready in about 30 Minutes | Serve 4 | Difficulty: Normal)

Ingredients
- 1 broccoli crown (8 ounces), cut into small florets, stalk peeled and chopped¾ cup quinoa
- 2 teaspoons olive oil
- ½ cup finely chopped yellow onion
- 1 clove garlic, chopped
- 1½ cups water
- ½ teaspoon kosher salt

Directions
1. Over high heat, bring a medium saucepan of water to a boil. Add the chopped broccoli and cook for about 4 minutes, until crisp-tender. Drain yourself and set aside. (There is no need for broccoli to be rinsed.)
2. Place the quinoa under cold running water in a fine-meshed wire sieve and rinse to remove its invisible bitter coating that occurs naturally. Drain thoroughly.
3. Over medium pressure, heat the oil in a medium saucepan. Add the onion and garlic and sauté for about 3 minutes, occasionally stirring, until tender. Add the quinoa, add the salt and water, and bring to a boil over high heat. Reduce the heat to medium-low, then tightly cover it. Simmer for about 20 minutes until the quinoa is tender and has absorbed the liquid. (If a little liquid is left, don't worry.)
4. Remove and add the broccoli from the sun. You don't stir. Tightly cover and let stand for 5 minutes for the broccoli to reheat. With a fork, fluff the quinoa and serve soft.

71. Creamed Spinach with Mushrooms
(Ready in about 30 Minutes | Serve 4 | Difficulty: Normal)

Ingredients
- 1 tablespoon unsalted butter
- 8 ounces white mushrooms, sliced
- 1 clove garlic, minced
- 2 (10-ounce) packages thawed frozen spinach, squeezed to remove excess liquid
- 2 tablespoons cornstarch
- 2 cups low-fat (1%) milk
- ½ teaspoon kosher salt
- ¼ teaspoon freshly ground black pepper
- Pinch of freshly grated nutmeg

Directions

1. In a large nonstick skillet over medium-high heat, melt the butter. Add the mushrooms and sauté for about 8 minutes, stirring periodically, before browning starts. Stir in the garlic and cook for about 1 minute until it is fragrant. Add the spinach and cook, constantly stirring, for about 2 minutes, to evaporate the excess liquid.
2. Sprinkle the cornstarch over the milk in a small bowl and whisk it to dissolve. Stir in the spinach mixture and cook for about 2 minutes, constantly stirring, until it boils and thickens. Using salt, pepper, and nutmeg to season. Serve hot, serve,

72. Sugar Snap Peas and Lemon Butter

(Ready in about 30 Minutes | Serve 4 | Difficulty: Normal)

Ingredients

- 12 ounces sugar snap peas, trimmed
- 1 tablespoon unsalted butter
- Freshly grated zest of ½ lemon
- 1 tablespoon fresh lemon juice
- 1 tablespoon finely chopped fresh chives
- Pinch of kosher salt
- Pinch of freshly ground black pepper

Directions

1. Over high heat, bring a medium saucepan of water to a boil. Add the sugar peas and cook for about 3 minutes, until crisp-tender. Scoop out 2 tablespoons of the cooking water and reserve it. In a colander, remove the sugar snap peas.
2. Add the reserved broth, butter, lemon zest and juice, chives, salt, and pepper, and place the sugar snap peas back in the saucepan. Mix well, allowing the water to mix with the melting butter. Switch to a serving bowl and serve hot

73. Summer Squash and Walnut Sauté

(Ready in about 30 Minutes | Serve 4 | Difficulty: Normal)

Ingredients

- 1 tablespoon olive oil
- ½ jalapeño, seeded and minced
- 1 medium zucchini, cut in half lengthwise and then into ¼-inch-thick slices
- 1 medium yellow summer squash, cut in half lengthwise and then into ¼-inch-thick slices¼ cup chopped walnuts
- 1 clove garlic, minced
- Pinch of kosher salt

Directions

1. Heat oil over medium-high heat in a large nonstick skillet. Add the jalapeño and sauté, frequently stirring, for about 1 minute, until softened.
2. Add the zucchini and the yellow squash and cook for 6 to 8 minutes, stirring occasionally, until brown and tender. Stir in the walnuts, garlic, and salt and cook for about 1 minute, until the garlic is fragrant. Serve it warm.

74. Squash and Bell Pepper Casserole

(Ready in about 30 Minutes | Serve 4 | Difficulty: Normal)

Ingredients

- 1 tablespoon plus
- 1 teaspoon olive oil
- 2 medium yellow squash, cut in half lengthwise and then into ½-inch-thick slices
- 1 small yellow onion, chopped
- ½ medium green bell pepper, cored and cut into ½-inch dice
- 1 teaspoon Italian Seasoning
- 1 clove garlic, minced¼ cup panko (Japanese-style bread crumbs), preferably whole-wheat panko

Directions

1. Preheat the oven to 350°F.
2. Heat 1 tablespoon oil over medium heat in an ovenproof medium nonstick skillet. Add the yellow squash and sauté for approximately 2 minutes, constantly stirring, until it starts to soften. Add the onion and bell pepper and cook, occasionally stirring, for about 5 minutes, until the onion is tender. Stir up the seasoning in Italy.
3. Stir in the remaining 1 teaspoon of oil and the garlic in a small cup. Attach the panko and combine thoroughly. Over the squash mixture, sprinkle uniformly.
4. Bake for about 15 minutes, until the squash is tender. From the skillet, serve hot.

75. Sweet Potato Steak Fries

(Ready in about 30 Minutes | Serve 4 | Difficulty: Normal)

Ingredients

- Olive oil in a pump sprayer
- 3 large orange-fleshed sweet potatoes (1½ pounds)
- ½ teaspoon kosher salt
- ¼ teaspoon freshly ground black pepper

Directions

1. Preheat the oven to 425 F. Using oil to spray a large rimmed baking sheet.
2. Peel the sweet potatoes and cut each one into 6 long wedges lengthwise. Spread out on the baking sheet in a single layer. Oil spray, toss and spray again. For 15 minutes, bake. Switch the fries and bake for about 15 more minutes, until lightly browned and soft. Use salt and pepper to season, toss well, and serve sweet.

Chapter 5: Dessert Recipes

In this chapter, we have compiled dessert recipes for DASH diet followers.

1. Berry Sundae

(Ready in 15min| serve6|Difficulty:Normal)

Ingredients

- 1 1/2 cups coarsely chopped strawberries
- 1 1/2 cups blueberries
- 1 1/2 cups raspberries
- 1 1/2 tablespoons balsamic vinegar
- Pinch of cracked black pepper
- 1 1/2 teaspoons grated lemon zest
- 1 1/2 teaspoons grated orange zest
- Juice of 1/2 orange
- 1/2 teaspoon vanilla extract
- 3 cups low-fat plain Greek yogurt
- 6 tablespoons sliced toasted almonds

Directions

1. In a big pot over medium heat, put all the ingredients except the yogurt and almonds and cook until the liquid starts to bubble.
2. Reduce the heat to low and simmer for about 15 minutes, or until the mixture thickens. The berries will break apart spontaneously, leaving a mildly chunky sauce.
3. Crush the berries with a fork or masher for a smoother sauce. Remove yourself from the sun. In six cups, add 1/2 cup of yogurt and finish with sauce and toasted almonds.

2. Grilled Apricots with Cinnamon

(Ready in 5min| serve4|Difficulty:Normal)

Ingredients

- 4 large apricots, halved and pitted
- 1 tablespoon extra-virgin olive oil
- 1/4 teaspoon ground cinnamon

Directions

1. Brush with oil on both sides of each apricot half, and put flat
2. On the hot grill or grill pan, side down. Grill for around 4 minutes, turn over the apricot halves and grill until soft for a few more minutes. Sprinkle with cinnamon and cut the apricots from the grill. Enjoy being wet or cold.

3. Grilled Peaches with Ricotta Stuffing and Balsamic Glaze

(Ready in 5min| serve4|Difficulty:Normal)

Ingredients

- 4 large peaches, halved and pitted
- 1 tablespoon extra-virgin olive oil
- 1 cup low-fat ricotta cheese
- 1/4 teaspoon ground cinnamon
- 1/8 teaspoon ground nutmeg
- 2 tablespoons low-fat milk
- 2 tablespoons Balsamic Glaze

Directions

1. Brush the two sides of each half of the peach with oil, and put them down. On the hot grill or grill pan, side down. Grill for about 4 minutes, turn over the peach halves and grill until soft for a few more minutes.
2. When the peaches are grilling, in a small bowl, mix the ricotta, milk, cinnamon, and nutmeg, stirring evenly to combine flavors.
3. Take the peaches from the grill and add 1/4 cup of the mixture of ricotta to the middle of each half of the peach. Drizzle and serve the balsamic glaze on each one.

4. Grilled Pineapple

(Ready in 5min| serve6|Difficulty:Normal)

Ingredients

- 1 large pineapple, sliced into rounds and cored

Directions

1. By laying it on its side and chopping off the pineapple, cut the pineapple bottom and top. On its freshly flat frame, stand it up. Cut the skin off in a downward motion, beginning from the top and moving to the root, operating in a circular direction.
2. Be careful not to take too much of the skin off the fruit. Cut out any brown stains until the skin has been removed. Then lay it again lengthwise, and split the rounds to the thickness you like. Cut out the inedible heart at the middle of each round with a cookie cutter or knife.
3. Place the rings directly on a hot grill with the pineapple. Grill for roughly three minutes, or before char marks emerge. Switch the rings over, then barbecue for an extra 2 to 3 minutes. Serve chilled or hot.

5. Red Sangria

(Ready in 5min| serve8|Difficulty:Normal)

Ingredients

- 1 (750 mL) bottle Spanish red table wine
- 1/4 cup brandy
- 1/4 cup Cointreau
- 1/2 cup orange juice
- 1 cup pomegranate juice
- 2 oranges, thinly sliced
- 2 Granny Smith apples, thinly sliced
- 1 1/2 cups seltzer, mineral water, or club soda

Directions

1. Stir together the champagne, brandy, Cointreau, and the fruit juices in a big pitcher.
2. Add the sliced fruit and chill for at least 30 minutes in the refrigerator before eating. Just prior to serving, add the seltzer, sparkling water, or club soda.

6. Baked Apples Stuffed with Cranberries and Walnuts

(Ready in about 30 Minutes | Serve 4 | Difficulty: Normal)

Ingredients

- Four baking apples, such as Braeburn or Rome½ lemon
- ⅓ cup dried cranberries
- ⅓ cup chopped walnuts
- 6 tablespoons grade B maple syrup
- ¼ teaspoon ground cinnamon
- ¼ teaspoon freshly grated nutmeg
- 4 teaspoons unsalted butter
- 1 cup boiling water

Directions

1. Preheat the oven to 350°F.
2. Break off the top inch of an apple one at a time to make a "lid." With a melon baller, scoop out the heart, stopping about half an inch from the bottom of the apple. Pick out the top half of the apple skin using a vegetable peeler. Rub the raw flesh with half of the lemon all over it.
3. Combine the cranberries, walnuts, 2 teaspoons of maple syrup, cinnamon, and nutmeg in a medium cup. Stuff the mixture into the apples. Top each one with 1 butter teaspoon. Replace the' lids of the fruit.'
4. In order to keep the apples, move to a baking dish only big enough. Squeeze half of the lemon juice from the lemon over the apples. Pour the boiling water in and securely cover it with aluminum foil. 20 minutes of baking. Uncover and baste with the liquid in the baking dish. Continue to bake until the apples are tender, 20 to 30 minutes longer, depending on the size of the apples when pierced with the tip of a small, sharp knife. Take it out of the oven and let it stand for 5 minutes.
5. Move each apple to a dessert bowl and add 1 tablespoon of maple syrup each to drizzle. Serve it sweet.

7. Buttermilk Panna Cotta with Fresh Berries

(Ready in about 30 Minutes | Serve 4 | Difficulty: Normal)

Ingredients

- 3 teaspoons unflavored gelatin powder
- ¼ cup plus 2 tablespoons low-fat (1%) milk
- 2¾ cups buttermilk
- ½ cup amber agave nectar or honey½ teaspoon vanilla extract
- Canola oil in a pump sprayer
- ½ cup fresh blueberries
- ½ cup fresh raspberries

Directions

1. Sprinkle the gelatin in a small heatproof bowl over the milk and let stand until the milk is absorbed by the gelatin, for about 5 minutes. To get ½ inch up the sides, add enough water to a small skillet and bring it to a simmer over low heat. Put the bowl in the water with the gelatin mixture and constantly stir with a

small heatproof spatula until the gelatin melts and dissolves completely around 2 minutes.
2. Meanwhile, over medium-low heat, heat the buttermilk in a medium saucepan, stirring continuously, only until it is warm to the touch. Do not overheat, or maybe it will curdle. Remove yourself from the sun. Attach the mixture of the gelatin and whisk until mixed. Agave and vanilla whisk. Transfer to a large measuring cup or pitcher of liquid.
3. Oil six 6-ounce custard cups or ramekins. Pour the buttermilk mixture into the ramekins in equal quantities. Cover with plastic wrap for each one. Refrigerate for at least 4 hours, or up to 2 days, until chilled and set.
4. Run a dinner knife around each ramekin's inside, making sure you hit bottom to crack the air seal. Place a plate over the top of the ramekin when working with one panna cotta at a time. Offer them a firm shake by holding the ramekin and plate together to unmold the panna cotta on the plate. Dip the ramekin (right side up) in a bowl of hot water if it is sbowlborn and keep it for 10 seconds, dry the ramekin, invert, and try again to unmold. The blueberries and raspberries are sprinkled and served chilled.

8. Cantaloupe and Mint Ice Pops

(Ready in about 30 Minutes I Serve 4 I Difficulty: Normal)

Ingredients

- 3 cups peeled, seeded, and cubed ripe cantaloupe
- ½ cup amber agave nectar
- 2 tablespoons fresh lemon juice
- 1 tablespoon finely chopped fresh mint

Directions

1. Have eight ice pop molds ready. In a food processor or blender, purée 2½ cups of the cantaloupe cubes. Transfer to a bowl. Pulse in the food processor or blender (or slice by hand) the remaining ½ cup of cantaloupe cubes until finely chopped, and add to the puree. Apply the agave, lemon juice, and mint to the whisk.
2. Divide the puree between the ice pop molds and cover the lid of each mold. Freeze for at least 4 hours, until the pops are strong. (The pops can be kept in the freezer for up to 1 week.)
3. Rinse the pop mold under lukewarm water to serve, then remove the pop from the mold. Frozen serve.
4. Cantaloupe and Mint Granita: In the freezer, put a metal baking dish or cake pan and a metal fork until very cold, approximately 15 minutes. The whole cantaloupe purée. To combine well, add the agave and the lemon juice and pulse. Only to mix, add the mint and pulse. Pour into the metal dish and freeze for around 1 hour until the mixture is icy along the sides of the bowl. Stir the ice crystals into the middle using the cold fork. Freeze again, around 1 hour more, until icy, and stir again; the mixture becomes more solid. Freeze for about 1 hour more, until the consistency is slushy. Freeze for up to 4 hours before serving. Using the fork's tines to scrape the mixture

into frozen slush just before serving. Serve in chilled bowls immediately.

9. Peach and Granola Parfaits

(Ready in about 30 Minutes I Serve 4 I Difficulty: Normal)

Ingredients

- 1 cup plain low-fat Greek yogurt
- 2 tablespoons amber agave nectar, honey, or grade B maple syrup
- ¼ teaspoon vanilla extract
- 8 tablespoons Make It Your Way Granola
- 4 ripe peaches or nectarines, pitted and cut into ½-inch dice

Directions

1. Stir the yogurt, agave, and vanilla in a small cup.
2. Layer 1 tablespoon of granola, 2 tablespoons of yogurt, and one-eighth of the diced peaches in a large parfait glass or wineglass for each serving, then repeat again. Immediately serve.

10. Easy Pear Crisp

(Ready in about 30 Minutes I Serve 4 I Difficulty: Normal)

Ingredients

- Canola oil in a pump sprayer
- 5 ripe, juicy pears, such as Comice or Anjou, peeled, cored, and cut into ½-inch pieces
- 2 tablespoons amber agave nectar or grade B maple syrup
- 1 tablespoon fresh lemon juice
- 2 teaspoons cornstarch
- ½ teaspoon freshly grated nutmeg1 cup Make It Your Way Granola.

Directions

1. Preheat the oven to 350°F. Lightly spray the oil on an 11 ?? 8½-inch baking dish.
2. In the baking dish, mix the pears, agave, lemon juice, cornstarch, and nutmeg. Bake for about 30 minutes, stirring every 15 minutes, until the pears are tender and have released their juices. Sprinkle the granola over the pear mixture and extract it from the oven. Go back to the oven and bake for about 5 minutes just to heat the granola. Remove from the oven and leave to stand at room temperature for 5 to 10 minutes.
3. Spoon into bowls for dessert and serve warm.

11. Roasted Pineapple with Maple Glaze

(Ready in about 30 Minutes I Serve 4 I Difficulty: Normal)

Ingredients

- 1 ripe pineapple
- Canola oil in a pump spray
- ¼ cup grade B maple syrup
- 1 tablespoon unsalted butter, melted

Directions

1. Preheat the oven to 425 F.

2. Cut the pineapple lengthwise into quarters using a big, sharp knife. To yield 8 wedges, cut each quarter lengthwise. For another use, reserve 4 of the wedges.
3. Using a paring knife to cut the flesh from the rind into one piece while dealing with 1 pineapple wedge at a time. Break the flesh into 5 large chunks vertically, holding them nestled in the rind.
4. Arrange the pineapple wedges in a baking dish and brush lightly with oil. Roast for about 15 minutes before it just begins to brown. In a small cup, whisk the maple syrup and butter together. Brush the mixture over the pineapple and bake for about 5 more minutes until the pineapple is glazed. Transfer to four large plates, drizzle with the baking dish liquid and serve warm.

12. Fresh Strawberries with Chocolate Dip

(Ready in about 30 Minutes I Serve 4 I Difficulty: Normal)

Ingredients

- ½ cup low-fat (2%) canned evaporated milk
- 5 ounces bittersweet chocolate (about 60% cacao content), finely chopped
- 24 strawberries, unhulled

Directions

1. In a tiny saucepan, carry the evaporated milk to a boil over medium heat. Remove from the heat and add the chocolate. Let it stand for about 3 minutes before the chocolate softens. Until smooth, whisk.
2. Divide the mixture of chocolate into four tiny ramekins. To dip, serve the strawberries with the chocolate mixture.

Chapter 6: Salad Recipes

In this chapter, we have presented DASH diet salad recipes.

1. Ambrosia with coconut and toasted almonds

(Ready in 20 min I Serve 2 I Difficulty: Easy)

Ingredients

- Slivered almonds 1/2 cup
- Unsweetened shredded coconut 1/2 cup
- Pineapple, cubed 1 small
- Oranges, segmented, 5
- Red apples, cored and sliced, 2
- Banana, halved lengthwise, sliced, and peeled 1
- Cream sherry 2 tablespoons
- Mint leaves for garnish, fresh

Directions:

1. Heat the oven to 325 F. On a baking dish, spread out the almonds and bake until golden and fragrant, occasionally stirring, for about 10 minutes. To cool, move it to a plate instantly. Attach the coconut to the baking sheet and cook for about 10 minutes, until lightly browned, stirring periodically. To cool, move it to a plate instantly.

2. In a big bowl, combine the grapes, pineapple, banana, strawberries, and sherry. To mix, kindly toss. Divide the fruit mixture into separate bowls similarly. Sprinkle generously with the toasted almonds and coconut, and garnish with mint. Serve instantly.

2. Apple lettuce salad

(Ready in 20 min | Serve 4 | Difficulty: Easy)

Ingredients

- Unsweetened apple juice 1/4 cup
- Lemon juice 2 tablespoons
- Canola oil 1 tablespoon
- Brown sugar 2 1/4 teaspoons
- Dijon mustard 1/2 teaspoon
- Apple pie spice 1/4 teaspoon
- Red apple, chopped, 1 medium
- Mixed salad greens 8 cups

Directions:

1. In a big cup, mix together the lemon juice, fruit juice, brown sugar, grease, apple pie, and mustard.
2. Attach and powder the apple for flipping. The salad greens are added and blended properly.

3. Apple salad with figs and almonds

(Ready in 20 min | Serve 4 | Difficulty: Easy)

Ingredients

- Red apples, cored and sliced, 2 larges
- Figs, chopped, 6 dried
- Carrots, peeled and grated 3/4 cup
- Ribs of celery, diced 2 cups
- Non-fat lemon yogurt 1/2 cup
- Slivered almonds 2 tablespoons

Directions:

1. Add the figs, onions, carrots, and celery to a little cup.
2. Apply the yogurt and blend well. Cover with slivered almonds and serve right away.

4. Apple-fennel slaw

(Ready in 20 min | Serve 4 | Difficulty: Easy)

Ingredients

- Fennel bulb, thinly sliced, 1 medium-sized
- Granny smith apple, cored and chopped thinly, 1 larges
- Carrots, 2 grated
- Raisins 2 tablespoons
- Olive oil 1 tablespoon
- Sugar 1 teaspoon
- Apple juice 1/2 cup
- Apple cider vinegar 2 tablespoons
- Lettuce leaves 4

Directions:

1. In a big cup, add the fennel, carrots, apple, and raisins to make the slaw. As you arrange the remaining ingredients, drizzle, coat, and refrigerate with olive oil.
2. In a small saucepan, mix the sugar and apple juice together. Place over medium heat and boil until reduced to about 1/4 cup, about 10 minutes. Take it from the sun and cool it. Incorporate the apple vinegar from the fruit. To blend right, stir in the apple juice mixture over the slaw and stir.

5. Artichokes alla Romana

(Ready in 20 min | Serve 8 | Difficulty: Easy)

Ingredients

- Breadcrumbs 2 cups fresh
- Olive oil 1 tablespoon
- Artichokes 4 large globe
- Lemons, 2 halved
- Grated Parmesan cheese 1/3 cup
- Garlic 3 cloves, finely sliced
- Sliced fresh flat-leaf Italian parsley 2 tablespoons
- Grated lemon zest 1 tablespoon
- Ground black pepper 1/4 teaspoon
- Low-sodium chicken or vegetable stock 1 cup
- Dry white wine 1 cup
- Minced shallot 1 tablespoon
- Chopped fresh oregano 1 teaspoon

Directions:

1. Heat the oven to 400 F. In a cup, blend the breadcrumbs and olive oil together. To powder it, toss it. Scatter the crumbs and bake in a shallow baking tray, stirring sometimes halfway through, until the crumbs are lightly brown, for about 10 minutes. Set it back now.

2. Snap off any rough outer leaves when working with 1 artichoke at a time and cut the stem flush with the root. Cut the top third of the leaves with a serrated knife and hack off any remaining thorns with scissors. To avoid discoloration, clean the cut edges with half a lemon. Separate the center from the inner leaves and draw out the tiny leaves. Using a melon baller or spoon, scoop out the fuzzy choke, then drive some lemon juice into the cavity. Trim the remaining artichokes in the same manner.

3. In a wide cup, toss the Parmesan cheese, garlic, parsley, lemon zest, and pepper with the breadcrumbs. Add 2 to 4 tablespoons of stock, 1 tablespoon at a time, using just enough to begin holding together in small clumps to begin stuffing.

4. Mound it gently, using 2/3 of the stuffing, into the center of the artichokes. Then spread the leaves open, starting at the bottom, then at the base of each leaf, spoon a rounded teaspoon of stuffing. Integrate the 1 cup stock, shallot, vinegar, and oregano with a tight-fitting cap into a Dutch oven (The artichokes can be prepared to this point several hours ahead and kept refrigerated.)

5. Bring it to a boil, then reduce it to medium heat. Arrange the artichokes, stem-end flat, in the milk, in one continuous layer.

Cover and simmer until the outer leaves are tender, for about 45 minutes (add water if necessary). Shift the artichokes to a shelf and let them cool slightly. It is necessary to cut each artichoke into quarters and eat it wet.

6. Asian vegetable salad

(Ready in 20 min | Serve 6 | Difficulty: Easy)

Ingredients

- Julienned carrot 1 1/2 cup
- Julienned red bell pepper 1/2 cup
- Julienned bok choy 1 1/2 cup
- Julienned yellow onion 1/2 cup
- Red cabbage 1 cup thinly sliced
- Spinach 1 1/2 cup thinly sliced
- Cilantro 1 tablespoon thinly sliced
- Minced garlic 1 tablespoon
- Chopped cashews 1 1/2 tablespoons
- Snow peas 1 1/2 cups
- Toasted sesame oil 2 teaspoons
- Low-sodium soy sauce 2 teaspoons

Directions:

1. You should wash all vegetables with running cold water. Only allow it to drain. Carrot Julienne, Cabbage, Bok Choy, and Onion (slice into very small strips like match sticks). Chiffonade the broccoli, cilantro, and lettuce (cut through the grain into very thin strips).
2. In a big bowl, toss the cut carrots, cashews, garlic, and snow peas together. Drizzle the sesame oil and soy sauce over the salad. To and serve.

7. Avocado salad with ginger-miso dressing

(Ready in 20 min | Serve 5 | Difficulty: Easy)

Ingredients
For the dressing

- Plain silken tofu 1/3 cup
- Low-fat soy milk 1/3 cup
- Peeled and minced fresh ginger 1 tablespoon
- Low-sodium soy sauce 1 1/2 teaspoons
- Light miso 1 teaspoon
- Dijon mustard 1 teaspoon
- Fresh cilantro (fresh coriander), 1 tablespoon chopped
- Green (spring) onion 1 tablespoon chopped

For the salad:

- Avocado, pitted, peeled, 1 small
- Fresh lemon juice 1 tablespoon
- Mixed baby lettuces 12 ounces
- Chopped red onion 1/4 cup
- Onion, including tender green top, 1 green (spring)
- Chopped fresh cilantro (fresh coriander) 1 tablespoon

Directions:

1. To create the seasoning, mix the tofu, ginger, soy milk, miso, soy sauce, and mustard in a blender. Just process until smooth and soft. In a dish, put the cilantro and the green onion and stir. Cover and refrigerate for at least 1 hour.
2. To stop browning, chuck the avocado slices with the lemon juice into a tiny cup. Set aside for it. In a big cup, mix the cabbage, green and red onions, and cilantro and toss to combine.
3. Add 2/3 of the dressing to cover and toss softly. Divide the lettuce into different dishes. Place 2 avocado slices on top of each piece in a crisscross-shape. Top each avocado cross with a drizzle of the remaining dressing. Serve instantly.

8. Baby beet and orange salad

(Ready in 20 min | Serve 4 | Difficulty: Easy)

Ingredients

- Baby beets with greens 2 bunches
- Ribs celery, chopped 1/2 cup
- Napa cabbage, sliced 1 1/2 cups
- Yellow onion, chopped (1/2 cup), 1 small
- Juice and zest of 1 orange
- 1 orange, peeled
- Olive oil 1/2 tablespoon
- Black pepper to taste

Directions:

1. Heat the oven to 400 F. Slice from the beets the greens. Clean the greens under cold flowing water; well drain, and reserve.
2. Make the beets rinsed. Drizzle your hands with a little olive oil and gently clean the beets to coat them. Cover the beets in foil for about 45 minutes or until soft, and fry before you can tolerate the outer skin and then take it off, cool. Slicing and resetting them.
3. Break the beet greens into strips and drop them in a mixing cup. Chop the celery, cabbage, and onion and add them to the dish, in a cup of zest and juice, 1 orange. Sliced and broken into pieces is the other orange. Drizzle 1/2 teaspoons of olive oil over the salad. Season with black pepper to blend, then toss.
4. Arrange the salad and end with sliced beets in chilled cups. Serve instantly.

9. Bean salad with balsamic vinaigrette

(Ready in 20 min | Serve 4| Difficulty: Easy)

Ingredients
For the vinaigrette:

- Balsamic vinegar 2 tablespoons
- Parsley, chopped 1/3 cup fresh
- Garlic 4 cloves, finely chopped
- Ground black pepper, pinch
- Olive oil 1/4 cup

For the salad:

- Low-sodium garbanzo beans, 1 can (15 ounces)
- Low-sodium black beans, 1 can (15 ounces)

- Red onion, diced, 1 medium
- Lettuce 6 leaves
- Celery, finely chopped, 1/2 cup

Directions:
1. In a small cup, whisk together the parsley, balsamic vinegar, garlic, and pepper to make the vinaigrette. Whilst whisking, gently apply the olive oil. Set aside for it.
2. In a big bowl, combine the beans and onion. Place the vinaigrette over the mixture and toss gently to blend properly and coat evenly. Protect, and then refrigerate until eaten.
3. To feed, put 1 leaf of lettuce on each plate. Divide the salad and garnish between the individual dishes with sliced celery. Serve instantly.

10. Beet walnut salad
(Ready in 20 min | Serve 8| Difficulty: Easy)

Ingredients
- Bunch beets, drained, 1 small
- Red wine vinegar 1/4 cup
- Balsamic vinegar 3 tablespoons
- Olive oil 1 tablespoon
- Water 1 tablespoon
- Fresh salad greens 8 cups
- Apple 1/4 cup chopped
- Celery 1/4 cup chopped
- Freshly ground pepper
- Chopped walnuts 3 tablespoons
- Gorgonzola cheese, crumbled, 1/4 cup

Directions:
1. In a saucepan of water, steam the raw beets until tender. Let the skin fall off. Break the 1/2-inch bullets through. Toss it into a medium dish of red wine vinegar.
2. In a big cup, add the olive oil, balsamic vinegar, and water. To the salad, add the vegetables and toss.
3. Add vegetables on individual salad plates. Cover with sliced beets and diced apples and celery. Using cheese, walnuts, and spices to sprinkle. Serve instantly.

11. Blue cheese, walnut spinach salad
(Ready in 20 min | Serve 8| Difficulty: Easy)

Ingredients
Dressing:
- Olive oil 4 teaspoons
- Balsamic vinegar 2 tablespoons
- Maple syrup 1 tablespoon
- Nutmeg 1/4 teaspoon
- Plain low-fat yogurt 1 tablespoon

Salad:
- Spinach, roughly chopped, 2 pounds
- Sliced red onion 1/2 cup
- Sliced cucumbers 1 1/2 cups
- Grape tomatoes 1 1/2 cups
- Chopped walnuts 1/4 cup
- Blue cheese crumbles 1/4 cup

Directions:
1. Mix all the ingredients in a mixer for dressing and chill out.
2. Along with dressing, throw the spinach greens and mound 2 cups on the chilled plates generously.
3. The top of the spinach crumbles with layers of walnuts, vegetables, and blue cheese. Just serve it.

12. Braised celery root
(Ready in 20 min | Serve 6| Difficulty: Easy)

Ingredients
- Vegetable stock or broth 1 cup
- 1 celery root (celeriac), peeled and diced
- Sour cream 1/4 cup
- Dijon mustard 1 teaspoon
- Salt 1/4 teaspoon
- Ground black pepper 1/4 teaspoon fresh
- Thyme leaves 2 teaspoons fresh

Directions:
1. In a large saucepan, carry the stock to a boil under high pressure. Stir the root of the celery in it. With the stock returning to a simmer, reduce the heat to low. Cover and simmer until the celery root is tender, stirring regularly, for 10 to 12 minutes.
2. Using a slotted spoon to move the celery root to a cup, cover, and keep it soft. Boost the fire under the saucepan to the full and bring the boiling liquid to a simmer. Cook for about 5 minutes, uncovered until reduced to 1 tablespoon.
3. Remove from the fire and sweep in the vinegar, sour cream, salt, and pepper. Add the celery root and thyme to the sauce and mix until warmed, over medium heat. Switch to a warmed serving plate and eat immediately.

13. Butternut squash and apple salad
(Ready in 20 min | Serve 6| Difficulty: Easy)

Ingredients
- 1 butternut squash, peeled and seeded, 8 cups
- Olive oil 2 teaspoons
- Apples cored 2 large cuts into 1/2-inch pieces
- Spinach, chopped, 6 cups
- Chopped celery 1 1/2 cups
- Arugula, chopped 6 cups
- Chopped carrots 2 cups

Dressing:
- Low-fat yogurt 1/2 cup
- Balsamic vinegar 2 teaspoons
- Honey 1 1/2 teaspoons

Directions:
1. Heat the oven to 400 F.
2. Mix the squash in the olive oil and cook in the oven for 20 to 30 minutes until lightly browned and tender. Fully cool them.
3. In a big bowl, combine all your vegetables.

4. Combine the vinegar, yogurt, and butter to prepare the dressing. Until smooth, whisk.
5. Pour the salad over the dressing. Toss yourself to watch it.

14. Chicken salad with pineapple and balsamic vinaigrette

(Ready in 25 min | Serve 5| Difficulty: Easy)

Ingredients

- Skinless chicken breasts, 4 boneless, each about 5 ounces
- Olive oil 1 tablespoon
- Unsweetened pineapple chunks 1 can (8 ounces)
- Broccoli florets 2 cups
- Baby spinach leaves 4 cups fresh
- Red onions 1/2 cup thinly sliced

For the vinaigrette:

- Olive oil 1/4 cup
- Balsamic vinegar 2 tablespoons
- Sugar 2 teaspoons
- Ground cinnamon 1/4 teaspoon

Directions:

1. Break each breast of a chicken into cubes. Heat the olive oil over medium heat in a big, nonstick frying pan. Connect the chicken and cook for about 10 minutes, until golden brown. Combine the fried chicken, broccoli, pineapple bits, spinach, and onions in a large serving bowl.
2. Mix the pineapple juice, olive oil, mustard, sugar, and cinnamon in a tiny cup to make the dressing. Pour the salad over. In order to disperse evenly, toss softly. Instantly serve.

15. Citrus salad

(Ready in 15 min | Serve 5| Difficulty: Easy)

Ingredients

- Oranges 2
- Red grapefruit 1
- Orange juice 2 tablespoons
- Olive oil 2 tablespoons
- Balsamic vinegar 1 tablespoon
- Spring greens 4 cups
- Pine nuts 2 tablespoons
- Sliced mint for garnish (optional), 2 tablespoons

Directions:

1. Act on 1 orange at a time, splitting a thin piece off the top and bottom, exposing the flesh. Stand the orange upright and, with a sharp knife, thickly cut off the peel, following the contour of the fruit and removing all of the white pith and membrane. Carefully cut down both sides of each segment, leaving the orange over a small cup, to free it from the membrane. When you work, discard any seeds and let the parts and any juice fall into the cup. Repeat for the other orange and for the grapefruit.
2. In a separate dish, whisk together the olive oil, orange juice, and vinegar. Load the mixture on the fruit segments to cover evenly and flip gently. Divide the greens of spring into individual dishes to feed. Cover each one with the fruit and dressing mixture and sprinkle each with 1/2 tablespoon of pine nuts. Serve instantly.

16. Couscous salad

(Ready in 15 min | Serve 5| Difficulty: Easy)

Ingredients

- Whole-wheat couscous 1 cup
- Zucchini, 1 cup cut into 1/4-inch pieces
- Red bell pepper, 1 medium cut into 1/4-inch pieces
- Red onion 1/2 cup finely chopped
- Ground cumin 3/4 teaspoon
- Ground black pepper 1/2 teaspoon
- Olive oil 2 tablespoons
- Lemon juice 1 tablespoon
- Sliced fresh parsley for garnish (optional)

Directions:

1. Cook the couscous according to instructions given on the box for preparation.
2. When you prepare couscous, fluff it with a fork. Combine the zucchini, cabbage, cumin, bell pepper, and black pepper. Set aside for it.
3. Blend the olive oil and the lemon juice together in a small cup. Pour the couscous mixture over and toss it in order to blend. Cover it and keep it refrigerated. Serve it refrigerated. Garnish it with herbs that are new.

17. Cucumber pineapple salad

(Ready in 15 min | Serve: 5| Difficulty: Easy)

Ingredients

- Sugar 1/4 cup
- Rice wine vinegar 2/3 cup
- Water 2 tablespoons
- Canned no-sugar-added pineapple chunks 1 cup
- Cucumber, 1 peeled and thinly sliced
- Carrot, 1 peeled and cut into thin strips
- Thinly chopped red onion 1/3 cup
- Torn salad greens 4 cups
- Sesame seeds, toasted 1 tablespoon

Directions:

1. In a big saucepan, put the vinegar, sugar, and water to a boil. Swirl constantly until reduced to approximately 1/2 cup, about 5 minutes. Switch to a large bowl and cool in the refrigerator before freezing. Add the pineapple, the carrot cucumber, and the red onion to the mixture. All right, toss well.
2. Divide the greens of the salad into separate dishes to eat. Sprinkle with the seeds of toasted sesame and top with the mixture of pineapple. Instantly, serve.

18. Dilled pasta salad with spring vegetables

(Ready in 35 min | Serve: 5| Difficulty: Normal)

Ingredients
For the dressing:

- Olive oil 1/4 cup
- Lemon juice 2 tablespoons
- Rice or white wine vinegar 2 tablespoons
- Dill weed 2 teaspoons
- Cracked black pepper, to taste

For the salad:
- Uncooked whole-grain shell pasta, 3 cups medium-sized
- Asparagus spears, 8 cut into 1/2-inch pieces
- Cherry tomatoes 1 cup halved
- Green peppers 1 cup sliced
- Green (spring) onions 1/2 cup chopped

Directions:
1. To make the dressing, mix the lemon juice, olive oil, vinegar, dill weed, and black pepper in a small cup. Brush to mix similarly. Just bring it back.
2. To build the salad and get it to a boil, fill a large pot 3/4 full of water. Attach the pasta and cook for 10 to 12 minutes, or until tender, according to the box directions (al dente). Please remove the pasta thoroughly and wash it under a cold mist.
3. In a small saucepan, coat the asparagus with water. Bring to a boil and cook until tender-crisp, around 3 to 5 minutes. Drain and shower under the cold spray.
4. In a large dish, he put the asparagus, pasta, tomatoes, onions, green peppers, and dressing. To similarly mix, toss.
5. Refrigerated. Secure and keep. Refrigerated serve.

19. Dilled shrimp salad on lettuce leaves
(Ready in 35 min I Serve: 5I Difficulty: Normal)

Ingredients
- Uncooked farfalle (bow tie) pasta, 2 cups
- Asparagus stalks, 4 fresh cuts into 1/2-inch pieces
- Reduced sodium 1/4 cup salad dressing
- Fresh dill 1 1/2 teaspoons
- Cooked shrimp 1/2 pound
- Cherry tomatoes, 8 halved
- Scallions or green onions, 4 diced
- Watercress 4 cups

Directions:
1. Load a big pot full of water with 3/4 and bring it to a boil. Connect the pasta and cook for 10 to 12 minutes, or until al dente, according to the package instructions (tender). Please remove the pasta thoroughly and wash it under a cold mist.
2. In a small saucepan, coat the asparagus with water. Carry to a boil, and simmer until tender-crisp, around 3 to 5 minutes. Drain and shower under the cold spray. In a little pan, apply the salad dressing and the dill. Brush to mix similarly.
3. In a large oven, add the spaghetti, lobster, asparagus, onions, and scallions. Apply the salad dressing mix and toss thinly to coat. Cover and refrigerate until fully cooled, for around 1 hour.fr
4. Divide between the plates to serve the watercress. Put the salad on top and eat it.

20. English cucumber salad with balsamic vinaigrette
(Ready in 35 min I Serve: 4I Difficulty: Normal)

Ingredients
- Cucumber with peel (8 to 9 inches in length), 1, washed and thinly chopped
- Cracked black pepper, to taste

For the dressing:
- Fresh rosemary 1 tablespoon finely sliced
- Balsamic vinegar 2 tablespoons
- Olive oil 1 1/2 tablespoons
- Dijon mustard 1 tablespoon

Directions:
1. In a small saucepan, apply the rosemary, vinegar, and olive oil. Heat over very low heat for around 5 minutes to blend and boost the flavors. Remove from the heat and blend until the mustard has blended well.
2. Attach the slices of the cucumber to a serving bowl. Over the cucumbers, pour the dressing and cover thinly with a flip. Apply the black pepper to taste. Refrigerate, until available, to feed.

21. Fattoush
(Ready in 25 min I Serve: 8I Difficulty: Normal)

Ingredients
For the dressing:
- Fresh lemon juice 1/4 cup
- Garlic 3 cloves, minced
- Ground cumin 1 teaspoon
- Ground sumac 1 teaspoon
- Salt 1/2 teaspoon
- Red pepper flakes 1/2 teaspoon
- Freshly ground black pepper 1/4 teaspoon
- Olive oil 2 tablespoons

For the salad:
- Whole-wheat pitas, 2, 6 inches in diameter
- Romaine lettuce, 1 head chopped (about 4 cups)
- Tomatoes, 2 seeded and diced
- Cucumbers, 2 smalls peeled, seeded, or diced
- Red bell pepper, 1 seeded and diced
- Green onions, minced 3
- Chopped fresh mint 1 tablespoon
- Flat-leaf Italian parsley 1/4 cup chopped

Directions:
1. Next, make the dressing. In a blender or food processor, combine the lemon juice, cumin, garlic, sumac (or lemon zest), cinnamon, red pepper flakes, and black pepper together. With the motor running until it is emulsified, slowly apply the olive oil in a thin stream. Set aside for it.
2. Next, have the pita croutons packed. Heat the oven to 400 F. Tear half-inch pieces of a single pita (or you may cut each into 8 triangles). Spread the bits in a single layer on a baking

sheet and bake until crisp and gently brown, around 8 minutes. Set aside for it.

3. Now, you are able to assemble the salad. In a big cup, combine the cabbage, tomatoes, cucumbers, green onions, bell pepper, mint, and parsley and toss. Apply the dressing to cover equally and toss softly. Divide the lettuce into different dishes. Top them up with the croutons.

22. French green lentil salad

(Ready in 25 min I Serve 6I Difficulty: Normal)

Ingredients

- Olive oil divided 4 tablespoons
- Onion, finely chopped 1/2 yellow
- Celery stalk, finely chopped 4-inch-piece
- Carrot, peeled and finely chopped 4-inch-piece
- Garlic, minced 3 cloves
- Mustard seed 1 teaspoon
- Fennel seed 1 teaspoon
- Vegetable stock, chicken stock or broth 2 cups
- Water 1/2 cup
- French green lentils, 1 cup
- Chopped fresh thyme 1 tablespoon or 1 teaspoon dried thyme
- 1 bay leaf
- Sherry vinegar or red wine vinegar 1 tablespoon
- Dijon mustard 1 tablespoon
- Flat-leaf Italian parsley, 2 tablespoons cut into strips
- Ground black pepper 1/4 teaspoon fresh

Directions:

1. Heat 2 teaspoons of olive oil over medium heat in a large saucepan. Attach the cabbage, the celery, and the carrot and sauté until the vegetables are softened for about 5 minutes. Add the mustard seeds, garlic, and fennel seeds, and sauté for around 1 minute before the spices are fragrant.

2. Add stock, water, lentils, bay leaf, and thyme. Improve the medium-high flame and bring it to a simmer. Reduce heat to low, cover partly and simmer for 25 to 30 minutes until the lentils are soft but still solid. Drain the lentils to conserve the liquid for frying. Shift the lentils and cut the bay leaf from a large cup.

3. Mix the vinegar, mustard, and 1/4 cup of the retained cooking liquid into a shallow bowl. Whisk in the remaining olive oil. (Discard any excess liquid or preserve it for another use.)

4. Apply the lentils to the parsley, vinaigrette, and pepper and shake gently to mix and uniformly coat. Wet to serve.

23. Greek salad

(Ready in 20 min I Serve 8I Difficulty: Normal)

Ingredients
For the vinaigrette:

- Red wine vinegar 1 tablespoon
- Fresh lemon juice 1 tablespoon
- Chopped fresh oregano 2 teaspoons or 3/4 teaspoon dried oregano
- Salt 1/4 teaspoon
- Ground black pepper 1/4 teaspoon
- Olive oil 2 1/2 tablespoons

For the salad:

- Eggplant, 1 large about 1 1/2 pounds
- Spinach, 1 pound stemmed or bite-sized pieces
- Cucumber, 1 English (hothouse) unpeeled, seeded, and diced
- Tomato, 1 seeded and diced
- Red onion, diced 1/2
- Pitted, chopped black Greek olives 2 tablespoons
- Crumbled feta cheese 2 tablespoons

Directions:

1. Place a rack in the lower third of the oven and heat it to 450 F. With a cooking spray of olive oil, coat the baking sheet loosely.

2. In a tiny mug, mix together the vinegar, oregano, lemon juice, salt, and pepper to make the vinaigrette. When whisking, add the olive oil slowly until it emulsifies in a thin stream. Set aside for it.

3. Spread the eggplant cubes into a single layer on the prepared baking sheet. To spray the eggplant, add the olive oil cooking spray. Bake for 10 minutes. Turn cubes and bake, 8 to 10 minutes longer, until lightly golden and softened. Set it back, leave it to chill.

4. In a big bowl, combine the lettuce, basil, cucumber, onion, and the cooled eggplant. Place the vinaigrette over the salad and toss gently to blend properly and coat evenly. Divide the lettuce into different dishes. Sprinkle with olives and feta. Serve instantly.

24. Grilled chicken salad with buttermilk dressing

(Ready in 30 min I Serve 4I Difficulty: Normal)

Ingredients
For the dressing:

- Fat-free mayonnaise 1/3 cup
- Low-fat buttermilk 1/4 cup
- Chopped tablespoons fresh dill 2 finely
- Minced garlic 1 teaspoon
- Cracked black pepper, to taste

For the salad:

- Boneless, 4 skinless chicken breasts (4 ounces each)
- Olive oil 2 teaspoons
- Torn salad greens 8 cups
- Red bell pepper, 1 sliced
- Onion sliced 1/2 sweet

Directions:

1. In a small dish, mix the mayonnaise, dill, buttermilk, garlic, and black pepper together. Whisk until smooth. Until possible, cover, then refrigerate.

2. Planning a hot fire on a barbecue grill or cooking a gas grill or broiler (grill). Brush the grill rack or broiler pan gently with cooking mist, away from the source of heat. It is necessary to position the cooking rack 4 to 6 inches from the heat source.

3. Clean the chicken breasts with the aid of olive oil. Grill or broil until browned and just cooked through, about 5 minutes on each side. Move the chicken to a cutting board and let it stand for 5 minutes before cutting it into strips.

4. In a big dish, add the salad greens, onion bell pepper, and most of the dressing together. To mix, toss well.

5. Move the salad to different dishes. Connect the sliced chicken to the drizzle and add the remaining sauce. Serve instantly.

25. Grilled chicken salad with olives and oranges

(Ready in 30 min | Serve 4| Difficulty: Normal)

Ingredients
For the dressing:
- Red wine vinegar 1/2 cup
- Garlic 4 cloves, minced
- Olive oil 1 tablespoon
- Red onion 1 tablespoon finely sliced
- Celery 1 tablespoon finely sliced
- Cracked black pepper, to taste

For the salad:
- Skinless chicken breasts, four boneless, each 4 ounces
- Garlic 2 cloves
- Leaf lettuce 8 cups
- Ripe (black) olives, 16 larges
- Oranges, peeled and sliced, 2 navels

Directions:
1. To make the dressing, mix the vinegar, olive oil, garlic, onion, celery, and pepper in a small cup. Stir evenly to mix. Until possible, cover, then refrigerate.

2. To make a hot fire or to heat a gas grill or broiler, use a barbecue grill. Brush the grill rack or broiler pan gently with cooking mist, away from the source of heat. It is necessary to position the cooking rack 4 to 6 inches from the heat source. To coat the chicken breasts, use garlic and cut the cloves. Grill or broil the chicken until browned, on either side, about 5 minutes, and then cooked through. Move the chicken to a cutting board and let it stand for 5 minutes before cutting it into strips.

3. On 4 plates, place 4 olives and 1/4 of the cut oranges, also place 2 cups of lettuce. On each plate, place 1 chicken breast cut into strips and drizzle it with seasoning. Serve instantly.

26. Grilled cod with crispy citrus salad

(Ready in 30 min | Serve 2| Difficulty: Normal)

Ingredients
- Cod 8 ounces
- Olive oil 1 teaspoon
- Chopped spinach 1 1/2 cups
- Shredded kohlrabi 1 1/2 cups
- Diced celery 1 cup
- Shredded carrot 1 1/2 cups
- Fresh basil 2 tablespoons chopped
- Fresh parsley 1 tablespoon chopped
- Red bell pepper 3/4 cup chopped
- Minced garlic (about 4 large cloves) 1 tablespoon
- Juice of 1 lemon
- Juice of 1 lime
- Juice of 1 orange
- Grapefruit 1 large cut into segments (about 1 cup)
- Orange 1 medium cut into segments (about 1/2 cup)
- Black pepper to taste

Directions:
1. Using cooking spray to spray a barbecue or broiler pan. Switch on a barbecue or broiler with hot water. Place the cod on the grill or broiler pan and gently brush it with oil.

2. Grill or broil for around 10 minutes 3 to 4 inches from the fire or before fish flakes easily with a fork. An internal temperature of 145 F. should be achieved by the trout. Only put aside.

3. Toss the remaining ingredients together in a large cup, except for the grapefruit and orange parts. Divide the salad into two pans. Top with bits of cod and citrus and, to taste, black pepper.

27. Mango tango salad

(Ready in 20 min | Serve 2| Difficulty: Easy)

Ingredients
- Mangoes pitted and cubed 3 ripe
- Juice of 1 lime
- Minced red onion 1 teaspoon
- Chopped fresh cilantro leaves 2 tablespoons
- Jalapeno pepper, half of 1 seeded and minced

Directions:
Mix and toss all ingredients in a bowl. Let stand 10 minutes. Toss just before serving.

28. Mixed bean salad

(Ready in 20 min | Serve 8| Difficulty: Easy)

Ingredients
- Unsalted green beans drained 1 can (15 ounces)
- Unsalted wax beans drained 1 can (15 ounces)
- Unsalted kidney beans drained 1 can (15 ounces)
- Unsalted garbanzo beans drained 1 can (15 ounces)
- White onion 1/4 cup chopped
- Orange juice 1/4 cup
- Cider vinegar 1/2 cup
- The sugar substitute, if desired

Directions:
1. Combine the beans and onion in a large bowl. Stir carefully to blend uniformly.

2. Whisk together the orange juice and vinegar in a separate dish. Add the substitution sugar for the desired sweetness.

3. Over the bean mixture, add in the orange juice mixture. To layer uniformly, stir. Before eating, let it stand for 30 minutes.

29. Pasta salad with mixed vegetables
(Ready in 40 min I Serve 3I Difficulty: Easy)

Ingredients
- Whole-wheat rotini (spiral-shaped) pasta 12 ounces
- Olive oil 1 tablespoon
- Low-sodium chicken broth 1/4 cup
- Garlic 1 clove, chopped
- Onions, chopped 2 mediums
- Unsalted diced tomatoes in juice 1 can (28 ounces)
- Mushrooms, sliced 1 pound
- Red bell pepper, sliced 1
- Green bell pepper, sliced 1
- Medium zucchini, shredded 2
- Basil 1/2 teaspoon
- Oregano 1/2 teaspoon
- Lettuce leaves 8 romaine

Directions:
1. Cook pasta according to the instructions on the box. Thoroughly drain the pasta. Place the pasta in a big bowl to eat. Stir in the olive oil and toss. Only put aside.
2. Heat the chicken broth in a big skillet over medium heat. Garlic, onions, and tomatoes are added. Saute for about 5 minutes until the onions are translucent. 3. Add the remaining vegetables and saute for about 5 minutes until tender-crisp. Stir in the oregano and basil.
4. To the pasta, apply the vegetable mixture. To combine equally, toss. Cover and refrigerate for around 1 hour, until well-chilled.
5. On individual plates, put lettuce leaves. Cover the pasta salad with it and serve immediately.

30. Pickled onion salad
(Ready in 20 min I Serve 4I Difficulty: Easy)

Ingredients
- Red onions, thinly sliced (about 2 cups) 2 larges
- (green) onions with tops, 4 spring chopped
- Cider vinegar 1/2 cup
- Olive oil 2 teaspoons
- Sugar 2 tablespoons
- Fresh cilantro, chopped 1/2 cup
- Lime juice 1 tablespoon
- Lettuce leaves 4

Directions:
1. Combine all the ingredients in a bowl. Refrigerate for 60 minutes before serving.

31. Potato salad
(Ready in 20 min I Serve 4I Difficulty: Easy)

Ingredients
- Potatoes, diced and boiled or steamed 1 pound
- Yellow onion, chopped (1 cup) 1 large
- Carrot, diced (1/2 cup) 1 large
- Ribs celery, diced (1/2 cup) 2
- Minced fresh dill (or 1/2 tablespoon dried) 2 tablespoons
- Ground black pepper 1 teaspoon
- Low-calorie mayonnaise 1/4 cup
- Dijon mustard 1 tablespoon
- Red wine vinegar 2 tablespoons

Directions:
1. Put all ingredients in a bowl and mix well. Chill before serving.

32. Quick bean and tuna salad
(Ready in 20 min I Serve: 4I Difficulty: Easy)

Ingredients
- Baguette, 1/2 whole-grain torn into 2-inch pieces (about 1 cup)
- Olive oil 2 tablespoons
- Cannellini beans, 1 can (16 ounces) no salt added, drained and rinsed
- Dill pickles, 2 small cuts into bite-size pieces (about 2 tablespoons)
- Red onion, 1 small thinly sliced (about 1/2 cup)
- Red wine vinegar 2 tablespoons
- Pepper 1/4 teaspoon
- Water-packed tuna, 1 can (7 ounces), drained, and rinsed, no salt added
- Fresh parsley 2 tablespoons finely chopped

Directions:
1. Heat the broiler. On a heavy baking sheet, put the baguette pieces and spray them with 1 tablespoon of oil. Place under the broiler until golden, around 1 to 2 minutes. Switch and broil the bread pieces for an extra 1 to 2 minutes.
2. Combine the remaining oil, beans, pickles, onion, vinegar, and pepper in a wide dish. Fold the bits of broiled baguette in. Divide the mixture into four bowls and apply the tuna and parsley to the tip.

33. Rice and beans salad
(Ready in 20 min I Serve 4I Difficulty: Easy)

Ingredients
- Uncooked brown rice 1 1/2 cups
- Water 3 cups
- Fresh parsley 1/2 cup chopped
- Shallots or spring onions 1/2 cup chopped
- Unsalted garbanzo beans 15-ounce can
- Unsalted dark kidney beans 15-ounce can
- Olive oil 1/4 cup
- Rice vinegar, 1/3 to 1/2 cup

Directions:
1. Put the water and rice in the stockpot. Cover and cook until the rice is tender, about 45 to 50 minutes, over medium heat. To room temperature, cool. Stir the remainder of the ingredients in. Refrigerate for 2 hours or more.

34. Salad greens with pears, fennel, and walnuts

(Ready in 20 min | Serve 4| Difficulty: Easy)

Ingredients

- Mixed salad greens 6 cups
- Fennel bulb, trimmed and thinly chopped, 1 medium
- Pears, cored, 2 medium quartered and thinly chopped
- Parmesan cheese 2 tablespoons
- Toasted walnuts, 1/4 cup coarsely chopped
- Olive oil 2 tablespoons
- Balsamic vinegar 3 tablespoons
- Freshly ground black pepper

Directions:

On 6 plates, evenly distribute the salad greens. Scatter the slices of fennel and pear over the greens. Sprinkle with walnuts and Parmesan cheese. Drizzle with vinegar and olive oil. Attach, to taste, black pepper. Immediately serve.

35. Salad greens with squash

(Ready in 20 min | Serve 4| Difficulty: Easy)

Ingredients

- Acorn squash (about 2 pounds total), 2 smalls
- Brown sugar 2 tablespoons
- Olive oil 1 tablespoon
- Leaf lettuce, such as spring mix, 4 cups
- Sunflower seeds 2 tablespoons
- Honey 4 teaspoons

Directions:

1. To encourage steam to escape during cooking, pierce the squash multiple times with a sharp knife. Microwave each squash for about 5 minutes, before soft. After 3 minutes, turn the squash to ensure the cooking is even.
2. On a cutting board, put the squash and break it in half. Scrape the seeds from each half of the middle and remove the seeds. Remove the squash pulp and place it in a mixing cup. For the other squash, repeat. Around 2 cups of pulp should be present. Sprinkle the brown sugar with the squash and apply some olive oil until flat, blend. To cool somewhat, set aside.
3. Divide the lettuce into four salad bowls. Cover with 1/2 cup of the mixture of squash, 1/2 tablespoon of sunflower seeds, and 1 teaspoon of honey each. Immediately serve.

36. Spiced melon salad

(Ready in 20 min | Serve: 4| Difficulty: Easy)

Ingredients

- Diced assorted melon 2 cups
- Plain or vanilla low-fat yogurt 1/2 cup
- Nutmeg 1/4 teaspoon
- Mace 1/4 teaspoon
- Clove 1/8 teaspoon
- Cinnamon 1/8 teaspoon
- Orange zest (about 1 tablespoon) and juice (about 3 tablespoons)

Directions

In a large bowl, mix all ingredients and toss well. Serve.

37. Spinach berry salad

(Ready in 20 min | Serve 4| Difficulty: Easy)

Ingredients

- Cups torn fresh spinach 4 packed
- Sliced fresh strawberries 1 cup
- Fresh or frozen blueberries 1 cup
- Sweet onion, sliced 1 small
- Pecans, toasted 1/4 cup chopped

Salad dressing:

- White wine vinegar or cider vinegar 2 tablespoons
- Balsamic vinegar 2 tablespoons
- Honey 2 tablespoons
- Dijon mustard 2 teaspoons
- Curry powder 1 teaspoon
- Pepper 1/8 teaspoon

Directions:

1. Mix all ingredients in a jar and top with dressing. Cover with the lid and toss well. 2. Serve immediately.

38. Steak salad with roasted corn vinaigrette

(Ready in 30 min | Serve 6| Difficulty: Normal)

Ingredients

- Fresh corn kernels 3 cups
- Water 1/2 cup
- Fresh lime juice 2 tablespoons
- Sliced red bell pepper 2 tablespoons
- Olive oil 2 tablespoons
- Salt 1/2 teaspoon
- Freshly ground black pepper 1/2 teaspoon
- Chopped fresh cilantro 1/4 cup
- Ground cumin 1 tablespoon
- Dried oregano 2 teaspoons
- Red pepper flakes 1/4 teaspoon
- Flank steak 3/4 pound (12 ounces)
- Romaine lettuce, 1 large head trimmed and torn into bite-sized pieces
- Cherry tomatoes, halved, 4 cups
- Thinly sliced red onion 3/4 cup
- Cooked black beans, no salt added, 1 1/2 cups

Directions:

1. Over medium-high heat, place a dry, large cast-iron or heavy nonstick frying pan. Attach the corn and cook, constantly stirring, for 4 to 5 minutes, before the corn starts to tan. Delete and set aside from the sun.
2. Combine the water, lime juice, bell pepper, and 1 cup of the roasted corn in a food processor, from pulse to puree. Apply olive oil, 1/4 of a teaspoon of cinnamon, 1/4 of a teaspoon of

black pepper, and cilantro to taste. Pulse for mixing. Set aside the vinaigrette.

3. On a barbecue grill, prepare a hot fire or heat a gas grill or broiler (grill). Lightly brush the grill rack or broiler pan with cooking spray, away from the heat source. The cooking rack should be placed 4 to 6 inches from the heat source.

4. Mix the cumin, oregano, red pepper flakes, and the remaining 1/4 teaspoon salt and 1/4 teaspoon black pepper together in a small cup. Rub in the steak on both ends. Place the steak on the grill rack or broiler pan and grill or broil each side for 4 to 5 minutes, rotating once, until browned. To scan for doneness, break into the middle (medium doneness is 160 F if using a meat thermometer). Let them stand for five minutes. Split into thin slices around the grain. Break the slices into 2 inch-long sections.

5. Combine the spinach, tomatoes, onion, black beans, and the leftover roasted corn in a large dish. To blend properly and cover equally, apply the vinaigrette, and toss gently.

6. Divide the salad into individual plates in order to eat. Top any serving with grilled steak slices.

39. Tabbouleh salad

(Ready in 30 min | Serve 8| Difficulty: Normal)

Ingredients

- Water 1 1/2 cups
- Bulgur (cracked wheat), 3/4 cup rinsed and drained
- Diced, seeded tomatoes 1 cup
- Chopped parsley 1 cup
- Chopped scallions or green onions 1/2 cup
- Dill weed 1 teaspoon
- Black olives, sliced 4
- Raisins 1/4 cup
- Lemon juice 1/4 cup
- Olive oil 2 tablespoons
- Freshly ground black pepper

Directions:

1. Bring the water to a boil in a shallow saucepan. Remove and add the bulgur from the sun. Cover and let stand before the bulgur is soft, for around 15 to 20 minutes, and the liquid is completely absorbed.

2. The bulgur and the remaining ingredients are added to a large dish. Just before the products are uniformly divided, toss gently. For 2 hours, cover and refrigerate to allow the flavors to blend. Serve refrigerated.

40. Tossed greens with pasta, fruit, and balsamic vinaigrette

(Ready in 30 min | Serve 6| Difficulty: Normal)

Ingredients

For the dressing:

- Dried rosemary 1 teaspoon or 1 tablespoon fresh rosemary
- Ground cinnamon 1/4 teaspoon
- Salt 1/4 teaspoon
- Balsamic vinegar 3 tablespoons
- Olive oil 1/4 cup

For the salad:

- Uncooked spiral whole-wheat pasta 4 ounces
- Mixed greens 6 cups
- Pears, cored and sliced, 2 large fresh
- Water chestnuts 1/2 cup sliced
- Golden raisins 1/2 cup
- Roasted unsalted soy nuts 3 tablespoons

Directions:

1. To make the dressing, use a tiny mug. Add the rosemary, cinnamon, salt, olive oil, and balsamic vinegar; combine thoroughly.

2. Fill 3/4 of a large pot full of water and bring it to a boil. Connect the pasta and cook for 10 to 12 minutes, or according to the packet instructions, until tender (al dente). Please thoroughly drain the pasta and clean it under the cool spray.

3. Combine the cooked spaghetti, mixed vegetables, pears, water, chestnuts, and raisins in a large dish. Whisk again briefly with the dressing and apply to the salad. To cover uniformly, toss. Divide the salad and finish with soy nuts on separate bowls. Immediately serve.

41. Warm coleslaw with honey dressing

(Ready in 30 min | Serve 6| Difficulty: Normal)

Ingredients

- Olive oil 6 teaspoons
- Yellow onion, 1 medium finely chopped (about 1/2 cup)
- Dry mustard 1 teaspoon
- Carrot, 1 large peeled and julienned
- Napa cabbage, 1/2 head cored and thinly chopped crosswise
- Cider vinegar 3 tablespoons
- Dark honey 1 tablespoon
- Salt 1/4 teaspoon
- Freshly ground black pepper 1/4 teaspoon
- Caraway seed 1/2 teaspoon
- Flat-leaf Italian parsley 1 tablespoon chopped fresh

Directions:

1. Heat 2 teaspoons of olive oil in a large nonstick saute pan over medium-high heat until hot yet smoke-free. Connect the onion and mustard and saute for about 6 minutes until the onion is soft and lightly golden. Transfer to a spacious bowl.

2. Reduce the heat to medium and apply to the pan 2 additional teaspoons of olive oil. Attach the carrot and toss and constantly stir for about 3 minutes until the carrot is tender-crisp. Shift the onion to the bowl.

3. Then, over medium heat, apply the remaining 2 teaspoons of oil to the pan. Attach the cabbage and toss and stir vigorously for about 3 minutes before the cabbage just starts to wilt. Shift the cabbage with the other vegetables to the bowl easily.

4. Over medium heat, rapidly apply the vinegar and honey to the pan, stirring until mixed and bubbly and the honey is dissolved. Pour the slaw on. Apply the pepper and salt and toss well. Garnish and eat warm with the caraway seeds and parsley.

42. Yellow pear and cherry tomato salad

(Ready in 30 min | Serve 6 | Difficulty: Normal)

Ingredients
For the vinaigrette

- Sherry vinegar 2 tablespoons or red wine vinegar
- Minced shallot 1 tablespoon
- Olive oil 1 tablespoon
- Salt 1/4 teaspoon
- Ground black pepper 1/8 teaspoon
- Yellow pear tomatoes, halved, 1 1/2 cups
- Orange cherry tomatoes, halved, 1 1/2 cups
- Red cherry tomatoes, halved, 1 1/2 cups
- Basil leaves, 4 large fresh cuts into slender ribbons

Directions:

1. Combine the vinegar and the shallot in a small bowl to make the vinaigrette and let it stand for 15 minutes. Stir in the olive oil, salt, and pepper and whisk until well mixed. Toss together all the tomatoes in a big serving or salad dish.
2. To blend properly and cover equally, pour the vinaigrette over the tomatoes, apply the basil shreds, and toss gently. Immediately serve the salad.

43. Roast Beef Salad with Beets, Apple, and Horseradish

(Ready in about 1hr | Serving 4 | Difficulty: Normal)

Ingredients

- 4 medium beets (1 pound), scrubbed but unpeeled
- 2 tablespoons cider vinegar
- 1½ tablespoons pared and freshly grated horseradish (use a zester, such as a Microplane)
- 2 tablespoons olive oil
- 1 large Rome apple, cored and cut into ½-inch dice
- 1 scallion, white and green parts, finely chopped
- 12 ounces thinly sliced Spiced Roast Eye of Round.

Directions

1. Preheat the oven to 400 ° F. Cover each beet in aluminum foil and place it on a rimmed baking sheet. When pierced with the tip of a tiny, sharp knife, bake until the beets are tender, around 1 1/4 hours. Unwrap and cool. Peel the beets and cut them into 1/2-inch cubes.
2. Whisk the vinegar and horseradish together in a medium cup, then whisk in the oil. Connect the scallion, apple, and beets and combine well. Cover and refrigerate for at least 1 hour or up to 1 day until chilled.
3. Divide the beet salad into four dinner plates, and top the sliced roast beef with equal quantities.

44. Classic Chicken Salad with romaine

(Ready in about 1hr | Serve 2 | Difficulty: Difficult)

Ingredients

- 2 tablespoons light mayonnaise
- 2 tablespoons plain low-fat yogurt
- ¼ teaspoon kosher salt (optional)
- ⅛ teaspoon freshly ground black pepper
- 8 ounces Basic Roast Chicken Breast 101 or Classic Poached Chicken cut into ½-inch dice (1½ cups)
- 2 small celery ribs, finely diced
- 1 scallion, white and green parts, finely chopped
- 4 romaine lettuce leaves, for serving

Directions

1. Combine the mayonnaise, yogurt, salt (if used and pepper in a medium dish. Connect the scallion, celery, and chicken and combine well. (For up to 2 days, the salad can be refrigerated in a sealed container.)
2. On two bowls, spoon equal portions of the chicken salad, add the lettuce, and serve.

45. Chinese Chicken Salad

(Ready in about 20 Minutes | Serve 2 | Difficulty: Normal)

Ingredients

- 2 cups packed, shredded Napa cabbage
- 8 ounces Basic Roast Chicken Breast 101 or Classic Poached Chicken, cut into ½-inch dice (1½ cups)
- 1 large carrot, shredded on the large holes of a box grater
- ½ medium red bell pepper, cored and cut into thin strips
- 2 tablespoons finely chopped fresh cilantro, plus more for sprinkling
- Asian Ginger Dressing

Directions

Combine the Napa cabbage, chicken, carrot, bell pepper, and 2 tablespoons of cilantro in a medium dish. Stir the dressing in. Divide between two bowls of salad, sprinkle with extra coriander and serve chilled.

46. Tarragon Chicken Salad with Grapes and almonds

(Ready in about 20 Minutes | Serve 2 | Difficulty: Normal)

Ingredients

- 3 tablespoons plain low-fat yogurt
- 2 tablespoons light mayonnaise
- 2 teaspoons finely chopped fresh tarragon
- Pinch of kosher salt

- ¼ teaspoon freshly ground black pepper
- 8 ounces Basic Roast Chicken Breast 101 or Classic Poached Chicken, cut into ½-inch dice (1½ cups)
- 1 cup halved red or green seedless grapes
- 2 medium celery ribs, thinly sliced
- ¼ cup sliced almonds, toasted
- 2 cups (2 ounces) mixed salad greens
- Lemon wedges, for serving

Directions

1. In a medium bowl, whisk the yogurt, mayonnaise, tarragon, salt, and pepper. Add the chicken, grapes, celery, and almonds and mix well.
2. Divide the salad greens between two salad bowls. Top each with half of the chicken mixture. Serve immediately with the lemon wedges for squeezing the juice over the salad.

47. Chipotle Chicken Chili Taco Salad

(Ready in about 20 Minutes I Serving 6 I Difficulty: Normal)

Ingredients
Baked tortilla chips

- Olive oil in a pump sprayer
- 3 (6-inch) corn tortillas, cut into eighths to make 24 wedges

Salad

- 1 tablespoon olive oil
- 1 pound boneless, skinless chicken thighs, trimmed, cut into 1-inch pieces
- 1 medium yellow onion, chopped
- 1 large red bell pepper, cored and cut into ½-inch dice
- 2 cloves garlic, minced
- 1 teaspoon dried oregano
- 1 teaspoon ground cumin
- ¼ teaspoon kosher salt 1 (14.5-ounce) can no-salt-added diced tomatoes, drained
- ⅓ cup of water
- 1 canned chipotle chili in adobo, minced
- 1 (15-ounce) can 50 percent reduced-sodium black beans, drained and rinsed
- 1 head iceberg lettuce, cored and torn into bite-sized pieces
- 6 tablespoons low-fat sour cream, for serving
- ½ cup chopped fresh cilantro, for serving Lime wedges, for serving

Directions

1. To make the chips for the tortilla: Preheat the oven to 400°F. Using oil to spray a rimmed baking sheet. Spread on the baking sheet with the tortilla strips and spray with oil. Bake, stirring periodically, until golden brown and crisp, for about 10 minutes. Let it cool. To make the salad: In a large nonstick skillet, heat 1 teaspoon of oil over medium-high heat. Add the chicken and cook for about 5 minutes, occasionally stirring, until lightly browned. Transfer to a dish.
2. Heat the skillet with the remaining 2 teaspoons of oil. Sauté the onion, bell pepper, and garlic, occasionally stirring, for around 5 minutes, until tender. Add the oregano, cumin, and salt and stir. Attach and carry the tomatoes, water, and chipotle to a simmer. Put the chicken back in the skillet. Reduce the heat to medium, cover the skillet, and cook until the chicken is tender and opaque about 35 minutes. Stir in the black beans for the last 5 minutes. Let the lettuce cool for 10 minutes.
3. Divide it into six serving bowls and cover it with chili. Garnish each bowl with 4 tortilla chips, top with 1 tablespoon of sour cream, and sprinkle with cilantro. Serve warm with wedges of lime,

48. Cobb Salad

(Ready in about 20 Minutes I Serve 2 I Difficulty: Normal)

Ingredients

- 5 cups (4 ounces) mixed salad greens
- 8 ounces cooked chicken breast, such as Basic Roast Chicken Breast 101, thinly sliced across the grain
- 1 ripe avocado, pitted, peeled, and sliced
- 1 cup Roasted Mushrooms with Thyme and Garlic
- 12 grape tomatoes 6 tablespoons Mustard Vinaigrette
- 2 tablespoons crumbled reduced-fat blue cheese

Directions

1. Divide into two deep salad bowls with the salad greens. Top each one with half the chicken, avocado, mushrooms, and tomatoes, arranging each of the ingredients in the bowl's own portion.
2. Add 3 tablespoons of Mustard Vinaigrette to each salad and sprinkle with 1 tablespoon of blue cheese. Immediately serve.

49. Autumn Turkey Salad with Apples and Dried Cranberries

(Ready in about 30 Minutes I Serve 4 I Difficulty: Normal)

Ingredients

- ¼ cup buttermilk
- 2 tablespoons light mayonnaise
- ¼ teaspoon kosher salt
- ¼ teaspoon freshly ground black pepper
- 10 ounces cooked turkey breast, such as Roast Turkey Breast with Root Vegetables, Lemon, and Garlic Cloves, cut into ½-inch dice (2 cups)
- 2 sweet apples, such as Gala or Fuji, cored and cut into ½-inch dice
- ¼ cup dried cranberries
- ¼ cup unsalted raw sunflower seeds
- 5 cups (4 ounces) mixed salad greens

Directions

1. Whisk together the buttermilk, mayonnaise, salt, and pepper in a medium cup. Mix well and add turkey, apples, dried cranberries, and sunflower seeds. (The salad can be kept refrigerated for up to 1 day in a sealed container.)
2. Divide the greens into four bowls of salad. Top each one with the same amount of salad and serve immediately.

50. Salmon Salade Ninoise
(Ready in about 30 Minutes | Serve 4 | Difficulty: Normal)

Ingredients
- 6 ounces green beans, trimmed and cut into
- 1-inch lengths
- 2 medium Yukon Gold potatoes (8 ounces), scrubbed, unpeeled, and cut into ½-inch-thick rounds
- 1 recipe Lemon Vinaigrette, divided
- 2 scallions, white parts finely chopped and green parts sliced
- 6 cups (5 ounces) mixed salad greens, such as mesclun
- 1 cup halved grape tomatoes
- 4 roasted salmon fillets

Directions
1. Over high heat, bring a medium saucepan of water to a boil. Attach the green beans and cook for about 3 minutes, until crisp-tender. Using a wire sieve or slotted spoon to lift them out of the water and move them to a colander. Rinse and set aside under cold running water.
2. Stir in the water with the potatoes and reduce the heat to mild. Cook for about 15 minutes, until the potatoes are just tender. Drain under cold running water and clean. Switch to a bowl. Apply 1 tablespoon of the vinaigrette and the whites of the chopped scallion and blend. Let it cool to room temperature with the potato salad.
3. With the remaining vinaigrette, toss the salad greens, tomatoes, and green beans in a wide bowl. Spread on a plate and top with the roasted salmon fillets. Arrange the four portions of the potato salad on a tray. Sprinkle and serve with the scallion greens

51. Warm Spinach Salad with Scallops and oranges
(Ready in about 30 Minutes | Serve 4 | Difficulty: Normal)

Ingredients
Vinaigrette
- 2 large navel oranges
- 2 tablespoons olive oil
- 2 tablespoons minced shallots
- 1 tablespoon balsamic vinegar
- ¼ teaspoon kosher salt
- ¼ teaspoon freshly ground black pepper

Salad
- ⅓ cup raw unsalted sunflower seeds
- Olive oil in a spray pump
- 1 pound sea scallops, cut in half crosswise
- 7½ cups (6 ounces) baby spinach

Directions
1. To make your vinaigrette: Grate 1 orange zest into a small cup. Cut the top and bottom off the other orange using a serrated knife, so it stands on the work table. To end up with a skinless disc, cut off the thick peel where it meets the flesh. Keep the fruit in one hand and cut through the thin membranes to release the segments, allowing them to fall into the bowl. Then work over a medium bowl to collect the juices. Repeat with the orange that remains. Through the cup, squeeze the juices from the membranes. Set aside the orange juice and orange segments, weigh, and reserve 2 tablespoons of orange juice.
2. Heat the oil over medium heat in a large nonstick skillet. Add the shallots and sauté for about 1 minute, until softened. Remove yourself from the sun. Stir in the orange juice and vinegar. Scrape the mixture into the bowl with the orange zest using a heatproof spatula. Add the pepper and salt and whisk well.
3. To make the salad: with paper towels, wipe the skillet clean. Over medium heat, heat the skillet. Add the sunflower seeds and cook for about 2 minutes, frequently stirring, until the seeds are fragrant and toasted. Onto plate, turn out.
4. Spray the skillet over medium-high heat with oil and heat it. Add the scallops and cook for about 3 minutes, turning halfway through cooking, until both sides are seared.
5. In a wide bowl, mix the spinach and orange segments. Attach the scallops, sunflower seeds, and vinaigrette and toss. Serve warm

52. Shrimp, mango, and Black bean Salad
(Ready in about 30 Minutes | Serve 4 | Difficulty: Normal)

Ingredients
- 2 tablespoons olive oil, plus more in a pump sprayer
- ¾ pound large shrimp (16 to 20), peeled and deveined
- 2 tablespoons fresh lime juice
- 2 ripe mangoes, pitted, peeled, and cut into ½-inch dice
- 1 (15-ounce) can reduced-sodium black beans, drained and rinsed
- ½ jalapeño, seeded and minced
- 2 tablespoons finely chopped fresh cilantro or mint
- 2 tablespoons minced red onion

Directions
1. Use oil to spray a large ridged grill pan and heat over medium heat. To the bowl, add the shrimp. (Place a broiler rack around 4 inches from the heat source and

preheat the broiler. Spray the broiler rack with oil and spread the shrimp on the rack.) Cook, turning periodically, 3 to 5 minutes throughout until the shrimp are opaque. Refrigerate for about 20 minutes to cool completely.
2. Whisk together the lime juice and the 2 tablespoons of oil in a wide serving dish. Gently toss and add the shrimp, pineapple, rice, jalapeño, cilantro, and onion. Instantly serve

53. Watermelon, Basin, and Shrimp Salad
(Ready in about 30 Minutes | Serve 4 | Difficulty: Normal)

Ingredients
- Olive oil in a pump sprayer
- 1 pound large shrimp (21 to 25), peeled and deveined
- 6 cups seedless watermelon cubes, cut into 1-inch squares, chilled
- ½ medium red onion, cut into thin half-moons
- 24 large basil leaves, cut into thin shreds (¼ cup packed)
- 1 recipe Lime Vinaigrette

Directions
1. Spray the broad nonstick skillet over medium-high heat with oil and heat. Attach the shrimp and cook for about 3 minutes, occasionally stirring, until opaque. Move and let cool to a tray. Cover and refrigerate for at least 1 hour until chilled.
2. Blend the watermelon, onion, and basil in a large serving dish. Apply the vinaigrette and shrimp and toss gently. Serve refrigerated.

54. Tuna and Vegetable Salad
(Ready in about 30 Minutes | Serve 2 | Difficulty: Normal)

Ingredients
- 1 (5-ounce) can low-sodium tuna in water, drained
- 2 small celery ribs, finely diced
- 1 small carrot, shredded
- 1 small scallion, white part only, finely chopped
- 2 tablespoons light mayonnaise
- 2 teaspoons chopped fresh parsley or dill (optional)

Directions
Mix all the ingredients, including the parsley, if used, in a small cup. (The salad can be refrigerated for up to 2 days in a sealed container.)

55. Tuna and White Beans Salad
(Ready in about 30 Minutes | Serve 2 | Difficulty: Normal)

Ingredients
- 2 tablespoons red wine vinegar
- 1 tablespoon water
- 1 small clove garlic, crushed through a press
- ¼ teaspoon dried oregano
- ¼ teaspoon kosher salt
- ¼ teaspoon crushed hot red pepper
- 1 tablespoon olive oil
- 1 (15-ounce) can no-salt-added cannellini beans, drained and rinsed
- 1 (5-ounce) can use very low-sodium tuna in water, drained
- 1 medium red bell pepper, roasted, seeded, and diced
- 2 tablespoons finely chopped fresh parsley
- 2 cups (2 ounces) mixed salad greens Lemon wedges, for serving

Directions
1. Whisk together the vinegar, sugar, garlic, oregano, salt, and hot pepper in a medium cup. In the grease, whisk. Add the beans, salmon, parsley, and red bell pepper (if used) and combine well. This salad can be refrigerated for up to 2 days in a sealed bowl.
2. Put 1 cup of salad greens into a large bowl for each serving. Place half of the tuna and bean mixture on top. To press the juice onto the salad, serve immediately with the lemon wedges.

56. Arugula, Peach, and Almond Salad
(Ready in about 30 Minutes | Serve 4 | Difficulty: Normal)

Ingredients
- 1 tablespoon balsamic vinegar
- 1 tablespoon olive oil, preferably extra-virgin
- 1 tablespoon water
- Pinch of kosher salt 6 cups (5 ounces) baby arugula, well washed and dried.
- 3 ripe peaches, pitted and sliced
- ½ cup sliced natural almonds,
- Freshly ground black pepper.

Directions
Whisk the vinegar, oil, water, and salt together in a large cup. Attach the peaches, arugula, and almonds and throw. Season yourself with pepper. Immediately serve.

57. Roasted Beet Salad with yogurt-Dill dressing
(Ready in about 1 hr | Serve 4 | Difficulty: Difficult I)

Ingredients
- 1½ pounds beets (6 medium) without leaves or stems, scrubbed but unpeeled
- ½ cup plain nonfat yogurt
- 1 tablespoon cider vinegar
- 1 tablespoon finely chopped fresh dill, tarragon, or parsley
- ½ teaspoon kosher salt
- ¼ teaspoon freshly ground black pepper
- 1 clove garlic, crushed through a press

- 1 cup halved grape tomatoes
- 2 scallions, white and green parts, trimmed and thinly sliced

Directions
1. Preheat the oven to 400 F. In aluminum foil, wrap each beet.
2. Put on a rimmed baking sheet and, depending on the size and age of the beets, roast until tender, around 1 1/4 hours. Unwrap it and let it cool until it is simple to treat. Peel and slice the beets into 1/2-inch-thick wedges.
3. Whisk together the milk, vinegar, dill, salt, pepper, and garlic in a medium cup. To coat, add the tomatoes, beets, and scallions and toss. Cover and refrigerate for at least 1 hour, up to 12 hours, until chilled. Serve refrigerated.

58. Apple Coleslaw with Buttermilk Dressing
(Ready in about 30 Minutes | Serve 4 | Difficulty: Normal)

Ingredients
- 1 (14-ounce) bag shredded coleslaw mix
- 1 large red bell pepper, cored and thinly sliced (a food processor with the slicing blade does the best job)
- 1 Granny Smith apple, unpeeled, shredded down to the core on the large holes of a box grater
- 2 scallions, white and green parts, finely chopped
- 1 tablespoon cider vinegar
- 1/3 cup plus
- 1 tablespoon buttermilk
- 3 tablespoons light mayonnaise
- 1/4 teaspoon kosher salt
- 1/2 teaspoon celery seed (optional)
- 1/4 teaspoon freshly ground black pepper

Directions
1. Combine a large bowl with the coleslaw blend, bell pepper, apple, and scallions. Sprinkle and toss well with the vinegar.
2. Mix the buttermilk, mayonnaise, salt, celery seeds (if used), and pepper in a small cup. Pour the mixture of cabbage over and mix well. For at least 1 hour and up to 1 day, cover and refrigerate. Serve chilled to serve with

59. Asian Slaw with Ginger Dressing
(Ready in about 1 hr. | Serve 4 | Difficulty: Difficult l)

Ingredients
- 1 (3-inch-long) piece of unpeeled fresh ginger, shredded on the large holes of a box grater
- 2 tablespoons unseasoned rice vinegar
- 1 clove garlic, crushed through a press
- 1/2 teaspoon kosher salt
- 1/4 teaspoon crushed hot red pepper
- 1 tablespoon Asian dark sesame oil
- 1 tablespoon canola oil
- 4 cups thinly sliced Napa cabbage (about 1/2 small head)
- 1 red bell pepper, cored and cut into 1/4-inch-wide strips
- 2 carrots, shredded
- 2 scallions, white and green parts, thinly sliced
- 2 tablespoons chopped fresh cilantro (optional)
- 1/4 cup coarsely chopped dry-roasted unsalted peanuts

Directions
1. In a large bowl, squeeze the shredded ginger to remove its juice. You need to have about two tablespoons of ginger juice. Apply the rice vinegar, garlic, salt, and hot pepper to the whisk. In the sesame and canola oils, whisking steadily.
2. Add the cabbage, bell pepper, carrots, cilantro, and scallions (if you use them) and combine well. Sprinkle and serve immediately with the peanuts. (For 1 day, the salad can be covered and refrigerated. Re-season before serving with more vinegar and sesame oil.) Serve immediately or cover and refrigerate with plastic wrap.

60. Crunchy, Broccoli Salad
(Ready in about 30 Minutes | Serve 6 | Difficulty: Normal)

Ingredients
- 1/2 cup dried cranberries
- 1 (12-ounce) bag broccoli slaw
- 2 scallions, white and green parts, finely chopped
- 1/4 cup sliced natural almonds,
- 1/4 cup nonfat sour cream
- 2 tablespoons cider vinegar
- 1/2 teaspoon kosher salt
- 1/4 teaspoon freshly ground black pepper

Directions
1. Cover the cranberries with hot tap water in a small bowl and let stand until softened, about 30minutes. (Or place the cranberries and water in a microwave-safe bowl and microwave for 1 1/2 minutes on high power.) Drain and pat dry.
2. In a medium bowl, combine the broccoli slaw, scallions, drained cranberries, almonds, sour cream, vinegar, salt, and pepper. Mix well to distribute the sour cream.
3. Cover with plastic wrap and refrigerate until the slaw is chilled and slightly wilted, about 1 hour and up to 12 hours. Serve chilled

61. Chopped Greek Salad
(Ready in about 30 Minutes | Serve 4 | Difficulty: Normal)

Ingredients
- 1 small red onion, cut into very thin half-moons
- 1 tablespoon red wine vinegar
- 1 tablespoon water

- 1 teaspoon dried oregano
- 1 clove garlic, minced
- ⅛ teaspoon freshly ground black pepper
- 1 tablespoon extra-virgin olive oil
- 1-pint grape tomatoes, cut in halves
- 1 medium cucumber, peeled, halved lengthwise, seeded, and cut into thin half-moons
- ½ cup diced (½-inch) green bell pepper
- 2 ounces (½ cup) crumbled regular rindless goat cheese

Directions
1. Soak the red onion for 30 minutes in a small bowl of cold water; drain and pat dry. (This move is optional, but it helps make the strong flavor of the onion mellow.)
2. Whisk together the vinegar, sugar, oregano, garlic, and pepper in a big cup. Whisk in the oil gradually. Connect the onion, peppers, cucumber, and bell pepper to the drained one and toss well. Sprinkle with the cheese from the goat and serve at once.

62. Iceberg Lettuce Wedge with Russian Dressing
(Ready in about 30 Minutes I Serve 4 I Difficulty: Normal)

Ingredients
- ½ head iceberg lettuce, cut in half lengthwise to make
- 2 wedges½ cup halved grape tomatoes
- ½ medium cucumber, peeled and thinly sliced
- ½ small sweet onion, cut into thin half-moons
- 1 recipe Russian Dressing

Directions
Put an iceberg wedge on a serving plate for each serving and surround it with the tomatoes, cucumber, and onion. With the dressing, top each wedge and serve

63. Kale, Pear, and Bulgur Salad
(Ready in about 30 Minutes I Serve 4 I Difficulty: Normal)

Ingredients
- ½ cup bulgur
- 1¾ cups boiling water
- 8 ounces curly kale
- 2 tablespoons fresh lemon juice
- ½ teaspoon kosher salt
- 2 ripe pears, such as Anjou or Comice, cored and thinly sliced
- ½ cup walnut pieces, and coarsely chopped
- 2 tablespoons extra-virgin olive oil Freshly ground black pepper

Directions
1. Put the bulgur in a heatproof medium bowl and add the boiling water to it. Let stand for around 30 minutes before the bulgur is tender is used. In a wire sieve, drain. Press off the bulgur's excess liquid. Only set aside.
2. Take the thick stems from the kale off and remove them. Stack the kale and coarsely slice crosswise into ½-inch-thick slices, taking a few bits at a time. Transfer to a large bowl of cold water to loosen some dust and agitate. Remove the kale from the water, and leave any dirt in the water behind. In the salad spinner, dry the kale or pat dry with paper towels.
3. Sprinkle lemon juice and salt on the kale. Rub the kale until tender, around 2 minutes, using your palms. Fluff the bulgur with a fork, and the pears and walnuts are added to the kale. Drizzle and toss with oil. Season yourself with pepper. Serve for up to 2 hours at once or refrigerate.

64. Potato Salad with Asparagus and Peas
(Ready in about 30 Minutes I Serve 10 I Difficulty: Normal)

Ingredients
- 3 large red-skinned potatoes (1½ pounds), scrubbed but unpeeled
- 8 ounces asparagus, woody stems discarded, cut into 1-inch lengths
- 2 tablespoons white wine or cider vinegar
- 3 celery ribs, thinly sliced
- ½ cup thawed frozen peas
- 2 scallions, white and green parts, finely chopped
- 2 tablespoons finely chopped fresh parsley
- ¼ cup plain low-fat yogurt
- 2 tablespoons light mayonnaise
- ½ teaspoon kosher salt
- ¼ teaspoon freshly ground black pepper

Directions
1. In a large saucepan, put the potatoes and add enough cold water to cover 1 inch. Cover and, over high heat, bring to a boil. Set and reduce the heat to medium-low with the lid ajar. Cook for about 30 minutes until the potatoes are tender when pierced with the tip of a sharp knife. Switch the potatoes to a colander using a slotted spoon; keep the water boiling. Under cold running water, clean the potatoes. Transfer to a chopping board and let stand to handle until cool enough.
2. Meanwhile, add the asparagus to the boiling water and cook for about 5 minutes, only until tender. Use paper towels to drain in the colander, clean under cold running water, and pat dry
3. Halve each potato and then cut it into ½-inch-thick slices. Move the warm potatoes to a medium bowl and sprinkle with the vinegar. Add asparagus, celery, peas, parsley, and scallions. Whisk together the yogurt, mayonnaise, salt, and pepper in a small cup. Pour the mixture of potatoes over and mix gently. Cover with plastic wrap and refrigerate for at least 1

hour, or up to 2 days, until chilled. Serve chilled to serve with

65. Lentil Goat Cheese Salad
(Ready in about 30 Minutes | Serve 10 | Difficulty: Normal)

Ingredients
- 1 cup green (Puy) or brown lentils
- 2 tablespoons sherry or cider vinegar
- 2 tablespoons water Freshly grated zest of 1 lemon
- ½ teaspoon kosher salt
- ¼ teaspoon freshly ground black pepper
- 2 tablespoons olive oil, preferably extra-virgin
- 1 medium red bell pepper, cored and cut into ¼-inch dice
- 2 celery ribs, cut into ¼-inch dice
- 1 medium carrot, peeled and cut into ¼-inch dice
- 2 tablespoons finely chopped fresh basil, oregano, or parsley
- 4 ounces (1 cup) crumbled goat cheese

Directions
1. Over high heat, bring a medium saucepan of water to a boil. Add the lentils and cook until tender, about 30 minutes (just like pasta). Drain, rinse under cold running water in a wire sieve, and drain well.
2. Whisk the vinegar, sugar, lemon zest, salt, and pepper together in a wide cup. Whisk in the oil gradually.
3. Add the bell pepper, lentils, celery, carrot, and basil, and toss well. (You can cover and refrigerate the salad for up to 1 day.) Sprinkle with the goat cheese and serve at room temperature or chilled.

66. Weeknight Tossed Green Salad
(Ready in about 30 Minutes | Serve 10 | Difficulty: Normal)

Ingredients
- 1 (5-ounce bag) mixed salad greens
- 1 cup halved grape tomatoes
- 1 cucumber, peeled, seeded, and sliced
- ½ cup sunflower or pumpkin seeds or sliced natural almonds American-Style French Dressing, Lemon Vinaigrette, Mustard Vinaigrette, Creamy Ranch Dressing, or Russian Dressing

Directions
1. In a wide bowl, toss the salad greens, tomatoes, and cucumber together. Sprinkle the seeds with them.
2. Drizzle and toss again with the dressing. Immediately serve.

67. Baby Spinach and Strawberry Salad
(Ready in about 30 Minutes | Serve 4 | Difficulty: Normal)

Ingredients
- 1 pound fresh strawberries, hulled
- 2 tablespoons balsamic vinegar
- 2 tablespoons olive oil, preferably extra-virgin
- 2 tablespoons water
- Pinch of kosher salt
- Pinch of freshly ground black pepper
- 2 teaspoons poppy seeds
- 7½ cups (6 ounces) baby spinach
- ½ cup toasted, skinned, and coarsely chopped hazelnuts
- 4 ounces (1 cup) crumbled goat cheese

Directions
1. Chop ¼ cup of the strawberries coarsely and move to a blender. Cut and set aside the remaining strawberries.
2. Purée the chopped strawberries, vinegar, grease, sugar, salt, and pepper in the blender until smooth. To mix, add the poppy seeds and pulse once or twice.
3. In a wide bowl, toss the baby spinach and strawberry dressing. Attach the reserved sliced strawberries and the hazelnuts and toss again. Sprinkle, if used, with goat cheese. At once, serve.

Chapter 7: Side Dish Recipes

In this chapter, we have compiled side dish recipes for DASH diet followers.

1. Acorn squash with apples

(Ready in 25 min | Serve: 2 | Difficulty: Easy)

Ingredients

- 1 Granny Smith apple, peeled, cored, and sliced
- 2 tablespoons brown sugar
- 1 small acorn squash, about 6 inches in diameter
- 2 teaspoons trans fat-free margarine

Directions:

1. Mix the apple and the brown sugar together in a shallow dish. Only put aside.
2. To let the steam escape while frying, pierce the squash multiple times with a sharp knife. Microwave on high, about 5 minutes, before tender. After 3 minutes, turn the squash to ensure the cooking is even.
3. On a cutting board, put the squash and break it in half. Scrape the seeds from each half of the middle and remove the seeds. Cover the hollowed apple mixture with the squash.
4. Send the squash to the microwave and cook it for about 2 minutes before the apples are softened.
5. To a serving plate, pass the squash. With 1 teaspoon of margarine, top each half and serve immediately.

2. Artichokes alla Romana

(Ready in 25 min | Serve: 8 | Difficulty: Easy)

Ingredients

- 2 cups fresh breadcrumbs, preferably whole-wheat
- 1 tablespoon olive oil
- 4 large globe artichokes
- 2 lemons, halved
- 1/3 cup grated Parmesan cheese
- 3 garlic cloves, finely chopped
- 2 tablespoons finely chopped fresh flat-leaf (Italian) parsley
- 1 tablespoon grated lemon zest
- 1/4 teaspoon freshly ground black pepper
- 1 cup plus 2 to 4 tablespoons low-sodium vegetable or chicken stock
- 1 cup dry white wine
- 1 tablespoon minced shallot
- 1 teaspoon chopped fresh oregano

Directions:

1. Heat the oven to 400 F. Mix the breadcrumbs and olive oil together in a dish. Toss it to coat it. In a shallow baking pan, scatter the crumbs and bake, stirring once halfway through, until the crumbs are softly golden, for about 10 minutes. Put aside to cool.
2. Snap off any rough outer leaves and trim the stem flush with the base while dealing with 1 artichoke at a time. With a serrated knife, hack off the top third of the leaves and slice off any remaining thorns with scissors. Clean the cut edges with half a lemon to reduce discoloration. Separate the inner leaves from the middle and pull the tiny leaves out. Scoop out the fuzzy choke using a melon baller or spoon, then squeeze some lemon juice into the cavity. In the same way, trim the remaining artichokes.
3. Toss the breadcrumbs with the Parmesan cheese, garlic, parsley, lemon zest, and pepper in a large cup.

Add 2 to 4 tablespoons of stock, 1 tablespoon at a time, using just enough to start holding together in small clumps for the stuffing to begin.
4. Mound it slightly into the middle of the artichokes using 2/3 of the stuffing. Then spread the leaves open, beginning from the bottom, and spoon a rounded teaspoon of stuffing at each leaf's base. (The artichokes can be cooked several hours in advance and held refrigerated to this point.)
5. Combine the 1 cup stock, wine, shallot, and oregano in a Dutch oven with a tight-fitting lid. (Note: Don't use cast iron, or it can turn brown with the cooked artichokes.) Bring to a boil, then reduce the heat to medium. Arrange the artichokes in one single sheet, stem-end flat, in the milk. Cover and cook for about 45 minutes until the outer leaves are tender (add water if necessary). Move the artichokes and let them cool slightly to a shelf. Every artichoke should be split into quarters and eaten wet.

3. Asparagus with hazelnut gremolata

(Ready in 35 min | Serve: 4 | Difficulty: Normal)

Ingredients

- 1 pound asparagus, tough ends removed, then peeled if the skin is thick
- 1 clove garlic, minced
- 1 tablespoon chopped fresh flat-leaf (Italian) parsley, plus sprigs for garnish
- 1 tablespoon finely chopped toasted hazelnuts (filberts)
- 1/4 teaspoon finely grated lemon zest, plus extra for garnish
- 2 teaspoons fresh lemon juice
- 1 teaspoon extra-virgin olive oil
- 1/4 teaspoon salt

Directions:

1. Carry some 1 inch of water to a boil in a large pot fitted with a steamer basket. Add the asparagus, cover, and steam for about 4 minutes before tender-crisp. Delete yourself from the pot.
2. Combine the asparagus, ginger, chopped parsley, hazelnuts, 1/4 teaspoon of lemon zest, lemon juice, salt, and olive oil in a large cup. To blend and cover, throw well.
3. On a serving platter, place the asparagus neatly and garnish with parsley sprigs and lemon zest. Immediately serve.

4. Baby minted carrots

(Ready in 35 min | Serve: 6 | Difficulty: Normal)

Ingredients

- 6 cups of water
- 1 pound baby carrots, rinsed (about 5 1/2 cups)
- 1/4 cup 100% apple juice
- 1 tablespoon cornstarch
- 1/2 tablespoon chopped fresh mint leaves
- 1/8 teaspoon ground cinnamon

Directions:

1. Through a large bowl, pour the water. Add the carrots and simmer for about 10 minutes, until tender-crisp. Drain the carrots in a serving bowl and set them aside.
2. Combine the apple juice and cornstarch in a shallow saucepan over moderate heat. Stir for about 5 minutes before the mixture thickens. Stir in the cinnamon and mint.
3. Pour over the carrots with the combination. Immediately serve.

5. Baked apples with cherries and almonds

(Ready in 45 min | Serve: 6 | Difficulty: Normal)

Ingredients:

- 1/3 cup dried cherries, coarsely chopped
- 3 tablespoons chopped almonds
- 1 tablespoon wheat germ
- 1 tablespoon firmly packed brown sugar
- 1/2 teaspoon ground cinnamon
- 1/8 teaspoon ground nutmeg
- 6 small Golden Delicious apples, about 1 3/4 pounds total weight
- 1/2 cup apple juice
- 1/4 cup water
- 2 tablespoons dark honey
- 2 teaspoons walnut oil or canola oil

Directions:

1. Preheat an oven to 350 F.
2. Toss the cherries, almonds, wheat germ, brown sugar, cinnamon, and nutmeg together in a small bowl, so all the ingredients are evenly spread. Only put aside.
3. If you like, the apples can be left unpeeled. To peel the apples in a decorative manner, extract the peel from each apple in a circular motion with a vegetable peeler or a sharp knife, missing every other row so that rows of peel overlap with rows of apple flesh. Core each apple, starting from the end of the stem, stopping 3/4 inch from the rim.
4. Divide the cherry mixture between the apples equally, pressing the mixture into each cavity softly. In a sturdy ovenproof frying pan or shallow baking dish, place the apples upright to keep them only big enough. Onto the bowl, pour the apple juice and water. Drizzle the honey and oil over the apples uniformly and carefully cover the pan with aluminum foil. Bake for 50 to 60 minutes, until the apples are moist when pierced with a knife.
5. Move the apples to separate dishes and drizzle with the juices from the pan. Serve at room temperature or hotter.

6. Black bean cakes

(Ready in 35 min | Serve: 4 | Difficulty: Normal)

Ingredients

- 2 cups dried black beans, picked over and rinsed, soaked overnight, and drained
- 4 cups of water
- 8 cloves garlic, chopped
- 1/2 cup chopped fresh cilantro
- 1/2 teaspoon salt
- 2 tablespoons olive oil

Directions:

1. Combine the black beans and water in a large saucepan over a high fire. Just get it to a boil. Reduce heat to medium, cover partly and simmer for around 60 to 70 minutes until the beans are tender. Drain thoroughly.
2. Mash the beans and garlic together in a large dish. Stir in the salt and cilantro. In 8 cakes, shape the mixture. For around 1 hour, switch to a plate and refrigerate.
3. Heat the olive oil in a big, non-stick frying pan over medium heat. Attach the cakes and cook until warm and the outside is slightly crisp, around 5 minutes, turning over once. Immediately serve.

7. Braised celery root

(Ready in 35 min | Serve: 4 | Difficulty: Normal)

Ingredients

- 1 cup vegetable stock or broth
- 1 celery root (celeriac), peeled and diced (about 3 cups)
- 1/4 cup sour cream
- 1 teaspoon Dijon mustard
- 1/4 teaspoon salt
- 1/4 teaspoon freshly ground black pepper
- 2 teaspoons fresh thyme leaves

Directions:

1. Bring the stock to a boil over high heat in a large saucepan. Stir the celery root in it. Decrease the heat to low if the stock returns to a boil. Cover and boil, stirring regularly, for 10 to 12 minutes, until the celery root is tender.
2. Switch the celery root to a bowl using a slotted spoon, cover, and keep warm. Boost the fire to the maximum under the saucepan and put a simmer of the boiling liquid. Cook, uncovered, for about 5 minutes, until reduced to 1 tablespoon.
3. Take the sour cream, mustard, salt, and pepper out of the heat and whisk in. To the sauce, add the celery root and thyme and stir over medium heat until heated. Switch to a serving dish that is warmed and serve immediately.

8. Braised kale with cherry tomatoes

(Ready in 35 min | Serve: 6 | Difficulty: Normal)

Ingredients

- 2 teaspoons extra-virgin olive oil
- 4 garlic cloves, thinly sliced
- 1 pound kale, tough stems removed and leaves coarsely chopped
- 1/2 cup low-sodium vegetable stock or broth
- 1 cup cherry tomatoes, halved
- 1 tablespoon fresh lemon juice
- 1/4 teaspoon salt
- 1/8 teaspoon freshly ground black pepper

Directions:

1. Over medium heat, heat the olive oil in a large frying pan. Add garlic and saute for 1 to 2 minutes, until lightly golden. Stir in the vegetable stock and kale. Cover, decrease the heat to medium-low and simmer for around 5 minutes until the kale is wilted and some of the liquid has evaporated.
2. Stir in the tomatoes and cook 5 to 7 minutes longer, uncovered, until the kale is tender. Remove and stir in the lemon juice, salt, and pepper from the sun. Immediately serve. Over medium heat, heat the olive oil in a large frying pan. Add garlic and saute for 1 to 2 minutes, until lightly golden. Stir in the vegetable stock and kale. Cover, decrease the heat to medium-low and simmer for around 5 minutes until the kale is wilted and some of the liquid has evaporated.
3. Stir in the tomatoes and cook 5 to 7 minutes longer, uncovered, until the kale is tender. Remove and stir in the lemon juice, salt, and pepper from the sun. Immediately serve.

9. Broccoli with garlic and lemon

(Ready in 35 min | Serve: 4 | Difficulty: Normal)

Ingredients

- 4 cups broccoli florets
- 1 teaspoon olive oil
- 1 tablespoon minced garlic
- 1 teaspoon lemon zest
- 1/4 teaspoon kosher salt
- 1/4 teaspoon ground black pepper

Directions:

1. Bring 1 cup of water to a boil in a shallow saucepan. In the boiling broth, add the broccoli and simmer for 2 to 3 minutes or until it is tender. Broccoli drain.
2. Heat the oil in a shallow, medium-high saute pan. Stir in the garlic and saute for about 30 seconds. Connect the broccoli, lemon zest, pepper, and salt. Combine to serve well.

10. Brown rice pilaf

(Ready in 45 min | Serve: 8 | Difficulty: Normal)

Ingredients

- 1 1/8 cups dark brown rice, rinsed and drained
- 2 cups of water
- 3/4 teaspoon salt, divided

- 1/4 teaspoon saffron threads or ground turmeric
- 1/2 teaspoon grated orange zest
- 3 tablespoons fresh orange juice
- 1 1/2 tablespoons pistachio oil or canola oil
- 1/4 cup chopped pistachio nuts
- 1/4 cup dried apricots, chopped

Directions:
1. Combine the rice, water, 1/4 of a teaspoon of salt, and saffron in a saucepan over high heat. Just get it to a boil. Reduce the heat to medium, cover, and simmer for about 45 minutes before the water is absorbed and the rice is tender. Transfer and hold warm in a big bowl.
2. Combine the orange zest and juice, the oil, and the remaining 1/2 teaspoon salt in a shallow cup. Whisk for mixing. Over the warm rice, pour the orange mixture. To mix and cover, add the nuts and apricots and toss gently. Immediately serve.

11. Brussels sprouts with shallots and lemon

(Ready in 45 min | Serve: 8 | Difficulty: Normal)

Ingredients
- 3 teaspoons extra-virgin olive oil, divided
- 3 shallots, thinly sliced (about 3 tablespoons)
- 1/4 teaspoon salt, divided
- 1 pound Brussels sprouts, trimmed and cut into quarters
- 1/2 cup no-salt-added vegetable stock or broth
- 1/4 teaspoon finely grated lemon zest
- 1 tablespoon fresh lemon juice
- 1/4 teaspoon freshly ground black pepper

Directions:
1. Heat 2 teaspoons of olive oil over medium heat in a large, non-stick frying pan. Connect the shallots and saute for about 6 minutes, until soft and softly golden. Incorporate 1/8 teaspoon salt. Transfer and set aside in a bowl.
2. Heat the remaining 1 teaspoon of olive oil over medium heat in the same frying pan. Add the Brussels sprouts and saute for 3 to 4 minutes before they begin to brown. Add the stock of vegetables and get it to a simmer. Cook, uncovered, for 5 to 6 minutes, until the Brussels sprouts are tender. Bring the shallots back to the pan. Add the lemon zest, juice, 1/8 of a teaspoon of salt and pepper, and stir. Immediately serve the dish.

12. Cauliflower mashed 'potatoes.'

(Ready in 45 min | Serve: 4 | Difficulty: Normal)

Ingredients
- 1 head cauliflower
- 1 clove garlic
- 1 leek, white only, split into 4 pieces
- 1 tablespoon soft-bowl margarine, non-hydrogenated
- Pepper to taste

Directions:
1. Break up little bits of cauliflower. Steam the cauliflower, garlic, and leeks in water in a large saucepan until fully tender, about 20 to 30 minutes.
2. To puree the vegetables, use a food processor until the texture resembles mashed potatoes. Just process a minor portion at a time.
3. Using a mixer if you want a finer finish. With a dishtowel, make sure to tightly keep the blender cap on. If the vegetables tend to be dusty, add a little hot water.
4. As per your taste, stir in margarine and pepper. Just serve.

13. Cheesy baked zucchini

(Ready in 35 min | Serve: 2 | Difficulty: Easy)

Ingredients
- 1 medium zucchini, about 6 inches long
- 1 teaspoon olive oil
- 1/8 teaspoon garlic powder
- 1/8 teaspoon onion powder
- 2 tablespoons grated Parmesan cheese

Directions:
1. Heat the oven to 375 F. Cut the zucchini from the sides. Cut part of the way into the zucchini at a half-inch along with the zucchini, but don't cut all of the ways down. It should look like the zucchini is cut in squares, but underneath, all the slices are still connected.
2. With a paper towel, gently pat the zucchini off. On a piece of foil wide enough to fit tightly around it, put the zucchini. Drizzle with olive oil over the top of the zucchini. Sprinkle of ground garlic and onion. In foil, seal the zucchini and pinch it closed. Place it on a tray to roast.
3. If you poke it with a fork, bake for 30 to 35 minutes or until the zucchini is tender. Take the foil out of the oven and open it. Over the zucchini, scatter the cheese. Leave open the foil. Return the zucchini to the oven for 1 to 2 minutes before the cheese is melted and a little brown. Serve it sweet.

14. Chinese-style asparagus

(Ready in 35 min | Serve: 2 | Difficulty: Easy)

Ingredients
- 1/2 cup water
- 1/2 teaspoon sugar
- 1 teaspoon reduced-sodium soy sauce
- 1 1/2 pounds fresh asparagus, woody ends removed and cut into 1 1/2-inch length

Directions:
1. Heat the water, sugar, and soy sauce in a large saucepan over high heat. Cook until it comes to a boil, then add the asparagus. Reduce heat to low and boil, around 3 to 4 minutes, until the asparagus

is tender-crisp. Move to a bowl for serving and eat immediately.

15. Classic Boston baked beans

(Ready in 35 min | Serve: 2 | Difficulty: Easy)

Ingredients

- 2 cups dried small, white beans (navy beans), picked over and rinsed, soaked overnight, and drained
- 4 cups of water
- 2 bay leaves
- 3/4 teaspoon salt, divided
- 1 yellow onion, chopped
- 1/2 cup light molasses
- 1 1/2 tablespoons dry mustard
- 3 strips thick-cut bacon, cut into 1/2-inch pieces

Directions:

Combine the beans, water, bay leaves, and 1/2 teaspoon salt over high heat in a big, ovenproof pot with a tight-fitting lid or in a Dutch oven. Just get it to a boil. Reduce the heat to medium, cover, and simmer partly until the beans are softened, 65 to 75 minutes, but still strong. Remove and discard the bay leaves from the sun. Don't let the beans drain.

Heat the oven to 350 F.

Stir in the beans with the onion, molasses, mustard, bacon, and the remaining 1/4 teaspoon salt. Cover and bake for 4 1/2 to 5 hours, until the beans are soft and covered with a thin syrup. Regularly check to ensure that the beans do not dry out, stirring and adding hot water as needed.

16. Corn pudding

(Ready in 35 min | Serve: 8 | Difficulty: Easy)

Ingredients

- 3 cups of water
- 3 cups skim milk
- 2 cups coarse cornmeal (or polenta)
- 1/4 cup maple syrup
- 1/4 teaspoon cinnamon
- 1/8 teaspoon nutmeg
- 1/8 teaspoon clove
- 1/8 teaspoon ginger
- 1/2 cup raisins

Directions:

1. Bring the water and milk to a boil in a saucepan. To extract lumps, add cornmeal, and stir. Get back to the boil. Then turn the heat to low and cover for 10 to 15 minutes, stirring periodically.
2. Shut the heat off and add the remaining ingredients. Enable 10 to 15 minutes to relax. Mix and serve.

17. Creamed Swiss chard

(Ready in 35 min | Serve: 8 | Difficulty: Easy)

Ingredients

- 2 tablespoons olive oil
- 1 1/2 tablespoons unbleached all-purpose flour
- 3 garlic cloves, finely chopped
- 1 1/4 cups low-fat plain soy milk
- 2 pounds Swiss chard, washed, stemmed, and cut crosswise into strips 1/2-inch wide
- 1/2 teaspoon freshly ground black pepper
- 1 tablespoon grated Parmesan cheese

Directions:

1. In a large frying pan, heat the olive oil over medium heat. Whisk in the flour to make a smooth paste. Continue whisking and add the garlic; cook for 30 seconds longer. Whisk in the soy milk and cook until the mixture thickens slightly.
2. Add the chard and stir to coat well. Cover and cook just until tender, about 2 minutes. Season with pepper. Sprinkle with the Parmesan and serve hot.

18. Creole-style black-eyed peas

(Ready in 35 min | Serve: 8 | Difficulty: Easy)

Ingredients

- 3 cups of water
- 2 cups dried black-eyed peas
- 1 teaspoon low-sodium vegetable-flavored bouillon granules
- 2 cups canned unsalted tomatoes, crushed
- 1 large onion, finely chopped
- 2 stalks celery, finely chopped
- 3 teaspoons minced garlic
- 1/2 teaspoon dry mustard
- 1/4 teaspoon ground ginger
- 1/4 teaspoon cayenne pepper
- 1 bay leaf
- 1/2 cup chopped parsley

Directions

1. Add 2 cups of water and the black-eyed peas to a medium saucepan over high heat. For 2 minutes, bring to a boil, cover, remove from the heat, and let stand for 1 hour.
2. Drain the water so that the peas are left in the saucepan. Add 1 cup of sugar, bouillon granules, tomatoes, cabbage, celery, garlic, mustard, ginger, bay leaf, and cayenne pepper to the remaining mixture. Stir and put to a boil. Cover, reduce heat, and simmer gently, stirring regularly, for 2 hours. To keep the peas covered with liquid, add water as needed.
3. Pour into a serving bowl and garnish with parsley; remove the bay leaf. Immediately serve.

19. Eggplant with toasted spices

(Ready in 35 min | Serve: 8 | Difficulty: Easy)

Ingredients

- 1 large eggplant, about 1 1/2 pounds
- 1 teaspoon mustard seed
- 1/2 teaspoon ground cumin

- 1/2 teaspoon ground coriander
- 1/2 teaspoon curry powder
- Pinch of ground ginger
- Pinch of ground nutmeg
- Pinch of ground cloves
- 1 tablespoon olive oil
- 1/2 yellow onion, finely chopped
- 2 cups cherry tomatoes, halved, or 1 cup tomato sauce
- 1 tablespoon light molasses
- 1 garlic clove, minced
- 1 teaspoon red wine vinegar
- 1/4 teaspoon salt
- 1/4 teaspoon freshly ground black pepper
- 1 tablespoon chopped fresh cilantro

Directions:

1. Using a barbecue grill to cook a hot fire or heat a gas grill or broiler. Lightly brush the rack or broiler pan with cooking spray, away from the heat source. The cooking rack should be placed 4 to 6 inches from the heat source.
2. Trim the eggplant and cut about 1/4-inch thick into round slices. Arrange the slices on a rack or pan and grill or broil for around 5 minutes on either side, rotating once, until the eggplant is soft and browned. Set yourself aside and keep warm.
3. Combine the first 7 spices in a small bowl. Heat the olive oil in a large frying pan until hot but not burning, over medium heat. Connect the spice mixture and simmer for about 30 seconds, stirring continuously. Add the onion and saute for about 4 minutes until it is soft and translucent. Tomatoes, molasses, garlic, and vinegar are added. Cook the sauce until it thickens, occasionally stirring, for about 4 minutes. Season with pepper and salt.
4. To a warmed serving dish or individual plates, pass the eggplant, pour the sauce over, and garnish with the cilantro.

20. Fresh fruit kebabs

(Ready in 35 min | Serve: 8 | Difficulty: Easy)

Ingredients

- 6 ounces low-fat, sugar-free lemon yogurt
- 1 teaspoon fresh lime juice
- 1 teaspoon lime zest
- 4 pineapple chunks (about 1/2 inch each)
- 4 strawberries
- 1 kiwi, peeled and quartered
- 1/2 banana, cut into 4 1/2-inch chunks
- 4 red grapes
- 4 wooden skewers

Directions:

1. Whisk together the yogurt, lime juice, and lime zest in a shallow dish. Cover until required, and refrigerate.
2. Into the skewer, thread 1 of each fruit. Repeat until the fruit is finished on the other skewers. Serve the lemon-lime dip with it.

21. Garlic mashed potatoes

(Ready in 35 min | Serve: 8 | Difficulty: Easy)

Ingredients

- 3 pounds russet potatoes, peeled and cubed
- 6 garlic cloves, separated and peeled
- 1/2 cup fat-free milk
- 1 tablespoon trans-fat-free margarine
- Ground black pepper, to taste
- 2 tablespoons chopped fresh parsley

Directions:

Cover the potatoes in a large stockpot with water. Just get it to a boil. Reduce the heat and simmer for about 15 minutes, before soft. Carefully rinse the potatoes and add to the stockpot.
Cover the garlic with water in a shallow saucepan. Just get it to a boil. Reduce the heat and simmer for about 10 minutes, until soft. Drain some garlic.
Combine the garlic and milk in a food processor or blender. Purée until it's smooth. To the potatoes, add the pureed garlic and the margarine. Mash to the consistency required. Season with, to taste, black pepper. Garnish with parsley and promptly serve.

22. Ginger-marinated grilled portobello mushrooms

(Ready in 35 min | Serve: 4 | Difficulty: Easy)

Ingredients

- 1/4 cup balsamic vinegar
- 1/2 cup pineapple juice
- 2 tablespoons chopped fresh ginger, peeled
- 4 large portobello mushrooms (about 4 ounces each), cleaned and stems removed
- 1 tablespoon chopped fresh basil

Directions:

1. Whisk together the balsamic vinegar, pineapple juice, and ginger in a small bowl.
2. Place the fungus in a glass dish, side up, stemless. Drizzle over the mushrooms with the marinade. Cover and marinate for about 1 hour in the refrigerator, turning the mushrooms over once.
3. Using a barbecue grill to cook a hot fire or heat a gas grill or broiler. Lightly brush the grill rack or broiler pan with cooking spray, away from the heat source. The cooking rack should be placed 4 to 6 inches from the heat source.
4. On medium heat, grill or broil the mushrooms, sometimes rotating, until tender, for around 5 minutes on each side. To stop drying out, baste it with marinade.

23. Glazed root vegetables

(Ready in 35 min | Serve: 3 | Difficulty: Easy)

Ingredients

- 1 1/2 cups water
- 1/2 cup onions, cut into 1-inch pieces (or pearl onions)

- 1/2 cup carrots, cut into 1-inch pieces (or baby carrots)
- 1/2 cup turnips, cut into 1-inch pieces
- 1/2 cup new potatoes, cut into 1-inch pieces
- 2 teaspoons sugar
- 1 teaspoon olive oil

Directions:

1. Add the water, onions, carrots, turnips, and potatoes into a saucepan. Simmer over medium heat until vegetables are soft, about 15 minutes, uncovered. Drain and dust with olive oil and sugar.
2. Shift the heat on and finish frying, rotating the pan until the vegetables are finely golden and glazed. Move to a bowl for serving and eat immediately.

24. Granola with raisins, apples, and cinnamon

(Ready in 35 min | Serve: 3| Difficulty: Easy)

Ingredients

- 1/4 cup slivered almonds
- 1/4 cup honey
- 1/4 cup unsweetened applesauce
- 1 tablespoon vanilla extract
- 1 tablespoon ground cinnamon
- 2 cups dry old-fashioned oatmeal
- 2 cups bran flakes
- 3/4 cup dried apple pieces
- 1/2 cup golden raisins

Directions:

1. Heat the oven to 325 F. Cover a baking sheet lightly with cooking oil.
2. Spread the almonds on a baking sheet and bake until crispy and fragrant, stirring periodically, for about 10 minutes. Switch it to a plate instantly to cool. Elevate the oven temperature to 350 F.
3. Whisk the sugar, applesauce, vanilla, and cinnamon together in a little cup. Just put aside.
4. Add the oatmeal and bran flakes into a big dish. To blend well, stir. Apply a combination of honey and toss with your mouth. Don't break up such clumps.
5. On a baking dish, distribute the cereal mixture uniformly. Put in the oven and bake until golden brown, stirring periodically, for around 30 minutes. Delete and cool slightly from the oven.
6. Mix the cereal mixture, the toasted almonds, the dried apple, and the raisins in a big bowl. Absolutely awesome. Store in a jar that is airtight.

25. Green beans with red pepper and garlic

(Ready in 35 min | Serve: 6| Difficulty: Easy)

Ingredients

- 1 pound green beans, stems trimmed
- 2 teaspoons olive oil
- 1 red bell pepper, seeded and cut into thin slices
- 1/2 teaspoon chili paste or red pepper flakes
- 1 clove garlic, finely chopped
- 1 teaspoon sesame oil
- 1/4 teaspoon salt
- 1/4 teaspoon freshly ground black pepper

Directions:

1. Split into 2-inch bits of beans. Bring 3/4 of a huge saucepan full of water to a boil. Attach the beans and simmer until they turn light green and, 1 to 3 minutes, are tender-crisp. To stop frying, rinse the beans, then plunge them into a bucket of ice water. Once again, rinse and put aside.
2. Over medium heat, heat the olive oil in a large frying pan. Attach the bell pepper and toss for about 1 minute, then stir. Stir in the beans and saute 1 minute longer.
3. Apply the paste and garlic to the chili and stir for 1 minute. The beans would be light green and tender. Stir in the sesame oil, then season with salt and pepper. Immediately serve.

26. Holiday green bean casserole

(Ready in 35 min | Serve: 6| Difficulty: Easy)

Ingredients

- 3 teaspoons olive oil, divided
- 1 medium onion, thinly sliced
- 1/4 cup finely chopped onion
- 1 clove garlic, finely chopped
- 2 tablespoons water
- 1 1/2 cups sliced mushrooms
- 3 tablespoons flour
- 1/2 teaspoon dried ground thyme
- 1 1/2 cups skim milk
- 1 pound fresh green beans, trimmed and cut into 1-inch pieces
- 1/3 cup fresh whole-grain bread crumbs

Directions:

1. Heat the oven to 350 F.
2. Over low heat, heat a large skillet and add 2 teaspoons of olive oil. Attach the sliced onion and saute, stirring regularly, for 15 to 20 minutes until the onions are golden. Take the onions out of the skillet and set them aside.
3. In a pan, add the remaining 1 teaspoon of olive oil, chopped onion, and garlic, and roast for 2 to 3 minutes. Add the water and mushrooms, and simmer for an estimated 5 minutes. Sprinkle the mixture with flour and thyme and stir. Stir the milk in steadily. Increase the heat to low and stir until the sauce thickens slowly.
4. Boil them in water for 8 to 10 minutes to roast the green beans. (Or cook the beans in the microwave for 5 minutes with 2 teaspoons of water to save time.)
5. Drain your beans and set them aside. With cooking spray, spray a 2-quart casserole and put the green beans in the casserole. Over the green beans, pour the mushroom sauce. Cover with slices of sauteed onion and crumbs of fresh bread. Bake for fifteen minutes, or until golden brown on top.

27. Honey sage carrots

(Ready in 35 min | Serve: 4 | Difficulty: Easy)

Ingredients

- 2 cups sliced carrots
- 2 teaspoons butter
- 2 tablespoons honey
- 1 tablespoon chopped fresh sage
- 1/4 teaspoon ground black pepper
- 1/8 teaspoon salt

Directions:

1. Load a medium saucepan with water and bring it to a boil. Attach the carrots and cook until the carrots are tender, for around 5 minutes. Drain yourself and set aside. 2. A medium saute pan is preheated, and butter is added. Add the carrots, sugar, sage, pepper, and salt until the pan is heated and the butter is melting. Saute for about 3 minutes, stirring regularly. Withdraw from the sun and serve.

28. Honey-glazed sweet potatoes

(Ready in 35 min | Serve: 4 | Difficulty: Easy)

Ingredients

- 1/4 cup water
- 2 tablespoons brown sugar
- 2 tablespoons honey
- 1 tablespoon olive oil
- 2 pounds sweet potatoes (about 4 large), peeled and cut into wedges
- Cracked black pepper or chopped herb of choice (rosemary, sage, or thyme), to taste

Directions:

1. Heat the oven to 375 F. Coat lightly with cooking spray on a 9-by-13-inch baking dish.
2. Put the water, brown sugar, honey, and olive oil in a small bowl to make the sauce. Until smooth, whisk.
3. Place the baking dish with a single layer of sweet potatoes. Over the sweet potatoes, pour the sauce. Turn back to powder them.
4. Cover and bake for about 45 minutes, until tender. Once or twice, turn the sweet potatoes over to finish coating them. Remove the cover when tender and continue to bake for about 15 minutes before the glaze is set.
5. Move to a serving dish and top with the preferred pepper or chopped herb. Immediately serve.

29. Lean country-style breakfast sausage

(Ready in 35 min | Serve: 4 | Difficulty: Easy)

Ingredients

- 1/2 pound lean ground pork loin
- 1/2 pound lean ground turkey breast
- 1 teaspoon sugar
- 1 teaspoon dry mustard
- 1 teaspoon onion powder
- 1 teaspoon sage
- 1 teaspoon ground black pepper
- 1/2 teaspoon red pepper flakes (optional)

Directions:

1. Blend all the ingredients together in a big bowl. Shape 12 patties of the mixture.
2. Using cooking spray to spray a big, non-stick skillet and put over medium heat.
3. Patties and cover are added. Cook until browned, about 5 minutes on either hand, and the juices run clear. When using a thermometer, cook until the temperature within exceeds 165 F. Move to a bowl for serving and eat immediately.

30. Lemon rice with golden raisins and almonds

(Ready in 35 min | Serve: 4 | Difficulty: Easy)

Ingredients

- 1/2 cup slivered almonds, coarsely chopped
- 1 cup uncooked brown rice
- 1 3/4 cup unsalted chicken broth
- 3 tablespoons lemon juice
- 2 teaspoons lemon zest
- 1/4 cup chopped onions
- 1/2 teaspoon ground cinnamon
- 1/4 teaspoon ground nutmeg
- 1 tablespoon trans-free margarine
- 1/3 cup water
- 1/2 cup golden raisins
- 1/2 cup frozen peas
- 2 tablespoons honey

Directions:

1. Heat the oven to 325 F. Cover a baking sheet lightly with cooking oil.
2. Spread the almonds on the baking sheet and bake until crispy and fragrant, stirring periodically, for about 10 minutes. Switch it to a plate instantly to cool.
3. Stir together the flour, broth, lemon juice, zest, onion, cinnamon, nutmeg, and margarine in a medium saucepan over medium heat. Cover and boil for 30 minutes or until the liquid is consumed, stirring regularly.
4. Combine the water and raisins in a shallow saucepan. Simmer, cover, and simmer for five minutes. Add the peas, then boil for another 1 minute. Connect to the rice and boil, about 15 to 20 minutes more, until all the liquid is absorbed.
5. The rice mixture is fluffed and moved to a serving bowl. Sprinkle with toasted almonds and add honey to drizzle. Immediately serve.

31. Lentil ragout

(Ready in 35 min | Serve: 6 | Difficulty: Easy)

Ingredients

- 1 teaspoon olive oil
- 1 cup chopped onions

- 6 medium tomatoes, chopped
- 5 cups of water
- 1 cup raw red lentils
- 1 tablespoon chopped fresh thyme
- 4 cloves garlic, minced
- 1 teaspoon kosher salt
- 1/4 teaspoon ground black pepper

Directions:

1. On medium-high heat, heat a medium saucepan. Put some gasoline. For 2 to 3 minutes, saute the onions. Attach the tomatoes and saute, constantly stirring, for another 3 minutes. Connect the water and lentils, then simmer for about 20 minutes before most of the water is absorbed.
2. Add the thyme, garlic, salt, and pepper and stir. Ragout is expected to be somewhat compact but not dry.

32. Parmesan roasted cauliflower

(Ready in 35 min | Serve: 6| Difficulty: Easy)

Ingredients

- 1/2 cup panko bread crumbs
- 1/4 cup finely grated Parmesan cheese
- 2 tablespoons olive oil
- 1 teaspoon fresh lemon zest
- 1 teaspoon finely chopped fresh basil
- 1/4 teaspoon paprika
- 1/4 teaspoon kosher salt
- 3 cups small cauliflower florets

Directions:

1. Load a medium saucepan with water and bring it to a boil. Heat the oven to 375 F. Lightly coat with cooking spray on an 8-by-8-inch baking dish.
2. Combine the bread crumbs, cheese, oil, lemon zest, basil, paprika, and salt in a shallow cup. To blend the mixture equally, use your palms.
3. Place the cauliflower for 3 minutes in boiling water; drain. In the baking dish, put the cauliflower and scatter the bread crumb mixture uniformly over the top. Bake until the crust is light brown or around 15 minutes.

33. Polenta with red pepper coulis

(Ready in 35 min | Serve: 6| Difficulty: Easy)

Ingredients

- 1 red bell pepper (capsicum), roasted and seeded
- 1 garlic clove
- 1 3/4 cups water
- 1 3/4 cups plain soy milk (soya milk) or 1 percent low-fat milk
- 1 tablespoon extra-virgin olive oil
- 1/4 teaspoon salt
- 1 cup polenta, preferably stone-ground
- 2 tablespoons grated Parmesan cheese
- 1 tablespoon chopped thyme

Directions:

1. Combine the roasted pepper, garlic, and 1 tablespoon of water in a blender or a food processor. To process until smooth; set aside the coulis.
2. Heat the oven to 450 F. Cover a 9-inch circular cake pan lightly with olive oil spray for frying.
3. Combine the soy milk, remaining water, olive oil, and salt in a broad saucepan. 4. Mix the polenta with a whisk and put over medium heat. Constantly whisk until the polenta continues to thicken. Reduce the heat to a low degree and stir with a wooden spoon again. Cook for about 15 minutes, constantly stirring, before the polenta pulls away from the sides of the bowl. To mix, add the coulis and stir.
5. In the prepared cake pan, add the mixture and top with the cheese. Bake until solid, 15 minutes roughly. Until eating, let it stand in the pan for 10 minutes. Break into six wedges and apply the thyme and sprinkle.

34. Potato salad

(Ready in 35 min | Serve: 8| Difficulty: Normal)

Ingredients

- 1 pound potatoes, diced and boiled or steamed
- 1 large yellow onion, chopped (1 cup)
- 1 large carrot, diced (1/2 cup)
- 2 ribs celery, diced (1/2 cup)
- 2 tablespoons minced fresh dill (or 1/2 tablespoon dried)
- 1 teaspoon ground black pepper
- 1/4 cup low-calorie mayonnaise
- 1 tablespoon Dijon mustard
- 2 tablespoons red wine vinegar

Directions:

1. Put all ingredients in a bowl and mix well. Chill before serving.

35. Quinoa risotto with arugula and Parmesan

(Ready in 35 min | Serve: 6| Difficulty: Normal)

Ingredients

- 1 tablespoon olive oil
- 1/2 yellow onion, chopped (about 1/2 cup)
- 1 garlic clove, minced
- 1 cup quinoa, well rinsed
- 2 1/4 cups low-sodium vegetable stock or broth
- 2 cups chopped, stemmed arugula (rocket)
- 1 small carrot, peeled and finely shredded
- 1/2 cup thinly sliced fresh shiitake mushrooms
- 1/4 cup grated Parmesan cheese
- 1/4 teaspoon salt
- 1/4 teaspoon freshly ground black pepper

Directions:

1. Heat the olive oil in a wide saucepan over medium heat. Connect the onion and saute for about 4 minutes until it is

smooth and translucent. Add the garlic and the quinoa and cook, stirring periodically, for about 1 minute. Don't make it brown the garlic.

2. Stir in the stock and get it to a boil. Reduce the heat to low and simmer for about 12 minutes until the quinoa is almost soft to the bite but slightly firm in the middle. The combination is going to be brothy. Incorporate the arugula, carrot, and mushrooms and boil until the grains of the quinoa turn white to translucent, about 2 minutes longer.

3. Stir in the cheese, then apply salt and pepper to the seasoning. Immediately serve.

36. Ratatouille with roasted tomato vinaigrette

(Ready in 35 min | Serve: 8| Difficulty: Normal)

Ingredients

- 1 eggplant, about 1 pound, cut into 1/2-inch cubes (about 4 cups)
- 7 teaspoons extra-virgin olive oil (divided)
- 2 zucchini, about 1/2 pound total weight, cut into 1/2-inch cubes (about 1 1/2 cups)
- 2 plum (Roma) tomatoes, halved lengthwise
- 1 yellow bell pepper, roasted and seeded
- 1 red bell pepper, roasted and seeded
- 1 shallot, coarsely chopped (about 2 tablespoons)
- 1/4 cup balsamic vinegar
- 1/2 teaspoon salt
- 1/2 teaspoon freshly ground black pepper
- 1 tablespoon grated lemon zest
- 1 tablespoon chopped fresh basil
- 1 tablespoon chopped fresh flat-leaf (Italian) parsley

Directions:

1. Position racks in the lower third and middle of the oven and heat to 450 F. Lightly coat 2 baking sheets with olive oil cooking spray.

2. In a bowl, toss the eggplant with 1 teaspoon of the olive oil. Spread the eggplant in a single layer on one of the prepared baking sheets.

3. In the same bowl, toss the zucchini with 1 teaspoon of the olive oil. On the second baking sheet, spread the zucchini in a single layer and arrange the tomato halves cut-side up. Rub a bit of olive oil left in the bowl on the top of the tomato halves. Place the eggplant on the lower rack and the zucchini and tomatoes on the middle rack of the oven. Roast for 8 minutes. Turn the eggplant, zucchini and tomatoes and roast until softened, about 8 minutes longer. Set aside to cool.

4. Peel the roasted bell peppers and dice into 1/2-inch pieces. Set aside.

5. To make the vinaigrette, in a blender or food processor, combine the roasted tomatoes, shallot, balsamic vinegar, salt and pepper. Process until smooth. With the motor running, slowly add the remaining 5 teaspoons olive oil in a thin stream until emulsified.

6. In a large bowl, stir together the roasted eggplant, zucchini, bell peppers and the lemon zest. Add the vinaigrette and toss just to combine. Sprinkle with the basil and parsley. Cover and refrigerate or serve at room temperature.

37. Roasted asparagus and wild mushrooms

(Ready in 35 min | Serve: 6| Difficulty: Normal)

Ingredients

- 1 pound asparagus, cut into 1-inch pieces
- 2 cups morel or other mushrooms, cut into quarters
- 1 teaspoon olive oil
- 2 tablespoons balsamic vinegar
- Zest of one lemon
- 1 teaspoon black pepper

Directions:

1. In a glass bowl or large sealable food container, combine all the ingredients. Toss it to coat it. Let it marinate in the refrigerator for 1 to 2 hours.

2. Place a non-stick baking sheet on it. Switch up the broiler. Cook, turning vegetables over once or until gently browned, for 2 to 3 minutes.

38. Roasted butternut squash fries

(Ready in 35 min | Serve: 6| Difficulty: Normal)

Ingredients

- 1 medium butternut squash
- 1 tablespoon olive oil
- 1 tablespoon chopped fresh thyme
- 1 tablespoon chopped fresh rosemary
- 1/2 teaspoon salt

Directions:

1. Heat the oven to 425 F. Cover a baking sheet lightly with non-stick cooking oil.

2. Peel the butternut squash skin and carve into even sticks, about 1/2 inch wide and 3 inches long. Combine the squash, milk, thyme, rosemary, and salt in a medium bowl; blend until the squash is covered evenly.

3. Spread and roast on the baking sheet for 10 minutes. Break the oven's baking sheet and shake to loosen the squash. Return to the oven and continue to roast until golden brown for another 5 to 10 minutes.

39. Roasted green beans

(Ready in 35 min | Serve: 4| Difficulty: Normal)

Ingredients

- 2 cups green beans, cleaned and trimmed
- 1 cup cherry tomatoes (about 20)
- 1 tablespoon minced garlic
- 2 teaspoons olive oil
- 1 teaspoon dried basil
- 1 teaspoon dried oregano
- 1 teaspoon onion powder
- 1/2 teaspoon salt

- 1/2 teaspoon pepper

Directions:
1. Heat the oven to 400 F. Grease the baking sheet slightly.
2. Combine the trimmed green beans, tomatoes, garlic, oil, basil, oregano, onion powder, salt and pepper in a medium bowl; blend until the beans are uniformly covered and flavored with olive oil.
3. On the baking sheet, put the green beans, making sure that they spread out equally. Roast for 10 to 15 minutes in the oven and stir after 10 minutes.

40. Roasted potatoes
(Ready in 35 min | Serve: 5| Difficulty: Normal)

Ingredients
- 1 pound large red or white potatoes with skins, cut into wedges 1/4-inch thick
- 1 tablespoon olive oil
- 1 teaspoon rosemary or oregano

Directions:
1. Heat the oven to 400 F. Cover a baking sheet lightly with cooking oil.
2. For 5 minutes, soak the potato wedges in ice water. Drain the potatoes under cool water and rinse thoroughly. To rinse, press in between paper towels. Move the potatoes to a large bowl, top the potatoes with olive oil and toss to coat.
3. On the prepared baking sheet, organize the potatoes into a single plate. For 15 minutes, roast. Turn over the potatoes and bake for an additional 5 minutes.
4. Sprinkle spices with them. Return the potatoes to the oven and roast for about 5 minutes until they are brown and crispy. Immediately serve.

41. Roasted potatoes with garlic and herbs
(Ready in 35 min | Serve: 4| Difficulty: Normal)

Ingredients
- 3/4 pound small (2-inch) white or red potatoes
- 4 garlic cloves
- 2 teaspoons olive oil
- 2 teaspoons chopped fresh rosemary
- 1/8 teaspoon salt
- 1/4 teaspoon ground black pepper
- 2 teaspoons butter
- 2 tablespoons chopped fresh parsley

Directions:
1. Heat the oven to 400 F. Coat the large baking dish lightly with cooking oil.
2. Add the entire potatoes, cloves of garlic, olive oil, rosemary, salt and pepper to a large mixing cup. Using your hands to blend until the oil and spices are mixed with the potatoes.
3. In the prepared baking dish, arrange the potatoes into a single plate. Use a lid or aluminum foil to protect and bake for 25 minutes.
4. Remove the foil or lid. Turn the potatoes and bake until the potatoes are soft and lightly browned, about 25 minutes, uncovered.
5. Place it in a serving bowl and mix it with butter. Sprinkle and serve with parsley.

42. Roasted winter squash with wild rice and cranberries
(Ready in 35 min | Serve: 4| Difficulty: Normal)

Ingredients
- 4 cups peeled and diced (1/2-inch pieces) winter squash
- 2 teaspoons canola oil, divided
- 1 cup diced onion
- 1 cup fresh cranberries
- 4 cups cooked wild rice
- 1/4 cup walnuts, chopped
- 1 small orange, peeled and segmented
- 1/2 tablespoon chopped Italian parsley
- 1/4 teaspoon thyme
- Black pepper to taste

Directions:
1. Heat the oven to 400 F. In a roasting pan, put the squash and toss it with 1 teaspoon of oil. For 40 minutes or until golden, roast it.
2. Brown the onions in a hot saute pan with the remaining oil. Garnish with cranberries and sauté for 1 minute. Connect the remaining ingredients and cook for 4 to 5 minutes or until fully cooked. Just serve.

43. Salad greens with squash
(Ready in 35 min | Serve: 4| Difficulty: Normal)

Ingredients
- 2 small acorn squash (about 2 pounds total)
- 2 tablespoons brown sugar
- 1 tablespoon olive oil
- 4 cups leaf lettuce, such as spring mix
- 2 tablespoons sunflower seeds
- 4 teaspoons honey

Directions:
1. To let the steam escape during cooking, pierce the squash multiple times with a sharp knife. Microwave each squash for about 5 minutes before soft. After 3 minutes, turn the squash to ensure the cooking is even.
2. On a cutting board, put the squash and break it in half. Scrape the seeds from each half of the middle and remove the seeds. Remove the squash pulp and place it in a mixing cup. For the other squash, repeat. Around 2 cups of pulp should be present. Sprinkle the brown sugar with the squash and apply some olive oil until flat, blend. To cool somewhat, set aside.
3. Divide the lettuce into four salad bowls. Cover with 1/2 cup of the mixture of squash, 1/2 tablespoon of sunflower seeds, and 1 teaspoon of honey each. Immediately serve.

44. Sauteed fresh corn
(Ready in 35 min | Serve: 6| Difficulty: Normal)

Ingredients
- 1 teaspoon olive oil

- 2 ounces prosciutto, cut into thin strips (about 1/2 cup)
- 2 cups fresh corn kernels (cut from about 4 medium ears of corn) or frozen corn
- 1 green bell pepper, seeded, cored, and diced
- 1 teaspoon minced garlic

Directions:

1. Heat the olive oil in a big skillet over medium heat. Connect the prosciutto and saute for about 5 minutes, until the meat is crisp. Add the corn, bell pepper, and garlic and stir. Saute, stirring regularly, for 5 to 7 minutes, until the kernels are tender. Immediately serve.

45. Sauteed zucchini coins

(Ready in 35 min | Serve: 4| Difficulty: Normal)

Ingredients

- 1 tablespoon olive oil
- 2 cups thinly sliced yellow zucchini
- 2 cups thinly sliced green zucchini
- 1 teaspoon dill weed
- 2 tablespoons fresh cilantro
- 2 scallions, chopped
- 2 tablespoons lemon juice

Directions:

1. Heat the oil in a big, non-stick frying pan over medium heat. Attach the slices of zucchini and saute for about 5 minutes before their colors escalate. Dill, cilantro, and scallions are added and stir until blended uniformly. Switch to a cooking cup. Sprinkle and eat directly with lemon juice.

46. Savory buckwheat pilaf with toasted spices

(Ready in 35 min | Serve: 6| Difficulty: Normal)

Ingredients

- 1 tablespoon olive oil
- 1 yellow onion, chopped (about 1 cup)
- 1 cup buckwheat groats
- 3 garlic cloves, minced
- 1/2 teaspoon cumin seed
- 1/2 teaspoon mustard seed
- 1/4 teaspoon ground cardamom
- 2 cups unsalted (no salt added) vegetable stock or broth
- 1 tomato, peeled and seeded, then diced (about 1 cup)
- 1/4 teaspoon salt
- 2 tablespoons chopped fresh cilantro (coriander)

Directions:

1. Heat the olive oil in a saucepan over medium heat. Connect the onion and saute for about 4 minutes until it is smooth and translucent. Add the buckwheat, garlic, cumin, mustard, and cardamom seeds. Saute, stirring continuously, for about 3 minutes, until the spices and garlic are fragrant and the buckwheat is gently toasted.

2. Pour the stock in carefully. Bring to a boil, then reduce heat to medium-low, cover, and simmer for around 10 minutes before the liquid is absorbed. Remove from the heat and let stand for 2 minutes, insulated.

3. Stir in the salt and tomatoes. Transfer and scatter with the cilantro in a serving cup. Immediately serve.

47. Seared endive

(Ready in 35 min | Serve: 6| Difficulty: Normal)

Ingredients

- 1 tablespoon water
- 8 heads of Belgian endive, washed and halved
- Juice from 1 lemon
- 1/4 teaspoon salt
- Ground black pepper, if desired
- 2 tablespoons chopped fresh parsley

Directions:

1. Heat the water in a large skillet over medium heat. Add endives, break down the sides when the outer leaves become transparent, cover, and simmer for several minutes.

2. Delete and expose from the sun. Squeeze over the endive with lemon juice and add salt and pepper to taste. Switch to a serving dish and apply parsley to garnish. Immediately serve.

48. Shrimp ceviche

(Ready in 35 min | Serve: 8| Difficulty: Normal)

Ingredients

- 1/2 pound raw shrimp, cut into 1/4-inch pieces
- 2 lemons, zest, and juice
- 2 limes, zest, and juice
- 2 tablespoons olive oil
- 2 teaspoons cumin
- 1/2 cup diced red onion
- 1 cup diced tomato
- 2 tablespoons minced garlic
- 1 cup black beans, cooked
- 1/4 cup diced serrano chili pepper and seeds removed
- 1 cup diced cucumber, peeled and seeded
- 1/4 cup chopped cilantro

Directions:

1. In a shallow pan, put the shrimp and cover it with lemon juice and lime, reserving the zest. Refrigerate until the shrimp is firm and white, for at least 3 hours.

2. Mix the remaining ingredients in a different bowl and set aside for cold cooking of the shrimp. Mix the shrimp and citrus juice with the remaining ingredients until they are ready to eat. Using baked tortilla chips to serve.

49. Southwest stuffed zucchini

(Ready in 35 min | Serve: 8| Difficulty: Normal)

Ingredients

- 2 poblano peppers

- 3 large ripe zucchinis (about 2 pounds)
- 2 cups fresh corn kernels (about 4 ears)
- 1 tablespoon chopped fresh oregano
- 1 tablespoon olive oil
- 1 tablespoon fresh lime juice
- 3/4 teaspoon ground cumin
- 1/4 teaspoon freshly ground black pepper
- 1/2 cup water
- 1/2 cup tomato sauce
- 1/2 cup uncooked quinoa
- 3 ounces soy cheese, shredded (about 1 cup packed)

Directions:

1. Heat up the broiler. Break the peppers lengthwise in half; remove the seeds and membranes. On a foil-lined baking sheet, put peppers on the side of the skin; flatten with your palm. Broil for 8 minutes or before they're roasted. Only let it cool. 2. Chop the peppers coarsely and put them in a bowl.
3. Break the zucchini in two. Scoop out each zucchini carefully, like a canoe, leaving the shells intact. Chop got his zucchini flesh cut. To the pan, add the zucchini, corn, and onion. 10 minutes of broiling, stirring twice.
4. To the diced peppers, add the zucchini and corn mixture, then whisk in the oregano, oil, lime juice, cumin, and black pepper.
5. Heat the oven to 350 F. In a fine sieve, place the quinoa and place the sieve in a wide bowl. Fill the water with the quinoa. Rub the grains together for 30 seconds with your fingertips. Drain and shower. Loop again for the treatment.
6. Combine the water, tomato sauce, and quinoa in a medium saucepan. Just get it to a boil. Cover, reduce heat and boil until liquid is consumed, or 15 minutes. Withdraw from the sun. Quinoa Fluff with a fork.
7. Connect the quinoa to the combination of zucchini and corn. Well, toss well. Spoon each zucchini shell with around 3/4 cup mixture. Sprinkle cheese over it. Bake for 20 minutes at 350 F, or until the cheese is golden brown.

50. Spicy red cabbage

(Ready in 35 min | Serve: 6| Difficulty: Normal)

Ingredients

- 1 1/2 pounds red cabbage, cored, quartered, and shredded (about 10 cups)
- 2 medium onions, chopped (about 1 1/2 cups)
- 1 tart apple, cored, peeled, and chopped (about 1 cup)
- 1 cup pitted prunes, chopped
- 1 garlic clove, crushed
- 1 teaspoon ground cinnamon
- 1/4 teaspoon ground cloves
- 1 teaspoon cumin seed
- 1 teaspoon coriander seed
- 2 tablespoons red wine vinegar
- Ground nutmeg, to taste
- 1/2 cup water

Directions:

1. Add both of the ingredients into a big jar. Stir thoroughly to blend. Cover and simmer, stirring regularly, until the vegetables are tender, around 1 hour over medium heat. To prevent the cabbage from drying out, add water as needed. Place it in a serving bowl and eat it either hot or cold.

51. Sweet carrots

(Ready in 35 min | Serve: 4| Difficulty: Normal)

Ingredients

- 1/2 cup water
- 1/4 teaspoon salt
- 2 cups shredded carrots
- 1 teaspoon trans-free margarine
- The sugar substitute, to taste
- 1 teaspoon lemon juice
- 4 tablespoons fresh parsley, chopped

Directions:

1. Bring the water to a boil in a shallow saucepan. Connect the shredded carrots and salt. Cover and simmer for another 5 minutes, until the water has evaporated. Extract the carrots from the sun. Stir in margarine, lemon juice, sugar substitute, and parsley. Immediately serve.

52. Sweet potatoes and roasted bananas

(Ready in 35 min | Serve: 6| Difficulty: Normal)

Ingredients

- 1 1/2 pounds sweet potatoes, washed
- 2 medium bananas, peeled and halved
- 2 tablespoons orange juice
- 1/2 teaspoon ground cinnamon
- 1/4 teaspoon ground cardamom
- 1/4 teaspoon ground nutmeg
- Red pepper flakes, to taste
- 3 tablespoons brown sugar
- Chopped parsley, for garnish

Directions:

Heat the oven to 375 F. Cover a baking dish lightly with cooking oil.
Poke many holes in the sweet potatoes with a fork. Bake for around 1 hour, until the potatoes are tender. Take it out of the oven and set it aside. When cold to the touch, peel.
In the prepared baking dish, put the banana halves. Bake for about 15 minutes, uncovered until the fruit is moist and juicy. Take it out of the oven and put the bananas over the orange juice. Stir in the drippings to scrape and mix the bananas properly.
Put the bananas, sweet potatoes, spices, and brown sugar into a large mixing cup. Blend until smooth, using an electric mixer. Transfer to a serving bowl that's ovenproof and return to the oven. Bake until completely warmed. Garnish with and serve the chopped parsley.

53. Tabbouleh salad

(Ready in 25 min | Serve: 6| Difficulty: Easy)

Ingredients
- 1 1/2 cups water
- 3/4 cup bulgur (cracked wheat), rinsed and drained
- 1 cup diced, seeded tomatoes
- 1 cup chopped parsley
- 1/2 cup chopped scallions or green onions
- 1 teaspoon dill weed
- 4 black olives, sliced
- 1/4 cup raisins
- 1/4 cup lemon juice
- 2 tablespoons extra-virgin olive oil
- Freshly ground black pepper, to taste

Directions:
1. Bring the water to a boil in a shallow saucepan. Remove and add the bulgur from the sun. Cover and let stand before the bulgur is soft, for around 15 to 20 minutes, and the liquid is completely absorbed.
2. The bulgur and the remaining ingredients are added to a large dish. Just before the products are uniformly divided, toss gently. For 2 hours, cover and refrigerate to allow the flavors to blend. Serve refrigerated.

54. Tangy green beans
(Ready in 25 min I Serve: 10I Difficulty: Easy)

Ingredients
- 1 1/2 pounds green beans, fresh, frozen or canned
- 1/3 cup diced sweet red bell peppers
- 4 1/2 teaspoons olive oil or canola oil
- 4 1/2 teaspoons water
- 1 1/2 teaspoons vinegar
- 1 1/2 teaspoons mustard
- 1/4 teaspoon salt
- 1/4 teaspoon pepper
- 1/8 teaspoon garlic powder

Directions:
1. In a steamer basket, cook the beans and red peppers over water until crisp-tender. In a small bowl, mix together all the remaining ingredients. Move the beans to a bowl for serving. Using dressing to apply and stir to coat.

55. Thyme roasted beets
(Ready in 25 min I Serve: 4I Difficulty: Easy)

Ingredients
- 2 medium golden or red beets, washed and trimmed
- 1 tablespoon olive oil
- 1 teaspoon fresh thyme
- 1/4 teaspoon salt
- 1/4 teaspoon ground black pepper

Directions:
1. Heat the oven to 400 F. Using aluminum foil to wrap the beets and roast for 40 minutes or until tender. To cool somewhat, set aside. Break the beets into medium-sized bits and peel the beets. Combine the cooked beets, oil, thyme, salt, and pepper in a medium dish. Put on a baking sheet and bake in the oven until hot for an extra 5 to 10 minutes.

56. Wild rice or quinoa stuffing
(Ready in 35 min I Serve: 12I Difficulty: Easy)

Ingredients
- 3/4 cup uncooked wild rice (or equal amount of uncooked quinoa)
- 2 1/2 cups water
- 1 tablespoon olive oil
- 3/4 cup chopped onion
- 1 cup sliced mushrooms
- 1 cup chopped apple (including peel)
- 1/4 cup dried cranberries
- 2 cups diced celery
- 1/2 teaspoon salt
- 1/4 teaspoon black pepper
- 1 tablespoon poultry seasoning
- 1/2 cup reduced-sodium chicken broth
- 1/4 cup slivered almonds, toasted

Directions:
1. Two or three times, rinse wild rice until the water runs clear.
2. Boil the wild rice and water in a 1 1/2-quart saucepan. Reduce to a boil, cover, and cook, stirring regularly, until all water is absorbed. You don't smoke. Cook the wild rice for 30 minutes or so. (Cook it for about 15 minutes if you're using quinoa.)
3. Heat olive oil over low heat in a skillet. Add the onion, mushrooms, apples, celery, and cranberries. Before tender, swirl and heat up. Add the seasoning of salt, pepper, and poultry. Continue to stir and cook gently, about 10 minutes overall, until fragrant.
4. Combine the cooked rice (or quinoa), the fruit-vegetable mixture, and the chicken broth in a large dish. Using it with turkey stuffing. Or bake until cooked through, in a baked dish sprayed with cooking spray (about 20 minutes). Serve with a sprinkle of toasted almonds and garnish.

57. Wild rice pilaf with cranberries and apples
(Ready in 35 min I Serve: 5I Difficulty: Easy)

Ingredients
- 1/4 cup slivered almonds
- 3 cups of water
- 1 1/2 cups wild rice, rinsed and drained
- 1/2 cup dried cranberries, no sugar added
- 2 tablespoons olive oil
- 1 tablespoon red wine vinegar
- 1 tablespoon sugar
- 2 Granny Smith apples, cored and diced

Directions:

1. Heat the oven to 325 F. Cover a baking sheet lightly with cooking oil.
2. Spread the almonds on the baking sheet and bake until crispy and fragrant, stirring periodically, for about 10 minutes. Switch it to a plate instantly to cool.
3. Bring 3 cups of water to a boil in a medium saucepan. Attach some rice. Decrease the heat and cover. To prevent the rice from drying out, keep adding water as needed. Simmer for about 45 to 60 minutes until the rice is tender. To drain, pour through a fine-mesh strainer. Put the rice back in the saucepan, then whisk in the dried cranberries. Cover and put aside.
4. Whisk together the oil, the vinegar, and the sugar in a small cup.
5. Combine the rice and the diced apples in a large dish. Apply the oil mixture and cover uniformly with a toss. Serve on individual dishes, wet or cold. And toasted almonds on top.

Chapter 8: Seafood Recipes

In this chapter, we have compiled seafood recipes that can be relished while following the DASH diet.

1. Spicy Cajun Salmon Bake

(Ready in 35 min | Serve: 4 | Difficulty: Normal)

Ingredients

- 1 tablespoon olive oil, plus more in a pump sprayer
- 2 medium Yukon Gold potatoes (8 ounces), scrubbed, unpeeled, and cut into ½-inch-thick slices 1 large red bell pepper, cored and cut into ½-inch dice
- 2 celery ribs, coarsely chopped
- 2 cloves garlic, coarsely chopped
- 2 plum (Roma) tomatoes, seeded and cut into ½-inch dice
- 3 scallions, white and green parts, chopped
- ½ teaspoon kosher salt
- 4 (5-ounce) salmon fillets
- 4 thin lemon slices, plus lemon wedges for serving
- 2 teaspoons Cajun Seasoning

Directions:

1. Preheat the oven to 400 F. Spray with oil on a 9 x 13-inch baking dish. Heat 1 tablespoon of oil over medium-high heat in a large nonstick skillet. Attach the potatoes and simmer for about 5 minutes, stirring regularly, before they begin to soften.
2. Add the bell pepper, celery, and garlic, and sauté for about 5 more minutes before the pepper softens. Stir in the scallions and tomatoes and sprinkle them with iodine. In the baking bowl, spread.
3. Bake, stirring regularly, for about 25 minutes, until the potatoes are almost tender. Take it out of the microwave. Using the vegetable mixture to arrange the salmon and finish each fillet with a lemon slice. Sprinkle the vegetables and fish with the
4. Seasoning of Cajun. Return to the oven and cook for 8 to 10 minutes until the catfish, when flaked with the tip of the knife, is opaque. Serve hot with wedges of lemon.

2. Salmon with Grapefruit, Avocado, and Fennel Salad

(Ready in 35 min | Serve: 4 | Difficulty: Normal)

Ingredients

Grapefruit, Avocado, and Fennel Salad

- 1 small fennel bulb
- 2 tablespoons fresh lemon juice
- 1 tablespoon extra-virgin olive oil
- ¼ teaspoon kosher salt
- ¼ teaspoon freshly ground black pepper
- 1 ripe avocado, pitted, peeled, and cut into ½-inch dice
- 1 pink or red grapefruit, peel removed, cut between the membranes into segments

Salmon

- 2 teaspoons olive oil
- 4 (5-ounce) salmon fillets

Directions:

1. To make the salad: Cut the fennel lengthwise in half. Cut them off if the fronds are attached and lock them. At the base of the bulb, cut out and remove the triangular heart. Break one fennel into small each-moons, each crosswise. Reserve the remaining half of the fennel and stalks for a different purpose.
2. Whisk the lemon juice and oil together in a medium cup, then season with salt and pepper. Apply the fennel, grapefruit, and avocado and blend gently. Set aside when the cod is being packed.
3. To cook the salmon: Heat the oil over medium heat in a large nonstick skillet.
Put in the salmon and protect. Cook until golden on the underside, about 3 minutes.
4. Switch and cook, uncovered, changing the heat if required, until golden brown is on the other side of each fillet and the cod looks barely opaque when golden brown is flaked in each fillet, and the cod looks barely opaque when flaked with the tip of a knife in the middle, about 3 minutes more.
5. Divide the salad with the fennel between four dinner plates. Cover each with a fillet of cod and serve right away.

3. Rice Paella with, Shrimp, and Asparagus

(Ready in 35 min | Serve: 4 | Difficulty: Normal)

Ingredients

- 8 ounces asparagus, woody stems discarded, cut into 1-inch lengths
- 1 tablespoon olive oil
- 1 medium yellow onion, chopped
- 1 medium red bell pepper, cored and cut into ½-inch dice
- 2 cloves garlic, minced
- 1 cup of rice
- 2 cups Homemade Chicken Broth (here) or canned low-sodium chicken broth 1
- (14.5-ounce) can no-salt-added diced tomatoes, drained
- ½ cup of water
- 1 teaspoon dried oregano
- ½ teaspoon crushed hot red pepper
- ¼ teaspoon crushed saffron threads
- 8 ounces large shrimp (21 to 25), peeled and deveined
- Lemon wedges, for serving

Directions:

1. Over high heat, put a small saucepan of water to a boil. Attach the asparagus and cook for about 2 minutes, until it's crisp and bright green. (Later on, it will finish cooking.) Drain, clean under running cold water, and then drain again. Only put aside. Heat the oil over low heat in a low Dutch oven or flameproof casserole.
2. Connect the onion, bell pepper, and garlic and simmer for about 3 minutes, stirring periodically, until tender. Stir in the rice, brown. Connect the broth, onions, water, oregano, saffron, and hot pepper, and bring to a boil. Reduce the heat to medium-low and cook until the rice has almost completely absorbed the liquid and cook until the rice has almost completely absorbed the liquid, around 40 minutes.
3. Using the Dutch oven to add the shrimp, and asparagus. Cover and cook until the entire cod is opaque, about 5 minutes. Remove and uncover from the heat.
4. Let the 3 minutes stand. Serve hot with wedges of lemon.

4. Shrimp Tacos with Lime-Cilantro Slaw

(Ready in 35 min | Serve: 4 | Difficulty: Normal)

Ingredients

Shrimp

- 2 tablespoons fresh lime juice
- 2 teaspoons chili powder
- 1½ pounds shrimps

Slaw

- Freshly grated zest of 1 lime
- 2 tablespoons fresh lime juice
- 2 tablespoons light mayonnaise
- 1 (12-ounce) bag coleslaw mix
- 2 plum (Roma) tomatoes, seeded and cut into ½-inch dice
- 2 scallions, white and green parts, finely chopped
- 2 tablespoons finely chopped fresh cilantro
- ½ teaspoon kosher salt
- Olive oil in a pump sprayer
- 12 (6-inch) corn tortillas, warmed
- Lime wedges, for serving

Directions:

1. To cook the fish: In a small glass or ceramic baking dish, whisk the lime juice and chili powder together. Marinate the shrimps. When making the slaw, cover, and refrigerate.

2. In a big bowl, whisk together the lime zest, juice, and mayonnaise to make the slaw. Apply the combination of coleslaw, onions, cilantro, scallions, and salt and blend well. Only put aside. Mix well. Only put aside.

3. Spray the broad nonstick skillet over medium-high heat with oil and heat. Remove the fish from the baking dish and let it drain back into the jar with the excess liquid.

4. Place in the skillet and cook for around 8 minutes, turning regularly. Switch to a serving bowl and flake with a fork into large chunks.

5. Spoon some shrimps and slaw onto a tortilla with each meal, then fold and enjoy, with a squeeze of lime juice if you like.

6. Limes and Shrimps Skewers

(Ready in 35 min | Serve: 4 | Difficulty: Normal)

Ingredients

- 1-pound shrimps, peeled
- 1 lime
- 1 teaspoon lemon juice
- ½ teaspoon white pepper

Directions:

1. Split into wedges with the lime.
2. Then add lemon juice and white pepper to the shrimps.
3. Loop the wedges of lime and lime onto the wooden skewers one by one.
4. To 400F, preheat the barbecue.
5. Place the shrimp skewers on the grill and cook on either side for 3 minutes or until the shrimps are light pink.

7. Crusted Salmon with Horseradish

(Ready in 35 min | Serve: 4 | Difficulty: Normal)

Ingredients

- 8 oz. salmon fillet
- 1 oz. horseradish, grated
- ¼ teaspoon ground coriander
- 1 teaspoon coconut flakes
- 1 tablespoon olive oil

Directions:

1. Mix up the flakes of horseradish, ground cilantro, and coconut.
2. Then, for 2 servings, split the salmon fillet.
3. Heat the skillet with olive oil.
4. In the pan, place the salmon fillets and finish with the horseradish mixture.
5. Over medium pressure, cook the fish for 5 minutes.
6. Then flip it on the other side and cook it for another 8 minutes.

8. Cucumber and Seafood Bowl

(Ready in 35 min | Serve: 4 | Difficulty: Normal)

Ingredients

- 2 cucumbers, chopped
- 1 teaspoon mustard
- ½ teaspoon ground coriander
- 1 teaspoon margarine
- 6 oz. shrimps, peeled
- 4 oz. salmon, chopped
- 1 tablespoon low-fat yogurt

Directions:

1. Heat the margarine in a saucepan. Attach the chopped salmon and roast on both sides for 2 minutes.
2. Then add the shrimps and sprinkle with ground coriander on the seafood. Cover the lid and cook the ingredients over low heat for 10 minutes.
3. Move them to the serving bowls, then. You incorporate cucumbers.
4. put the yogurt and mustard together.
5. Sprinkle the mustard mixture with the food.

9. Fish Tacos

Servings: 4 | Prep time 10 minutes | Cook time 10 minutes

Ingredients

- 4 corn tortillas
- 1 cup white cabbage, shredded
- ¼ cup low-fat yogurt
- 1 teaspoon taco seasonings
- 1-pound cod fillet, chopped
- 1 tablespoon coconut oil

Directions:

1. Sprinkle with taco seasonings on the sliced egg.
2. In the pot, melt the coconut oil.
3. Attach the cod and cook on either side for 5 minutes, or until the fish is light brown.
4. Then, on the corn tortillas, put the fried cod.
5. Shredded cabbage is added.
6. Sprinkle with low-fat yogurt ingredients and seal in taco style.

10. Tuna and Pineapple Kebob

(Ready in 35 min | Serve: 4 | Difficulty: Normal)

Ingredients

- 12 oz. tuna fillet
- 8 oz. pineapple, peeled
- 1 teaspoon olive oil
- ¼ teaspoon ground fennel

Directions:

1. On medium cubes, chop the tuna and pineapple and brush with the olive oil and ground fennel.
2. Then loop them in the skewers and put them on the 400F grill in the preheated one.
3. Cook the kebabs on either side for 4 minutes.

11. Paprika Tilapia

(Ready in 25 min | Serve: 4 | Difficulty: Easy)

Ingredients

- 2 tilapia fillets

- 1 teaspoon ground paprika
- ½ teaspoon chili powder
- 2 tablespoons avocado oil

Directions:
1. Sprinkle with ground paprika and chili powder on the tilapia fillets.
2. Then heat the avocado oil for 2 minutes in a skillet.
3. Place the fish fillets in the hot oil and cook each side for 3 minutes.

12. Herbed Sole
(Ready in 35 min | Serve: 4 | Difficulty: Normal)

Ingredients
- 10 oz. sole fillet
- 2 tablespoons margarine
- 1 tablespoon dill weed
- 1 teaspoon garlic powder
- ½ teaspoon cumin seeds

Directions:
1. In the skillet, toss the margarine.
2. Add cumin seeds and grow with dill.
3. For 30 seconds, boil the mixture and cook it.
4. Then slice 2 servings of the single fillet and dust it with garlic powder.
5. In the molten margarine mixture, put the fish fillets.
6. Cook the fish on both sides for 3 minutes.

13. Rosemary Salmon
(Ready in 35 min | Serve: 4 | Difficulty: Normal)

Ingredients
- 1-pound salmon fillet
- 4 teaspoons olive oil
- 4 teaspoons lemon juice
- 1 tablespoon dried rosemary

Directions:
1. Cut the salmon fillet into 4 servings.
2. Then rub the fillets with olive oil, lemon juice, and dried rosemary.
3. Put the salmon on the tray and bake it for 12 minutes at 400F.

14. Tuna Stuffed Zucchini Boats
(Ready in 35 min | Serve: 4 | Difficulty: Normal)

Ingredients
- 1 zucchini, trimmed
- 6 oz. tuna, canned
- 2 oz. low-fat cheese, shredded
- 1 teaspoon chili flakes
- 1 teaspoon olive oil

Directions:
1. Cut the zucchini into halves and scoop the zucchini meat from them to get the zucchini boats.
2. Fill the zucchini boats with tuna and shredded cheese.
3. Sprinkle the zucchini with olive oil and transfer to the oven.
4. Cook the meal at 385F for 20 minutes.

15. Baked Cod
(Ready in 35 min | Serve: 4 | Difficulty: Normal)

Ingredients
- 10 oz. cod fillet
- 1 teaspoon Italian seasonings
- 1 tablespoon margarine

1. Rub the baking pan with margarine.
2. Then chop the cod and sprinkle with Italian seasonings.
3. Put the fish in the baking pan and cover with foil.
4. Bake the meal at 375F for 30 minutes.

16. Basil Halibut
(Ready in 35 min | Serve: 4 | Difficulty: Normal)

Ingredients
- 1-pound halibut, chopped
- 1 tablespoon dried basil
- 1 teaspoon garlic powder
- 2 tablespoons olive oil

Directions:
1. In a pan, add in the olive oil and heat it up.
2. Meanwhile, combine the halibut, the dried basil, and the ground garlic.
3. Combine the fish in the hot oil and cook on each side for 3 minutes.

17. Tilapia Veracruz
(Ready in 35 min | Serve: 4 | Difficulty: Normal)

Ingredients
- 1 cup tomatoes, chopped
- 1 teaspoon dried oregano
- 1 onion, diced
- ½ cup bell pepper, chopped
- ¼ cup of water
- 1 tablespoon olive oil
- 4 tilapia fillets

Directions:
1. Heat up olive oil in the skillet and add tilapia fillets.
2. Roast the fish for 4 minutes per side. Remove the fish from the skillet.
3. Add the onion in the skillet and cook it for 2 minutes.
4. Then add bell peppers, oregano, and tomatoes. Stir the ingredients well and cook them for 5 minutes.
5. After this, add water and fish.
6. Close the lid and cook the meal for 5 minutes more.

18. Lemon Swordfish
(Ready in 35 min | Serve: 4 | Difficulty: Normal)

Ingredients
- 18 oz. swordfish fillets
- 1 tablespoon margarine
- 1 teaspoon lemon zest
- 3 tablespoons lemon juice
- 1 teaspoon ground black pepper

- 2 tablespoons olive oil
- ½ teaspoon minced garlic

Directions:
1. Cut the fish into 4 servings.
2. After this, in the mixing bowl, mix up lemon zest, lemon juice, ground black pepper, and olive oil. Add minced garlic.
3. Rub the fish fillets with lemon mixture.
4. Grease the baking pan with margarine and arrange the swordfish fillets.
5. Bake the fish for 25 minutes at 390F.

19. Spiced Scallops
(Ready in 35 min | Serve: 4 | Difficulty: Normal)

Ingredients
- 1-pound scallops
- 1 teaspoon Cajun seasonings
- 1 tablespoon olive oil

Directions:
1. Rub the scallops with Cajun seasonings.
2. Heat up olive oil in the skillet.
3. Add scallops and cook them for 2 minutes per each side.

20. Shrimp Putanesca
(Ready in 35 min | Serve: 4 | Difficulty: Normal)

Ingredients:
- 5 oz. shrimps, peeled
- 1 teaspoon chili flakes
- ½ onion, diced
- 1 tablespoon coconut oil
- 1 teaspoon garlic, diced
- 1 cup tomatoes, chopped
- ¼ cup olives, sliced
- ¼ cup of water

1. Heat up coconut oil in the saucepan.
2. Add shrimps and chili flakes. Cook the shrimps for 4 minutes.
3. Stir them well and add diced onion, garlic, tomatoes, olives, and water.
4. Close the lid and sauté the meat for 15 minutes.

Per serving: 128 calories, 11.7g protein, 5.8g carbohydrates, and 6.7g fat, 1.5g fiber, 100mg cholesterol, 217mg sodium, 255mg potassium.

21. Curry Snapper
(Ready in 35 min | Serve: 4 | Difficulty: Normal)

Ingredients
- 1-pound snapper fillet, chopped
- 1 teaspoon curry powder
- 1 cup celery stalk, chopped
- ½ cup low-fat yogurt
- ¼ cup of water
- 1 tablespoon olive oil

Directions:
1. Roast the snapper fillet in olive oil for 2 minutes per side.
2. Then add celery stalk, curry powder, low-fat yogurt, and water.
3. Stir the fish until you get the homogenous texture.
4. Close the lid and simmer the fish for 10 minutes on medium heat.

22. Grouper with Tomato Sauce
(Ready in 35 min | Serve: 4 | Difficulty: Normal)

Ingredients
- 12 oz. grouper, chopped
- 2 cups grape tomatoes, chopped
- 1 chili pepper, chopped
- 1 tablespoon margarine
- 1 teaspoon ground coriander

Directions:
1. Toss the margarine in the saucepan.
2. Add chopped grouper and sprinkle it with ground coriander.
3. Roast the fish for 2 minutes per side.
4. Then add grape tomatoes and chili pepper.
5. Stir the ingredients well and close the lid.
6. Cook the meal for 10 minutes on low heat.

23. Braised Seabass
(Ready in 35 min | Serve: 4 | Difficulty: Normal)

Ingredients
- 10 oz. seabass fillet
- 1 cup tomatoes, chopped
- 1 yellow onion, sliced
- 1 tablespoon avocado oil
- 1 teaspoon ground black pepper

Directions:
1. Heat the skillet with olive oil.
2. Attach the sea bass fillet and roast it on each side for 4 minutes.
3. Remove the cod and add the sliced onion from the skillet.
4. For 2 minutes, cook it.
5. Include the tomatoes and ground black pepper after that.
6. Get it to a boil with the mixture.
7. Close the lid and add the fried sea bass.
8. For 15 minutes, prepare the dinner.

24. Five-Spices Sole
(Ready in 35 min | Serve: 4 | Difficulty: Normal)

Ingredients
- 3 sole fillets
- 1 tablespoon five-spice seasonings
- 1 tablespoon coconut oil

Directions:
1. Rub the sole fillets with seasonings.
2. Then heat up the coconut oil in the skillet for 2 minutes.
3. Place the sole fillets in the hot oil and cook them for 4.5 minutes per side.

25. Clams Stew

(Ready in 35 min | Serve: 4 | Difficulty: Normal)

Ingredients

- 1-pound clams
- 1 teaspoon dried thyme
- 1 teaspoon ground paprika
- ½ cup light cream (low-fat)
- 1 tablespoon lemon juice

Directions:

1. Place the dried thyme, paprika, and cream on the ground.
2. Get it to a boil with the liquid.
3. Then apply the lemon juice and whisk well into the mixture.
4. Cover the lid and apply the clams.
5. Simmer the stewed clams for 5 minutes.

26. Salmon in Capers

(Ready in 35 min | Serve: 4 | Difficulty: Normal)

Ingredients

- 2 tablespoons avocado oil
- 1-pound salmon fillet, chopped
- 1 tablespoon capers, drained
- ½ cup low-fat milk

Directions:

1. Heat up a pan with the oil over medium-high heat, add salmon, and roast it for 5 minutes.
2. Add capers and milk and sauté the meat for 10 minutes over medium heat.

27. Horseradish Cod

Servings: 4 | Prep time: 10 minutes | Cook time: 10 minutes

Ingredients

- 1 tablespoon avocado oil
- 12 oz. cod fillet
- ½ cup low-fat cream cheese
- ¼ teaspoon ground black pepper
- 2 tablespoons dill, chopped
- 1 tablespoon horseradish

Directions:

1. Heat up a pan with the oil over medium-high heat, add cod, season with black pepper, and cook for 5 minutes on each side.
2. In a bowl, combine the cream cheese with the dill and horseradish.
3. Top the cooked cod with a horseradish mixture.

Per serving: 180 calories, 17.8g protein, 2.3g carbohydrates, 11.4g fat, 0.5g fiber, 74mg cholesterol, 154mg sodium, 108mg potassium

28. Salmon and Corn Salad

(Ready in 35 min | Serve: 4 | Difficulty: Normal)

Ingredients

- 2 tablespoons canola oil
- ½ teaspoon lemon juice
- 1 cup corn kernels, cooked
- 1-pound salmon, canned, shredded
- 1 tablespoon scallions, chopped

Directions:

1. Put all ingredients in the bowl and mix up the salad.

29. Spicy Cajun Catfish Bake

(Ready in about 30 Minutes | Serve 4 | Difficulty: Normal)

Ingredients

- 1 tablespoon olive oil, plus more in a pump sprayer
- 2 medium Yukon Gold potatoes (8 ounces), scrubbed, unpeeled, and cut into ½-inch-thick slices
- 1 large red bell pepper, cored and cut into ½-inch dice
- 2 celery ribs, coarsely chopped
- 2 cloves garlic, coarsely chopped
- 2 plum (Roma) tomatoes, seeded and cut into ½-inch dice
- 3 scallions, white and green parts, chopped
- ½ teaspoon kosher salt
- 4 (5-ounce) catfish fillets
- 4 thin lemon slices, plus lemon wedges for serving
- 2 teaspoons Cajun Seasoning

Directions

1. Preheat the oven to 400 F. Spray with oil on a 9 x 13-inch baking dish.
2. Heat 1 tablespoon of oil over medium-high heat in a large nonstick skillet. Add the potatoes and cook for about 5 minutes, occasionally stirring, until they begin to soften. Add the bell pepper, celery, and garlic; and sauté for about 5 more minutes before the pepper softens. Stir in the scallions and tomatoes and sprinkle them with salt. In the baking dish, spread.
3. Bake, stirring periodically, for about 25 minutes, until the potatoes are almost tender. Take it out of the oven. Use the vegetable mixture to arrange the catfish and top each fillet with a lemon slice. Sprinkle the Cajun seasoning with the fish and vegetables. Return to the oven and cook for 8 to 10 minutes until the catfish, when flaked with the tip of the knife, is opaque. Serve hot with wedges of lemon.

30. Cod with Grapefruit, Avocado, and Fennel Salad

(Ready in about 30 Minutes | Serve 4 | Difficulty: Normal)

Ingredients

Grapefruit, Avocado, and Fennel Salad

- 1 small fennel bulb
- 2 tablespoons fresh lemon juice
- 1 tablespoon extra-virgin olive oil
- ¼ teaspoon kosher salt
- ¼ teaspoon freshly ground black pepper
- 1 ripe avocado, pitted, peeled, and cut into ½-inch dice
- 1 pink or red grapefruit, peel removed, cut between the membranes into segments

Cod
- 2 teaspoons olive oil
- 4 (5-ounce) cod fillet

Directions
1. To make the salad: Cut the fennel lengthwise in half. Cut them off if the fronds are attached and reserve them. At the base of the bulb, cut out and discard the triangular heart. Break one half-cross-wise fennel into thin half-moons. Reserve the remaining half of the fennel and stalks for a different purpose.
2. Whisk the lemon juice and oil together in a medium cup, and season with salt and pepper. Apply the fennel, grapefruit, and avocado and blend gently. Set aside while the cod is being prepared.
3. To cook the cod: Heat the oil over medium heat in a large nonstick skillet. Put in the cod and cover. Cook until golden on the underside, about 3 minutes. Turn and cook, uncovered, adjusting the heat as required, until golden brown is on the other side of each fillet and the cod looks barely opaque when flaked with the tip of a knife in the middle, around 3 more minutes.
4. Divide the salad with the fennel between four dinner plates. Cover each one with a fillet of cod and serve immediately.

31. Brown Rice Paella with Cod, Shrimp, and Asparagus
(Ready in about 30 Minutes | Serve 6 | Difficulty: Normal)

Ingredients
- 8 ounces asparagus, woody stems discarded, cut into 1-inch lengths
- 1 tablespoon olive oil1 medium yellow onion, chopped
- 1 medium red bell pepper, cored and cut into ½-inch dice
- 2 cloves garlic, minced
- 1 cup of brown rice
- 2 cups Homemade Chicken Broth or canned low-sodium chicken broth
- 1 (14.5-ounce) can no-salt-added diced tomatoes, drained
- ½ cup water1 teaspoon dried oregano
- ½ teaspoon crushed hot red pepper
- ¼ teaspoon crushed saffron threads
- 12 ounces cod fillets, cut into 1-inch pieces
- 8 ounces large shrimp (21 to 25), peeled and deveined
- Lemon wedges, for serving.

Directions
1. Over high heat, bring a small saucepan of water to a boil. Add the asparagus and cook for about 2 minutes, until it's crisp and bright green. (Later on, it will finish cooking.) Drain, rinse under running cold water and drain again. Only set aside.
2. Heat the oil over medium heat in a medium Dutch oven or a flameproof casserole. Add the onion, bell pepper, and garlic and cook for about 3 minutes, occasionally stirring, until tender. Stir in the rice, brown. Connect the broth, tomatoes, water, oregano, saffron, and hot pepper, and bring to a boil. Reduce heat to medium-low and cook, covered, until the liquid is almost completely absorbed by the rice, about 40 minutes
3. Using the Dutch oven to add the cod, shrimp, and asparagus. Cover and cook until the whole cod is opaque, about 5 minutes. Remove and expose from the sun. Let the 3 minutes stand. Serve warm with wedges of lemon.

32. Fish Tacos with Lime-Cilantro Slaw
(Ready in about 30 Minutes | Serve 6 | Difficulty: Normal)

Ingredients
Fish
- 2 tablespoons fresh lime juice
- 2 teaspoons chili powder
- 1½ pounds cod fillets

Slaw
- Freshly grated zest of 1 lime
- 2 tablespoons fresh lime juice
- 2 tablespoons light mayonnaise
- 1 (12-ounce) bag coleslaw mix
- 2 plum (Roma) tomatoes, seeded and cut into ½-inch dice
- 2 scallions, white and green parts, finely chopped
- 2 tablespoons finely chopped fresh cilantro
- ½ teaspoon kosher salt
- Olive oil in a pump sprayer
- 12 (6-inch) corn tortillas, warmed
- Lime wedges, for serving

Directions
1. To prepare the fish: In a shallow glass or ceramic baking dish, whisk the lime juice and chili powder together. Attach the cod, then turn the coat on. When making the slaw, cover, and refrigerate.
2. In a big bowl, whisk together the lime zest, juice, and mayonnaise to make the slaw. Apply the mixture of coleslaw, onions, cilantro, scallions, and salt and blend well. Only set aside.
3. Spray the broad nonstick skillet over medium-high heat with oil and heat. Remove the fish from the baking dish and let it drain back into the dish with the excess juice. Place in the skillet and cook for about 8 minutes, turning periodically, until opaque when flaked with the tip of a knife in the thickest portion. Switch to a serving bowl and flake with a fork into large chunks.
4. Spoon some fish and slaw onto a tortilla with each serving, then fold and eat with a squeeze of lime juice, if you wish.

33. Halibut with Spring Vegetables
(Ready in about 30 Minutes | Serve 4 | Difficulty: Normal)

Ingredients

6. 8 baby red-skinned potatoes (about 1 ounce each), scrubbed but unpeeled, cut in halves
7. 32 baby carrots, preferably not baby-cut carrots, trimmed
8. 1 tablespoon unsalted butter
9. 1 cup chopped leeks, white and pale green parts only
10. 1 cup Homemade Chicken Broth or canned low-sodium chicken broth
11. ½ cup of water
12. ¼ cup dry vermouth or white wine
13. 4 (5-ounce) skinless halibut fillets
14. ¼ teaspoon kosher salt
15. ¼ teaspoon freshly ground black pepper
16. Finely chopped fresh chives, parsley, or a combination, for serving.
17. Lemon wedges, for serving.

Directions

1. Over high heat, bring a medium saucepan of water to a boil. Add the potatoes, reduce the heat to medium and cook for 5 minutes, simmering steadily. Attach the carrots and cook until the vegetables, when pierced with a thin, sharp knife tip, are almost, but not yet, tender, about 3 more minutes. Drain under cold running water and clean.
2. In a large skillet over medium heat, melt the butter. Attach and cover the leeks. Cook, stirring periodically, for about 5 minutes, until tender. Bring to a boil and add the broth, sugar, and vermouth. To mix the flavors, reduce the heat to medium-low, cover partially with the lid and simmer for 5 minutes.
3. In a single layer, spread the potatoes and carrots in the skillet. Arrange the vegetables with halibut fillets and season with salt and pepper. Cover tightly and simmer for 10 to 12 minutes until the vegetables are tender, and when pierced with the tip of a small, sharp knife, the halibut is opaque in the middle.
4. Divide the vegetables and the broth equally between four bowls of deep soup. Using a halibut fillet to top each one and sprinkle with the herbs. Add wedges of lemon and serve warm.

34. Roasted Salmon Fillets with Basil Drizzle

(Ready in about 30 Minutes | Serve 4 | Difficulty: Normal)

Ingredients

Salmon

- Olive oil in a pump sprayer
- 4 (6-ounce) skinless salmon fillets
- ¼ teaspoon kosher salt
- ¼ teaspoon freshly ground black pepper

Basil Drizzle

- 1 clove garlic, peeled
- ½ cup packed fresh basil leaves
- 3 tablespoons coarsely chopped fresh parsley leaves
- 2 tablespoons water1 tablespoon balsamic vinegar
- Pinch of kosher salt
- Pinch of freshly ground black pepper
- ¼ cup extra-virgin olive oil

Directions

1. For the salmon to be prepared: Preheat the oven to 400 °F. Spray with oil on a 9 x 13-inch baking dish.
2. In a baking dish, put the salmon fillets, spray them with oil, and season with salt and pepper. Roast until the salmon, when prodded with the tip of a knife in the thickest portion, looks scarcely opaque, around 10 minutes.
3. Meanwhile, make the basil drizzle: drop the garlic clove through the feed bowle to mince the garlic with a food processor working. (Or drop the garlic into the lid of a blender through the hole.) Stop the food processor or blender, add the basil, parsley, water, vinegar, salt, and pepper, and pulse to chop the herbs a few times. With the engine going, apply the oil gradually. Pour the mixture into a small bowl and drizzle.
4. Move the fillets to dinner plates using a metal spatula and drizzle with equal quantities of the basil mixture. Serve it warm.

35. Salmon and Edamame Cakes

(Ready in about 30 Minutes | Serve 4 | Difficulty: Normal)

Ingredients

- 2 cups flaked cooked salmon (about 13 ounces), such as Roasted Salmon Fillets with Basil Drizzle
- ¼ cup panko (Japanese-style bread crumbs), preferably whole-wheat panko
- 2 large egg whites
- 1 tablespoon peeled and minced fresh ginger
- 1 scallion, white and green parts, finely chopped
- 1 tablespoon finely chopped fresh cilantro1 clove garlic, crushed through a press½ cup thawed frozen edamame
- Canola oil in a pump sprayer
- Lime wedges, for serving.

Directions

1. Mix the salmon, panko, egg whites, ginger, scallion, cilantro, and garlic in a medium dish. Stir the edamame in. Form the mixture into four cakes that are 3½-inch tall. Move for 15 to 30 minutes to a waxed paper-lined plate and refrigerate.
2. Spray a large nonstick skillet over medium heat with oil and heat. Attach the salmon cakes and cook for 3 to 4 minutes until the underside is browned. Flip the cakes over and cook for 3 to 4 more minutes until the other sides are browned. Serve hot, with wedges of lime,

36. Sea Scallops and Vegetables with Ginger Sauce

(Ready in about 30 Minutes | Serve 4 | Difficulty: Normal)

Ingredients

- 1 pound sea scallops, each cut in half horizontally
- ¾ cup low-sodium chicken broth
- 1 tablespoon reduced-sodium soy sauce
- 1 tablespoon rice vinegar
- ¼ teaspoon crushed hot red pepper
- 2 teaspoons cornstarch
- 1 tablespoon canola or vegetable oil
- 8 ounces sugar snap peas, trimmed
- 1 large red bell pepper, cored and cut into 2 × ¼-inch strips
- 2 scallions, white and green parts, 1 minced and 1 finely chopped
- 1½ tablespoons peeled and minced fresh ginger
- 2 cloves garlic, minced

Directions

1. Over high heat, bring a medium saucepan of water to a boil. Attach the scallops and cook for around 30 seconds before they become opaque around the edges. Uh, drain.
2. Combine the broth, soy sauce, vinegar, and hot pepper in a glass measuring cup. Sprinkle with the cornstarch and whisk until it dissolves with a fork. Only set aside.
3. Over high heat, heat a large wok or skillet. Drizzle in the oil and cover the entire surface by tilting the wok. Add the peas and bell pepper to the sugar snap and stir-fry until softening starts, around 1 minute. Stir in the minced scallion, ginger, and garlic and stir-fry for about 30 seconds until fragrant. Attach the mixture of scallops and broth and bring it to a boil, stirring regularly. Cook for about 1 minute until the scallops are opaque throughout and the sauce is thickened.
4. Divide the mixture of scallops equally between four bowls, sprinkle with the chopped scallion and serve wet.

37. Shrimp with Corn Hash

(Ready in about 30 Minutes | Serve 4 | Difficulty: Normal)

Ingredients

- 4 teaspoons olive oil
- 1 pound large shrimp (21 to 25), peeled and deveined
- ½ cup chopped red onion
- ½ medium red bell pepper, seeded and cut into ½-inch dice
- 1½ cups fresh corn kernels, cut from 2 large ears of corn
- 1 cup halved cherry or grape tomatoes
- ¼ teaspoon crushed hot red pepper
- ¼ cup of water
- 1 tablespoon fresh lemon juice
- 2 tablespoons coarsely chopped fresh basil

Directions

1. Heat 2 teaspoons of oil over medium-high heat in a large nonstick skillet. Add the shrimp and cook, stirring periodically, for 3 to 5 minutes, until it is opaque. Transfer to a dish.
2. In the skillet, heat the remaining 2 teaspoons of oil over medium to high heat. Add the onion and bell pepper and cook for about 1 minute, frequently stirring, until tender. Connect the hot pepper, tomatoes, and corn and cover. Cook, stirring periodically, for about 3 minutes until these vegetables are cooked through.
3. Connect the shrimp and reheat for about 1 minute, stirring sometimes. Stir in the water and lemon juice and cook, using a wooden spoon to scrape up any browned bits in the pan. Move and sprinkle with the basil in a serving bowl. Serve hot.

38. Greek Shrimp with Zucchini and Grape Tomatoes

(Ready in about 30 Minutes | Serve 4 | Difficulty: Normal)

Ingredients

- 3 teaspoons olive oil
- 1 pound large shrimp (21 to 25), peeled and deveined
- 1 large zucchini, halved lengthwise and cut into ¼-inch-thick half-moons
- 2 tablespoons minced shallot
- 1 clove garlic, minced
- 1-pint grape or cherry tomatoes halved lengthwise
- ¼ teaspoon freshly ground black pepper
- 2 tablespoons dry vermouth
- Grated zest of 1 lemon
- 2 tablespoons fresh lemon juice
- 1 tablespoon finely chopped fresh oregano or 1 teaspoon dried oregano
- ¼ cup (1 ounce) crumbled goat cheese, for serving

Directions

1. Heat 1 teaspoon of oil over medium-high heat in a big, nonstick skillet. Add the shrimp and cook, stirring periodically, for about 3 minutes, until it becomes opaque. At this point, the shrimp will be slightly undercooked. Transfer to a dish.
2. Heat the skillet with the remaining 2 teaspoons of oil. Attach the zucchini and sauté until crisp-tender and lightly browned, occasionally stirring, for about 5 minutes. Stir in the shallot and garlic and cook for about 30 seconds until it is fragrant. Add the tomatoes and pepper and cook for about 3 minutes, frequently stirring, until thoroughly cooked.
3. Add the vermouth, lemon zest and juice, and oregano, and return the shrimp to the skillet. Cook, sometimes stirring, for around 1 minute to reheat the shrimp.
4. Switch to a serving bowl and top with the cheese from the goat. Serve it warm.

39. Crispy Tilapia with Mediterranean Vegetables

(Ready in about 30 Minutes | Serve 4 | Difficulty: Normal)

Ingredients

- 1 tablespoon olive oil, plus more in a pump sprayer
- 1 medium yellow onion, chopped
- 2 cloves garlic, minced
- 1 medium zucchini, cut in half lengthwise and then into ½-inch-thick slices
- 1 medium yellow squash, cut in half lengthwise and then into ½-inch-thick slices4 plum (Roma) tomatoes, seeded and cut into ½-inch dice
- Freshly grated zest of 1 lemon
- 2 tablespoons fresh lemon juice
- 1 tablespoon chopped fresh oregano or 1 teaspoon dried oregano
- ¼ teaspoon crushed hot red pepper4 (5-ounce) tilapia fillets
- 3 tablespoons panko (Japanese-style bread crumbs), preferably whole-wheat panko

Directions

1. Preheat the oven to 350°F.
2. Heat 1 tablespoon oil over medium heat in a large ovenproof nonstick skillet. Add the onion and garlic and cook for about 3 minutes, occasionally stirring, until tender. Add the zucchini and the yellow squash and cook for about 3 minutes, until tender. Stir in the tomatoes, juice and lemon zest, oregano, and hot pepper. Remove yourself from the sun. Arrange the vegetables with tilapia fillets. Using the panko to sprinkle and spray with oil.
3. When flaked in the thickest part with the tip of a knife, bake until the tilapia is opaque, about 12 minutes. Serve it warm.

40. Tuna with Fennel and Potatoes

(Ready in about 30 Minutes | Serve 4 | Difficulty: Normal)

Ingredients

Vegetables

- 1 tablespoon olive oil, plus more in a pump sprayer
- 1 head fennel (about 1 pound)
- 3 medium potatoes, scrubbed but unpeeled, cut in halves and then crosswise into ¼-inch-thick slices
- 1 large red bell pepper, cored and cut into ¼-inch-wide strips
- 4 cloves garlic, chopped
- Freshly grated zest of 1 lemon
- 1 teaspoon kosher salt
- ½ teaspoon crushed hot red pepper
- 2 tablespoons freshly grated Parmesan cheese

Tuna

- Olive oil in a pump sprayer
- 4 (6-ounce) tuna steaks, about 1 inch thick
- ½ teaspoon freshly ground black pepper
- Lemon wedges, for serving

Directions

1. Preheat the oven to 400°F.
2. To prepare the vegetables: Spray a 9 × 13-inch baking dish with oil. Cut the fronds (leaves) off the fennel. Chop 2 tablespoons of fennel fronds and reserve. Cut the fennel head in half lengthwise, and cut out the thick triangular core at the bottom of the head. Cut the head and stalks crosswise into ¼- to ½-inch-wide strips.
3. Heat the 1 tablespoon oil in a large nonstick skillet over medium-high heat. Add the potatoes and cook, occasionally stirring, until they begin to soften around the edges, about 5 minutes. Stir in the fennel, bell pepper, garlic, lemon zest, salt, and hot pepper. Spread in the baking dish. Bake, occasionally stirring, until the potatoes are tender, about 30 minutes. During the last 5 minutes, sprinkle with the Parmesan. Remove from the oven and let stand while preparing the tuna.
4. To prepare the tuna: Wipe the skillet clean with paper towels. Spray the skillet with oil and heat over medium-high heat. Season the tuna with pepper. Place the tuna steaks in the skillet and cook until the undersides are seared about 2 minutes. Flip the tuna and cook until the other sides are seared, about 2 minutes more for rare tuna. Divide the vegetables equally among four dinner plates, and top each with a tuna steak. Sprinkle with the reserved chopped fronds. Serve hot, with the lemon wedges

Chapter 9: Beef, Pork and Lamb Recipes

In this chapter, we have compiled beef, pork and lamb recipes that can be relished on DASH diet.

1. Curry-Rubbed Sirloin with Peanut Dipping Sauce

(Ready in about 30 Minutes | Serve 8 | Difficulty: Normal)

Ingredients

Sirloin

- 1 teaspoon curry powder
- ½ teaspoon ground ginger
- ½ teaspoon granulated garlic
- ½ teaspoon kosher salt
- ½ teaspoon freshly ground black pepper
- Canola oil in a spray pump
- 1¾ pounds sirloin steak, about
- 1 inch thick, excess fat trimmed

Peanut Dipping Sauce

- ¼ cup smooth peanut butter
- 3 tablespoons brewed cold black tea
- 3 tablespoons light coconut milk
- 2 teaspoons peeled and minced fresh ginger
- 2 teaspoons reduced-sodium soy sauce
- 1½ teaspoons rice vinegar
- 2 teaspoons curry powder
- 1 clove garlic, crushed through a press
- Chopped fresh cilantro or mint for garnish

Directions

1. Mix the curry powder, ground ginger, granulated garlic, salt, and pepper in a small bowl to prepare the sirloin. Spray the oil with the curry mixture on both sides of the steak and season. Let the peanut sauce stand at room temperature when making it.
2. To make Peanut Dipping Sauce: Mix peanut butter, tea, coconut milk, ginger, soy sauce, vinegar, curry, and garlic in a medium dish.
3. Place a broiler rack about 4 inches from the heat source and preheat to high. Oil the rack for the broiler and add the steak. Broil, turning over the steak after 3 minutes until browned on both sides, and when pressed in the middle, the meat just feels slightly robust, around 6 minutes for medium-rare. Switch to a carving board and quit for 3 minutes to stand.

2. Sirloin, Shiitake, and Asparagus Stir-Fry

(Ready in about 30 Minutes | Serve 6 | Difficulty: Normal)

Ingredients

Sauce

- ¾ cup Homemade Chicken Broth or canned low-sodium chicken broth

- 2 tablespoons dry sherry or dry vermouth
- 1 tablespoon rice vinegar
- 1 tablespoon low-sodium soy sauce
- 1 tablespoon cornstarch
- ½ teaspoon freshly ground black pepper

Stir fry

- 4 teaspoons canola oil
- 1 pound sirloin steak, excess fat trimmed, cut across the grain into
- ¼-inch-thick slices and then into 2-inch strips
- 1 tablespoon peeled and minced fresh ginger
- 2 cloves garlic, minced
- 12 ounces thin asparagus, woody stems discarded, cut into 1-inch lengths
- 6 ounces shiitake mushroom caps, sliced
- 6 ounces sugar snap or snow peas, trimmed
- ½ cup of water
- 3 scallions, white and green parts, cut into 1-inch lengths

Directions

1. To make the sauce: whisk the broth, sherry, vinegar, soy sauce, corn starch, and pepper together in a small cup.
2. Heat 2 teaspoons of oil in a large nonstick skillet or wok over medium-high heat to create a stir-fry. Add the steak and cook in two batches, stirring periodically, until seared, for around 2 minutes. Transfer to a dish.
3. In the skillet, heat the remaining 2 teaspoons of oil over medium to high heat. Apply the ginger and garlic and mix for about 30 seconds, until fragrant. Add the snap peas, asparagus, shiitake, and sugar and mix well. Add the water and cook for about 3 minutes, stirring regularly, until the water has evaporated and the vegetables are crisp-tender. Stir in the scallions at the last minute.

3. Beef and Mushrooms with Sour Cream–Dill Sauce

(Ready in about 30 Minutes | Serve 4 | Difficulty: Normal)

Ingredients

- 2 teaspoons canola oil, plus more in a pump sprayer
- 1 pound sirloin steak, excess fat trimmed, cut across the grain in ½-inch-thick slices and then into 2-inch-wide pieces
- 12 ounces cremini mushrooms, sliced
- ¼ cup finely chopped shallots
- 2 teaspoons cornstarch
- ¾ cup Homemade Beef Stock
- ½ cup reduced-fat sour cream
- 1 tablespoon finely chopped fresh dill
- ½ teaspoon kosher salt
- ½ teaspoon freshly ground black pepper

Directions

1. Spray the broad nonstick skillet over medium-high heat with oil and heat. Attach half of the sirloin and cook until browned on both sides, turning the sirloin pieces halfway through cooking, about 2 minutes. Transfer to a dish. Repeat with the sirloin that remains.
2. Heat 2 teaspoons of oil over medium heat in a skillet. Add the mushrooms and cook until the liquid evaporates and they begin to brown, occasionally stirring, for about 6 minutes. Stir in the shallots and cook, around 1 minute, until softened.
3. Sprinkle the cornstarch over the broth in a small bowl and stir to dissolve. Stir in the mushrooms and cook until they are cooked and thickened. Add the sour cream, dill, salt, and pepper and stir. Return the sirloin and any juices to the skillet on the plate and cook for about 30 seconds until heated. Serve it wet.

4. Filet Mignon au Poivre with Bourbon-Shallot Sauce

(Ready in about 30 Minutes | Serve 4 | Difficulty: Normal)

Ingredients

- 1 tablespoon four-peppercorn blend (a commercial blend of black, white, red, and green peppercorns)
- 4 (6-ounce) filets mignons
- 1 teaspoon canola oil, plus more in a pump sprayer
- ¼ cup finely chopped shallots
- ¼ cup bourbon, brandy, or Cognac
- 1 cup Homemade Beef Stock or canned low-sodium beef broth
- 1 tablespoon cold unsalted butter
- Pinch of kosher salt

Directions

1. Crush the peppercorns coarsely in a mortar and pestle or under a large skillet on a working surface. Scatter the crushed peppercorns on a tray. Sprinkle the peppercorns uniformly over the mignons on both sides of the fillets, pressing them to stick to the skin.
2. In a large nonstick skillet, spray enough oil to thinly coat the bottom and heat over medium-high heat. Add the mignons and cook until the undersides are well browned around 4 minutes. For medium-rare beef, turn and brown the other sides until the meat feels slightly durable about 4 minutes. Move to a plate.
3. Combine the shallots and 1 teaspoon of oil in the skillet and cook for about 2 minutes over medium heat, frequently stirring, until the shallots soften. Add the bourbon and cook for around 1 minute, until almost completely evaporated. Add the stock and bring it to a boil over high heat, scraping the browned bits with a wooden spatula in the skillet. Boil until reduced, around 2 minutes, to ½ cup. Remove from the heat and whisk in the salt and butter.
4. Serve each steak, topped with a spoonful of sauce, on a dinner plate.

5. Spiced Roast Eye of Round
(Ready in about 30 Minutes | Serve 12 | Difficulty: Normal)

Ingredients
- 1 teaspoon cumin seeds
- 1 teaspoon coriander seeds
- ½ teaspoon whole black peppercorns
- ½ teaspoon kosher salt
- ½ teaspoon ground ginger
- ¼ teaspoon freshly ground black pepper
- ⅛ teaspoon cayenne pepper1 (3-pound) beef eye of round roast, tied
- 1 clove garlic, cut into about 12 slivers
- Olive oil in a pump sprayer

Directions
1. In the center of the oven, position a rack and preheat the oven to 400 °F.
2. In a mortar, in an electric spice grinder, or on a work counter under a large skillet, crush the cumin, coriander, and peppercorns together coarsely. Move the salt, ginger, pepper, and cayenne to a dish.
3. Make 1-inch-deep incisions in the beef using the tip of a tiny knife and stuff a garlic clove sliver into each slit. Spray the oil on the beef and sprinkle the spice mixture with it. Place the roast in a roasting pan on a meat rack.
4. For 10 minutes, roast. Reduce the temperature of the oven to 350 ° F and proceed to roast until an instant-read thermometer inserted in the beef center reads 125 ° F for a medium-rare duration of about 1 hour. Transfer the beef and let stand for 10 minutes on a carving board.
5. Remove the string and cut into thin slices with the meat crosswise. Move to a serving dish and pour over the beef with the carving juices. Immediately serve.

6. Beef Fajitas with Two Peppers
(Ready in about 30 Minutes | Serve1 | Difficulty: Normal)

Ingredients
- 2 teaspoons olive oil, plus more in a pump sprayer
- 1 pound sirloin steak, excess fat trimmed, cut across the grain into ½-inch-thick slices and then into 2-inch-wide pieces
- 1 large red bell pepper, cored and cut into ¼-inch-wide strips
- 1 large green bell pepper, cored and cut into ¼-inch-wide strips
- 1 medium red onion, cut into thin half-moons
- 2 cloves garlic, minced
- 1 tablespoon Mexican Seasoning
- 12 (8-inch) flour tortillas or Boston lettuce leaves, for serving
- Lime wedges, for serving.

Directions
1. Spray the broad nonstick skillet over medium-high heat with oil and heat. Attach half of the sirloin and cook until browned on both sides, turning the sirloin pieces halfway through cooking, about 2 minutes. Transfer to a dish. Repeat with the sirloin that remains.
2. Heat 2 teaspoons of oil over medium-high heat in a skillet. Add the bell peppers, onion, and garlic. Cook for about 7 minutes, occasionally stirring, until tender. Stir in the beef and the Mexican Seasoning with some juices. Move it to a bowl.
3. Fill a flour tortilla or lettuce leaf with the beef mixture to serve and squeeze on top with lime juice. Roll up, serve up.

7. Ground Sirloin and Pinto Chili
(Ready in about 30 Minutes | Serve 6 | Difficulty: Normal)

Ingredients
- 1 tablespoon olive oil
- 1 medium yellow onion, chopped
- 1 medium green bell pepper, cored and chopped
- 2 cloves garlic, minced
- 1¼ pounds ground sirloin
- 2 tablespoons chili powder
- ½ teaspoon pure ground chipotle chili, or 1 minced canned chipotle chili with its clinging adobo, or ¼ teaspoon cayenne (optional)
- ½ teaspoon kosher salt
- 1 (28-ounce) can reduced-sodium chopped tomatoes in juice, undrained
- 2 (15-ounce) cans reduced-sodium pinto beans, drained and well rinsed
- Optional toppings: shredded low-fat Cheddar cheese, nonfat sour cream, chopped fresh cilantro leaves

Directions
1. Over medium heat, heat the oil in a big saucepan. Attach the onion and bell pepper and cook for about 3 minutes, occasionally stirring, until tender. Stir in the garlic and cook for about 1 minute until it is fragrant. Add the sirloin and cook until it loses its raw appearance, stirring regularly and breaking the meat with the side of the spoon, for around 6 minutes. Add chili powder, ground chipotle (if used), and salt and cook for 1 minute, stirring frequently.
2. Connect the tomatoes and their juice to the mixture and bring to a boil over high heat. Return the heat to medium and simmer for about 15 minutes, stirring periodically, until the juices have thickened slightly. Connect the beans and cook for about 5 minutes, until heated. If you prefer a thicker chili, use a large spoon to mash some of the beans into the cooking sauce. Spoon into cups, add the toppings and serve hot if desired.

8. Sirloin and Black Bean Burgers with Fresh Tomato Salsa

(Ready in about 30 Minutes | Serve 6 | Difficulty: Normal)

Ingredients
Salsa
- 2 plum (Roma) tomatoes, seeded and cut into ¼-inch dice, or 1 cup coarsely chopped grape or cherry tomatoes
- 2 tablespoons minced white or yellow onion
- 1 tablespoon fresh lime juice
- 1 tablespoon minced fresh cilantro
- 1 small jalapeño or serrano chili, seeded and minced
- 1 clove garlic, minced Pinch of kosher salt

Burgers
- 1 pound ground sirloin1 (15-ounce) can reduced-sodium black beans, drained and rinsed
- 1 teaspoon chili powder
- ½ teaspoon kosher salt
- ½ teaspoon freshly ground black pepper
- ¼ teaspoon granulated garlic or garlic powder
- ¼ teaspoon granulated onion or onion powder
- Olive oil in a pump sprayer
- 4 whole-wheat buns, toasted (optional)
- 2 ripe avocados, halved, pitted, peeled, and sliced

Directions
1. To make the salsa: Combine the tomatoes, onion, lime juice, cilantro, jalapeño, garlic, and salt in a medium serving dish. Set aside while the burgers are being made.
2. Mix together the ground sirloin, beans, chili powder, salt, pepper, granulated garlic, and granulated onion in a medium bowl to make the burgers. Shape the meat mixture into four 3½-inch burgers by using hands rinsed under cold water. Press them back into position if the beans poke through the ground sirloin.
3. Spray the broad nonstick skillet over medium-high heat with oil and heat. Add the burgers and cook until browned on both sides, turning after 2 minutes, about 5 minutes for medium burgers. Transferring to The dish.
4. Place a burger on a bun for each serving, if necessary, and top with a spoonful of salsa and a few avocado slices. Serve at once, on the side with the remaining salsa.

9. Beef and Bulgur Meat Loaf

(Ready in about 30 Minutes | Serve 8 | Difficulty: Normal)

Ingredients
- 1 cup boiling water½ cup bulgur
- 2 teaspoons canola oil, plus more in a pump sprayer
- 1 medium yellow onion, chopped
- 1 medium red bell pepper, cored and cut into ¼-inch dice
- 2 cloves garlic, minced¼ cup plus
- 2 tablespoons low-salt tomato ketchup
- 1 tablespoon Worcestershire sauce
- 1 teaspoon kosher salt
- ½ teaspoon freshly ground black pepper
- 2 large egg whites1 pound ground sirloin

Directions
1. Combine the boiling water and bulgur in a heat-resistant medium bowl and leave to stand for around 20 minutes until the bulgur has softened and absorbed the water.
2. Preheat the oven to 350°F meanwhile. Cover with aluminum foil on a rimmed baking sheet and spray with oil.
3. Heat 2 teaspoons of oil over medium heat in a medium nonstick skillet. Add the onion, bell pepper, and garlic and cook for about 6 minutes, occasionally stirring, until tender. Transfer and cool slightly in a bowl.
4. In a wire sieve, drain the bulgur, pressing firmly on the bulgur to remove the excess water. Add the vegetables to the bowl, then mix in ¼ cup of the ketchup, Worcestershire sauce, salt, and pepper. (At this stage, adding these ingredients helps cool the vegetables so that the egg whites don't cook from the heat.) Stir in the whites of the egg. Only add the ground sirloin and blend until mixed. Form the foil-lined baking sheet into an 8 x 4-inch loaf.
5. Bake for about 40 minutes until the loaf is golden brown and an instant-read thermometer inserted in the center reads 165 °F. Spread the top of the loaf with 2 teaspoons of ketchup over the last 5 minutes.

10. Beef Ragù with Broccoli Ziti

(Ready in about 30 Minutes | Serve 6 | Difficulty: Normal)

Ingredients
- 1 tablespoon olive oil
- 8 ounces ground sirloin
- 1 medium yellow onion, chopped
- 1 medium carrot, cut into ¼-inch dice
- 1 medium celery rib, cut into ¼-inch dice
- 2 cloves garlic, minced
- 1 (28-ounce) can no-salt-added crushed tomatoes
- 2 teaspoons Italian Seasoning
- ¼ teaspoon crushed hot red pepper broccoli Ziti
- 6 tablespoons freshly grated Parmesan cheese

Directions
1. Heat oil over medium-high heat in a medium saucepan. Add the beef and cook until the meat loses its raw appearance, stirring regularly and breaking the ground sirloin with the side of the spoon, for around 7 minutes. Add the onion, carrot, celery, and garlic and stir. Reduce and cover the heat to medium. Cook,

stirring periodically, for about 5 minutes, until the vegetables soften.
2. Stir in the onions, hot pepper, and Italian Seasoning and bring to a boil. Reduce the heat to medium-low and simmer until the sauce is slightly reduced, stirring regularly around 45 minutes.
3. Divide the hot Ziti broccoli into 6 deep bowls. Top each one with the same amount of sauce and, if used, sprinkle with 1 tablespoon of Parmesan cheese. Serve it wet.

11. Pork Chops in Mustard Sauce

(Ready in about 30 Minutes | Serve 1½ chops each| Difficulty: Normal)

Ingredients

- Canola oil in a pump sprayer
- 6 (4-ounce) boneless pork loin chops, about ½ inch thick
- ½ teaspoon kosher salt
- ½ teaspoon freshly ground black pepper
- 2 teaspoons cornstarch
- ½ cup Homemade Chicken Broth or canned low-sodium chicken broth
- ½ cup low-fat (1%) milk
- 1 tablespoon Dijon mustard
- 1 tablespoon unsalted butter
- 2 tablespoons minced shallots
- 2 teaspoons chopped fresh tarragon, rosemary, or chives

Directions

1. Spray a large nonstick skillet over medium heat with oil and heat. Season the salt and pepper with the pork and apply it to the skillet. Cook for about 3 minutes, until the underside, is golden brown. Flip the pork and cook until the other sides are golden brown, and when pressed with a fingertip in the thickest section, the meat feels strong, around 3 minutes more. Transfer to a dish.
2. Meanwhile, whisk the cornstarch into the broth in a small cup. Add the mustard and milk and whisk again; set aside.
3. Over medium heat, melt the butter in the skillet. Add the shallots and cook, constantly stirring, for about 2 minutes, until tender. Again, whisk the broth mixture, pour it into the skillet and bring it to a boil. Return the pork and any juices to the skillet on the plate and cook for about 1 minute, turning periodically, until the sauce thickens. Shift the pork to a deep dish and split it in half with each chop. Over the pork chops, pour the sauce and sprinkle with the tarragon. Serve it wet.

12. Pork Chops with Sweet-and-Sour Cabbage

(Ready in about 30 Minutes | Serve 4 | Difficulty: Normal)

Ingredients
Red Cabbage

- 1 slice reduced-sodium bacon, coarsely chopped
- 1 teaspoon canola oil
- 1 medium yellow onion, chopped
- 1 small red cabbage (1¼ pounds), cored and thinly sliced
- ¼ cup cider vinegar
- 2 Granny Smith apples, cored and cut into ½-inch dice
- ¼ cup water
- 3 tablespoons grade B maple syrup
- 1 teaspoon kosher salt
- ¼ teaspoon freshly ground black pepper

Pork chops

- Canola oil in a pump sprayer
- 4 (4-ounce) boneless center-cut pork chops, excess fat trimmed
- ¼ teaspoon kosher salt
- ¼ teaspoon freshly ground black pepper

Directions

1. Red cabbage preparation: Cook the bacon in the oil in a medium saucepan over medium heat, occasionally stirring, until the bacon is crisp and brown, around 5 minutes. Add the onion and cook, periodically stirring, until golden, about 5 minutes. Stir in the cabbage in three or four additions, sprinkling each addition with a tablespoon or so of the vinegar. Apples, water, maple syrup, salt, and pepper are added. Reduce the heat to medium-low, then tightly cover it. Cook until the cabbage is very soft, occasionally stirring, for about 1 hour. Apply a few tablespoons of water if the liquid cooks out.
2. To cook the pork: spray a large nonstick skillet over medium heat with oil and heat. Season the salt and pepper with the pork and apply it to the skillet. Cook until golden brown on the underside, about 3 minutes. Flip the pork and cook until the other sides are golden brown, and when pressed with a fingertip in the thickest section, the meat feels strong, around 3 minutes more. In order to stay warm, switch to a plate and tent with foil.
3. Enhance the heat to strong under the skillet. Apply to the skillet the red cabbage mixture and any liquid, and cook, scraping the browned bits with a wooden spoon in the skillet. Cook for about 3 minutes until the juices have thickened. Return the pork and any juices to the skillet on the counter. Serve it hot.

13. Rosemary Pork Chops with Balsamic Glaze

(Ready in about 30 Minutes | Serve 4 | Difficulty: Normal)

Ingredients

- Olive oil in a pump sprayer
- 4 (4-ounce) boneless pork loin chops, about ½ inch thick
- 1 tablespoon finely chopped fresh rosemary
- ½ teaspoon kosher salt
- ½ teaspoon freshly ground black pepper

- ¼ cup balsamic vinegar

Directions

1. Spray a large nonstick skillet over medium heat with oil and heat. Season the rosemary, salt, and pepper with the pork. Add to the skillet and cook for around 3 minutes until the underparts are golden brown. Flip the pork and cook, adjusting the heat as needed so that the pork cooks continuously without burning until the other sides are browned, and when pressed with a fingertip in the middle, the pork feels firm, around 3 minutes more. Move each chop to a plate for dinner.
2. When the heat is off, apply the vinegar to your skillet. (Do not inhale the fumes, as they are powerful.) Scrape the browned bits at the bottom of the skillet with a wooden spoon. For the vinegar to evaporate to around 2 teaspoons, the residual heat of the skillet should be appropriate. To reduce the vinegar slightly, return the skillet to medium heat if needed. Drizzle over each chop with the glaze and serve sweet.

14. Pork Chops with White Beans

(Ready in about 30 Minutes | Serve 4 | Difficulty: Normal)

Ingredients

- 3 teaspoons olive oil
- 4 (4-ounce) boneless pork loin chops, about ½ inch thick
- ½ teaspoon kosher salt½ teaspoon freshly ground black pepper
- 1 medium yellow onion, chopped
- 1 medium carrot, cut into ½-inch dice
- 1 medium celery rib, cut into ½-inch dice
- 2 cloves garlic, minced
- ½ cup Homemade Chicken Broth or canned low-sodium chicken broth
- 1 (15-ounce) can no-salt-added cannellini beans, drained and rinsed
- 2 ripe plum (Roma) tomatoes, seeded and cut into ½-inch dice
- ½ teaspoon herbes de Provence, Italian Seasoning or dried rosemary Chopped fresh parsley, for serving

Directions

1. Heat 1 teaspoon of oil over medium heat in a large nonstick skillet. With salt and pepper, season the pork. Add to the skillet and cook for around 3 minutes until the underparts are golden brown. Flip the chops and cook for about 3 more minutes, until the other sides are browned. Transfer to a dish.
2. Heat the skillet with the remaining 2 teaspoons of oil. Add the onion, carrot, celery, and garlic and cover. Cook, stirring periodically, for about 5 minutes, until the vegetables soften. Add the broth and bring it to a boil, stirring the brown bits with a wooden spoon in the skillet. Add the beans, onions, and herbs from Provence. Cover and boil for about 15 minutes to mix the flavors.
3. Return the pork and any juices to the skillet on the counter. Simmer, uncovered, for about 3 minutes, until the pork feels firm when pressed with a fingertip in the middle.
4. Divide the bean mixture equally between four large bowls of soup and cover each with a chop of pork. Sprinkle and serve with the parsley

15. Pork Tenderloin with Easy BBQ Sauce

(Ready in about 30 Minutes | Serve 6 | Difficulty: Normal)

Ingredients

- 1½ pounds pork tenderloin, sinew, and excess fat trimmed
- 1 teaspoon kosher salt
- ½ teaspoon freshly ground black pepper
- 1 tablespoon canola oil
- 2 tablespoons all-fruit peach spread
- 2 tablespoons no-salt-added tomato ketchup
- 1 tablespoon cider vinegar
- 1 teaspoon chili powder
- ½ teaspoon hickory liquid smoke flavoring (optional)

Directions

1. Preheat the oven to 350°F.
2. With salt and pepper, season the pork. Fold the tenderloin's thin ends and tie them down with kitchen twine so that the meat is uniformly thick. Heat the oil with an ovenproof handle over medium heat in a large nonstick skillet. Attach the tenderloin and cook for about 5 minutes, occasionally turning, until browned on all sides.
3. Mix the peach spread, ketchup, vinegar, chili powder, and liquid smoke in a small bowl (if used). Spread over the tenderloin. Move the skillet to the oven with the tenderloin and bake for 12 to 15 minutes until an instant-read thermometer inserted in the center of the tenderloin reads 145°F. Put the pork on a carving board and let it stand for five minutes.
4. Break the strings and cut into 1/2-inch-thick slices of the tenderloin crosswise. Arrange on plates for dinner and pipe on top of any carving juices. Serve it hot.

16. Grilled Pork and Vegetable Souvlaki with Oregano-Lemon Marinade

(Ready in about 30 Minutes | Serve 6 | Difficulty: Normal)

Ingredients
Marinade

- ½ cup coarsely chopped yellow onion
- 2 tablespoons fresh lemon juice
- 2 tablespoons olive oil, preferably extra-virgin
- 2 teaspoons dried oregano
- 2 garlic cloves, crushed under a knife and peeled

- ¼ teaspoon kosher salt
- ¼ teaspoon freshly ground black pepper

Souvlaki

- 1½ pounds center-cut pork loin, trimmed, and cut into eighteen
- 1½-inch pieces1 medium red onion, peeled and cut into twelve 1½-inch pieces
- 1 large zucchini, trimmed, cut lengthwise, and then crosswise into 12 pieces
- Olive oil in a pump sprayer
- Lemon wedges, for serving

Directions

1. Purée the onion, lemon juice, oil, oregano, garlic, salt, and pepper together in a blender to make the marinade. Pour it into a big plastic zipper bag.
2. To make the souvlaki: Add the pork to the bag and toss in the marinade to coat. For at least 2 hours and up to 8 hours, seal the bag and refrigerate.
3. Place the broiler rack approximately 4 inches from the heat source and preheat the broiler.
4. Have six metal kebab skewers ready. Remove the pork from the marinade, allowing the meat to cling to the marinade. On each of six metal skewers, thread 3 pork bits, 2 red onion pieces, and 2 zucchini pieces, rotating the ingredients without tightly packing them together. With oil, spray the vegetables.
5. Lightly spray a broiler rack with gasoline. Broil the souvlaki until the pork is porky, turning periodically, Lightly browned and, when pierced with the tip of a thin, sharp knife, just barely pink for 8 to 10 minutes. Take it out of the broiler and let stand for 3 minutes. Serve hot with wedges of lemon.

17. Pomegranate-Marinated Leg of Lamb

(Ready in about 30 Minutes I Serve 6 I Difficulty: Normal)

Ingredients

Marinade

- ½ cup bottled pomegranate juice
- ½ cup hearty red wine, such as Shiraz
- 1 teaspoon ground cumin
- 1 teaspoon dried oregano
- ½ teaspoon crushed hot red pepper
- 3 cloves garlic, minced

Lamb

- 1¾ pounds boneless leg of lamb, butterflied and surface fat trimmed
- ½ teaspoon kosher salt
- Olive oil in a pump sprayer

Directions

1. To make the marinade: whisk the pomegranate juice, wine, cumin, oregano, hot pepper, and garlic together in a medium cup. Transfer to a large plastic bag with a zipper.
2. To make the lamb ready: add the lamb to the bag, squeeze the air out, and close the bag. Refrigerate for at least 1 hour and no more than 8 hours, turning periodically.
3. Place a broiler rack approximately 8 inches from the heat source and preheat the broiler.
4. Remove the lamb from the marinade, letting it drain off the excess marinade. Using paper towels to blot, but do not dry absolutely. Season with a little salt. Using oil to spray the broiler rack. Place the lamb on the rack and broil, turning periodically, until inserted in the thickest part of the lamb, browned and an instant-read thermometer reads 130 ° F for medium-rare, around 20 minutes. Switch to a carving board and allow 5 minutes to stand.
5. Break the lamb into thin slices all over the grain. Switch to a dish and pipe on the top of the carving juices. Serve hot, serve,

Chapter 10: Appetizer Recipes

This chapter comprises of amazing appetizer recipes that can be enjoyed by those following DASH diet for a healthy lifestyle

1. Artichoke dip
(Ready in about 30 Minutes I Serve 8 I Difficulty: Normal)

Ingredients
- 1 can (15.5 ounces) artichoke hearts in water, drained
- 4 cups chopped raw spinach
- 2 cloves garlic, minced
- 1 teaspoon ground black pepper
- 1 teaspoon minced fresh thyme (or 1/3 teaspoon dried)
- 1 tablespoon fresh minced parsley (or 1 teaspoon dried)
- 1 cup prepared unsalted white beans (or half a 15.5-ounce can of unsalted white beans, rinsed and drained)
- 2 tablespoons grated Parmesan cheese
- 1/2 cup low-fat sour cream

Directions
1. Combine the ingredients in a mixing dish. Switch to a glass or ceramic dish that is oven-safe and bake for 30 minutes at 350 F. Serve it warm.

2. Artichoke, spinach, and white bean dip
(Ready in about 30 Minutes I Serve 8 I Difficulty: Normal)

Ingredients
- 2 cups artichoke hearts
- 1 tablespoon black pepper
- 4 cups chopped spinach
- 1 teaspoon minced dried thyme

- 2 cloves garlic, minced
- 1 tablespoon minced fresh parsley
- 1 cup cooked white beans
- 2 tablespoons grated parmesan cheese
- 1/2 cup reduced-fat sour cream

Directions

1. Heat the oven to 350°C.
2. Mix together all of the ingredients. Put it in a ceramic or glass dish and bake it for 30 minutes.
3. Using vegetables or whole-grain bread or crackers to serve.

3. Artichokes alla Romana

(Ready in about 30 Minutes | Serve 8 | Difficulty: Normal)

Ingredients

- 2 cups fresh breadcrumbs, preferably whole-wheat
- 1 tablespoon olive oil
- 4 large globe artichokes
- 2 lemons, halved
- 1/3 cup grated Parmesan cheese
- 3 garlic cloves, finely chopped
- 2 tablespoons finely chopped fresh flat-leaf (Italian) parsley
- 1 tablespoon grated lemon zest
- 1/4 teaspoon freshly ground black pepper
- 1 cup plus 2 to 4 tablespoons low-sodium vegetable or chicken stock
- 1 cup dry white wine
- 1 tablespoon minced shallot
- 1 teaspoon chopped fresh oregano

Directions

1. Heat the oven to 400 F. Mix the breadcrumbs and olive oil together in a dish. Toss it to coat it. In a shallow baking pan, spread the crumbs and bake, stirring once halfway through, until the crumbs are softly golden, for about 10 minutes. Set to cool aside.
2. Snap off any rough outer leaves and trim the stem flush with the base while dealing with 1 artichoke at a time. With a serrated knife, cut off the top third of the leaves and slice off any remaining thorns with scissors. Clean the cut edges with half a lemon to avoid discoloration. Separate the inner leaves from the middle and pull the tiny leaves out. Scoop out the fuzzy choke using a melon baller or spoon, then squeeze some lemon juice into the cavity. In the same way, trim the remaining artichokes.
3. Toss the breadcrumbs with the Parmesan cheese, garlic, parsley, lemon zest, and pepper in a large cup. Add 2 to 4 tablespoons of stock, 1 tablespoon at a time, using just enough to start sticking together in small clumps for the stuffing to begin.
4. Mound it slightly into the middle of the artichokes using 2/3 of the stuffing. Then spread the leaves open, beginning from the bottom, and spoon a rounded teaspoon of stuffing at each leaf's base. (The artichokes can be prepared several hours in advance and held refrigerated to this point.)
5. Combine the 1 cup stock, wine, shallot, and oregano in a Dutch oven with a tightly fitted lid. (Note: Don't use cast iron, or it will turn brown with the cooked artichokes.) Bring to a boil, then reduce the heat to low. Arrange the artichokes in one single sheet, stem-end down, in the liquid. Cover and boil for about 45 minutes, until the outer leaves are tender (add water if necessary). Move the artichokes and let them cool slightly to a rack. Every artichoke should be cut into quarters and served warm.

4. Avocado dip

(Ready in about 30 Minutes | Serve 8 | Difficulty: Normal)

Ingredients

- 1/2 cup fat-free sour cream
- 2 teaspoons chopped onion
- 1/8 teaspoon hot sauce
- 1 ripe avocado, peeled, pitted, and mashed (about 1/2 cup)

Directions

1. Mix the sour cream, onion, hot sauce, and avocado together in a small bowl. Mix to uniformly combine the ingredients. Serve with sliced vegetables or fried tortilla chips.

5. Baba ghanoush

(Ready in about 30 Minutes | Serve: 8 | Difficulty: Normal)

Ingredients

- 1 bulb garlic (about 8 cloves)
- 2 eggplants, sliced lengthwise, skin removed
- 1 red bell pepper, halved and seeded
- Juice of 1 lemon (about 4 tablespoons)
- 1 tablespoon chopped fresh basil
- 1 tablespoon olive oil
- 1 teaspoon black pepper or to taste
- 2 rounds of whole-wheat pita or other flatbread

Directions

1. Spray the cooking spray on the cold grill. Heat one side to high on the grill. (Or, on one side of the grill, shift the coals.)
2. Slice the garlic bulb off the end, wrap it in foil, and put it on the cooler part of the grill. 20 to 30 minutes to roast. Place the eggplant slices and bell pepper on the hot portion of the grill. Grill on each side for 2 to 3 minutes.
3. Squeeze out the roasted garlic and put it in the food processor. Connect the eggplant and red bell pepper to the grill. Add lemon juice, basil, pepper, and olive oil until smooth, pulse. Place the dip in the bowl for serving.
4. A few seconds of warm bread on either side of the grill. With dip, serve.

6. Baked brie envelopes

(Ready in about 30 Minutes | Serve: 8 | Difficulty: Normal)

Ingredients

- 1/2 cup fresh or frozen cranberries
- 1/2 medium orange, quartered
- 2 tablespoons sugar
- 1 cinnamon stick
- 1 sheet puff pastry dough, cut into 12 1/4-ounce squares
- 6 ounces Brie cheese, cut into 1/2-ounce cubes
- 2 tablespoons water
- 1 egg white

Directions

1. Heat the oven to 425 F.
2. Heat a small saute pan over medium-high heat; brush with cooking spray lightly. Reduce heat to low levels. Place in the pan the cranberries, orange, sugar, and cinnamon stick and cook for about 10 minutes, stirring continuously until the cranberries are tender and the mixture begins to thicken. Remove from the heat and quit to cool down. Remove the orange quarters and cinnamon stick.
3. Roll each puff pastry square out. On every puff pastry square, place one cube of cheese and 1 teaspoon of cooled cranberry mixture. Combine the water and the white egg in a small cup. Dab a small amount of the egg mixture onto the inside of the puff pastry using a pastry brush. Pull around the cheese and cranberry mixture like an envelope, one corner of the pastry at a time. Baste the egg mixture on the top of the pastry. Place the envelopes on a baking sheet and bake until golden brown or for 10 to 12 minutes.

7. Basil pesto stuffed mushrooms

(Ready in about 30 Minutes | Serve: 8 | Difficulty: Normal)

Ingredients

- 20 crimini mushrooms, washed and stems removed

Topping:
- 1 1/2 cups panko breadcrumbs
- 1/4 cup melted butter
- 3 tablespoons chopped fresh parsley

Filling:
- 2 cups fresh basil leaves
- 1/4 cup fresh Parmesan cheese
- 2 tablespoons pumpkin seeds
- 1 tablespoon olive oil
- 1 tablespoon fresh garlic
- 2 teaspoons lemon juice
- 1/2 teaspoon kosher salt

Directions

1. Heat the oven to 350 F. On a baking sheet, line the mushroom caps upside down.
2. Combine the panko, butter, and parsley in a small bowl to prepare the topping; set aside.
3. Place the basil, cheese, pumpkin seeds, oil, garlic, lemon juice, and salt in a food processor to prepare the filling. Process until blended evenly.
4. Stuff the mushroom caps generously with the basil pesto filling. Sprinkle about 1 teaspoon of panko topping on each mushroom. Gently pat the topping on it. Bake until golden brown or for 10 to 15 minutes.

8. Black bean and corn relish

(Ready in about 30 Minutes | Serve 8 | Difficulty: Normal)

Ingredients

- 1 can (15.5 ounces) black beans, rinsed and drained (about 2 cups)
- 1 cup frozen corn kernels, thawed to room temperature
- 4 tomatoes, seeded and diced (about 3 cups)
- 2 garlic cloves, chopped
- 1/2 medium red onion, diced (about 1/2 cup)
- 1/2 cup chopped parsley
- 1 green, yellow or red bell pepper, seeded and diced (about 1 cup)
- 2 teaspoons sugar
- Juice from 1 lemon

Directions

1. Combine all of the ingredients in a large bowl. For mixing, toss gently. For at least 30 minutes, cover and refrigerate to allow the flavors to blend.

9. Chickpea polenta with olives

(Ready in about 30 Minutes | Serve 8 | Difficulty: Normal)

Ingredients
For the polenta:

- 1 3/4 cups chickpea flour
- 2 cups plain soy milk
- 1 cup chicken stock, vegetable stock, or broth
- 1/2 tablespoon extra-virgin olive oil
- 3 cloves garlic, chopped
- 1 tablespoon chopped fresh thyme, oregano, or basil, or 1 teaspoon dried
- 1 teaspoon dry mustard
- 1/4 teaspoon freshly ground black pepper
- 3 egg whites

For the topping:

- 1/2 tablespoon extra-virgin olive oil
- 1/2 yellow onion, minced
- 1/4 cup coarsely chopped pitted Kalamata olives
- 1/4 cup dry-packed sun-dried tomatoes, soaked in water to rehydrate, drained, and chopped
- 2 tablespoons grated Parmesan cheese

- 2 tablespoons finely chopped fresh flat-leaf (Italian) parsley

Directions

1. Put the flour, soy milk, stock, olive oil, garlic, thyme, mustard, and pepper together in a blender or food processor until smooth operation. Through a broad bowl, pour the batter. Let it stand in the refrigerator for 1 hour.
2. Heat the oven to 425 F. Using cooking spray to thinly coat a 9-by-13-inch baking pan.
3. Beat the egg whites in a big, spotlessly clean cup, using a high electric mixer, until stiff peaks develop. Fold the egg whites into the batter gently.
4. In the prepared bowl, pour the batter into it. Bake for about 15 minutes, until puffed and lightly browned around the edges. Leave for 15 minutes to cool.
5. Heat your broiler. Place the rack 4 inches from the source of the sun.
6. Make the topping while the polenta is cooling. Heat the olive oil over medium-high heat in a small frying pan. Add the onion and cook for about 6 minutes, until soft and softly golden. Connect the tomatoes and olives and cook for 1 minute. Remove yourself from the sun.
7. Spoon the onion mixture equally over the baked polenta carefully and sprinkle with the cheese. Broil until finely browned at the tip. Watch carefully; it only takes about 1 minute to do this. Sprinkle parsley with it. Switch to a wire rack and leave for 10 minutes to cool. Cut 8 squares, then cut the diagonal squares into 16 wedges. Immediately serve.

10. Chipotle spiced shrimp

(Ready in about 30 Minutes | Serve: 4 | Difficulty: Normal)

Ingredients

- 1 pound uncooked shrimp, peeled and deveined
- 2 tablespoons tomato paste
- 1 1/2 teaspoons water
- 1/2 teaspoon extra-virgin olive oil
- 1/2 teaspoon minced garlic
- 1/2 teaspoon chipotle chili powder
- 1/2 teaspoon chopped fresh oregano

Directions

1. In cold water, clean the shrimp. Pat dry and set aside on a plate with a paper towel.
2. To make the marinade, whisk the tomato paste, water and oil together in a small cup. Garlic, chili powder, and oregano are added. Mix thoroughly.
3. Spread the marinade (it will be thick) on both sides of the shrimp using a brush. Place it in the fridge.
4. Using a barbecue grill to prepare a hot fire or heat a gas grill or broiler. Lightly brush the grill rack or broiler pan with cooking spray, away from the heat source. The cooking rack should be placed 4 to 6 inches from the heat source.
5. In a grill basket or on skewers, put the shrimp and place on the grill. After 3 to 4 minutes, turn the shrimp over. Depending on the heat of the fire, the cooking time varies, so watch carefully.
6. Switch to a plate and quickly serve.

11. Coconut shrimp

(Ready in about 30 Minutes | Serve 4 | Difficulty: Normal)

Ingredients

- 1/4 cup sweetened coconut
- 1/4 cup panko breadcrumbs
- 1/2 teaspoon kosher salt
- 1/2 cup coconut milk
- 12 large shrimp, peeled and deveined

Directions

1. Heat the oven to 375 F. Cover a baking sheet lightly with cooking oil.
2. In a food processor, put the coconut, panko, and salt and process until the mixture has an even consistency. In a small bowl, put the panko mixture. In another small cup, put the coconut milk in it. In the coconut milk and then in the panko mixture, dip each shrimp and put them on the baking sheet. Coat the top of the shrimp loosely with cooking oil. Bake for about 10 to 15 minutes, until golden brown.

12. Crispy potato skins

(Ready in about 30 Minutes | Serve: 4 | Difficulty: Normal)

Ingredients

- 2 medium russet potatoes
- Butter-flavored cooking spray
- 1 tablespoon minced fresh rosemary
- 1/8 teaspoon freshly ground black pepper

Directions

1. Heat the oven to 375 F.
2. Clean and pierce the potatoes with a fork. Place in the oven and bake for about 1 hour, until the skins are crisp.
3. Carefully cut the potatoes in half and scoop out the pulp, leaving about 1/8 inch of the potato flesh attached to the skin. The potatoes will be very hot. For different usage, save the pulp.
4. Using butter-flavored cooking spray to spray the inside of each potato skin. Press the pepper and rosemary in. Put the skin back in the oven for 5 to 10 minutes. Immediately serve.

13. Fresh fruit kebabs

(Ready in about 30 Minutes | Serve 4 | Difficulty: Normal)

Ingredients

- 6 ounces low-fat, sugar-free lemon yogurt
- 1 teaspoon fresh lime juice
- 1 teaspoon lime zest
- 4 pineapple chunks (about 1/2 inch each)
- 4 strawberries
- 1 kiwi, peeled and quartered
- 1/2 banana, cut into 4 1/2-inch chunks
- 4 red grapes
- 4 wooden skewers

Directions

1. Whisk together the yogurt, lime juice, and lime zest in a small cup. Cover until required, and refrigerate.
2. Into the skewer, thread 1 of each fruit. Repeat until the fruit is gone, on the other skewers. Serve the lemon-lime dip with it.

14. Fresh tomato crostini

(Ready in about 30 Minutes | Serve 4 | Difficulty: Normal)

Ingredients

- 4 plum tomatoes, chopped
- 1/4 cup minced fresh basil
- 2 teaspoons olive oil
- 1 clove garlic, minced
- Freshly ground pepper
- 1/4 pound crusty Italian peasant bread, cut into 4 slices and toasted

Directions

1. In a medium cup, mix the tomatoes, basil, oil, garlic, and pepper. Cover them and make them stand for 30 minutes. Divide the tomato mixture between the toast and any juices. At room temperature, serve.

15. Fruit salsa and sweet chips

(Ready in about 30 Minutes | Serve 4 | Difficulty: Normal)

Ingredients

For tortilla crisps:

- fat-free whole-wheat tortillas
- Cooking spray
- 1 tablespoon sugar
- 1/2 tablespoon cinnamon

For the fruit salsa:

- 3 cups diced fresh fruit, such as apples, oranges, kiwi, strawberries, grapes, or other fresh fruit
- 2 tablespoons sugar-free jam, any flavor
- 1 tablespoon honey or agave nectar
- 2 tablespoons orange juice

Directions

1. Heat the oven to 350 F. Break the tortilla into 8 wedges each. On two baking sheets, lie bits. Make sure that they do not overlap. Spray with cooking spray on the tortilla bits.
2. Combine the sugar and cinnamon in a small dish. Over the tortilla wedges, sprinkle uniformly. Bake until the bits are crisp or for 10 to 12 minutes. Place and let cool on a cooling rack.
3. Get the fruit sliced into cubes. In a mixing bowl, mix the fruits together gently. Whisk the jam, honey, and orange juice together in another cup. Over the diced fruit, pour this. Gently mix. Using plastic wrap to cover the bowl and refrigerate for 2 to 3 hours.
4. Serve as a dip for the cinnamon tortilla chips or a topping.

16. Ginger-marinated grilled portobello mushrooms

(Ready in about 30 Minutes | Serve 4 | Difficulty: Normal)

Ingredients

- 1/4 cup balsamic vinegar
- 1/2 cup pineapple juice
- 2 tablespoons chopped fresh ginger, peeled
- 4 large portobello mushrooms (about 4 ounces each), cleaned and stems removed
- 1 tablespoon chopped fresh basil

Directions

1. Whisk together the balsamic vinegar, pineapple juice, and ginger in a small cup.
2. Place the fungi in a glass dish, side up, stemless. Drizzle over the mushrooms with the marinade. Cover and marinate for about 1 hour in the refrigerator, turning the mushrooms over once.
3. Using a barbecue grill to prepare a hot fire or heat a gas grill or broiler. Lightly brush the grill rack or broiler pan with cooking spray, away from the heat source. The cooking rack should be placed 4 to 6 inches from the heat source.
4. On medium heat, grill or broil the mushrooms, sometimes turning, until tender, for about 5 minutes on each side. To stop drying out, baste it with marinade.
5. Move the mushrooms to a serving platter using tongs. Garnish with basil and quickly serve.

17. Gluten-free hummus

(Ready in about 30 Minutes | Serve 4 | Difficulty: Normal)

Ingredients

- 2/3 cup dried chickpeas (garbanzos), picked over and rinsed, soaked overnight, and drained
- 3 cups of water
- 2 cloves garlic
- 1 bay leaf
- 1/2 teaspoon salt
- 1 tablespoon olive oil
- 3/4 cup plus 2 tablespoons sliced green (spring) onion
- 2 tablespoons sherry vinegar
- 3 tablespoons chopped fresh cilantro (fresh coriander)
- 1 teaspoon ground cumin

Directions

1. Combine the chickpeas, water, garlic cloves, bay leaf, and 1/4 teaspoon salt in a large saucepan over high heat. Just bring it to a boil. Reduce the heat to medium, cover partially and simmer for 50 to 60 minutes until the beans are very tender. The bay leaf is drained and discarded, reserving the garlic and 1/2 cup of the cooking fluid.
2. Mix the chickpeas, cooked garlic, olive oil, 3/4 cup green onion, vinegar, cilantro, cumin, and the

remaining 1/4 teaspoon salt in a blender or food processor. Purée method. Add the reserved cooking liquid until the mixture has the consistency of a dense spread, 1 tablespoon at a time.
3. Stir the chickpea mixture and the remaining 2 tablespoons of the green onion together in a shallow serving dish. Serve immediately or, until ready to serve, cover, and refrigerate. Create 1 1/2 cups or so.

18. Grilled pineapple
(Ready in about 30 Minutes | Serve 8 | Difficulty: Normal)

Ingredients
For the marinade
- 2 tablespoons dark honey
- 1 tablespoon olive oil
- 1 tablespoon fresh lime juice
- 1 teaspoon ground cinnamon
- 1/4 teaspoon ground cloves
- 1 firm, ripe pineapple
- 8 wooden skewers, soaked in water for 30 minutes, or metal skewers
- 1 tablespoon dark rum (optional)
- 1 tablespoon grated lime zest

Directions
1. On a barbecue grill, prepare a hot fire or heat a gas grill or broiler (grill). Lightly brush the grill rack or broiler pan with cooking spray, away from the heat source. The cooking rack should be placed 4 to 6 inches from the heat source.
2. Combine the honey, olive oil, lime juice, cinnamon, and cloves in a small bowl to create the marinade, and whisk to combine. Only set aside.
3. Cut off the leaf crown and the pineapple foundation. Stand the pineapple upright and cut down just below the surface in long, vertical strips and leave the tiny brown 'eyes' on the fruit. Using a big, sharp knife, pare off the skin. Sit on its side the pineapple. Cut a shallow furrow, using a spiral pattern around the pineapple, to detach all the eyes by aligning the knife blade with the diagonal rows of eyes. Stand upright with the peeled pineapple and cut it lengthwise in half. Place each pineapple half cut-side down and cut it into four long wedges lengthwise; slice the core away. Break each wedge into three parts crosswise. Thread onto each skewer the three bits of pineapple.
4. With the marinade, gently clean the pineapple. Grill or broil, turning once and basting with the remaining marinade once or twice, until tender and golden, approximately 5 minutes on each hand.
5. Remove the pineapple from the skewers and put it on a serving dish or individual plates. If used, brush with the rum and sprinkle with lime zest. Serve warm or hot.

19. Hummus
(Ready in about 30 Minutes | Serve 14 | Difficulty: Normal)

Ingredients
- 2 cans (16 ounces each) reduced-sodium chickpeas, rinsed and drained except for 1/4 cup liquid
- 1 tablespoon extra-virgin olive oil
- 1/4 cup lemon juice
- 2 garlic cloves, minced
- 1/4 teaspoon cracked black pepper
- 1/4 teaspoon paprika
- 3 tablespoons tahini (sesame paste)*
- 2 tablespoons chopped Italian flat-leaf parsley

Directions
1. Purée the chickpeas using a blender or food processor. Add the lemon juice, olive oil, garlic, pepper, paprika, tahini, and parsley. Blend thoroughly.
2. Add the reserved liquid until the mixture has the consistency of a thick spread, 1 tablespoon at a time.
3. Serve immediately or, until ready to serve, cover, and refrigerate.

20. Marinated portobello mushrooms with provolone
(Ready in about 30 Minutes | Serve 14 | Difficulty: Normal)

Ingredients
- 2 portobello mushrooms, stemmed and wiped clean
- 1/2 cup balsamic vinegar
- 1 tablespoon brown sugar
- 1/4 teaspoon dried rosemary
- 1 teaspoon minced garlic
- 1/4 cup grated (1 ounce) provolone cheese

Directions
1. Heat the broiler (grill). Position the rack 4 inches from the heat source. Lightly coat a glass baking dish with cooking spray. Place the mushrooms in the dish, stemless-side (gill-side) up.
2. In a small bowl, whisk together the vinegar, brown sugar, rosemary, and garlic. Pour the mixture over the mushrooms. Set aside for 5 to 10 minutes to marinate.
3. Broil (grill) the mushrooms, turning once, until they're tender, about 4 minutes on each side. Sprinkle grated cheese over each mushroom and continue to broil (grill) until the cheese melts. Transfer to individual plates.

21. Peanut butter hummus
(Ready in about 30 Minutes | Serve 14 | Difficulty: Normal)

Ingredients
- 2 cups garbanzo beans
- 1 cup of water
- 1/2 cup powdered peanut butter
- 1/4 cup natural peanut butter
- 2 tablespoons brown sugar
- 1 teaspoon vanilla extract

Directions

1. In a food processor, put all of the ingredients. Until smooth operation. For up to 1 week, refrigerate.

22. Pickled asparagus

(Ready in about 30 Minutes | Serve 14 | Difficulty: Normal)

Ingredients

- 1 pound fresh asparagus, trimmed (about 3 cups)
- 1/4 cup pearl onions
- 1/4 cup white wine vinegar
- 1/4 cup cider vinegar
- 1 sprig fresh dill (or 2 teaspoons dried)
- 1 cup of water
- 2 whole cloves
- 3 cloves garlic, whole
- 8 whole black peppercorns
- 1/4 teaspoon red pepper flakes
- 6 whole coriander seeds

Directions

1. Trim off the asparagus' woody ends and cut the spears into lengths that fit into the jars. In a strainer, put spears, wash well and drain. Trimming the onions. In airtight containers, combine all ingredients. Please refrigerate for up to 4 weeks.

23. Roasted butternut squash fries

(Ready in about 30 Minutes | Serve 14 | Difficulty: Normal)

Ingredients

- 1 medium butternut squash
- 1 tablespoon olive oil
- 1 tablespoon chopped fresh thyme
- 1 tablespoon chopped fresh rosemary
- 1/2 teaspoon salt

Directions

1. Heat the oven to 425 F. Cover a baking sheet lightly with nonstick cooking spray.
2. Peel the butternut squash skin and cut into even sticks, roughly 1/2 inch wide and 3 inches long. Combine the squash, oil, thyme, rosemary, and salt in a medium bowl; blend until the squash is coated evenly.
3. Spread and roast on the baking sheet for 10 minutes. Remove the oven's baking sheet and shake to loosen the squash. Return to the oven and continue to roast until golden brown for another 5 to 10 minutes.

24. Roasted potatoes with garlic and herbs

(Ready in about 30 Minutes | Serve 14 | Difficulty: Normal)

Ingredients

- 3/4 pound small (2-inch) white or red potatoes
- 4 garlic cloves
- 2 teaspoons olive oil
- 2 teaspoons chopped fresh rosemary
- 1/8 teaspoon salt
- 1/4 teaspoon ground black pepper
- 2 teaspoons butter
- 2 tablespoons chopped fresh parsley

Directions

1. Heat the oven to 400 F. Coat the large baking dish lightly with cooking spray.
2. Add the whole potatoes, cloves of garlic, olive oil, rosemary, salt, and pepper to a large mixing bowl. Using your hands to blend until the oil and spices are mixed with the potatoes.
3. In the prepared baking dish, arrange the potatoes into a single layer. Use a lid or aluminum foil to cover and bake for 25 minutes.
4. Remove the foil or lid. Turn the potatoes and bake until the potatoes are soft and lightly browned, about 25 minutes, uncovered.
5. Put it in a serving bowl and mix it with butter. Sprinkle and serve with parsley

25. Roasted red pepper hummus

(Ready in about 30 Minutes | Serve 14 | Difficulty: Normal)

Ingredients

- 2 cups chickpeas
- 1 cup roasted red bell pepper, sliced, seeded
- 2 tablespoons white sesame seeds
- 1 tablespoon lemon juice
- 1 tablespoon olive oil
- 1 1/4 teaspoons cumin
- 1 teaspoon onion powder
- 1 teaspoon garlic powder
- 1 teaspoon kosher salt
- 1/4 teaspoon cayenne pepper

Directions

1. Process all ingredients in a food processor until smooth.

26. Shrimp ceviche

(Ready in about 30 Minutes | Serve 14 | Difficulty: Normal)

Ingredients

- 1/2 pound raw shrimp, cut into 1/4-inch pieces
- 2 lemons, zest, and juice
- 2 limes, zest, and juice
- 2 tablespoons olive oil
- 2 teaspoons cumin
- 1/2 cup diced red onion
- 1 cup diced tomato
- 2 tablespoons minced garlic
- 1 cup black beans, cooked

- 1/4 cup diced serrano chili pepper and seeds removed
- 1 cup diced cucumber, peeled and seeded
- 1/4 cup chopped cilantro

Directions
1. In a shallow pan, put the shrimp and cover it with lemon juice and lime, reserving the zest. Refrigerate until the shrimp is firm and white, for at least 3 hours.
2. Mix the remaining ingredients in a separate bowl and set aside for cold cooking of the shrimp. Mix the shrimp and citrus juice with the remaining ingredients until they are ready to eat. Using baked tortilla chips to serve.

27. Shrimp marinated in lime juice and Dijon mustard
(Ready in about 30 Minutes | Serve 8 | Difficulty: Normal)

Ingredients
- 1 medium red onion, chopped
- 1/2 cup fresh lime juice, plus lime zest as garnish
- 2 tablespoons capers
- 1 tablespoon Dijon mustard
- 1/2 teaspoon hot sauce
- 1 cup of water
- 1/2 cup rice vinegar
- 3 whole cloves
- 1 bay leaf
- 1 pound uncooked shrimp, peeled and deveined (about 24)

Directions
1. Mix together the onion, lime juice, capers, mustard, and hot sauce in a shallow baking dish. Only set aside.
2. Add the sugar, vinegar, cloves, and bay leaf into a large saucepan. Bring it to a boil, then add the shrimp to it. Cook for 1 minute, continuously stirring. Drain and pass the shrimp to the shallow dish that holds the mixture of onions, making sure the cloves and bay leaf are discarded. Stir to blend. Cover and refrigerate for about 1 hour, until well-chilled.
3. Divide the shrimp mixture into small individual bowls to serve, and garnish each with lime zest. Only serve it cold.

28. Smoked trout spread
(Ready in about 30 Minutes | Serve 8 | Difficulty: Normal)

Ingredients
- 1/4 pound smoked trout fillet, skinned and broken into pieces
- 1/2 cup 1 percent low-fat cottage cheese
- 1/4 cup coarsely chopped red onion
- 2 teaspoons fresh lemon juice
- 1 teaspoon hot pepper sauce
- 1/2 teaspoon Worcestershire sauce
- 1 celery stalk, diced

Directions
1. Combine the salmon, cottage cheese, red onion, lemon juice, sweet pepper sauce, and Worcestershire sauce in a blender or food processor. Process until smooth, stopping as necessary to scrape down the bowl's sides. Fold the diced celery in. Cover until just before serving, and refrigerate.

29. Southwestern potato skins
(Ready in about 30 Minutes | Serve 8 | Difficulty: Normal)

Ingredients
- 6 large baking potatoes
- 1 teaspoon olive oil
- 1 teaspoon chili powder
- 1/8 teaspoon hot pepper sauce
- 6 slices turkey bacon, cooked until crisp, chopped
- 1 medium tomato, diced
- 2 tablespoons sliced green onions (scallions)
- 1/2 cup shredded cheddar cheese

Directions
1. Heat the oven to 450 F. Cover a baking sheet lightly with cooking oil.
2. Scrub and poke each of the potatoes with a fork several times. Microwave uncovered on high until tender, about 10 minutes. Remove the potatoes from the microwave and put them to cool on a wire rack. Cut each potato in half lengthwise when it is cooled to the touch and scoop out the flesh, leaving around 1/4 inch of the flesh attached to the skin. (Save the flesh of the potato for another meal.)
3. Whisk the olive oil, chili powder, and hot sauce together in a small cup. Brush a mixture of olive oil on the inside of the skin of the potato. Break each half of the skin of the potato in half crosswise once again. On a baking sheet, put the potatoes.
4. Mix the turkey bacon, tomatoes, and onions gently in a small bowl. Fill this mixture with each potato skin and sprinkle each one with cheese.
5. Bake for about 10 minutes until the cheese is melted and the potato skins are cooked through. Immediately serve.

30. Sweet and spicy snack mix
(Ready in about 30 Minutes | Serve 8 | Difficulty: Normal)

Ingredients
- 2 cans (15 ounces each) garbanzos, rinsed, drained, and patted dry
- 2 cups wheat squares cereal
- 1 cup dried pineapple chunks
- 1 cup raisins
- 2 tablespoons honey
- 2 tablespoons Worcestershire sauce
- 1 teaspoon garlic powder

- 1/2 teaspoon chili powder

Directions

1. Heat the oven to 350 F. Using butter-flavored cooking spray to thinly coat a 15 1/2-inch-by-10 1/2-inch baking dish.
2. Spray a strong skillet generously with butter-flavored cooking spray. Add the garbanzos to the skillet and cook over medium heat until the beans begin to brown, frequently stirring around 10 minutes. To the prepared baking sheet, move the garbanzos. With cooking oil, gently spray the beans. Bake, frequently stirring, for about 20 minutes, until the beans are crisp.
3. Cover a roasting pan lightly with a cooking spray flavored with butter. Measure into the pan the cereal, pineapple, and raisins. Add garbanzos roasted. Stir to blend uniformly.
4. Honey, Worcestershire sauce, and spices are mixed in a big glass measuring cup. Stir to blend uniformly. Over the snack mix, pour the mixture and toss gently. Spray the mixture with the cooking spray once more. Bake for about 10 to 15 minutes, stirring regularly to avoid the burning of the mixture.
5. Remove and let cool from the oven. Store in a container that is airtight.

31. Tomato basil bruschetta

(Ready in about 30 Minutes | Serve 8 | Difficulty: Normal)

Ingredients

- 1/2 whole-grain baguette, cut into six 1/2-inch-thick diagonal slices
- 2 tablespoons chopped basil
- 1 tablespoon chopped parsley
- 2 cloves garlic, minced
- 3 tomatoes, diced
- 1/2 cup diced fennel
- 1 teaspoon olive oil
- 2 teaspoons balsamic vinegar
- 1 teaspoon black pepper

Directions

1. Heat the oven to 400 F. Toast slices of baguette until lightly browned. Mix with all of the other ingredients. Blend the spoon uniformly over the toasted bread. Immediately serve.

32 White bean dip

(Ready in about 30 Minutes | Serve 8 | Difficulty: Normal)

Ingredients

- 1 can (15 ounces) white (cannellini) beans, rinsed and drained
- 8 garlic cloves, roasted
- 2 tablespoons olive oil
- 2 tablespoons lemon juice

Directions

1. Connect the beans, roasted garlic, olive oil, and lemon juice to the blender or food processor. Blend until perfectly smooth. Serve on top of thin slices of French toasted bread or triangles of pita. This is also perfect on top of red (sweet) bell peppers that are cut into squares.

33. Bruschetta

(Ready in about 30 Minutes | Serve 8 | Difficulty: Normal)

Ingredients

- 1/2 whole-grain baguette, cut into six 1/2-inch-thick diagonal slices
- 2 tablespoons chopped basil
- 1 tablespoon chopped parsley
- 2 cloves garlic, minced
- 3 tomatoes, diced
- 1 teaspoon olive oil
- 2 teaspoons balsamic vinegar
- 1 teaspoon black pepper

Directions

1. Toast baguette slices until finely browned in a 400 F oven.
2. Mix with all of the other ingredients.
3. Blend the spoon uniformly over the toasted bread.
4. Dust on top of a little Parmesan cheese.
5. While warm, serve.

34. Flatbread Pizza

(Ready in about 30 Minutes | Serve 8 | Difficulty: Normal)

Ingredients

- 1 multi-grain flatbread, round or rectangular
- 1/3 cup organic crushed tomatoes
- 1 clove fresh garlic, finely chopped
- Red pepper flakes to taste
- 1/2 cup shredded mozzarella cheese, reduced-fat
- 1/2 red bell pepper, cut into 2" slices
- 1/2 cup sliced mushrooms
- 1 tablespoon extra-virgin olive oil
- 3 tablespoons freshly chopped basil

Directions

1. Preheat the oven to 400°C. Place the flatbread on a baking sheet lined with parchment.
2. Spread on top of the bread with crushed tomatoes. Sprinkle lightly with chopped garlic and a flake of red pepper.
3. Sprinkle on top with cheese, bell pepper, and mushrooms. Drizzle with the olive oil, extra virgin. Lightly add salt and pepper.
4. Bake for 15-20 minutes, or until the cheese starts bubbling around the edges and turns golden.
5. Remove and slightly cool. Add fresh chopped basil to the garnish. Enjoy!

35. Spaghetti Pie

(Ready in about 30 Minutes | Serve 8 | Difficulty: Normal)

Ingredients

- 12 oz. spaghetti (keep ½ cup of the cooking water for later)

- 1 yellow onion, chopped
- ½ red capsicums
- ½ green capsicums
- 1 lb of ground turkey (or chicken or beef)
- 1 cup tomato paste
- 3 large eggs
- 1 cup of 2% shredded mozzarella
- 1 cup of 2% grated Parmesan cheese
- 1 tablespoon of dried mixed herbs (3 tablespoons of fresh)
- 1 teaspoon Chia Seeds
- 2 tablespoon olive oil

Directions

1. Preheat the oven to 350.
2. Sauté the onions in a large skillet until tender. Add beef or ground turkey and 3⁄4 cup tomato paste. Add half the pasta water and stir well with the capsicums and chia seeds.
3. Consistency, adding more cooking water as needed, should be like a thick Bolognese sauce.
4. Mix the cooked pasta, eggs, parmesan cheese, 1 cup of the mozzarella, and 1⁄4 cup of the tomato paste in a wide bowl.
5. Using olive oil to grease a 9 or 10-inch pie pan. Spread over the bottom of the pan with half the meat mixture. To level, it, apply the spaghetti mixture and press it down. Spread the remaining mozzarella on top, along with the remaining meat mixture.
6. Bake the pie for 30 to 35 minutes in the oven. Remove from the oven and leave to stay for 10 minutes or so. Using a sharp knife or pizza slicer to carve, like a pie, into wedges. Using a green salad to serve.

36. Pita Pizza

(Ready in about 50 Minutes | Serve 8 | Difficulty: Normal)

Ingredients

- 1 whole wheat pita
- Tomato sauce
- Low-fat mozzarella
- Red bell peppers

Directions

1. Assemble and toast the pizza for 5 minutes in the oven.

Chapter 11: Poultry Recipes

This chapter comprises of mouth-watering DASH diet poultry recipes.

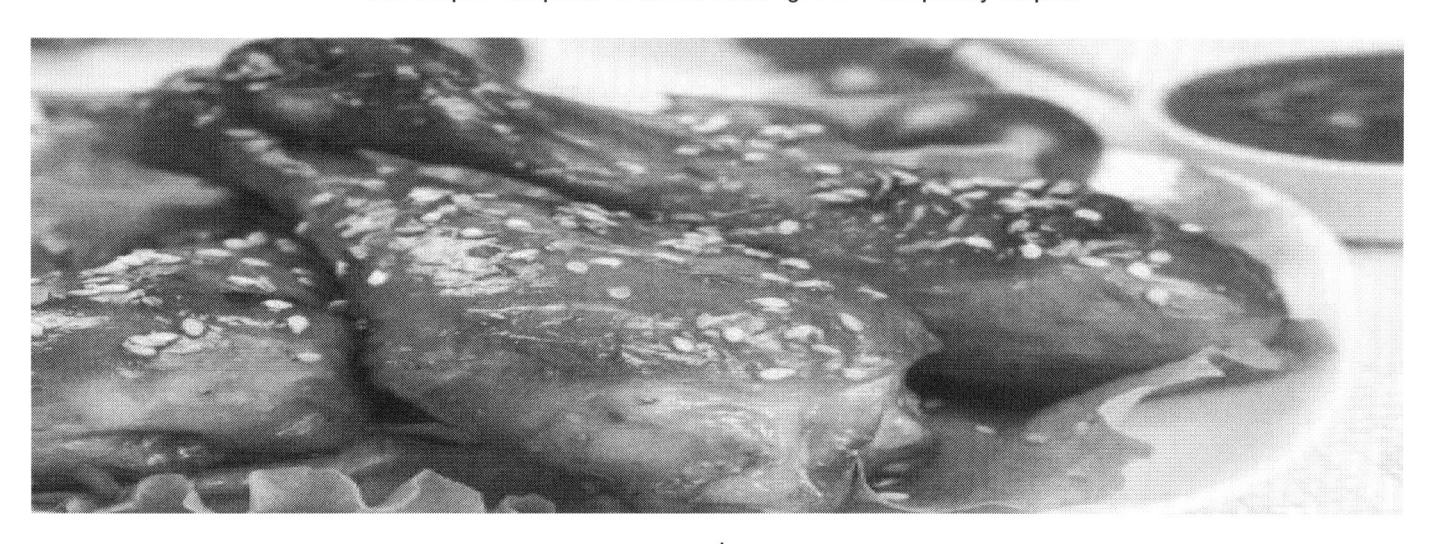

1. Basic Roast Chicken Breast

(Ready in about 30 Minutes | Serve 6 | Difficulty: Normal)

Ingredients

- 2 (10-ounce) chicken breast halves, with skin and bone
- ½ teaspoon kosher salt
- ¼ teaspoon freshly ground black pepper
- Olive oil in a pump sprayer 1 tablespoon minced shallot
- t⅔cup Homemade Chicken Broth or canned low-sodium chicken broth; or ½ cup chicken broth plus 2 tablespoons dry vermouth or dry white wine
- 1 tablespoon cold unsalted butter (optional)

Directions

1. Preheat the oven to 400 F.
2. Use a small, sharp knife to cut the skin off the meat and pull back the skin, leaving it attached to the large side of the chicken half. Deal on one breast half at a time:

beginning at the rib cage. Season the salt and pepper with the raw skin. Replace the flesh-covering skin.

3. Arrange the side of the chicken skin in a small roasting pan (a 9 ?? 13-inch metal baking dish works well) and spray the oil. Roast for 35 to 40 minutes before an instant-read thermometer inserted into the thickest part of the chicken registers 165 ° F. Switch the chicken to a carving board for 5 minutes and let it stand. (Let it cool fully if you prepare the chicken specifically for salads and sandwiches. You can want to skip the next step.)
4. Pour all but 1 teaspoon of the pan's fat off. Add the shallot to the pan and cook over medium heat, frequently stirring, for about 1 minute, until the shallot is tender. Connect the broth and bring it to a boil over high heat, scraping with a wooden spoon the browned bits in the pan. Boil until one-third, around 2 minutes, of the broth, is reduced. Remove yourself from the sun. Apply the butter to the pan sauce and whisk until the butter melts, if you want to thicken the sauce slightly.
5. Carve the chicken meat, discarding the skin and bones. Move and drizzle to dinner plates.
6. Over each serving, equal quantities of sauce. Serve hot.

2. Classic Poached Chicken

(Ready in about 30 Minutes I Serv: 2½ Cups diced chicken meat I Difficulty: Normal)

Ingredients

- 2 (10-ounce) chicken breast halves, with skin and bones
- 1 small onion, thinly sliced
- 2 sprigs of fresh parsley (optional)Pinch of dried thyme
- A few black peppercorns½ bay leaf

Directions

1. Place the chicken and onion in a medium saucepan and add ample water to cover 1 inch (about 1quart). Bring over high heat to a simmer, skimming off any foam growing to the surface.
2. Attach the parsley, thyme, peppercorns, and bay leaf (if used). Simmer for 15 minutes and reduce the heat to medium-low. The chicken won't be cooked fully.
3. Remove from the heat and tightly cover. When pierced in the thickest part with the tip of a knife, let stand till the chicken is opaque, about 20 minutes. Put the chicken on a cutting board and let it cool until it is easy to handle.
4. Pull the bones and skin off. (Return the skin and bones to the saucepan if you want to make chicken broth. Boil over low heat until the liquid is reduced to around 2 cups, around 1 hour. Drain into a heatproof bowl and cool. Refrigerate for up to 3 days in an airtight jar or freeze for up to 2 months.) Cover and refrigerate the meat for up to 2 days.

3. Chicken Mediterranean with Artichokes and Rosemary

(Ready in about 30 Minutes I Serve: 6 I Difficulty: Normal)

Ingredients

- 1 tablespoon olive oil, plus more in a pump sprayer
- 2 (12-ounce) boneless, skinless chicken breasts, pounded to even thickness, each cut in half crosswise to make 4 serving piece
- 1 teaspoon kosher salt
- ¼ teaspoon freshly ground black pepper
- ½ small yellow onion, chopped
- ½ large red bell pepper, seeded and cut into ½-inch dice
- 1 clove garlic, minced1 (14.5-ounce) no-salt-added diced tomatoes in juice, drained1 (9-ounce) box thawed frozen artichoke hearts, coarsely chopped
- 2 teaspoons cornstarch
- 1 cup Homemade Chicken Broth or canned low-sodium chicken broth
- 2 teaspoons chopped fresh rosemary or sage, or 1 teaspoon dried rosemary or sage
- ¼ teaspoon crushed hot red pepper

Directions

1. Spray a large nonstick skillet over medium heat with oil and heat. With salt and pepper, season the chicken. Add the chicken to the skillet and cook for about 6 minutes, turning halfway through the cooking process, until golden brown on both sides. Transfer to a dish.
2. Heat 1 tablespoon oil over medium heat in a skillet. Add the onion, bell pepper, and garlic and cook for about 5 minutes, occasionally stirring, until tender. Stir in the artichokes and tomatoes. Dissolve the cornstarch into the broth in a small bowl. Stir, along with the rosemary and hot pepper, into the skillet mixture. Put the chicken back in the skillet and bring the liquid down to a simmer. Lower the heat to medium-low and cover the skillet with the garlic lid. Cook until the juices are slightly thickened, and the chicken is opaque when pierced with the tip of a knife in the thickest portion, around 6 minutes, stirring occasionally. Serve it warm.

4. Chinese Chicken with Bok Choy and Garlic

(Ready in about 30 Minutes I Serve 4 I Difficulty: Normal)

Ingredients
Sauce

- ¾ cup Homemade Chicken Broth or canned low-sodium chicken broth
- 2 tablespoons rice vinegar
- 1 tablespoon reduced-sodium soy sauce
- 1 teaspoon amber agave nectar or sugar
- ½ teaspoon crushed hot red pepper
- 2 teaspoons cornstarch

Chicken

- 4 teaspoons canola oil
- 1 pound boneless, skinless chicken breast halves, cut across the grain into ¼-inch-thick slices

- 4 cloves garlic, minced
- 2 tablespoons peeled and minced fresh ginger
- 1 large head bok choy (1½ pounds), cut crosswise into ½-inch-thick pieces, well washed, but not dried
- 3 scallions, white and green parts, cut into 1-inch lengths

Directions

1. To make the sauce: Combine the broth, vinegar, soy sauce, agave, and hot pepper in a small cup. Sprinkle and whisk in the cornstarch to dissolve. Put aside the mixture for the sauce.
2. To cook the chicken: Heat 2 teaspoons of oil over medium-high heat in a large wok or nonstick skillet. Add the chicken and cook for about 2 minutes, occasionally stirring, until lightly browned. Transfer to a dish.
3. Heat the skillet with the remaining 2 teaspoons of oil. Apply the garlic and ginger and mix for about 30 seconds until it is fragrant. Add the bok choy and the scallions and cook for about 3 minutes, frequently stirring, until the bok choy is crisp-tender. Return the chicken and any juices to the skillet on the counter. Cook, constantly stirring, until the whole chicken is opaque, around 1 minute. Stir in the mixture of the sauce and cook, constantly stirring, until cooked and slightly thickened. Serve it warm.

5. Chicken with Mushroom Cacciatore Sauce

(Ready in about 30 Minutes | Serve 4 | Difficulty: Normal)

Ingredients

- 1 tablespoon olive oil, plus more in a pump sprayer
- 2 (12-ounce) boneless, skinless chicken breast halves, pounded to even thickness, each cut in half cross wise to make 4 serving pieces
- ½ teaspoon kosher salt
- ¼ teaspoon freshly ground black pepper
- 1 medium yellow onion, chopped
- ½ medium green bell pepper, cored and cut into ½-inch dice
- 1 clove garlic, minced
- 1 (14.5-ounce) can no-salt-added diced tomatoes with juice, undrained
- ¼ cup hearty red wine, dry vermouth, or water
- 1 teaspoon Italian herb seasoning or dried oregano

Directions

18. Spray a large nonstick skillet over medium heat with oil and heat. Season the chicken with salt and pepper, add to the skillet, and cook until golden brown on both sides, around 6 minutes, turning halfway through cooking. Transfer to a dish.
19. Heat 1 tablespoon oil over medium heat in a skillet. Add the onion, bell pepper, and garlic and cook for about 5 minutes, occasionally stirring, until tender. Add the tomatoes and their juice, the wine, and the seasoning of the herbs. Bring to a boil, and scrape with a wooden spoon the browned bits in the skillet. Decrease the heat to medium-low and simmer for around 5 minutes until the liquid is slightly reduced.
20. Put the chicken back in the skillet and cover it with a garlic lid. When pierced in the thickest part with the tip of a sharp knife, boil until the chicken becomes opaque, 6 to 8 minutes. Serve it wet.

6. Mexican Chicken Breast with Tomatillo Salsa

(Ready in about 30 Minutes | Serve 4 | Difficulty: Normal)

Ingredients
Tomatillo Sauce

- 8 ounces tomatillos (preferably all the same size), husked
- 2 scallions, white and green parts, coarsely chopped
- ½ jalapeño, seeded and minced
- 1 tablespoon fresh lime juice
- 1 tablespoon coarsely chopped fresh cilantro
- 1 clove garlic, crushed under a knife and peeled
- Pinch of kosher salt

Chicken

- Olive oil in a pump sprayer
- 2 (10-ounce) boneless, skinless chicken breast halves, pounded to the ¾-inch thickness and cut in half to make 4 portions
- 1 tablespoon Mexican Seasoning
- Lime wedges, for serving

Directions

1. To make the sauce: Over high heat, bring a medium saucepan of water to a boil. Tomatillos are added, and the heat is reduced to mild. Cook only until they turn olive green at a moderate boil, using a slotted spoon to move the tomatillos when they are ready, around 5 minutes, from the water to a bowl. Don't overcook, nor will the tomatillos burst. Drain the tomatillos carefully.
2. Puré the drained tomatillos, scallions, jalapeño, lime juice, cilantro, garlic, and salt in a food processor (or a blender with its lid ajar). Only set aside.
3. To cook the chicken: spray a large nonstick skillet over medium heat with oil and heat. Spray with the oil on both sides of the chicken and sprinkle with the Mexican seasoning. Add the chicken to the skillet and cook for about 6 minutes, turning halfway through the cooking process, until golden brown on both sides.
4. Pour in the tomatillo salsa and simmer for 6 to 8 minutes until the chicken is opaque when pierced with the tip of a sharp knife in the thickest region. Serve hot with wedges of lime,

7. Chicken and Apple Curry

(Ready in about 30 Minutes | Serve 4 | Difficulty: Normal)

Ingredients

5. 2 teaspoons canola oil, plus more in a pump sprayer
- 2 (10-ounce) boneless, skinless chicken breast halves, trimmed, pounded to ¾-inch thickness, and cut into 4 equal serving portions

- 1 medium yellow onion, chopped
- 2 medium celery ribs, chopped
- 2 Granny Smith apples, peeled, cored, and cut into ½-inch dice
- 1 tablespoon curry powder
- ¾ cup light coconut milk
- ½ cup of water
- 2 tablespoons fresh lime juice
- ½ cup sliced natural almonds, for serving

Directions
1. Spray the broad nonstick skillet over medium-high heat with oil and heat. Add the chicken and cook for about 6 minutes, flipping halfway through cooking, until lightly browned on both sides. Transfer to a dish.
2. Heat 2 teaspoons of oil over medium heat in a skillet. Add the onion, celery, and apples and cook for about 5 minutes, frequently stirring, until the onion is tender. Sprinkle and stir well with the curry powder.
3. Stir in the coconut milk, lime juice, and water and bring to a boil, stirring frequently. Stir in the chicken and cover. When pierced in the center with the tip of a small, sharp knife, reduce the heat to medium-low and simmer until the chicken is opaque around 6 minutes.
4. Move the chicken to a serving platter that is deep. Increase the heat to high under the skillet and boil the sauce for around 1 minute until slightly thickened. Over the chicken, pour in the sauce mixture and sprinkle with the almonds. .Serve hot

8. "Moo Shu" Chicken and Vegetable Wraps
(Ready in about 30 Minutes | Serve 6 | Difficulty: Normal)

Ingredients
Sauce
- ⅓ cup Homemade Chicken Broth or canned low-sodium chicken broth
- 1 tablespoon rice vinegar
- 1 tablespoon no-salt-added tomato ketchup
- 1 tablespoon reduced-sodium soy sauce
- 1 teaspoon Asian sesame oil
- 2 teaspoons cornstarch

Chicken
- 4 teaspoons canola oil
- 1 (8-ounce) boneless, skinless chicken breast half, cut across the grain into ¼-inch-thick bite-sized pieces
- 10 ounces shiitake mushroom caps, sliced
- 1 (12-ounce) package broccoli slaw
- 3 scallions, white and green parts, cut into 1-inch lengths
- 1 (8-ounce) can sliced water chestnuts, drained and rinsed
- 1 tablespoon peeled and minced fresh ginger
- 2 cloves garlic, minced

Wraps
- 12 Boston or Bibb lettuce leaves

Directions
1. To make the sauce: whisk the broth, vinegar, ketchup, soy sauce, sesame oil, and cornstarch together in a small bowl.
2. To cook the chicken: In a large nonstick skillet, heat 2 teaspoons of oil over medium to high heat. Add the chicken and cook, stirring periodically, for about 4 minutes, until it becomes opaque. Transfer to a dish. In the skillet, heat the remaining 2 teaspoons of oil over medium to high heat. Add the mushrooms and cook for about 5 minutes, occasionally stirring, until tender. Add the broccoli slaw, scallions, and water chestnuts and cook for about 3 minutes, frequently stirring, until the slaw is hot and wilted. Add the ginger and garlic and cook for another 1 minute, until fragrant. Stir in the reserved sauce and chicken.
3. Blend and apply to the skillet. Stir for about 30 seconds until the sauce is thickened and heated.
4. Move the chicken mixture to a mixing bowl to eat. Let each person spoon the mixture of chicken onto a lettuce leaf, roll it up and enjoy it.

9. Roast Turkey Breast with Root Vegetables, Lemon, and Garlic Cloves
(Ready in about 30 Minutes | Serve 6 | Difficulty: Normal)

Ingredients
- 1 (2¾-pound) turkey breast half, with skin and bones
- 1 teaspoon herbes de Provence or Italian Seasoning
- 1 teaspoon kosher salt
- ¾ teaspoon freshly ground black pepper
- 2 pounds red-skinned potatoes, cut into 1-inch pieces
- 3 large carrots, cut into 1-inch pieces
- 2 medium parsnips, peeled and cut into 1-inch pieces
- 1 medium turnip, peeled and cut into 1-inch pieces
- 1 head garlic, separated into unpeeled cloves
- 1 tablespoon olive oil
- Grated zest of 1 lemon
- 2 tablespoons fresh lemon juice
- 1 tablespoon cornstarch
- 1½ cups Homemade Chicken Broth or canned low-sodium chicken broth
- Chopped fresh parsley for garnish

Directions
1. Preheat the oven to 350°F.
2. Make a narrow incision in the turkey breast to remove the skin from the rib bones, using a thin, sharp knife. To create a pocket, slip your fingers under the skin. Season the flesh with the herbs of Provence, half a teaspoon of salt, and half a teaspoon of pepper under the surface.

3. Mix the potatoes, carrots, parsnips, turnips, and garlic in a broad roasting pan. Drizzle and toss well with the grease. Spread with the turkey in the pan and roof.
4. In the thickest section of the breast half, roast until the turkey is golden brown and an instant-read thermometer inserted registers 165 °F, around 1½ hours. Switch the turkey to a carving board and tent with carving
5. Foil with aluminum.
6. Increase the temperature of the oven to 450°F. In the roasting pan, continue cooking the vegetables, stirring periodically, until tender and lightly browned, for approximately 10 minutes. Take it out of the oven. Add the lemon zest and juice, ½ teaspoon salt remaining, and ¼ teaspoon pepper remaining and toss well. Transfer to an aluminum foil serving platter and tent to stay warm.
7. In the pan, pour out and discard the fat. Sprinkle the cornstarch over the broth in a small bowl and whisk until it is dissolved. Heat the roasting pan until sizzling, over medium-high heat. Pour in the mixture of the broth and bring to a boil, scraping with a wooden spoon the browned bits in the pan. Reduce the heat to low and simmer for about 2 minutes until slightly thickened. Pour the sauce into a boat with the gravy.
8. Discard the skin of the turkey. In ½-inch-thick slices, cut the turkey meat from the bone around the grain. Over the carrots, arrange the turkey and sprinkle with the parsley. With the sauce, serve sweet.

10. Turkey Cutlets with Lemon and Basil Sauce

(Ready in about 30 Minutes | Serve 4 | Difficulty: Normal)

Ingredients

- 1 pound turkey cutlets, cut into 8 serving pieces
- ½ teaspoon kosher salt¼ teaspoon freshly ground black pepper
- ¼ cup whole-wheat flour
- 4 teaspoons olive oil
- 1 cup Homemade Chicken Broth or canned low-sodium chicken broth grated zest of ½ lemon
- 3 tablespoons fresh lemon juice
- 2 tablespoons dry vermouth
- 1 tablespoon cold unsalted butter
- 2 tablespoons finely chopped fresh basil

Directions

1. Season the turkey with pepper and salt. Spread the flour on a plate and cover the flour with the turkey and shake off the excess. Heat 2 teaspoons of oil over medium heat in a large nonstick skillet. Add half the turkey to the skillet and cook for about 4 minutes, flipping the turkey halfway through the cooking process, until lightly browned on both sides. Transfer to a dish. Repeat with the remaining 2 teaspoons of oil and turkey, and put on the plate with the turkey.
2. Combine in the skillet the broth, lemon zest and juice, and vermouth and bring to a boil over high heat. Cook until half the volume is depleted, around 5 minutes. Put the whole turkey back in the skillet and reduce the heat to medium. When the turkey is pierced in the center with the tip of a sharp knife, cook, turning the turkey in the sauce, until the sauce is lightly thickened and the turkey is opaque, around 2 minutes, move the turkey to a bowl for serving.
3. Take the skillet away from the sun. In the sugar, whisk, then 1 tablespoon of the basil. Pour over the turkey, and sprinkle with 1 tablespoon of basil remaining. Serve it wet.

11. Sloppy Toms

(Ready in about 30 Minutes | Serve 4 | Difficulty: Normal)

Ingredients

- 1 tablespoon canola oil
- 1 medium yellow onion, chopped
- 2 large celery ribs, cut into ½-inch dice
- 1 large green bell pepper, cored and cut into ½-inch dice
- 1¼ pounds ground turkey1 (8-ounce) can no-salt-added tomato sauce
- ½ cup no-salt-added tomato ketchup
- 1 tablespoon Worcestershire sauce
- 1 tablespoon balsamic vinegar
- 1 teaspoon kosher salt
- ½ teaspoon freshly ground black pepper
- 6 whole-wheat sandwich buns, toasted

Directions

1. Heat the oil over medium heat in a large nonstick skillet. Add the onion, celery, and bell pepper and sauté for about 5 minutes, occasionally stirring, until tender. To one side of the skillet, switch the vegetables. Cook, stirring regularly and breaking up the meat with the side of a wooden spoon until the turkey loses its raw look, about 6 minutes. Add the ground turkey to the cleared side of the skillet. Combine the vegetables and turkey.
2. Bring to a boil, stir in tomato sauce, ketchup, Worcestershire sauce, vinegar, salt, and pepper. Reduce heat to medium-low and simmer until slightly thickened, frequently stirring for around 10 minutes.
3. Spoon ⅔ cup of the turkey mixture onto half a bun on a plate for each serving, then cover with the top half of the bun. Serve it wet.

12. Turkey-Spinach Meatballs with Tomato Sauce

(Ready in about 30 Minutes | Serve 6 | Difficulty: Normal)

Ingredients

Turkey-Spinach Meatballs

- 1 (10-ounce) box frozen chopped spinach, thawed and squeezed to remove excess liquid1 medium yellow onion, shredded on the large holes of a box grater

- 2 cloves garlic, minced
- ⅓ cup whole-wheat bread crumbs, made from day-old bread pulsed in the blender
- 2 large egg whites or ¼ cup seasoned liquid egg substitute
- 1 teaspoon Italian seasoning or dried oregano
- 1 teaspoon kosher salt
- ½ teaspoon freshly ground black pepper
- 1¼ pounds ground turkey
- Olive oil in a pump sprayer
- ½ cup of water

Tomato Sauce
- 1 tablespoon olive oil
- 1 medium yellow onion, chopped
- 2 cloves garlic, minced
- 1 (28-ounce) can no-salt-added crushed tomatoes
- 2 teaspoons Italian Seasoning or dried oregano
- ¼ teaspoon crushed hot red pepper
- 6 tablespoons freshly grated Parmesan cheese

Directions
1. Combine the spinach, onion, garlic, bread crumbs, egg whites, Italian seasoning, salt, and pepper in a big bowl to make the meatballs. Attach and thoroughly mix the ground turkey. To firm the mixture and make it easier to treat, refrigerate it for 15 to 30 minutes.
2. Roll up 18 meatballs with the turkey mixture. Spray a large nonstick skillet over medium heat with oil and heat. In batches, add the meatballs and cook for around 6 minutes, occasionally turning, until lightly browned. Transfer to a dish. Connect the water to the skillet and bring to a boil, using a wooden spoon to stir up the browned bits in the pan. Remove yourself from the sun.
3. To make the sauce: Heat the oil over medium heat in a medium saucepan. Attach the onion and sauté for about 5 minutes, occasionally stirring, until golden and tender. Stir in the garlic and cook for about 1 minute until it is fragrant. Add the skillet sauce, onions, Italian seasoning, and hot pepper; thoroughly mix and bring to a boil. Reduce heat to medium-low and simmer until mildly thickened, occasionally stirring, for about 15 minutes. Bury the meatballs in the sauce and cook until the meatballs, when pierced to the middle with the tip of a sharp knife, show no sign of pink, about 15 more minutes. Divide 6 bowls of meatballs and sauce, sprinkle each with 1 tablespoon of Parmesan cheese (if used), and serve warm.

13. Cajun Turkey Burgers with Pickled Red Onions
(Ready in about 30 Minutes | Serve 4 | Difficulty: Normal)

Ingredients
Pickled Red Onions
- 1 small red onion, cut into thin half-moons
- ½ cup cider vinegar, as needed

Turkey Burgers
- 2 teaspoons canola oil, plus more in a pump sprayer
- 2 celery ribs, finely chopped
- ½ cup finely chopped red bell pepper
- 2 cloves garlic, finely chopped
- 2 scallions, white and green parts, finely chopped
- 1 teaspoon Cajun Seasoning
- 1¼ pounds ground turkey
- ½ teaspoon kosher salt
- 4 whole-wheat hamburger buns, toasted
- 4 tomato slices
- 4 red lettuce leaves

Directions
1. To pickle the onions: In a small bowl, put the onions and add enough vinegar to cover the onions. Let it stand for at least 30 minutes and up to 6 hours at room temperature.
2. To make turkey burgers: Heat 2 teaspoons of oil over medium heat in a large nonstick skillet. Add the celery, bell pepper, and garlic and cook for about 5 minutes, occasionally stirring, until tender.
3. Attach the scallions and cook for about 2 minutes until they are wilted. Stir in the Spice of the Cajun. Put it in a big bowl and let it cool. To the vegetable mixture, add the ground turkey and salt and thoroughly blend. Shape into four burgers, 3½-inch. Place it on a plate lined with waxed paper and cook for 15 to 30 minutes.
4. Using paper towels, wash the skillet out. With the grease, spray the skillet and heat over medium heat. Attach the burgers and cook for about 5 minutes until the undersides are golden brown. Flip the burgers and cook until the other sides are browned, and when pushed on top with a finger, the burgers feel resilient, about 5 minutes more. Withdraw from the skillet
5. Place a burger in a bun with each serving and top with some red onions, a tomato, and a lettuce leaf. Serve hot, serve,

14. Turkey Mini Meat Loaf with Dijon Glaze
(Ready in about 30 Minutes | Serve 4 | Difficulty: Normal)

Ingredients
- 2 teaspoons canola oil, plus more in a pump sprayer
- 1 medium yellow onion, finely chopped
- 1 medium carrot, cut into ¼-inch dice
- 1 medium celery stalk, cut into ¼-inch dice
- 1 tablespoon water
- 1¼ pounds ground turkey
- ¾ cup old-fashioned (rolled) oats
- 1 large egg, beaten
- 1 teaspoon dried rosemary
- ½ teaspoon kosher salt
- ¼ teaspoon freshly ground black pepper

- 1 tablespoon Dijon mustard
- 1 tablespoon honey

Directions

1. Preheat the oven to 350°F. Line with aluminum foil on a large baking sheet and spray with oil.
2. Heat 2 teaspoons of oil over medium heat in a medium nonstick skillet.
3. Add the onion, carrot, water, and celery. Cook, stirring periodically, for about 10 minutes, until the vegetables are tender. Place in a medium bowl and leave to cool slightly. Apply the ground turkey, oats, egg, rosemary, salt, and pepper and blend until mixed, gently but thoroughly. Divide into four equal portions and form each, about 2 inches apart, into a 5 ?? 3-inch loaf on the prepared baking sheet.
4. Bake until lightly browned and placed in the center of a loaf; an instant-read thermometer reads about 160°F, about 35 minutes. Take it out of the oven. In a small bowl, combine the mustard and honey, then spread the top of each loaf with one-quarter of the mustard mixture. Return to the oven and continue baking for about 5 more minutes until the mustard mixture is glazed. Leave to stand before serving at room temperature for 5 minutes.

Chapter 12: Main Dishes, Soups and Chowders

In this chapter, we have compiled recipes of main dishes, soups and chowders.

1. Grain hot cereal

(Ready in about 30 Minutes | Serve: 8 | Difficulty: Normal)

Ingredients

- Uncooked pearl barley 1/2 cup
- Uncooked red wheat berries 1/2 cup
- Uncooked brown rice 1/2 cup
- Uncooked steel-cut oats 1/4 cup
- Uncooked quinoa 3 tablespoons
- Flaxseed 2 tablespoons
- Kosher salt 1/2 teaspoon
- Water 1 1/2 quarts

Directions

1. Mix the barley, wheat berries, corn, beans, quinoa, flaxseed, and salt in a large saucepan. Pour water over the ingredients, stir and, over medium heat, bring to a boil. Reduce the heat to low and simmer, stirring periodically, for 45 minutes.

2. Asian pork tenderloin

(Ready in about 30 Minutes | Serve: 8 | Difficulty: Normal)

Ingredients

- Tablespoons sesame seeds
- 1 teaspoon ground coriander
- 1/8 teaspoon cayenne pepper
- 1/8 teaspoon celery seed
- 1/2 teaspoon minced onion
- 1/4 teaspoon ground cumin
- 1/8 teaspoon ground cinnamon
- 1 tablespoon sesame oil
- 1 pound pork tenderloin, sliced into 4 portions

Directions

1. Heat the oven to 400 F. Lightly brush a baking dish with cooking oil.
2. Add the sesame seeds to a single layer in a heavy frying pan. Over low heat, cook the seeds, constantly stirring until they look golden and give off a noticeably toasty aroma, around 1 to 2 minutes. Remove the seeds from the pan to cool.
3. In a cup, add the coriander, cayenne pepper, celery seed, minced onion, cumin, cinnamon, sesame oil, and toasted sesame seeds. To mix evenly, stir.
4. Place the pork tenderloin in the prepared baking dish. Rub the spices on both sides of the pork bits. Bake until no longer pink, around 15 minutes. Or bake until a meat thermometer hits 165 F (medium) or 170 F

3. Baked chicken and wild rice with onion and tarragon

(Ready in about 40 Minutes | Serve: 6 | Difficulty: Normal)

Ingredients

- 1 pound boneless, skinless chicken breast halves
- 1 1/2 cups chopped celery
- 1 1/2 cups whole pearl onions
- 1 teaspoon fresh tarragon

- 2 cups unsalted chicken broth
- 3/4 cup uncooked long-grain white rice
- 3/4 cup uncooked wild rice
- 1 1/2 cups dry white wine

Directions

1. Heat the oven to 300 F.
2. Cut the breasts of the chicken into 1-inch pieces. In a nonstick frying pan, mix the chicken, celery, onions, and tarragon with 1 cup of the unsalted chicken broth. Cook until the chicken and vegetables are tender, about 10 minutes, over medium heat. Set to cool aside.
3. In a baking dish, whisk together the rice, wine, and remaining 1 cup chicken broth. Leave for 30 minutes to soak.
4. To the baking dish, add the chicken and vegetables. For 60 minutes, cover and bake. Check periodically and, if the rice is too dry, add more broth. Immediately serve.

4. Baked cod with lemon and capers

(Ready in about 40 Minutes | Serve: 6 | Difficulty: Normal)

Ingredients

- 4 cod fillets, each 6 ounces
- 1 lemon
- 1 teaspoon low-sodium chicken-flavored bouillon granules
- 1 cup hot tap water
- 1 tablespoon butter, softened
- 1 tablespoon all-purpose flour
- 4 teaspoons capers, rinsed and drained

Directions

1. Heat the oven to 350 F. Spray with cooking spray on 4 squares of foil.
2. On each foil square, position 1 cod fillet. Break the lemon in half. Squeeze half of the juice over your trout. Break the other half into strips, bring the foil over the fish and seal it.
3. When checked with the tip of a knife, bake in the oven for around 20 minutes until the fish is opaque throughout.
4. Apply the granules of the chicken bouillon and the hot tap water to a small bowl. Before the granules dissolve, stir. Only set aside.
5. Mix the butter and flour together in another small bowl. Move it to a heavy casserole. Till the butter-flour mixture melts, whisk over moderate heat. Add the butter mixture to the bouillon and proceed to stir until it thickens. Attach the capers and detach them from the sun. Pour the fish over and eat.

5. Baked macaroni with red sauce

(Ready in about 40 Minutes | Serve: 6 | Difficulty: Normal)

Ingredients

- 1/2 pound extra-lean ground beef
- 1 small onion, diced (about 1/2 cup)
- 1 box (7 ounces) whole-wheat elbow macaroni
- 1 jar (15 ounces) reduced-sodium spaghetti sauce
- 6 tablespoons Parmesan cheese

Directions

1. Heat the oven to 350 F. Cover a baking dish lightly with cooking oil.
2. Cook the ground beef and onion in a nonstick frying pan until the meat is browned and the onion is translucent. Well, drain and set aside.
3. Fill 3/4 of a large pot full of water and bring it to a boil. Connect the pasta and cook for 10 to 12 minutes, or according to the package instructions, until al dente. Thoroughly drain the pasta.
4. Connect the beef and onions to the cooked pasta and spaghetti sauce. Stir to blend uniformly. In the prepared baking dish, spoon the mixture into it. Bake for approximately 25 to 35 minutes until bubbly.
5. Break the macaroni into individual plates. Sprinkle 1 tablespoon of Parmesan cheese for each one. Immediately serve.

6. Baked oatmeal

(Ready in about 40 Minutes | Serve: 6 | Difficulty: Normal)

Ingredients

- 1 tablespoon canola oil
- 1/2 cup unsweetened applesauce
- 1/3 cup brown sugar
- Egg substitute equivalent to 2 eggs or 4 egg whites
- 3 cups uncooked rolled oats
- 2 teaspoons baking powder
- 1 teaspoon cinnamon
- 1 cup skim milk

Directions

1. Stir together the oil, applesauce, sugar, and eggs in a good-sized cup. Add milk and dry ingredients. Mix thoroughly.
2. Using cooking spray to generously spray a 9-by-13 baking pan. Spoon the mixture of oatmeal into the pan. Bake at 350 F for 30 minutes, uncovered.

7. Baked salmon with Southeast Asian marinade

(Ready in about 40 Minutes | Serve: 6 | Difficulty: Normal)

Ingredients

- 1/2 cup pineapple juice (no sugar added)
- 2 garlic cloves, minced
- 1 teaspoon low-sodium soy sauce
- 1/4 teaspoon ground ginger
- 2 salmon fillets, each 4 ounces
- 1/4 teaspoon sesame oil
- Freshly ground black pepper, to taste

- 1 cup diced fresh fruit, such as pineapple, mango, and papaya

Directions
1. Add the pineapple juice, garlic, soy sauce, and ginger into a small cup. Stir to blend uniformly. In a tiny baking dish, place the salmon fillets. Pour over the top of the pineapple juice mixture. Put them in the fridge and marinate for 1 hour. Turn the salmon around regularly as needed.
2. Heat the oven to 375 F. Lightly coat 2 aluminum foil squares with cooking spray. On the aluminum foil, put the marinated salmon fillets. Sift each with 1/8 of a teaspoon of sesame oil. Cover each with 1/2 cup of diced fruit and sprinkle with pepper. Wrap the foil around the salmon, securing the edges by folding. When checked with the tip of a knife, bake until the fish is opaque all through, about 10 minutes on each side. Move the salmon to individual plates that are warmed and serve immediately.

8. Balsamic roast chicken
(Ready in about 40 Minutes | Serve: 6 | Difficulty: Normal)

Ingredients
- 1 whole chicken, about 4 pounds
- 1 tablespoon fresh rosemary or 1 teaspoon dried rosemary
- 1 garlic clove
- 1 tablespoon olive oil
- 1/8 teaspoon freshly ground black pepper
- 8 sprigs fresh rosemary
- 1/2 cup balsamic vinegar
- 1 teaspoon brown sugar

Directions
1. Heat the oven to 350 F.
2. Mince the rosemary and garlic together. Remove the meat from the skin of the chicken and rub the flesh with olive oil and then the herb mixture. Using black pepper to sprinkle. Put 2 sprigs of rosemary into the chicken cavity. The Chicken Truss.
3. Put the chicken in a roasting pan and roast for around 1 hour and 20 minutes, for 20 to 25 minutes per pound. The entire chicken should be cooked at an internal minimum temperature of 165 F. Baste pan juices regularly. Move the chicken to a serving platter when the chicken is browned and the juices run clear.
4. Combine the balsamic vinegar and the brown sugar in a shallow saucepan. Heat until hot and brown sugar is dissolved in the mixture, but don't boil.
5. Carve the chicken and the skin is removed. With the vinegar mixture, top the bits. Garnish and serve immediately with the remaining rosemary.

9. Barbecue chicken pizza
(Ready in about 40 Minutes | Serve: 6 | Difficulty: Normal)

Ingredients
- 1 cup tomato sauce, no salt added
- One 12-inch thin, whole-grain pizza crust
- 1 green pepper, cut into rings
- 1 tomato, sliced
- 1 cup mushrooms, sliced
- 4 ounces cooked chicken breast, sliced about 1-inch thick, with all visible fat removed
- 4 tablespoons barbecue sauce
- 1 cup shredded, reduced-fat mozzarella cheese (about 4 ounces)

Directions
1. Heat the oven to 400 F.
2. Spread the sauce uniformly over the crust of the pizza. Add pepper, tomato, chicken, and mushrooms. Drizzle over the pizza with barbecue sauce and cover with cheese.
3. Bake for 12 to 14 minutes or so. Break into 8 slices of pizza and serve.

10. Barley and roasted tomato risotto
(Ready in about 40 Minutes | Serve: 6 | Difficulty: Normal)

Ingredients
- 10 large plum (Roma) tomatoes, about 2 pounds total weight, peeled and each cut into 4 wedges
- 2 tablespoons extra-virgin olive oil
- 1/2 teaspoon salt, divided
- 1/2 teaspoon freshly ground black pepper, divided
- 4 cups low-sodium vegetable stock or broth
- 3 cups water
- 2 shallots, chopped
- 1/4 cup dry white wine, optional
- 2 cups pearl barley
- 3 tablespoons chopped fresh basil, plus whole leaves for garnish
- 3 tablespoons chopped fresh flat-leaf (Italian) parsley
- 1 1/2 tablespoons chopped fresh thyme
- 1/2 cup grated Parmesan cheese, plus extra ungrated Parmesan for making curls for garnish

Directions
1. Heat the oven to 450 F.
2. On a nonstick baking sheet, arrange the tomatoes. Drizzle with 1 tablespoon of olive oil and add 1/4 of a teaspoon of salt and 1/4 of a teaspoon of pepper. For mixing, toss gently. Roast for 25 to 30 minutes until the tomatoes soften and begin to brown. Set aside 16 wedges of tomatoes to use for garnishing.
3. Combine the vegetable stock and water in a saucepan and bring it to a boil over high heat. Lower the heat to a low level and keep it simmering.
4. In a big, heavy saucepan, over medium heat, heat the remaining 1 tablespoon of olive oil. Add the chopped shallots and saute for 2 to 3 minutes, until soft and translucent. Stir in the white wine, if used, and cook for 2 to 3 minutes until most of the liquid evaporates. Stir in the barley and cook for 1 minute, stirring. Stir in 1/2 cup of the stock mixture and cook, stirring

periodically, until the liquid is fully absorbed. Continue to stir in 1/2-cup intervals in the stock mixture, cooking each time until the liquid is absorbed before adding more, until the barley is tender, for a total of 45 to 50 minutes. Take the tomatoes, chopped basil, parsley, thyme and grated cheese out of the heat and fold in. To mix, add the remaining 1/4 teaspoon salt and 1/4 teaspoon pepper and stir.

5. Divide the risotto into individual shallow bowls that are warmed. Garnish with the reserved wedges of the roasted tomato and the whole leaves of basil. Cut a curl or two of Parmesan cheese using a vegetable peeler to top each serving.

11. Bean salad with balsamic vinaigrette

(Ready in about 40 Minutes | Serve: 6 | Difficulty: Normal)

Ingredients

For the vinaigrette:

- 2 tablespoons balsamic vinegar
- 1/3 cup fresh parsley, chopped
- 4 garlic cloves, finely chopped
- Ground black pepper, to taste
- 1/4 cup extra-virgin olive oil

For the salad:

- 1 can (15 ounces) low-sodium garbanzo beans, rinsed and drained
- 1 can (15 ounces) low-sodium black beans, rinsed and drained
- 1 medium red onion, diced
- 6 lettuce leaves
- 1/2 cup celery, finely chopped

Directions

1. To make the vinaigrette, whisk the balsamic vinegar, parsley, garlic and pepper together in a small cup. Whilst whisking, add the olive oil slowly. Only set aside.
2. Combine the beans and onion in a large bowl. Over the mixture, add the vinaigrette and toss gently to blend well and coat evenly. Cover and, once eaten, refrigerate.
3. To eat, place on each plate 1 leaf of lettuce. Divide the salad and garnish with chopped celery between the individual dishes. Immediately serve.

12. Beef and vegetable kebabs

(Ready in about 40 Minutes | Serve: 6 | Difficulty: Normal)

Ingredients

- 1/2 cup brown rice
- 2 cups water
- 4 ounces top sirloin (choice)
- 1 tablespoon fat-free Italian dressing
- 1 green pepper, seeded and cut into 4 pieces
- 4 cherry tomatoes
- 1 small onion, cut into 4 wedges
- 2 wooden skewers, soaked in water for 30 minutes, or metal skewers

Directions

1. In a saucepan over high heat, combine the rice and water. Bring to a boil. Reduce the heat to low, cover and simmer until the water is absorbed and the rice is tender, about 30 to 45 minutes. Add more water if necessary to keep the rice from drying out. Transfer to a small bowl to keep warm.
2. Cut the meat into 4 equal portions. Put the meat in a small bowl and pour Italian dressing over the top. Rub the dressing into each piece. Cover and place in the refrigerator for at least 20 minutes to marinate, turning as needed.
3. Prepare a hot fire in a charcoal grill or heat a gas grill or a broiler. Away from the heat source, lightly coat the grill rack or broiler pan with cooking spray. Position the cooking rack 4 to 6 inches from the heat source.
4. Thread 2 cubes of meat, 2 green pepper pieces, 2 cherry tomatoes and 2 onion wedges onto each skewer. Place the kebabs on the grill rack or broiler pan. Grill or broil the kebabs for about 5 to 10 minutes, turning as needed.
5. Divide the rice onto individual plates. Top with 1 kebab and serve immediately.

13. Beef and vegetable stew

(Ready in about 40 Minutes | Serve: 6 | Difficulty: Normal)

Ingredients

- 1 pound beef round steak
- 2 teaspoons canola oil
- 2 cups diced yellow onions
- 1 cup diced celery
- 1 cup diced Roma tomatoes
- 1/2 cup diced sweet potato
- 1/2 cup diced white potato with skin
- 1/2 cup diced mushrooms
- 1 cup diced carrot
- 4 cloves of garlic, chopped
- 1 cup chopped kale
- 1/4 cup uncooked barley
- 1/4 cup red wine vinegar
- 1 teaspoon balsamic vinegar
- 3 cups low-sodium vegetable or beef stock
- 1 teaspoon dried sage, crushed
- 1 teaspoon minced fresh thyme
- 1 tablespoon minced fresh parsley
- 1 tablespoon dried oregano
- 1 teaspoon dried rosemary, minced
- Black pepper, to taste

Directions

1. Grill or broiler heat (medium heat). Cut the fat and gristle out of the steak. Grill or steak grill for 12 to 14 minutes, rotating once. Don't overcook anymore.

Remove from the heat and allow to rest during vegetable preparation.
2. Saute the vegetables in oil over medium-high heat in a large stock pot until lightly browned, about 10 minutes. Attach the barley and cook for a further 5 minutes.
3. Dry Pat Steak with paper towels. Cut the bits into half an inch and add them to the pot. Then add some vinegar, stock, herbs, and spices.
4. Bring to a boil and simmer for 1 hour, until the barley is cooked and the stew thickens significantly.

14. Beef brisket
(Ready in about 40 Minutes | Serve: 6 | Difficulty: Normal)

Ingredients
- 1 tablespoon olive oil
- 2 1/2 pounds beef brisket, trimmed of fat and cut into 8 pieces of roughly equal size
- Course ground pepper
- 1 1/2 cups chopped onions
- 4 garlic cloves, smashed and peeled
- 1 teaspoon dried thyme
- 1 can (14.5 ounces) no-salt-added tomatoes and liquid
- 1/4 cup red wine vinegar
- 1 cup low-sodium beef stock or red wine

Directions
1. Heat the oven to 350 F.
2. Heat 1 tablespoon of oil over medium-high heat in a large Dutch oven or a heavy pot. A seasonal pepper brisket. Cook the meat in batches, turning regularly, until all sides are dark brown. Move the brisket to a tray.
3. Attach a pot of onions. Cook and stir until golden brown. Add the garlic and thyme and cook for about 1 minute and stir until fragrant.
4. Add the (undrained) tomatoes, vinegar, and stock or wine. Just bring it to a boil. Put the beef back in the pot, cover it, then place the pot in the oven. Cook for 3 to 3 1/2 hours, until the beef is tender.

15. Beef stew with fennel and shallots
(Ready in about 40 Minutes | Serve: 6 | Difficulty: Normal)

Ingredients
- 3 tablespoons all-purpose (plain) flour
- 1 pound boneless lean beef stew meat, trimmed of visible fat and cut into 1 1/2-inch cubes
- 2 tablespoons olive oil or canola oil
- 1/2 fennel bulb, trimmed and thinly sliced vertically
- 3 large shallots, chopped (about 3 tablespoons)
- 3/4 teaspoon ground black pepper, divided
- 2 fresh thyme sprigs
- 1 bay leaf
- 3 cups no-salt-added vegetable stock or broth
- 1/2 cup red wine, optional (not included in analysis)
- 4 large carrots, peeled and cut into 1-inch chunks
- 4 large red-skinned or white potatoes, peeled and cut into 1-inch chunks
- 18 small boiling onions, about 10 ounces total weight, halved crosswise
- 3 portobello mushrooms, brushed clean and cut into 1-inch chunks
- 1/3 cup finely chopped fresh flat-leaf (Italian) parsley

Directions
1. On a tray, put the flour. Dredge in the flour with the beef cubes. Heat oil over medium heat in a big, heavy saucepan. Add the beef and cook until browned on all sides, turning as required, for about 5 minutes. Remove the beef with a slotted spoon from the pan and set it aside.
2. Over medium heat, add the fennel and shallots to the pan and saute until softened and softly golden, 7 to 8 minutes. Apply 1/4 of a teaspoon of pepper, sprigs of thyme and bay leaf. For 1 minute, saute.
3. Send the beef back to the pan and, if used, add the vegetable stock and wine. Bring to a boil, then reduce the heat to medium, cover and simmer gently, 40 to 45 minutes, until the meat is tender.
4. Stir in the carrots, potatoes, mushrooms and onions. The liquid will not completely cover the vegetables, but as the mushrooms soften, more liquid will collect. Simmer gently, about 30 minutes longer, until the vegetables are tender.
5. Discard the bay leaves and thyme sprigs. Stir in the parsley and 1/2 teaspoon of pepper left. Ladle it into individual warmed bowls and eat it immediately.

16. Beef stroganoff
(Ready in about 40 Minutes | Serve: 6 | Difficulty: Normal)

Ingredients
- 1/2 cup chopped onion
- 1/2 pound boneless beef round steak, cut 3/4-inch thick, all fat removed
- 4 cups uncooked yolkless egg noodles
- 1/2 can fat-free cream of mushroom soup (undiluted)
- 1/2 cup of water
- 1 tablespoon all-purpose (plain) flour
- 1/2 teaspoon paprika
- 1/2 cup fat-free sour cream

Directions
1. Saute the onions in a nonstick frying pan over medium heat until translucent, around 5 minutes. Attach the beef and continue cooking for another 5 minutes or until the whole of the beef is tender and browned. Well drain and set aside.
2. Fill 3/4 of a large pot full of water and bring it to a boil. Add the noodles and cook for 10 to 12 minutes, or according to package instructions, until al dente (tender). Thoroughly drain the pasta.
3. Whisk together the soup, water and flour in a saucepan over medium heat. Stir for about 5 minutes before the sauce thickens. In the frying pan, add the

soup mixture and paprika to the beef. Stir the mixture over medium heat until fully heated. Remove and add the sour cream from the heat. Until combined, stir.

4. Divide the pasta between the plates for serving. Cover with the mixture of beef and immediately serve.

17. Black bean wrap

(Ready in about 40 Minutes | Serve: 6 | Difficulty: Normal)

Ingredients

- 1 1/2 cups canned low-sodium black beans, rinsed and drained
- 1 1/2 cups frozen corn kernels, thawed to room temperature
- 3 tablespoons chopped fresh cilantro
- 2 tablespoons chopped green chili peppers (seeds removed)*
- 4 green onions, diced (including green stems)
- 1 tomato, diced
- 1 tablespoon chopped garlic
- 6 fat-free whole-grain tortilla wraps, 10 inches in diameter
- 3/4 cup shredded cheddar cheese
- 3/4 cup salsa

Directions

1. Add the black beans, peas, cilantro, chilli peppers, onions, tomato and garlic to a microwave-safe dish. Stir to blend uniformly. Microwave for 30 seconds to 1 minute on high power. For 30 seconds to 1 minute, stir and heat again. Repeat until there is a hot mixture.
2. Put 2 tortillas between paper napkins or paper towels and keep warm for 20 seconds in the microwave. Repeat with the tortillas that remain.
3. Place about 1/2 cup of bean mixture on 1 tortilla to eat. Placed 2 tablespoons of cheese and 2 tablespoons of salsa on top. Open the sides and fold the tortilla's bottom over the filling, then roll to close. Repeat with the tortillas that remain and serve immediately.

18. Broccoli, garlic and rigatoni

(Ready in about 40 Minutes | Serve: 6 | Difficulty: Normal)

Ingredients

- 1/3 pound whole-wheat rigatoni
- 2 cups broccoli florets (tops)
- 2 tablespoons Parmesan cheese
- 2 teaspoons olive oil
- 2 teaspoons minced garlic
- Freshly ground black pepper, to taste

Directions

1. Fill 3/4 of a big water-filled pot and bring it to a boil. Add the pasta and cook for 10 to 12 minutes, or until al dente, as per package instructions (tender). Drain the pasta thoroughly.
2. Bring 1 inch of water to a boil in a pot fitted with a steamer basket while the pasta is cooking. Add the broccoli, cover and steam until tender, for about 10 minutes.
3. In a big pot, combine the cooked pasta and broccoli. Mix with the parmesan cheese, olive oil and garlic. Season with pepper to taste. Serve instantly.

19. Broiled White Sea bass

(Ready in about 40 Minutes | Serve: 6 | Difficulty: Normal)

Ingredients

- 2 white sea bass fillets, each 4 ounces
- 1 tablespoon lemon juice
- 1 teaspoon garlic, minced
- 1/4 teaspoon salt-free herb seasoning blend
- Ground black pepper, to taste

Directions

1. Heat up your broiler (grill). Place the rack 4 inches from the source of the sun. Spray a baking pan lightly with cooking spray. In the pan, position the fillets.
2. Sprinkle the fillets with lemon juice, garlic, herbal seasoning and pepper. When measured with the tip of a knife, broil (grill) until the fish is opaque, around 8 to 10 minutes. Immediately serve.

20. Buckwheat Pancakes

(Ready in about 40 Minutes | Serve: 6 | Difficulty: Normal)

Ingredients

- 2 egg whites
- 1 tablespoon canola oil
- 1/2 cup fat-free milk
- 1/2 cup all-purpose (plain) flour
- 1/2 cup buckwheat flour
- 1 tablespoon baking powder
- 1 tablespoon sugar
- 1/2 cup sparkling water
- 3 cups sliced fresh strawberries

Directions

1. Whisk the egg whites, canola oil and milk together in a small cup.
2. Combine the flour, baking powder and sugar in another dish. Apply the mixture of egg white and sparkling water and whisk until slightly humidified.
3. Over medium heat, position a nonstick frying pan or a griddle. Spoon 1/2 cup of pancake batter into the pan as a drop of water sizzles when it strikes the pan. Cook until bubbles cover the top surface of the pancake and the edges are lightly browned, for around 2 minutes. Turn and cook until well-browned on the bottom and cooked through the pancake, 1 to 2 minutes longer. Repeat with the pancake batter that remains.
4. The pancakes are moved to individual plates. Cover each one with 1/2 cup of sliced strawberries and serve right away.

21. Chicken and asparagus tossed with penne

(Ready in about 40 Minutes | Serve: 6 | Difficulty: Normal)

Ingredients

- 1 1/2 cups uncooked whole-grain penne pasta
- 1 cup asparagus, cut into 1-inch pieces
- 6 ounces boneless, skinless chicken breasts, cut into 1-inch cubes
- 2 cloves garlic, minced
- 1 can (14.5 ounces) diced tomatoes, no salt added, including juice
- 2 teaspoons dried basil or oregano
- 1 ounce soft goat cheese, crumbled (about 1 tablespoon)
- 1 tablespoon Parmesan cheese

Directions

1. Fill 3/4 of a large pot full of water and bring it to a boil. Add the pasta and cook for 10 to 12 minutes, or according to the package instructions, until al dente (tender). Thoroughly drain the pasta. Only set aside.
2. Bring 1 inch of water to a boil in a pot fitted with a steamer basket. Add some asparagus. Cover and steam for about 2 to 3 minutes, before tender-crisp.
3. Using cooking spray to spray a large nonstick frying pan. Add the garlic and chicken and saute over medium-high heat. Cook for about 5 to 7 minutes, until the chicken is golden brown. Add the tomatoes, including the juice, basil or oregano, and cook for another 1 minute.
4. Put the cooked pasta, steamed asparagus, chicken mixture, and goat cheese in a large dish. To blend uniformly, toss gently.
5. Divide the pasta mixture into 2 plates in order to serve. Sprinkle a 1/2 tablespoon of Parmesan cheese with each serving. Immediately serve.

22. Chicken brats

(Ready in about 40 Minutes | Serve: 6 | Difficulty: Normal)

Ingredients

- 1 cup minced yellow onion
- 4 cloves garlic, minced
- 1/2 teaspoon canola oil
- 1 cup cooked brown rice
- 1 pound ground chicken breast
- 2 teaspoons fennel seed
- 1 teaspoon cumin seed (or caraway, which has a milder flavor)
- 1 teaspoon ground paprika
- 1 teaspoon ground black pepper
- 1/2 teaspoon ground white pepper
- 1/2 teaspoon ground cayenne pepper
- 1 teaspoon minced fresh rosemary (or 1/4 teaspoon dried)
- 1/4 teaspoon nutmeg
- 1 teaspoon ground mustard seed
- 1 teaspoon celery seed

Directions

1. Sauté the onion and garlic in the canola oil in a frying pan until it is browned. Mix with the cooked rice, ground chicken breast, and the remaining ingredients in a big bowl. 1 hour refrigerator.
2. Break the mixture into six equal parts. Roll the sausage into shape. Or you could pipe the mixture into 6 sausage forms, if you prefer. Place the pan on a tray.
3. Roast for 5 to 10 minutes in an oven at a temperature of 350 F, until the internal temperature is 125 F. Transfer to the grill to finish the cooking process. The brats are not completely cooked until the internal temperature of 165 F is reached.

23. Chicken quesadillas

(Ready in about 40 Minutes | Serve: 6 | Difficulty: Normal)

Ingredients

- 4 boneless, skinless chicken breasts, each 4 ounces
- 1 cup chopped onions
- 1/2 cup smoky or hot salsa
- 1 cup chopped fresh tomatoes
- 1 cup chopped fresh cilantro
- 6 whole-wheat tortillas, each 8 inches in diameter
- 1 cup shredded reduced-fat cheddar cheese

Directions

1. Heat the oven to 425 F. Cover a baking sheet lightly with cooking oil.
2. Slice each breast of chicken into cubes. Add the chicken and onions and saute until the onions are tender and the chicken is fully cooked, around 5 to 7 minutes, in a big, nonstick frying pan. Withdraw from the sun. Stir in the cilantro, tomatoes and salsa.
3. Lay a tortilla flat to assemble and brush the outer edge with water. Spread about 1/2 cup of the mixture of chicken onto the tortilla, leaving the outer rim about 1/2 inch free. Sprinkle the melted cheese with a spoonful. Fold and seal the tortilla in half. Place a cookie sheet on it. Repeat with the tortillas that remain.
4. Coat the top of the tortillas lightly with cooking oil. Bake until the quesadillas, about 5 to 7 minutes, are lightly browned and crispy. Break in half and quickly serve.

24. Chicken salad with pineapple and balsamic vinaigrette

(Ready in about 40 Minutes | Serve: 6 | Difficulty: Normal)

Ingredients

- 4 boneless, skinless chicken breasts, each about 5 ounces
- 1 tablespoon olive oil

- 1 can (8 ounces) unsweetened pineapple chunks, drained except for 2 tablespoons juice
- 2 cups broccoli florets
- 4 cups fresh baby spinach leaves
- 1/2 cup thinly sliced red onions

For the vinaigrette
- 1/4 cup olive oil
- 2 tablespoons balsamic vinegar
- 2 teaspoons sugar
- 1/4 teaspoon ground cinnamon

Directions
1. Slice each breast of chicken into cubes. Heat the olive oil in a big, nonstick frying pan over medium heat. Add the chicken and cook for approximately 10 minutes, until golden brown. Combine the cooked chicken, pineapple chunks, broccoli, spinach and onions in a large serving bowl.
2. In a small cup, whisk together the olive oil, vinegar, pineapple juice, sugar and cinnamon to make the dressing. Pour the salad over. To cover uniformly, throw gently. Immediately serve.

25. Chicken tamales
(Ready in about 40 Minutes | Serve: 6 | Difficulty: Normal)

Ingredients
- 12 dried corn husks
- 1 tablespoon canola oil
- 2 boneless skinless chicken breasts, about 12 ounces total (9 ounces cooked)
- 1 large yellow onion, diced
- 2 red bell peppers, roasted and diced
- 2 ribs celery, diced
- 1 fresh chili pepper, finely diced
- 4 cloves garlic, finely diced
- 2 cups vegetable stock
- 1 tablespoon ground black pepper
- 1 tablespoon cumin seed
- 1 tablespoon minced fresh oregano
- 1/2 cup plus 2 tablespoons stone-ground cornmeal (masa)

Directions
1. Soak the corn husks for one hour in a tank of water.
2. Heat the large skillet over medium heat, stir in the oil and sauté the chicken breasts on each side for 2 minutes, or until golden brown. Remove the chicken from the casserole. Add the vegetables (except garlic) to the pan and sauté until lightly browned for 10 minutes. Add the garlic, then saute for another 2 minutes.
3. Add the chicken back to the pan and add the spices and vegetable stock. Lower the flame to simmer. Cover and cook for 20 minutes, until 165 F is the internal temperature of the chicken. Remove the chicken, then let it cool.
4. Add the remaining liquid to the stone-ground cornmeal (masa) and cook until the liquid is completely absorbed. Only set aside.
5. Pull aside the chicken. Drain the husks of corn well, pat dry. Lay husks out flat and spread on each one the masa mixture. Split the pulled chicken between them. Top with vegetables then. Fold and roll yourself like a burrito.
6. Bake the tamales for about 15 minutes at 375 F or steam them over boiling water in a sealed colander for about 30 minutes. You can wrap tamales in nonstick foil alternately and grill them for around 5 minutes. Be sure to cook until the internal temperature is at least 165 F. To feed, unwrap.

26. Chipotle spiced shrimp
(Ready in about 40 Minutes | Serve: 4 | Difficulty: Normal)

Ingredients
- 1 pound uncooked shrimp, peeled and deveined
- 2 tablespoons tomato paste
- 1 1/2 teaspoons water
- 1/2 teaspoon extra-virgin olive oil
- 1/2 teaspoon minced garlic
- 1/2 teaspoon chipotle chili powder
- 1/2 teaspoon chopped fresh oregano

Directions
1. In cold water, clean the shrimp. Pat dry and set aside on a plate with a paper towel.
2. To make the marinade, whisk the tomato paste, water and oil together in a small cup. Garlic, chilli powder and oregano are added. Mix thoroughly.
3. Spread the marinade (it will be thick) on both sides of the shrimp using a brush. Place it in the fridge.
4. Using a barbecue grill to prepare a hot fire or heat a gas grill or broiler. Lightly brush the grill rack or broiler pan with cooking spray, away from the heat source. The cooking rack should be placed 4 to 6 inches from the heat source.
5. In a grill basket or on skewers, put the shrimp and place on the grill. After 3 to 4 minutes, turn the shrimp over. Depending on the heat of the fire, the cooking time varies, so watch carefully.
6. Switch to a plate and quickly serve.

27 Cinnamon French toast
(Ready in about 40 Minutes | Serving 2 | Difficulty: Normal)

Ingredients
- 4 egg whites
- 1 teaspoon vanilla
- 1/8 teaspoon ground nutmeg
- 4 slices cinnamon bread
- 1/4 teaspoon ground cinnamon
- 1/4 cup maple syrup

Directions
1. Stir together the egg whites, vanilla and nutmeg in a small cup. To combine uniformly, whisk. In the egg mixture, dip the bread, covering both sides.

2. Over medium heat, position a nonstick frying pan or a griddle. Add the bread if a drop of water sizzles when it reaches the pan. Sprinkle cinnamon on it. Cook until it is golden brown on both sides, about 4 to 5 minutes on either side.

3. On warmed individual plates, put 2 slices of French toast. To each one, add 1 teaspoon of powdered sugar and 2 tablespoons of maple syrup. Immediately serve.

28. Corn tamales with avocado-tomatillo salsa

(Ready in about 40 Minutes | Serve: 6 | Difficulty: Normal)

Ingredients

For the tamales:
- 18 dried corn husks, plus extra husks to make ties
- 3 cups fresh or frozen corn kernels (thawed), divided
- 2 cups masa harina
- 1/2 cup lukewarm water
- 1 teaspoon baking powder
- 1/4 teaspoon salt
- 3 tablespoons canola oil
- 1/4 cup diced red bell pepper
- 1/4 cup diced green bell pepper
- 2 tablespoons diced yellow onion
- 1/8 teaspoon red pepper flakes

For the salsa:
- 1/4 cup chopped avocado
- 4 medium tomatillos, husked and chopped (about 2 cups)
- 1 tablespoon fresh lime juice
- 2 tablespoons chopped fresh cilantro (coriander)
- 1/2 teaspoon seeded, minced jalapeno pepper
- 1/4 teaspoon salt

Directions

1. Place the corn husks in a bowl of water to soften for 10 minutes to create the tamales. Drain well and rinse. Dry and set aside, Pat.
2. Please process 2 1/2 cups of the corn kernels in a food processor until coarsely pureed.
3. Combine the pureed maize, masa harina, lukewarm water, baking powder, 1/4 teaspoon salt and oil in a large dish. Mix until well-blended, if necessary, using your hands. Only set aside.
4. Over medium heat, position the dry nonstick frying pan. Add the bell peppers, onion and the remaining 1/2 cup of corn kernels and sauté for 6 to 8 minutes until tender-crisp. Stir in the flakes of red pepper and remove them from the sun.
5. Place 3 tablespoons of masa mixture in the centre of a soaked corn husk to assemble a tamale. Flatten and create a small well in the centre with your hand. To the well, add 1 tablespoon of the sauteed vegetables. Fold over the filling to cover the long side of the corn husk, then fold over the ends, overlapping them. Tie with a thin strip torn from a husk that is extra soaked. To make 18 tamales in all, repeat.
6. Bring 2 inches of water to a boil in a large pot fitted with a steamer basket. Layer the wrapped tamales in the basket of the steamer. Cover until the filling is firm and the tamales are heated through, 50 to 60 minutes with a damp kitchen towel and steam. As required, add more water.
7. Create the salsa while the tamales are steaming. Mix the avocado, tomatillos, lime juice, cilantro, jalapeno and 1/4 of a teaspoon of salt in a small cup. Gently toss.
8. To eat, put on each plate 3 tamales. A generous spoonful of salsa on the side follows each serving.

29. Creole-style black-eyed peas

(Ready in about 40 Minutes | Serve: 8 | Difficulty: Normal)

Ingredients

- 3 cups water
- 2 cups dried black-eyed peas
- 1 teaspoon low-sodium vegetable-flavored bouillon granules
- 2 cups canned unsalted tomatoes, crushed
- 1 large onion, finely chopped
- 2 stalks celery, finely chopped
- 3 teaspoons minced garlic
- 1/2 teaspoon dry mustard
- 1/4 teaspoon ground ginger
- 1/4 teaspoon cayenne pepper
- 1 bay leaf
- 1/2 cup chopped parsley

Directions

1. Add 2 cups of water and the black-eyed peas to a medium saucepan over high heat. For 2 minutes, bring to a boil, cover, remove from the heat and let stand for 1 hour.
2. Drain the water so that the peas are left in the saucepan. Add 1 cup of sugar, bouillon granules, tomatoes, onion, celery, garlic, mustard, ginger, bay leaf and cayenne pepper to the remaining mixture. Stir and carry to a boil. Cover, reduce heat and simmer slowly, stirring periodically, for 2 hours. To keep the peas covered with liquid, add water as needed.
3. Pour into a serving bowl and garnish with parsley, remove the bay leaf. Immediately serve.

30. Curried pork tenderloin in apple cider

(Ready in about 40 Minutes | Serve: 8 | Difficulty: Normal)

Ingredients

- 16 ounces pork tenderloin, cut into 4 pieces
- 1 1/2 tablespoons curry powder
- 1 tablespoon extra-virgin olive oil

- 2 medium yellow onions, chopped (about 2 cups)
- 2 cups apple cider, divided
- 1 tart apple, peeled, seeded and cut into chunks
- 1 tablespoon cornstarch

Directions
1. Season the curry powder with the pork tenderloin and let it stand for 15 minutes.
2. Heat the olive oil in a big, heavy skillet over medium to high heat. Attach the tenderloin and cook until browned on both sides, around 5 to 10 minutes, turning once. Remove the skillet meat and set aside.
3. In a pan, add the onions and saute until soft and golden. Add 1 1/2 cups of cider, reduce the heat and boil until half the amount of the liquid is added.
4. Remove the chopped apple, cornstarch and the 1/2 cup of cider left over. Stir and cook for about 2 minutes until the sauce thickens. For the final 5 minutes, return the tenderloin to the skillet and simmer.
5. Arrange the tenderloin on a serving platter or break it into separate plates to serve. Pour the thickened sauce over the meat and serve straight away.

31. Easy pizza for two
(Ready in about 40 Minutes | Serve: 8 | Difficulty: Normal)

Ingredients
- 1/2 cup chunky no-salt-added tomato sauce
- 1 ready-made whole-wheat flatbread (about 10-inch diameter)
- 2 slices of onion, 1/4-inch wide
- 4 slices red bell pepper, 1/4-inch wide
- 1/4 cup shredded low-fat mozzarella
- 2 tablespoons chopped fresh basil

Directions
1. Heat the oven to 350 F. Cover a baking pan lightly with cooking oil. Over the flatbread, spread the tomato sauce. Place the onion, tomato, mozzarella and basil on top. Place the pizza on a baking sheet and bake for 5 to 7 minutes, until the cheese is melted and golden brown.

32. Fettuccine with clams, basil, tomato, corn and garlic
(Ready in about 40 Minutes | Serve: 8 | Difficulty: Normal)

Ingredients
- 10 ounces (about 5 cups) uncooked fettuccine
- 2 tablespoons minced garlic
- 2 large tomatoes, seeded and chopped
- 2 cups corn kernels, fresh or frozen
- 1/2 cup white wine
- 1 tablespoon olive oil
- 4 tablespoons chopped fresh basil
- 2 cans (4 ounces each) clams, drained
- 1/4 teaspoon salt
- Ground black pepper, to taste

Directions
1. Fill 3/4 of a large pot full of water and bring it to a boil. Add the pasta and cook until al dente (tender), about eight minutes or as directed by the packet. Thoroughly drain the pasta.
2. Garlic, onions, corn, wine, olive oil, and basil are added to a large saucepan. Cover and put, stirring regularly, to a boil. Add the clams and pasta and reduce the heat. To coat, throw gently. Season with pepper and salt and serve immediately.

33. Fish Veracruz
(Ready in about 40 Minutes | Serve: 8 | Difficulty: Normal)

Ingredients
- 2 pounds whitefish fillets, such as tilapia, cod, sole, pollock or halibut
- 1/4 cup lime juice
- 1/2 tablespoon canola oil
- 1 small onion, peeled and sliced
- 1 small green bell pepper, seeded and cut into strips
- 1/4 cup jalapeno pepper, seeded and sliced
- 2 cups fresh salsa or pico de gallo
- 1/2 cup no-salt-added tomato sauce
- 1/2 cup sliced ripe olives
- 1 tablespoon capers
- 4 tablespoons fresh cilantro, chopped, or 4 teaspoons dried cilantro
- 1 lime cut into 8 wedges

Directions
1. In a 9-by-13-inch baking pan, place the fish. Sprinkle the juice with lime. Cover for at least 20 minutes and refrigerate.
2. Heat the oven to 425 F. Heat oil over medium-high heat in a big, nonstick skillet. Add the bell pepper, onion and jalapeno pepper. Cook and stir regularly for 2 minutes or until the vegetables are soft yet crisp.
3. Stir in the tomato sauce, olives, capers, and salsa. Just bring it to a boil. Lower the heat and simmer for around 1 minute.
4. Pour the sauce over the fish and bake for about 20 minutes in the preheated oven, or until the fish flakes easily with a fork.
5. With a slotted spatula, remove the fish and vegetables from the pan. Serve with lime wedges and cilantro.

34. Five spice pork medallions
(Ready in about 40 Minutes | Serve: 8 | Difficulty: Normal)

Ingredients
- 2 tablespoons low-sodium soy sauce
- 1 tablespoon green (spring) onion, including tender green top, minced
- 3 garlic cloves, minced

- 1 tablespoon olive oil
- 3/4 teaspoon five-spice powder
- 1 pound pork tenderloin, trimmed of visible fat
- 1 tablespoon olive oil
- 1/2 cup water, plus 1 to 3 tablespoons as needed
- 1/4 cup dry white wine
- 1/3 cup chopped yellow onion
- 1/2 head green cabbage, thinly sliced (about 4 cups)
- 1 tablespoon chopped fresh flat-leaf (Italian) parsley

Directions

1. Combine the soy sauce, green onion, garlic, olive oil and five-spice powder in a shallow baking dish to make the marinade. Whisk for mixing. To coat, add the pork and turn once. Cover and marinate for at least 2 hours in the refrigerator, preferably overnight, turning the pork around periodically.
2. Heat the oven to 400 F.
3. Remove the marinade from the pork and pat it dry. Put the marinade away. Heat the olive oil in a big, oven-proof frying pan over medium-high heat. Add the pork and cook until lightly browned on all sides, turning as required, for about 5 minutes. To the pan, add 1/2 cup of water.
4. Switch the hot pan to the oven and roast until the inside of the pork is slightly pink and an inserted instant-read thermometer reads 160 F. Switch the pork to a cutting board, cover with a towel in the kitchen, and let stand for 10 minutes.
5. Meanwhile, over medium-high heat, position the pan. Using a wooden spoon to clean up any browned pieces, add the wine and deglaze the pan. Attach the yellow onion, then cook for 1 minute or so. Cabbage and 1 tablespoon of the remaining water should be applied. Stir well, reduce the heat to medium, cover and simmer for around 4 minutes until the cabbage wilts. If required, add 1 to 2 tablespoons of additional water.
6. Slice the tenderloin of pork into eight medallions. Divide the wilted cabbage and medallions between individual plates and garnish with parsley. Immediately serve.

35. Fresh puttanesca with brown rice

(Ready in about 40 Minutes | Serve: 8 | Difficulty: Normal)

Ingredients

- 4 cups chopped ripe plum tomatoes
- 4 Kalamata olives, pitted and sliced
- 4 green olives, pitted and sliced
- 1 1/2 tablespoons capers, rinsed and drained
- 1 tablespoon minced garlic
- 1 tablespoon olive oil
- 1/4 cup chopped fresh basil
- 1 tablespoon minced fresh parsley
- 1/8 teaspoon red pepper flakes
- 3 cups cooked brown rice

Directions

1. Combine the tomatoes, olives, capers, garlic and oil in a wide bowl. Then apply the flakes of basil, parsley and red pepper, stirring to mix.
2. Cover and leave to stand for 20 to 30 minutes at room temperature, stirring periodically. Serve over rice that is cooked.

36. Fried rice

(Ready in about 40 Minutes | Serve: 8 | Difficulty: Normal)

Ingredients

- 2 cups cooked brown rice
- 3 tablespoons peanut oil
- 4 green onions with tops, chopped
- 2 carrots, finely chopped
- 1/2 cup finely chopped green bell pepper
- 1/2 cup frozen peas
- 1 egg
- 2 tablespoons low-sodium soy sauce
- 1 tablespoon sesame oil
- 1/4 cup chopped parsley

Directions

1. Heat the peanut oil over medium-high heat in a big, heavy skillet or wok. Put the cooked rice together and saute until softly golden. Add the carrots, green onions, green pepper and peas. Stir-fry for about 5 minutes, until the vegetables are tender-crisp.
2. Push the vegetables and rice to the sides by hollowing out a circle in the middle of the skillet. Break the hollow egg and cook, scrambling the egg gently as it heats. In the rice mixture, whisk the scrambled egg. Sprinkle with sesame oil, soy sauce and chopped parsley. Immediately serve.

37. Glazed turkey breast with fruit stuffing

(Ready in about 40 Minutes | Serve: 8 | Difficulty: Normal)

Ingredients

- One 5 pound whole, bone-in turkey breast (thawed)

Rub:

- 2 tablespoons chopped fresh rosemary
- 2 tablespoons chopped fresh thyme leaves
- 2 tablespoons olive oil

Stuffing:

- 1 small onion, thinly sliced
- 1 apple, peeled and thinly sliced
- 1 pear, peeled and thinly sliced
- 1/4 cup dried cranberries (or raisins)

Glaze:

- 2 cups apple juice, divided
- 1 tablespoon brown sugar
- 1 tablespoon brown mustard

- 1 tablespoon olive oil

Directions
1. Heat the oven to 325 F.
2. Place the turkey breast on a rack in a roasting pan, skin-side-up.
3. Mix the herbs and olive oil together in a small bowl to make a paste. With your fingers, gently loosen the skin from the meat, leaving deep pockets between the skin and the meat. Directly smear half of the paste on the beef. Eared uniformly over the surface of the skin with the remaining paste.
4. Mix the sliced onions and fruit together in another small bowl. With the mixture, stuff each bag.
5. Through the bottom of the roasting pan, pour 1 cup of the apple juice. Roast the turkey breast for 1 3/4 to 2 hours until the skin is golden brown and, when inserted into the thickest and meatiest areas of the breast, an instant-read thermometer registers 165 F. Top the breast loosely with aluminium foil if the skin is overbrowned.
6. Create the glaze in the meantime. Mix the remaining cup of apple juice, brown sugar, mustard and olive oil in a saucepan. Heat to boiling, reduce heat and simmer until thickened and decreased to around 3/4 cup in volume. Using this during the last 30 minutes of cooking to baste the turkey.
7. Cover with foil when the turkey is finished and allow it to rest for 15 minutes at room temperature. Carve, serve and spoon over the turkey with any remaining glaze

38. Grilled Asian salmon

(Ready in about 40 Minutes | Serve: 8 | Difficulty: Normal)

Ingredients
- 1 tablespoon sesame oil
- 1 tablespoon reduced-sodium soy sauce
- 1 tablespoon fresh ginger, minced
- 1 tablespoon rice wine vinegar
- 4 salmon fillets, each 4 ounces

Directions
1. Mix the sesame oil, soy sauce, ginger and vinegar together in a shallow glass bowl. To coat both sides, add the salmon and turn. Refrigerate, turning periodically, for 30 to 60 minutes.
2. Grill lightly with oil and then fire over medium-high heat. Put the salmon on the grill and cook on one side for 5 minutes. If a knife blade inserted in the middle reveals that the pink flesh is almost invisible, the fish is primed. Serve it sweet.

39. Grilled chicken salad with olives and oranges

(Ready in about 40 Minutes | Serve: 8 | Difficulty: Normal)

Ingredients

For the dressing:
- 1/2 cup red wine vinegar
- 4 garlic cloves, minced
- 1 tablespoon extra-virgin olive oil
- 1 tablespoon finely chopped red onion
- 1 tablespoon finely chopped celery
- Cracked black pepper, to taste

For the salad:
- 4 boneless, skinless chicken breasts, each 4 ounces
- 2 garlic cloves
- 8 cups leaf lettuce, washed and dried
- 16 large ripe (black) olives
- 2 navel oranges, peeled and sliced

Directions
1. Combine the vinegar, garlic, olive oil, onion, celery and pepper in a small bowl to make the dressing. Stir to blend uniformly. Cover until required, and refrigerate.
2. Using a barbecue grill to prepare a hot fire or heat a gas grill or broiler. Lightly brush the grill rack or broiler pan with cooking spray, away from the heat source. The cooking rack should be placed 4 to 6 inches from the heat source. Use garlic to coat the chicken breasts, then remove the cloves. Grill or broil the chicken until browned, about 5 minutes on each side, and only cooked through. Switch the chicken to a cutting board and let stand before cutting into strips for 5 minutes.
3. Arrange 2 cups of lettuce on 4 plates with 4 olives and 1/4 of the sliced oranges. Put 1 chicken breast cut into strips on each plate and drizzle with dressing. Immediately serve.

40. Grilled cod with crispy citrus salad

(Ready in about 40 Minutes | Serve: 8 | Difficulty: Normal)

Ingredients
- 8 ounces cod
- 1 teaspoon olive oil
- 1 1/2 cups chopped spinach
- 1 1/2 cups shredded kohlrabi
- 1 cup diced celery
- 1 1/2 cups shredded carrot
- 2 tablespoons chopped fresh basil
- 1 tablespoon chopped fresh parsley
- 3/4 cup chopped red bell pepper
- 1 tablespoon minced garlic (about 4 large cloves) or to taste
- Zest and juice of 1 lemon
- Zest and juice of 1 lime
- Zest and juice of 1 orange
- 1 large grapefruit cut into segments (about 1 cup)
- 1 medium orange cut into segments (about 1/2 cup)
- Black pepper to taste

Directions

1. Using cooking spray to spray a grill or broiler pan. Switch on a grill or broiler with hot water. Put the cod on the grill or broiler pan and gently brush it with oil.
2. Grill or broil for around 10 minutes 3 to 4 inches from the fire or until fish flakes easily with a fork. An internal temperature of 145 F. should be achieved by the fish. Only set aside.
3. Toss the remaining ingredients together in a large bowl, except for the grapefruit and orange parts. Divide the salad into two pans. Top with bits of cod and citrus and, to taste, black pepper.

41 Grilled pork fajitas

(Ready in about 40 Minutes | Serve: 8 | Difficulty: Normal)

Ingredients

- 1 teaspoon ground cumin
- 1/2 teaspoon oregano
- 1/2 teaspoon paprika
- 1/4 teaspoon ground coriander
- 1/4 teaspoon garlic powder
- 1 pound pork tenderloin, cut into strips 1/2 inch wide and 2 inches long
- 1 small onion, sliced
- 8 whole-wheat flour tortillas, about 8 inches in diameter, warmed in the microwave
- 1/2 cup shredded sharp cheddar cheese
- 4 medium tomatoes, diced (about 3 cups)
- 4 cups shredded lettuce
- 1 cup salsa

Directions

1. On a barbecue grill, prepare a hot fire or heat a medium-high or 400 F gas grill or broiler.
2. Stir together the cumin, oregano, paprika, coriander and garlic powder in a small cup. Dredge the pork parts in the seasonings, absolutely covering them.
3. In a cast-iron pan or barbecue basket, put the pork strips and onions. At medium-high heat, grill or broil, turning several times, until browned on all sides, around 5 minutes.
4. To eat, spread on each tortilla an equal amount of pork strips and onions. Top each with 1 tablespoon of cheese, 1/2 cup of shredded lettuce, 2 tablespoons of tomatoes, and 2 tablespoons of salsa. Fold the tortilla's sides over the filling, then roll to close.

42. Grilled snapper curry

(Ready in about 40 Minutes | Serve: 8 | Difficulty: Normal)

Ingredients

- 1/2 teaspoon coconut extract
- 1 cup low-fat soy milk (or skim milk)
- 1 teaspoon cornstarch
- 1/2 teaspoon fennel seed
- 1 tablespoon turmeric
- 1 teaspoon ground coriander
- 1 teaspoon ground cumin
- 1 teaspoon paprika
- 1 teaspoon canola oil
- 2 tablespoons minced ginger
- 2 cloves garlic, minced
- 1 cup sliced onion
- 1 cup sliced red bell pepper
- 1 poblano pepper, sliced
- 2 cups sliced celery
- 2 cups sliced bok choy
- 4 six-ounce red snapper fillets
- Black pepper to taste

Directions

1. Mix together the coconut extract, soy milk, cornstarch and spices in a small cup. Only set aside.
2. Add the oil and saute ginger, garlic, onion, peppers, celery and bok choy for a few minutes in a large skillet over medium-high, until softened and lightly browned. Apply the mixture of milk and spices to the pan and whisk to blend. Heat softly. Do not cook. Withdraw from the sun.
3. Grill or grill a snapper until the internal temperature exceeds 145 F (about 10 minutes). With 1 1/2 cups of vegetables and sauce, serve each fillet. Season with black pepper to taste according to.

43. Grouper with tomato-olive sauce

(Ready in about 40 Minutes | Serve: 8 | Difficulty: Normal)

Ingredients

- 4 grouper fillets or steaks, each 5 ounces and about 1-inch thick
- 1/4 teaspoon freshly ground black pepper, divided
- 1 1/2 tablespoons extra-virgin olive oil
- 1 yellow onion, finely chopped
- 2 cloves garlic, minced
- 3 tomatoes, peeled and seeded, then diced
- 5 large pimento-stuffed green olives, sliced
- 1 tablespoon capers, rinsed
- 1 jalapeno chili, seeded and cut into 1-inch julienne
- 2 tablespoons fresh lime juice

Directions

1. Sprinkle 1/8 of a teaspoon of pepper with the grouper steaks on both sides. Heat 1 1/2 teaspoons of olive oil in a large, nonstick frying pan over medium-high heat. Add the fish to the pan and sear on both sides, about 2 minutes per side, until lightly browned. Transfer to and hold warm on a tray.
2. Lower the heat to medium and apply to the pan the remaining 1 tablespoon of olive oil. Add the onion and saute for about 6 minutes until it is soft and softly golden. Add the garlic and saute for around 1 minute, until tender. To allow the flavours to blend, add the tomatoes, olives, capers and jalapeno and simmer for 10 minutes. Apply the remaining 1/8 of a teaspoon of pepper. Take the fish back to the bowl. When

measured with the tip of a knife, cover and simmer for 6 to 8 minutes until the fish is opaque throughout.
3. Move the grouper steaks to individual plates that are warmed. Stir in the vegetables and pan juices with the lime juice. Over each steak, spoon some sauce. Immediately serve.

44. Halibut with tomato basil salsa

(Ready in about 40 Minutes | Serve: 8 | Difficulty: Normal)

Ingredients

- 2 tomatoes, diced (about 1 1/2 cups)
- 2 tablespoons fresh basil, chopped
- 1 teaspoon fresh oregano, chopped
- 1 tablespoon minced garlic
- 2 teaspoons extra-virgin olive oil
- 4 halibut fillets, each 4 ounces

Directions

1. Heat the oven to 350 F. Using cooking spray to thinly coat a 9-by-13-inch baking pan.
2. Mix the tomato, basil, oregano and garlic in a small cup. Apply the olive oil and blend thoroughly.
3. In the baking pan, arrange the halibut fillets. Spoon over the fish with the tomato mixture. Place in the oven and bake for around 10 to 15 minutes, until the fish is opaque throughout when checked with the tip of a knife.
4. Transfer to individual plates and quickly serve.

45. Hearty chicken bowl

(Ready in about 40 Minutes | Serve: 8 | Difficulty: Normal)

Ingredients

- 1 tablespoon canola oil, divided
- 2 cups sliced carrots
- 1 cup diced yellow onion
- 1 cup fresh mushrooms
- 2 tablespoons minced fresh parsley
- 1 cup uncooked fancy wild rice
- 2 tablespoons chopped walnuts
- 1 tablespoon fresh ground black pepper
- 2 1/2 cups no-salt-added chicken stock
- 2 boneless skinless chicken breasts (4 ounces each)
- 1 cup diced red beets
- 1 cup peeled and diced butternut squash
- 2 cups chopped beet tops (greens)
- 1 tablespoon balsamic vinegar
- 2 tablespoons dried cranberries

Directions

1. Over medium heat, heat the sauce pan, add half the oil and the carrots, onion, mushrooms and parsley. Saute for 10 minutes or until the onions start to brown. Add wild rice, walnuts, chicken stock and black pepper. Bring to a boil, simmer and reduce. Cover and leave for 40 minutes to cook.
2. Meanwhile, add the rest of the oil to a saute pan. On both sides, add chicken breasts and brown, around 3 minutes a side. Cook until the temperature inside is 165 F. Set aside, keep warm, and remove the chicken from the pan.
3. To the hot pan, add the diced beets and squash. Saute for 15-20 minutes on medium heat, until the squash starts to brown and both products are tender. Add the chopped greens, balsamic vinegar, blend of cranberries and rice, toss to combine and loosen the cooked bits from the bottom of the plate.
4. Divide into four bowls, top with chicken breast slices and serve.

46. Herb-crusted baked cod

(Ready in about 40 Minutes | Serve: 8 | Difficulty: Normal)

Ingredients

- 3/4 cup herb-flavored stuffing
- 4 cod fillets, 4 ounces each
- 2 tablespoons honey

Directions

1. Heat the oven to 375 F. Using cooking spray to thinly coat a 9-by-13-inch baking pan.
2. Place the stuffing and seal in a jar. Crush it until it has the texture of a crumb.
3. Brush with honey on a fillet. Place the fillet in the stuffing bag. To uniformly coat the cod, shake the bag gently. Place the fillet and repeat it with the remaining fillets in the baking dish. Discard any honey that is unused.
4. When checked with the tip of a knife, bake for about 10 minutes until the fish is opaque throughout. Instantly serve.

47. Herb-rubbed turkey au jus

(Ready in about 40 Minutes | Serve: 8 | Difficulty: Normal)

Ingredients

- 1 whole turkey (about 15 pounds), thawed
- 1 tablespoon olive oil
- 1/2 cup water
- Herb rub:
- 2 teaspoons dried sage
- 1 tablespoon dried thyme
- 2 tablespoons chopped fresh parsley

Au jus:
- 2 teaspoons dried sage
- 1 tablespoon dried thyme
- 2 tablespoons chopped fresh parsley
- 2 tablespoons honey
- 1/2 cup apple juice
- 1 cup defatted pan drippings

Directions

1. Heat the oven to 325 F.
2. Combine the sage, thyme and parsley in a small bowl to make the rub. Mix thoroughly and set aside.

3. Remove the turkey's neck and giblets and discard them. In cool water, clean the turkey inside and out. Pat with paper towels to rinse.
4. Place fingers or a spoon between the skin layer and the meat, beginning at the neck area, to gently loosen the skin. On a rack in a roasting pan, put the turkey breast-side up. Under the skin of each breast, add about 1 tablespoon of the herb mixture. Rub the olive oil on the exterior of the turkey. Brush over the exterior of the bird the remaining herb mixture. Bind the legs together loosely. Place it in the centre of the oven.
5. Cover the turkey with a tent of foil after around 1 1/2 hours to prevent the skin from being overcooked. After the bird has roasted for 3 to 3 1/2 hours, check the doneness. When the thigh is deeply pierced and juices run clear (180 to 185 F) or when the muscle of the breast reaches 170 to 175 F, the turkey is finished.
6. From the oven, remove the turkey. Let it stand for 20 minutes. Add 1/2 cup of water; scrape the drippings and browned bits into the bowl. Pour or skim away the fat into a gravy separator. Only set aside.
7. Combine the sage, thyme, parsley, honey and apple juice in a saucepan. Simmer over medium heat until half is reduced. Add the drippings from the degreased pan and bring to a low boil, stirring frequently.
8. Carve the turkey and drizzle the sauce over the turkey slices. Immediately serve.

48. Honey crusted chicken
(Ready in about 40 Minutes | Serve: 2 | Difficulty: Normal)

Ingredients
- 8 saltine crackers, each about 2 inches square
- 1 teaspoon paprika
- 2 boneless, skinless chicken breasts, each 4 ounces
- 4 teaspoons honey

Directions
1. Heat the oven to 375 F. Cover a baking dish lightly with cooking oil.
2. Crush those crackers. In a small cup, put the crackers and add the paprika. To blend well, stir.
3. Add the chicken and honey to a separate dish. To cover uniformly, toss. Add the mixture of crackers. In the cracker mixture, blend and press the chicken until it is evenly coated on both sides.
4. In the prepared baking dish, put the chicken in it. Bake for about 20 to 25 minutes, until lightly browned and baked. Immediately serve.

49. Italian chicken and vegetable packet
(Ready in about 40 Minutes | Serve: 2 | Difficulty: Normal)

Ingredients
- 1 skinless, boneless chicken breast, about 3 ounces
- 1/2 cup diced zucchini
- 1/2 cup scrubbed and diced potato
- 1/4 cup diced onion
- 1/4 cup sliced baby carrots
- 1/4 cup sliced mushrooms
- 1/8 teaspoon garlic powder
- 1/4 teaspoon Italian seasoning or oregano

Directions
1. Heat the oven to 350 F.
2. Break off a sheet of heavy-duty aluminium foil or parchment paper measuring 12 inches. Fold in half the foil or parchment paper, unfold and spray with the spray for cooking.
3. The chicken breast should be focused on the sheet. Place the zucchini, potato, onion, carrots and mushrooms on top. Sprinkle the chicken and the vegetables with garlic powder and Italian seasoning.
4. Bring together the foil and make small, overlapping folds down the packet length to be sealed. To make a strong seal, twist the two ends many times so that the liquid won't escape during cooking.
5. Place the packet on a cookie sheet and bake until the chicken and vegetables are tender, for 45 minutes.

50. Lasagna
(Ready in about 40 Minutes | Serve: 2 | Difficulty: Normal)

Ingredients
- 1 pound extra-lean ground beef
- 1 onion, chopped
- 1 1/2 teaspoons dried basil
- 3/4 teaspoon oregano
- 3/4 teaspoon garlic powder
- 1 can (6 ounces) unsalted tomato paste
- 1 can (8 ounces) unsalted tomato sauce
- 3 1/2 cups water
- 3/4 pound uncooked lasagna noodles
- 1 cup low-fat cottage cheese
- 3 cups shredded low-fat mozzarella cheese

Directions
1. Heat the oven to 325 F. Cover a 9-by-13 pan lightly with cooking spray.
2. Combine the ground beef and onion in a wide saucepan to make the sauce. Until the ground beef is browned and the onion is translucent, cook over medium heat. Drain thoroughly. Add the basil, oregano, garlic powder, tomato paste, water, and tomato sauce. Stir to blend uniformly. Bring to a boil, reduce heat and cook for 10 minutes to simmer.
3. At the bottom of the prepared pan, add 1/2 cup of the sauce. Cover with 1/3 of the remaining sauce, 1/3 cup of cottage cheese and 1 cup of mozzarella cheese, with a layer of uncooked lasagna noodles. Repeat until they have used up the ingredients. Cover with aluminium foil and bake for about 1 hour and 20 minutes, until the noodles are soft and the cheese is lightly browned.

51. Linguine with roasted butternut squash sauce
(Ready in about 40 Minutes | Serve: 2 | Difficulty: Normal)

Ingredients

- 1 medium butternut squash (about 2 pounds), split and seeded
- 2 tablespoons olive oil, divided
- Freshly ground black pepper to taste
- 12 ounces whole-wheat linguine or other pasta
- 1 1/2 cups reduced-sodium vegetable broth
- 8 sage leaves, cut into thin strips
- 1/4 cup diced yellow onion
- 1/2 cup chopped red bell pepper
- 2 cloves garlic, minced
- 1 tablespoon cider vinegar
- 1/8 teaspoon ground nutmeg
- Parmesan cheese

Directions

1. Heat the oven to 400 F. With 1 tablespoon of oil, brush the squash and season generously with pepper. Roast for approximately 60 minutes or until soft. Take it out of the oven and let it cool to room temperature.
2. To a boil, put a big pot of water. Add the pasta and cook according to the instructions on the box.
3. Place the cooked butternut squash in a big blender or food processor. Purée until it's smooth. The broth and puree are added slowly until the sauce achieves the desired consistency. Depending upon the size of your squash, you might need to add a little water.
4. Heat the remaining olive oil in a small skillet over medium-high heat until it shimmers slightly. Add the sage and cook for about 30 seconds until it is bright green. Add the garlic, red pepper and onion. Saute for 3 to 5 minutes until it is smooth. Add the butternut squash, which is pureed. Using vinegar, nutmeg and more black pepper to season. Attach the pasta and stir until it is well covered with the pasta. Sprinkle, if needed, with Parmesan cheese. Just serve.

52. Mango salsa pizza

(Ready in about 40 Minutes | Serve 2 | Difficulty: Normal)

Ingredients

- 1 cup chopped red or green bell peppers
- 1/2 cup minced onion
- 1/2 cup chopped mango
- 1/2 cup pineapple tidbits
- 1 tablespoon lime juice
- 1/2 cup chopped fresh cilantro
- 1 12-inch prepared whole-grain pizza crust, purchased or made from a mix

Directions

1. Heat the oven to 425 F. Cover a 12-inch round pan lightly with cooking oil.
2. Mix the tomatoes, onions, mango, pineapple, lime juice and cilantro together in a small bowl. Only set aside.
3. Roll the dough out, then press it into the bowl. Place them in the oven and cook for 15 minutes or so.
4. Remove the crust of the pizza from the oven and spread it with the mango salsa. Place the pizza back in the oven and cook for around 5 to 10 minutes, until the toppings are hot and the crust is browned.
5. Break the pie into eight slices and immediately serve.

53. Mediterranean-style grilled salmon

(Ready in about 40 Minutes | Serve: 2 | Difficulty: Normal)

Ingredients

- 4 tablespoons chopped fresh basil
- 1 tablespoon chopped fresh parsley
- 1 tablespoon minced garlic
- 2 tablespoons lemon juice
- 4 salmon fillets, each 5 ounces
- Cracked black pepper, to taste
- 4 green olives, chopped
- 4 thin slices lemon

Directions

1. Using a barbecue grill to prepare a hot fire or heat a gas grill or broiler. Lightly brush the grill rack or broiler pan with cooking spray, away from the heat source. The cooking rack should be placed 4 to 6 inches from the heat source.
2. Combine the basil, parsley, minced garlic and the lemon juice in a small cup. Spray with cooking spray on the fish. Using black pepper to sprinkle. With equal quantities of the herb-garlic mixture, top each fillet. Place the herb-side fish down on the grill. Over high heat, barbecue. When the edges turn white, turn the fish over after around 3 to 4 minutes and put it on aluminum foil. Shift the fish or reduce the heat to a cooler section of the grill. When measured with the tip of a knife, grill until the fish is opaque throughout and an instant-read thermometer inserted into the thickest part of the fish reads 145 F (about 4 minutes longer).
3. Remove and put the salmon on warmed plates. Add green olives and lemon slices to garnish.

54. New York strip steak with whiskey-mushroom sauce

(Ready in about 40 Minutes | Serve: 2 | Difficulty: Normal)

Ingredients

1. Using a barbecue grill to prepare a hot fire or heat a gas grill or broiler. Lightly brush the grill rack or broiler pan with cooking spray, away from the heat source. The cooking rack should be placed 4 to 6 inches from the heat source.
2. Grill or broil steaks until slightly pink on the inside, around 10 minutes on each side, or until 145 F (medium rare), 160 F (medium) or 170 F (medium) or 170 F (medium rare) is indicated on the food thermometer (well-done).
3. Heat the margarine over medium heat in a tiny saucepan. Garlic, mushrooms, thyme and rosemary should be included. Saute lightly, for around 1 to 2 minutes, until the mushrooms are tender. Remove and carefully add the whiskey from the heat and (be

careful not to let the alcohol flame). For another minute, stir. Cover the mushroom mixture with the steaks and serve immediately.

55. Orange roughy with lemon and thyme
(Ready in about 40 Minutes | Serve: 2 | Difficulty: Normal)

Ingredients
- 2 orange roughy fillets, each 4 ounces
- 1 lemon, cut into 4 wedges
- 1 teaspoon fresh thyme, chopped

Directions
1. Heat up your broiler (grill). Place the rack 4 inches from the source of the sun. Cover a baking dish lightly with cooking oil. Place the fish on the baking dish that has been prepared. Over the fillets, squeeze the juice from 2 lemon wedges. Sprinkle thyme on it.
2. When measured with the tip of a knife, broil (grill) until the fish is opaque, around 8 to 10 minutes. Take it out of the oven. Garnished with the remaining two lemon wedges, serve immediately.

56. Orange-rosemary roasted chicken
(Ready in about 40 Minutes | Serve: 2 | Difficulty: Normal)

Ingredients
- 3 skinless, bone-in chicken breast halves, each 8 ounces
- 3 skinless, bone-in chicken legs with thigh pieces, each 8 ounces
- 2 garlic cloves, minced
- 1 1/2 teaspoons extra-virgin olive oil
- 3 teaspoons fresh rosemary or 1 teaspoon dried rosemary, minced
- 1/8 teaspoon freshly ground black pepper
- 1/3 cup orange juice

Directions
1. Heat the oven to 450 F. Cover a baking pan lightly with cooking oil.
2. Rub garlic on each slice of chicken. Sprinkle your fingers with oil, brush them with oil, and sprinkle them with rosemary and pepper. In the baking dish, put the chicken bits. Over the chicken, pour the orange juice. For 30 minutes, cover and bake. Turn the chicken and return it to the oven until browned, about 10 to 15 minutes longer, using tongs. To prevent it from drying out, baste the chicken with the orange juice from the pan as needed.
3. To individual serving plates, pass the chicken. Spoon orange juice over the top of the chicken from the pan and serve right away.

57. Overnight refrigerator oatmeal
(Ready in about 40 Minutes | Serve: 2 | Difficulty: Normal)

Ingredients
- 1/3 cup skim milk (or soy milk)
- 1/4 cup unsweetened applesauce
- 1/4 cup old-fashioned rolled oats
- 1/4 cup Greek low-fat plain yogurt
- 1/4 cup diced apples
- 1 1/2 teaspoons dried chia seeds
- 1/4 teaspoon cinnamon

Directions
- Place all the ingredients in a mason jar with 1 pint. Screw and shake the lid on until well-combined. Refrigerate and eat chilled overnight.

58. Paella with chicken, leeks and tarragon
(Ready in about 40 Minutes | Serve: 2 | Difficulty: Normal)

Ingredients
- 1 teaspoon extra-virgin olive oil
- 1 small onion, sliced
- 2 leeks (whites only), thinly sliced
- 3 garlic cloves, minced
- 1 pound boneless, skinless chicken breast, cut into strips 1/2 inch wide and 2 inches long
- 2 large tomatoes, chopped
- 1 red pepper, sliced
- 2/3 cup long-grain brown rice
- 1 teaspoon tarragon, or to taste
- 2 cups fat-free, unsalted chicken broth
- 1 cup frozen peas
- 1/4 cup chopped fresh parsley
- 1 lemon, cut into 4 wedges

Directions
1. Heat the olive oil in a big, nonstick frying pan over medium heat. Add strips of onions, leeks, garlic and chicken. Saute for about 5 minutes, until the vegetables are translucent and the chicken is lightly browned. Attach the tomatoes and slices of red pepper and saute for another 5 minutes. Add the rice, tarragon and broth and blend well together. Just bring it to a boil.
2. Decrease the heat, cover and simmer for 10 minutes or so. Stir in the peas and proceed to simmer uncovered for 45 to 60 minutes until the broth is absorbed and the rice is soft.
3. Split into individual plates in order to serve. Garnish with 1 tablespoon parsley and 1 slice of lemon each.

59. Pasta primavera
(Ready in about 40 Minutes | Serve: 2 | Difficulty: Normal)

Ingredients
- 2 cups broccoli florets
- 1 cup sliced mushrooms
- 1 cup sliced zucchini or yellow squash
- 2 cups sliced red or green peppers

- 1 tablespoon extra-virgin olive oil
- 1/2 cup chopped onion
- 2 garlic cloves, minced
- 1 teaspoon butter
- 1 cup evaporated fat-free milk
- 3/4 cup freshly grated Parmesan cheese
- 12 ounces whole-wheat pasta (angel hair or spaghetti)
- 1/3 cup finely chopped fresh parsley

Directions

1. Carry about 1 inch of water to the boil in a large pot fitted with a steamer basket. Add the broccoli, zucchini, mushrooms and peppers. Cover and steam for about 10 minutes, before tender-crisp. Remove yourself from the pot.
2. Heat the olive oil in a large saucepan, then saute the onion and garlic over medium heat. To coat the vegetables with the onion and garlic mixture, add the steamed vegetables and stir or shake. Remove from heat, keep warm though.
3. Heat the butter, the evaporated milk and the Parmesan cheese in another large saucepan. Stir until somewhat thickened and heated through, over moderate heat. Continually stir and don't scald. Remove from heat, keep warm though.
4. In the meantime, fill a 3/4 full large pot with water and bring it to a boil. Add the pasta and cook until al dente (tender), about 10 to 12 minutes or as directed by the packet. Thoroughly drain the pasta.
5. Divide the pasta equally between individual plates. Top with the vegetables and pour the vegetables and pasta over the sauce. Garnish with fresh parsley, then serve right away.

60. Pasta salad with mixed vegetables

(Ready in about 40 Minutes | Serve: 2 | Difficulty: Normal)

Ingredients

- 12 ounces whole-wheat rotini (spiral-shaped) pasta
- 1 tablespoon olive oil
- 1/4 cup low-sodium chicken broth
- 1 garlic clove, chopped
- 2 medium onions, chopped
- 1 can (28 ounces) unsalted diced tomatoes in juice
- 1 pound mushrooms, sliced
- 1 red bell pepper, sliced
- 1 green bell pepper, sliced
- 2 medium zucchini, shredded
- 1/2 teaspoon basil
- 1/2 teaspoon oregano
- 8 romaine lettuce leaves

Directions

1. Cook pasta according to the instructions on the box. Thoroughly drain the pasta. Place the pasta in a big bowl to eat. Stir in the olive oil and toss. Only set aside.
2. Heat the chicken broth in a big skillet over medium heat. Garlic, onions and tomatoes are added. Saute for approximately 5 minutes until the onions are translucent. Add the remaining vegetables and saute for about 5 minutes, until tender-crisp. Stir in the oregano and basil.
3. To the pasta, apply the vegetable mixture. To combine uniformly, toss. Cover and refrigerate for around 1 hour, until well-chilled.
4. On individual plates, put lettuce leaves. Cover the pasta salad with it and serve immediately.

61. Pasta with grilled chicken, white beans and mushrooms

(Ready in about 40 Minutes | Serve: 2 | Difficulty: Normal)

Ingredients

- 2 boneless, skinless chicken breasts, each 4 ounces
- 1 tablespoon olive oil
- 1/2 cup chopped white onion
- 1 cup sliced mushrooms
- 1 cup white beans, canned or cooked (no salt added)
- 2 tablespoons chopped garlic
- 1/4 cup chopped fresh basil
- 12 ounces uncooked rotelle pasta
- 1/4 cup grated Parmesan cheese
- Ground black pepper, to taste

Directions

1. Using a barbecue grill to prepare a hot fire or heat a gas grill or broiler. Lightly brush the grill rack or broiler pan with cooking spray, away from the heat source. The cooking rack should be placed 4 to 6 inches from the heat source. Grill or broil the chicken until browned, about 5 minutes on each side, and only cooked through. Switch the chicken to a cutting board and let stand before cutting into strips for 5 minutes.
2. Heat the olive oil in a big, nonstick frying pan over medium heat. Add the onions and mushrooms and saute for about 5 minutes, until tender. Add the white beans, garlic, basil and strips of grilled chicken. Just keep wet.
3. Fill 3/4 of a large pot full of water and bring it to a boil. Add the pasta and cook for 10 to 12 minutes, or according to the package instructions, until al dente (tender). Thoroughly drain the pasta. Place the pasta back in the pot and add the mixture of chicken. To combine uniformly, toss. Between the bowls, divide the pasta. Garnish each one with 1 tablespoon of black pepper and Parmesan cheese. Immediately serve.

62. Pasta with marinara sauce and grilled vegetables

(Ready in about 40 Minutes | Serve: 2 | Difficulty: Normal)

Ingredients

- 2 tablespoons extra-virgin olive oil, divided

- 10 large fresh tomatoes, peeled and diced
- Salt (optional)
- 1/2 teaspoon minced garlic
- 2 tablespoons chopped onion
- 1 tablespoon chopped fresh basil or 1 teaspoon dried basil
- 1 teaspoon sugar
- 1/2 teaspoon dried oregano
- 1/8 teaspoon freshly ground black pepper
- 2 red peppers, sliced into chunks
- 1 yellow summer squash, sliced lengthwise
- 1 zucchini, sliced lengthwise
- 1 sweet onion, sliced into 1/4-inch-wide rounds
- 8 ounces whole-wheat spaghetti

Directions

1. Heat 1 tablespoon of olive oil in a heavy skillet over medium-high heat to make the marinara sauce. Combine the tomatoes, salt, garlic, chopped onions, basil, sugar, black pepper and oregano. Simmer uncovered, for about 30 minutes, until the sauce thickens.
2. Using a barbecue grill to prepare a hot fire or heat a gas grill or broiler. Lightly brush the grill rack or broiler pan with cooking spray, away from the heat source. The cooking rack should be placed 4 to 6 inches from the heat source.
3. Using the remaining tablespoon of olive oil to brush the red peppers, squash, zucchini and sweet onion. On the grill rack or broiler pan, put the vegetables. Grill or broil, turning as needed, about 5 to 8 minutes until the vegetables are tender. To a cup, move the vegetables and set aside.
4. Fill 3/4 of a large pot full of water and bring it to a boil. Connect the pasta and cook for 10 to 12 minutes, or according to package instructions, until tender (al dente). Thoroughly drain the pasta.
5. Divide the pasta equally between individual plates. Top it with grilled vegetables and marinara sauce. Immediately serve.

63. Pasta with pumpkin sauce

(Ready in about 40 Minutes I Serve: 2 I Difficulty: Normal)

Ingredients

- 2 cups whole-wheat bow tie pasta
- 2 teaspoons olive oil
- 1 medium onion, chopped
- 4 cloves garlic, minced
- 8 ounces fresh mushrooms, sliced
- 1 cup low-sodium chicken or vegetable broth
- 1 can (15 ounces) pumpkin
- 1/2 teaspoon rubbed sage
- 1/8 teaspoon salt
- 1/4 teaspoon ground black pepper
- 1/4 cup grated Parmesan cheese
- 1 tablespoon dried parsley flakes (or 3 tablespoons chopped fresh parsley)

Directions

1. Cook pasta according to the instructions for the kit.
2. Meanwhile, over medium to high heat, put a large skillet. Connect the olive oil, garlic, onion, and mushrooms. Cook for approximately 10 minutes or until the onion is tender.
3. Add the broth, sage, pumpkin, salt and pepper. Lower the heat and simmer for 8 minutes or so.
4. Drain and apply to the pumpkin sauce when the pasta has finished cooking. Stir to blend.
5. Until serving, sprinkle it with Parmesan cheese and parsley.

64. Pasta with spinach, garbanzos and raisins

(Ready in about 40 Minutes I Serve: 2 I Difficulty: Normal)

Ingredients

- 8 ounces (about 3 cups) dry bow tie pasta
- 2 tablespoons olive oil
- 4 garlic cloves, crushed
- 1/2 of a 19 ounces can of garbanzos, rinsed and drained
- 1/2 cup unsalted chicken broth
- 1/2 cup golden raisins
- 4 cups fresh spinach, chopped
- 2 tablespoons grated Parmesan cheese
- Cracked black peppercorns, to taste

Directions

1. Fill 3/4 of a large pot full of water and bring it to a boil. Add the pasta and cook for 10 to 12 minutes, or according to the package instructions, until al dente (tender). Thoroughly drain the pasta.
2. Heat the olive oil and garlic over medium heat in a wide skillet. Garbanzos and vegetable broth are added. Stir until warmed through. Add the spinach and raisins. Heat until the spinach is wilted, 3 minutes or so. Don't overcook anymore.
3. Between the bowls, divide the pasta. Apply 1/6 of the sauce, 1 teaspoon of Parmesan cheese and peppercorns to each serving to taste. Immediately serve.

65. Penne tossed with cherry tomatoes, asparagus and goat cheese

(Ready in about 40 Minutes I Serve: 2 I Difficulty: Normal)

Ingredients

- 1/3 pound whole-wheat penne pasta
- 1/2 cup chopped asparagus, 1-inch pieces
- 1 tablespoon water
- 1/2 cup halved cherry tomatoes

- 1/4 cup chopped fresh basil, plus whole leaves for garnish
- 1 tablespoon minced garlic
- 1/8 teaspoon freshly ground black pepper
- 2 ounces goat cheese

Directions
1. Fill a 3/4 big pot full of water and bring it to a boil. Connect the pasta and cook for 10 to 12 minutes, or according to the package instructions, until tender (al dente). Thoroughly drain the pasta.
2. Put the asparagus and the water in a microwave-safe bowl while the pasta is cooking. Heat the asparagus until tender-crisp, around 3 minutes, on high power.
3. Mix the cherry tomatoes, basil, garlic and pepper together in a dish. Connect the asparagus, goat's cheese and pasta and toss until well-mixed. Place it in the refrigerator to cool for at least 20 minutes.
4. Between the bowls, divide the pasta. Add new basil leaves to garnish and serve with.

66. Polenta with fresh vegetables

(Ready in about 40 Minutes | Serve: 2 | Difficulty: Normal)

Ingredients
- 1 cup coarsely ground cornmeal (polenta)
- 4 cups water
- 1 teaspoon garlic, chopped
- 1 cup sliced fresh mushrooms
- 1 cup sliced onions
- 1 cup broccoli florets
- 1 cup sliced zucchini
- 2 tablespoons grated Parmesan cheese
- Chopped fresh oregano, basil or rosemary, to taste

Directions
1. Heat the oven to 350 F. Cover a 3-quart ovenproof dish lightly with cooking spray.
2. In a prepared oven, combine the polenta, water and garlic. Bake uncovered until the polenta pulls away, about 40 minutes, from the sides of the baking dish. The polenta should be moist.
3. Spray a nonstick frying pan with cooking spray while the polenta is cooking. Add the onions and mushrooms. Saute over medium heat for about 5 minutes, until the vegetables are tender.
4. Bring 1 inch of water to a boil in a pot fitted with a steamer basket. Add the zucchini and broccoli. Cover and steam for 2 to 3 minutes, before soft-crisp.
5. Top with the cooked vegetables when the polenta is finished. Sprinkle, to taste, with Parmesan cheese and herbs. Immediately serve.

68. Polenta with roasted Mediterranean vegetables

(Ready in about 40 Minutes | Serve: 2 | Difficulty: Normal)

Ingredients
- 1 small eggplant, peeled, cut into 1/4-inch slices
- 1 small yellow zucchini, cut into 1/4-inch slices
- 1 small green zucchini, cut into 1/4-inch slices
- 6 medium mushrooms, sliced
- 1 sweet red pepper, seeded, cored and cut into chunks
- 2 tablespoons plus 1 teaspoon extra-virgin olive oil
- 6 cups water
- 1 1/2 cups coarse polenta (corn grits)
- 2 teaspoons trans-free margarine
- 1/4 teaspoon cracked black pepper
- 10 ounces frozen spinach, thawed
- 2 plum (Roma) tomatoes, sliced
- 6 dry-packed sun-dried tomatoes, soaked in water to rehydrate, drained and chopped
- 10 ripe olives, chopped
- 2 teaspoons oregano

Directions
1. Heat up your broiler (grill). Place the rack 4 inches from the source of the sun.
2. Brush 1 tablespoon of olive oil with the eggplant, zucchini, mushrooms and red pepper. On a baking sheet, put in a single layer and broil under low pressure. Turn as needed and brush with 1 tablespoon olive oil occasionally. Remove from the broiler when tender and lightly browned (grill). Use immediately or cover for later use and refrigerate.
3. Preheat a 350 F microwave. Using cooking spray to cover a decorative, ovenproof 12-inch flan or quiche baking dish.
4. Bring water to the boil in a medium saucepan. Reduce the heat and whisk the polenta slowly. For around 5 minutes, continue to stir and cook. Stir in margarine and season with 1/8 of a teaspoon of black pepper when polenta falls off the side of the pan. Withdraw from the sun.
5. Spread polenta into the base of the baking dish and the sides. Brush the olive oil with 1 teaspoon. Put the mixture in the oven and bake for ten minutes. Remove it and stay warm.
6. Drain the spinach and press the paper towels between them. Superior polenta with spinach. Put together a sheet of sliced tomatoes, sun-dried chopped tomatoes, and olives. Put the remaining roasted vegetables on top. Sprinkle the remaining 1/8 of a teaspoon of black pepper with oregano. For another 10 minutes, return to the oven. Remove from the oven when fully hot. Split and serve into 6 wedges.

69. Pork chops with black currant jam sauce

(Ready in about 40 Minutes | Serve: 2 | Difficulty: Normal)

Ingredients
- 1/4 cup black currant jam
- 2 tablespoons Dijon mustard

- 2 teaspoons olive oil
- 6 center cut pork loin chops, trimmed of all visible fat, each 4 ounces
- 1/3 cup wine vinegar
- 1/8 teaspoon freshly ground black pepper
- 6 orange slices

Directions
1. Whisk the jam and mustard together in a small bowl.
2. Heat the olive oil in a big, nonstick frying pan over medium-high heat. Add the chops of pork and cook, turning once, until both sides are browned, about 5 minutes per side. Put 1 tablespoon of the jam-mustard mixture on top of each pork chop. Cover and cook for an additional 2 minutes. To warmed plates, pass the pork chops.
3. Cool the frying pan to a temperature that is warm, not acidic. To extract the bits of pork and jam, add wine vinegar into the pan and stir. Over each pork chop, pour the vinegar sauce. Garnish with orange slices and sprinkle with pepper. Serve immediately

70. Pork medallions with herbes de Provence
(Ready in about 40 Minutes | Serve: 2 | Difficulty: Normal)

Ingredients
- 8 ounces pork tenderloin, trimmed of visible fat and cut crosswise into 6 pieces
- Freshly ground black pepper, to taste
- 1/2 teaspoon herbes de Provence
- 1/4 cup dry white wine

Directions
1. Sprinkle with black pepper over the bits of pork. Place the pork between waxed paper sheets. Pound with a mallet or roll until roughly 1/4-inch thick with a rolling pin.
2. Cook the pork over medium-high heat in a large, nonstick frying pan until the meat is browned, 2 to 3 minutes on each side. Remove from the heat and sprinkle with the Provence herbs. On individual plates, put the pork and keep warm.
3. Through the frying pan, pour the wine. Cook until it boils. From the bottom of the pan, remove the brown pieces. Over the meat, pour the wine sauce and serve immediately.

71. Pork tenderloin with apples and balsamic vinegar
(Ready in about 40 Minutes | Serve: 2 | Difficulty: Normal)

Ingredients
- 1 tablespoon olive oil
- 1 pound pork tenderloin, trimmed of all visible fat
- Freshly ground black pepper, to taste
- 2 cups chopped onion
- 2 cups chopped apple
- 1 1/2 tablespoons fresh rosemary, chopped
- 1 cup low-sodium chicken broth
- 1 1/2 tablespoons balsamic vinegar

Directions
1. Heat the oven to 450 F. Cover a baking pan lightly with cooking oil.
2. Heat the olive oil in a large skillet over high heat. Sprinkle with black pepper and substitute pork. On all sides, cook until the tenderloin is browned, about 3 minutes. Place in the prepared baking pan and remove from the sun. Roast the pork for 15 minutes or until 165 F is indicated by a food thermometer (medium).
3. Meanwhile, in the skillet, incorporate the onion, apple and rosemary. Saute over medium heat for around 3 to 5 minutes until the onions and apples are tender. Stir in the vinegar and broth. Increase the heat and simmer for about 5 minutes until the sauce is reduced.
4. Place the pork on a large platter for serving. On the diagonal, slice and position on 4 warmed plates. Scoop over the top with the onion-apple sauce and serve immediately.

72. Pork tenderloin with apples and blue cheese
(Ready in about 40 Minutes | Serve: 2 | Difficulty: Normal)

Ingredients
- 1 pound pork tenderloin
- 1/2 teaspoon white pepper
- 2 teaspoons black pepper
- 1/4 teaspoon cayenne pepper
- 1 teaspoon paprika
- 2 teaspoons canola oil
- 2 apples, sliced
- 1/2 cup white wine or 1/2 cup unsweetened apple juice
- 1/4 cup (about 1 ounce) crumbled blue cheese

Directions
1. Heat the oven to 350 F. Trim all the fat and silvery membrane on the tenderloin. With spices season.
2. Add oil and put the tenderloin in the pan in a broad skillet over medium-high heat. Sear each side, turning the meat using tongs. Move the meat to the roasting pan and cook in the oven until the internal temperature reaches 155 F for 15 to 20 minutes. Remove the tenderloin from the oven and transfer it to a platter. Cover with tape, then leave to rest.
3. Add the apples to the roasting pan and saute until dark brown on the stovetop. Stir in the wine (or juice) and boil until the liquid has halved.
4. Slice the bacon, top with a spoon of apples and sprinkle with the blue cheese. Just serve.

73. Pork tenderloin with fennel sauce
(Ready in about 40 Minutes | Serve: 2 | Difficulty: Normal)

Ingredients

- 4 pork tenderloin fillets, each 4 ounces
- 2 tablespoons olive oil
- 1 teaspoon fennel seeds
- 1 fennel bulb, cored and thinly sliced
- 1 sweet onion (Vidalia), thinly sliced
- 1/2 cup dry white wine
- 1 can (12 ounces) low-sodium chicken broth
- Fennel fronds, for garnish
- Orange slices, for garnish

Directions:
1. Place the pork between wax paper sheets. Pound each with a mallet or roll to around 1/4-inch thick with a rolling pin.
2. Heat oil over medium heat in a thick, nonstick skillet. Apply the fennel seeds and swirl for about 3 minutes, until fragrant. Add the pork and cook until browned, on each side, for about 3 minutes. To remain warm, remove the pork from the skillet and cover it.
3. To the skillet, add the fennel and onion slices. Saute before tender, 5 minutes roughly. Remove the skillet from the vegetables and cover them to stay warm.
4. To the skillet, add the wine and chicken broth. Boil over high heat until half the volume is reduced. Put the pork back into the skillet, cover and cook for 5 minutes over low heat. Remove the cover and the mixture of fennel and onion is applied. Cover and cook for an additional 2 minutes. Serve on warmed plates garnished with orange slices and fennel fronds.

74. Prawns puttanesca
(Ready in about 40 Minutes | Serve: 2 | Difficulty: Normal)

Ingredients
- 1 tablespoon olive oil
- 1 1/4 pounds prawns (about 16 large shrimp), peeled and deveined
- 1/2 teaspoon freshly ground black pepper
- 2 tablespoons dry white wine
- 4 tomatoes, peeled and seeded, then diced (about 2 1/2 cups)
- 1/4 cup dry-packed sun-dried tomatoes, soaked in water to rehydrate, drained and chopped
- 3 cloves garlic, minced
- 1/4 cup chopped pitted Nicoise olives
- 1 tablespoon capers, rinsed and chopped
- 2 anchovy fillets, rinsed and finely chopped
- 1 tablespoon grated lemon zest
- 1 tablespoon chopped fresh flat-leaf (Italian) parsley
- 1 tablespoon chopped fresh basil
- 1/2 teaspoon red pepper flakes (optional)

Directions:
1. Heat the olive oil in a big, nonstick saute or frying pan over medium-high heat. Add the sprinkled prawns and black pepper, and cook for about three minutes. Turn the prawns over and cook for about 2 minutes longer, until opaque and pink. Transfer and hold warm in a mug.
2. To scrape up any browned pieces, add the wine and deglaze the plate, stirring with a wooden spoon. Add the tomatoes, fresh and sun-dried, and add the garlic. Reduce the heat to medium and simmer for about 3 minutes, until the tomatoes are tender.
3. To allow the flavours to blend, add all the remaining ingredients and cook for about 2 minutes longer. Put the prawns back in the pan and toss well to coat them. Immediately serve.

75. Quick bean and tuna salad
(Ready in about 40 Minutes | Serve: 2 | Difficulty: Normal)

Ingredients
- 1/2 whole-grain baguette, torn into 2-inch pieces (about 1 cup)
- 2 tablespoons olive oil
- 1 can (16 ounces) cannellini beans, no salt added, drained and rinsed
- 2 small dill pickles, cut into bite-size pieces (about 2 tablespoons)
- 1 small red onion, thinly sliced (about 1/2 cup)
- 2 tablespoons red wine vinegar
- 1/4 teaspoon pepper
- 1 can (7 ounces) water-packed tuna, no salt added, drained and rinsed
- 2 tablespoons finely chopped fresh parsley

Directions:
1. Broiler with Fire. On a heavy cookie sheet, put the baguette pieces and brush them with 1 tablespoon of oil. Place under the broiler until golden, around 1 to 2 minutes. Turn and broil the bread pieces for an additional 1 or 2 minutes.
2. Combine the remaining oil, beans, pickles, onion, vinegar and pepper in a wide bowl. Fold the bits of broiled baguette in. Divide the mixture into four bowls and add the tuna and parsley to the tip.

76. Quinoa risotto with arugula and Parmesan
(Ready in about 40 Minutes | Serve: 2 | Difficulty: Normal)

Ingredients
- 1 tablespoon olive oil
- 1/2 yellow onion, chopped (about 1/2 cup)
- 1 garlic clove, minced
- 1 cup quinoa, well rinsed
- 2 1/4 cups low-sodium vegetable stock or broth
- 2 cups chopped, stemmed arugula (rocket)
- 1 small carrot, peeled and finely shredded
- 1/2 cup thinly sliced fresh shiitake mushrooms
- 1/4 cup grated Parmesan cheese
- 1/4 teaspoon salt
- 1/4 teaspoon freshly ground black pepper

Directions:

1. Heat the olive oil in a big saucepan over medium heat. Add the onion and saute for about 4 minutes until it is soft and translucent. Add the garlic and the quinoa and cook, stirring occasionally, for about 1 minute. Don't let it brown the garlic.
2. Stir in the stock and bring it to a boil. Reduce the heat to low and simmer for about 12 minutes, until the quinoa is almost tender to the bite but slightly firm in the middle. The mixture is going to be brothy. Incorporate the arugula, carrot and mushrooms and boil until the grains of the quinoa turn white to translucent, about 2 minutes longer.
3. Stir in the cheese and apply salt and pepper to the seasoning. Immediately serve.

77. Rice and beans salad

(Ready in about 40 Minutes | Serve: 2 | Difficulty: Normal)

Ingredients

- 1 1/2 cups uncooked brown rice
- 3 cups water
- 1/2 cup chopped fresh parsley
- 1/2 cup chopped shallots or spring onions (approximately 2 shallots or several spring onions)
- 15-ounce can unsalted garbanzo beans
- 15-ounce can unsalted dark kidney beans
- 1/4 cup olive oil
- 1/3 to 1/2 cup rice vinegar, according to your taste

Directions:

1. Place the water and rice in the stockpot. Cover and cook until the rice is tender, about 45 to 50 minutes, over medium heat. To room temperature, cool. Stir the rest of the ingredients in. Refrigerate for 2 hours or longer.

78. Rice noodles with spring vegetables

(Ready in about 40 Minutes | Serve: 2 | Difficulty: Normal)

Ingredients

- 1 package (8 ounces) rice noodles
- 1 tablespoon peanut oil
- 1 tablespoon sesame oil
- 1 tablespoon grated fresh ginger
- 2 garlic cloves, finely chopped
- 2 tablespoons reduced-sodium soy sauce
- 1 cup small broccoli florets
- 1 cup fresh bean sprouts
- 8 cherry tomatoes, halved
- 1 cup chopped fresh spinach
- 2 scallions, chopped
- Crushed red chili flakes (optional

Directions:

1. Fill 3/4 of a large pot full of water and bring it to a boil. Add the noodles and cook for 5 to 6 minutes, or according to package instructions, until tender. With cold water, drain and clean the noodles thoroughly. Only set aside.
2. Heat the oils over a medium heat in a large pot or frying pan. Add the garlic and ginger and stir-fry until it is fragrant. Stir in the soy sauce and broccoli and continue cooking for about 3 minutes over medium heat. Attach the remaining vegetables and the cooked noodles and toss until thoroughly warmed.
3. Divide the noodles between warmed plates and, if desired, cover with crushed red chilli flakes. Immediately serve.

79. Roasted salmon

(Ready in about 40 Minutes | Serve: 2 | Difficulty: Normal)

Ingredients

- Two 5-ounce pieces salmon with skin
- 2 teaspoons extra-virgin olive oil
- 1 tablespoon chopped chives
- 1 tablespoon fresh tarragon leaves (optional)

Directions:

1. Heat the oven to 425 F. Top a board with foil for baking.
2. Rub the salmon with 2 teaspoons of oil all over it. On a foil-lined baking sheet, roast the skin side down until the fish is cooked through, about 12 minutes. Check if the fish flakes easily with the fork after 10 minutes. Continue baking for 2 more minutes if it doesn't.
3. Lift the salmon off the skin with a metal spatula and put the salmon on a serving plate. Discard your skin. Sprinkle the herbs with the salmon and eat.

80. Roasted salmon with maple glaze

(Ready in about 40 Minutes | Serve: 2 | Difficulty: Normal)

Ingredients

- 1/4 cup maple syrup
- 1 garlic clove, minced
- 1/4 cup balsamic vinegar
- 2 pounds salmon, cut into 6 equal-sized fillets
- 1/4 teaspoon kosher or sea salt
- 1/8 teaspoon fresh cracked black pepper
- Fresh mint or parsley for garnish

Directions:

1. Preheat a 450 F oven. Cover a baking pan lightly with cooking oil.
2. Mix together the maple syrup, garlic and balsamic vinegar in a small saucepan over a low heat. Heat up until the heat is hot and drain the heat. To be used for basting, pour half of the mixture into a small cup, and leave the remainder for later.
3. Dry the salmon Pat. Place on the baking sheet, skin-side down. With the maple syrup mixture, clean the salmon. Bake for 10 minutes or so, brush again with a mixture of maple syrup, and bake for another five minutes. Continue to baste and bake, around 20 to 25 minutes in all, until the fish flakes easily.

4. Move the fillets of the salmon to plates. Sprinkle with black pepper and salt, and top with the mixture of reserved maple syrup. Add new mint or parsley to garnish and serve immediately.

81. Old fashioned chicken and brown rice soup

(Ready in about 1hr | Serve: 8 | Difficulty: Difficult)

Ingredients

- ⅔ cup brown rice
- 1 tablespoon canola oil
- 1½ pounds boneless, skinless chicken thighs, excess fat trimmed, cut into bite-sized pieces
- 2 medium leeks, white and pale green parts only, chopped and well rinsed (2 cups), or 1 large yellow onion, chopped
- 2 medium carrots, cut into
- ½-inch dice
- 2 large celery ribs, cut into
- ½-inch dice
- 1 quart Homemade Chicken Broth or canned low-sodium chicken broth
- 2 cups of water
- 2 tablespoons finely chopped fresh parsley
- 1 teaspoon kosher salt
- ½ teaspoon freshly ground black pepper
- ¼ teaspoon dried thyme
- 1 bay leaf

Directions:

1. Over high heat, bring a medium saucepan of lightly salted water to a boil.
2. Add the rice and reduce the heat to a low-medium level.
3. Cook until the rice is tender at a low boil, about 40 minutes.
4. Drain, rinse under cold water, and set aside in a wire sieve. Meanwhile, heat the oil over medium-high heat in a large pot. Add the chicken and cook in two batches, occasionally stirring, until lightly browned, for around 6 minutes. Transfer to a dish.
5. Add to the pot the leeks, carrots, and celery. Reduce and cover the heat to medium.
6. Cook, uncovering and stirring with a wooden spoon periodically, loosening the browned bits with the spoon at the bottom of the pot, until the vegetables soften, about 5 minutes.
7. Add the broth and water and bring to a boil over high heat, skimming away any foam that rises to the surface. Return the chicken to the pot. Add the parsley, salt, pepper, thyme, and bay leaf and mix well. Return the heat to medium-low and simmer, uncovered, until the chicken, pierced with the tip of a sharp knife, is tender and opaque around 40 minutes.
8. Stir in the brown rice and cook for about 5 minutes, until heated. Dispose of the Bay Leaf. Ladle it into bowls, and serve warm.

82. Chicken and Spring vegetable soup

(Ready in about 1hr | Serve: 8 | Difficulty: Difficult)

Ingredients

- 1 tablespoon olive oil
- 1½ pounds boneless, skinless chicken thighs, excess fat trimmed, cut into bite-sized pieces
- 1 large leek, white and pale green parts only, chopped (1 cup)
- 1 quart Homemade Chicken Broth (here) or canned low-sodium chicken broth
- 1-quart water
- 2 large red-skinned potatoes, scrubbed but unpeeled, cut into ½-inch pieces
- 1 teaspoon kosher salt
- ½ teaspoon freshly ground black pepper
- 1 pound asparagus, woody stems discarded, cut into 1-inch lengths 1 cup thawed frozen peas
- 8 tablespoons light sour cream, for serving

Directions:

1. Heat oil over medium-high heat in a kettle. Add the chicken and cook in two batches, occasionally stirring, until lightly browned, for around 6 minutes. Transfer to a dish.
2. Add the leek to the pot and cook for about 3 minutes, occasionally stirring, until it is softened. Add the broth and stir, loosening the brown bits with a wooden spoon at the bottom of the jar. Then stir in the water, potatoes, salt, and pepper and bring to a boil over high heat, skimming off any foam that rises to the top.
3. Decrease the heat to a medium-low level. Simmer for about 40 minutes, until the chicken is soft and opaque when pierced with the tip of a sharp knife. Stir in the asparagus and peas for the final 5 minutes.
4. Ladle into soup cups, add 1 tablespoon of sour cream to each serving, and serve hot

83. Mexican Chicken Tortilla soup

(Ready in about 1hr | Serve: 8 | Difficulty: Difficult)

Ingredients

Baked tortilla strips

- Olive oil in a pump sprayer
- 3 (6-inch) corn tortillas, cut into strips about ½ inch wide and 1 inch long

Soup

- 1 tablespoon olive oil

- 1½ pounds boneless, skinless chicken thighs, excess fat trimmed, cut into bite-sized pieces
- 1 medium yellow onion, chopped
- 1 medium red bell pepper, cored and cut into
- ½-inch dice
- 1 large zucchini, trimmed and cut into
- ½-inch dice
- 2 cloves garlic, minced
- 1 jalapeño, seeded and finely chopped
- 3 cups Homemade Chicken Broth or canned low-sodium chicken broth
- 3 cups of water
- 1 (14.5-ounce) can no-salt-added diced tomatoes with juice, undrained
- 1 cup fresh or thawed frozen corn kernels
- 2 tablespoons chopped fresh cilantro, plus more for serving
- Lime wedges, for serving

Directions:

1. To make strips of tortilla: Preheat the oven to 400°F. Using oil to spray a rimmed baking sheet. On a baking sheet, spread the tortilla strips and spray them with oil. Bake, occasionally stirring, until golden brown and crisp, for 7 to 10 minutes. Just let it cool.
2. To make the soup: In a large pot, heat the oil over medium to high heat. Add the chicken and cook in two batches, occasionally stirring, until lightly browned, for around 6 minutes. To reduce the heat to mild, add the onion, red pepper, zucchini, garlic, and jalapeño. Cook, stirring periodically, until tender, around 5 minutes.
3. Stir in the broth and scrape the brown bits with a wooden spoon into the bottom of the jar. Stir in the water and the tomatoes and bring them to a boil over high heat with their juice. Decrease the heat to a medium-low level. Simmer until the chicken, when pierced with the tip of a sharp knife, is opaque in the center, about 35 minutes. Stir in the corn and 2 teaspoons of cilantro for the last 5 minutes.
4. Sprinkle each serving with about 1 tablespoon of tortilla chips and extra cilantro. Ladle into soup bowls. Serve hot with lime wedges to squeeze as desired into the broth.

84. Hearty beef vegetable soup

(Ready in about 1hr | Serve: 8 | Difficulty: Difficult)

Ingredients

- 1 tablespoon vegetable oil
- 1 large yellow onion, chopped (2 cups)
- 2 medium carrots, cut into ½-inch dice
- 2 large celery ribs, cut into ½-inch dice
- 2 medium parsnips, cut into ½-inch dice
- 1½ pounds ground sirloin
- 1-quart Homemade Beef Stock or canned low-sodium beef broth
- 2 cups of water
- 1 (14.5-ounce) can no-salt-added canned diced tomatoes in juice, undrained
- 2 tablespoons chopped fresh parsley
- 1 teaspoon kosher salt
- ½ teaspoon freshly ground black pepper
- ½ teaspoon dried thyme
- 1 bay leaf
- 2 cups cooked macaroni (optional)

Directions:

1. Over medium heat, heat the oil in a large pot. Add the onion, carrots, celery, and parsnips and cook for about 5 minutes, occasionally stirring, until the onion has softened. To one side of the pot, push the vegetables. Put the beef in the empty side of the pot and cook until the beef loses its raw look, stirring regularly and breaking up the meat with the side of a spoon, for about 5 minutes. Combine the vegetables and beef.
2. Mix the broth with the water, the tomatoes and their juice, the parsley, the salt, the pepper, the thyme, and the bay leaves. Bring it to a boil over high heat. Reduce the heat to medium-low and simmer for about 20 minutes, until the vegetables are tender. Dispose of the Bay Leaf. Ladle it into bowls, and serve it warm.

85. Lentil and Sausage soup

(Ready in about 1hr | Serve: 15 | Difficulty: Difficult)

Ingredients

- 1 tablespoon olive oil
- 1 large yellow onion, chopped (2 cups)
- 2 medium carrots, chopped
- 2 medium celery ribs, chopped
- 4 cloves garlic,5 minced
- 1 pound sweet or hot turkey sausage, casings removed
- 1 pound lentils, sorted, rinsed, and drained
- 1 quart Homemade Chicken Broth or canned low-sodium chicken broth
- 1-quart water, plus more as needed
- ½ teaspoon dried rosemary
- 1 teaspoon kosher salt
- ½ teaspoon crushed hot red pepper
- 1 (14.5-ounce) can no-salt-added diced tomatoes in juice, undrained
- 2 cups whole-wheat rotini or other bowlular pasta

Directions

1. Over medium heat, heat the oil in a large pot. Add the onion, carrots, celery, and garlic and cook for about 5 minutes, occasionally stirring,

until tender. Attach the turkey sausage and cook until the sausage loses its raw look, stirring regularly and breaking up the meat with the side of a wooden spoon, around 6 minutes.
2. Stir in the lentils, broth, water, rosemary, salt, and hot pepper, and bring to a boil over high heat. Reduce the heat and simmer, stirring periodically, around 45 minutes, until the lentils are softened. Add the tomatoes and their juice and simmer until the lentils are tender, adding more hot water to barely cover the lentils, about an additional 45 minutes.
3. Add enough hot water to cover with 1/2 inch of lentils and bring to a simmer. Stir in the pasta and cook for about 15 minutes, until the pasta is really tender. Ladle it into bowls of soup and serve it warm.

86. Sausage milestone with Kale and Beans

(Ready in about 1hr | Serve: 8 | Difficulty: Difficult)

Ingredients

- 1 tablespoon olive oil
- 1¼ pounds sweet turkey sausage, casings removed
- 1 large yellow onion, chopped
- 2 medium carrots, cut into ½-inch dice
- 2 medium celery ribs, cut into ½-inch dice
- 2 medium zucchini, trimmed and cut into ½-inch dice
- 2 cloves garlic, minced1 quart Homemade Chicken Broth
- 2 cups water1 (14.5-ounce) can no-salt-added diced tomatoes in juice, undrained
- 1 teaspoon dried oregano
- ½ teaspoon crushed hot red pepper
- 1 bay leaf
- 4 packed cups thinly sliced black kale (wash well and remove tough stems before slicing)
- 1 (15-ounce) can no-salt-added cannellini beans, drained and rinsed

Directions:

1. Over medium heat, heat the oil in a large pot. Attach the turkey sausage and cook until the sausage loses its raw look, stirring regularly and breaking up the sausage with the side of a wooden spoon, around 6 minutes. Add the onion, carrots, celery, zucchini, and garlic and cook for about 5 minutes, occasionally stirring, until the onion softens.
2. Bring to a boil and bring to a boil over high heat. Stir in broth, sugar, tomatoes and their juice, oregano, hot pepper, and bay leaf. Simmer for 30 minutes and reduce the heat to medium-low. Stir in the kale and beans and simmer for about 15 more minutes until the vegetables are very tender.
3. Dispose of the Bay Leaf. Ladle it into bowls of soup and serve it sweet.

87. Homemade clam Chowder

(Ready in about 35 Minutes | Serve: 8 | Difficulty: Normal)

Ingredients

- 1 large red-skinned potato (8 ounces), scrubbed but unpeeled, cut into ½-inch cubes
- 2¼ cups water, divided
- 1 teaspoon canola oil
- 2 strips reduced-sodium bacon, cut into 1-inch pieces
- 1 tablespoon unsalted butter
- 1 medium onion, chopped1¾ cups Homemade Chicken Broth or 1 (14.5-ounce) can low-sodium chicken broth
- 2 cups low-fat (1%) mil
- k¼ teaspoon dried thyme
- ¼ teaspoon freshly ground black pepper
- 2 tablespoons cornstarch1 cup chopped clams with juice

Directions:

1. In a medium saucepan, put the potatoes and 2 cups of water to a boil. Reduce the heat and simmer for about 15 minutes, until the potatoes are barely tender.
2. Meanwhile, over medium heat, heat the oil in a large saucepan. Add the bacon and cook, sometimes flipping the bacon until browned, for around 5 minutes. Switch it to a cutting board, let it cool, and chop the bacon coarsely.
3. Melt the butter over medium heat in a large saucepan, add the onion and sauté, occasionally stirring, until tender, for about 3 minutes. Return the bacon and the potatoes and their soup, broth, milk, thyme, and pepper to the saucepan. Bring to a boil and cook over medium-low heat, around 10 minutes, to mix the flavors.
4. Sprinkle the cornstarch over the remaining ¼ cup of water in a small bowl, stir until it dissolves, and whisk into the simmering soup. Attach the clams and the juice, then bring it to a boil. Serve it wet.

88. Cod and Corn Chowder

(Ready in about 30 Minutes | Serve: 6 | Difficulty: Normal)

Ingredients

- 1 teaspoon canola oil
- 2 reduced-sodium bacon strips, cut into 1-inch pieces
- 1 small yellow onion, chopped
- 2 celery ribs, cut into ½-inch dice

- ½ large red bell pepper, cored and cut into ½-inch dice
- 3 tablespoons all-purpose flour
- 3 cups Homemade Chicken Broth) or canned low-sodium chicken broth
- 1½ cups low-fat (1%) milk
- ½ teaspoon kosher salt
- ⅛ teaspoon freshly ground black pepper
- Pinch of dried thyme
- 1 pound skinless cod fillets, cut into bite-sized pieces
- 2 cups fresh or thawed frozen corn kernels
- Chopped fresh parsley for serving

Directions:

1. Over medium heat, heat the oil in a big saucepan. Cook the bacon until browned, occasionally stirring, for around 6 minutes. Switch the bacon to paper towels to drain using a slotted spoon, leaving the fat in the saucepan.
2. Add the onion, celery, and red pepper to the saucepan and cook over medium heat for about 5 minutes, occasionally stirring, until tender. Sprinkle and whisk in the flour for 30 seconds. Bring to a boil and stir in the broth, milk, salt, pepper, and thyme. To mix the flavors, reduce the heat to medium-low and simmer for around 15 minutes.
3. Add the cod, bacon, and corn, and cook for about 5 minutes until the cod becomes opaque. Sprinkle with the parsley, and serve sweet. Ladle it into soup bowls.

89. Manhattan Snapper chowder

(Ready in about 35 Minutes | Serve: 10 | Difficulty: Normal)

Ingredients

- 1 tablespoon olive oil
- 1 medium yellow onion, chopped
- 2 medium carrots, cut into ½-inch dice
- 2 large celery ribs, cut into ½-inch dice
- 2 large red potatoes (about 1 pound), scrubbed but unpeeled, cut into ½-inch dice
- 1 quart Homemade Chicken Broth or canned low-sodium chicken broth
- 2 cups of water
- ½ teaspoon freshly ground black pepper
- r½ teaspoon dried basil
- ¼ teaspoon dried thyme
- 1 bay leaf
- 2 (14.5-ounce) cans no-salt-added diced tomatoes in juice, undrained
- 1 pound skinless snapper fillets, cut into bite-sized pieces
- Chopped fresh parsley for serving (optional)

Directions:

1. Over medium heat, heat the oil in a large pot. Add the onion, carrots, celery, and potatoes and cook for about 5 minutes, frequently stirring, until the onions are tender. The broth, wine, pepper, basil, thyme, and bay leaf are added. Carry it over high heat to a boil. Reduce the heat and simmer for about 15 minutes, until the potatoes are almost tender. Stir in the tomatoes with their juice and simmer for about 10 more minutes, until the potatoes are softened.
2. Add the snapper and cook for about 3 minutes until it's opaque. Dispose of the Bay Leaf. Ladle into cups, sprinkle (if using) with parsley, and serve wet.

90. Sweet potato, Collard, and black-eyed Pea Soup

(Ready in about 30 Minutes | Serve: 8 | Difficulty: Normal)

Ingredients

- 1 tablespoon canola oil
- 1 (7-ounce) ham steak, cut into bite-sized pieces
- 1 large yellow onion, chopped
- 2 cloves garlic, minced
- 1 quart Homemade Chicken Broth
- 3 cups of water
- 1 pound sweet potatoes (yams), peeled and cut into ½-inch dice
- ½ teaspoon salt
- ½ teaspoon crushed hot red pepper
- 4 packed cups thinly sliced collard greens (wash well and remove thick stems before slicing)
- 1 cup frozen black-eyed peas

Directions:

1. Over medium heat, heat the oil in a large pot. Add the ham and cook, stirring periodically, until lightly browned, around 3 minutes. Add the onion and garlic and cook, stirring, until the onion softens, around 5minutes.
2. Bring to a boil over high heat and add broth, water, sweet potatoes, salt, and hot pepper. Return the heat to medium and cook at a low boil until the sweet potatoes begin to soften about 10 minutes. Stir in the collards and black-eyed peas and cook until the greens and sweet potatoes are tender, about 10 minutes longer. Ladle it into bowls of soup and serve it sweet.
3.

91. Homemade Chicken Broth

(Ready in about 1hr | Serve: 3 quarts | Difficulty: Normal)

Ingredients

- 3½ pounds of chicken wings or backs

- 1 tablespoon vegetable oil
- 1 medium yellow onion, chopped
- 1 medium carrot, chopped
- 1 medium celery rib, chopped
- About 4½ quarts water, divided
- 4 fresh parsley sprigs
- ½ teaspoon black peppercorns
- ¼ teaspoon dried thyme
- 1 bay leaf

Directions:
1. Preheat the oven to 450°F.
2. Chop the wings into chunks between the joints using a cleaver or a heavy knife. (It is optional to cut the back into 2- or 3-inch chunks.) Spread in a large roasting pan. Roast until the wings have browned beautifully, about 40 minutes.
3. Meanwhile, over medium heat, heat the oil in a broad stockpot. Add the onion, carrot, and celery and cook for about 5 minutes, occasionally stirring, until softened. Switch the wings to the pot using tongs.
4. In the roasting pan, pour out some fat. Put the pan on high heat and heat over two burners until the pan is sizzling. Add 2 cups of water and bring to a boil, applying a wooden spoon to the browned bits in the pan. Pour into the saucepan and add enough cold water (about 4 quarts) to cover 1 inch of the ingredients. Using a large spoon to skim off any foam that rises to the top, raise the heat underneath the pot and bring it to a boil.

92. Summer Berry Soup
(Ready in about 1hr | Serve: 3 quarts | Difficulty: Normal)

Ingredients:
- ½ cup apple juice
- ¼ cup strawberries
- ¼ cup raspberries
- ¼ cup blackberries
- ¼ cup blueberries
- 1 teaspoon potato starch
- ¼ teaspoon ground cinnamon

Directions:
1. In the saucepan, pour in the apple juice.
2. Add all the berries and cinnamon from the field. Cover the lid and cook the ingredients.
3. In a bottle, apply three tablespoons of apple juice mixture, apply potato starch and whisk until smooth.
4. Then pour the berry soup into the starch mixture and stir until the soup is thickened.
5. Cover the lid and leave the soup for 10 minutes to recover.

93. Green Beans Soup
(Ready in about 1hr | Serve: 3 quarts | Difficulty: Normal)

Ingredients
- ½ onion, diced
- 1/3 cup green beans, soaked
- 3 cups of water
- ½ sweet pepper, chopped
- 2 potatoes, chopped
- 1 tablespoon fresh cilantro, chopped
- 1 teaspoon chili flakes

Directions:
1. In the saucepan, put all the ingredients and close the lid.
2. On medium heat, cook the soup for 40 minutes or until the ingredients are all tender.

94. Turkey Soup
(Ready in about 1hr | Serve: 3 quarts | Difficulty: Normal)

Ingredients
- 1 potato, diced
- 1 cup ground turkey
- 1 teaspoon cayenne pepper
- 1 onion, diced
- 1 tablespoon olive oil
- ¼ carrot, diced
- 2 cups of water

Directions:
1. In a saucepan, heat the olive oil and add the diced onion and carrot.
2. For 3 minutes, prepare the vegetables. Then stir them well and add the cayenne pepper and ground turkey.
3. Attach the diced potato and stir well with the spices. Cook them for an extra 2 minutes.
4. Add water, too. Check if all the ingredients have been put in.
5. Cover the lid and simmer for 20 minutes to make the broth.
6. Lower the heat to a low level. Attach the parsley, peppercorns, bay leaf, and thyme. Simmer, uncovered, for at least 2 hours and up to 4 hours, until the stock is well flavored.
5. In a very large heatproof bowl, position a colander. In the bowl, strain the broth, discarding the solids.

95. Pasta Soup
(Ready in about 1hr | Serve: 3 quarts | Difficulty: Normal)

Ingredients:
- 2 oz. whole-grain pasta
- ½ cup corn kernels
- 1 oz. carrot, shredded
- 3 oz. celery stalk, chopped
- 2 cups low-sodium chicken stock
- 1 teaspoon ground black pepper

Directions:
1. Bring the chicken stock to boil and add shredded carrot and celery stalk. Simmer the liquid for 5 minutes.
2. After this, add corn kernels, ground black pepper, and pasta. Stir the soup well.
3. Simmer it on the medium heat for 8 minutes.
4. Place the bowl of broth in a larger bowl of water with ice. Let the broth stand until soft, stirring periodically, for around 30 minutes. Remove the ice water from the cup, put it on a kitchen towel, and dry the bowl's sides. Refrigerate overnight, uncovered.

5. Scrape off the fat from the top of the broth by using a spoon. (The broth may be refrigerated or moved to airtight containers for up to 3 days and frozen for up to 3 months.)

Conclusion

Your go-to book for safe, tasty food will become the DASH Diet Cookbook. The DASH diet is rich in foods dependent on plants, including fruits, berries, beans, nuts, seeds, whole grains, and vegetable fats that are good for the heart. Add low-fat and non-fat milk (a main DASH diet food) and protein to this base (fish and seafood, lean beef, pork, and poultry). You will no longer have to pick between the recipes you want and eating more healthily with this wide array of choices for preparing outstanding meals. The DASH Diet Cookbook, based on the incredibly popular DASH diet, is designed to make living a DASH lifestyle as easy and tasty as possible. The quicker the meal is to make, the more likely you are to make it a part of your favorite recipes' daily rotation. You will abandon the concept of a "diet," as I always do, so cooking the DASH way will become a way of life, as normal as breathing... or feeding! So, what's a diet for DASH? As part of a study to find ways to reduce blood pressure without drugs, this innovative perspective on healthy eating was originally developed. DASH, which was the name of the initial report, is an acronym for Nutritional Methods to Stop Hypertension. The organizers of the study decided to take the best aspects of vegetarian diets that were proven to be correlated with lower blood pressure to create a strategy that would be versatile enough to cater to the vast majority of devoted meat eaters in the Americas. They built what they thought was the healthiest eating plan for omnivores. And this dream has been borne out by research. As well as first-line hypertension treatment, the DASH diet helps reduce blood pressure. It decreases cholesterol as well.

The DASH eating style has been found to help lower the risk of multiple diseases and life-threatening medical problems or accidents, including stroke, cardiac attack, heart failure, type 2 diabetes, renal disease, kidney stones, and certain forms of cancer, when measured over very long periods of time. Not only is DASH prescribed for those who have or are at risk for certain disorders, but in the Food Guidelines for Americans, it is recommended for all. And for weight loss, the DASH diet is fabulous, as it is filled with voluminous fruits and vegetables and has plenty of protein to ensure satiety. In reality, the plan is so rich in nutritious foods that people find it easy to follow without being tempted to "cheat." In 2011, 2012, and 2013, the DASH diet was ranked by the U.S. as the "Number 1 Best Overall Diet" News & Report on the Planet. Doctors and nutritionists commonly hail it as the best and healthiest diet schedule. As tests have shown that children who adopt a DASH feeding routine are more likely to be at a good weight and have healthier blood pressure, even kids get a health advantage. This makes DASH a perfect idea for the whole family.

Printed in Great Britain
by Amazon